The Writer's Handbook

Edited by
SYLVIA K. BURACK
Editor, *The Writer*

Publishers   THE WRITER, INC.   Boston

CONTENTS

PART I—BACKGROUND FOR WRITERS

PART II—HOW TO WRITE: Techniques

GENERAL FICTION

III

SPECIALIZED FICTION

NONFICTION: BOOKS AND ARTICLES

POETRY, PLAYS, AND TELEVISION

JUVENILE AND TEEN-AGE WRITING

PART III—EDITORS, AGENTS, AND BUSINESS

PART IV—WHERE TO SELL

THE WRITER'S HANDBOOK

1

CREATIVE TRUST

By John D. MacDonald

The writer and the reader are involved in a creative relationship. The writer must provide the materials with which the reader will construct bright pictures in his head. The reader will use those materials as a partial guide and will finish the pictures with the stuff from his own life experience.

I do not intend to patronize the reader with this analogy: The writer is like a person trying to entertain a listless child on a rainy afternoon.

You set up a card table, and you lay out pieces of cardboard, construction paper, scissors, paste, crayons. You draw a rectangle and you construct a very colorful little fowl and stick it in the foreground, and you say, "This is a chicken." You cut out a red square and put it in the background and say, "This is a barn." You construct a bright yellow truck and put it in the background on the other side of the frame and say, "This is a speeding truck. Is the chicken going to get out of the way in time? Now you finish the picture."

If the child has become involved, he will get into the whole cut-and-paste thing, adding trees, a house, a fence, a roof on the barn. He will crayon a road from the truck to the chicken. You didn't say a word about trees, fences, houses, cows, roofs. The kid puts them in because he knows they are the furniture of farms. He is joining in the creative act, enhancing the tensions of the story by adding his uniquely personal concepts of the items you did not mention, but which have to be there.

Or the child could cross the room, turn a dial and see detailed pictures on the television tube. What are the ways you can lose him?

You can lose him by putting in too much of the scene. That turns him into a spectator. "This is a chicken. This is a fence. This is an apple tree. This is a tractor." He knows those things have to be there. He yawns. And pretty soon, while you are cutting and pasting and explaining, you hear the gunfire of an old western.

You can lose him by putting in too little. "This is a chicken," you say, and leave him to his own devices. Maybe he will put the chicken in a forest, or in a supermarket. Maybe the child will invent the onrushing truck, or a chicken hawk. Too much choice is as boring as too little. Attention is diffused, undirected.

You can put in the appropriate amount of detail and still lose him by the way you treat the chicken, the truck, and the barn. Each must have presence. Each must be unique. *The* chicken. Not *a* chicken. He is eleven weeks old. He is a rooster named Melvin who stands proud and glossy in the sunlight, but tends to be nervous, insecure and hesitant. His legs are exceptionally long, and in full flight he has a stride you wouldn't believe.

If you cannot make the chicken, the truck, and the barn totally specific, then it is as if you were using dingy gray paper for those three ingredients, and the child will not want to use his own bright treasure to complete the picture you have begun.

We are analogizing here the semantics of image, of course. The pace and tension and readability of fiction are as dependent upon your control and understanding of these phenomena as they are upon story structure and characterization.

Here is a sample: The air conditioning unit in the motel room had a final fraction of its name left, an "aire" in silver plastic, so loose that when it resonated to the coughing thud of the compressor, it would blur. A rusty water stain on the green wall under the unit was shaped like the bottom half of Texas. From the stained grid, the air conditioner exhaled its stale and icy breath into the room, redolent of chemicals and of someone burning garbage far, far away.

Have you not already constructed the rest of the motel room? Can you not see and describe the bed, the carpeting, the shower? O.K., if you see them already, I need not describe them for you. If I try to do so, I become a bore. And the pictures you have composed in your head are more vivid than the ones I would try to describe.

No two readers will see exactly the same motel room. No two children will construct the same farm. But the exercise of the need to create gives both ownership and involvement to the motel room and the farm, to the air conditioner and to the chicken and to their environments.

Sometimes, of course, it is useful to go into exhaustive detail. That is when a different end is sought. In one of the Franny and Zooey stories, Salinger describes the contents of a medicine cabinet shelf by shelf in such infinite detail that finally a curious monumentality is achieved, reminiscent somehow of that iron sculpture by David Smith called "The Letter."

Here is a sample of what happens when you cut the images out of gray paper: "The air conditioning unit in the motel room window was old and somewhat noisy."

See? Because the air conditioning unit has lost its specificity, its unique and solitary identity, the room has blurred also. You cannot see it as clearly. It is less real.

AND WHEN THE ENVIRONMENT IS LESS REAL, THE PEOPLE YOU PUT INTO THAT ENVIRONMENT BECOME LESS BELIEVABLE, AND LESS INTERESTING.

I hate to come across a whole sentence in caps when I am reading something. But here, it is of such importance, and so frequently misunderstood and neglected, I inflict caps upon you with no apology. The environment can seem real only when the reader has helped construct it. Then he has an ownership share in it. If the air conditioner is unique, then the room is unique, and the person in it is real.

What item to pick? There is no rule. Sometimes you can use a little sprinkling of realities, a listing of little items which make a room unique among all rooms in the world: A long living room with one long wall painted the hard blue of Alpine sky and kept clear of prints and paintings, with a carved blonde behemoth piano, its German knees half-bent under its oaken weight, and with a white Parsons table covered by a vivid collection of French glass paperweights.

5

I trust the reader to finish the rest of that room in his head, without making any conscious effort to do so. The furnishings will be appropriate to his past observations.

How to make an object unique? (Or where do I find the colored paper for the rooster?) Vocabulary is one half the game, and that can come only from constant, omnivorous reading, beginning very early in life. If you do not have that background, forget all about trying to write fiction. You'll save yourself brutal disappointment. The second half of the game is input. All the receptors must be wide open. You must go through the world at all times looking at the things around you. Texture, shape, style, color, pattern, movement. You must be alert to the smell, taste, sound of everything you see, and alert to the relationships between the aspects of objects, and of people. Tricks and traits and habits, deceptive and revelatory.

There are people who have eyes and cannot see. I have driven friends through country they have never seen before and have had them pay only the most cursory attention to the look of the world. Trees are trees, houses are houses, hills are hills—to them. Their inputs are all turned inward, the receptors concerned only with Self. Self is to them the only reality, the only uniqueness. Jung defines these people in terms of the "I" and the "Not I." The "I" person conceives of the world as being a stage setting for Self, to the point where he cannot believe other people are truly alive and active when they are not sharing that stage with Self. Thus nothing is real unless it has a direct and specific bearing on Self.

The writer must be a Not-I, a person who can see the independence of all realities and know that the validity of object or person can be appraised and used by different people in different ways. The writer must be the observer, the questioner. And that is why the writer should be wary of adopting planned eccentricities of appearance and behavior, since, by making himself the observed rather than the observer, he dwarfs the volume of input he must have to keep his work fresh.

Now we will assume you have the vocabulary, the trait of constant observation plus retention of the telling detail. And at this moment—if I am not taking too much credit—you have a new appraisal of the creative relationship of writer and reader. You want to begin to use it.

The most instructive thing you can do is to go back over past work, published or unpublished, and find the places where you described something at length, in an effort to make it unique and special, but somehow you did not bring it off. (I do this with my own work oftener than you might suppose.)

Now take out the subjective words. For example, I did not label the air conditioner as old, or noisy, or battered, or cheap. Those are evaluations the reader should make. Tell how a thing looks, not your evaluation of what it is from the way it looks. Do not say a man looks seedy. That is a judgment, not a description. All over the world, millions of men look seedy, each one in his own fashion. Describe a cracked lens on his glasses, a bow fixed with stained tape, tufts of hair growing out of his nostrils, an odor of old laundry.

This is a man. His name is Melvin. You built him out of scraps of bright construction paper and put him in front of the yellow oncoming truck.

The semantics of image is a special discipline. Through it you achieve a reality which not only makes the people more real, it makes the situation believable, and compounds the tension.

If a vague gray truck hits a vague gray man, his blood on gray pavement will be without color or meaning.

When a real yellow truck hits Melvin, man or rooster, we feel that mortal thud deep in some visceral place where dwells our knowledge of our own oncoming death.

You have taken the judgment words out of old descriptions and replaced them with the objective words of true description. You have taken out the things the reader can be trusted to construct for himself.

Read it over. Is there too much left, or too little? When in doubt, opt for less rather than more.

We all know about the clumsiness the beginning writer shows when he tries to move his people around, how he gets them into motion without meaning. We all did it in the beginning. Tom is in an office on one side of the city, and Mary is in an apartment on the other side. So we walked him into the elevator, out through the foyer, into a cab, all the way across town, into another foyer, up in the elevator, down the corridor to Mary's door. Because it was motion without meaning, we tried desperately to create interest with some kind of ongoing interior monologue. Later we learned that as soon as the decision to go see Mary comes to Tom, we need merely skip three spaces and have him knocking at Mary's door. The reader knows how people get across cities, and get in and out of buildings. The reader will make the instantaneous jump.

So it is with description. The reader knows a great deal. He has taste and wisdom, or he wouldn't be reading. Give him some of the vivid and specific details which you see, and you can trust him to build all the rest of the environment. Having built it himself, he will be that much more involved in what is happening, and he will cherish and relish you the more for having trusted him to share in the creative act of telling a story.

2

THREE ESSENTIALS FOR A
SUCCESSFUL WRITING CAREER

BY JOHN JAKES

TO SUCCEED, any writer must master the tools of his trade. A fiction writer, for example, must learn plot construction; how to characterize by showing instead of telling; how to write dialogue that is functional and natural at the same time; and so on.

Those are matters of craft, and fairly technical. But they are by no means the whole story. Over the years, I've become convinced that three less technical, but no less important, factors play a vital part, not to say a crucial one, in determining the long-term course of a writing career.

Since I am primarily a fiction writer, I have thought about the three factors from that point of view. But all three can apply just as easily to the writing of nonfiction, plays, or even poetry. When I speak to writers' groups, I call these factors "the three P's." By any name, I believe they spell the difference between failure and success in making the great leap from amateur ambition to a career as a part-time or full-time professional.

I. PRACTICE

Some writers prefer to have outsiders think of writing not as a skill but as some form of sorcery, forever incomprehensible to the "layman." And it's true that you can never reduce the work of a Dickens, a Zola, a Faulkner to a formula, or a list of technical do's and don'ts. There are certain forever-indefinable attitudes and abilities that set the genius apart from those of us of lesser literary ability.

Genius aside, however, the literary protectionist is wrong; writing is in part a skill, and certain technical aspects of it can be learned by any reasonably intelligent person.

Even more fundamental to success is practice. There is nothing mysterious about it, either. Writing is a lot like playing golf, or the piano. To lift yourself out of the amateur class, you must do more than dabble; and once launched, you cannot, I believe, sustain a professional career without a continuing commitment to practice.

Top golfers on the pro tour continue to practice, no matter how much money they've won. A Broadway actress with a role in a hit play continues to take acting and voice lessons in her spare time because she knows you can never do too much of what you do best. It's the same with a writer. Whether you're a beginner or a selling professional, you should write so much material, on a set schedule, every day, or every week, almost without fail.

These thoughts are by no means original. They are, in fact, re-statements of the old writing adage about the seat of the pants and the seat of the chair. To me, however, the word practice expresses that idea in a simpler and more meaningful way, because implicit in the word is an added benefit: IMPROVEMENT.

Consider golf and piano playing again. The more you do of either one, however poorly at first, the better you become. Sometimes you are not even aware of this improvement, but it's there. Thus, for a writer, practice does much more than guarantee that you will produce a certain amount of material every week or every month. It actually helps you get better at what you're doing.

Admittedly, such practice isn't always pleasant. Many times you'd probably rather be doing other, less taxing things. During the years in which our children were growing up, I set a writing schedule of 2½ to 3 hours, three nights a week. I tried to stick to that schedule regardless of the demands of my full-time job in advertising, sometimes even the demands of my family—and to do it no matter how tired I was at 7 o'clock in the evening.

Of course, if there was an important school program one night, or if someone in the family was sick, or I absolutely had to go back to the office for a couple of hours, no writing got done. But I always tried to make up for it at another time during the week.

Unless you have the determination to practice, which would improve your work consciously and through the sheer act of repetition, you do not really want to be a writer. Rather, you probably just want to be *known* as a writer. There's a vast difference between the two, and you would be better off doing something else.

II. PERSISTENCE

Beginning writers who are too easily discouraged will never achieve the big breakthrough to the professional ranks. I've known would-be writers who gave up after the third or fourth rejection of a story, never dreaming that factors *outside the material itself* sometimes influence a decision to accept or not.

This first dawned on me some years ago, when my then-agent requested a new, clean copy of a detective story I had all but forgotten. I wrote to ask what had happened to the first manuscript. Too grubby and dog-eared for further submissions, was the answer. "But we'll keep trying it at market; there's always a buyer somewhere for a salable story."

And there was. Ultimately the story wound up in a cheap pulp-paper men's magazine—just about what it deserved—and I was paid $30. The point is, I would have retired the manuscript long before the agent did. He knew the realities of publishing better than I.

Editorial tastes change, sometimes with incomprehensible rapidity; *editors* change, sometimes with even greater rapidity. Editor "A" may take an instant and illogical dislike to your material and never buy anything from you, no matter how expertly your manuscripts are put together. Then editor "A" moves on to another job, and editor "B" snaps up your first offering—the same piece editor "A" rejected twice!

That is, editor "B" snaps it up if you haven't given up on that particular publisher—even on writing itself—and have resubmitted the manuscript after noting in a writers' magazine that the name on the editorial door has changed.

You must always be dispassionate enough to understand that your material *probably* fails to click because it isn't up to professional standards—but confident enough to realize that other factors could be playing a part.

How to strike that balance? It isn't easy, and there are no rules anyone can give you. It's something you must feel. I failed again and again with given stories and novels—still do—yet I always believed the fault was in the specific piece and my handling of it; the rejection never signaled to me that I had no business trying to be a writer.

True enough, I came close to feeling that way many times; discouragement is part of every writer's emotional baggage. Offsetting that is belief in your own ability, a belief that pushes you ahead. My shorthand term for this state of constant forward movement is persistence.

11

Alas, the lesson of persistence is lost on many beginning writers—if indeed they ever hear it at all. If beginners did not give up so easily, the writing trade would be far more crowded and competitive than it is. That is a professional secret you should never forget.

So keep your faith in yourself, and don't retire a script after five rejections. Refuse to settle for anything less than six to twelve and realize even then that the sale might not come until submission number thirteen.

A final, purely personal aside. Keep your self-confidence internal, silent. Too many amateur writers (too many professionals, I might add) are basically insecure people; this inclines them toward conversation almost exclusively centered around themselves and their work. I dislike socializing with most writers because their talk tends to be little more than a tiresome variation on one theme: "I."

Avoid that sort of thing. Let others pay you the compliments. People will like you better for it, and the compliments will have some meaning.

III. PROFESSIONALISM

This is not a "do" or "don't" as much as a state of mind, an attitude toward your work.

For me, the true professional is exemplified by the playwright. Typically, in the thick of rehearsals for a new show, he is forced to edit, refocus, often completely destroy and rebuild his script because it is failing its ultimate test: It is not working on stage, and the actors, the director, and the tryout audiences keep telling him so.

In such a situation, the writer can't hide from the truth about his work. Unless he wishes to withdraw the script, he is forced to search for and confront its weaknesses, then struggle to shore them up, or eliminate them. He is professional when he chooses to do this, rather than withdraw and sulk.

Narrative writing, too, either "works" or it doesn't. The difference is, the writer of narrative material is far removed from his audience; he is cushioned from the shock of watching his material fail. This distance makes it easier for the writer to find scapegoats: The editor gave the book a bad title. The cover was terrrible. The publisher's salesmen didn't push the book hard enough. All of which may be perfectly true—or, alternatively, such excuses may represent the writer's understandable, but unprofessional, protection of his own ego.

About the only time a writer of narrative prose confronts an uncompromising "audience" is when he submits his manuscript to an editor. And if the editor expresses dissatisfaction with some or all of it, that lone opinion is more easily overridden by the writer's rationalization than are the scowls of the playwright's cast, or the snickers and coughs of his disapproving audience.

Hence, since it's easier for a narrative writer to dodge the truth, he must work twice as hard to develop a professional attitude.

I have known a lot of writers who will never realize their full potential because they haven't made the effort. Although they sell material, I wouldn't consider any of them professionals in the fullest and best sense. Most of these writers, not surprisingly, belong to the "Don't-touch-a-comma-of-mine" school.

Such an attitude is a protective device, and to some extent understandable. Publishing is a business like any other; not all people who hold jobs in it are competent. I have sat in enough publishing and advertising meetings to know that even highly intelligent, apparently reasonable men and women can come up with a great many silly, stupid, or downright harmful ideas, given the right circumstances and enough time to deliberate.

I am not suggesting that you surrender your work and your principles to any and every criticism. On the other hand, without a willingness to accept—indeed, to seek—competent advice, you are not professional. But if you are, you will usually find yourself asking silent questions about a finished piece: "What's wrong with it? How can I fix it?"

Because of the writer's inevitable psychic closeness to his work, answering the first question is often hard, if not downright impossible. Hence the professional usually asks a third question as well: "Since I feel something's wrong, but I can't find the flaw, who can?"

I've always believed that you should at all costs avoid "criticism" from well-meaning amateurs such as friends or relatives. Aunt Nell may be able to tell you that your story "doesn't interest me"—but is it because there's no narrative hook? No sympathetic protagonist? No dramatic irony? No suspense?

Aunt Nell doesn't know, and what's more, she probably couldn't care less. You're no better off than you were before you showed her the manuscript. Seek help from those qualified to give it. A good teacher.

An agent. Or, most often, an editor whose judgment you trust—and who is looking for material.

On the Kent family novels, I was blessed with two such editors, both of whom spotted numerous weak points in the manuscripts and suggested (but never dictated) ways in which these might be eliminated, with a resulting improvement of the final product. The specifics of this repair work they left to me—assuming, I imagine, that I knew the materials and techniques needed to effect them.

You begin to mature as a writer, and to deserve the name, when you not only sense something wrong in your work, but can figure out how to fix it. This didn't happen to me until I was about thirty-five—or some sixteen years after I made my first sale.

Many times during those first sixteen years, when an editor would ask for changes in a script, I panicked because I wasn't sure I knew how to bring off the requested improvements. Now I know how to strengthen motivation, develop more sympathy for a protagonist, alter the style of a character's dialogue, underplay a scene, and so on.

I don't mean I do it perfectly; I mean I am usually confident that I know how to approach a repair job, and can bring it off. Parenthetically, I might note that this is the sort of technical control you acquire through practice.

Moreover, I'm usually anxious to do the fixing. I have learned a simple lesson that eluded me for too many years. The better the writer makes his material, the better his rewards.

So cultivate an objective attitude. Ruthlessly examine your own work for deficiencies. Study acknowledged masters, or contemporaries whose writing you admire, to see how they achieve their effects.

Welcome—encourage—comments from an experienced critic whose opinions you respect, and do this no matter how painful the criticism may be. Reflect on each suggestion, weigh its merits (I have seldom if ever turned down a suggestion from a good editor), then make your plan for reworking the material, and carry it out with all the technical skills at your command.

All of this can be called professionalism. But the core of it is the objective attitude about yourself and your work. When you achieve that, you have left the ranks of the amateur forever, and you stand an excellent chance of success in your writing career.

3

FIRST, YOU ARE A SPONGE

By Roger Caras

It would be impossible to estimate the number of times I have been approached by students (and non-students) who wanted to be writers and asked, *What courses should I take?* Very often the terrifying question asked is, *How did you do it?* I find that question terrifying simply because I don't like telling strangers that indeed I haven't done "it," not yet, at least.

What do you tell people who want to be writers or at least think they do? (One is as bad as the other.) In fact, I have tried to answer their questions. I like to think that some of them may have listened.

These are the points I try to make sound like a kind of gospel. In my experience gospels generally are easier to sell than suggestions. Gospels seem to carry their own secret power. If you don't listen, look out!

1. *There is no way to become a successful writer.* Your dream is as impossible as wanting to be a senator or a movie star. It can't be done. There is no way into that sanctum of all sanctums. One hitch—if you ignore this point and really want it badly enough, you will do it despite the fact that it is impossible. In short, stop asking and start doing. The only difference between a writer and a non-writer is that the writer writes.

2. *Don't be in a hurry.* The world can wait and probably will. Impatience is understandable but seldom productive. If you want to write, be prepared to schlog. Learn your craft slowly by doing. Write.

3. *Read.* Then read some more, and more and more. Never stop reading. Early in your career, at least, read everything through even

when you know it is bad. Figure out why it is bad. Being able to toss a bad book aside after ten pages is a luxury good writers can afford. Beginners can learn as much from a poor book or article as from a good one, or almost as much.

4. *Travel.* Anywhere you can afford to go. It can be cheaper than you think, you can save up, you can get out of your normal setting and see who lives where and how. The number of would-be writers who remain fixed in a limiting atmosphere is nothing less than amazing. Learn to feel a place, learn the meaning of ambience, learn to taste and smell and touch and see and hear. Listen to voices, human voices, bird calls, wind sounds, learn to *listen*. It is one thing a lot of writers do rather poorly.

5. *Spread out.* Dilettante is not an evil word. I would rather know something about good wine, a little about erotic poetry, a fair bit about health care in South America and perhaps even some basic facts about Japanese martial arts than nothing about all of them. Learn to taste everything. Follow any lead, walk down any alley, attend every lecture for which you can find the time. Look, listen, again, listen.

In short, my advice to beginning writers, would-be writers and even writers who are doing less than they feel they should be doing is the same: Be a sponge. First you are a sponge. You have to soak up the world. When it comes time, wring yourself out on paper. But, you can't wring out a dry sponge. It has to soak "it" up before it can release "it." *It* being everything, anything, all things worth the writer's and the reader's time.

So, back to the initial question: What courses would I take? If I were starting school over again and could design a curriculum for myself, this would be the kind of program I would try for:

History: American (in depth), African, Russian, and English; as many courses as possible in the history of science; histories of the Blacks and Asians in America, and the American Indian; the Second World War, the Roman Republic and the Roman Empire.
Literature: English and American, as much as possible.
Social science: Basics of physical and cultural anthropology, archaeology, ethnology, abnormal psychology, criminology, physical and political geography.
The urban scene: City planning and urban problems, public health and health care problems.

Science: The human body, comparative zoology, botany, forensic medicine.
The arts: The history of film, theater arts, broadcasting, acting technique.
Basic skills: Spelling, punctuation, grammar, typing (and changing ribbons!).

(It's never too late: Most of these courses are available in adult education and university extension programs.)

I've probably left out a few things; any of the courses suggested (except the last) might trigger a reflex for hot pursuit. That urge should never be suppressed. A writer should always go where his or her curiosity leads. One *starts* as a dilettante, one should not remain one. Early in the sponge stage there will be foci. They are not to be denied.

My remarks may seem to take this question of how writers should train themselves with less seriousness than the subject calls for, but in fact that is not so. I really do believe that the pyramidal shape of education today is hazardous for writers; it is not good for their intellectual or financial health. Explain that pyramid? O.K.

We start off in nursery school and there is nothing we do not want our teachers to tell us about. As pre-readers we are interested in stories about everything and anything.

In kindergarten it is pretty much the same. All through grammar school, in fact, we remain curious little animals. A visit to a warehouse, a factory (heaven only knows), a kennel, a museum of any description, all of it is rich and wonderful.

But, then comes junior and senior high school. We are beginning to focus more narrowly. No more kid stuff like curiosity. Now it is academics! We have to get into college. There is pressure to set aside hobbies like music and baseball in favor of French, although French will probably have a great deal less to do with our future than either music or baseball.

And then we go to college—with a major. We find less and less time for electives. Between required courses and glandular disturbances, our pyramid is coming to a point. There is too little time to be curious, except about our own libidos. All through our educational experience, we have come to know more and more about less and less. But, what happened to curiosity? It was phased out, not allowed for, and if that isn't the death of good writing, what in heaven's name could be? We live, think and speak jargon. Creativity has become a waste of time.

And so, again, my advice has always been, first you are a sponge, and if the gods are good, you will remain a sponge until the day you die.

A writer should listen until the end and never stop wondering about most of the things he hears. When a writer stops listening, stops learning, cashes in his or her curiosity, the good days have passed. It is all hack work from there on or, worse yet, rote.

4

OUTSIDE THE IVORY TOWER

A Letter to a Young Writer

By B. J. Chute

My dear, discouraged, young friend: Thank you for your letter. I am delighted that your new story is going well, that the characters are clear in your mind, the narrative on the move and the prose marching with it. However, I am not delighted that your next sentence begins with a large BUT.

"But," you say, "I am feeling very discouraged. The manuscripts are piling up, and, although I send them out faithfully, they come back just as faithfully. I shall never feel like a writer until one of my stories is accepted, and I have sold *nothing*. Am I," you ask dejectedly, "living in an ivory tower?"

My first impulse was to write you a letter of warm sympathy—there, there, of course you're depressed, who wouldn't be? My second impulse was to write you a letter of warm encouragement—hang in there, patience and fortitude, remember that the darkest hour is just before the editor dawns. But my third impulse is to offer neither pats nor pep talks but some practical advice. And, also, I shall offer a warning.

I have been a professional writer for more than fifty years. I have published fourteen books and hundreds of short stories. Almost everything I have written has eventually appeared in print, but often only after many rejections. My work has been paid for, but sometimes as little as ten dollars. It has appeared in book form and in magazines, on radio and TV, and once on Broadway. Sometimes I have been blessed with a wide audience, but sometimes my public appears to consist of one lighthouse-keeper and his pet goldfish.

However, let us agree that I have had a modestly successful career. To an unpublished writer like you, it may seem very successful; to a blockbuster bestseller, very modest indeed. To me? A successful career, and this is why.

19

What I mean by success is: *The freedom to write what I want to write in the way I want to write it.*

I think this is what you mean, too. I don't think you want a writing career because you believe that fame and fortune lie at the end of the rainbow. Fame and fortune are perfectly good things, and some splendid writers have pursued them without sacrificing quality, but obviously you can't count on their arrival. And, at the moment, you are feeling that not only is your footing on the bottom rung of the success-ladder very precarious but also that the entire ladder may be about to slip out from under you. So you ask dejectedly, "Am I living in an ivory tower?"

And my answer is, "Of course you are! That's where you belong."

A writer's ivory tower is the place where he is free to do his writing. Far from being an escape from the "real" world, it *is* the writer's real world, the place where he puts his words on paper. It is by these words that a writer ultimately stands or falls—published or unpublished, paid for or not paid for, recognized or unknown.

A serious writer (and *serious* does not mean *solemn*—ask P. G. Wodehouse or Geoffrey Chaucer) is simply a writer who takes his work as seriously as he takes himself, and perhaps even more so. He also takes his ivory tower seriously, because all his writing equipment is inside its ivory walls.

Basically, this equipment consists of three essentials. Number One, obviously, is creative ability, a broad term which ranges from a small talent to a great genius. Number Two is the alphabet. It is awesome to realize that *Hamlet* was composed from twenty-six letters which form all those words that Shakespeare arranged and rearranged until they fell gloriously into the shape of a man and his world. Number Three combines the first two and puts them into visible form—stone, parchment, paper; chisel, pen, typewriter, word processor—whatever method the writer uses to fasten down his words so that they can be read.

Now, as a writer, you already have these three essentials, and they are available to you at all times. Your creative ability made you write your stories in the first place. The alphabet has been yours from childhood, and it is not only a miracle, it is a portable miracle. And the physical tools of your craft are easy to come by, and they build the bridge between the writer and the "real" world.

20

At this point, I shall drop the quotation marks around the word *real,* because the world inside the ivory tower and the world outside it are both real. Your problem is not to choose between them but to learn to live in both, to maintain the realities of the ivory tower (the freedom to write what you want to write in the way you want to write it) and, at the same time, to cope with the realities of daily living.

For a writer, there are always plenty of realities to cope with—lack of money, lack of time, rejections, personal problems, and many, many more. Every professional struggles with these at one time or another and sometimes with all of them at once, but somehow most professionals find a way to cope. Unhappily, too many would-be writers give up early, too discouraged to keep on fighting.

Someone once said that discouragement is the only weapon the Devil needs, and I agree wholeheartedly. It can be paralyzing. But you are young, energetic and talented, and the problems you face now should be challenges, not threats. You should not be asking, "Am I living in an ivory tower?" You should be asking, "Since the ivory tower is where I do my writing, how can I maintain it?"

Well, the first thing you have to accept is that, with ivory towers as with so many things, it isn't the initial cost, it's the upkeep. The chinks in the walls let in drafts, the turrets are in constant need of repair, the drawbridge has to be oiled, and the moat goes dry. The ceilings fall, and the taxes rise. But it is the home of your writing, and you are the one who will have to defend it.

If money is a problem, find a way to support your habit. Most writers do not make a living from their writing, and you probably will not, or at least not for some time. My own income has always borne a marked resemblance to a yo-yo, and in some years I have had no income from writing at all.

If time is a problem, plan to write in the early mornings, late at night, on weekends, on park benches, buses, subways. I wrote my first two books and dozens of short stories in the ten years, right after graduation from high school, when I was employed as a full-time secretary.

As to rejections, recognize the simple fact that all writers get them. The only difference is that, for an established writer, the rejections come live in the form of an editor's personal regrets, instead of canned with a postage stamp on them. I am still having manuscripts rejected, and I expect I always will. So what's new?

21

As to the personal problems—the unavoidable interruptions, the domestic crises, the worries and troubles—everyone has them, including librarians and truck drivers, politicians and parents. The only way to deal with them is to put first things first, and sometimes the writing will have to give way temporarily to other priorities. Endure this as gracefully and as patiently as possible, and remember that your ivory tower will wait for your return.

All these ways of coping are merely ways of defending your work, and I think that, even when you are most discouraged, you really know that if you hold fast, you will come through. The best practical advice I can offer you then is summed up in a very old-fashioned injunction: *Persevere.* If the Devil's weapon is discouragement, the writer's weapon is steadfastness.

However, I told you at the beginning of this letter that, besides advice, I would offer a warning. In your own letter, just before you asked if you were living in an ivory tower, you made a statement which may have seemed reasonable to you but which is actually very foolish indeed. You said, "I shall never feel like a writer until one of my stories is accepted."

Nonsense! What does it matter whether you feel like a writer or not? Does the story that is now in your typewriter care about whether you are lunching with an editor, being interviewed on TV, or opening a stack of fan mail? Does it even care about whether it gets printed? No, it does not.

Writing well is hard enough without cluttering the ivory tower with personal ambition. There is nothing wrong with ambition, with the natural human desire to be recognized and appreciated, but the ivory tower is not the place for it, and it will only interfere with your work. Remember that it is the words on the paper that matter, and you will have to put them there with all the craft and patience and intelligence and care and love that you can summon up. When you have those words on paper in such a way that you have created real people, painted real landscapes, roused real emotions, pinned life down on the stage of your blank piece of paper, then—oh, then!—you will feel like a writer. When you have done that, a hundred rejections will make no difference, nor will a hundred acceptances.

More writing careers fail from lack of the writer's own support than from lack of public or editorial support. And that is why you must find all the ways possible to keep your work free inside the tower and to guard it outside. You will need money to pay the upkeep and to buy time. You will need time to do the work right, time to experiment, time to tear up the pages and throw them away and start all over again if you have to. Most of all, through your whole career, you will need time to learn your craft (and I hope, someday, it will be your art). Right now, you have a lot to learn, and you will never stop learning.

Inside the ivory tower, only the writing matters. Time enough and space enough outside its walls for all the so-called rewards of success. It is not that these are not to be enjoyed when they come; it is that they probably will not (and certainly should not) come until the work is done and done right. Curiously enough, when they do come, you may find that they are not as rewarding as you thought they would be. You may find yourself eager only to get on with the next ivory-tower job. That eagerness can be the greatest pleasure of all.

Does my advice to you seem too idealistic to be useful? Am I offering directives from an ivory tower? I hope so. Let me give the last word to a brilliant playwright who had more than his share of struggle in both the world of the ivory tower and the world outside. Tennessee Williams said once, in an interview, "The only honor that can be conferred on a writer is a good morning's work."

The ivory tower rests its case.

5

NOTES FOR A YOUNG WRITER

By Shirley Jackson

IN THE country of the story, the writer is king. He makes all the rules, with only the reservation that he must not ask more than a reader can reasonably grant. Remember, the reader is a very tough customer indeed, stubborn, dragging his feet, easily irritated. He will willingly agree to suspend disbelief for a time: he will go along with you if it is necessary for your story that you both assume temporarily that there really is a Land of Oz, but he will not suspend reason, he will not agree, for any story ever written, that he can see the Land of Oz from his window.

You would do well to picture your typical reader as someone lying in a hammock on a soft summer day, with children playing loudly near by, a television set and a radio both going at once, a sound truck blaring past in the street, birds singing and dogs barking. All you have to do with your story is catch his attention and hold it. Your story is an uneasy bargain with your reader. Your end of the bargain is to play fair and keep him interested; his end of the bargain is to keep reading. It is terribly easy to put a story down half-read and go off and do something else. Nevertheless, for as long as the story does go on, you are the boss. You have the right to assume that the reader will accept the story on your own terms. You have the right to assume that the reader, however lazy, will exert some small intelligence while he is reading. Suppose you are writing a story about a castle. You do not need to describe every tower, every man at arms, every stone; your reader must bring his own complement of men at arms and towers; you need only describe one gardener to imply that the castle is well stocked with servants. In your stories, then, set your own landscape with its own horizons, put your characters in where you think they belong, and move them as you please.

24

Your story must have a surface tension, which can be considerably stretched but not shattered; you cannot break your story into pieces with jagged odds and ends that do not belong. You cannot begin a story in one time and place, say, and then intrude a major flashback or a little sermon or a shift in emphasis to another scene or another character, without seriously marring the story, and turning the reader dizzy with trying to keep up. Consider simple movement from one place to another; if some movement is necessary and inevitable—as of course it is in most stories—then let the reader come along with you; do not jolt him abruptly from one place to another; in other words, let your story move as naturally and easily as possible, without side trips into unnecessary spots of beauty. Suppose you are writing a story about a boy and a girl meeting on a corner; your reader wants to go to that very corner and listen in; if, instead, you start your boy and girl toward the corner and then go off into a long description, you will lose your reader and your story will fall apart. Always, always, make the duller parts of your story work *for* you; the necessary passage of time, the necessary movement must not stop the story dead, but must push it forward.

Avoid small, graceless movements. As much as possible, free yourself from useless and clumsy statements about action. "They got in the car and drove home" is surely too much ground to cover in one short simple sentence; assuming that your characters did get into the car and did have to drive home, you have wasted a point where your action might work for your story; let the process of their getting home be an unobtrusive factor in another, more important action: "On their way home in the car they saw that the boy and the girl were still standing talking earnestly on the corner." Let each such potentially awkward spot contribute to your total action. In almost every story you will face some unwanted element, something your characters *have* to do to keep the story going at all; people have to get from one place to another, or get dressed, or eat their dinners, before the story can continue; try always to make these actions positive. For instance: "She dealt the cards; her fingers clung to each card as though unwilling to let go of anything they had once touched," or, "During all of dinner, the singing went on upstairs, and no one said a word." (I would like to see someone write that story.)

In every story there comes a time when you have to let your reader know what something looks like, or that your hero and heroine said good-morning-how-are-you-today-isn't-the-weather-lovely-how's-your-mother before they got on to the most important business of the story. With description, you must never just let it lie there; nothing in your story should ever be static unless you have a very good reason indeed for keeping your reader still; the essence of the story is motion. Do not let your chair be "a straight chair, with no arms and a hard wooden seat." Let your heroine go over and take a firm hold of the back of a straight wooden chair, because at the moment it is stronger than she. Naturally, it is assumed that you are not going to try to describe anything you don't need to describe. If it is a sunny day let the sun make a pattern through the fence rail; if you don't care what the weather is, don't bother your reader with it. Inanimate objects are best described in use or motion: "Because his cigarette lighter was platinum, he had taken to smoking far too much."

Conversation is one of the most difficult parts of the story. It is not enough to let your characters talk as people usually talk, because the way people usually talk is extremely dull. Your characters are not going to stammer, or fumble for words, or forget what they are saying, or stop to clear their throats, at least not unless you want them to. Your problem is to make your characters sound as though they were real people talking (or, more accurately, that this is "real" conversation being read by a reader; look at some written conversation that seems perfectly smooth and plausible and natural on the page, and then try reading it aloud; what looks right on the page frequently sounds very literary indeed when read aloud; remember that you are writing to be read silently). The sounds and cadences of spoken speech are perfectly familiar to you; you have been talking and listening all your life. Most people speak in short sentences, tending to overuse certain words. Whenever anyone gets the floor and a chance to tell a story or describe an incident, he will almost always speak in a series of short sentences joined by "and"; this is of course a device to insure that his audience will have no chance to break in before he has finished his story. In a conversation, people do say the same things over and over; there is very little economy in spoken speech. There is a great deal of economy in written speech. Your characters will use short sentences, and will tell long stories only under exceptional circumstances, and even then only in the most carefully stylized and rhythmic language; nothing can dissolve a short story quite so effectively as some bore who takes up

26

the middle of it with a long account of something that amuses him and no one else. A bore is a bore, on the page or off it.

Listen always to people talking. Listen to patterns of talking. Listen to patterns of thinking displayed in talking. Think about this: If a husband comes home at night and says to his wife, "What do you think happened to me? When I got onto the bus tonight I sat down next to a girl and when the conductor came along he had a live penguin riding on his head, a live penguin, can you imagine? And when I looked at it, it turned out it was a talking penguin and it said 'Tickets, please,' and there was this guy across the aisle and you really won't believe this but it turned out *he* had a parrot in his pocket and the parrot put out his head and he and the penguin got to talking and I never heard anything like it in my life," don't you know that after the husband has said all this his wife is going to say, "What did the girl look like?" Your characters will make their remarks only once unless there is a good reason for repeating them; people hear better in stories than in real life. Your characters will start all their conversations in the middle, unless you have a very good reason for their telling each other good morning and how are you. Remember the importance of the pattern, as important on paper as in real life; a character who says habitually, with one of those silly little laughs, "Well, that's the story of my life," is not ever going to turn around and say, with a silly little laugh, "Well, that's my life story."

Look at this device: " 'I hate fresh asparagus,' she said to her kitchen clock, and found herself saying it again ten minutes later to Mrs. Butler in the grocery; 'I hate fresh asparagus,' she said, 'it always takes so long to cook.' " You are, at this moment, well into a conversation with Mrs. Butler. Your reader, being a common-sense type, no doubt assumes that before the remark about asparagus, your heroine and Mrs. Butler said good-morning-my-aren't-you-out-early-and-isn't-that-a-charming-hat. Your reader may also assume, if he is perceptive, that your heroine in some fashion turned away from her kitchen clock, got her hat and coat on, picked up her pocketbook, forgot her shopping list, and in some fashion either walked or drove or bicycled to the store. She is there, she is in the middle of a conversation with Mrs. Butler; not ten words ago she was at home talking to the clock. The transition has been relatively painless; your reader has been required to read only one sentence and get around one semicolon, and the asparagus remark has been repeated simply to tie together the two halves of the sentence.

Your characters in the story, surely, are going to be separate and widely differing people, even though they are not necessarily described to the reader. You yourself have some idea of what they are like and how they differ; there is, for instance, in almost everyone's mind, an essential difference between the hero and the heroine. They don't look alike, even if you are the only one who knows it; your reader will assume it; after all, he has seen people before. They don't dress alike, they don't sound alike. They have small individualities of speech, arising naturally out of their actions and their personalities and their work in the story.

Use all your seasoning sparingly. Do not worry about making your characters shout, intone, exclaim, remark, shriek, reason, holler, or any such thing, unless they are doing it for a reason. All remarks can be *said*. Every time you use a fancy word your reader is going to turn his head to look at it going by and sometimes he may not turn his head back again. My own name for this kind of overexcited talking is the-other-responded. As in this example: " 'Then I'm for a swim,' cried Jack, a gallant flush mantling his cheek. 'And I am with you!' the other responded."

Your coloring words, particularly adjectives and adverbs, must be used where they will do the most good. Not every action needs a qualifying adverb, not every object needs a qualifying adjective. Your reader probably has a perfectly serviceable mental picture of a lion; when a lion comes into your story you need not burden him with adjectives unless it is necessary, for instance, to point out that he is a green lion, something of which your reader might not have a very vivid mental picture.

Someone—I forget who—once referred to the easier sections of his work as "benches for the reader to sit down upon," meaning, of course, that the poor reader who had struggled through the complex maze of ideas for several pages could rest gratefully at last on a simple clear paragraph. Provide *your* reader with such assistance. If you would like him to rest for a minute so you can sneak up behind him and sandbag him, let him have a little peaceful description, or perhaps a little something funny to smile over, or a little moment of superiority. If you want him to stop dead and think, do something that will make him stop dead;

use a wholly inappropriate word, or a startling phrase—"pretty as a skunk"—or an odd juxtaposition: "Her hair was curly and red and she had great big feet." Give him something to worry about: "Although the bank had stood on that corner for fifty years it had never been robbed." Or something to figure out: "If John had not had all that tooth trouble there would never have been any question about the rabbits." In all this, though, don't let the reader stop for more than a second or he might get away. Catch him fast with your next sentence and send him reeling along.

And if you want your reader to go faster and faster make your writing go faster and faster. "The room was dark. The windows were shaded, the furniture invisible. The door was shut and yet from somewhere, some small, hidden, precious casket of light buried deep in the darkness of the room, a spark came, moving in mad colored circles up and down, around and in and out and over and under and lighting everything it saw." (Those adjectives are unspeakable in every sense of the word, and wholly unnecessary; this is an example, not a model.) If you want your reader to go slower make your writing go slower and slower: "After a wild rush of water and noise the fountain was at last turned off and the water was gone. Only one drop hung poised and then fell, and fell with a small musical touch. Now, it rang. Now."

Remember, too, that words on a page have several dimensions: they are seen, they are partially heard, particularly if they seem to suggest a sound and they have a kind of tangible quality—think of the depressing sight of a whole great paragraph ahead of you, solidly black with huge heavy-sounding words. Moreover, some words seem soft and some hard, some liquid, some warm, some cold; your reader will respond to "soft laughter" but not to "striped laughter"; he will respond more readily to "soft laughter" than to "sweet laughter," because he can hear it more easily. There are also words like "itchy" and "greasy" and "smelly" and "scratchy" that evoke an almost physical response in the reader; use these only if you need them. Exclamation points, italics, capitals, and, most particularly, dialect, should all be used with extreme caution. Consider them like garlic, and use them accordingly.

If you keep your story tight, with no swerving from the proper path, it will curl up quite naturally at the end, provided you stop when you have finished what you have to say. One device is beginning and ending on what is essentially the same image, so that a story beginning, say,

"It was a beautiful sunny day," might end, "The sun continued to beat down on the empty street." This is not a bad policy, although it can be limiting. There is no question but that the taut stretched quality of the good short story is pulled even tighter by such a construction. You can tie your story together, however, with similar devices—how about a story which opens on a lady feeding her cat, and ends on a family sitting down to dinner? Or a story which opens on your heroine crying and closes on her laughing? The beginning and ending should belong together; the ending must be implicit in the beginning, although there have been stories which were defeated because the author thought of a wonderful last line and then tried to write a story to go with it; this is not wrong, just almost impossible.

I am not going to try to tell you how to set up a plot. Just remember that primarily, in the story and out of it, you are living in a world of people. A story must have characters in it; work with concrete rather than abstract nouns, and always dress your ideas immediately. Suppose you want to write a story about what you might vaguely think of as "magic." You will be hopelessly lost, wandering around formlessly in notions of magic and incantations; you will never make any forward progress at all until you turn your idea, "magic," into a person, someone who wants to do or make or change or act in some way. Once you have your first character you will of course need another to put into opposition, a person in some sense "anti-magic"; when both are working at their separate intentions, dragging in other characters as needed, you are well into your story. All you have to do then is write it, paying attention, please, to grammar and punctuation.

6

EXPLORE YOUR OWN WORLD

By Sloan Wilson

Long ago, when I was about nineteen years old, a professor of philosophy at Harvard shouted these words at me: "You have no imagination and you can create nothing!" At the time, I thought him, to say the least, unkind, and I hotly denied the charge in front of the whole class. With a smile, the professor told me to go to a blackboard and draw an imaginary beast.

The beast I concocted had the head of the professor, more or less, the body of a pig, the wings of an eagle, the tail of a fish and the legs of a deer. The students giggled, but the professor regarded it with mild disdain.

"You see," he said, "you have imagined nothing and you have created nothing. All you have done is to take parts you have observed and rearranged them. Don't feel bad about it. That's all anyone can do. Only God creates. Man rearranges."

That is one of the very few pieces of wisdom I remember from my four years at Harvard — besides the fact that one shouldn't call a dinner coat a tuxedo, and it's all right to wear a soft shirt with it. When I teach classes in creative writing, I usually start by pointing out that only God creates — man rearranges. The religious people like it, but very few understand what I'm trying to get at.

What I'm trying to say is that writers really have nothing with which to work but their own experience, their own memories. That is their clay, their plaster of Paris, their block of marble. Unlike sculptors, writers can find no more modern material from which to fashion their work.

Now, as soon as I say this, several pupils challenge me. They point out that Stephen Crane wrote a great war novel without going to war. They ask what Tarzan is, if not a work of the imagination. What about science fiction? What about historical novels and other books based on research? What about detective stories, which usually are written by people

31

who have never worked as a detective or tried to solve an actual murder?

If there is an exception to the philosopher's rule, it is probably Crane's *The Red Badge of Courage.* Consider, however, the fact that Crane grew up in the generation that immediately followed the Civil War and in a small town where that conflict was still the central topic of conversation. From early childhood, he breathed in the war — not only the relevant facts, but also the emotions. Although his material was secondhand, it was as close to firsthand as he could get.

In a sense, Crane did a disservice to thousands of would-be writers who followed him. Whenever a youngster who has never heard a shot fired in anger, or even at a target range, tries to write about war, he uses Crane as license. In desperation, I finally asked a student trying to write about the Spanish Revolution what kind of canteens the soldiers used. Were they aluminum, steel, leather, or what? Did the caps screw on or were they corks?

The young woman did not know. My point is that Stephen Crane did know everything about the equipment of Civil War soldiers. That may not be important, but if a writer does not know the outside of his characters, he doesn't inspire the reader with much faith in his knowledge of the inside.

About the other so-called exceptions to the philosopher's rule, I have two answers. Daydreams can become as much a part of a person as memories. Tarzan is every little boy's fantasy, every puny man's impossible dream. Edgar Rice Burroughs' un-African Africa exists under almost everyone's hat. I doubt very much that Burroughs just imagined Tarzan, created him for money. The components had been observed, but the inspired combination itself may have been a memory of youth as valid as memories of riding no-hands on a bicycle. The strength of Tarzan, which has made him last far longer than books dearer to the hearts of the critics, is that he is as recognizable as an old friend to every generation of boys who discover him. In a way, we are all authors of Tarzan. He is what we thought about when we were supposed to be doing our arithmetic.

About the other kinds of book I mentioned — historical novels, science fiction, detective stories — I can say that the trappings may be borrowed from research, but the author is still in there, walking around in his funny clothes. If his idea of history is one bedroom scene after another, with plenty of beheadings at the proper dates, he has given us,

32

perhaps, more of his personality than he knows, more of his own day-dreams. The characters from outer space in science fiction act out dreams that are remarkably human. Some detective stories are little more than puzzles, but the best of them superimpose that game on a believable background peopled by many interesting characters. I enjoy the dozens of detective stories by John D. MacDonald because better than anyone else he write about parts of Florida that I know well. He, of course, lives there.

Writers whose stories always have a large element of sadism may be meek little men who would not step on a bug, but I doubt whether they created sadistic emotions without ever feeling them. Not everyone can make a sadistic scene convincing, no matter how profitable it might be. Writers are often engaged in more interior reporting than they like to admit.

Although some novels don't fit easily into the theory that literature is based on experience, this does not disprove the theory. My own feeling is that the more directly it comes from the wellspring of the author's life, the better the book. Melville did, after all, go whaling. Faulkner did not write about the Deep South from the vantage point of Newark, New Jersey, and Fitzgerald was not married to a fat, ugly woman who spent her life trying to be elected chairman of the Connecticut PTA. In their dramas, they gave us themselves, their own histories, their own excitement, their own heartbreaks, their own vision of life.

Hemingway is perhaps a little different. He gave us his exuberance, his machismo, his grace under pressure, all right. He was what millions wanted to be, a sort of thinking man's Tarzan. Perhaps his tragedy was that he could not wrestle in public with the demons that killed him. That might have made his best book.

It is perhaps necessary to emphasize here that when I talk about writing from memory, I mean remembered emotions much more than remembered backgrounds, and the characters of one's personal story who elicited the strongest emotions.

My friend, Robert Newton Peck, had written many good books when he began *A Day No Pigs Would Die,* but none as moving as that account of the death of a pig butcher in Vermont. Because he had lived in Vermont, the author had all the details of rural life at his fingertips. Beyond that, he had been intensely devoted to his own father, and, when he started to write from the son's point of view about a pig butcher trying to get through hard times on a hard-scrabble farm, his pen took off. In writing with such honest love about a father, the author reversed the stereotype we see so much these days about sons who hate their fathers. The reason the story is so poignant, however, is that it's just as much a part of Peck's living flesh as his strong right hand. He didn't just sit down and make it up.

When I say that most good books are based on remembered emotion and experience, I do not mean, of course, that one would have a great novel if only one could keep a tape recorder at hand from childhood on. The fact that art is based on experience does not mean it is the same thing. A blob of clay is not considered a statue in even the most *avant-garde* museums. A novel is, of course, a drastic condensation of life. Unlike some lives, it must be given form — a climax somewhere before the end.

The morality that must be applied to a novel is much stricter than the one many people apply to their lives. You may suffer from racial prejudice, bitterness, and chronic depression. You can have people in your books who reflect these attitudes, but that is very different from writing a novel that in its total effect is anti-black and depressive.

There is probably much more boredom, tedium, and depression in most lives than would be tolerated in books. Perhaps all art must in some sense elate, even be a little manic. The dancer does not go onstage looking glum, and though a singer may sing doleful songs, she usually manages to smile between numbers. People want an emotional charge from art. If the writer is not "charged," it is perhaps wise for him to wait for a better day before sitting down at the typewriter.

When students of writing accept the fact that most good novels are based on experience, many of them still hesitate to try turning their own lives into fiction. One of the diseases of youth is the conviction that one's own life is far less glamorous than that of anyone else. The late Kenneth P. Kempton, in my opinion the best teacher of writing that Harvard ever had, used to complain that all his rich students wanted to write about the dramas of the slums, while all the scholarship students were trying to write about high society. Endless battle scenes were penned by those who reached maturity between wars, and fuzzy-chinned virgins wrote sex scenes so explicit they needed only diagrams to become manuals. Kempton tried to get us to respect our own backgrounds enough to write about them. All backgrounds, of course, have dramatic potential.

Another reason some people are afraid of using their memories in writing their novels is the fear of hurting the people from their past or present. But this can be avoided, if writers become adept at disguising the real people who have suggested their fictional characters. A shift in geographical location, altered physical characteristics, and a change of name can do wonders.

It also is wise to remember that a writer's view of the past is much more subjective than he may think. If he has hated a man named Mike all his life, Mike may not even recognize the portrait of himself as an ogre, nor will many of Mike's friends. Our idea of people is shaped by how they treated us, and they may have treated others quite differently. This, more than the laws of libel, is reason for presenting our views of people as fiction, rather than as objective truth. This is why no author likes to be asked on what "actual people" he has based his fictional characters. He has drawn them from personal memories that in their original form could not be sold.

Another reason many writers don't want to base a novel on personal experience is sheer humility, too much modesty. Isn't the guy in the bar who tries to unload his life history on the other patrons a classic bore?

Yes — but not because he is trying to give you his life story. These talkers are bores because they lie about themselves, making themselves the downtrodden heroes of every encounter. Anyone who tries to tell the truth about himself is interesting. The land of truth, of course, is dangerous territory, where only the brave dare to tread. How wrong and how right was I, the author must ask himself, in recalling any dispute, from a divorce to a business blowup? The writer who must constantly portray himself or herself as a moral winner, or who resorts constantly to *mea culpa,* had better stick to writing fantasy.

Nobody said writing is easy, and it isn't all that typing that is so hard. Attempting to write a fair portrait of one's mother can be as harrowing as psychoanalysis. Trying to get oneself into perspective as a young man on the make, or as a none-too-brave soldier, can rip away all kinds of protective curtains that we have dropped to shield ourselves from the past.

If a writer does this job well, he can be sure of an audience. People hunger to know the truth about each other. In America we are brought up to respect the idea that each of us is unique. In one way that's true, of course, but it obscures the equally important fact that we are all brothers, not so different from one another as we sometimes think. I have written eleven books, all of which are taken from my own experiences, but it is surprising how often people write to say, "How did you know so much about *me*?" We are all grains of sand on the same beach, and this makes novels based on personal experience a legitimate kind of geological research. Some people study mountains, but those who study a grain of sand may end up knowing more about the essential makeup of the continent.

Some students are afraid they will run out of autobiographical material. Writers do dry up, but lack of personal experience is not the reason. The loss of excitement about life can strike any writer dead. If he retains his capacity for elation, he will find that the older he gets, the more his perceptions of his past keep changing. I did not imagine my own life, and I did not create it, but my mind can now rearrange all the parts of the puzzle in ways beyond the comprehension of my younger selves.

Finally, of course, a writer must be an egotist, but a good writer is too egotistical and too skillful to allow himself to appear that way on paper. The writer's false cloak of charming modesty is one deceit that is permitted!

7

THE PROLIFIC WRITER

By Isaac Asimov

There are grave disadvantages to being a prolific writer and if you are seriously interested in writing, it may very well be that prolificity is the last thing you want.

To be prolific means that you must be able to write quickly, facilely, and without much concern as to what improvements you might possibly introduce if you took enough time. That is precisely what you *don't* want to do if your interest is in writing well.

To write quickly and to write well are usually incompatible attributes, and if you must choose one or the other, you should choose quality over speed every time.

But suppose you do write pretty well. Isn't it possible to write quickly and easily, *too?* Surely, it is legitimate to dream of that. Any writer who has perspired his way through some bit of creation, who has worked his way through endless crossing-outs and crumplings, and who has ended uncertainly with something whose virtues seem to dim perceptibly as he gives it a final reading, must wonder what it might feel like to dash something off between yawns, so to speak, and have it read perfectly well.

Not only will a mind-wrenching job then become simple, but you will be able to turn out many more items, charge for each one, and improve your bank balance enormously.

What do you need to achieve that?

1) You have to like to write.

Without that, everything else falls to the ground, and you will have to seek other daydreams. Prolificity isn't for you.

Mind you, I don't say you must have the urge to write or the deep ambition to write. That is not enough. Everyone who tries to write must obviously have the urge and the ambition to do so, and everyone would just love to have a finished manuscript on the desk.

What about the in-between, though? What about the actual mechanical process of scribbling on paper, or beating on typewriter keys, or speaking into a mouthpiece? If that is just an agonizing intermediate between the original urge and the final ecstasy, then you may be a good writer, you may even be a writer of genius — but you will never be a prolific writer. No one could stand that much agony.

No, the very act of turning it out must be actively pleasurable.

2) You must not like much of anything else *but* writing.

After all, most of us are constantly torn between desires, but for the writer who wants to be prolific, there should be no room for doubt. It's writing you must want to be doing, not anything else.

If you look out at one of those perfect days, when all nature is smiling and calling to you to get out there and enjoy life, and you say, "Oh, hell, I'll write tomorrow," then abandon all dreams of prolificity.

If you can look out at such a day and feel a sudden pang of apprehension that some loved one is going to come over and say, "What a perfect time for a pleasant walk" or "What a perfect time to go out and do thus-and-so!" then there's hope for you. (Frankly, what I do is keep the shades down at all times and pretend there's a blizzard outside.)

3) You have to have self-assurance.

If your sentences never seem perfect to you and if you are never happy unless you have revised and revised and revised until the sentence disappears altogether under the weight of erasures and interlineations, or until you have restored it full-circle to what it was originally, then how can you hope to be prolific?

You may ask, "But what if the sentence isn't good? I can't just leave it, can I?"

Of course not, but the assumption here is that you're a reasonably good writer to begin with and that it's your dream to be prolific, also. As a reasonably good writer, you have undoubtedly written a reasonably good sentence, so let it go. Once you are finished with the piece, you can go over it and change anything that really *needs* changing, and then type the whole thing to get clean copy. But then, that's it.

Remember, change only what *needs* changing. You must cultivate an active dislike for changing and never do it without a sigh of regret.

Undoubtedly, you have read over and over again that there is no such thing as writing, only rewriting; that it's the polish that does it. Sure, but that's if you want to be a *great* writer. We're talking prolific here.

4) Never lose time.

You can replace money, if you lose a wallet. You can buy a new type-writer, if your apartment is ransacked. You can marry again, if a divorce overtakes you. But that minute that has vanished unnecessarily will never come back, and what's more, it was the best minute you will ever have, for all future minutes will come when you are older and more nearly worn out.

There are a variety of ways of saving time and every prolific writer chooses his own. Some become completely asocial, tearing the phone out of the wall and never answering mail. Some establish a family member as dragon to stand between themselves and the world. Some turn off their senses and learn to write while activity swirls all about them.

My own system is to do everything myself. I have no assistants, no secretaries, no typists, no researchers, no agents, no business managers. My theory is that all such people waste your time. In the time it takes to explain what you want, to check what they do, to point out where they did it wrong — you can do at least three times as much by yourself.

So there you are. If you want to be a prolific writer, you have to be a single-minded, driven, nonstop person. — Sounds horrible, doesn't it?

Well, then, concentrate on being a *good* writer, and leave prolific for those poor souls who can't help it.

8

OWED TO THE PUBLIC LIBRARY

By Lesley Conger

YESTERDAY I fell in love with the public library all over again.

It was a mild, sweet day, not bright, not gloomy; faintly misty, but not wet. A perfect day, really. And because I had had an errand elsewhere, I approached the library from a direction I don't ordinarily use. It was like seeing a familiar, beloved face in a new and enchanting light. WALK, the traffic signal commanded me, but I stood bemused on the curb, just looking, until I found myself disobeying WAIT and loping across as the red turned green.

It's a middle-aged building, our library, rose brick and gray stone, built in a style that reminds me of some children's blocks I must have had when I was small, the kind that came with doors and windows and chimneys and arches. Georgian, Colonial? I don't know enough about architecture to tell you. But it's a lovely building, with tall windows arched at their tops, and broad stone steps leading up to the doors.

I usually take those steps two at a time. But yesterday I hesitated, and then I walked around the block. There are large elms lining the street, and on the inner edge of the sidewalk, a low concrete balustrade with a rail of the perfect width for young wall-walkers. Between the balustrade and the building grow rhododendron and other greenery, but along the walk concrete benches are set at intervals, each with a name chiseled upon its backrest: Henry Fielding, George Eliot, William Makepeace Thackeray. . . . On Henry Fielding an old man dozes, knobby hands resting on top of his knobby cane. Behind George Eliot, inside the balustrade, a young man sits on the grass reading. Charles Dickens, Charlotte Brontë, Victor Hugo. . . . There is a girl in a long patchwork skirt sitting on Victor Hugo; she looks at me through great, round, violet sunglasses, which she doesn't really need. Edgar Allan Poe, Mark Twain, Bret Harte . . . I wonder, do people always notice

40

whose lap they are occupying? Is the girl with the violet glasses waiting for someone, and did she say she'd meet him at the Victor Hugo bench? Oliver Wendell Holmes, Robert Louis Stevenson. . . . Can you remain utterly indifferent to Charlotte Brontë once you've sat leaning against her, eating an apple, feeling the spring sunshine?

Dumas, Hawthorne, Irving. Trollope, Sterne, Austen. . . . There are over twenty benches—twenty-two, I think. Sir Walter Scott, Charles Kingsley, James Fenimore Cooper. And if you approach from the southwest corner, the first two benches you see are Charles Reade and George Borrow. . . . Reade and Borrow, borrow and read. Yes, of course, that's what I'm here for!—and I stop to tie my shoe on Borrow's knee.

On the building itself there are more names, clusters of names, engraved large and clear high up on the gray blocks of the frieze. Not only writers, there, but inventors, musicians, explorers, scientists, painters, religious leaders. Palestrina, Aeschylus, Zoroaster, Copernicus, Raphael. I am dizzy, but less from looking up than from thinking of them: all of them, inside the library, waiting for me—all mine, all just for the asking!

Someone once wrote me to comment on my knowledge of literature. *Enviously.* But there is nothing to envy. The truth is that I never studied literature, certainly not in college, where for some mysterious reason I spent half my time grubbing about in exotic languages, most of which I haven't used since. My college education stands me in no good stead when it comes to writing this chapter—or anything else, for that matter.

Let me confess something—though, indeed, it's not a confession if confessing means admitting to something I'd rather conceal. When I write about books and writers, I am a great deal of the time writing about books and writers I have myself just that moment encountered, and the greatest part of my enthusiasm is the joy of recent discovery.

For finding out is the most delightful part of knowing. And fresh knowledge, even be it concerning things old to others, is my favorite commodity.

Not long ago I pointed out that writing is an occupation with free entry. You need no diploma, no union card, no previous experience. It doesn't matter who you are; everyone's eligible.

Well, unlike most colleges and universities, the public library doesn't care who you are, either. Victor Hugo doesn't care. Jane Austen doesn't care. Euripides doesn't care, and he is waiting there for you as much as he waits for me. To those who have asked me what kind of education a writer should have, and to those who have bemoaned their lack of an education, let me say that the best of *my* education has come from the public library—and still does, week after week. My tuition fee is bus fare and once in a while, five cents a day for an overdue book.

But despite the engraved names and despite the emotions they inspire in me, the library is not a pantheon, not some kind of temple dedicated to these gods of intellect and achievement, not a sterile memorial or a musty tomb. It holds not dry bones but still viable thoughts that can leap from a mind long dead to yours, through the agency of the printed page. And more—because of course it isn't Euripides that I seek out every time, or Thackeray, or Brontë or Poe. Last week it turned out to be Barbara Pym, Russell Baker, and John Updike; next week, who knows? Henry James, Jean Auel, and Shirley MacLaine? Or how about *The Cloister and the Hearth* (that's Reade) and *The Romany Rye* (that's Borrow)?

I rounded the block. Oh, it's a beautiful building, warm and mellow in the sunshine. For the sun is out now, and the girl with the violet glasses needs them after all. I look up at the frieze once more—Molière, Voltaire!—and I take the steps by twos and push my way through the heavy doors.

You don't need to know very much at all to start with, if you know the way to the public library.

9

FORMULA FOR SUCCESS

By Marjorie Holmes

WHENEVER I teach a class in writing I insist on a blackboard where I put the following formula:

IF YOU HAVE THESE	AND WILL DO THESE
Talent	Write every day
Belief in your own ability	Keep a notebook
Patience, persistence	Study your writers' magazine
Self-discipline	Send your work out

YOU CANNOT FAIL!

I am absolutely convinced from personal experience that this hypothesis is true. You can become a selling writer, *if you first have certain essentials,* and *if you will then proceed to do certain things.*

Let's examine the basic qualifications:

First and foremost, *Talent.* The talent for writing is a must. It includes imagination and originality, plus an inborn ability to use words gracefully and effectively in written form. Talent is a gift—and this is true of music, painting, any of the arts. It is something that can't be acquired; and although talent can and must be developed through study and practice, it can't be taught.

Talent, especially for writing, usually shows up in childhood, and seldom goes unnoticed. The neighbor kids are an eager audience for your incessantly scribbled stories. Parents and teachers are impressed. While the others in the room worriedly chew their pencils, you are already halfway through a writing assignment. Yours is the paper read before the class. This continues through college, if you go; and if there is a campus magazine your work appears in it. People tell you (as if you didn't know) you should be a writer, you have talent!

Even talent, however, must be backed up by: *A burning belief in your own ability.* The deep inner conviction that you can and will do it.

43

A force that will drive you to the typewriter come hell or high water, no matter how many people interrupt you, discourage you, or more commonly, simply don't care. Because, alas, the hallelujah chorus about your talent is silent once you are out of school. Swept into marriage and/or a job, the mere *time* to write is scarce, and when you try, the rejections are often quick and cruel. This is a time when your own faith can be seriously threatened, but it is *not the time to quit*.

I was lucky. My college writing instructor made us send our stuff out. This confirmed the fact that I should not quit, by way of a few small checks (the first, $7.00 from *Weird Tales* Magazine for a poem). I married right after graduation, in the depths of the Depression; but again the gods smiled. Two weeks before our first child was born, I sold my first story (the $200.00 paid for the baby). Two weeks later, I sold another. World, here I come! Then, seemingly, it was all over. I was to "beat my knuckles bloody against the wall," as Thomas Wolfe said, before I sold again.

These are the times that wring a writer's soul. *To know you can do it, and yet fail.* Why, why, why? Even so, it never occurred to me *not* to do it. And however brutal the pain of failing, you never *really* fail at something until you stop trying. For me, to abandon my gift would be unthinkable. The guilt would be intolerable. . . . "Defeat new-forges the chosen among men," wrote Romain Rolland in *Jean Christophe.* "It sorts out the people. It winnows out those who are purest and strongest and makes them purer and stronger." I make no claims to be pure, but in periods like this, a writer soon finds out whether or not he or she is strong.

Patience and persistence. If you have enough faith in yourself, these will follow. You will refuse to give up, you will keep trying. Through sheer stubborn persistence, I gradually broke into the magazines, first the small ones, then the more prestigious, meanwhile working on a novel. When stories and articles came back I revised and retyped them, if necessary, and sent them out again. Eventually most of them landed somewhere, sometimes after numerous rejections. One piece had been rejected so often (17 times!) I was on the verge of offering it to a local paper for five dollars when, to my amazement, it was accepted by *Nation's Business* for $150.00.

As for that first novel, *World by the Tail,* it was revised and rejected repeatedly over a period of at least ten years. We were finally using the manuscript as a perch for our little girl at the breakfast table, when a few pages fell out one day. I picked them up, started reading and decided it had to have one more chance. After one more revision, following the advice of a professional critic, it sold to Lippincott, on condition that I revise *again*. More months of patient persistent work before publication. The book enjoyed marvelous reviews, but modest sales, then was out of print so long I almost neglected to renew the copyright. But lo, after all those years along came Bantam, who brought it back to life in paperback with a first printing of 250,000 copies! Later the in-print figure approached a million. . . .

Another novel, *Two From Galilee,* written long after I'd become an "established writer" (which means only that you've published enough to feel more secure), took six years to sell. It was turned down by practically every publisher extant, including the firm for whom I'd already written two best sellers. In fact, they had the distinction of rejecting it twice! Yet when Fleming H. Revell finally took the gamble, it made *The New York Times* best seller list and was listed by *Publishers Weekly* as one of the ten best sellers of 1972.

You've got to believe in yourself and your own ideas. If the project is valid, the writing good, and you are patient and persistent, it will succeed.

Self-discipline. The will to work, whether you feel like it or not. Making a schedule and sticking to it. The courage to say, "No!" to temptations—coffee klatches, luncheons, bridge parties, or to the dozens of civic duties other people are always trying to get you to perform. The only duties that should take precedence over your writing are duties to your family. And make sure even these are not simply your own excuses to procrastinate.

I was lucky enough to have four children. Yes, lucky, although it didn't always seem so at the time. Children are the perfect excuse *not* to leave home for the presumed freedom of "working." I'd had that, in law offices while working my way through college. After years of pounding somebody else's typewriter, it was almost an indulgence to pound my own. Also, kids have to be bathed, fed and gotten off to school pretty much on schedule. This gives you a framework into which to fit your writing. Time was too precious to waste; I raced to accomplish as much as possible before they woke up or got home.

People with plenty of time on their hands seldom feel this urgent need to get *at* it. This I found true of several childless friends who were always talking about writing; yet they took jobs, joined clubs, chaired committees, held office—did everything else but write. In short, they *invented* interruptions to keep from it. I think when life itself provides the interruptions you are far more likely to make the effort to overcome them.

So you have the basic qualifications, some of which will, by their very nature, guide you in getting the audience a talented writer's work should have. But what are the specific steps to take?

First, *Write every day.* This, of course, is part of discipline; but here are some things that have helped me:

Have your own place where you do nothing else but write. The psychology of having your own writing desk or table and going to it at the same time every day will help you develop the habit. And once you get there don't sit waiting for ideas; get something *down—write*!

That's almost a direct quote from a lecture I heard years ago by Ruth Suckow, an Iowa novelist I very much admired. The advice was invaluable. During the Depression my husband and I moved a lot. My "place" was indeed often only a card table in a bedroom corner, but it was sacrosanct to my writing, and I went there, insofar as humanly possible, at the same time every day. Later, we always managed a proper well-equipped study. This, too, encourages the attitude of self-confidence and determination so important to a writer. You're not simply playing at a hobby; you are a professional writer.

Write at least two hours or more. But let no day pass without writing *something*. If only a page, a paragraph, or even a sentence on your current project. Incredibly, and however slowly, words add up to finished articles and stories, even books. If you just stay with something long enough, the day will come when you finish it! That this is important should be obvious. One completed piece of work, however dissatisfied you may be with it, is better than ten or twenty dazzling starts. Remember, there is no earthly way to publish anything, no matter how good, unless it's done.

Keep a notebook. I echo every word. A notebook is a valuable treasure house wherein to store ideas, bits of dialogue, characters observed, scenes from life you may not need right now but simply can't bear not to record. My own notebook began with daily assignments to "write a paragraph or two about anything you want to express." How glorious, this freedom to write as you please about whatever you please! This too helps develop the writing habit; while sheer immediacy and spontaneity will accumulate priceless material, and bring forth some of your best writing.

My notebook, begun when I was a college freshman, was to be the inspiration and chief source of material for the column I began years later for the *Washington (D.C.) Star*. One day, poring over that bulging notebook, wondering if there weren't *some* way to utilize its many scenes of family life, I decided to try them as a column. The result, *Love and Laughter,* not only appeared for twenty-five years, there were spin-offs by way of books: A collection called *Love and Laughter* (Doubleday), *To Treasure our Days* (Hallmark), and two from EPM Publications, *As Tall as My Heart* and *Beauty in Your Own Backyard*. I also drew on the notebook for many stories and articles.

Send your work out. As the old but true saying goes, "Nothing ever sold in a desk drawer!" If you will write and rewrite and polish, bringing to every piece of work, however small, your finest artistry; if you will follow the rules of submission (a clean, double-spaced, easy-to-read manuscript, accompanied by a stamped, self-addressed envelope); and if you market intelligently, choosing publications appropriate to your material, then, other things being equal, the time will come when you will succeed.

In short, if you first have the qualifications for becoming a writer and will do the things I've stated, *you cannot fail!*

10

TAMING YOUR MUSE

By Mary Hedin

EVERY writer knows that writing well is difficult. But getting published is even more difficult. Most writers cannot make a living by writing—certainly short story writers can't—and they must therefore find another source of income. The difficulties of writing and the need to work at other tasks often keep fiction writers from writing. They mean to write, they passionately want to write, but other demands and duties seem to consume all their available time. There are would-be writers working in almost every field and profession: In my creative writing classes, there have been a clothing salesman, a counselor in the suicide prevention center, an import-export salesman, a computer operator, a nursery school teacher, a beautician, an advertising executive—all of them frustrated by the problem of finding time for their writing.

An often unrecognized part of their problem is one of focus. The apparent lack of time and energy is often a lack of motivation.

My life has often been hectic, but I have discovered a number of things I can do to help me produce my work. Before I discuss these, I want to state an absolutely essential first principle: *Writing is worthwhile, and you are worthy of the task.*

You must have faith in yourself, or writing will be impossible. Of the many beginning writers I've known during the past decade, I have rarely seen one who wanted to write but had no talent for it at all. If you have the need to write, you probably have talent. Although you may have problems with aspects of the craft, you can overcome these with study and practice. My experience makes me believe that only writers want to write.

Given that and assuming faith in the art and in yourself, there are ways you can encourage your gift and get to the task of writing, no matter how busy you are.

First, *keep a notebook.*

Carry the notebook with you, at all times, if possible. Your notebook should not be too small. Small pages invite brief synoptic entries, crabbed ideas. An 8″ × 10″ is a good size, and a spiral-bound notebook is good for commuters since it will lie flat on the knees and is firm enough to write on through joggling rides. I prefer the old-fashioned composition notebooks with sewn backs. I'm kept from tearing out pages I judge inferior, and I am less likely to use my notebook for grocery lists. It is helpful to develop an attitude of reverence toward this notebook: It is the keeper of your artistic soul!

Enter something in the notebook every day. Describe a person near you on the bus. Later enter notes on his imagined life. Record bits of conversation you overhear. People do say the most fascinating and revealing things in public places. Make weather entries: try to catch the changes in sights and sounds during rain, during snow; the precise images about you on a bright spring morning, during sunset in early winter. These things you'll need when a fully conceived story is under-way.

Enter in your notebook every idea for a story that comes into your mind. This is so very important that I repeat: *Enter every idea for a story you encounter.* Inspirations for stories are often flashes, quick flarings of the imagination that can and do drop into the gray routines of our daily lives and get lost, forever forgotten. Those gifts of inspirations must be recorded immediately. Sometimes a long interval will pass before the idea for a story is developed into a story, but if recorded its possibilities will be kept for you, there in your notebook.

Record odd items you find in newspapers and magazines. One of my narrative poems grew from a short filler I found in the middle of the long news stories in a daily paper—a mere half-inch item about a woman lost in a snowstorm. One of my most successful stories had its beginnings in a letter in the "Dear Abby" column.

Also enter into your notebook every significant memory from your childhood. Those early experiences provide some of the richest mate-rial for stories. You need only think of some of the classic tales of literature to realize how deeply archetypal childhood experiences touch readers, how such tales live on: Folk tales and fairytales like "Snow White and Rose Red," "The Little Match Girl," "Jack and the Beanstalk"; Mark Twain's and Louisa May Alcott's stories of childhood experiences will live as long as people read; the popular Laura Ingalls Wilder book series, *Little House on the Prairie,* became a source and basis of a television series. Almost every good contemporary writer has written stories based on his childhood—Frank O'Connor's "First Communion," Kay Boyle's "A Member of the Family," William Faulkner's "The Bear" are a few that come to mind.

Dreams, too, should be entered in the writer's notebook. Dreams can be the basis for stories of fantasy, for surreal tales that reflect the fears and anxieties, the absurdities and ironies of our contemporary lives.

From time to time, read old entries in your notebook. Write down your responses to some of the old material. Spend a little space discussing with yourself the story ideas or news clippings that caught your eye and your interest. Explore the dreams, add clusters of memory material to those earlier entries. Encourage your imagination to build on those small foundations by adding detail, posing complications, considering consequences. Ask yourself, "What if?" Jot down, "Suppose . . ."

The chief function of the writer's notebook is to keep one focused on writing, to keep the creative imagination lively, to make continually available the resources for eventual stories. At all costs, keep a notebook.

A second factor in keeping oneself focused on writing is reading. It is important to read and read a lot. Read as many short stories as you can get your hands on. You will learn a lot about the craft through reading. How to start your story? Where to start? Whose voice to use in telling the tale? How to handle time, how to use the flashback? How to describe a scene full of swift action? How to deal with sex subtly? How to present facing or reacting to death without being maudlin or morbid? All such problems have been handled by writers before you—writers around you. The best teaching tool is the well-written story. You learn by observing, by imitating another writer's craftsmanship. Best of all, a fine short story will inspire you to get working on your own.

Each year I check out of the library the two best-known collections of short stories—*The Best American Short Stories* and *Prize Stories: O. Henry Awards.* Reading this range of varied, often brilliant stories, I find myself stimulated to new efforts with my own work.

I believe there is a renaissance of interest in the short story. A number of fine collections have appeared recently, among them Raymond Carver's *Cathedral,* Gail Godwin's *Mr. Bedford and the Muses,* Bobbie Ann Mason's *Shiloh and Other Stories,* and Dianne Benedict's *Shiny Objects.* Each of these writers is highly skillful. In their stories, you'll find deft and rich revelation of character, keenly explored conflicts and dilemmas, admirable control of style. I recommend them.

Use as models the writers whose way of telling a story and whose subjects and story ideas and themes seem relevant to your own. Study their craft, analyze and try to imitate their style until you feel you can do as well. Then apply the skills you have learned to your own subjects and stories.

It is also important for the time-pressured, distracted writer to nurture his unconscious. Though most people may take no special notice as the unconscious performs its tasks or exercises its powers, the creative writer should do everything he can to put this vital aspect of the self to full use. The unconscious can carry a large amount of the work involved in writing stories. I'm often asked how I can teach full time, keep my home operating, and write as continuously as I do. The answer lies in the use I make of this underground creator. To enhance the effectiveness of my unconscious, I read my current work the last thing before I turn out the light at night. I hold the work in my mind as I drift off to sleep, considering an elusive character, a misty plot, or a troublesome dramatic scene. In giving over to the sleeping mind the problems of creating, I find that the unconscious seems to grow attentive and to function specifically through the night and on through my next day's busy schedule.

But I believe the unconscious needs enrichment, fertilization. For some writers, the other arts provide such enrichment—music, painting and sculpture, drama, film. Other writers find meditation or solitary walks or fishing a source of nourishment. I find reading fairy tales, old myths, the *I Ching* and *Upanishad Chronicles,* and good poetry helpful. Willa Cather read the Bible before each day's stint of writing, not so much, it is said, for its content, as for the effect of that cadenced ancient prose on her own work. William Faulkner also perused the Bible and Shakespeare as well though he read nothing contemporary in his mature years since he felt that did not encourage his writing. Sylvia Plath pored over her thesaurus, finding that exotic words and phrases enhanced her creativity.

To find out what will nurture your unconscious and free your creative energies, you should try to perceive what kinds of reading and activity act as compost for your creative ground. Then make those activities part of your life, regularly. Your writing will be easier, your stories will have more depth and vitality.

The last advice I offer to those writing under conditions of limited time is both the hardest and the easiest. Stay up an hour later than everyone else in your household or get up an hour earlier, whichever your biological clock finds easier. That hour of solitude and peace given over to what you most love—writing—will make you feel wonderfully wealthy. What you can accomplish in that time can be great. If you write only one page in that hour, you will have thirty pages done in one month. In a year? Why, even a dozen stories might result.

Always, the fact remains that writing well is not easy and does take time. Many of our great writers have struggled in ways similar to ours. T. S. Eliot said that for him it had been useful to work in a bank or in publishing, that the difficulty of time had given a "greater pressure of concentration" to his work. He felt that to have nothing else to do might cause one to write too much, rather than concentrating on perfecting smaller amounts. Katherine Ann Porter reported that she had spent ninety percent of her time in "little dull jobs" that "didn't take her mind" in order to keep her head above water. Anthony Trollope worked as a postal clerk all day and wrote his numerous novels at night.

With such luminaries as inspiration and with devotion to the tricks and habits that keep one's gift alive, one can write even when "there isn't any time."

11

STRINGS THAT TOUCH THE SKY

BY JANE YOLEN

I COME from a family of string savers and kite fliers. It is an easy connection: kites/strings. Taking what is left over and used up and making it touch the sky is a good metaphor for writing.

If I were a scientist, I would remind myself that matter can never be lost. If I were a gardener, I would call it the great recycle of life. If I had a religious vocation, I would call it the second coming. But I am a writer from a family of string savers and kite fliers, so I see my writing in terms of a series of loops. What you have researched and written about once, you can use again and again in brand new ways. Loop upon loop. A veritable cat's cradle of ideas. Let me give you an example.

I wrote a book about the Quakers, a biography of the founding father of the religion, entitled *Friend: The Story of George Fox.* And because it was successful, another publisher asked me to do a book about the history of the Shakers, for they were a bizarre and radical outgrowth of the Society of Friends.

Loop 1. Simple Gifts, the Shaker book, was built upon some of the history I had already researched for the Quaker book. The earlier work had also prepared me to understand the group religious mind as well as persecuted religious minorities and their behavior. However, as I researched this particular nonfiction book project, I kept thinking that there were surely many stories in that history. I had already found dozens of them in the journals of believers and apostates. One that interested me especially (probably because my then fourteen-year-old daughter was beginning to get interested in boys) was a Romeo and Juliet story set in a Shaker community, made more interesting by the central fact that Shakers were celibate! This led me to write a novel.

Loop 2. The Gift of Sarah Barker was that novel. Sarah greatly resembled my daughter in both looks and character: headstrong, passionate, self-doubting, but always questioning authority. Set *that* girl down in a community of would-be angels in nineteenth century Massachusetts, and there's bound to be an interesting explosion.

Loop 3. For that Shaker novel about Sarah, I used the great round barn of Hancock Shaker Village as the central meeting place for her and the boy Abel Church. I loved that barn and had spent many quiet moments meditating there when I was doing my research. I longed to make use of that peculiar, fascinating barn again. But how? I didn't want to write another Shaker book. For the moment, two were enough. But a year later, when I was in the midst of writing a science fiction novel, *Dragon's Blood,* the Shaker material surfaced again. *Dragon's Blood* takes place in the 24th century on an ex-penal colony planet called Austar IV. The dragon farm on which my young hero worked as a bond slave quite naturally began to resemble a Shaker farm community—*without* the celibacy. And the stud barn where the great cock dragons were kept was, not surprisingly, built around a round central mow. The description of the steam rising from the stored grasses in that mow comes directly from a period description of the Hancock barn.

Loop 4. Dragon's Blood grew into a trilogy. *Heart's Blood* is the second book. I'm currently writing the third, tentatively called *Dragon's Eyes.* I am thinking about new ways to transform all that I have learned in the writing of this particular series of loops, all involving Shakers in some way. Another novel about religious communities—this time the millennial kind who sit on mountain tops waiting for the predicted end of the world—is already beginning to take shape in my mind.

Loops within loops within loops.

Nothing is lost in research or writing, though it may take years before any one idea is rediscovered, disinterred. This is personal literary archeology.

English teachers in school writing classes always caution their students to "write about what you know." They always neglect to add (indeed they may not realize) that there are many ways to "know" something. By looping and re-looping, an author gets to know a lot of characters and settings in a very deep way. To reuse them, melting them down in the furnace of the heart and mind, then reshaping them into something new, is what writing is all about. We are, after all, craftspeople, and the heart-metal is tempered by that cooling process between books and stories.

Whether you call it crafting or the great recycle or the second coming or the fact that matter cannot be lost, it is the same. All writers are savers of string, and the best writers know instinctively that pieces of string tied together can make a line long enough, eventually, to touch the sky.

12

REAL WRITERS EAT AARDVARK

By Joan Lovan LeClere

REAL writers accumulate professional attitudes along their paths from "would-be" to "real." They are persistent—dogged to the point of masochism. Real writers revise and retype until either their fingers get stuck between the keys or they get it right. They are precise—obsessed with absolute authenticity about everything. For example, real writers, in describing a particular taste or texture, would even eat aardvark to be sure their description was accurate.

Would-be writers do a lot of guessing. They think, "That's close enough." But real writers approach their work as critically and fastidiously as did Michelangelo when he created *David* from a marble block. This distinction makes the difference between a hobby and a career, a rejection and a check.

A real writer knows that each reader is an expert on something, so every written fact better be true. Real writers amass a varied library from second-hand bookstores and garage sales. If writing about the twenties, they actually listen to their grandmas' reminiscences and spend hours reading 1920s newspapers on microfilm at the library.

Real writers do not try to sell their work before its time. They rewrite until completely satisfied, and never shrug off an error assuming that the editor will catch it. Today's overworked editor in an understaffed office will indeed catch it and send the piece zinging back. Real writers act on that nagging doubt. How long does it take to retype a page so that awkward sentence can be made to shine and soar like a butterfly in sunlight? Ten minutes? Real writers take ten minutes.

A real writer uses a dictionary and thesaurus, choosing words to make the reader think "Oh!" instead of "Huh?"

Real writers banish clichés from their thoughts as if they were inexpiable sins. Clichés are so apt, so easy, so fatal.

A real writer is master of the semicolon; he labors with Strunk and White until he recalls most of his eighth-grade grammar. Real writers read works well written and some that are not, to see how they got that way. A real writer views writing as a craft responsive to instruction, practice, and correction, like ballet dancing or tuba-tooting.

Real writers don't use drugstore typing paper or erasable bond for final copies, but buy twenty-pound, twenty-five per cent cotton bond from an office supply store. Of course, for first, fifth, or however many drafts, they use whatever they can find, taking into account that paper towels don't feed well through a typewriter.

Real writers submit manuscripts typed professionally, ideally with carbon ribbons, free of typos, misspellings, and cross outs. They keep copies and proofread relentlessly.

Real writers acquire accoutrements that make them feel like writers. They rope off a corner of their living quarters as a private domain where, amidst a glorious clutter of clippings and unintelligible notes, nestles that plastic and metal god: the Typewriter. Contrary to public opinion, leather patches, alcoholism, and cats are not absolutely essential.

The real writer keeps a low profile until published, realizing that everyone and his cousin is a would-be writer. After publication, however, the real writer has the world's permission to hire the local high school marching band.

Real writers do not hoard manuscripts in file folders; they mail them (with a self-addressed stamped envelope) to editors. When a manuscript comes back, a real writer mails it to another editor, knowing that rejections are part of the game and that a manuscript in a drawer is dead. A real writer reads *The Writer's Handbook* instead of *Reader's Digest,* recognizing that marketing is eight-tenths of professional writing. Real writers keep index cards on each submission so they know where everything is and don't submit the same work twice to the same magazine. The real writer is a marketing expert.

Real writers have so many works submitted they don't stew about any one creation. The real writer does not write just one piece, send it out, and sit back placidly, waiting to see what happens to it before writing the next piece or story. Writing generates writing. Real writers write every day—no excuses. No—the dog doesn't have to be washed. No—rejection slips don't have to be alphabetized. Yes—words have to be written. To real writers, writing is not a sometime thing; it's a profession.

Real writers know the only way they can fail is if they quit. The real writer persists while would-be writers dump their words on a table for Scrabble. Real writers take six rejections in one day and resolutely send the works out again. A real writer studies writing articles and attends workshops and conferences, knowing one bit of good advice may be all he needs to make the difference. He heeds those rare, precious notes from editors and rewrites, never assuming his creation is perfect. A real writer refuses to give up.

Real writers know in their hearts they are potentially the greatest writers in the world, only presently operating on an interim level. Each story or article is better than the last, written more fluently, developed more convincingly.

Real writers observe trends and best-seller lists. They take advantage of a current craze if it strikes their interest and they think they can break into print with a coattail piece.

Real writers know when to end.

13

CREATIVITY LIMITED

By Katherine Paterson

I HAD been writing fiction for years with hardly anyone noticing, when, suddenly, a book of mine won a National Book Award, and overnight I seemed to have opinions worth consulting. "Dear Mrs. Paterson," one correspondent asked, "Do you think civilization as we know it will survive the twentieth century?" "Dear Mr. So-and-so," I replied, "I don't know at four o'clock what I'll be having for supper at six, a matter that is almost entirely under my control."

Most questions were less cosmic and more relevant, like the one asked me by an editor friend at the end of a business call: "Oh, by the way," she said, "while I have you on the phone, what is your theory of creativity?" She wanted a quotation for an article she was writing. What she got was several minutes of stammering at the prime daytime rate.

In order not to be caught like that again, I began to read articles and books about creativity. Incidentally, the word "creativity" doesn't even appear in my *Oxford English Dictionary,* 1971 edition. Aside from the fact that the word didn't exist until quite recently, the chief thing I learned about creativity is that students of human behavior seem to know very little about what it is. Psychiatrists writing about it were either reduced to poetry or else sought to explain it as some kind of neurosis. The one point that seemed to make sense to me out of my research was a point Rollo May makes in *The Courage to Create.* That is—there is no such thing as unlimited creativity. It is within limits, often very narrow limits, that a creative work comes into being.

I am as concerned about freedom as the next American, but freedom is quite different from the lack of limitations. Let me illustrate. Very often people ask me, "How do you find time to write?" The first time I remember being asked this question it was by a woman who worked a forty-hour week outside her home. I was puzzled. "How do *you* find time to work?" I asked, feeling her life was far more complex than mine. But she didn't see it as the same thing at all. Instead, she began to list what she saw as my limitations. You have four lively children. Your husband is a church pastor. You have three PTA's, choir, church activities, etc., etc., etc. At last I realized that the questioner was assuming that my husband's work and my children's activities were limitations that enslaved me, whereas I felt that they were the very boundaries that gave form to my life.

Boris Pasternak (author of *Doctor Zhivago*) had a great dread of being deported. He felt that if he were forced out of Russia, he would no longer be able to write. Russia was for him a necessary limitation. "Don't you wish," I am asked, "don't you wish you could just sail away alone to a Caribbean isle and write all day?" Never. "What? No, never?" Well, hardly ever. The more perceptive question came from a critic who knows my work almost better than I do. "Your writing is so bound up with your children," she said. "What are you going to do when they all grow up?" For a moment I had a hint of the panic Pasternak must have felt when threatened with deportation. But only for a moment. I've lived long enough to know that in this world there is rarely a shortage on limitations. There'll be more when I need them.

Life is often a parable for art. Many of the same people who worry that I don't have time to write are bothered by my choice of form. "Don't you feel constricted writing for children?" they'll ask. William, don't you find fourteen tightly rhymed lines an absolute prison? Ah, Pablo, if you could just yank that picture off that lousy scrap of canvas! You get the point. Form is not a bar to free expression, but provides the boundaries within which writers and artists freely choose to work.

You choose an art form, says C.S. Lewis, in one of his most quoted sentences, because it is the best form for something you have to say. It seems to me, therefore, more than a little silly to complain that your freedom has been restricted by the form you chose.

The library promotion staff at Crowell Junior Books say that I write novels for ages ten and up. When I examine books intended for this audience, my first observation is how few special limitations there seem to be.

There is, for example, no apparent limitation on vocabulary or sentence structure. A writer for *The Washingtonian Magazine* did a reading level test on my book, *The Master Puppeteer*. He reported to his readers that it fell comfortably between the seventh- and eighth-grade levels, which is just where my publisher claims it belongs. But the writer went on to say that he had applied the same test to Erica Jong's *Fear of Flying*. *Flying*, he said, had come out at the sixth-grade level. These are matters beyond my knowledge, but I do know that I spend an inordinate amount of time with my nose in dictionaries trying to develop a vocabulary worthy of my readers.

O.K., O.K., you can use big words if you want to. But, the protester cries from the back row, you'll have to admit that your subject matter is restricted. I can only speak from experience. My editor has never tried to restrict me. Let me offer a brief and brutal survey of my already published novels for children and young adults. In the first, the hero is a bastard, and the chief female character ends up in a brothel. In the second, the heroine has an illicit love affair, her mother dies in a plague, and most of her companions commit suicide. In the third, which is full of riots in the streets, the hero's best friend is permanently maimed. In the fourth, a central child character dies in an accident. In the fifth, turning away from the mayhem in the first four, I wrote what I refer to as my "funny book." In it the heroine merely fights, lies, steals, cusses, bullies an emotionally disturbed child, and acts out her racial bigotry in a particularly vicious manner.

You may not be surprised to know that I do from time to time receive letters of protest from teachers and librarians. You may be amazed to know that the only element in any of my books that any of these adults has complained to me about is the occasional profanity. Characters in young people's novels should be permitted to do anything, it would seem, except cuss. I can perceive this only as a testimony to the power of words.

But back to subject matter. When I examine a bald recitation of the events depicted in my books, I come away slightly shocked. What could I have been thinking of? Yet, somehow, when a story is coming to life, I'm not judging it as appropriate or inappropriate, I'm living through it.

In my teen-age novel, *The Sign of the Chrysanthemum,* Akiko ended up in a brothel not because I wanted to scandalize my readers, not because I was advocating legal prostitution, but because in twelfth-century Japan, a beautiful thirteen-year-old girl with no protector would have ended up in a brothel. And the penniless boy who loved her would indeed have been powerless to save her. I didn't want to make Akiko a prostitute, but there was no way out. It did occur to me afterward that I hadn't seen a lot of books for young readers along this line, but more than twelve years ago when I was writing this story, I was being torn apart that such a thing did and does happen to children in this world. If

61

we compare subject matter as my friend at *The Washingtonian Magazine* compared reading levels, I note that at the time my book was being readied for market, the adult best seller that was breaking every sales record since *Gone with the Wind* was the story of an overachieving sea gull.

If the limitations inherent to my form are not in reading level or subject matter, where are they? I am going to tell you where the boundaries are for me, realizing that you will be able to cite a gate for every fence.

First, a book for young readers has to tell a story. This may seem self-evident, but the truth is some people ignore it because plotting is very hard work. When I hear myself being introduced as a "great natural storyteller," it is all I can do to keep from leaping to my feet to object. "Great natural storytellers" don't spend countless days hewing a story line out of rock with a straight pin, now do they? Yet it has to be done. I received an anguished letter from a yet unpublished writer in which she asked, "Isn't there any place for the plotless teen-age novel?" I could only think of one. As burdensome as the limitation of plot may seem to be, it is not one I'm willing to circumvent. I simply don't like novels that aren't going anywhere, and I can't imagine many readers who do.

A second limitation on the novel for the young is length. There are, of course, plenty of exceptions to this. *Watership Down* (Richard Adams) and *The Lord of the Rings* (Tolkien) were written by the authors as stories for their own children. But these days a novel for the young usually runs under two hundred pages. Unlike plotting, this length limitation suits my natural tendencies. I am one of those people who write short. A great deal of my revision time is spent fleshing out and very little in cutting. When I first began to think seriously about writing, I assumed that my tendency to "write short" would lead me into the world of the short story. So I wrote short story upon short story, selling practically nothing. I think the truth of the matter is that I am not basically a short story writer. I am a novelist who writes short novels.

This is closely related to what I see as a third limitation. Intricacy, density, design—I'm not sure what to call it, but when I read *Blood Tie* (Mary Lee Settle), *Celestial Navigation* (Anne Tyler) or *Daniel Martin* (John Fowles), I hear a symphony orchestra. When I read my own *Bridge to Terabithia,* I hear a flute solo, unaccompanied. Occasionally, to be sure, you get a decent adult novel along the flute solo line, but most truly fine adult novels are extremely complex works of art. Some eleven-year-olds are reading Dickens and Austen, but most are not. And even when I'm dealing with an almost impossibly complicated situation like the Gempei War in twelfth-century Japan, I tend to hear through all the storm and clamour a rather simple melody.

A writer is also limited, you see, by who she is. As Flannery O'Connor wrote to a young writer friend: "There is only one answer . . . and that is that one writes what one can. Vocation implies limitation but, few people realize it who don't actually practice an art."* So when people ask me why I write what I do, I take comfort from one of my heroes. Flannery O'Connor wrote what she could; I write what I can.

A fourth limitation has to do with characters. They may be any age, and, indeed, any species, but they must be characters a reader can care about. This is another of those limitations I can rejoice in. When I am reading a novel and discover that the author has contempt for the people he has created, I am furious. If he despises these who are flesh of his flesh, what right does he have to inflict them on me? I don't want to waste my energy reading, and certainly not my energy writing, about people I hate. Even if I start a book with a satisfying villain, I seem doomed to care for her before the end.

There is certainly room in the world of books for entertainment, but for the serious writer of fiction for the young there is a fifth limitation, that of theme, for she will want to write not only a story that is going somewhere but a story about something that matters deeply. I would like to share with you the best explanation of the importance of theme in books for young people that I have ever heard. It comes from Jill Paton Walsh's 1978 Whitthall Lecture at the Library of Congress:

> When I was young my grandfather tried to teach me to play chess, which he deeply loved and wanted to share with me. And he got me horribly confused. Like most good players, he was not really interested in opening games. No sooner did I get far enough to advance a king's pawn timidly two paces than he was telling me about six thousand possibilities in the middle game opened up by such a beginning and six thousand others by the same act excluded. The more he spoke the less I understood him.
>
> How often I recollect that situation when I read adult novels. They are treatises on the complexities of the middle game, written by and for players of some skill. My grandfather was not wrong to point out to me the consequences of an opening game, which does indeed condition the middle game. But he had forgotten to tell me about checkmate, and you cannot play at all unless you know how the game is won and lost and what will count as an ending. That is why it is necessary in chil-

---

*The Habit of Being (Farrar, Straus and Giroux).

dren's books to mirror death, to show a projected end, and to teach that nothing is forever, so that the child may know the nature of the game he is playing and may take a direction, make purposeful moves. It is the plain truth that human life is passing and that we must find what we will value in the world, and how we will live in the light of that.†

That is why, you see, I do find the strong themes of my books appropriate for young readers. Like Jill Paton Walsh, I want my readers to see the nature of the game we are all engaged in so that they may make purposeful moves.

And in the shadow of this rather grand limitation, I find a more personal one. I will not take a young reader through a story and in the end abandon him. That is, I will not write a book that closes in despair. I cannot, will not, withhold from my young readers the harsh realities of human hunger and suffering and loss, but neither will I neglect to plant that stubborn seed of hope that has enabled our race to outlast wars and famines and the destruction of death.

If you think that this is the limitation that will keep me forever a writer for the young, perhaps it is. I don't mind. I do what I can and do it joyfully.

---

†"The Lords of Time" (*The Quarterly Journal of the Library of Congress,* Vol. 36, No. 2, Spring 1979).

14

THE FACTS ABOUT FICTION
A Written Interview

WITH IRVING WALLACE

Q. *We've read somewhere that you draw your ideas for topical novels from the headlines. Is that true? If so, explain.*

A: What you've read is absolutely untrue. It must have been written by a journalist or critic who knows nothing about the making of books. Generally, if an author were to base his novels on daily headlines, he would write and publish books that were terribly dated, almost historical.

Let us presume you decide to base a book on today's major headline because you want to write about a current event. How would you do it? The headline has given you an idea for a theme, subject, background. You begin to develop it in your mind as a novel and you make notes. You evolve some fictional characters, decide where they came from, what they are going through, and where they are headed. Out of these characters and the overall theme you begin to develop a story line or plot. Once you have that, you begin to research the subject of your headline, read all you can about it, interview experts on it, even travel to the sites of the story to guarantee authenticity and get a feel for the background. In my case, this process takes six months to a year.

Now you are ready. You begin writing the first draft of the novel. For me, this creative part may take a half year of writing, writing daily—even Saturdays, Sundays, Mother's Day—at least five or six hours a day. With the first draft completed, you begin to rewrite and revise it, to delete scenes that do not work, to write new scenes that work better, to strengthen a character, to improve sentence structure. For my novel, *The Almighty,* I did six rewrites after I had a first draft. I don't mean I completely rewrote every page each time. But on every go-through I revised at least half the pages.

O.K. Now you have a finished book ready for submission to a publisher. Your literary agent reads it and comments. A publisher reads it, likes it, buys it, and prepares it for publication. Your editor will want some more revisions (because your novel may need revisions, or perhaps the editor must justify his or her job, or simply wishes to impose his or her point of view on the manuscript). With this done there follows copyediting (inconsistencies are spotted, semicolons inserted). Next, your book goes to the printer, and back come the first galley proofs, which your publisher and you collaborate on correcting, even revising some more. Finally, page proofs, which most writers don't see. To the printer, to the bindery, to the reviewers, to the bookstores, and certainly a bound copy to you. Publishers like to say this process takes eight months.

Remember, you wrote a topical book based on a headline. But here it is possibly two-and-a-half years since you saw that headline. Your topical book about a current event is no longer topical or current. No, that is definitely not the way to develop a topical book.

Q. *Well, if not from headlines, how do you get book ideas on subjects that will be current when the novel appears?*

A: By finding a subject of continuing and ongoing interest—a good example, *Space,* by James Michener. Another example, my novel *The Prize,* which deals in fiction with the behind-the-scenes story of Nobel Prize judges and Nobel Prize winners. The subject is in the news annually. It never dates. The other approach: By selecting a subject you sense and anticipate will be in the news and much on readers' minds three or four years from now.

Instinctively, I've used both approaches. A subject that is always news? The so-called Kinsey Report came out. Most people bought it but did not read it. It was too dense, too academic. People read *about* it. Some time after, I read another sex survey and was inspired to look into the subject. I learned there had been many sex surveys before Kinsey made them news. And there have been almost countless ones since. I wondered how a sex survey really worked, what kind of humans were involved in conducting it, why ordinary persons cooperated by giving personal answers, and how these answers affected them. So I researched the subject in depth. Along the way, I developed fictional characters. I blended facts with imagined fiction. The result was my novel, *The Chapman Report,* fortunately an international best seller. The central subject of the novel remains in the news constantly. Sex surveys are always news. More important, love and sex, the relationship between men and women, the emotions of the characters, remain timeless.

As to anticipating the news, can that really be done? I can only say that I have done it (and I can't say I'm psychic, although my daughter Amy—the co-author of *The Psychic Healing Book*—is). I don't know how you anticipate what readers will be interested in three or six or ten years from now. If you write about human emotions and problems, you are surely safe and will write a timely book. But we are discussing subject matter. Well, it has to do with reading, listening, thinking, imagining, above all *sensing* what you might be interested in and what future readers might be interested in some years from now.

When I published *The Man* in 1964, many persons, even in my publishing house, thought I was crazy. A black man who becomes President of the United States, even accidentally? Really crazy. I wrote the book because I had strong feelings about racism in America, and I felt such a novel could dramatize for millions of white readers what they were doing to the black minority. But I also sensed—anticipated—this would be an even more newsworthy or topical subject through the 1970's and 1980's and after.

I had the same instinct when I wrote *The Word,* published in 1972. It seemed to me that religion, faith, belief in a Supreme Being would be of growing interest in a confused world in the years to come. I guessed that my story, centered on the discovery of a previously unknown fifth gospel that might be added to the New Testament, could be an overall subject of continuing interest to me, as well as—hopefully—future readers. This proved to be true. The Born Agains are only one manifestation of the public's non-ending need for order, belief in something, belief in anything.

Q. *In your novel,* The Almighty, *you seem to have reached straight into the current news about terrorists for the subject. True, it is a continuously topical subject, but it was also a contemporary news subject. What do you say about that?*

A: *The Almighty* is not about terrorism. It is about the way the media misuse and manipulate the day-to-day news, and thus keep the reading public misinformed. I employ terrorists in the story largely to make my point and because this means of telling the story had a good dramatic feel to it.

Let me tell you how I got the inspiration for *The Almighty*. One evening, some years ago, I was watching the national network news on television. The anchorman was reporting some event concerning a subject upon which I was well informed at first hand. I realized that the news he was reporting was being utterly distorted, sensationalized, warped, to grab viewers and ratings. I was dismayed by the false picture of the world this was giving viewers. Then I thought about the hundreds of press interviews I had given this past decade in cities across the country, and how reporters who had interviewed me had exaggerated, omitted, rearranged statements I had made in order to produce more attention-getting features. More distortions. Immediately, I saw the subject for a new novel. The new publisher of a floundering Manhattan daily wants to top his competitors, wants to headline exclusive beats that no one else has. So he does the ultimate thing in manipulating the news: He invents it. He hires a terrorist gang to create front-page stories only for him. Until a woman reporter he has employed gets onto his trail. So you can see. My novel is not about terrorists. It is about the manipulation of events by the media. It was a statement I had to make. It was also a challenging drama to plot and write.

Q. *All right, let's talk about the use a novelist can make of fact in fiction. Several of your works of fiction have been called factions, because of the way you blend fact with make-believe. Why do you do it? How do you do it? How did you do it in* The Prize?

A: Novelists have always blended fact and fiction. Some were better at it than others. Charles Dickens was a past master. Leo Tolstoi and Stendhal were good at it, also. When I came to write novels, my experience as a writer had been largely in nonfiction. When I turned to fiction, I became fascinated by the technique of intermingling factual material with imagined material. It was, indeed, a technique. To thread fact through fiction was one more means of making the fiction absolutely believable, and even more colorful and interesting, as long as the use of facts did not obstruct the flow of story narrative. In *The Chapman Report* the members of the Chapman sex-survey team discuss their fictional findings, but they also compare their findings to earlier real-life sex surveys I had researched and studied. In *The Prize* two fictional Nobel laureates from different countries, sharing the same scientific discovery, are at odds, antagonists, because one believes that the other has stolen his work and does not deserve to share the honor. I worried that readers might not accept this conflict as possible in real life, so to enable readers to suspend disbelief I had a wise Swedish official, who sensed the antagonism, relate to the pair some historical disputes and disagreements between famous Nobel laureates who did not like sharing the prize.

Actually, *The Prize* grew out of a visit I had made to Stockholm to write some articles on advances in Swedish science—and when one Swedish scientist, Dr. Sven Hedin, told me he was a judge on three different Nobel Prize committees, I was astounded. The reason I was astounded was that Dr. Hedin was not only pro-Nazi and pro-Hitler, but he was highly political, prejudiced, and utterly uninformed in certain areas in which he voted. (Since he was a judge for the literature award, I asked him whether James Joyce's name had ever come up as a contender for the Nobel Prize. Dr. Hedin said to me, "James Joyce? Joyce? Who's he?") This encounter led me to further research, interviews with other Nobel judges and even prizewinners, and they taught me about the human element in the annual prize-giving. That inspired me to write a work of fiction, *The Prize,* about the awards. It took me fifteen years before I found out how to write it, but write it I did, weaving incredible factual information with my fiction throughout. I even wrote a documentary book about how I wrote this work of fiction. It is called *The Writing of One Novel* and recounts in detail the whole process of how I used facts to underline and accent my fiction. Needless to say, in *The Word,* employing factual material I had obtained in interviews with clergymen, theologians, biblical scholars, I helped clarify and heighten the fiction I had written.

Q. *If, as many novelists believe, truth is too strange for fiction, how do you modify it to make it believable, real, true?*

A: You don't modify facts, you never tamper with them. A fact is a fact. Fiction *is* fiction. But the twain does meet, can meet. You use facts as support for your fiction, when helpful, when necessary. But you don't distort the facts. As my one-time agent, Paul R. Reynolds, used to say, "If truth is too unusual and strange, don't use it in fiction; use it only in nonfiction, where you can authenticate it with more facts."

Q. *Do you feel factual research is necessary for the writing of a novel?*

A: Of course not. We've been discussing fact in relation to a certain kind of novel. Most novels, some of the very best, require no research at all. The characters and plot come out of the author's own personal experiences, observations, readings, feelings. The trap here—in writing only about what you know or have experienced in your life—is that after a while, after many books, you can run out of first-hand material. You might tend to repeat yourself. You also limit yourself. I know one published author who always wanted to write a novel about an attorney, but he told me he simply couldn't because he wasn't an attorney and had never known one well. I told him that was no excuse. I told him to do some research on attorneys, meet some and interview them, find out about their professional and personal lives. I told him to research and broaden his horizon.

I remember when I was preparing my novel *The Seven Minutes*. It was about an attorney and an obscenity trial. I happened to know quite a few lawyers, and I questioned them closely about their lives and obscenity law and censorship. But I didn't know a thing about how an obscenity trial was conducted—this was to be the climax of my novel—and there were no trials in progress I could observe. So what I did was track down a copy of the transcript of the last great obscenity trial held in Los Angeles. It dealt with a Henry Miller book then banned. All transcripts had been destroyed save one, still in the hands of a court clerk at that trial. I rented his transcript and Xeroxed it. It came to twenty thick manuscript volumes, and I spent months studying these volumes to learn obscenity trial procedure. Several renowned attorneys, among them F. Lee Bailey, told me my resultant novel was the best trial book of its kind ever written and one without a single inaccuracy.

Another important value of factual research is that it gives you ideas for your fictional plotting. For *The Almighty*, I planned a fictional heist at the Dead Sea scrolls museum. I went to Jerusalem twice to research the scene and the scrolls. Just as I was leaving the museum on the second visit, I said casually to the expert who had been guiding me,

"Well, I guess this is just about the most valuable collection of authentic ancient documents on earth." And he said to me, "Not quite. The scrolls here aren't all authentic. One of them, the main one, is a phoney." This information was a stunner, and I was able to use it twice in *The Almighty*.

I had my protagonist write a feature story about the scrolls after he visits the museum:

> With reluctance Ramsey attended to his job, made notes for his story, noted everything from the fact that the museum's interior architecture was in the form of the cave in which the scrolls had been found to the fact that the scrolls were enshrined behind thick glass in ten display cases to the fact that the fragments of the main scroll, the Isaiah, were not the originals but clever photocopies, since the fragile real fragments might be destroyed by exposure to light in the building.

Later, when this tidbit is passed on to a terrorist leader on his way to attack and rob the museum, the leader instructs his cohorts:

> After the entrance hall and souvenir area in the museum, there's a tunnel with its lighted glass showcases. Ignore those. Don't bother with them . . . Those are not the great treasures. Go on past them into the main circular central hall. Avoid the elevated pedestal in the center of the room. It contains leaves of the Isaiah scroll, but these are photocopies, fakes, not the original. Go for the ten showcases around the room.

Q. *Is there one piece of advice you can give to an aspiring writer, one who wants to write but is finding it difficult to do so?*

A: There are many things I could say, but there is one thing I must say. The most difficult, even frightening, step for an aspiring writer is transforming the marvelous creative imaginings in his head into words on a blank sheet of paper. Somehow, the imagined words become clumsy and awkward when written down. Yet, writing them down is what writing is basically all about—putting black on white, as de Maupassant used to say it. The best way to ease into that is to keep a daily journal. I've kept a daily journal, one page a day, for many, many years. My children, David and Amy, used to watch me fill that journal. Eventually, both of them started keeping daily journals in their own manner. It was wonderful practice for them. It got them used to setting their thoughts down on paper. It made them comfortable about working with words. When it came to writing actual books, neither of them was blocked. To date, David has published more than ten books, and Amy has published more than six. Go thou and do likewise.

15

IMAGERY AND THE THIRD EYE

By Stephen King

SOME CRITICS have accused me—and it always comes out sounding like an accusation—of writing for the movies. It's not true, but I suppose there's some justification for the idea; all of my novels to date have been sold to the movies. The assumption seems to be that you can't do that sort of thing without trying, but as some of you out there will testify, it's the sort of thing you very rarely can do by consciously trying.

So, you're saying, why is this guy talking about movies when he's supposed to be talking about writing? I'll tell you why. I'm talking about movies because the most important thing that film and fiction share is an interest in the image—the bright picture that glows in the physical eye or in the mind's eye. I'm suggesting that my novels have sold to the movies not because they were written for the movies, but simply because they contain elements of vivid image that appeal to those who make films—to those for whom it is often more important to see than it is to think.

Novels are more than imagery—they are thought, plot, style, tone, characterization, and a score of other things—but it is the imagery that makes the book "stand out" somehow; to come alive; to glow with its own light. I'm fond of telling my writing classes that all the sophistries of fiction must follow story, that simple caveman invention ("I was walking through the forest when the tiger leaped down on me . . .") that held his audience spellbound around a fire at night—and perhaps he even got an extra piece of meat for his efforts if the story was a good one, the first writer's royalty! But I also believe that story springs from image: that vividness of place and time and *texture*. And here the writer is always two steps ahead of the film director, who may have to wait for the right weather, the right shadows, or the right lens (and when the real world gives way, as it so often does in my books, he must then turn to the special effects man).

72

Where does good imagery come from? Rather than that tiresome question, *What does it mean?* that always seems to come up when an image is presented, a better and more profitable question might be, *What does it make you think of?*

Sometimes would-be writers will say to me, "I know what I mean but I don't know how to describe it." What this usually means is, "I can't describe it because I can't quite see it."

An example: A beginning writer may put down, "It was a spooky old house," and let it go at that, knowing it doesn't convey any real punch or immediacy, but not knowing what to do about it. The writer has a sense that "It was a spooky old house" is somehow wrong, but he or she doesn't quite . . . know why. It's like that maddening itch in the middle of your back that you just can't scratch. Well, I'll tell you what's wrong with "It was a spooky old house." It isn't an image; it's an idea. Ideas have no emotional temperature gradient; they are neutral. But try this, from the early going in my novel, *'Salem's Lot:*

The house itself looked toward town. It was huge and rambling and sagging, its windows haphazardly boarded shut, giving it that sinister look of all old houses that have been empty for a long time. The paint had been weathered away, giving the house a uniform gray look. Windstorms had ripped many of the shingles off, and a heavy snowfall had punched in the west corner of the main roof, giving it a slumped, hunched look. A tattered no-trespassing sign was nailed to the right-hand newel post.

Nowhere in the paragraph does it say the house being described is "spooky"; the closest I come is the use of the word "sinister" to describe the boarded-up windows. If I've succeeded, readers will not need me to supply the adjective "spooky"; they will come to that decision on their own.

Now you might think of some details the above description (and I'm using that word, not "image," quite deliberately—come along with me for another couple of minutes and I think you'll see why) does *not* supply. What sort of a walk leads up to this house? Any? How many storeys does it have? What style is it—Jacobean? Victorian? Is there a driveway? A garage? A weather vane on the roof? None of these details is here; that is what the reader brings to it.

The point is, I think, that imagery is not achieved by overdescription—a Roget's full of adjectives by your typewriter may not be the answer to your problems with imagery. A good artist may be able to impress you with a young girl's beauty in a line sketch that takes only minutes to do—a curve of cheek, a wavy S-curve indicating the fall of hair, the tilt of a single eye. A painting that the artist labors over for weeks or months may be able to achieve no more—and may achieve much less because the artist has overkilled his subject.

If I can say anything important to writers who are still learning the craft of fiction, it's this: imagery does not occur on the writer's page; it occurs in the reader's mind. To describe everything is to supply a photograph in words; to indicate the points which seem the most vivid and important to you, the writer, is to allow the reader to flesh out your sketch into a portrait. Since 'Salem's Lot was originally published several years ago, I've seen maybe three dozen different pictures of the Marsten House, all based on the description I gave in that short paragraph quoted above; no two are the same, and none of them is quite the picture I had in my own mind—and I wouldn't have it any other way.

Good description produces imagery, then. The next question that always comes is, "How do I know what details to include and which to leave out?" The answer to the question is simply stated but more difficult to apply: Leave in the details that impress you the most strongly; leave in the details you see the most clearly; leave everything else out.

Our eyes convey images to our brains; if we are to convey images to our readers, then we must see with a kind of third eye—the eye of imagination and memory. Writers who describe poorly or not at all see poorly with this eye; others open it, but not all the way. Here is a paragraph from The Shining that I still like pretty well (it's funny how books recede from you, like people you once shared long and not particularly comfortable journeys with; you promise you'll stay in touch but somehow never do. And yet, from every book I've ever written, there are a few passages with which I'm still on friendly terms, and this is one of those):

His father would sweep him into his arms and Jacky would be propelled deliriously upward, so fast it seemed he could feel air pressure settling against his skull like a cap made out of lead, up and up, both of them crying 'Elevator! Elevator'; and there had been nights when his father in his drunkenness had not stopped the upward lift of his slabmuscled arms soon enough and Jacky had gone right over his father's flattopped head like a human projectile to crash-land on the hall floor behind his dad. But on other nights his father would only sweep him into a giggling ecstasy, through the zone of air where beer hung around his father's face like a mist of raindrops, to be twisted and turned and shaken like a laughing rag, and finally to be set down on his feet, hiccupping with reaction.

I saw this scene played in my own head; I saw it with that third eye as clearly as I now see this dark green typewriter I sit before, with its black keys and its bright white letters. I saw it as image; translated as much as I felt I needed to into description; and then turned it over to the reader. The details that impressed me the most strongly as I imagined the scene were: 1) that peculiar sensation of weight on the boy's head as he is swept up (not air-pressure, of course, but gravitational pull); 2) the father's huge arms (fair skin, fine fair hairs, and freckles, although none of those are in the description); 3) the father's short haircut; 4) that smell of beer, which is, in its own way, as unmistakable as the smell of lemon or vinegar or roses. And of all of them, the two that seemed to fill the image up for me best were the smell of beer and the boy *looking down from above* on his father's crewcut, seeing the white scalp through the bristly hairs.

I left out the fair skin, the freckles, the hallway where the Elevator game always took place, the fact that there was an umbrella stand there—a brass one that used to be a shell casing—because none of them seemed to make the image stronger. The reader may have seen different furnishings: a light fixture casting shadows of father and son on the wall; the sound of a television or radio in the other room. But the idea of imagery is not to set the picture by giving everything (that is for photographers, not writers), but to give enough to suggest a texture and a feel. And the writer must be confident enough in his or her own imaging ability to stop when it's time to stop, because as we all know, the joy of reading novels, which no movie can equal, is the joy of seeing in the mind, feeling the fantasy flower in the way that is unique to each individual reader. The reader has his or her own third eye; the job of the writer is only to provide a spectacle for it.

Too many beginning writers feel that they have to assume the entire burden of imagery; to become the reader's seeing-eye dog. That is simply not the case. Use vivid verbs. Avoid the passive voice. Avoid the cliché. Be specific. Be precise. Be elegant. Omit needless words. Most of these rules—and the four hundred I haven't quoted—will take care of themselves almost automatically if you will, from this point on, take two pledges: First, not to insult your reader's interior vision; and second, to see everything before you write it.

The latter may mean you'll find yourself writing more slowly than you've been accustomed to doing if you've been passing ideas ("It was a spooky old house'') off as imagery. The former may mean more careful rewriting if you've been hedging your bets by overdescription; you're going to have to pick up those old pruning shears, like it or not, and start cutting back to the essentials.

Let's say you want to describe (and thereby create an image of) a rainy day in a big city; and further, let us say that the mood you want to pass along to the reader is one of dreariness. When you finish this sentence, lean back—I mean physically lean back—and see that city, that rain, that mood.

You opened your eyes too soon. Close them and try again—give yourself thirty seconds, maybe even a minute. O.K. Go ahead.

How widely did your eye see? Did you see a skyline? Many buildings? An aerial view? Was the sky white or dark? Did you see people? Men holding their hats, bending forward a little, the wind belling out the backs of their coats? Women with umbrellas? Taxis splashing water? All of these are good; they offer a sort of description that bears the fruit of imagery. But now suppose you sharpen your focus; suppose I ask you to see *one street corner* in that gray, rainy, dismal city. It's three o'clock in the afternoon and now that rain is really coming down—look at it! And it's Monday, too; what a bummer. Now, close your eyes again, this time for a full minute, and see what's happening on that corner. And if you peek before the minute's up, you lose your Writers Guild card. O.K. Do it now.

Did you see it? The bus that droned by and splashed the women, driving them back? The faces looking out indifferently or tucked away behind newspapers? There was an ad for jeans on the back of the bus—it showed a girl bending over and the slogan, blurry with rain, read: THE ENDS JUSTIFY THE JEANS. Did you see the awning of the small grocery store across the way running with rivulets of water? Could you hear water gushing into the sewer gratings? And when the cars braked for the light, could you see their tail lights reflected up from the pavement in long scarlet streaks? Did you see the man with the newspaper on his head?

Some of them, maybe. Probably not all. You maybe saw other things, just as interesting; perhaps you even caught the tag end of a story in the image—a man running through the rain, looking back over his shoulder, or a child in a yellow slicker being pulled abruptly into a car with DPL plates—or perhaps you just saw the image itself. But, believe this: if you saw the image, you can put it on paper. If you doubt it, go to your typewriter *this minute* and write down what you saw. You know the feeling: to write is to re-experience, and as you write, that image will grow brighter and brighter, becoming something that is very nearly beautiful in its clarity. Do a paragraph; do two. And then give someone a rainy Monday afternoon in the city. Or, if you caught that tantalizing tag of story, chase it before it gets away. Follow the running man or get into that car and see what's in there; see who grabbed the child, and try to find out why. You can do it, if you care to open that inner eye just as wide as it will go.

Last word: Don't ever become totally transported with imagery. The eye sees everything, but the mind behind the eye must make the judgments on what to keep and what to throw away. "Always leave the table while there's still a little edge on your hunger," my mother used to say, "and you'll never have to worry about making a glutton of yourself, Stevie." The same is true of imagery. Once you've trained that third eye to see well, the hand itches to write down everything. If you're writing fiction, you don't want to drown your reader in textures; remember that image leads to story, and story leads to everything else. But also remember that a writer's greatest pleasure is in seeing, and seeing well.

What that third eye—that inner eye—can see is infinite. It's a little bit like having a whole amusement park in your head, where all the rides are free.

16

BECOMING THE CHARACTERS IN YOUR NOVEL

By Gail Godwin

THE frontiers of my writing life expanded remarkably when I discovered what good writers before me always knew: I could be anybody—if I was willing to work hard and be patient and trust my intuitions and disregard my fears.

Paradoxically, it was a knowledge I had as a child writer, but I had to re-learn it as an adult. At the age of nine, of twelve, I took it for granted I could enter the mind of any character I wanted to. I did not hesitate. I sat down and wrote a story about a henpecked husband, about a rich and lonely little boy who lived behind an ornate fence, about a dog on holiday, written from the dog's point of view.

Then I entered the age of self-consciousness and self-doubt and lost my innocent confidence. The writing teachers of the moment were preaching Write About What You Know, and I cringed at my childhood folly (What did I know about husbands, about being rich, about being a little boy, about being a *dog*?) and obediently shrank my horizons. I wrote about a girl like myself, and then I wrote about a woman like myself; and though I discovered some interesting insights and techniques in the process, I often raged against the fence I had built around myself and wondered how I could tear it down.

It was not easy, because the Spirit of the Time was trumpeting "consciousness" and self-consciousness and, above all, the self. And, as every literary historian knows, the Spirit of the Time shapes the style and the content of its Literature. Out of style were the old Victorians with their baggy monsters of novels and their devout assumptions that it was their *duty* to create a world and populate it with multiple and varied characters. The new rule was: Keep a chaste point of view and explore one's own inner processes; don't go populating worlds!

Now you can do a lot with a single point of view, provided you make your central character intelligent, sensitive, and compassionate, capable of having fascinating thoughts and meeting a fascinating array of other people. I stretched each heroine as far as I could: made her travel far from home, get involved with complex or unusual people, made her suffer, think and grow.

But something in me was longing to leap that point-of-view barrier and be more than one person at a time.

The turning point came with my novel, *A Mother and Two Daughters*. Its subject matter—three strong and different women bound in the closest of ties—demanded three points of view, if I were to show the subjective reality of each character, complete with her history, her style of behavior and speech and thought, the important people in her life, and—most crucial, perhaps—the mysterious way in which she had shaped and been shaped by the other two heroines.

I wanted the reader to identify equally with each of the three characters. I wanted to strike such an authentic and distinctive tone with each protagonist that a reader could open any page of the novel at random and know whose point of view was being expressed.

I myself was none of these women—nor was my mother or my sister. (The idea for the novel had come from a friend who told about a disastrous vacation she and her sister and her mother had taken six months after the father's death. There was a fight, and the sisters did not speak for two years afterwards.) So I would have to work hard to imagine myself into them, without the props of personal experience or memory. I would have to create *their* experiences, *their* memories, *their* social worlds.

As I wrote this novel, two unexpected things happened: first, I realized that, though none of the women was based on me, I could be any of them. When we as writers create characters, we are in the process stretching our own identities. We begin each new character with the warm clay of sympathy, some feeling in common, and, before we know it, we are that character. Concerning Nell, the mother, I did not know what it is like to be 63, or to be a widow, or even to have daughters of my own, but I did know what it feels like to be an ironic personality, always a little apart from my surroundings—as Nell is, by nature; and I knew, as Nell knows, what it is like to be lonely and yet to treasure one's aloneness for the freedom it allows you to be "nobody," just an awareness committed to the universe of which you are a part.

Concerning Cate, the older daughter, I knew what it feels like to rail against complacency and rebel against the status quo; I have never been particularly brave, or even very much of a rebel, but I could start Cate on her way to being one, with the basis of those feelings rooted in my own experience. Concerning Lydia, the proper younger daughter, so nervous with her sense of responsibility, so aching with her need to accomplish something for herself, I could bond myself to her with those shared feelings and set her on her course of cautious, but ardent, self-emancipation.

The second unexpected revelation that came to me as I wrote this novel was that I was not only telling the story of these three women, I was also creating a society. And, as the book grew thicker with characters, each with a need to express himself or herself, I discovered what I wish for every developing writer to discover: I discovered that I knew more than I thought I knew, about a great variety of people.

Ironically, I often came to this knowledge by listing all the things I *didn't* know about a certain character. I knew that Cate was going to meet a man who would tempt her spirit of independence as it had never been tempted before. But what would that man be like?

The intuition that flashed upon my mind was: Cate enjoys conflict; so this man would do something Cate would disapprove of. What would she disapprove of? Well, she mistrusts people with a great deal of money. So, make my man a millionaire. How did he make those millions? My intuition flashed again: pesticides. Those would certainly be out of favor with an idealist like Cate, who championed fair distribution, whether in economy or biology.

And so I began to see Roger Jernigan. First I had to research pesticides, about which I knew next to nothing. Furthermore, I had to research them *from their positive side,* as a man like Jernigan would see them. Thus I could speak from inside him when he tells Cate at their first dinner together, "When I started my business, it was considered a safeguard industry. We were the saviors; now we're the villains. But I've never made a product thinking, Let's hope this wipes out all the robins." Jernigan is sincere. He believes in what he does. And, in spite of herself, Cate is attracted to his authenticity.

But I had to learn who he was before I could make him authentic.

"Who are they?" Turgenev used to ask himself this about his characters before starting a story or novel. His second question was: *"What can I make them do that will show them completely?"*

During the writing of this novel, I often asked about a new character who had just walked onstage, What can I show this person doing, how can I describe this person, so his or her essence, or function, is immediately evident to the reader?

For instance, in the first chapter, which describes a party, there is a very minor character, Lucy Bell, who has made it her function in life to grease the wheels of society so events can run smoothly. What quick vision can I give of Lucy as she enters the party with her belligerent, alcoholic husband? I chose to personify Lucy Bell *as her function:* "Latrobe Bell was preceded into the room by the plucky Lucy, who was smiling and blinking rapidly, like one of those small cars with flashers that escort an oversized vehicle which might prove dangerous on its own."

Don't be afraid if some of your characters come to you shadowed in their own mysteries. Don't retreat, saying, "Maybe I'd better imagine somebody closer to home." Be courageous. Say, it is my job as a fiction writer to bring them out. Your impetus for wanting to write about just these characters may be that their mystery attracts you. Don't you often walk down the street and feel perfectly free to imagine the lives of all kinds of people who pass by? You do it naturally, without thinking. But, in writing, we often lose confidence because we draw ourselves up suddenly and say: "What right have I to imagine what is in that person's mind or heart? Of course I can't know." Maybe you don't know *exactly,* but people reveal worlds in their gestures, their clothes, the set of their mouths, the words they speak, the way they live, the friends (and enemies) they choose.

If you find yourself going blank about a character, don't think it a waste of time to sit down with a notepad and ask questions about him. This process often yields more than you'll be able to use in your story. But that's not a waste, either. What you know and don't tell will often be evident in a kind of richness of texture that envelops that character.

Start anywhere. How does _____ speak? In long, rambling sentences or in short, decisive ones? What does that tell you about _____? Is there a note of apology? Irony? What about pet expressions? (If a character prefaces his remarks habitually with, "I wouldn't lie to you about this," what could that mean?) Does the way _____ speaks tell you anything about his deepest beliefs? If you listen carefully enough, it will.

How does _____ look? Not so much whether the eyes are brown

or blue or the hair blonde or red, but what does that character's appearance tell you about his or her mode of life?

How does _____ feel about the other people in this scene? What kind of things does _____ notice or fail to notice?

During the writing of *A Mother and Two Daughters,* I also kept a special notebook with a page for each character's chronology. When born. When married. Important dates. Characters are influenced by their times, just as we are. If a character is born into the Great Depression, that may influence his subjective reality as well as his objective fortunes.

These are some of the techniques that helped me escape that terribly limiting enclosure of one point of view. And every time I succeeded in entering the special reality of another character, it expanded my vision of human life. After all, Point of View remains the eminent domain of fiction: no other medium has succeeded quite as well at getting into the minds of its characters. As writers, we ought to explore and exploit our privileged territory for all it is worth. Dickens did not hesitate to describe the viewpoint of a dog—or of a lamp post!—and I was on the right track with those childhood stories of other realities. So remember: You know more about those others than you think. Bond yourself to each mysterious new character with compassion, and then cling to him with all the tentacles of your curiosity. Pretty soon you'll surprise yourself by looking at the world through his eyes.

17

WHAT MAKES A FICTION WRITER?

By B. J. Chute

The other day, an interviewer asked me, "What makes a fiction writer?" and I could only answer, "I have no idea." It is a time-honored and shopworn question, and there are as many answers to it as there are writers, because all writers are different.

The interviewer, being neither time-honored nor shopworn but, on the contrary, young and lively, changed her question to "What makes *you* a fiction writer?" I felt I could answer that question reasonably well, and I did so by offering such (time-honored and shopworn) reasons as a natural bent for storytelling, a life-long habit of reading, a love of words, and all the etcetera of halfway answers which I hope were useful to her but which really did not satisfy me.

Thinking now about her question, I have been turning it over and over in my mind until I arrived, like Alice, at my looking-glass destination by walking away from it. I do not believe I know what makes me a fiction writer, but I do believe that there are four qualities without which one cannot write fiction at all.

The first, of course, is *imagination*. Imagination is as necessary to a novelist or short-story writer as the spinning of webs is to a spider and just as mysterious. It defies analysis (either one is a spider, or one isn't), and it has been quite properly called "the creative impulse." It has also been called the Muse, and, when the Muse vanishes, that yawning void she leaves behind her is known as "writer's block."

Imagination cannot be created, but it can be fostered, and this fostering is part of the writer's duty. It is not enough to congratulate oneself on having been gifted (lovely word!) with imagination, though it is certainly a major cause for rejoicing. The imagination, like the intellect, has to be used, and a creative writer ought to exercise it all the time. There is no idea, however insignificant or vague it may be, that the imagination cannot touch to new beginnings, turning it around and around in different lights, playing with it, *listening* to it. One of the most marvelous things about spiders (and writers) is the way they will launch themselves into space on a filament so infinitely slender as to be nearly invisible, and, lo, there is suddenly a bridge flung over the chasm, across which any fly (or any reader) can walk with perfect confidence.

The second quality I believe to be essential for writing fiction is *empathy,* which the dictionary properly defines as "mental entering into the feeling or spirit of a person or thing." As with imagination, one is to a degree born with empathy; but, like imagination, it can be fostered. Writers of fiction write from inside themselves, but they also write from inside other people, and, again, this is a kind of gift. It is what produces strong and believable characterization. *Madame Bovary* was written from the inside out. Flaubert seems to know not only the passion, the boredom, the despair and the terrible loneliness of that pitiful woman, but he also seems to know the most trivial light or shadow that falls across her mind. Imagination could create her, and her world, and the people around her, but it is Flaubert's empathy that makes his unhappy Emma not just credible but totally real. This is Melville's "subterranean miner that works in us all," and, although we cannot expect to be Melvilles or Flauberts, we can mine what we have. And if we do that, with honesty and intensity, who knows what lode of treasure we may strike?

The third quality is *style.* In its simplest form, style in writing can be defined as the way in which a thing is said. It is a much abused word, and it sometimes seems to me that it is woefully misunderstood by writers and readers alike. Style does not exist apart from the story, and, if five people tell an identical story, each one will tell it in a different style. The best style will produce the best story, and the listeners will turn to it even if they do not know why they turn. Style is a great preservative of writing, and no writer ought ever to think that a really good style is beyond his reach. But many writers do think so, and too many settle for second best when, in fact, they ought to be working all the time against any such preposterous limitation of their own capacities.

Once I ran across a description of style as applied to architecture, which is just as true of writing—"What is style? Clear thinking,

84

really; the ability to use your head before you do anything with your hands." Sloppy thinking will produce sloppy style, and I am certain there is not a writer among us who has not stared hopelessly at the written page which reflects the muddy results. What to do? Go back, of course. Find out what you are trying to say, and, having found it, select the words that will make the reader see what you are seeing. Selection is vital to style. Because English is an incredibly rich language, there are many bad ways of saying something, and many good ways, but there is usually only one right way. This right way will be the writer's *own* way—in short, his style, or what Proust called "the underlying tune" which distinguishes one writer from another. This should represent the very best the writer has to offer. "Second best" will not do.

Take, as an example, a description from Nathaniel Hawthorne. He is introducing a minister, and all he wishes to say about him is that he is a serious person, wears a beard, and is dressed in the kind of dark clothes and tall hat that would have been affected by a clergyman of his time. There are perhaps a hundred ways of putting all these details together so that the reader can visualize the character sharply, and most such descriptions would probably take a paragraph, certainly several sentences. Hawthorne does it in seven words; his minister is "grave, bearded, sable-cloaked and steeple-crowned."

This is perfectly beautiful writing, and it is as exact as it is beautiful. The picture is instantaneous and vivid, and the tone is faultless. I do not know whether Hawthorne got those seven words right the first time, or whether he labored over them in rewrite after rewrite. Even successive drafts of his manuscript would tell us nothing, because the majority of a writer's work goes on in his mind. What matters is that every word in Hawthorne's description is the right one: *grave,* with its sonorous double meaning; *bearded,* just the simple piece of information to balance the poetic images that follow; *sable-cloaked,* concealing, mysterious, and darker than darkness itself; and, finally, the triumph of *steeple-crowned,* which makes us see not only the minister in his tall hat, but Church, Authority and Heaven as well.

It is true that the average writer is not a Nathaniel Hawthorne, but it is also true that none of these seven words is in the least obscure or recondite or self-conscious; each one would be available to any writer who was craftsman enough to persist in finding it. If a writer is willing to work all the time and in everything he writes to achieve the best style of which he is capable, the words will be there for him as they were for Hawthorne.

And this brings us, inevitably, to the fourth quality, which is *patience.*

Patience in a writer is many things, but most of all, I think, it is characterized by concern for the words on the page. The aim of this concern is "to see the thing and throw the loop of creation around it," as Joyce Cary said. (And notice how riveting the phrasing of that statement is; there's style for you!) What Cary calls "the thing" is the idea, the initial impulse, the product of imagination and empathy. The "loop of creation" is the finding of the right words that will make it possible for the reader to share the writer's special vision, and such words can be very evasive, very slow to come.

At rare and wonderful intervals, the stars in their courses do seem to join together, and the writer finds himself writing so effortlessly and with such precision that it almost seems as if he were taking dictation. These are the best of times, but they are certainly not ordinary. In ordinary times, the words on the page are merely adequate: they move the story along; the second draft will be easier; experience lends hopefulness. The worst of times are when the words will not come at all, and the writer feels as if he were floundering in a swamp or gasping for air in a desert. This can be really frightening, and it is here—in swamp or desert—that the quality of patience will spell the difference between disaster and survival.

In the dictionary, the second definition for the word *patience* is "calmness in waiting." I like this definition very much indeed, because there is a steadiness about it and a good deal of faith, and any writer needs both.

When the final draft of a manuscript is on paper, the words are all that really matter. Money, status, and fame are by-products; nice to have, but nothing permanent. If that statement seems idealistic, of course it is. It is meant to be. To call upon the dictionary once more, idealism is "the cherishing or pursuing of ideals, as for attainment." For the writer of fiction, the pursuit is through imagination and empathy, the cherishing is through style, and the attainment is through patience.

Excellence is simply idealism in action, and so high an aim is bound to fall short of the mark many times. I call to your attention the words of John Adams, written in February of 1776—"We cannot ensure success, but we can deserve it."

18

HOW TO WRITE A NOVEL

By Morris L. West

YOU buy two reams — one thousand pages — of blank paper. You sit down, and you write one complete page every day for one year. At the end of that time, you have a book — good, bad or indifferent! You also have a wastebasket full of rejected pages.

The prescription sounds simple. In practice it is very difficult because it demands industry and continuity. Besides, like a sentence of death, the mere act of writing concentrates the mind most wondrously.

In a longish life as a professional writer, I have heard a thousand masterpieces talked out over bars, restaurant tables and love seats. I have never seen one of them in print. Books must be written, not talked.

Writing is like making love. You have to practice to be good at it. Like the best love-making, it has to be done in private and with great consideration for your partner in the enterprise, who in this case is the reader.

A novel is a story. It is a story about people. People live and die in a dimension of space and time. People have a past, a present and some promise of a future.

If you want to be a novelist you have to know people. You have to know the dimensions in which they have lived, do live, or may live. Again it sounds like an elementary proposition. But, try writing a novel without adequate preparation, and you will find that the people of your dreams have no bones to hold them up. The country in which they live is vague and featureless; and the time dimension is an evanescent moment.

To tell a story you need an audience. Have you ever tried talking to a blank wall? Have you ever tried writing a letter to a nonexistent lover? Both experiences are extremely frustrating. Every act of communication presupposes a communicator and an audience, whether the audience be actual or putative. If you want an audience, you have to have enough art to be able to command its attention for a single instant, which is the beginning of your story, and hold it thereafter for the duration of your narrative.

It's a kind of social contract. One doesn't pay $10.00 for a book in order to be bored. One pays for the classic experience of being purged by pity, terror, laughter and vicarious living and loving.

Do you want examples? Go back to the fairy tales of your childhood: "Once upon a time there were three bears who lived in a little house in the forest...." Go back to the Bible: "One day Saul was sitting in his house, spear in hand, with the evil spirit upon him, and David was playing the harp before him. He tried to pin David to the wall and David escaped from his presence whilst the spear stuck in the wall...."

Are you interested? Of course you are. Do you want to continue? Of course you do. Child or adult, you are instantly involved. The personages are real and vivid. The time, the place, the action are instantly defined. Disbelief is suspended. You cry to know what happened next.

What happens next constitutes the plot and the theme of the novel. For me, the theme always develops before the plot. The plot is the framework within which the theme is exposed and expounded. For example, in *The Shoes of the Fisherman* I tried to understand how the world might look through the eye of a loving creator; a single unified purview of the constant struggle between good and evil. The plot grew out of the theme. The Pope claims to be the vicar of Christ on earth. In theory, at least, from the moment he is elected, he must look upon the world with the loving and caring eye of the creator. But a Pope is only human; he is limited by the historic circumstance and by his own personality. How, therefore, will he comport himself?

I began *The Ambassador* in a different fashion. I knew a great deal about the circumstances that led to the assassination of President Diem and his family in South Vietnam. I knew of the American involvement in the assassination. I knew many of the political complexities involved. I asked myself how would I, a supposedly moral man, act if I were asked directly or indirectly to sign a death warrant?

The Salamander was a different case again. I had lived a long time in Italy. I had developed a profound love/hate relationship with the country, its culture, and its passionate people. I decided that I wanted to express this relationship in the form of a novel. I decided first to write an historical novel — the story of one Italian, born in 1900, who had survived the First World War, the Fascist period, and the Second World War, to become a leading industrialist.

I made four attempts at this historical treatment. I wrote nearly a hundred thousand words and threw most of them away. The theme was very clear to me. I knew everything I wanted to say. However, I had chosen the wrong vehicle through which to say it. I discovered that I was not an historical novelist. I am a novelist of the immediate drama. I had to construct my plot in the now. I had to begin with a trigger incident in the present, with characters existing in the present, and show the past through their eyes.

The experience was a salutary one: I had finally discovered the "why" and the "how" of what previously had been a purely instinctive method of working.

The "why" was essentially simple. I am a man, deeply involved in the business of living. I am hungry for all sorts of experiences. I cannot live at secondhand; therefore I cannot write at secondhand. I must write now about things which I know now, feel now, suffer now, enjoy now.

The "how" also became very clear. I must begin in a single moment of potential drama. I must be able to state this moment wholly and completely in a single sentence or, at most, a single paragraph. *The Devil's Advocate* begins with such a sentence: "It was his profession to prepare other men for death. It shocked him to be so unready for his own." The opening of *The Shoes of the Fisherman* was even shorter: "The Pope was dead." *Summer of the Red Wolf* begins: "Suddenly I was sick of the savagery of the world." *The Ambassador* commences: "As a diplomat I have a good record. In his valedictory letter the President called it, 'a distinguished and meritorious career, the sum of whose service represents a great profit to the United States of America.'"

Until this opening statement is made, I cannot begin the book, no matter how clear the rest of it is in my mind. Once the statement is made, the book proceeds by a logical process based on one question, "What if...?"

Think about this for a moment. It is the end of the day. You are leaving the office as usual. A number of choices are open to you: You can turn right and go downtown to catch the subway; you can turn left and walk half a block uptown to the neighborhood bar; you can cross the street to buy an evening newspaper; you can go back into your office to pick up a file which you have forgotten. Each of these choices will have a different consequence for the narrative.

Back in your office, you will find an ambitious colleague ransacking your filing cabinet. In the neighborhood bar, you will find an attractive woman with whom you may be tempted to start a love affair. On the subway, you may be mugged or you may be conned into a bad business deal. As you cross the street to buy a newspaper, you may be run down by a car. Whichever course you choose, you are committed to it for the rest of your story.

All of which brings me to the *selective process* of the novelist. You can't tell or show everything within the compass of a book. If you try to tell or show everything, your reader will die of boredom before the end of the first page. You must, therefore, ask yourself what is the core of the matter you wish to communicate to your reader? Having decided on the core of the matter, all that you tell him must relate to it and illustrate it more and more vividly.

Example: A story from the Hindu epic, *The Ramayana.* Rama and his two brothers were trained in archery by a great master. One day the master said to them:

"You are now ready to be tested as marksmen."

He took them to a clearing in the forest and showed them a tall tree upon one of whose branches was a beautiful colored bird. To the first brother he said:

"Stand to the mark, take aim and, before you fire, tell me what you see."

The first brother said:

"I see the tree and the bird."

The master said:

"Stand down."

The second brother stood to the mark, took aim and said:

"I see the bird on the branch."

The master said:

"Stand down."

Then Rama stood to the mark and took aim. The master asked:

"What do you see, Rama?"

Rama answered:

"I see the blue feathers on the neck of the bird."

Twentieth-century readers are assaulted at every hour of the day and night by audio impressions, visual impressions, subliminal solicitations. They see everything, hear everything. They perceive too much, reflect too little, and their imaginations become atrophied for want to use. It is a test of our skills that we, with nothing more strident than black print on white paper, can force them to concentrate on the blue feathers on the neck of the bird, and yet be aware, without our telling, of the myriad wonders of the surrounding forest.

19

THE MAGICAL WORLD OF THE NOVELIST

By Sidney Sheldon

ONE OF the questions I am frequently asked is, "How does one write a best seller?" My answer is that I don't know. If someone deliberately sets out to write a best seller, what he is really saying is that he is going to try to write a book that will appeal to everyone. In essence, he is looking for the lowest common denominator. I believe when you try to appeal to everyone, the result is that you end up appealing to almost no one. Every good writer that I know writes to please himself, not to please others. He starts with an idea that excites him, develops characters that interest him, and then writes his story as skillfully as he knows how. If one worries about quality rather than success, success is much more likely to follow.

How does one get started as a writer? The best advice I ever heard of came from Sinclair Lewis. After his Pulitzer Prize for *Main Street,* he was besieged by requests to speak to writing classes at various universities. He turned them all down until one day, after frantic importuning from an Ivy League college, he consented to speak. At the appointed time the auditorium was packed with eager would-be writers, waiting to hear words of wisdom from the master. Sinclair Lewis strode out on the stage and gazed upon his audience. He stood there for sixty seconds of absolute silence, and then said, "Why aren't you home writing?" And he turned and walked off the stage.

I started as a script reader in Hollywood when I was seventeen, then went on to write motion picture scenarios, Broadway plays and television series.

I was a producer at Columbia Studios when I got the idea for *The Naked Face,* my first novel. I contemplated writing it as a motion picture or a Broadway play, but hesitated because the plot called for a great deal of introspection on the part of the protagonist. Because so much of the story was cerebral, there seemed to be no way to let the audience know what the character was thinking. Then it occurred to me that if I wrote it as a novel I could do exactly that. Every morning from nine to twelve I dictated the book to one secretary, while another kept the outside world at bay. At twelve o'clock, I put on my producer's hat and worked on other projects until the following morning. The book was finished a year later. Irving Wallace sent me to his agent, who liked the book and sold it to William Morrow. Most of the reviews on *The Naked Face* were excellent, but the sales were minor. Since I had turned down other projects while writing the book, it proved to be an expensive experiment for me. It would have been easy to have returned to the dramatic rather than the narrative form of writing; but I was hooked. I immediately began another novel with no expectation that it would be any more rewarding financially than was *The Naked Face.* But I was not looking for financial reward. I had found something better: Freedom.

When you are writing for television, theatre or motion pictures, you have a hundred collaborators. There is the star who complains, "I can't read those lines. You'll have to change them"; the director who says, "That scene you wrote in the tea room—let's change it to having them climb the Matterhorn"; the cameraman who filters your story through his lens; the musicians who will finally create moods for your words with their music. I had been used to working with such collaborators all my professional life. It is part of the system. When a writer is under contract to a studio and he's told to change something, he changes it. He is an employee who receives a weekly check, just like the grips and the hairdressers.

Now, with my first novel, I had a taste of freedom—complete and total freedom. No one was looking over my shoulder, no one was telling me how or what to write, no one was second-guessing me. It was an exhilarating experience. I knew that what I wrote might fail, but at least it would be *my* failure.

My second novel was *The Other Side of Midnight,* and it turned out to be one of the ten best-selling novels of the past decade. *Turned out to be.* I did not set out to write a best seller. It began as an idea that I liked, and I went to work on it. Two and a half years later I turned it over to a publisher.

When I begin a book, I start out with a character. I have no plot in mind. The character begets other characters, and soon they begin to take over the novel and chart their own destinies.

A caveat: Even though it works for me, I strongly advise beginning writers not to write without an outline. Writing without some kind of blueprint can lead to too many blind alleys. (While writing *Bloodline*, I found that the character of old Samuel was taking over the book, and since he was not a major character, I had to throw 250 pages into the wastebasket to bring the story back into perspective.)

I dictate the first draft of my novels to a secretary. When the first draft is typed—and it usually runs between 1,000 and 1,200 pages—I go back to page one and start a rewrite. Not a polish—a complete rewrite. I will often throw away a hundred pages at a time, get rid of half a dozen characters and add new ones. Along the way, I constantly refine and tighten. When I get to the end of the book again, I go back to page one. I repeat this process as many as a dozen times, spending anywhere from a year to a year and a half rewriting and finally polishing, until the manuscript is as good as I know how to make it. When I have done my final polish, instead of sending it to the publisher, I start out at the beginning once more and cut ten out of every hundred pages so that the book will read ten percent faster.

The only one beside my secretary who sees my work while it is in progress is my wife, who is a brilliant editor. She reads the second drafts of my books, and I incorporate her comments into the following drafts. When the finished manuscript is ready, my editor and I meet to discuss any changes. He makes suggestions, but he emphasizes that they are *only* suggestions. If there is a difference of opinion, mine is allowed to prevail. Try that at MGM!

I think it is important to set up a disciplined schedule. If you write only when the muse sits on your shoulder, it is unlikely that your project will ever get completed. I work five or six days a week from ten in the morning to six in the evening, with a short break for lunch. I live with my characters, as they live with me.

There are two kinds of writers: Those who want to write and those who have to write. *Wanting* to write is not enough, for it is a painfully difficult profession filled with rejections, disappointments, frustrations. *Having* to be a writer is something else again. If that is the case with you, then I pity you and I envy you. I pity you because you are without a choice. There is no way for you to escape from the agonies and despair of creation, for you will find that what you write will never be good enough to satisfy you. You will always be striving to reach that impossible perfection. You will be Orpheus, using the music of your words to try to reach the unattainable Eurydice.

I envy you because you are going to reach heights that you never dreamed possible. You will create your own exciting worlds and people them with your own wonderful creatures. You will burden them with sorrows and disasters, fill them with joy, give them love, destroy them. What a fantastic and awesome thing it is to play God!

Perhaps, in this, is the clue to writing successfully. Make your characters live, make them real. If your readers do not empathize with your characters, your story, no matter how clever, must surely fail. Make them love your characters or hate them. Let the reader be envious of them or repelled or fascinated; but make the reader *believe*. There is only one way to do that: *You* must believe.

And when you have created that magic world, with characters that move and breathe and feel joy and sorrow, as you feel joy and sorrow, then, ah, then, you will have come as close as any mortal can to reaching out and touching the stars.

20

LEAVING THE READER SATISFIED

By Phyllis A. Whitney

THE conclusion of any piece of fiction is as important, if not more important, than the opening. True, if we lack a good opening, the reader will probably never reach the end of the story, but if we don't provide an ending that will seem right, our story or novel will bring no satisfaction to the reader. The best way to build success as a writer is to develop a following of satisfied readers who will come back for more of your written words.

"Satisfied" doesn't necessarily mean "happy." The reader must feel that the ending of a story or novel grows naturally from the events that have been evolving and from the particular characters he has been reading about.

I've noticed in my writing classes that very young writers tend to kill off their characters at the end of a story, while older writers prefer to keep them alive. Perhaps this is more a commentary on age than on art. Either way can be right, provided the reader feels that the ending is justified and grows logically from what has gone before. "Grows logically" is the key phrase. Gratuitously unhappy endings — chosen because the writer believes they are more "artistic" — never satisfy.

Before going on with our discussion, a word about the examples I'll be using in this chapter. Some of them will be drawn from books for young people, because I know this field so well. But whether you write adult or juvenile fiction, there is no difference in the techniques of telling a good story and interesting a reader.

In old books on writing technique, there was a type of story known as "the biter bit." Here, the main character is so thoroughly unpleasant that readers follow him eagerly to the end in order to see him get the awful punishment that is coming to him. The ending can thus be tragic and satisfying at the same time.

(At this point, permit me a Victorian aside: Dear Reader, please allow me to use the pronoun "him" instead of the awkward and self-conscious "him or her" that is being nervously interposed these days. Until someone comes up with a usable pronoun to cover both, may we follow the more customary convention that implies that "she" is included in "he.")

To resume...There is another kind of punishment story besides the one in which the main character seems to be asking to be punished. This second type may bring the reader deep regret, even to tears, yet it leaves him with a feeling of rightness at the end.

A good example of this is Kin Platt's gripping young adult novel, *Head Man*. The boy in the story, a member of a Los Angeles street gang, is picked up and sent for two years to a rehabilitation camp in California. There he begins to make it toward a better sort of life, and we become so emotionally involved in following his story that we plug for him all the way. When he is on the outside again, the good effects of the camp, the counseling of men who have become his friends, stay with him for a while. He almost makes it. The choice is his. He weakens, chooses the wrong course, and meets a brutal death at the end of the book. The reader feels devastated. Yet we know that this ending is right. He *had* a choice. And in this case it is a more effective ending because of the punch it delivers than it would have been had the boy been "saved."

Another "sad" ending occurs in Norma Mazer's sensitive young adult novel, *A Figure of Speech*. The girl in this story opposes the intention of her family to send a beloved grandfather to an old people's home. Her efforts to prevent this lead to a touching but unsentimentalized story. The old man dies at the end — a tragedy that needn't have happened. But because of the young woman's own clear and honest vision, we are left with a clearer vision of old people and their treatment than we had before reading the book. There is satisfaction as well as regret in the ending, because she *tried,* when others did not. She has grown as a human being.

A totally different sort of ending is suitable in a good tale of action and adventure, in which disappointment is seldom allowable. An excellent example of this may be found in a marvelous novel for young people — *Snowbound*, by Harry Mazer (husband of Norma Mazer).

In *Snowbound* a boy and a girl who heartily dislike each other are trapped in a car in a blizzard and must stay alive until rescued. This is breathless reading, as both must use ingenuity to help each other and themselves. The faults and strengths of each character surface under these primitive conditions, and by the time they are rescued they have learned respect for each other and for themselves. No other ending but rescue is possible, and it is enormously satisfying to have these two people come through their terrible ordeal. They *deserve* to win.

That is one of the measuring sticks one can apply to an ending. In most cases, what happens to the main character or characters should be deserved because it has been earned. When that is the case, reader satisfaction is guaranteed. The boy in *Head Man* made the wrong choice, and though the ending is grim, he could have escaped by earning a different ending. The young reader is poignantly aware of this and, perhaps, carries the lesson over into his own life.

Scarlett O'Hara in *Gone With the Wind* gets exactly what she deserves in the course of the novel. She deserves to save Tara, because that is the one thing she has always worked for unselfishly and wholeheartedly. But she also deserves to lose Rhett Butler at the end.

On the other hand, Norma Mazer's young heroine in *A Figure of Speech* deserves to save her grandfather, but fails because reality defeats her. There is sadness and grief in the ending, yet the book is entirely satisfying. The reader is forced to admit sadly that the world is like that — and perhaps he is prompted to try to change what is wrong.

Sometimes the criterion for the ending must be found in what we are trying to say to the reader. In the examples I've given, there may be greater satisfaction in an "unhappy" ending because of the painful truth that has been revealed.

I am reminded of two film versions of the same story — *That Hamilton Woman,* produced by Alexander Korda in 1941, starring Laurence Olivier and Vivien Leigh; and *The Nelson Affair,* produced by Hal Wallis, starring Glenda Jackson and Peter Finch. In the first, the true-to-life ending seems shocking and wrong. In the second, it feels right. They are totally different in treatment. My favorite is the lovely, romantic, earlier version in which Emma Hamilton is portrayed as a beautiful and gracious woman who has risen above her rough beginnings to become Lord Nelson's love and very much a lady. The film and the acting are perfect in their romantic way, until the end when we see Emma in prison, having been picked up as a drunken slut on the street.

Even though we have been warned in the prologue that this is coming, it is a shock, because the character as portrayed has never seemed to deserve such an ending. It doesn't seem justified by the character's actions as revealed to us. In the second, less romanticized Hal Wallis production, Emma is capable of being rough and crude, given to disgracing herself on various occasions. Despite her love for Nelson, she is often tipsy, and the same ending as in the first picture comes as no surprise. It is what she has been heading for and probably deserves. For me, the Korda film thus seems flawed in its ending.

Some years ago in an interview on television, I heard director Joshua Logan recount a conversation he'd had with Maxwell Anderson about Anderson's successful plays. Was there some one thing, Logan asked him, that had worked for him above all else, one bit of advice he could give young playwrights? Anderson responded that the main character must learn something *about himself* before the end of the play, and that this must be something that would *change his life forever*. Only then would an audience feel satisfied enough to make the play a success. Logan asked why there must be such satisfaction, and Anderson said, ". . . because otherwise they walk out."

Such change is equally important in a short story or novel. The most satisfying endings always involve change. If the main character remains the same at the end as he was at the beginning, he hasn't gone anywhere. He needs to change — either to grow or to deteriorate. Which brings us to the come-to-realize ending.

Because the come-to-realize ending, in which the main character sees the error of his ways and changes (grows), can so easily fail, it has often been frowned upon by editors. However, it can be one of the most useful and satisfying endings, once we understand the technique of using it. To be used properly, there must be three steps:

1. Character becomes aware of how wrong he has been because something *happens* to shock him into realization.

2. He thinks about this, and tries to understand, to recognize and accept that he was wrong.

3. He proves *through action* that he has changed.

If you omit any one of these three simple steps, the ending will fail. Under Step 1, you can't have your character merely *told* in an undramatic way that he is wrong. It may be that someone has tried to tell him all through the story, and he hasn't believed or listened. Telling isn't strong enough unless it comes through dramatic action.

Once the shock that wakes him up has been administered, there should be a pause — a quieter moment in which he considers what has happened and makes the change-over in his own mind. Omit this pause, and the change won't be convincing. If you end the story at this point, however, it will sink, and the reader will be left unbelieving.

So there must be a third step. Now the character must *prove* that he has changed. It is the omission of this step that most often causes editors to condemn this type of story. Now the character must take some positive course of action to show that he has changed. Only then can the ending be completely satisfying to the reader — who will only be convinced by action. Words and thoughts are not sufficient proof.

To use an example from my own writing, where, in retrospect, I think the ending could have been improved, let's look at my novel *Spindrift*. I had written the ending twice, and finally let the third version go into print. After publication, a number of readers told me that they didn't entirely believe in the ending, even though they liked the rest of the book. I now know what was wrong: I had left out a step.

The heroine of *Spindrift* has spent most of the book falling out of love with her husband (for reasons she thinks justifiable), and being attracted to another man. There was no difficulty about waking her up to the truth of the situation and letting her come-to-realize how wrong she had been. The man she was attracted to is the villain, who holds her in a dangerous situation at the end of the story and is threatening her life. There is plenty of dramatic action to change her mind. The second step is taken care of when she realizes that her husband is a far stronger and more worthy person than she has lately given him credit for being. She knows that she still loves him.

Events move furiously toward the end, with her husband rescuing her against odds from the other man. The third step is missing. All the protagonist does to prove that she has changed is to fling her arms about her husband at the end, the equivalent of walking happily into the sunset. The reader is left questioning. Will she be satisfied? How do we *know* she has changed? How do we know that her husband will now hold her love? She hasn't proved a thing. And I think that particular ending is weak because I didn't heed my own rules. What the main character does to prove change doesn't have to be something tremendously dramatic. It can be a very simple thing the character does. I'm sure that if I had "come to realize" myself what I was doing, I would have sought out some earlier element in the story that could have been used to give the heroine a bit of convincing action to prove to the reader that she had really changed.

101

The type of ending you prefer to write will, of course, grow from your own nature and life experience. I have always believed in fighting no matter what the odds. It isn't my nature to be easily defeated, and I am always optimistic, so my heroines put up a very good fight. My role is that of an entertainer, and thus my endings are always upbeat — though, I hope, not unrealistic.

There are a few other things to be said about fiction endings. Certainly the conclusion should surprise. If the reader guesses all along exactly what is going to happen, we fail. I don't mean the old-fashioned O. Henry twist, but nevertheless something unexpected. Part of the fun (and reading should first of all be entertainment) is not being able to tell how the story will come out. That doesn't hold for mysteries alone. Every story should keep the reader guessing and anticipating. If we can't stay one step ahead and furnish surprise, we will leave a so-what reader to put aside our books and never remember our names.

Another thing that the author must take care of is picking up any loose ends. This becomes particularly difficult in the mystery novel, where there can be all sorts of unanswered questions in the reader's mind. So much that is complex has gone before that a great deal of explanation may be needed. When I read a mystery or suspense novel in which the writer goes on and on *after the story is over,* I am bored. This type of explanatory ending (at great length) used to be more common than it is now, but I still see it from the hands of writers who should know better. We must work in as much explanation ahead of time as possible. Often this can be done just before the climax scene, when the reader is willing to stand still for a moment because he knows excitement is coming. The idea is to explain as much as possible well in advance, yet still hold out something that the reader is eager to know. You don't give up this tidbit of answer until the last page. Last paragraph is even better, but seldom possible.

One more word — and it is one that returns us to the opening and the very backbone of our story: The main character must have a strong desire for something he wants tremendously. (Weak *want,* weak *story.*) It will be something he wants enough to give him drive and purpose and goal all the way through. In the end, he will either get what he desires, or lose it — depending mainly on what he deserves. When you come to the ending, don't overlook that purpose, which must be attained or be lost in the last pages. If you keep in mind where you are going with this from the very beginning, you will be likely to leave a satisfied reader at the end of your novel or short story.

Which brings us to an ending here and now. *My* purpose and desire were to tell you what I know about endings. I hope I can leave you satisfied.

21

MYTHS AND REALITIES ABOUT SHORT STORY WRITING

BY CATHERINE BRADY

THE first time I submitted my short story "Home" to a magazine for publication, it was accepted—as the winner of *Redbook*'s Fifth Annual Young Writers Contest. That's *not* what happens with most of my short stories. Most of them, dog-eared and tattered, have traveled across the country several times over—I've sent one story out at least twenty times. Rejection is the standard fate for beginning writers, and one feels lucky if the Xeroxed form letter accompanying the manuscript has a few lines of criticism or advice scrawled across the bottom.

That confident advice can be confusing as well as intimidating: "Needs more plot"; "Feels static"; "Sorry, we see too many stories on this subject." While there may be buried truth in such generalizations, they offer little in the way of practical advice and often reduce stories to their lowest common denominator. When you're striving hard for your first publication, it's hard to remember to take such advice with a grain of salt. The following paragraphs are an attempt to offer just that—a few qualifications on the classic generalizations writers constantly hear from editors and other writers.

Stories depend on plot. It would be more accurate to say that a story is a complete dramatic event. "Dramatic event" implies that something hangs in the balance—i.e., neither the reader nor the central character is certain of the outcome—and "complete" means that every element of the story bears on that outcome in such a way that the reader anticipates it without being able to predict it. Endings that come as a total shock, no matter how plotted, don't work for the reader.

A whole cartload of shoot-'em-outs and love scenes won't make a story dramatic; plot is not simply a string of events. Particularly in a short story—which in its condensed construction resembles a lyric poem more than a novel—the writer must carefully select a few scenes that develop character rather than pack a story with events. The adage that character is action implies the reverse; the most exotic plot proves ineffectual if it doesn't test a character's perception of events against the reader's. This helps to explain why so many short stories treat the basic human experiences, such as love and marriage, family life, and death. Every reader brings to such stories a wealth of personal experience with which to compare the events in the story and to respond emotionally.

Rather than stuffing a story with action as if it were a Thanksgiving turkey, a writer should pare the story down to its essentials. Simplicity leaves far more room for evocation than action-packed narrative. For example, the first draft of "Home" included many more scenes than the final draft. Originally, I made the mistake of taking the narrator, Deirdre, through her day, rather than selecting scenes which amplified the central subject of the story, marriage. In the final draft, I reduced the story to the three essential scenes: Deirdre introducing her fiancé, Paul, to her family; the wedding of her cousin, which was the occasion for their visit; and the brief final scene, in which Deirdre watches her father and Paul in her family's garden. Single-mindedness is an advantage in a short story: the parents' marriage, Deirdre's impending marriage, and the crude wedding rituals at the cousin's wedding, while they seem to repeat the point, allow for all the dramatic tension I could pack into the story.

The central character must experience a revelation. Although generally true, this maxim deflects attention from the real impetus of a short story: to challenge the *reader's* perceptions. A character's change of heart is important only insofar as the reader experiences a change of heart along with the character. People read for self-centered reasons, and if your character's revelation produces no corresponding revelation for the reader, you've lost a reader. Stories must be set up around a dilemma which cannot be readily resolved. The writer can afford a character who doesn't "see the light," as long as the reader's view of the character changes radically. Novelty depends on more than exotic characters; the writer can introduce the reader to a character who's just like Joe next door, if the reader discovers something he or she never guessed about Joe before reading the story. The reader has to believe in and recognize Joe before he or she can accept the unfamiliar or unexpected from Joe, and as a consequence change some preconceptions about how people act and feel. This kind of surprise—unlike involved plot complications—is the way really to hook your reader.

Irony can be a powerful source of just such a revelation for the reader. Deirdre, the narrator of "Home," must learn to accept the risks and failures that accompany marriage if she is to have the courage to persevere in her own relationship. But how could I make this a dilemma for the reader? I had to present marriage as a problem, convincingly portray her parents' marriage as a negative lesson, a "failure" Deirdre hopes to avoid. Then I had to turn this failure on its head, when Deirdre learns that her parents' perseverance in a bad marriage is ironically the very quality a good marriage requires. She also discovers that the mistakes she fears so much often constitute the flesh and bone of a marriage, the history that binds two people together.

Hook your reader with a surprising twist of the plot. Tricks and surprise endings don't seem to produce as powerful a reader response as the subtle accumulation of details, those clues to the outcome that make a drama feel "complete." In this sense, all stories are detective stories, and a good writer withholds until the last minute the piece of evidence which will make the other clues fall into place. In "Home," I tried to drop clues that Deirdre clung suspiciously hard to the belief in control over her own fate. Her resentment of her fiancé for not sharing her pessimistic view of her parents' marriage—for having a storybook attitude which exactly mirrors her hopes for her own marriage— provides another clue to her misjudgment, and the placid camaraderie of Paul and Deirdre's relationship seems bloodless beside the destructive but passionate relationship of her parents. The full implications of these clues aren't brought out until the conclusion. Only then does Deirdre admit that she and Paul are as vulnerable as her parents, and only then can she move toward real love and away from the sterility that characterizes her "nice" relationship with Paul.

Plot surprises that fail to draw on what precedes them violate the "completeness" so crucial to the success of a story. Most of us have been annoyed at detective novels that drop clues that are never used, and the same principle applies to short stories. Every detail and character must contribute to the outcome, and sense details provide the most compelling evidence. Clear metaphors and images compress so much information that, rather than slowing down a story, they contribute to the development of the action. In a scene from "Home," Deirdre's parents dance at a wedding:

Deirdre's father led her mother onto the dance floor. As dancers they were well-matched, not simply because of their skill but also because they knew each other's movements as only long-practiced partners could. She calculated the number of inches beween her mother's body and her father's, both of them in perfect synchronization, and still their bodies seemed somehow wrong, withheld.

The dance itself comes to represent *in every detail* what's wrong with the marriage, and because it occurs at a wedding, it draws the reader's attention to the larger question of marriage as a long-standing tradition. Metaphors derive their power from complete identification; if you describe a character as being like a fox, then he should not only be cunning, but he should also have beady eyes, a sharp nose, and a sleek form.

Show, don't tell. A good rule, and one that a writer should almost never break. But it is not an absolute. Taken to its extreme, this rule produces stories in which the reader flounders in search of clues. Telling can be treated like a lawyer's summation: resort to it only after the evidence is in. At the conclusion of "Home," when Deirdre watches Paul trying to coax her father into small talk, she stumbles onto an insight that can only be told but that clearly derives from the scene she witnesses: that inevitability that she and Paul will hurt each other is not simply to be feared but must be risked as the price of love.

Another good rule of thumb for deciding when to step in and tell a character's thoughts is to compare how long it would take to try to show those thoughts through indirection and detail. If one sentence can tell what it would take two paragraphs to show, opt for conciseness. When you choose to tell, don't make the mistake of doing so in abstract language; telling can become a kind of detail if the words you choose accurately reflect the speaking voice. Better to explain in the rich language of speech than to tack onto a story abstractions more suited to a social science tract than to ordinary conversation.

Be original. The effort to be original can throw into shadow the more important concerns of storytelling. Readers don't ask themselves whether a story is original; they ask whether it rings true in light of their own experience, and whether it moves them. Striving for an unusual effect or subject—a common mistake of beginning writers—

107

nearly always results in a story that feels strained to the reader. Style that attracts attention to itself calls attention away from the story.

The sum of what I've tried to say here is that simplicity and directness are the most reliable tools for any writer. In the effort to write for a particular market or audience, one can easily lose sight of this, probably the oldest of truisms about writing. To write simply and directly requires conviction in the value of the story you want to tell, and that conviction must be the measure for all criticism and advice, regardless of its source.

22

IN THE BEGINNING . . .

By Lee Smith

To my mind the beginning of any story is the most important part: The beginning determines whether we have a reader or whether we don't. If the reader is not sufficiently caught up in what's going on at the outset, he'll stop reading, turn the page, maybe put that particular magazine or collection of stories back on the shelf and pick up something more interesting.

The question is this: Just what, exactly, is this reader looking for, anyway—this pretty blond in the blue jeans, this balding guy in the white short-sleeved shirt, this earnest high school boy, this dimpled blue-haired lady with the alligator shoes, this mythical fiction reader who comes in all shapes and sizes?

I think this reader is looking for *fiction*. This reader does not want to read biography, travelogue, history, or memoir. This reader does not want to know any more, right now, about the real world. If he did, he wouldn't have picked up that story in the first place. However—and paradoxically—we have to catch him up in our tale, we have to give him another world real enough to walk around in for a little while, an alternative reality strong enough to live and breathe in—at least for the duration of our story.

To do this, we need to concentrate in the beginning on those shopworn terms—but still as valid now as they ever were—of character, setting, and conflict.

All the characters who are going to be important to the story ought to show up at, or close to, the beginning, and their relationships need to be defined. It's very disconcerting for the reader if we have a traveling salesman stroll in on the last page and provide the ending. If we want to do this—and we can, of course, do anything we want to—we must at least mention this traveling salesman early on: show him cresting the top of a hill in the distance, with his case of samples, or mention that Aunt Louise bought a vacuum cleaner from him last week.

We should also try to develop these characters well enough to let our reader know what kind of people they are, what problems they face, what they're likely to do. To my mind, good character development is intrinsic to making the reader care about the story. It doesn't really matter how interesting the plot is. Plot is *not* the story. A story happens at the point at which plot and character intersect. A story is about the ways in which events shape and change people, and the ways in which people influence events. The reader simply does not care what's happening unless he knows whom it's happening to.

Imagine: We're reading a vivid newspaper account of Mrs. X, who jumped out the second-story window of her lovely Georgian home, landed in a hydrangea, and is now under intensive care at a local hospital. Now this is interesting, granted; these events are unusual, gripping. But we would be much more likely to search the next day's paper avidly for a follow-up on the incident if we were acquainted with Mrs. X and had some idea why she did it; if Mrs. X were our Aunt Louise whose daughter has become a Moonie, say; or if Mrs. X were our old college roommate. The more we know about Mrs. X, the more likely we are to care about what happens to her.

But a distinction needs to be made here. The reader of fiction wants to participate in the story. He wants to know all about the characters, but he doesn't want to be told. We have to *show* him. Our characters must act, speak, think. We can give relevant details about their past, descriptions of clothing and mannerisms. But we can't do this all at once. We have to concentrate on action and dialogue, weaving in the narrative detail, and this is the reason it's often easier to start a story with a scene than with narration. Throw that reader right into the midst of things, give him plenty of clues, but make *him* figure out what's happening and why, and what it means.

The setting should be clarified in the beginning, too. No matter how interesting and well-developed our characters are, no matter how suspenseful our plot, none of it will seem real if we allow it to happen in thin air. The reader wants to know where, when, and under what circumstances; often, this information is necessary to his understanding of the story itself. And we can use details of setting to develop character. (A description of the items on Mr. Brown's desk, for instance, could tell the reader all he needs to know about Mr. Brown. Does Mr. Brown have an almost bare working surface, with only a ballpoint pen in a holder and three lucite boxes saying Out, In, and Pending? Or is there a jumble of papers, bills, and memos on his desk, a picture of Charlie Chaplin on the wall, and two tickets for the 1964 World Series in the top drawer?) Setting may also be used to foreshadow events and set the mood for the whole story. (But we have to watch it here: We don't want a cloudburst to break at exactly the moment Jim tells Laura the relationship is over.)

We have our characters and our setting. Now the next thing to make sure we have is conflict. This term is bandied about so freely that it's hard to keep in mind what in the world it means. (Once I assigned a junior high school class to write a scene with plenty of conflict in it. I got three fights, eight family arguments, two football games, one demolition derby, and one instance of child abuse.) No, no, I said. But what does conflict *mean*? they said.

It's a hard question. I think it means, quite simply, that something in the story is up for grabs. The *status quo* of one or more of the people involved is threatened in some way. *A possibility for change exists.* Perhaps the main character has to make a decision; perhaps events are causing a change in his or her life; maybe a longstanding situation or relationship is faltering; or, more usually, the main character simply feels, for one reason or another, out of sync with the world. In terms of conflict, however, a short story starts at a different point from a novel. A novel may start way, way back there at the beginning of things, but a story starts where an old conflict becomes apparent.

I try to introduce some element of conflict into a story as soon as I can, in the first or second paragraph if I can figure out a way to get it in. I wasn't able to do it in my first version of a story named "Heat Lightning," which started off this way:

Geneva moves in a dream. She sits in a straightback kitchen chair on the front porch, stringing pole beans on a newspaper on her lap and looking up every now and then at the falling-down sidetrack up on the mountain across the road, at the dusty green leaves the way they curl up in the heat, at nothing. It is real hot. The black hair on Geneva's forehead sticks to her skin and she keeps pushing it back. She strings the beans and breaks them in two and drops them back in the pot by her side without once looking down. From where she sits she can see the dirt road in front of her house beyond the fence.

After revision, it went like this:

Geneva moves through a dream these days. Right now she sits in a straightback kitchen chair on the front porch, stringing pole beans on a newspaper on her lap and looking up every now and then at the falling-down side-track up on the mountain across the road, at the dusty green leaves the way they curl up in the heat, at nothing. It is real hot. The black hair on Geneva's forehead sticks to her skin and she keeps on pushing it back. She strings the beans and breaks them in two and drops them into the pot by her side without once looking down. She feels a change coming on. Geneva has known that something is up ever since last Wednesday night when she hollered out in church.

I think Number Two is better. It brings in an element of time ("these days"—"Right now") not present in Number One, indicating that *today*, the day of the story, is going to be different from all the other days in Geneva's life. I tried to have the last sentence pique the reader's curiosity and make him want to find out what's going to happen next.

Here's another example from the beginning of a short story named "All the Days of Our Lives":

It's been a real bad week for Helen. She drives her big Riviera home from work, quickly, carelessly, flipping it around the corners and curves of the town that she has lived in all her life. Almost. Except for the time she ran away with Joe, a time that seems so long ago now, all stretched out in a big arch over years and years like a giant rainbow only of course it wasn't long at all, only two months actually, or one month and three weeks to be exact.

The same two crucial things, I hope, come across here: (1) that this week, the week of the story, is unusual in some way for Helen, and (2) the mention of "the time she ran away with Joe" ought to intrigue the reader enough to make him want to learn more about it and what it has to do with how Helen lives now.

In other words, good news is no news: Everything running along smoothly, a happy day in Middletown, is rarely the stuff of fiction. The conflict needs to be established in the beginning, escalated and complicated in the middle, resolved or (more usually) clarified in the ending, where some moment of recognition often occurs. Things might change or they might not change, but the *possibility* for change (occasioned by the conflict) has occurred.

Beginning a story sounds simple enough: Clarify the setting, develop the characters, set the conflict in motion as soon as possible. Why, then, are beginnings so hard to write? For the same reason, I think, that writing fiction is so hard in the first place. Words on paper involve a commitment, an investment of the emotional intellectual ephemeral *self* right there in black and white. That's risky. And the greatest risk lies in starting the story at all; it's so much easier to go to the movies, or plant some herbs, or pay the bills. Because what if, once started, we can't finish the story? Then we have *failed,* and we're worse off than we were before. The beginning is the hardest part of the whole thing.

Given this fact, I try not to expect too much of myself the first time around. I know I have a tendency to describe the setting forever before I can get the action going; I know that in most stories I'll have to cut several paragraphs of lovely description of some old barn. But I describe that barn *anyway,* first time around, because I'll do just about anything to get the story started. I know I can—and will—cut it later.

I've found a similar tendency among my students, who often write what fiction writer Doris Betts has dubbed "The Toothpaste Story." The toothpaste story starts with a ringing alarm clock, then the obligatory groan, the stumbling to the bathroom, the showering, the brushing of the teeth, dressing for the day, coffee, then the long drive to the office where—Bingo!—the story starts. The first 2½ pages should be cut. But that's OK. Writing is so hard to do that any way we can get into a story is, I think, legitimate. We can let people brush their teeth for five pages, if we want to, as long as we cut those pages eventually: Get the beginning under control, pare it down, concentrating on those old basics of character, setting, and conflict. If we can do this, our reader will be drawn into the story. He'll sit down, take off his shoes (those tennis shoes, those cordovans, those alligator heels), put up his feet and start to *read.*

23

WHY DID MY STORY GET REJECTED?

By Marion Zimmer Bradley

ONE of the hardest things a young writer—one who has made maybe two or three sales, but cannot sell *regularly*—must cope with, is to distinguish between the story which sells first time out, and the other story he or she has written, which is "just as good" but for one reason or another does not sell.

A story may be bad in all kinds of ways, and still be salable, if it has some things the editor finds important (because he knows from experience that this is what his readers want). But a story may be good in all kinds of ways, excellently written, with warm, lovable characters and wonderful style, plus a philosophical outlook, and it is still going to get rejected if it doesn't give the editor those few things the editor wants and needs.

When I was editing two recent anthologies, I tried very hard to analyze the "gut feelings" I had about why one story worked and another one didn't. In general, I rejected stories for one or more of the following reasons, and this had nothing to do with how well written the stories were.

1. The pace was wrong. 2. The story was not complete in itself. 3. Main character was not identifiable. 4. Editor could not get interested in the characters. 5. Nothing happened in the story. 6. Character did not have a serious enough problem. 7. The story was just too grim. 8. The story was offensive, or the editor thought it was offensive.

Nine out of ten stories that are rejected fall into one or another of these eight categories; there is some big hole in the plotting of your story; or it is told in a way which is unclear, confusing, or offensive to your editor's idea of his preferred reader. But there is always the tenth story, which has absolutely nothing wrong with it, but gets rejected anyway. You can say it isn't your fault, but in a very serious way it *is* your fault, because all of the following "no-fault rejections" are *preventable*.

1. *The editor couldn't read your story* because it was typed on a dim ribbon, was a sloppy unreadable Xerox, or because your spelling was so bad he didn't want to be bothered figuring out what you meant. Or the editor never got a chance to read your story because you didn't address it right, or because the label fell off and it went to the dead letter office. Or he read it, and loved it, but he never got a chance to tell you so because you hadn't put your name and address on the story, only on the envelope, and the envelope got thrown away in the mail room. Or he couldn't write you and tell you about it because you didn't send enough postage and his magazine has a firm policy not to answer any manuscripts not accompanied by return postage.

2. *The story was a perfectly good, well-plotted story,* but this particular editor doesn't buy sword and sorcery, or high-technology space opera, or post-doomsday stories, or horror stories. Next time, *read the market requirements.*

3. *The story was a pretty good story,* but the editor just didn't happen to like the end, and he wasn't enthusiastic enough about it to write and ask if you would mind if he changed it.

4. *The story was a pretty good story,* but your opening was a little slow and the editor got bored before he could find out how good it was and ask you to change the first page a little.

5. *The story was a perfectly good story,* but something about this story pushed one of the editor's personal buttons—maybe he is a devout Roman Catholic and the story spoke favorably of abortion, or he is a dedicated environmentalist and the story dealt with something which hit one of his personal fears, neuroses or emotional convictions. It's even possible that you had a character in the story who reminded the editor of his hated stepmother, or the college professor who flunked him out of Integral Calculus and wrecked his chances of getting into grad school. Try another editor.

6. *The story was a perfectly good story,* but the editor was going to press tonight and needed a story exactly 7,500 words long to fill a spot vacated by an ad that cancelled or a column that missed its deadline, and your story was 8,500 words long. Or he needed a story 10,000 words long and yours was only 7,500.

7. *The story was a perfectly good story,* but the editor had just bought another story on the same theme by Harlan Ellison, Ben Bova, or Ursula K. LeGuin. Tough luck, and that's the breaks.

It is all too easy, when the editor sends back your story, to flatter yourself that your story is really pretty good, and that it was rejected for one of these no-fault reasons. In general, your first dozen or three dozen rejections will be for cause: Your story just isn't well enough plotted, the characters are too tangled, the plot doesn't make sense, there is something wrong with the end or the beginning, or for some reason, the editor just can't care enough about your characters.

The difference between the amateur and the professional is that the professional *assumes* that the editor knows his job, and if his story is rejected, he must have done something wrong. (And once an editor respects you as a professional and assumes *you* know your job, he will *tell* you if it's not your fault: "Dear Joe—sorry, this is too long for me," or "I'm overbought," or . . .

Try your story again if it's rejected. But if it's rejected *everywhere,* assume there was some reason nobody liked it, and try another story. . . . And listen to that sneaking little voice that tries to tell you where that first one really fell apart.

24

BOOKS THAT ENCHANT AND ENLIGHTEN

By Ken Follett

WHY are good books so boring?

We wondered about this as students, plodding through Henry James or Virginia Woolf while we longed to get back to *My Gun Is Quick*. Perhaps we were afraid to ask, for fear of seeming naive. As writers I think we should be asking the question still. It could turn out to be the most important question around.

Literature wasn't always so dull: this is a truism. *Oliver Twist* was a magazine serial. I read somewhere that one episode ended as Bill Sikes began to beat up Nancy; and when the ship carrying the next issue of the magazine arrived in New York, there was a crowd on the quay waiting to find out if Nancy died. The story may be apocryphal, but it makes a point: the greatest novelist in the English language used melodrama as liberally as any writer of soap opera.

Nowadays melodrama is unfashionable. Or is it? The literary phenomenon of the decade is the romantic-historical blockbuster — the kind of book my English agent calls a Sweet Savage Hysterical. There's melodrama — but it doesn't get reviewed in the *New York Times*. All right, I know — Kathleen Woodiwiss isn't in the Dickens class. Actually, that's the point. Nobody that good writes melodrama any more. Nobody that good writes mass-market fiction any more. This is a catastrophe. How did it happen?

In England the Education Act of 1870 made everyone go to school. No doubt something similar happened in the USA. Anyway, soon there was a literate population and a mass market for fiction. Publishers, writers and readers then divided into two camps: the elite, who until then had been the only readers, turned to increasingly rarefied intellectual fiction; and the newly literate mass went for sensation. The highbrows read Henry James while the rest of us devoured Tarzan. This is history. What I want to say is that both camps suffered because of the dichotomy.

117

First, character became the only permissible subject for a serious novel. (This was new: *Robinson Crusoe* was no more about *character* than *Raise the Titanic*.) Second, after the publication in 1922 of James Joyce's *Ulysses,* introspection became the paramount literary technique. Today the tail end of that movement is in a bad way (which is what people mean when they say the novel is dead). Although occasionally capable of touching an exposed nerve — as did *Fear of Flying,* for example — the light-comic approach of intellectual fiction today generally can't cope with much more than the trivia of middle-class life. Revolution, tragedy, passion, power, death: Thomas Hardy and Emily Brontë could write about these, but Kingsley Amis and John Updike can't; and when Gore Vidal writes about the end of the world he does it as a comedy. This, I think, is why friends of mine who like their novels deep at all costs read nineteenth-century stuff all the time. Serious fiction today is up a blind alley and banging its head against the wall.

I realize all this is not too terrifically scholarly: I'm just saying how it looks to me as a working storyteller.

While the intellectuals were plodding through Evelyn Waugh the rest of us were gasping with Mickey Spillane and swooning with Daphne du Maurier. And, just as they had to eat an awful lot of pudding to get at the plums, so we found — didn't we? — that cotton candy may be sweet but it nourishes not at all.

What went wrong (stick with it, now, I'm getting to the point) was that both fiction markets set themselves low standards. So long as they gave us thrilling tales the great mass-market writers, from Edgar Rice Burroughs to Dennis Wheatley, were permitted cardboard characters, sloppy writing, and texture as bland as Formica. The elite, who could get away with none of that, were allowed to dispense with plot, story, excitement, sensation, and the world outside the mind, so long as they were deep.

Well, what's to be done? I hope it's clear by now that this isn't going to be another plea for thrillers to be treated with critical seriousness: most of them, mine included, don't merit it because they aren't good enough (and it's small consolation that most serious novels aren't either). But our profession won't produce too many great writers while we continue to opt either for exciting trash or thoughtful tedium.

Will the intellectuals learn to enchant as well as enlighten us? It *can* be done. *One Flew Over the Cuckoo's Nest* satisfies the intellect without boring the pants off us. There are a few others: *The Grapes of Wrath, 1984, Lord of the Flies.* They're all mavericks, though: freaks, offshoots from the literary mainstream; each of them is about something more than character, and none of the authors produced a body of mass-market hits. Being an intellectual usually involves belonging to a social sub-group of intellectuals, and we get our standards of excellence from our social peers. Anyone who swallows the idea that character is all there is to write about starts the race with one leg in a plaster cast.

For the writer of popular fiction it's different: and here's where I get around to technique, which is what I was asked to discuss.

Yes, people will sometimes buy a weepy romance or an exciting thriller even if it's as shallow as Mickey Mouse and written like a Maoist press release. But our readers don't actually *prefer* trashy writing. On the contrary.

Look: the underwater knife fight is more exciting, not less, if it's described in graceful, powerful prose; the plot has more drama if it depends on character development as much as external events; the romance is more thrilling if the tall, dark hero nurses a genuine, credible sadness behind that handsome-but-cruel smile.

Some examples. There are lots of fine police procedurals, but Ed McBain's 87th Precinct mysteries stand out, not because of their authenticity or ingenuity, but because Steve Carella and Meyer Meyer and Bert Kling are funny and worried and clever and brave and *real*. *The Spy Who Came in from the Cold* hasn't got a terrific plot, but it is written with such grace, insight and conviction that it was the thriller of the decade. Stephen King's *Salem's Lot* keeps us awake at night, not because of the vampires in the story — Vampires? Is he kidding? — but because we believe in and care for the small town where they strike. There have been many Mafia novels, but only one made us feel how it is to be part of the Family; only one explained how murder and Catholicism can be reconciled in the prayer of the Mafia wives.

Take note: these four examples have virtues we expect of serious fiction — and those virtues gave them mass-market success.

What's more, serious novels which (perhaps accidentally) have the merits of pulp fiction are often both critical and commercial hits: *The Forsyte Saga* is a soap opera, *Fear of Flying* is an old romance in radical-feminist clothes, *Sons and Lovers* is a family saga, *Intruder in the Dust* is a detective story.

So here comes the message. I don't, as you've guessed, want us all to start writing heavy stuff: God forbid. Let's concentrate on the need to thrill readers, move them, and scare them half to death. When we need a standard by which to measure our plots, we'll look to Robert Ludlum, not Saul Bellow. For construction we'll emulate *The Day of the Jackal* rather than *Nicholas Nickleby*. We'll learn how to make people cry by reading *Love Story*, not *Women in Love*.

But let's learn other things from the intellectuals. Watch how Faulkner creates a rural community, and forget *Peyton Place*. We know how Agatha Christie creates suspense on stage, but what is Harold Pinter's trick? If there's an adolescent in the story, compare him with the boy in *Catcher in the Rye*, not the girl in *The Exorcist*.

I know, it's a depressing experience. It tells us how shallow our work is. But it also tells us how good fiction *can* be. Writing successful fiction is a matter of getting lots of different things right (which is why there's no formula for a best seller) and the way to get better, I suspect, is to discover new things to get right.

O.K., let's get something practical out of all this theorizing. The hero of your thriller has a streak of ruthlessness. They generally do: perhaps they have to, to be thriller heroes. But let's not leave it at that. What were the events, who were the people, who shaped his personality? Why did he, as a sixteen-year-old, decide that the thing to be is *tough*, when others were picking *clever* or *sexy* or *rich?*

Your passionate melodrama is set in eighteenth-century England, and all the main characters are wealthy. You think this means you don't have to worry about where their money comes from. Worry about it. Do they own land? Then they need to know the price of corn. Are they in politics? Then which party, and why do they get elected? Are they merchants? Are they richer or poorer than they were a generation ago? Why? These things aren't as important as their gowns and their manners and their weddings, but you should know about both.

The spymaster has a mentally retarded son. You put this in to make him more human: good idea. Now, what happens to a family when a child like this is born? If you don't know, find out. You went to the trouble to research the gun he carries and the unbreakable book code he uses to communicate with the double agent; now think about his home life. And when you've developed that idea so well that it's beginning to get in the way of that tricksy little plot you've got all figured out, then you know you're writing a better book.

Writers have something of a responsibility. People get an awful lot of their ideas about life from fiction. Like it or not, one or two of us will probably change the way our contemporaries think — and it's mass-market stuff that does this. My generation learned about Nazi Germany from the TV show "Holocaust." The popular view of life under communism comes from George Orwell's *1984,* not *The Gulag Archipelago.* British people never understood Watergate until we saw the movie *All the President's Men.* And then there's *Roots.*

It's often said that a romance or a mystery can't be well characterized, true to life and beautifully written because everything has to be subordinate to the plot. I think that's like saying verse will never have the impact of prose because the choice of words is constrained by metre and rhyme. In fact the rules of formal poetry give the words *more* impact. Plot ought to do the same for character.

"When that spymaster's everyday life begins to make the plot implausible, which do you sacrifice — story or realism?"

Sorry, you don't get off the hook that easily. The object is to have a plot and a character that fit together like ball and socket. It is terribly difficult to write beautiful rhyming verse, because the rules are so restricting. Similarly, the need for a happy ending, a violent climax, a ludicrously ambitious theft, or a love interest for the hero — all of these make it harder to write real people and credible events and sensitive prose. Anyone can write: it's writing *well* that is so tough.

But then, who told you it was easy?

25

ABOUT THAT NOVEL

By Evan Hunter

STARTING: If you haven't got an idea for one, forget it. If you haven't got an idea you want to express on paper, in words, forget it. If you prefer putting paint on canvas, or rolls on your pianola or in your oven, forget it. You're going to be with this novel for a long, long time, so you'd better have *thought* about it before you start writing it. When it's ready to be written, you'll know. You'll know because you can't get it out of your mind. It'll be with you literally day and night. You'll even *dream* about it, but don't get up and rush to your type-writer. Go back to sleep. Only in movies do writers get up in the middle of the night with an inspiration. The time to go to the type-writer is when you're fresh and ready to do battle. There *will* be a battle, no question, a siege that will seemingly go on forever. So sit down, make yourself comfortable, and begin.

No outline at first, except the loose one in your head, draped casually around the idea. The thing you are trying to find is the voice. This is the single most important thing in any novel. The voice. How it will *sound*. Who is telling the story? Why is he telling it? If you're sixty years old and writing in the first person singular about a sixteen-year-old high school student, beware of the voice. It may be your own, and that is wrong. If you're writing in the third person, you can change the *tone* of the voice each time you switch to another charac-ter, but the *voice* itself must remain consistent throughout. The voice is your style. Except in my mystery series, I try to change my style to suit the subject matter of any novel I'm writing. I've come a hundred pages into a novel using the wrong voice, and I've thrown those pages away and started a new search for the right voice. Don't worry about spending days or weeks trying to find a voice. It will be time well spent. You'll know when you hit upon it. Things will suddenly *feel* right.

Once you've found the voice, write your first chapter or your first scene. Test the water. Does it still feel right? Good. *Now* make your outline. First of all, determine how long the book will be. The average mystery novel runs about 200 pages in manuscript, but a straight novel can be something as slim as *Love Story* or as thick as *Gone With the Wind*. You are the only person who knows in advance what your story is about. You are the only one who can figure how many pages you will need to tell this story. Take out your calculator. Are you writing a 300-page novel? O.K., how many chapters will you need? The length of each chapter will be determined by how much you have to *say* in that chapter. If you're depicting the Battle of Waterloo, it might be a trifle difficult to compress it into ten pages. If you're writing about a man putting out the garbage, you probably have only a scene, and you'll need additional scenes to make a full chapter.

Outline the novel in your own way, never mind freshman high-school English courses. I've outlined a forty-page chapter with just the words "Father-son confrontation." The outline is you, talking to yourself on paper. Get friendly with yourself. Tell yourself what you, as the writer, want to accomplish in any given chapter. "O.K., now we want a big explosion in the garage, and we want to see all these goddamn flames, and smell the smoke, and we want neighbors running over with garden hoses. Bring the little girl in at the end of the scene, shocked by what she's done." Got it? *Talk* to yourself. You don't have to outline the whole book. Just take the outline as far as your invention will carry it. Later, when you've written all the chapters you've already outlined, you can make another outline of the *next* several chapters. If a chapter is needed between something that has happened before and something that will happen later, and you don't know what to put between those two slices of bread, just type in the words, SCENE MISSING. You'll come back to it later. You're going to be here awhile.

MOVING: Set yourself a definite goal each day. Tack it on the wall. Ten pages? Five pages? Two pages? Two paragraphs? It doesn't matter. *Set* the goal, make it realistic, and *meet* it. If you're writing a planned 400-page novel, it will seem impossible ever to get it finished.

400 pages may be a year away. But your daily goal is here and now, and it's important to set that goal and meet it so that you'll have a sense of immediate reward. At the end of each week, on your calendar, jot down the number of pages you've already written. Store your kernels. Watch the cache grow. Keep the thing moving. If it bogs down, if you're supposed to write a tender love scene and you've just had a fight with your accountant, put the anger to good use. Jump ahead and write the Battle of Waterloo chapter. *Don't stop writing!* It's easier to go fishing or skiing—but sit at that damn typewriter, and look at the four walls all day long if you have to. There is nothing more boring than looking at the walls. Eventually, if only to relieve the boredom, and because you've made a deal with yourself not to get out of that chair, you'll start writing again. At the end of the day, read over what you've written. If you think it's lousy, don't throw it away. Read it again in the morning. If it still looks lousy, do it over again. Or if it's still bothering you, and you don't know why, move on. Keep it *moving*. The nice thing about writing, unlike public speaking, is that you can correct all your mistakes later.

CHANGING: The only true creative aspect of writing is the first draft. That's when it's coming straight from your head and your heart, a direct tapping of the unconscious. The rest is donkey work. It is, however, donkey work that must be done. Whether you rewrite as you go along—taking that bad chapter from the night before and putting it through the machine again from the top—or whether you rewrite everything only after you've completed the book, you *must* rewrite. But be careful. You can hone and polish something until it glows like a diamond, but you may end up with something hard and glittering and totally without the interior spark that was the result of your first commitment to paper. You're only a virgin once, but try to bring to each rereading of your own material the same innocence you brought to it the first time around. You will be rereading it *twenty* times before you're finished. Each time, ask yourself what you intended. Do you want me to cry when I read this scene? Well, are *you* crying? If you're not, why aren't you? Find out why you aren't. Did someone say something that broke the mood of the scene? Is that field of daffodils too cheerful for the tone of the scene? Has your heroine stamped her foot when she should be tearing out her hair? Work it, rework it. When you yourself begin crying, you've got it.

ENDING: How do you know when you're finished? You're finished when you're satisfied. If a scene is right the first time around, leave it alone. Tell yourself, "Terrific, pal," and leave it alone. You'll know you're getting to the end because you'll suddenly slow down. When that happens, set smaller goals for yourself. Instead of those five pages today, make it three. Your pace is slower because you don't want to let go of this thing. You've been living together for a long, long time, you've let this smelly beast into your tent, and you've grown to love it, and now you're reluctant to have it gallop out over the sands and out of your life forever. The temptation is to keep it with you forever, constantly bathe it and scent it, groom it and curry it, tweeze its lashes and tie a bow on its tail. *Recognize* the temptation and recognize too that everything eventually grows up and leaves home. When you've done the best you can possibly do at this time (there *will* be other books, you know) put it in a box, give it a farewell kiss, and send it out into that great big hostile world.

SENDING: Where do you send it? Be exceedingly careful in choosing your agent or your publisher. Don't send the book to anyone who charges a fee for reading it or publishing it. In the real world of publishing, people pay *you* for your work. The Society of Authors' Representatives (if you decide to go the agent route) will send you on request a list of reputable agents in the United States. The address is 101 Park Avenue, New York, New York 10017. Just write and ask, enclosing a self-addressed, stamped envelope. If you decide to submit your manuscript directly to a publisher instead, a long list of publishers looking for various kinds of novels appears in *The Writer* Magazine, or in the market list in Part IV of this volume. Although some book publishers today have given up reading unsolicited manuscripts, many others still maintain reading staffs, and their sole purpose is to search for publishing possibilities. Send the novel manuscript out. One publisher at a time. Multiple submissions are frowned upon except when an agent is conducting a huge auction, and then the publishers are made aware beforehand that the book is being submitted simultaneously all over the field. Choose a publisher who has previously published your sort of book. Don't shotgun it around blindly. If your novel espouses atheism, don't send it to a religious publisher.

WAITING: So now your monster is out roaming the countryside, trying to earn a living. No, there it is in the mailbox. Damn thing. Wish you hadn't given it life at all. Tear open the package. Nice little noncommittal note. Thanks a lot, but no thanks. Despair. Chin up, kiddo, send it out again. But here it is *back* again. And *again.* And *yet* again. Plenty of publishers in the world, just keep trying. Pack it, send it, wait again. Why? Why wait? Why set up a vigil at the mailbox? Why hang around the post office looking like someone on the Wanted posters? You should be *thinking* instead. You should be mulling a new idea. *Don't* wait. What you *should* be doing is—

STARTING: If you haven't got an idea for one, forget it. If you haven't got an idea you want to express on paper, in words, forget it. If you prefer putting paint on canvas, or rolls on your pianola or in your oven, forget it. You're going to be with this novel for a long, long time, so you'd better have *thought* about it before you start writing it. When it's ready to be written, you'll know.

Write it.

26

VISUALIZING FICTION ON PAPER

By Dorothy Uhnak

WRITING began so far back in childhood that I literally cannot remember a time when I was *not* writing. I spent fourteen years of my adult life as a police officer in New York City. During all that time, I wrote continually, drawing on everything around me: the unique, exciting situations, the deadly boredom, the brutality, sadness, pain, humor (often macabre), the courage, cowardice, intelligence, stupidity, greed, anger, danger, and intense loyalty which characterize the working life of a police officer.

I was a capable police officer: I was promoted three times and awarded medals twice. I worked hard, was dedicated and earnest and concerned. Yet all the time, the writer in me was compiling events, feelings, atmosphere, emotions, situations for future use. *Policewoman,* semi-autobiographical, semi-fictional, was published during my tenure as a police officer and was my first attempt to set forth some things I had observed, learned, experienced, been a part of.

My first novel, *The Bait,* was published after I resigned from police work in order to devote myself more fully to writing and to continue my education. It was awarded the Edgar for the Best First Mystery of 1968, which I felt was somewhat ironic, for I never considered myself a "mystery writer." People are my main concern as a writer, and the task I set myself is to dig into the "mystery" of human behavior in given circumstances.

I have used the police world in all my books to date in order to explore certain events occurring between people, rather than to tell a "cop story" per se.

The Bait dealt with a sex murderer. On a deeper level, it explored the tormented world of a tragically demented man and his impact on a bright, sensitive young policewoman.

The Witness, second in my trilogy set in the Manhattan District Attorney's Squad, was a straightforward story about black organized crime and corruption. It was also a story about youthful idealism, hopes and energies that were misused and betrayed. It was part of the education-in-life of young Detective Christie Opara.

The Ledger, third in the trilogy, could be described as the story of the beautiful mistress of a crime lord. It was also a character study of two apparently opposite young women: one the worldly mistress, the other the idealistic Christie Opara. It was a probing of the painful, hidden truths each girl had to face about herself.

When I undertook my latest novel, *Law and Order,* I realized it was a radical departure from anything I had previously attempted. It was to span three generations, through four decades which have seen more social, political, moral upheaval than most of the rest of our history all put together. For one solid year, I did nothing but research. I probed back more than a hundred years to gain a fuller understanding of the immigrants who came to populate New York City, to lead and dominate not only the Police Department but the political and religious structure of the city for so many years. While the main characters are Irish, I also had to study all the important ethnic groups who comprise New York, to understand their aspirations, backgrounds, influences, self-image. I immersed myself in reading and discussion not only about politics, religious and ethnic history and folklore, but in economics and the effects of the Great Depression, World War II, the post-war world, the Korean War, Vietnam, the youth movement, generation gap, emergence of the drug culture.

I spent three weeks in Ireland wandering at random through that lovely tortured country: spoke to people, listened to them, read as much Irish writing as I could absorb until I could *feel* the rhythm of Irish thought and emotion. I allowed myself to get caught up and carried by the Irish idiom.

My characters grew out of the research. Certain strong characters began to dominate the other members of their family. And it was a "family" that grew into the story. They were at the hub and center of all the changing times of their city and their world. Through the three generations of O'Malleys, my aim was to present some of the social and moral questions with which we are confronted

128

in these complex times. My hero, Brian O'Malley, is first introduced as a young, inexperienced boy of eighteen, faced with the sudden responsibility of caring for his mother, grandmother, brothers and sisters on the violent death of his policeman-father. The book ends when Brian is a fifty-two-year-old Deputy Chief Inspector in the New York City Police Department, dealing as best he can with forces of corruption, coming to terms with his own policeman son, a Vietnam veteran, trying to live in a rapidly changing and always puzzling world.

One of the most exciting things about writing *Law and Order* was when the characters "took off" on their own. This hasn't happened to me as a writer very often. It is a rare, exciting, heady, exhilarating experience and occurs only when the characters are so well known, so well loved, that they can be trusted to act and react instinctively true to themselves.

The worst moment came when the manuscript was totally completed—all polished and ready to be set in galleys. I experienced the most dreadful sense of loss imaginable. All those warm, exciting, wildly active, strong and familiar people with whom I had shared my life for so long were suddenly taken from me, to be thrust out into the large and critical world.

The solution to this feeling of loss, for me at any rate, was to let a little time go by, enjoy the fruits of my labor, involve myself in other facets of the work, i.e., promotion and publicity—to relax, enjoy, take a deep breath, and begin the whole process all over again.

It must be admitted that no matter how many books I've written, how many characters created and lived with and let go, when I put the blank white paper in my machine, it is no easier for me to begin the written word than it ever has been. Publicity tours and best-seller lists, and book club and movie and TV sales are all very exciting and rewarding and lucrative. However, at the beginning of the day I am a pauper before the blank white paper. The trick is, I guess, just to keep at it from ground zero and to build on it during each session at the machine. Happily, it has started again for me; tentatively, fragilely, hopefully, I've begun a new book. Thankfully.

Since I've always been curious about other writers' work habits,

I will set down some of my own with hopes that my example will warn others to adopt other methods. Sometimes I wonder how in the world I've ever accomplished *any* body of work: I never seem to do all those things I'm positive a writer *should* do.

I've never kept notebooks filled with valuable phrases, impressions, observations. Oh, I've stacks of notebooks of all kinds— spiral ones with businesslike brown covers and spiral ones with pretty flowers on the cover. Somber little black looseleaf notebooks that fit into the palm of my hand and large ones that fill up my lap. They are all filled with empty pages, because I've never really known what to put in them. Once or twice, I've jotted down phrases which I conjured in the middle of the night, or en route somewhere on the subway, but somehow that never seemed pertinent to anything, and I spent too much time wondering what in the world I had in mind when I wrote them down in the first place. There are also pencil sketches of advertisements and some interesting doodles, not one of which is helpful.

A long time ago, I came to a strange conclusion relative to me and note-taking. Mysteriously, it has worked for me, but I do not recommend it to anyone else, merely report on it. If the thought, impression, idea, phrase, situation, or whatever is important enough for me to remember and use somewhere in my writing, I will retain it in cell x-y-or-z of my brain. If it isn't worth using, I will forget it. I don't remember how many flashing, brilliant thoughts might have been retained had they been jotted down. I do know that many conversations between characters in my stories give me a strong sense of *déjà vu*, because they were carried on in my head at some unconnected time in the past.

Another thing I don't do and feel I should: I don't have any work schedule. I mean, *I don't have any work schedule at all.* For a person who spent so many years in a structured work-situation, this leaves much room for feelings of guilt. I know I *should* sit at the machine and accomplish at least *that* much work each day, but I don't. I frankly don't know *when* I work. Sometimes, I leap out of bed at six in the morning, jump into my clothes, gulp my cup of tea and hammer out scene after scene after scene. Then, for days at a time, I avoid the top floor, which is where I work. At about three in the afternoon, the urge might hit again, and I hammer away at the next scene. I will point out that no matter how remiss I am about regulating my work schedule, at least this much is structured: I work a scene through, beginning to end, whether it runs for four pages or forty, whether it takes twenty-three minutes or six hours. Maybe it's those six-hour binges that get the job done for me.

In between actually sitting and pounding the keys, the story does go on inside my head, regardless of what else I am, physically, doing. I rake the leaves, play with the dogs, feed the cats, forget to defrost the supper, stare at daytime television (which is a horrible admission, I realize). The saving grace is that the story process continues, sometimes in some subterranean, unknown manner, because solutions to story problems sometimes take place when least expected. For example: in the shower, riding in a car at night, folding laundry, dusting the furniture, painting a wall.

When I'm well into a manuscript—in fact, during all stages of the manuscript—I rarely if ever rewrite. Probably because I wait so long before actually sitting down to the task, forming sentences in the air before I form them on paper, by the time I actually *do* sit down to work (whenever that is!), the phrases are ready and generally come out the way I want them to. Not always, but more often than not.

Generally, I am amazed at the way the pages of a manuscript pile up, given a particular period of time, because although I complain continuously about working too hard, when it's all over, I have very little remembrance of having worked *at all*.

Given one magic wish as a writer, I would want to be gifted with some kind of power to transform the scene in my head immediately into a bound, printed form without the ever-present struggle to find the words to frame and form the thought. My constant struggle as a writer is to zero in on the exact words that will enable my reader to see, feel, experience a particular scene with as much concern and intensity as I experience while visualizing and writing it.

I don't know what advice to offer young writers. I'm not even sure anyone should presume to offer any advice beyond that one tormenting, beautiful, obvious, obscure, demanding, torturous ecstasy: WRITE. Don't talk about it, whine about it, rap about it, agonize over it, dissect, analyze, study or anything else: Just do it. WRITE.

27

TWENTY QUESTIONS TO ASK A CHARACTER

By Winifred Madison

Dig deeper! How many times does an author hear this advice? Characters are the life and breath of a story. Get your reader to care about what happens to them and you have won him over. But how do you do this?

First, most important of all, the character must seem alive to you, so very much alive that you feel as though you were inside his skin. This may happen instantly as you pass someone on the street or meet someone at a party and immediately you know something instinctively about this person and you feel you must use him in one of your stories. It may be a matter of luck that has no logical explanation. It simply happens.

The source does not matter so much as the *depth* and *insight* you develop. I get to know and understand my characters the same way I discover those individuals who come into my life. It's a mixture of first impressions, concrete factual knowledge, that mysterious "knowing" that comes about when you spend time with a person. Time is the key word.

Make up a dossier for each of your principal characters, either before you write your story or after you've completed the first draft. The twenty questions that follow will help you "dig deep," to probe the depths of your characters so you will get to know them.

1. Pretend you are walking down the street and you see your character for the very first time. Quick now—what word or phrase leaps to your mind? It may be one word: tyrant, drudge, darling, dreamer, flirt, macho, slob . . . anything at all. It may be a phrase, a warning, such as "Watch out!" or "Me first!" It could be a foolish giggle or a friendly hello or a plaintive, "I really wouldn't know . . ." No matter how far-

fetched or illogical this initial impact may be, it may prove a valuable insight into the essence of that particular person.

One day a young woman came to my door—attractive, blonde, smiling easily. The first words that filled my mind were "California, country sun, remarkably good health in every way." I made her sixteen years old, a capable 4-H girl, and she became the heroine of my young adult novel, *Dance With Me*. As I wrote it, that first impression stayed in my mind.

Some authors, attracted by a photograph or illustration in a newspaper or magazine, will clip it and use it as a model. A good idea.

2. Quickly following the initial impact will be the general physical impression of the person. Again, do not try to think of the words you may ultimately use when you write the story; let them come freely to your mind: "a burly block of a man," "a sunbeam," "a weed," "a wisp," "a full-blown cabbage rose about to shed its petals." The posture, the stance, the stride and rhythm of movement, possibly some body gestures, as well as the bulk and density of the physical build, will immediately give you clues to your character.

3. Are you reminded of an animal or an object? If a comparison happens to come to mind, explore it. Some people definitely resemble birds, cats, rodents, or monkeys, and in the case of inanimate objects such disparate things as a bus, or a feather duster, or a fragile wine glass. Be careful about clichés, the too frequent "birdlike woman" or the "China doll heroine."

4. Can you sense a color in your character, something beyond skin color or purely physical features? Certain psychics claim to see colors emanating from personalities. We cannot always go that far, but we may have the impression of an insistent color, a "brown personality," or a radiant red-gold, or a dismal blue-gray. One person may make you think of bright primary colors, while a subtle shifting of gray tones characterizes another.

5. What kinds of clothes does your character wear? Here is an important key to his psyche. Often people dress to conform to what they

believe is their social status: We all wear uniforms. However, we may be fooled, as individuals sometimes dress according to their fantasies and unconscious or unfulfilled desires—interesting and worthwhile for a fiction writer to explore. And use. For example, the middle-aged woman who wears too much makeup and designer jeans meant for her daughter or even for her granddaughter, may be saying she doesn't want anyone to know her age, or that she has a real dread of getting old and unattractive to young people (young men?), or that she wants to relive her youthful, romantic experiences. A businessman who wears western boots, shirt, and string tie and carries his attaché case to his big-city office is saying something important about himself and his dreams. It can be a defiance of convention or a yearning for a carefree youth he never had.

6. The person's voice is also revealing. Can you describe its tonal quality in one word, such as, soft, soothing, abrasive, enthusiastic, energetic, etc.? Does your character speak with an accent, a lisp, a certain eccentricity? How does he use words? What does he say, and what does he leave unsaid? As you learn more about this man, you should be able to imitate him, the quality of voice, the expression, suggest the very words he would use. Become an actor or actress as you write, saying out loud your character's speeches until you are convinced that is exactly how they must sound.

7. Where does your character live during the course of the story? How much of his immediate environment is forced on him and how much of it does he control? Does he like it? What does it mean to him? Is it possible he wants to leave it and if so, why?

You will not need and should not include in your story or novel every detail of your hero or heroine's life, but the more you know about it, the more you will understand some of the reasons for his or her actions.

8. Where and when was he born? Where did he live during his childhood? What country? What environment, i.e., a city, a small town, a rural area, mountains, the coast? How has this background shaped his personality? Was anything in particular happening historically?

9. What were the earliest and theoretically the most important influences? What of his parents, his siblings, relatives, friends, teachers, early loves? Here is where you will find many keys to the personality you are studying.

10. Every decade has new problems, changing standards, different moods. The forties are not like the fifties, nor are the fifties like the sixties, and so on. Does the one in which your hero formed his personality influence him in his actions and philosophy? Does he accept the standards of his time or does he rebel?

We have progressed beyond our first impression, although it should always stay with us. Can you imitate your character, walk like him, talk as he would, know exactly what he would think and how he would react to almost anything at all? If so, he is taking physical shape. Now try to get inside him. Know him better than he knows himself.

11. What is most important to him? What does he want more than anything else? Do you know his fantasies, his daydreams?

12. What is his conflict? If he has no problem, chances are he won't be interesting. Is his conflict imposed by circumstances, or does it emanate from within him? Suppose, for example, he is a young man who detests war and yet wishes to defend his country, a common dilemma for many young people today.

What of a woman who wants to get out and live by herself and yet fears she will lose her family if she does so?

Do you want your character to settle his conflict by himself, or will fate or circumstances do it for him?

13. How far will he go to get what he wants? Will he steal, commit a crime or perform an immoral act to achieve his goal? You may hook your reader by getting him to wonder about it along with you.

14. Here is a most telling question: What does your character fear the most? Does this keep him from achieving his ends?

15. More revealing areas. Cards, money, love. How much does winning matter to your character? How does he handle competition?

16. How does he react to children, and animals, foreigners, old people? How do you know? Would he kick his wife's dog if she weren't there to defend it? Would he carry a spider outside rather than kill it when it had crept into his bedroom? Would this woman refuse to rent a room to an oriental or a black or to someone who had children?

17. How does your character shape the plot? How does the plot shape him or her? Does he grow or change during the course of the story? If by any chance he remains the same, which should be unlikely, can you explain that?

18. How does this character interact with other members of the cast? Who acts as his foil? Who contrasts or complements your hero or heroine? Who or what threatens him?

19. By this time you've made quite a study of this character. Do you like him or her? What is undesirable or negative about him? What, no faults? Then such a character is likely to be b-o-o-ring. And not quite human. The same theory will hold for the villains of the piece. A person who is completely bad is only slightly less boring than one who is entirely good. Rembrandt used to advise mixing a little darkness in the light areas and a little light in the dark sections of a drawing. The same principle will make your characters more interesting.

20. Finally, what is there in your character that will make the reader care about what happens to him? Whether you are writing "the great American novel" or something more modest, your reader must be touched by your hero or heroine, or you have lost him. And what about you? Do you find yourself so involved that you hate to make your characters suffer? (Although you will have to do it anyway, because without suffering there is no story.)

A human being can be endlessly complicated. Twenty questions are only the first of many questions you will want to ask your character. What does he do on a stormy day? Does he cheat on his income tax? What does he like to eat? Where would he go on a vacation if he had a free choice and didn't have to think about money?

"Digging deeper" means living with your character day and night. It's one way of meeting interesting people!

28

CREATING THE "OUTCAST" CHARACTER

BY EVELYN WILDE MAYERSON

FROM EARLIEST times, the aberrant among us have held a strange fascination. Our literature is rich with Calibans and Quasimodos, and modern fiction has countless examples of characters who are impaired or have psychopathic personalities. William Faulkner's Benjy in *The Sound and the Fury,* Steinbeck's Lenny in *Of Mice and Men,* Mary Shelley's creature in her novel *Frankenstein,* Edgar Allan Poe's crippled dwarf in *Hopfrog,* Conrad Aiken's schizophrenic child Paul in "Silent Snow, Secret Snow," Saul Bellow's *Herzog,* and playwright Bernard Pomerance's *The Elephant Man,* all represent an earnest quest of the writer to explore the aberrant.

We are both attracted and repulsed by the deprived or emotionally and physically impaired. For the novelist or story writer to whom characterization may be the single most important element of his work, dealing with a character who both attracts and repels presents problems that the creation of other characters does not. Writers who would create offbeat or oddball characters and make them not only come alive but also have appeal for readers, have a few strikes against them. It is easier for readers to identify with characters favored with youth, talent, and beauty, attributes that our society holds in high regard. Even if readers are not so endowed, they like to believe that they could become so. Further, readers like to live vicariously through the experiences of the advantaged. The world of the beautiful and the healthy, where one has presumably sufficient attractiveness to garner all the sexual partners and material goods one wants, offers fulfillment of the most audacious daydreams and fantasies.

In creating an aberrant character, however, writers have to know before they put down their first word that there is natural reader resistance to this character from the start. No reader wants to live vicariously through such a person's experiences.

137

Writers, then, are dealing not only with their art, but also with human emotion on a very elemental level. It is not enough that they be talented craftsmen, they must also understand that readers are not only rational thinking beings, but irrational feeling beings with enough private fears to choke a typewriter. Responding to this is a challenge and also the first step.

The next step is an examination of the novelist's own motivation in choosing the character. Is the decision an honest one? Is the selection made because of its inherent shock value, or is it a natural part of the writer's statement, his philosophy, question, story line, or even metaphor? Writers must ask themselves why they want to use this character as opposed to another more closely approximating the normal. For example, if the writer plans to do a piece about someone grossly fat, that person's obesity must be intrinsic to the story. There has to be a valid reason for the choice: What problem does the writer intend to construct that requires a fat character? Why fat and not thin; why either extreme; and would a person of average weight do as well?

In my novel *Sanjo,* I first set out to write about contrasts in perspective. To demonstrate this conflict, I chose a severely retarded adult woman as my protagonist. I did not want to write about a retarded child, a character who would have naturally endearing qualities simply because we think children are appealing. Neither did I want to create a physically attractive woman; because of the sexual significance, such a main character would soften the problem and not allow it to be stated as starkly as I wished—a situation without remedy. The factors that would cause the reader to care about Sanjo would not stem from her physical qualities, but from her day-to-day activities, her responses and her feelings, her triumphs and her despairs.

It is an interesting sidelight to note that most aberrant fictional characters (with the exception of a few, including Marjorie Kellogg's Junie Moon in *Tell Me That You Love Me, Junie Moon,* and Joanne Greenberg's schizophrenic adolescent in *I Never Promised You A Rose Garden*) have been men. I don't think that this is a reflection of a greater number of aberrant males than females in our society. Rather it has to do with what our society will and will not accept in women. Carson McCullers says that the oddball is a revelation of ourselves. I think that the preponderance of the aberrant male in fiction is a revelation of how our society sees women.

It is harder to evoke sympathy for the impaired female because of such attitudes—something to do with the rigidly determined position of women in our society as either adornment, sexual partner, or mother. Until recently, there was little place for the female who was none of these. My selection of Sanjo and Hester the bag woman in my novel *If Birds Are Free* was a deliberate attempt to expose some of these deep-rooted prejudices.

The writer who is confident that this selection of an aberrant character is an honest one, must care about the character. I don't mean with a bleeding heart leaking all over one's copy, but with an intelligent empathy for the difficulties such a character must face in a world that reveres the normal. Although most writers care about all their characters, they are more likely to be able to influence the readers' sympathy and understanding and make them worry about what will happen to their protagonist if their concern is genuine.

The best way I know to achieve this is to recognize one's limitations. Some of us are more richly endowed than others, some of us less. No matter how good we think we are, we are sure to meet someone better in some respects.

The writer must be free from taboo and the convention of who is and who is not a proper subject for a fictional character. In a recent study of creativity, it was found that there was a correlation between inhibition and creativity: The more creative persons, defined as those actively producing the arts—writers, composers, painters, sculptors, and the like—inhibit themselves and monitor their thoughts less than the noncreative. Propriety and inhibition have no place in literature. Writers must be confident that all human experience is suitable material for their explorations.

Writers must also avoid style and treatment taboos. Much of *Sanjo* and of my later novel *If Birds Are Free* is funny. I didn't design it that way. That's the way both stories naturally developed. If I had been inhibited, I would have censored myself with thoughts like, it's not O.K. to be writing about a retardate and a schizophrenic derelict in the first place, so I'd better be serious, even funereal, and hope that in so doing I have expiated my transgression.

If a subject with which he is unfamiliar interests the writer, he can research it. Ignore the caveat that one can only write about what he has experienced. One of the best battle scenes ever written was by Stephen

Crane in *The Red Badge of Courage,* and he was never on a battlefield. I am an avid researcher and a believer in finding out what I don't know. There are many sources for information, including libraries, newspaper morgues, and people to telephone. I can spend days checking out a single fact that I consider significant to my story or to my character. While researching the medical and legal problems in *If Birds Are Free,* in addition to weeks spent sitting in a courtroom, I spoke to a doctor in Oregon who is an expert on the treatment of frostbite, to a lawyer in Philadelphia who is an expert on the legal rights of the indigent insane, and to two experts on the endangered falcon, one in New Jersey and one in Miami. I enjoy researching, particularly in the dusty corners of the library where investigation becomes detective work.

In addition to clarifying facts in libraries and through consultation with experts, the writer must meet people who share the impairments of the fictional character. If they are not part of the writer's personal experience, he has only to find them and spend some time with them. When I needed to know more about shopping bag ladies, I went into the streets of Philadelphia, spent four days in a hostel, spent more time dishing out food in another hostel (potatoes and bread were my responsibility; for some reason my portions were never consistent enough for me to serve the meat), and talking and listening to whoever would stick around me long enough to do so. It meant that I left my preconceptions at home with my briefcase, sat on stone steps for hours, and walked miles, waiting for the right time to speak, the right time to question—with not too much direct eye contact, or too much smiling, a social contrivance at once distrusted by the wary. I knew that if I moved in too fast, my bag ladies would hustle themselves and their bags away.

Writers can simulate the experience of some handicapped characters. For example, to create my blind character Augie, I put layers of gauze over my eyes so that my vision, like his, was limited to light and shadow, and vague general outlining of shapes. I do not presume to say that my single day's experience with bandaged eyes lets me fully understand the blind experience, but it does bring me one step closer than before I bruised my shins, fell down twice, and spilled coffee on my blouse.

Armed with background to give him a clear idea of his character, the writer is ready to bring the character to life. Characterization deals with three major components: *physical description* (age, sex, height, weight, walk, speech, facial expressions, etc.); *the inner mind* (memory, motiva-

140

tion, self-image, intelligence, sensibilities—in short, the psyche of the character); and *behavior* (habits, mannerisms of the character, and his responses to situations and to other people).

The physical description of the mentally or physically impaired requires a deft but delicate hand. The writer must be careful not to hit the reader with too much too soon. In the construction of Sanjo, the retarded victim of Down's syndrome, I used almost no physical description at all in the first chapter other than that of her stubby fingers. The reader's first picture of Sanjo comes from the responses of others around her, from her father, who looks at her in "the way he looked at a scab on his elbow that never healed," from an insurance agent who couldn't touch her, and whose hands . . . "flopped beside him, hypotonic appendages that had lost their will . . . like the only time he had been with a prostitute," and from little four-year-old Penny, who tells her to " 'put your tongue back in your mouth.' "

Physical description is delayed until the second chapter where it is divided, occurring naturally in the narration as part of the story line. On page 31, "Her skirt covering her stubbly legs . . . and her straight, sparse brown hair cut to her ears." Again, on page 35, "Her body looked like a wedge. Wide triangular cartilage gave her a flattened saddle nose. Her eyes had a hooded look, the lids with an epicanthic fold which made her look, to some people, Oriental." Her "customary, unsteady gait, stooped, her head hanging forward and her feet spread wide apart. Her arms hung straight down from her shoulders with her palms facing behind her."

Physical description is only one dimension of characterization. We have to round the character in other ways, so that we show not only what this person looks like, but also the clothes he wears, if he eats breakfast or grabs a Clark's Bar on the run and downs it with a swig of coffee from a thermos, his social class, vernacular, schooling, occupation, age, the kind of neighborhood he grew up in, his hopes and fears, and that special collection of traits that makes him unique. It is with these details that we bring the character closer to the reader's experience and make identification possible.

To describe the inner mind, we have only to step into the character's shoes. All of us have felt alone, intimidated, jubilant, hopeful, inadequate, and frightened. The writer has to invest his character with these feelings and demonstrate them to the reader. It is easier then for readers to identify with that character, when it is evident that they share the experience of being human. For example, all of us can recall anguish at the loss of a loved one. Sanjo experiences that anguish after her mother has a stroke and lies in the intensive care unit of a hospital, and Sanjo is sent to live with Mrs. Cervitano, the neighbor across the street.

Sanjo's house had a heliotropic pull for her. She continued to face in its direction like a leaf drawn to the sun. The house was her biography. It brought to mind the events of the day before as well as her whole life. This was the first time in her experience that she had not awakened in it. It was also the first time in her experience that she had not been with at least one of her parents.

She sat on the curb to stare at her house, her heart pounding, her hands sweating, and her stomach turning. She had a strong need to go to the bathroom. The worried feeling was back. "Ma! Poppy! Come out!" There was no answer. She hugged her knees.

The third component of characterization—behavior—is what makes the character unique. Habits and mannerisms give him individuality. Knowing something about his background enables us to give him unique traits of personality when we put him into situations to which he must respond. His behavior is what results naturally.

In the following conversation, in which Hester the bag woman is told by her doctor that he wants to amputate her feet, she demonstrates her tenacity.

"You want to cut my feet off. I don't want you to cut my feet off."
"That's essentially it. It's something we don't like to do, but we believe very strongly we have to do it, and soon. Time is an important factor here. Do you know why we need to amputate your feet?"
"You have a quota."
"No. That's not the reason."
"You think I'm going to die."
"That's right. That's what we think. That's what we're all afraid of."
"Leave me alone."
"Does that mean you want to die? . . . "
"It means I don't want to be short."

Finally, writers have to resist the temptation to sentimentalize their aberrant characters. Pity can get in the way, and it is not pity one wants, anyway, certainly not from the reader. I made Augie, the legally blind street hustler in *If Birds Are Free,* a rogue, a sniveling opportunist, and a liar. I wanted no saintly beggars tapping around my street corners, and decided instead that Augie would be no more, no less virtuous than the general population.

What the writer is looking for is to make the reader identify with the character, feel empathy, not pity. The writer wants the reader to feel, not that there but for the grace of God go I, but there in another guise go I.

29

CHECKPOINTS FOR YOUR SHORT STORY

By Margaret Chittenden

Every day, hundreds of writers hurl short stories at beleaguered magazine editors, who hurl most of them back at about the same rate. Yet editors are not our enemies. They are vitally interested in publishing the best material they can. That's why many of them are willing to plough through 10,000 to 30,000 submissions searching for the twelve to twenty-four short stories they need.

How can we get our stories to be among the chosen few? Obviously, with today's odds, it's not enough just to write a good story. It has to have something extra to make it stand out from the rest.

I can't claim to have all the answers. But I can share with you the questions I ask of every story I write before I type the final draft, questions whose answers, I think, determine whether or not my stories will make it in the marketplace.

First, I look at the CHARACTERS. Are they alive? Do they walk off the page and into the reader's heart? If they aren't alive, can I bring them to life? Most important, can I bring them to life in the limited space of a short story?

I make a practice of studying people in supermarkets, restaurants, libraries, airports, wherever I happen to be. As I watch them (discreetly, I hope), I make up one-liners that capture not only something of their appearance, but also something of what I imagine their characters to be. I use these one-liners in my stories. Like this. "Only her eyes give her away— such sad, lost eyes, too big for her small face." ("Three's A Family," *Good Housekeeping*) or this: "Dave was a Sagittarian, born old, dark eyes full of memories from the day he was born, but hope there too, always hope." ("The Shooky Bridge," *P.I. Northwest*)

Once I can *see* my characters clearly, I listen to them talk. If I've done my job right, they don't talk the way most of us do. They don't ramble around the subject. They aren't—*boring!* Good dialogue is crisp and to the point. It should not only communicate; it should tell something about the speaker, and if possible, the listener.

My story, "What's A Nice Girl Like Me Doing?" (*Ladies' Home Journal*) is a lighthearted look at a fairly serious problem. A mother is overwhelmed by the noise and commotion of her children. This is not the life she intended to have. One of the ways I showed this to the reader was through dialogue.

"When I was in High School," I reminisced, "I meant to become a female Albert Schweitzer. How did I end up here?"
Rob patted my hand. "Look at it this way. Out in the jungle you'd be coping with witch doctors and drums. Not a lot of difference."

While I'm still dealing with my characters, I take a look at their motivation. Have I let the reader know *why* there is conflict between them? There has to be conflict. There has to be a reason.

In my story, "Three's A Family," a woman and her stepdaughter are not getting along. I let the reader know why in this way:

I was nurtured on television myths of beribboned little girls, cuddling close to mothers, listening to fairy tales, sharing shampoo. But Patty doesn't like to read. "That's kid stuff," she says. She won't let me wash her hair. "I can manage myself," is her favorite phrase.

If I've motivated my characters properly, the reader will understand them. And if he understands them, he will believe in them. They will have come to life.

Now let's move on to the writing itself. Is it lively? Full of energy and life—vigorous? Writing like that would be sure to sell. It's certainly something to strive for.

I look at the nouns first. Are they specific? Did I write, "The car ran over the dog in the street." Or did I write, "The Volkswagen ran over the Saint Bernard in the middle of Picadilly Circus."

Whenever possible I try to be specific. "The bungalow," "the farm-house," "the three-story brownstone." Not "the house."

Verbs are next up for scrutiny. Are they active? "He strolled" is better than "He was walking slowly." "He sauntered" is even more effective. "Claire *attacked* her oysters." "The sailboats *scudded* across the blue water." "Dan *scuffed* sand with his bare toes."

What else can I do to make my writing lively? How about the sentences? Are they varied enough, or do too many begin with "the" or consist simply of subject, predicate, object? Suppose I try to wake the reader up with a change in rhythm? Here's an example:

> Discouragement filled her as he escorted her, oh so gallantly, back to the table. The wineglasses were still there. So was the bug. ("Memory of Love," *Good Housekeeping*)

I often use one or two words set between periods for the sake of effect. "I walked back into my house with a feeling of disbelief. Silence. Complete and utter silence."

Punctuation can also make a difference in liveliness. I'm fond of the dash. (Too fond, copy editors tell me.)

> How often I'd moved along this hall, listening at bedroom doors, checking that the children were all in there—breathing. ("Nice Girl.")

Next checkpoint: PACE—the rate of movement, progress, development. A short story shouldn't gallop along, of course, but it should move fairly rapidly to hold the reader's interest. If my story seems too slow-paced, it probably needs to be cut. I examine every·word in every sentence, asking myself, "Is this *necessary* to the story?" If it's not, out with it.

Most of my stories are short-shorts of about 1500 words. But they don't start out that way. My first draft is invariably 6000 words. Write long, cut short, is my motto.

I check for pace first at the beginning of the story. Am I explaining too much, leading in to the story instead of starting *in medias res,* as the ancient Romans put it? Here are a couple of my beginnings that I feel passed this test:

> Every young wife must have moments of discontent. I'd had quite a few before Joel and I visited Anita Lane's apartment. ("After The Wedding," *Good House-keeping*)

> Standing bareheaded beside the open grave, I'm trying not to think that—my God—that's Dave in the casket, trying not to listen to the ash-dry voice of the Chaplain droning, because it can't be Dave, Dave is my friend. ("The Shooky Bridge.")

Pace is just as important in the middle of the story. That is where the story develops. A story should not be a string of unrelated events; one incident should arise logically out of another. So I check to see if the story middle follows the rule of cause and effect. In "After The Wedding," *because* Ellen and Joel go to visit Anita's perfect apartment, Ellen begins to worry that she's cheated Joel by marrying him before he was established and had a chance to make money. *Because* of her worry, she is subdued, and Joel thinks she's upset because he hasn't provided the things Anita owns. *Because* of this, he becomes quiet and thoughtful which makes Ellen afraid—and so on.

Pace is vital to the ending of a story. There isn't room to explain everything. I have to show the resolution of the story and finish as gracefully and quickly as possible. In my stories I want the main character to solve his/her problem, fail to solve it, or come to a new understanding of it; if it's a literary-type story, let the *reader* come to a new understanding of the problem. But something must have changed if the reader is to feel satisfied.

And I must show this to the reader in as few words as possible.

I ended "Nice Girl," this way:

> He pulled me into his arms and I relaxed against him, feeling warm and understood. "Tell me," he murmured into my hair, "what's a nice girl like you doing in a place like this?"
> I smiled against his shoulder. "Living," I said. "Just living."

Here the main character shows she has reached a new understanding of her problem. She has realized that in a few years the children will be gone and the house will be silent, so she'd better enjoy the sounds of her children while she can.

And that's a sneaky way to introduce theme. The above sentence was also the theme of the story. For some reason, theme is often disregarded entirely by writers. But no story will leap off the stack into the editor's hands if it doesn't have a theme, if it doesn't *say* something. Read one of your stories. What does it say? Put it in one sentence.

The theme doesn't have to be world-shaking. Some of mine are the following: "A practical husband is better than a romantic one." "Living with the right person is more important than having a lot of *things.*" "Rudeness in a child can be a cover-up for fear."

Next checkpoint: Does the SYMBOLISM work? Do you use symbolism in your stories? If you are a poet, you are used to thinking in symbols. In my soul I am a poet, but in my brain I am as pedestrian as they come. I have to hunt consciously for symbols.

147

I've used a lot of birds. Birds are interesting. Starlings do not behave in the same way as pelicans or ducks or swallows or hawks.

Bridges are a good bet, too. A bridge can be the line between life and death, or the period between childhood and maturity.

Animals can be used for analogies. I have a gerbil that refuses to leave her cage. If I open the door, she huddles in a back corner, trembling. Symbol for a story.

I can't of course drop a symbol into a story and let it lie there. In "Three's A Family," the stepmother puts up a birdhouse to attract swallows. Starlings move in. (She had wanted a cuddly, pretty daughter—she got a rough, tough tomboy of a stepdaughter.) Mother and stepdaughter watch the starlings (hinting at possible future closeness). They see the father starling struggling to get a large twig into the birdhouse, battering it over and over, determined to get it in. (The daughter has the same attitude toward life.) All through the story, starlings are contrasted with swallows to show the difference between the mother's expectations and the reality of the child.

It's a good idea to look for symbolism in stories you read. And work at using it in your own. Remember, editors are looking for that extra edge—that certain something that makes your story special.

Sometimes I decide a light touch will improve a story. More often, the entire story is written with a light touch. This is my personal extra edge, I think. I do have an upbeat (some say irreverent) view of life, and I deliberately bring that into play in my work. Every writer should speak with his or her own voice, of course. It is possible, I've found, to treat the most serious problem with a light touch and still make the point I want to make:

> I collapsed beside him (Rob) on the stairs. "Did you ever wonder what our lives would be like if we didn't have children?"
> "Frequently. But unfortunately there's no way to make birth control retroactive." ("Nice Girl.")

In the first draft, Rob's reply was "Frequently, but there's not much we can do about it now!" The light touch made the same point, but in a livelier way, I think.

Sometimes I exaggerate a situation to give it humor (though it has to be believable). In "Nice Girl," I had all three children making some kind of noise. Randy is playing his trumpet. Kristen is watching "Sesame

148

Street." Tammy is playing, "I'm a little teapot," on her record player. Mother is going crazy. The reader, I hope, is identifying—and smiling.

I often spend days—*weeks,* going over and over stories so that they will read in a light, breezy, easy way. I like leaving readers with a smile—albeit a rueful smile. Humor can even enliven a sad story and give it poignancy. It's a device worth trying, though it should not be added gratuitously. It has to belong to the story. *Everything* has to belong to the story.

Not all my stories are light, though the light ones outsell the more serious ones five to one. But whatever I write, I want my reader to feel some kind of emotion. Many of my stories came about because of a moment of emotion. The time I suddenly noticed my young son's hands were bigger than mine. The time my daughter told me not to chase starlings away from the birdhouse. "Starlings have to live, too," she said. The time a man told me the only choice he'd ever had in life was the choice between living and dying. "I chose to live," he told me. I didn't write a story about him, but I did write about a man in the same situation who chose to die. ("The Shooky Bridge.")

For the reader to have an emotional reaction, the writer must have one first. Do you smile while reading parts of your stories? Do you feel a lump in your throat here, a wave of nostalgia there? Do you feel anger, sorrow, happiness, love? Let the reader in on your feelings, on your story people's feelings. Reach for the heart. If you can make your story lively and well-paced, bring your characters to life and motivate them believably so that they move the reader emotionally, then your story will be greeted by that beleaguered editor with the grateful words, "Yes, this is the story I've been looking for."

30

CREATING A "REJECTION-RESISTANT" NOVEL

By Shelly Lowenkopf

THERE IS nothing to match first the outrage and then the dismay of the beginning writer who discovers how much of a book-length manuscript an editor or agent will read before reaching the decision to send the manuscript back to the author.

Three pages.

If you haven't caught their interest by then, you aren't likely to, and they know it. I'm here to tell you what has to go into the first three pages of your manuscript to make sure editors, agents, and prospective readers stay with you.

Start with important action. Involve someone of consequence in an event of consequence or with a threat of significant impact. A major complaint among editors who read the work of unpublished novelists and of agents who screen potential clients is the blunt, often fatal verdict: Nothing happens. Make sure something happens in your opening, even if it is only an artful promise that something momentous is building and *will* explode soon.

Amazing how many beginners include "warm-up exercises," bits and pieces of background and detail the author needs to know in order to back off and let the characters tell the story. More often than not, the reader doesn't care about these bits of trivia and resents being told them. Warm-up exercises and needless descriptions are the first things to pare after you've finished your first draft.

Think stress. Fiction demands conflict, the yeast of all drama. Make sure your opening action has a stressful effect on one or more of your major characters. If all your characters are happy or agree or get on well together or like the same flavor of ice cream, what chance is there for excitement and conflict? Disagreement, change, pressures, and fear force issues.

Make promises you intend to keep. Each genre or category of novel carries an inherent promise of a special feature. Mystery readers expect an intriguing puzzle or an opportunity to match wits with a skilled sleuth. Romance readers expect to see an interesting heroine who is being pressured into making difficult choices about career, love interest, and family loyalties. Adventures promise the reader fast-paced action. Historicals promise rich background and a sense of a particular time in the past. Fantasies promise imaginative use of magic and seemingly insurmountable barriers. Science-fiction novels promise a convincing extrapolation of the unknown from the known. Juvenile fiction promises to discuss the problems of young readers without patronizing them.

Get to know the promise expected by the readers of the genre you intend to write. Make that promise in a dramatic way, and keep hammering away at it by additional plot pressures on the main characters. Tolstoi's classic beginning to his novel *Anna Karenina*—"Happy families are all alike; every unhappy family is unhappy in its own way"—promises a story of heart-wrenching sadness. Generations and countless Kleenex later, no serious critic has yet come forth to suggest that Tolstoi reneged on his promise.

The prolific writers who have learned their craft well get to the basics fast in the first three pages. A tantalizing promise is one of the staples of fiction. Check out the big names in the categories that interest you. Note carefully how these authors set up the opening promise sometimes as early as the first paragraph.

Introduce or foreshadow your major characters. They don't necessarily have to appear on stage right at the beginning; minor characters can be talking about them instead. However you introduce your major characters, make sure they are doing something or something is being done to them. The first few pages of a novel is no place for sitting around and speculating.

Protagonist/antagonist. Let the reader know the loyalties and sympathies of your major characters. Help the reader choose someone to root for and identify with, and recognize whom to fear, suspect, or dislike.

Point-of-view. Who is telling your story and why? The narrator of your novel can materially effect the dramatic impact on the reader. F. Scott Fitzgerald chose Nick Carraway—exactly the right person—to "tell" *The Great Gatsby*. Anyone else as narrator and the ironic effect of Gatsby's life and his second attempt to woo Daisy would have been blunted, possibly lost. And imagine how forced and irritating Sherlock Holmes would have sounded if he'd narrated his own deeds in the first person. Dr. Watson was the perfect choice of foil and narrator. Look carefully at your own characters and the demands of a particular genre, then choose the narrator or narrators for the best possible effect.

What's at stake? Establish what your major characters have to gain or lose. What are their goals? What obstacles have to be cleared? What milestones have to be reached? Some novels in the adventure and espionage categories literally deal with the fate of an entire nation. Some novels focus on an individual career or the outcome of an election or the results of a horse race. If the reader sees what the stakes are, there is a greater likelihood that the reader will empathize with your protagonists, applaud their successes, and suffer at their setbacks.

Establish the setting. Show where your novel will take place and when. If your work is a fantasy, your setting will most likely be an entirely imaginary world, the results of your own creation. Give the reader immediate help; show the surroundings, refer to flora and fauna. Wherever your novel is set and whatever the historical perspective, show the reader as quickly as possible as much as necessary to grasp the nuances of plot.

Establish the arena. Beginners often mistake this element for setting. Every novel has a dramatic collision or confrontation between protagonist and antagonist. The arena for a sports novel is the playing field, stadium, race course, or ring. The arena for the Western is the open range or desert. Historicals have arenas in castles, battlefields, country manors, government buildings, or cities. Romances frequently have their arenas in the home, while science fiction often uses the confines of a space craft or a colony on a real planet, an orbiting space station, or an imaginary locale. A novel of the legal profession will be likely to feature a courtroom clash, and a novel about doctors could have the arena in the operating room or the laboratory. The arena is the place where an epic confrontation between the opposing forces takes place. This confrontation leads directly to the conclusion.

The beginning must foreshadow the conclusion. However spontaneous and flexible a novel may seem, its inner workings are quite fixed and rigid. A novel is not a series of random events; all activities are carefully linked. There may be happy accidents of creativity on the way to the conclusion, but the author who does not see the beginning as a means of

152

reaching the conclusion is an author who is losing control of pace, conflict, and suspense. If the conclusion comes from somewhere outside the framework of the story, the reader will feel cheated. At the very least, the beginning hints at the arena where the opposing forces will collide.

Set the tone. Romances and historicals move at a more leisurely pace to allow the reader to absorb background and to luxuriate in the richness of relevant description. Clothing, architecture, gardens, meals, music, and the like get more emphasis. Mysteries and adventures tend to get right down to the business of establishing the puzzle or problem.

Often, tone is an overall personality. Sometimes it may reflect the feelings of the narrator. It is permissible—even desirable—to vary the tone from narrator to narrator in a multiple point-of-view book.

Study the genre you wish to write. The wrong tone could become a fatal flaw. No tone at all—a detached, impersonal approach—could rob a clever plot and strong characters of a unifying personality by making them appear to be part of a journalistic report. Don't try to force an elegant style, don't try to set records for the number of figures of speech used, resist the temptation to use puns or throw-away humor. If you are having trouble setting a proper tone, it is probably because you are getting in the way of your characters. Go back to your protagonist and antagonist, take more time to know them, then listen to what they tell you.

Establish interest. This is often confused with plot, what's at stake, or suspense, but is really directed at your own sense of interest and participation in the novel you are writing. The work currently in your typewriter may be the most tightly plotted mystery since Dashiell Hammett, or it may be an historical with the sweep and background that would make Mary Renault groan with envy. But if it is not interesting to you—if you are having to force it—you will not carry the vital life forces through to the editor and your hoped-for audience. If you find your interest waning, stop and take a survey of the missing elements. You must ask yourself in all candor what it will take to restore your interest. Then you must listen very carefully for the answer and build the elements suggested by that answer into your story. There is no such thing as an obligatory boring scene, where it is all right to pile on the background or description. If you can't find an interesting way to get it—whatever *it* is—into your novel, chances are great that it doesn't belong.

No free rides. Nothing should be permitted in your novel that doesn't carry its own weight. This applies uniformly to characters, descriptions, motives, exchanges of dialogue, jokes, red herrings, plot twists. Choose

153

every element with care; if you aren't going to use it later, if it doesn't make some material contribution to the development and outcome of the story, forget it. The famous "Flitcraft" story Sam Spade tells Brigid O'Shaugnessey in *The Maltese Falcon* seems thrown in for padding at first, but on later consideration, the reader can see how it provides valuable insights into the characters and the problem at hand.

By now, you're probably ready with the big question: How am I supposed to cram all these elements into three or four manuscript pages for later development? The good news is that it can be done. Top professionals are doing it all the time. The bad news is that it may take you several drafts before you have your opening well enough in mind to contain all the vital elements. But look at it this way: by working with your opening until you hone it to the point at which the reader feels he *has* to see more, you are protecting the investment you put into the remaining two or three hundred pages. You are making it easier for yourself when the time comes to plan your next novel, and you are eliminating those dangerous reefs and shoals waiting to hang you up when you reach the halfway point of your manuscript.

Use the italicized items I've discussed when you start your first draft. Make sure you have something in mind for each element. Try experimenting with different places to begin your story and remember that there is no law stating that a novel has to be in perfect chronological order.

Just as some of your special effects and plot twists will surprise and intrigue your readers, the point in your plot that you eventually select for your opening may surprise you. It may be the one place where all these vital elements fall into place as if they belonged.

Then you will be on your way, and so will your reader.

31

THE FLASHBACK ALTERNATIVE

By John Ball

Of all of the literary devices in common use, the flashback can be, and very frequently is, the most annoying. To use one successfully is not only very difficult, but also runs a strong risk of killing reader interest dead on the spot.

Every professional who even occasionally appears before the public is invariably asked to tell "some of the secrets of writing." As we all know, there aren't any such secrets, but here is a clue that may be helpful: Never, under any circumstances, use a flashback if you can find any way to avoid it. The good news is that almost always you can.

Speaking as an author who has also done his stint as an editor, reviewer, and publisher, I have seen more good stories ruined by flashbacks than by any other single cause. Note that I said, "good stories." By this I mean properties that otherwise would be very publishable and of real interest to the reader, which is essentially the same thing.

Think about the logic of it. A book begins with a chapter filled with exciting action. There is a violent car chase, shots are fired; the pavement is rich with the pungent smell of burning rubber. The reader is fully gripped and urgently wants to know what is going to happen next. With interest high, he turns the page, and what's there? That ol' debbil flashback ready to intercept his interest with a long detour back through history, while his involvement with the arresting opening steadily diminishes to the vanishing point.

Several years ago I saw a film that starred David Wayne. It opened with a Fourth of July scene in a small town. Up the street came the local band and in it, playing the trombone, was an old man tottering along. He was played by Wayne. Then the scene dissolved into flashback which, incredibly, lasted for the rest of the film. A train pulled into the station of that same town and an energetic young man got off. It was David Wayne. The story soon settled around his high hopes for his future, his ambitious plans.

155

But none of this interests the viewer, because he already knows that this promising young man, who hopes eventually to go to the big city and make his fortune, is going to end up in this same small town, the elderly wearer of a hand-me-down uniform in the town band.

There went another wasted evening, despite the fact that David Wayne is a fine and usually entertaining actor.

Whereupon some writer will wring his or her hands and say, "But I just *have* to flash back."

No, you don't. There are many ways to avoid it, and the better you are as a writer, the more adept you will become at utilizing the alternatives. Here are some of them:

Start earlier. Often you can start your story earlier in time and grab your reader's interest in the events that are to follow. A brief prologue will often do the trick here. A young girl sits on top of a cliff, looking out to sea, and dreaming of the far places of the world. We see that wanderlust already has a firm hold on her, and we know that she is born for adventure. In chapter one, as the story proper opens, we discover her as a young woman riding a pedicab through the streets of Singapore. Already we know something about her, her character, and why she is in this exotic, oriental setting.

Start later. Consider the David Wayne picture I just described for you. Suppose it had opened just a little later, with the young man getting off the train, full of ideas and ambition. We could then take a real interest in his career without the foreknowledge that he is already doomed. Now we have at least a small element of suspense: Will he make good or not? There was no need whatever for the opening scene; it was deadly because it robbed the viewer of any hope that the likable young protagonist would beat the odds and become a man of importance.

Dialogue. The car chase we just witnessed is over; a dead body is taken away. The police inspector, saddened, goes into a restaurant for a cup of coffee with the new young detective he is breaking in. They sit down at a table together . . .

"Inspector, you knew the dead man, didn't you?"

"Yes, Sammy, I did, in a way of speaking. I've been after him, off and on, for almost ten years."

"Why—what did he do?"

"He started off by attacking a fourteen-year-old girl in a public park. She just happened to be Captain Hargreaves' daughter. He was Sergeant Hargreaves then, but that doesn't matter."

"Was he busted for it?"

"Yes, he was. But the defense attorney confused the poor girl hopelessly; the accused was given a six months' suspended sentence."

"I bet every cop in town was watching him after that."

"No, Sammy, we left him entirely alone, that is until . . . "

This is only the bare bones; the actual dialogue would contain movement, background, the sounds in the restaurant, the hot acid taste of the coffee, and all of the other things that give reality to a scene.

This is a very useful method, but it can be easily overdone. Be careful that it fits properly in the story. Whatever you do, avoid that scene often used in plays in which the maid tells the butler at great length all about the goings-on.

The dossier method. This one works like a charm when it fits into the story. The character killed in the car chase is a European, so Interpol is asked for a full report. When it comes back, in teletype form, the reader is only too anxious to read it in detail, particularly if it is headed CONFIDENTIAL. Labeling a document TOP SECRET is almost as exciting as hearing these words over the air: "We interrupt this program to bring you a special news bulletin."

The sudden thought technique. The police inspector, tired but still on the job, stops for a moment to light a cigarette. As he does so, he remembers for a moment when, as a young patrolman, he first saw a dead body lying bleeding in the street. He shakes out the match and goes on his way.

You may ask, "Isn't this really a miniature flashback?" No, because it doesn't break the continuity of the story. The reader's interest isn't derailed and forced to adjust to another time and place. We all have thoughts that flash into our minds, which we consider for a bare moment and then thrust aside, thoughts that do not interrupt the flow of our lives—unless we let them prey on our nerves. If that happens, it is in the present, not the past, and it's the present that is engaging the reader's interest.

The investigation way. After the car chase the police investigator begins to dig into the past of the man suspected of being the driver of the fatal car. As he goes to the newspaper files, conducts interviews, and follows the other steps of an organized investigation, the reader follows him, listens in, and learns the man's past history along with the detective. Properly done this can be not only an interesting, but also an exciting technique; and it keeps the story events flowing in sequence.

Interrogation. The wanted man has been captured and is brought in for questioning. Three or four people surround him in a small room, while others watch through one-way glass and listen over a speaker. The reader is allowed to listen in also as the suspect is questioned. Sometimes he lies, sometimes he finally gives true information when he is confronted with what the police already know. A lot of very good surprises can be sprung this way. There are hundreds of possibilities in interrogation scenes. Quite often when a suspect is being questioned, someone will slip a note in to one of the interrogating officers. He reads it and then springs something that is a complete surprise to the suspect, and to the reader as well. This actually happens.

Also, interrogation scenes give an exceptional opportunity for pointed characterizations as people are revealed under stress.

Many times I have been asked, "But isn't just a *little* flashback all right?"

Is just a little curare all right in your morning coffee?

The surprise revelation. This is a very good one if you handle it well. We all, for instance, dislike a stuffy, obvious snob. We long for the moment that he or she will come a cropper. Suppose that we have a holier-than-thou woman who is leading a campaign to have certain books she considers improper taken off the library shelves. She may object to the poems of Walt Whitman, or even to unexpurgated Shakespeare.

Let us slip into the town meeting where our self-appointed guardian of the public morals is holding forth, condemning some flaming regency romances for their vivid sexual scenes. Just about the time it seems as if she will carry the day, a reporter stands up and asks quietly, "Isn't it true, Mrs. Gotrocks, that the very books you are speaking about so harshly are in actuality *your own works*?"

The reader is stunned for a moment until he realizes that Mrs. Gotrocks is using this method to try to make herself famous under her pseudonym.

Or the reporter may ask, "Mrs. Gotrocks, since you are so against any sort of sexual description, how is it that twenty-six years ago, under the name of Vivian France, you were a carnival stripper with the XYZ Shows?"

Of course he has to prove that he is right, but everyone in that hall, and the reader, is only too anxious to have him do so. They are now most happy to listen to the details of her past, but note that these details are being told in the present, without interrupting the smooth flow of the story.

These are a few of the techniques that will substitute for a flashback: there are many more. You may very well invent some of your own. Please, for the sake of good writing and the satisfaction of our precious readers, stop short every time you are tempted to flash back and see if you can find another and better way.

32

LIVING OTHER LIVES

By Caroline Leavitt

I'VE always resisted using the word "character." To me, "character" just isn't a good enough fit for all the living, breathing presences populating a novel, those people who stubbornly persist in living, who haunt and hurt me even after I close the book cover. And why shouldn't they? After all, I've shared their lives, I've suffered and bled and celebrated, too; I've really lived right alongside of them, and sometimes even died alongside of them, too. It's a most wonderful, cathartic magic for any reader when this occurs, when you can live another life. But being on the reader's end is one thing; sitting down at the writer's lonely expanse of desk is quite another. Having actually to create this magic, to write life and breath into characters so that readers care about them is a process as slow and elusive and difficult as getting to know and care about people in real life.

And it's just as marvelous.

Remember that old literary adage about always, always, writing with a particular audience in mind? Well, forget it. If you apply this dictum to your characterizations, then you just might be spending much of your time trying to explain your characters to your readers instead of trying to understand them yourself, being a constant interpreter instead of letting your characters do their own living. Always thinking about a particular reader sets up a kind of barrier between you and your character; and for the reader, it might mean the difference between being introduced to a person secondhand, and simply, delightedly, meeting the person all on his own.

I really think it's important to start selfish, to work with how you yourself feel about your characters, with what kinds of things make *you* feel close to a person. If you can come to love a character, to feel that he has a life of his own and is as real as you are, then chances are that the reader will, too.

But where does the writer start? Probably just where he does with anyone. Characters, after all, *are* people, real people, as soon as you suspend your disbelief and enter the printed page. As with real people, you enter their lives slowly; you know them as they begin to reveal themselves to you. This revelation process can be broken down into three parts—physical descriptions, actions, and thoughts.

What initially attracts me to people and makes me want to know them isn't so much how they look, as how they seem to feel about those looks, how they either express themselves or hide through their appearance. Style, for me, is really just another facet of personality, and as such, is another way to get to know someone.

For example, Duse, the palmist in my second novel, *Lifelines,* is beautiful, wildly exotic, with masses of crazy red hair. That's fine, but at this stage, that sentence is nothing more than descriptive filler. I don't know much about the woman other than this lovely shell that she inhabits. What jolts Duse alive for me, what makes her endearing, is how she acts on that wild beauty, what she lets it make of her. Duse lets you see that she is concerned about her looks only to the extent that they are uniquely *hers,* and therefore, like any sort of identity, they are not to be tampered with. I turned Duse's looks into a kind of action as much as I could; I tried virtually to make those looks have a life of their own, a story line. Duse won't wear clothing that belongs to anyone else, because she somehow feels the identity of the past owner riding right through the weave of the cloth. It's a trauma she passes on to her daughter Isadora. You get to *see* Duse shopping for her baby daughter, letting the girl pat her hands along a rack of dresses, as if a baby can choose, as if a baby knows. You *see* Duse not interfering with her daughter's choice, buying a garish dress for a baby because it's all part of her daughter's sense of self.

I tried, too, to get some sort of emotional response from any physical description, because I remember emotions; they touch me, more than images. In one case, I did this by trying to show the effects on Duse when her physical appearance—her sense of self—is tampered with. Duse has a stroke and is left paralyzed, unaware of her surroundings. A friend cuts back all her marvelous hair, making it look like every other

161

woman's hairdo, all in a good-natured attempt to make things easier for Duse. Duse can't react. Perhaps, in her condition, she doesn't even realize what has happened, but the passages that were set up before, that carefully showed how Duse kept making sure she always looked like nobody but herself, like nobody else, help make this particular scene especially poignant, make the reader feel for her.

Action *is* character. You'd no more want to get involved with a real person who just stands around doing nothing than you would with such a fictional character. People moving, doing things, striving for goals, are living. But life is three pronged, made up of the past, the present and the future, time schemes you need to be aware of.

You never meet people in a vacuum. People don't spring out at twenty or forty like new postage stamps. There were things going on in their pasts, forces and memories that continue to drive them. A character's past defines his present, shapes his future, and can give motivations for behavior that might be less than admirable. This sense of time also helps to move the story along and give life to it. For example, Duse's past created her present, made her who she was. That past—a life in which her father never took her photograph or celebrated her birthday, in which her mother wanted her to make something of herself as long as that something was different from what she was already— gave birth to Duse's fierce self-protecting spirit. And that spirit was what she tried to pass on to her own unwilling daughter.

Moving characters from one time to another involves goals. What makes you feel close to people is often what they believe in, what they want, and how desperately they want it. You can get wrapped up in a character's obsessive quest; you can root for the character, or even become the character himself.

The goal should really be a kind of journey that helps reveal character, that lets you discover him at the same time that he is discovering himself. My first novel, *Meeting Rozzy Halfway,* chronicled a sister's devotion to her mentally ill sibling. Bess's goal was supposedly to free her sister from insanity, a quest that made her very sympathetic, something readers could identify with. And because we shared this quest, we later share Bess's pain and confusion when she realizes how much more she really needed her sister's illness for her own survival. We feel her pain as tragically as she herself does.

It's difficult to express intimate feelings and emotions. People usu-

162

ally tend to keep things like that cemented up inside rather than risk hurting someone or being hurt themselves. There's no way to know when a person is hiding something from you, no clues, and so, unfortunately, a valuable facet of that person remains hidden, and you are distanced, when you might have become very close.

Writing gives you the chance to rectify that situation. Oh, maybe your hero will never be able to come out and tell his wife that she makes him feel small and low and mean, but he can think out loud, he can let the reader in on how he feels. In this way, he will gain the reader's sympathy and get him involved with his life. An inability to act can be as poignant as the act itself—if you know the reasons behind the inaction.

Again in *Lifelines,* Duse is married to Martin, a practical-minded dentist, who will never believe in his wife's ability to read palms or predict anything more dramatic than the weather. Duse knows this, and as a result there's a terrible underlying sadness in their relationship. Martin can't talk about his feelings, can't work them out. I opened Martin up, though, by letting him think out loud, in a worried, impassioned soliloquy. He remembers his own parents, his crazy mother who spoke in tongues, his father's contempt for anything religious. Martin remembers, too, how his father would still drive his mother to those meetings, how they'd both sit outside at night holding hands, having a wonderful loving marriage anyway. Martin talks to no one, but it is during this remembering that he decides that he will just have to accept Duse, that she can bay at the moon, and he'll still love her. He may not have revealed himself to Duse, but he has revealed himself to the readers and that certainly endears him to them and makes them care.

People in life have quirks and funny habits, which you don't notice unless you are around those people a great deal. Well, characters are pretty much the same. These quirks and habits may not be especially crucial to plot development, but they help flesh out a character to make him real.

The writer needs to observe. Where does a character live? What does he like to binge on late at night when he's watching the late movie? Tiny details create a sense of reality, of life going on; things like using salt to brush your teeth, like squirreling away movie magazines. All these details are simply ways of opening up a life, of letting readers live that life right along with the characters. And if those habits are quirks which are shared by the reader, are things the reader can identify with, so much the better.

You know, there really isn't any one formula for creating characters people will care about. I really wish there were. Then I wouldn't be struggling over the characters in my latest novel the same erratic way I did over the people in my first books. But what I can say, what I do somehow intrinsically know, is that when you do manage to create a character who is real, he exists totally on his own. He doesn't need your help any more, he somehow takes off without you, and you know it, and then he is as mysterious and wonderful and *alive* as anyone.

33

THE SHORT STORY HEROINE

By Marlene Fanta Shyer

SOME WRITERS are fond of saying that they create characters who then assume their own life and "take over" their plot, but for a writer of short stories, this is about as pragmatic as buying carpeting and building a house around it. In a word, it's an indulgence, and if you want to sell to the women's "slicks," don't be tempted to meander.

The parameters are rigid. Your characters must move along, resolving the problems you've created for them in the space of six to sixteen pages, with no detours and no time-outs. It's a fast and undeviating track, and you've got to keep your eye hard on the destination.

As you push your characters along, the challenge is to compress without squeezing the life's breath out of them, turning them into no-frills stereotypes. Most important is the heroine, because she is the motor that generates the direction your story will take. You must get her moving and breathing within a few lines, and you must make her likable, someone to whom all American women between 18 and 35 can relate and with whom editors will immediately fall in love—in twenty-five words or less!

O.K., I'm exaggerating, but you get the idea—no heavy narrative, no anecdotal history. Go very easy on physical descriptions, too. (The magazines hire illustrators, so let them figure out whether your heroine is a blonde or a redhead—I've never spawned an Elephant Woman yet!) You can describe her most economically by not describing her at all, but by letting her actions reveal her personality. In a short story, degrees earned, childhood foibles, and food preferences may be mentioned only if they bear directly on the present plot. For example, don't say, "Mary took piano lessons for four years," unless Mary's piano playing is relevant now, as in "Four years of piano lessons, and Mary's only audience was now pounding his fist against the wall of her apartment." In other words, Mary's playing describes Mary *and* moves the plot.

I will not admit to using a "formula" for my fictional women, but I do have a few techniques I use to improve my chances for sales, since I'm convinced that the empathic protagonist is the most important single factor in selling any story. It's my experience that editors feel plot flaws are like the tracks that can be relaid, but that heroines, however economically described, are the engines that can never be overhauled.

So, since word-wasting is out, my first rule is never to clutter. The fewer characters in any story, the better. I limit names and cut out the underbrush of personal biography. It clears the center stage for the all-important heroine.

Second, I try to imbue my leading lady with small flaws. I myself have never been able to identify with too-perfect people and find little faults endearing. In "A Dream Come True" *(Good Housekeeping),* my heroine compares herself with the photos of the women in the fashion magazine that has arrived in the mail this morning, resisting the urge to throw it into the garbage pail "which was too full to accommodate it anyhow"—(she's not a perfect housekeeper). "I don't have time for marinating *poulets,* decorating with silk handkerchiefs, or even blow-drying my hair every day. Mostly it just lies there flat and would never go with a $400 blouse anyway." (She's not a perfect cook, decorator, looker, either.)

Who of us has not been frustrated at the never-neverland of the glossy pages of the fashion press? My heroine continues, "With three children I seem incapable of even small gestures of elegance and style and . . . despite heroic efforts, we are living a disordered, imperfect existence, filled with flaws and dailiness." Ah, who isn't? The reader (and editor) hopefully establishes an unconscious "Hey, that's how *I* feel too!" bond with Ms. Imperfect. Which brings me to another desirable character trait: Universality.

My heroines are never rich or famous. I do suppose rich or famous sells well in many quarters, but the women's magazines seem to prefer someone like the heroine in my story, "Change of Plans" *(Good Housekeeping),* who once had her foot on the first step of the diamond ladder and had dropped off to have a family. (Despite the ever-growing number of career-comes-first women, the old-value heroine is still going strong, and it's still safer to write about wives with kids, than

166

divorcées.) In "Change of Plans," my leading lady cries every year as she watches the Academy Awards, because she knows an Oscar will never stand on her fireplace mantel. She once had her chance—I describe *very briefly* the years of struggle and the break that finally came just when she'd learned she was pregnant—and she's missed out. It's O.K.; the kids send a paper airplane on which they've written their mother a love note, and she sticks that on the mantel instead.

If you detect in this outline a *déjà vu* plot quality, you may be right, but that's the tricky part. Freshening up new-old ideas and hoary heroines in a skimpy space is not easy. In "Change of Plans," it was a little touch, the inclusion of a small accident at the roller-skating rink (roller skating was all the rage at the time the story appeared). In "A Dream Come True," in which my heroine yearned to look and live like the models in *Vogue*, I added a bit about a decision she made to have a small mole removed. When she calls the dermatologist for an appointment, the secretary puts her on "hold" and plays recorded music in her ear, a very "today" touch and also a situation the heroine considers a metaphor for her own life. (She feels shunted aside, overlooked and sentenced to be very ordinary.) Here I have combined character delineation and plot development, and have moved both along the same track without losing sight of my destination for a moment.

Personality and warmth can be hard to come by in twenty-five words or less, but most of the time if one of my stories fails, it's because my leads are lacking in that department, as in one of my recent flops, in which the mother of two allowed her husband to play favorites with one of her two sons (revealing herself to be wishy-washy). It never sold. In another old story of mine that did the rounds and always came back, my main character came on too aggressively towards her man, which is still a no-no, despite our current, supposedly sexually egalitarian climate. Men are still permitted to be more aggressive; the heroine still is the one pursued, still does not make the calls, or pay for the dinners. Don't be *too* contemporary!

Changing times are more likely to brush up against the perfect heroine than to overhaul her. In my love story, "Someone With a Heart" *(Ladies' Home Journal)*, Leslie is afraid of crime in her city and affected by a certain pervasive urban heartlessness. I've used a transit strike as a plot device, to get her walking past a building, in a window of which she spots her beloved lost dog. A contemporary dog lover

167

walking forty blocks to work is another example of the intertwining of heroine with action/plot.

In this story, dialogue says most of it. I've saved the most important facet of character delineation till last. What goes between the quotation marks is the passport that gets your heroine to her destination—and don't forget her picture is forever in there between its pages. When Leslie's crosspatch boss demands, "Is a dog more important than Tech-Electric?" she, the modern woman, speaks right up. "Yes," she says, revealing herself not only as a warm and loyal dog lover, but assertive as well. But then, she adds, "I'll stay [overtime] tomorrow, but I can't stay tonight."

Now she is revealing herself to be soft, compliant, not insensitive to the demands of the company/boss, and also cooperative.

A lot to ask of your heroine in twenty-five words or less?

Sure, but remember, you're the engineer. The people who live in the magazine's pages are *yours*. Get *them* on the right track to get your story on the right track. Bon voyage and full speed ahead!

34

WRITING FROM RESEARCH

By David Westheimer

Many years ago, when I was a student at Rice University, George Williams, a professor of English, used to tell us, "Write about what you know."

Now, with many years of writing experience behind me, I still think this was excellent advice, especially for beginners. A new writer has enough problems grappling with a project as large as a novel, without suffering the labor and insecurity of working with unfamiliar material. It is so much simpler to draw the material from your own background and ideas and concentrate on getting your characters developed and your story told.

But, if you have a theme so compelling to you that you simply must develop it in a novel, and that theme requires research, then research you must. If Margaret Mitchell had been put off by the amount of research necessary to do a book set in the Civil War era, we would not have *Gone with the Wind*.

Even if you are writing about what you know, it may still require a certain amount of research. My first novel, *Summer on the Water*, was set in an area I knew well, the little bayshore communities not far from Houston, Texas. But I realized I did not know enough about this setting to capture it fully in fiction. I went to some of the places I thought I knew well to refresh my memory. I looked at things through the eyes of a prospective novelist rather than of a casual visitor and discovered much that was significant in the light of fiction but which I had overlooked when I was visiting for recreation. This was research in every sense, even though this setting was one I had known since childhood. (I even looked at the area from the air, but how many fledgling writers have a brother-in-law who is a licensed private pilot and will take them up for nothing?)

You're writing something based on your own youth or childhood and set right in your own hometown, and what do you need with research? Can you really remember what was on the corner of Travis and Lamar fifteen or twenty years ago, or what an ice cream cone or a pair of Keds cost then, or what the hit song was in July of a certain year? Such little details may be useful to your story, and you'll have to look them up somewhere. That's research. If you haven't realized such little details are useful, think about it now. Ordinary facts such as those can contribute a strong sense of place and time and often react with the personal recollections of the reader to enhance the effect of your narrative.

I've mentioned two major disadvantages of writing from research —the amount of work and time involved and the insecurity of dealing with unfamiliar material. There are also advantages: You broaden your range of subject matter, you have the use of material with which to enrich your narrative, and you engage your reader's interest in what you have to say apart from, and in addition to, the story you're telling. You learn things from your research, and your reader learns them from your novel—the reader unaware and painlessly so if you use your material correctly.

Where do you find research materials? The most accessible and, unless you live in a small town, richest source is usually the public library. It has shelf after shelf of books all indexed by subject, one of which may be yours. It has encyclopedias and reference works, bound magazines and journals, often files of major newspapers. When you do research from a book, be sure to check the bibliography. It almost invariably will lead you to other works on your subject or related ones. Do not overlook the periodical files. Periodicals publish a lot of material that never finds its way into hardcovers. Periodicals, too, have subject-matter indexes.

If you live in a university town, get to know its school library. On some subjects a university library may have better research sources than the public library. If non-students are not permitted access to the stacks, it is likely you may be able to get a library card by paying a small annual fee.

Newspaper files are invaluable sources of the details of daily life and of history in the making. If the library does not have bound files of back issues, your local paper should at least have its own files. The repository of a newspaper's files was once called the morgue. Now I think it's called the library. By either name, it is usually open to the average citizen and almost certainly to a writer doing research. Just tell the librarian who you are and why you want to use the files, and you'll have no problem. Nowadays the back issues are generally on microfilm. The library will have a microfilm reader. If you don't know how to operate the machine, the librarian will show you. Never, never clip anything from a paper's bound files.

The Library of Congress and the National Archives in Washington have, of course, an immense range of books, photographs, and documents. You can get a certain amount of information by mail, including some microfilm or page copies, but really to dig into their resources, it's better to go there.

You can get information on a lot of different subjects from government agencies. Some of it is free. Some pamphlets and brochures may require a small fee. You can get long lists of available publications, including expensive hardcover books, from the Government Printing Office, Washington, D.C. 20402. Or you can write a specific department of government, say Defense, Interior or Agriculture, for information in their purview.

You can get information from industry. Want to know how an oil refinery operates? Write the public relations department of any major oil company. If you're persuasive enough and/or they're on the ball enough, you'll get an answer. This is generally true of any firm large enough to employ a public relations staff or have a company library.

There's information to be had from your local government and business firms, as well. The Chamber of Commerce is often a good place to begin a search for information. The local police department and crime lab can fill you in on crime and punishment; someone in the mayor's office can tell you how a city is run or where to find out exactly what happens after a fire alarm goes off.

People are an inexhaustible source of information. People with special knowledge, such as college professors, old-timers or your family doctor, or people in trades who can tell you how to repair or sabotage a truck, build a house or dig a well. (I made extensive use of truckers and mechanics in research for my last novel, *The Olmec Head*.) Don't be afraid to ask. They can only say no but will usually say yes when they learn you're writing a book. For *The Olmec Head*, among the many things I learned from truckers were fuel consumption, fuel capacities, load limits, cruising speeds, descriptions of equipment, truckers' jargon. A dispatcher who helped me told me that the load I was hauling would put the gross weight over the Texas limit of 78,000 pounds if transported by the usual tractor-trailer rig. But, he added, if I used a "ragtop" trailer, it would get the weight down below the maximum allowed. So I used that little detail in the novel: "That means our rig can't weigh more than thirty thousand pounds empty," Bell said. "The people renting it to you can tell you the weight. Get a ragtop trailer. That's one with a fabric cover instead of a solid top. It's lighter." (*The Olmec Head*, p. 235.)

As the above demonstrates, some informants may get involved in your project and volunteer information you did not have enough knowledge of the subject to ask about. (The mechanic who told me what could cause a diesel truck to run poorly without actually stopping it, later told me after reading the book I could have done a much better job than I did in switching a heavy load from one truck to another.)

As for researching a physical setting, the best thing to do is visit the area, study it, take pictures to use later to refresh your memory. If you can't get there, you'll have to read about it. For foreign locations, travel agencies, tourist bureaus and consulates can usually provide illustrated brochures. I used a lot of such materials for areas of Italy I did not know in writing *Von Ryan's Express*. One of the travel brochures I got from the Italian consulate mentioned the fact that a spire in Modena was visible for many miles. In the novel, the train bearing Colonel Ryan and his fellow POWs was approaching Modena at dawn. This is how I used that bit of seemingly insignificant information in the book. Ryan had to finish killing off the German guards before they reached the next town. He was not sure just when that would be. And then, "Far up ahead a slender column glistened like a white thread dangling from the rim of the sky." Ryan now knew they were getting close to Modena.

How much research do you do? For something based on your own background, probably not much. Just enough to confirm your recollections or to provide information you could not have known about. That big fire downtown was in 1953, not 1954. The President of the United States came to your town in 1948, but you didn't know that because at the time you were too young to be aware of it. Or one of your characters works in a bottling plant. You've never been in a bottling plant. Now is the time to visit one.

For work, based chiefly on research, a historical novel, for example, or a story about prospecting for gold in Brazil when you haven't even any gold in your teeth and have never been farther than the county seat, of course you must do a whole lot of research. Just remember to steep yourself in it, not drown yourself. Some writers get so involved in their subject that they research endlessly and never do get around to writing the book. Or they wear themselves out with the research and haven't the energy or will to do any writing. Either way, the book never gets written. Also, there is a tendency to continue the research beyond the point where you have enough material, simply because you feel too insecure about actually writing the book. You have to start writing, insecurities and all. If you find you don't know enough about your subject after all and were right to feel insecure, call a brief halt to your writing and do some more research. Now, however, you may find you know exactly what information you lack and can go directly to a source instead of following a lot of blind trails.

Never let research become an excuse not to sit down and write instead of a means to an end. I know "writers" who are not only unpublished but also unwritten because of that.

When you've got all this research material, how do you use it? *Sparingly.* Don't give your reader gobs of undigested information, or even crumbs of facts, merely for the sake of using something you're pleased with yourself for having learned. Your research material should enhance the narrative, or make it move, or make it more real, or reveal something about your characters and their times or life styles. Often a few significant details will suffice to establish an entire era or place or way of life.

By selecting your details carefully you can avoid bogging your story down and telling your reader more than he wants to know, and you can still create the illusion that you know everything worth knowing about your subject.

I once read an otherwise good novel about a World War II bomber pilot by a man who knew nothing of pilots or bombers except what he had learned from research. Which was a great deal— and which he found it necessary to share. He told everything he had learned about how to run through the checklist, start the engines, taxi, take off and get into formation. And it was dull, dull, dull, stopping his story in its tracks. A writer more discriminating in his use of research material would have mentioned only the most significant details of the procedures, those the reader might be expected to find interesting, and written a much shorter and far more exciting scene.

What I wish to stress is, do not use material just because you know it, or because it was so much trouble to obtain. In writing *Lighter Than a Feather,* a novel about what might have happened if the U.S. had invaded Japan instead of using the atom bomb, I sometimes spent weeks trying to obtain documents I'd heard about, and then when I had them, I realized there was nothing in them worth using in the story. When this happens, there is a tendency to force some of the material into your story just because it was hard to come by. It is a tendency that must be resisted.

Naturally, there was an enormous amount of information I could use in the many U.S. and Japanese documents I amassed in my *Feather* research. Tides and weather conditions in the invasion areas on specific dates, for example, and the location and composition of U.S. and Japanese units, descriptions of U.S. and Japanese tanks and weapons, the training of Japanese civilian "volunteer" forces, the way Japanese soldiers addressed their superiors, what Japanese soldiers ate, why Japanese soldiers did not surrender, how much Japanese soldiers of all ranks were paid. These are but a few samples chosen at random. I used literally thousands of bits of information because *Feather* depended so heavily on research. To sum up:

Try to write about what you know.

If you must write on subjects or backgrounds you don't know, do your homework thoroughly and utilize all available sources.

Don't spend so much time and energy on research that you never get around to writing your novel.

Use your material sparingly; don't smother your reader or your novel with masses of raw information.

Try for the significant detail, the one that will engage the reader's interest, add to your story and give the impression you could say a great deal more on the subject if you wished.

35

THE LISTENING EAR

By Anne Chamberlain

Dumb!" The unseen woman in the next booth exclaimed, "about as dumb as a coon in a tree, that's my opinion, and who knows better'n me?"

"You're the one as knows," an eager girlish voice supplied.

"More brains than you can shake a stick at, and turns them all the wrong way, that's my opinion. Why, let me tell you now what she done last Wednesday afternoon, nobody home, and in she snaked and I think she got into my parlor table drawer, read my postcards—my bills too, electric and the gas, she read, and that weren't the worst of it. Let me tell you . . . ." The narrative slipped into a tantalizing whisper, incoherent to the casual listener. I was that listener, a traveler, enjoying a quick stopover meal at the village restaurant. Not having previously noticed the two women, I now realized that I probably wouldn't catch a good look if I left before they did. Fascinated, I lingered for a few minutes, and was rewarded with the suddenly loud, dramatic final line: "And then she ate the *whole* watermelon!"

Over the mountainous miles of the homeward drive, over the years since, this delectable tidbit remains one of the small treasures in my memory. A "treasure" it can be justly termed, for, with the intimate village atmosphere, the rural idiom and emphasis of the narrator, the avid (perhaps fawning?) attendance of her companion, this fragment limns a scene, hints at characterization, suggests numerous stories. What a sneaky, spiteful, absurd act, eating somebody's watermelon! And why would the marauder, obviously well known to the victim, indulge in so barbaric a feast? Were they feuding neighbors, rivals in quilting club contests, jealous sisters-in-law, or simply harborers of a longtime natural animosity? A humorous situation, certainly, which— as always with comedy—would be seasoned with sound psychological undertones. Over the countless possibilities, the listener/writer can muse, fantasize, and, in due time, select that which seems most suitable to his particular talents.

For me as an author, cultivating an astute ear for dialogue is a lifelong process. Having grappled with the task of presenting dramatic scenes on paper, of distilling ordinary speech for extraordinary effects, yet of preserving the tones and rhythm of natural talk, I have become a student, a collector, and a connoisseur. Mine is not a calculated eavesdropping. The phrases, fragments of discussion, and sometimes complete anecdotes that reach my ears by chance are tossed into the air wherever people gather and talk, free to any and all who pay attention. They are often delightfully unexpected, and in afterthought, may lend themselves to fascinating interpretations.

In restaurants, airports, stores, hotel lobbies, elevators, the listener finds rich fields to explore. Settings for arrivals and departures may be especially fruitful:

"Please," a woman clutches at the arm of her escort; they are standing in line at the airport, he with a gleaming briefcase, she—apparently—about to say goodbye: "I ask you once more, Arthur, please . . ." He does not answer, nor does he look at her. Her fingers tighten on his sleeve. "Arthur, I'm asking," she murmurs, her voice sinking into a whisper.

For what is she pleading? That he phone at the customary time tonight, forgetting this morning's argument? That he look up the wayward son, who in the city of the father's destination, has recently moved in with an objectionable girl friend? That he think more carefully before he accepts the promotion that will take them from the home and neighborhood she has learned to love? Is he usually "Arthur" to her or, in more relaxed moments, "Art"? Does he remain silent because he is angry, or merely bored?

The listener knows only that she is serious about something, that he is adamant. An alert ear learns the importance of inflection. How many dozens of ways there are of saying "please"! Politely, as a vocal punctuation, urgently, sardonically, savagely, humbly, sometimes a mixture of emotions pour into the single syllable. "It isn't what he said, it's the way he said it," is the frequent plaintive tagline of an anecdote, when the narrator remembers the direct quote but realizes that—in itself—this fails to capture the impact. It is the desperate, last-minute

177

quality of the airport woman's utterance, the breathlessness, the sleeve-clutching, the fading into a whisper that dramatizes her words. Were the writer to develop a story line from this episode, he would use the verbs, adjectives, and action detail to present the dialogue within its emotional context.

Perhaps Arthur is indeed expecting to be offered a promotion, his acceptance of which will take them and their children to a much larger city, a strange and—to Millicent, his wife—a frightening environment. It means transplanting their two youngsters, in sensitive early teen years, to more urban schools and (she suspects) more hazardous temptations. Ashamed as she is to admit it, she hates leaving the house she has cherished for years, the garden she has lovingly tended, the church and the women's clubs; oh, she loves him far more than any *place,* he surely knows this, but isn't she human, doesn't her own life, don't the lives of the children count? The present action, which seems to have evolved easily from Millicent's point of view, could be unfolded within the airport setting, as they arrive, check in, wait, continue the discussion that may have previously waxed into an argument, softened into mutual understanding, flared again into anger. Brief flashbacks, dramatizing the tensions, could be woven into the immediate scene, which builds to the last few minutes, as they stand in line. At this point, even though the situation may have been artfully developed, it would be temptingly easy to overwrite:

"Please," she begged wistfully, clutching at his sleeve, pouring her heart into this last minute entreaty, "I ask you once more, Arthur, please . . ."
Stone-faced, stubbornly silent, he stood, refusing to look at her.
"Arthur," tears surged into her voice. Her fingers tightened on his sleeve, as though she would hold him, draw him to her, fold him into her arms, "I'm asking . . ." Her voice sank into a whisper, a strangled sob.
He stared coldly and mutely into space.

This has too much trimming. Overembellishment is a weakness common to the writing of dialogue. If the author astutely employs other techniques, descriptions of characters and of setting, perhaps subjective delineation of the unspoken feelings of one or more of those concerned, the actual spoken exchange should need little adornment. Knowing Millicent and Arthur, through their airport wait and through the thoughts and the flashback episodes that have illuminated their tensions, the reader understands much of what is not spoken at their

178

parting. Seeing him board the plane, Millicent knows that some day she and the children will be boarding with him. Or she realizes, only dimly yet, as she turns from waving goodbye, that this time he is truly leaving, she is going home. One story possibility; airports bustle with them.

The listening author discriminates. It would impossible to hear, much less to heed, the countless words that may be spoken around one in the course of a crowded day. As a fiction writer, I have a built-in tape recorder, which, for my purposes, is more convenient and dependable than its mechanical counterpart. It receives constantly; it erases the superfluous; it may splice; it will store what seems worth keeping.

"I went downtown this morning—oh the loveliest day, I just can't tell you! Sunshine and breeze and spring everywhere, I danced, danced on my toes all the way, and right at the corner by the mailbox, you can't imagine who I saw, I ran right into her, I hadn't seen her for—you can't imagine how long!— centuries! And you'll never guess what she told me, she came right out with it—" the young woman babbles merrily to her hairdresser, a captive but not uninterested audience, "on the street, on the corner by the mailbox, I'll have you know, she told me, might have been saying, 'it's a nice day,' she was that nonchalant, she came right out with it—"

An individual's speech is as unique as his handwriting, his manner of dress, his voice, walk, gestures, his smile and his eyes. This woman talks in hyperbole, loves to prattle, and contrives through suspenseful hints to keep her audience attentive:

"She was divorced, that's what she said, cool as a cucumber, and then before I got over *that,* I mean I'd barely begun to digest it, she goes right on to say she's married again. Can you imagine! And all within five minutes, well no more than ten, and here I am, my jaw just dropping and she says, 'I thought you knew, didn't you know,' and I said no I didn't know, how could I, hadn't seen, hadn't heard a word about her in centuries and—" to a murmured question from the beautician, "didn't I tell you *who* she is? Well-l-l . . ." Into a genealogical chart she spins, spilling names, father, grandfather, uncle, aunts, first husband and, "a Hardquist, of course, and you do, well maybe you don't know the Hardquists but he, number one husband I mean, he was a chip off the old block, his father Jedson, *the* Jedson, and what I couldn't tell you, my dear, about Jedson Hardquist—"

Seated two chairs away in the beauty salon, I reflect that shocking news, delivered bluntly by a mailbox, might—for a minute or two— silence the babbler's torrential monologue. And I ponder over that woman, "as cool as a cucumber," with the mixed-up marital history. And what about Jedson? I will be hearing more, for I, too, am a captive audience.

In dramatizing the speech mannerisms of the babbler, who can rapidly become a loquacious bore, the writer must aim to convey her effect on others without producing a similar tedium in the reader. One quoted paragraph, like that above, can characterize her compulsive gushiness, and additional phrases will suggest all that is not on paper. While the incessant talker is particularly difficult to harness in dialogue, the need for pruning and culling applies to the speech of all characters.

"No, I didn't know about the Hardquists," the beautician interposes pointedly. She is tired of the monologue. Perhaps she dislikes scurrilous gossip; too much of it whirls around her shop. And is there, in the weary but gentle rebuke of her tone, a distaste for the whole carefree society, the smug, prosperous, much-married and divorced people about whom she hears so much? A story, a hundred or more stories could be written from the point of view of a skilled and patient beautician.

In contrast with the fluent monologuist, the terse speaker, who favors a form of verbal shorthand, poses a different challenge to the writer. Often his reticence can be dramatized through the speeches addressed to him. In the hotel lobby, I notice the young wife greeting her husband enthusiastically:

"How was your morning?"
"Same as ever." He kisses her amiably and takes her arm, steering her to the dining room.

She has come into town from suburbia. They will lunch together, and I reflect that she is hungry for excitement and news.

"Same?" She pouts, teasing him. "Oh, you, it's always the same, same, same," and pats his arm, "but what about Chalmers? Anything happen?"
He motions toward the hostess, they are conducted to a table, sit down, order cocktails.

From this overheard exchange, I spin an imaginative continuation, just enough to suggest more:

"You haven't told me about Chalmers. . . ."

"Fired," he lights a cigarette.

"Oh no! Oh how terrible, was he upset, how did he take it? Oh poor Lydia—"

He has opened the menu. "Think I'll have the steak."

"Did he come in? Did you see him? What did he *do?*"

"Yes," he smiles to the waitress, as she places the cocktails before them, "I think we'll order now."

With this taciturn man, who may have excellent reasons for not wanting to tell his wife about Chalmers, the problem is to convey what he does not choose to say; much can be achieved through action detail.

Fine stories have been written without a scrap of dialogue; others have consisted entirely of spoken words. Most authors use direct quotes at high dramatic points, emphasizing and advancing the narrative. Often, I become so absorbed with other aspects of the story that I do not give enough consideration to the question: Would this character say this in this way? By cultivating the listening ear, I am more aware of natural speech and more alert to those weaknesses that may be distilled into direct quotes.

I have learned to be wary of the overly structured sentence, the too complete and well-rounded paragraph. It is not inconceivable (in writing, nothing is!) for the anguished husband, leaving his wife, suitcase packed and hand on doorknob, to address her: "Much as I love you and always will, our marriage has become totally incompatible, is beyond the help of counselors, and is mutually erosive to our respective personalities." Not inconceivable, as this husband may be a person addicted to eloquence; one does imagine that, if he used such terms, his wife willingly opened the door for him. It is more likely that he would speak briefly, might shout, mumble, lunge out of the house. Under intense emotional pressure, a character's talk is usually jagged, sentences incomplete, feelings too deep for balanced, measured phrases.

A vehement discussion may go on for thousands of words, lasting a whole evening, and to report it literally would not only cover dozens of pages but would bury the story in the process. I am, therefore, aware that I must delete and, if I listen as an author may, I find myself deleting swiftly, editing what I hear, saving what is worthwhile.

"I told him in no uncertain terms," said the portly man at the bus stop, "that his attitude was depressing, demoralizing, and disappointing." He paused, groped for another alliterative adjective, exploded triumphantly, "destructive." He bit at his cigar. "Yes," I told him—"destructive!"

His companion nodded sagely and stroked his drooping moustache. "You told him off, Fred, you surely did. I wish I had your gift for language. But what'd he say? Fred, what *did* he say?"

The bus arrived, they climbed on together, still talking. . . .

The listening bystander will not know what he said. Or how he managed to be all of those adjectives, rolled into one, or were these faults pure imaginings of a pompous fellow worker? Was our denouncer guilty of the very accusations he so relished? A distinct possibility. A story? I muse.

Cultivating the listening ear is an educational process that helps me write dialogue I have never heard until I imagine the characters and what they are saying; it is also a rich source, an inexhaustible mine of material. Of perhaps a thousand tidbits that I overhear and speculate about, only one or two may combine within the ever mysterious creative self to produce a story. Constant entertainment is at my command. I can turn on that tape recorder which, in the depths of memory, is always waiting, brimming with ideas.

How did matters finally work out for Arthur and Millicent? Maybe he wasn't considering a promotion, after all. She might have been pleading because, in the city of his destination, there lived that former secretary, the golden-haired and lynx-eyed, the sly and determined, with whom Arthur was still in touch. He had said it would be stupid, plain unfriendly not to look her up, at least to telephone; why, she and Millicent had been on good terms, hadn't they? She had made the mistake of protesting and had lighted the match—or had the fire been simmering already? Another story.

The babbler in the beauty shop prates on. In the next chair may be Old Jedson Hardquist's third wife, young, sharp-eared, new to town, rapidly absorbing important information. Or the patient beautician, scissoring deftly, may have had, as her last client, the carefree "cool as a cucumber" woman who had met the babbler at the mailbox. Anything can happen; the listener can pick and choose.

How did poor Chalmers react to being fired? Will the eager wife ever learn details from her cautious husband? Was the portly man's unknown target actually "depressing, demoralizing, disappointing, and destructive"? Delectable, that phrasing, in its pompous smugness.

Come to think of it, how big was that watermelon?

36

BUILDING TENSION IN
THE SHORT STORY

By Joyce Carol Oates

THE most important aspect of writing is characterization—does a character come alive, is he memorable in some way? But the means of disclosing character is also important, for if a story lacks a strong narrative line, an editor or reader might not be patient enough to discover even the most stunning of fictional characters.

Novels are complex matters; the density of interest has to go up and down. Short stories, however, are generally based on one gradual upward swing toward a climax or "epiphany"—moment of recognition. A good chapter in a novel should probably be based on the same rhythmic structure as a short story. The novel, of course, can be leisurely while the average short story must be economical. Certain modern stories are so economical that single words or phrases are used to reveal the story's meaning—for instance, John Collier's "The Chaser," which ends with the words "au revoir" and not "goodbye."

While I think the best kind of contemporary story is much more rich and complex and daring than the Chekhovian-type stories so fashionable a few decades ago, still the writer must be careful to limit the range of his "secondary" material—descriptions, background. If he succeeds in winning the reader's attention by dramatic means, then the more important aspects of his story will be appreciated. We have all written wonderful little stories that are "hidden" somewhere in overlong, awkward, unsatisfactory masses of words.

Here are two examples of short story beginnings, each leading into a different kind of story:

1) "Let me tell you something about the Busbys," the old gentleman said to me. "The Busbys don't wash themselves—not adequately. And especially not as they grow older."

2) Just around the turn, the road was alive. First to assault the eye was a pro-
fusion of heads, black-haired, bobbing, and a number of straw hats that
looked oddly professional—

The stories following these beginnings are to be found in *Prize
Stories 1965: The O. Henry Awards,* edited by Richard Poirier and
William Abrahams. The first story, "There," by Peter Taylor, invites the reader to listen in on a confidential, gossipy conversation:
the words "Let me tell you" are intriguing enough, but the surprise
comes in the second line. And we are introduced to a strange little
town, "There," where each family seems to have a peculiar trait all
its own—not washing properly, eating too much, narrow-minded
complacency—and dying. Peter Taylor, the author of many excellent short stories of a rich, complex type, builds tension in a highly
refined manner. We listen in on this old man's monologue, amused by
his portraits of people back "there," and gradually we become emotionally involved in the pathos of his love for a girl who belonged to
a family with a secret common trait—and then we find out, along
with the narrator, that this common trait is dying. The girl has died
young; the lover, now an aged man, has married someone else; there
is no tragedy here, everything is muted and understated. But the
story is unforgettable because Taylor has built so very gradually and
unobtrusively the tension that arises out of the girl's impending
death. Everything is past tense, but vitally alive.

The second beginning is from a story of mine, "First Views of the
Enemy." Beginning with a near-accident, this story relies on tension
building up within the main character's mind. A bus carrying migrant fruit pickers has broken down at the roadside, and when a
young mother with her child drives by, one of the Mexican children
darts in front of the car to frighten her. The tension between the
young, American, rather materialistic woman and the socially-
marginal people is the theme of this story. The woman arrives home
safely, but she carries the image of this "enemy" with her into her
expensive home, which now seems to her vulnerable. Her realization
that she could lose everything she owns drives her to an orgy of selfishness as she locks things up, closes her drapes, even picks her most
beautiful flowers and forces food upon her child. The tension is psychological, not active; the "enemy" does not appear after the first

encounter. We see that the true "enemy" is the woman's hysterical selfishness, which she is forcing upon her child also.

Franz Kafka's classic, "The Metamorphosis," begins like this:

> As Gregor Samsa awoke one morning from uneasy dreams he found himself transformed in his bed into a gigantic insect.

Incredible, of course. Unbelievable. But Kafka's mild-mannered prose proceeds on as if an event of no great dimensions has taken place. You, the reader, find out about Gregor's metamorphosis at the same time he does. You are surprised, yes, but so is Gregor—a quite ordinary young man, devoted to his family and his work. This surrealistic story is much more "realistic" in its ability to convince and emotionally involve than most slick fiction with its easily-recognizable people. But Kafka thrives on tension. He builds it from his first sentence on. Kafka is always asking, "What happens next?" and then he asks, "After that, what happens?" Like Simenon, he drives his characters to extremes and tests them. "The Metamorphosis" is beautifully constructed in three sections, each dealing with the tense relationship between the stricken Gregor and his family, until Gregor dies in order to release his loved ones. Tension is achieved on the literal level—what is going to happen to the insect-man?—and on the symbolic level—what will be the outcome of the "love" between members of a family when one of them is mysteriously stricken and is no longer "human"?

These three stories, widely differing in technique, build up tension through an accumulation of detail. If violence erupts in fiction, it should be the outcome of tension; it should not come first, nor should it be accidental. Action stories are of interest to certain audiences, but quality stories usually refine action onto a psychological level. There is "action"—movement—but it takes place in a person's mind or in a conversation. If someone finally kills someone else, it is simply the climax of a rhythmic building of tension that lasts long enough to be convincing but is short enough to be interesting.

Remember that tension created for its own sake is cheap; no one will read your story more than once. The tension is part of your technique but technique is only a means to an end; it is never the end itself. That is why the French "new novel" is so boring—it has no capacity to move us—while older, stormy works like *Wuthering*

Heights (which could only be "camp" to today's *avant-garde*) will be interesting to all imaginable future generations. I think the stress placed today on technique is misleading. A writer should imagine his scenes dramatically, as if they were to take place on the stage. There, empty, wordy passages are found out at once. It isn't "words" or "style" that make a scene, but the content behind the words, and the increase of tension as characters come into conflict with one another. "Words" themselves are relatively unimportant, since there are countless ways of saying the same thing.

A final suggestion: be daring, take on anything. Don't labor over little cameo works in which every word is to be perfect. Technique holds a reader from sentence to sentence, but only content will stay in his mind.

37

THE WILLING SUSPENSION OF DISBELIEF

By Elizabeth Peters

ALTHOUGH Coleridge coined the useful phrase, "the willing suspension of disbelief," it has been the goal of storytellers since the pre-literate dawn of time and of writers since fiction began. Writers of suspense fiction particularly depend upon this gesture of good will on the part of the reader, but successful achievement of that goal depends upon the writer as well as the reader. Presumably, the reader of thrillers or novels of suspense starts each book in the proper mood of suspended disbelief, but he cannot sustain this mood if the author taxes his intelligence too much. How, then, does the writer of suspense fiction create an aura of plausibility which will allow readers to accept his creation, "for the moment," as Coleridge adds?

The so-called Gothic novel is a sub-category of the novel of suspense. In most cases, the term "Gothic" is a misnomer, for the romantic, "damsel-in-distress" thrillers which publishers label "modern Gothics" are not Gothics at all. Their ancestors are not Mrs. Ann Radcliffe's *The Mysteries of Udolpho* or Horace Walpole's *The Castle of Otranto,* but Wilkie Collins' *The Moonstone* and Charlotte Brontë's *Jane Eyre.* The true Gothic novel requires an atmosphere of brooding supernatural horror and a setting that includes ruined castles and desolate moors. I don't consider my books to be true Gothics, but it would be pedantic of me to object to the term, which is certainly more succinct than more accurate designations. I may then be forgiven if I refer henceforth to this form of fiction as "Gothic."

The most important thing for a writer of Gothics to recognize is that the genre is inherently incredible, almost as unlikely as a fantasy novel. Personally, I find it as easy to believe in the green Martians of Barsoom as I do in the adventures of Gothic heroines. Some writers of Gothics seem to feel that because their plots are fantastic, they need not be logical. The converse is true. The more fantastic the plot, the more important are those factors that invite belief, or, at least, the suspension of disbelief.

What are these factors? Some may be seen in the three elements of plot, character and setting.

The plot of a Gothic novel must be tight, consistent, and logical —within the given framework. Like the fantasy novel, which starts with a single fantastic premise, the Gothic begins with what I like to call an "initiating coincidence." The heroine happens to overhear a conversation between two people who are planning a murder; or she happens to accept a job as governess in an isolated household whose inhabitants all suffer from severe neuroses. None of these situations is very likely, but we can admit one such fortuitous occurrence in order to get our plot moving. From that point on, however—no coincidences, no lucky accidents. If the hero is walking down Main Street at the moment when the heroine, cornered by the villain, screams for help, the hero must have a reason for being on Main Street at that vital moment. It will not suffice to explain that he keeps in shape by jogging down Main Street every fine afternoon. If the heroine is to be rescued—and Gothic heroines always are—the rescuer must be brought to the spot by hard work and/or logical deductions.

Plausibility of character is as important as consistency of plot. The two are related, of course. A stupid heroine's foolish behavior can lead to plot complications. Indeed, the plots of the poorer Gothics seem to depend wholly on the heroine's incredible naïveté, as she falls into one pitfall after another. But it is difficult for the reader to identify, or even sympathize, with heroines of such consummate imbecility. Admittedly, Gothic heroines have a propensity for getting into trouble. It is one of the important elements of the Gothic plot, but it can also be one of the great weaknesses of the genre. Critics justifiably jeer at the dim-witted girls who take nocturnal strolls around grim old mansions. If you must get your heroine out of her nice, safe, locked room in the middle of the night, after two murders have already been committed, do give her a good reason for leaving that security. (I cannot think of anything that would induce me to leave my room under those circumstances, except perhaps the voices of my children screaming for help.) Your heroine must have an equally pressing motive. Better yet, have her stay in her room and get into trouble in some less conventional manner. And no mysterious notes asking for a midnight rendezvous in the castle crypt, please. Critics sneer at that one, too. A heroine ought to have sufficient intelligence to check with the hero to make sure he actually sent the note before she ventures into a crypt.

The characters of Gothic novels are not profound or complex; in two-hundred-odd pages we do not have space for such luxuries, since we must spend a good deal of verbiage on plot and atmosphere. But if our characters are cardboard, they need not be absurd. They must not exhibit flagrant personality aberrations, or behave so idiotically that the reader begins to hope they will be murdered in the crypt, as they deserve to be.

Of course, the more fully developed and realistic your characters, the more plausible their actions will seem. One of the classics in the field, Daphne du Maurier's *Rebecca*, has a heroine who has always exasperated me by her timidity and docility; but she is believable, because she behaves in a way that is consistent with her background and her personality.

Atmosphere and setting are particularly important to thrillers of this type, and the same rule applies: the more unusual or exotic the setting, the harder you must work to give it an appearance of authenticity. In these days of jets and travel books, Samarkand is no more exotic than Paris or Rome. But you must make sure that your descriptions of these cities are accurate, and that you include enough details to convince the reader of the reality of the setting in which your heroine's wild adventures are to take place. I do not subscribe to the theory that a writer can write only about things he or she has personally experienced. I have personally visited all the cities and countries I have used in my books; but I could not have written about them without the aid of maps, photographs, and detailed notes taken on the spot. Perhaps a conscientious writer can do this with a city he or she has never seen—but it will require a great deal of work.

The rule holds even when you are inventing a setting. In one of my books, the action takes place in Rothenburg, a small German town I know fairly well, but for various reasons I decided to add an imaginary castle to that city instead of using an existing structure. I did almost as much research on the castle as I did on the city, reading about medieval castles and Franconian architecture, so that the description of my imaginary castle would agree with details of real structures of that period. If your characters do a lot of running around, draw floor plans. Readers love to spot discrepancies, and will write irritated letters if you have your heroine descend a staircase where no staircase can conceivably exist.

One useful trick to make sure that the reader will accept your devices of plot or of setting is to prepare him for them well in advance. A strategically located doorway, through which the hero gains entrance to the conference room—a secret passage whereby your characters can escape when danger threatens—these, and other devices, will seem more plausible if they are mentioned before you actually need them. Again, the more unusual the prop, the more carefully you must explain its presence. A secret passage in a medieval castle needs only a sentence or two of description, since the reader knows that medieval castles abound in such conveniences. A secret passage in a modern split-level house requires considerable explanation—and perhaps a brief character sketch of the eccentric individual who had it built.

Plot props require the same advance preparation. If the heroine's knowledge of Urdu is going to save her from a fate worse than death, or expose the master criminal, you must tell the reader early in the book that she is an expert in this abstruse language. If you do not, she will resemble Superwoman when she comes up with the information. And for pity's sake, if she or the hero is to be an expert in ichthyology or Egyptology, learn something about those subjects before you talk about them. I was once put off an otherwise readable Gothic because it involved a reincarnated Egyptian princess named Cha-cha-boom, or something equally absurd. No reincarnated Egyptian, fake or genuine, would have such a name, and the repetition of the inane syllables grated on me so strongly that I never finished the book. The author could easily have found an authentic ancient Egyptian name in the encyclopedia. I remember another book I never finished reading because the villain, a German sea captain, kept shouting "Grüss Gott!" in frenzied moments. If you do not know that "Grüss Gott" is a friendly greeting in southern Germany, have your villain stick to English.

You may think that few readers have much knowledge of Egyptology or other abstruse subjects. This would be a dangerous assumption. Archaeology is a popular field, and for some odd reason, which I mean to investigate one day, archaeology buffs seem to be especially addicted to thrillers. But that is not the important thing. The important thing is that plausibility depends upon the accumulation of consistent, accurate details. They really do add verisimilitude to an otherwise bald and unconvincing narrative. The reader may not consciously note all your errors; but a series of careless inconsistencies will tax the reader's willingness to accept your imaginary world, and a single glaring error may be enough to snap that fragile thread on which the suspension of disbelief depends.

Of course, you are bound to slip up occasionally, no matter how conscientiously you research your book. As I work through revision after revision, I come across howlers I can't believe I missed the first and second times. To my chagrin, a few of them escape me even in the third and fourth revisions and get into print, despite the additional efforts of my intelligent editors. In one of my books, written under another name, an integral plot prop was an old family Bible. Long after the book was published, a reader wrote to me inquiring how the Bible happened to survive the conflagration that had destroyed the equally ancient family mansion and most of its contents. "I can imagine several possible solutions," she added charitably, "but I do think you ought to have *told* us."

She was absolutely correct. I should have told her. And I would have done so, if I had noticed the discrepancy. However, errors of this sort are not in the same category as careless mistakes or poorly developed characters. An occasional gap in the plot or an error of fact will not be serious if the rest of the plot is as tight as you can make it, and if the other facts have been checked and rechecked.

I could go on, giving examples of the basic rule, but if you read many Gothics, you will spot plenty of other cases, of success and of failure. Of course there are some writers who seem to be able to break all the rules and get away with it. Don't bother writing to tell me about them. I know about them. I only wish I knew how they do it.

191

38

POINT OF VIEW: EXPERIMENT IN LIVING

By Marjorie Franco

A few years ago I walked into a New York office, gave my name to the receptionist and sat down. The receptionist, a young girl, turned to me and inquired, "Are you an actress?" "No," I said, disappointing her, "I'm a fiction writer." I had the feeling she wanted me to be an actress—it's more glamorous, I suppose—and to make amends I said, "Inside many a writer lives an actor." Nodding agreeably, but clearly dissatisfied, the girl returned to her work. Had she been interested I could have explained that writing, like acting, is an experiment in living, and that the writer (and the actor), by lifting himself out of his own particular life, looks at life from another point of view.

What is point of view, and what does it have to do with writing, or acting, or the persons behind either of these creative arts? The dictionary says point of view is a "position from which something is considered or evaluated." All right; that seems clear. The writer takes up a position from which to tell a story. What position? A reader might say, "That's simple; he tells a story in either the first or third person." It might seem simple, but for the writer it is not.

There are at least six third-person viewpoints and five first-person viewpoints, some rarely used. To discuss all of these or to discuss technique without a story to hang it on can be confusing. Even though the writer has an intellectual mastery of viewpoint techniques, he may not create a good viewpoint character. Writers learn by doing. Did Chekhov sit down and ask himself, "Should I adopt the position of concealed narrator and third-person protagonist narrator restricted, or what?" Or did he simply write "The Kiss"?

This is not to say that it is unimportant to learn technique, for a writer needs to learn as much as he can about the tools of his craft. But tools are only a means to something more, and a preoccupation with them can lead to mechanical writing. Viewpoint, then, is not a matter of manipulation, of attaching oneself, willy-nilly, to a position, to a character, and then telling the story through that character's mind and feelings. Viewpoint is organic, and writers have in common with the actor the method to make it work.

An actor trained in the Stanislavski method knows the psychology of his character; he knows *how* he does things because first he knows *why*. The actor tries to put himself in his character's place, to enter his world, live his life, master his actions, his thoughts and feelings. His truth. It is not enough merely to think of an emotion. Abstract emotions don't come across, or they fall into clichés. It is better to imagine what a character might think or do in a *certain situation*. Then the emotion comes of itself.

A writer uses a similar method of organic viewpoint. He puts himself in his character's place, enters his world, indeed creates his world, suffers his pains and celebrates his joys. If a writer has never laughed or cried at his typewriter, then I doubt if he has ever been deeply inside a character.

Before a writer takes up a viewpoint position he might do well to consider his own temperament and personality and the limitations these impose on his choices. Fiction is personal, as personal as the writer's imagination and emotional experience. New writers are often told, "Write what you know." I would broaden that by saying, "Write what you know emotionally." Love, hate, anger, joy, fear—these are universal. They become unique when they are connected to experience. Our emotional experiences are stored within us. Filtered through memory and a well-developed imagination, they can be called up, made fresh and organized into the work at hand. Creative imagination is the writer's valuable gift, and even though it is somewhat limited by his experience, within that sphere of experience it is unlimited in variety and combination. Hopefully the writer is always enlarging his sphere, adding to his storehouse with outward experience in reality.

Out of the sphere of my emotional experience I wrote "The Poet of Evolution Avenue" (*Redbook*), the story of a young wife and mother who was, also, a bad poet. She believed her creative gift was being hampered by the intrusion of her family. She had neither the time nor the privacy to write a real poem. Time and privacy are practically forced on her in the form of a vacation alone in her father's California apartment, but it isn't until she is ready to go home that she is able to write a real poem, and then only because she doesn't want to go home empty-handed.

This story is based on the old Ivory Tower idea: a poet is more productive when isolated from the world. My poet discovered that she had been making excuses for herself, that her world was her stimulus, and that she had trouble producing poetry without it.

The idea for that story came out of my own emotional experience. Some years earlier I had gone to California to be near my father while he was in the hospital undergoing surgery. For three weeks I lived alone in his apartment, a large, tight-security building in which I rarely saw the other residents. I had brought my typewriter, thinking I would turn out a volume or two between hospital visits. It didn't work. I was accustomed to working with people around. Interruptions. Interruptions can be marvelous. They take the place of pacing, a necessary activity of some writers. I learned that I am not an Ivory Tower writer, ideal as that may seem; I need the stimulus of family and friends.

Every writer has his own voice, and it is up to him to find it and use it with authority. That voice comes through as male or female, child or adult, humorous or serious, but behind it, within it, is the author's brooding presence, his vision of life. He describes the world from his point of view. He is on intimate terms with his viewpoint characters. Henry James could imagine what his focal character (he is never named) in *The Aspern Papers* might think and do when he is forced to admit to the woman who loves him that he has been using her for his personal gain. But I doubt if James could have lived inside Bigger, as Richard Wright did in *Native Son*, and chased and killed the huge rat in a Chicago tenement. Who is to say one view is better or worse than another? Each is different, unique.

Recognizing his limitations, an author adopts a viewpoint position he can understand emotionally as well as intellectually. My story, "Miss Dillon's Secret" (*Redbook*), is about a teacher. I have never been a teacher, but teaching is within the sphere of my emotional experience. I have been a student, of course, and my husband, now a principal, was once a teacher. His experiences have rubbed off on me. I believe that a natural teacher is born, not made, that the qualities in such a person work together to make learning exciting. The title character in my story, Miss Dillon, is drawn from a real person, an experienced teacher whose students come back to visit her with their husbands and wives and children and grandchildren.

I adopted the viewpoint position of a young teacher who had worked with Miss Dillon. There were more decisions for me to make. Will I place myself inside or outside the viewpoint character? And how far inside or outside? This can be a difficult choice, for each character has its own limitations, and the author, to keep his voice appropriate to the viewpoint, puts limits on his "knowledge" accordingly. He seems to know less than he does. Consider, for example, Hemingway's camera-eye view which limits his "knowledge" to what can be seen from the outside. Or, at the other extreme, Joyce's deep internalizing, which limits him in the other direction.

For my viewpoint character I adopted a position somewhere in between. With the story told in the third person, my character's problems are external, but her discovery of Miss Dillon's secret is internal, brought about by an emotional experience with one of her former students.

We might ask ourselves certain questions concerning viewpoint: 1) Who will be the narrator? author, in first or third person? character, in first person? or nobody (omniscient narrator)? 2) From what angle does the narrator tell the story? Above, center, front, periphery, shifting? 3) Where does the author place the reader? Near, far, shifting?

Sometimes an author adopts a viewpoint position instinctively, and all goes well. The voice flows from a stable position. At other times an author finds himself tangled in clumsy sentences and tedious explanations, surrendering his surprises too early, battling predictability, placing his best scenes offstage. When this happens, the problem could very well be the viewpoint he chose. He may be looking from the wrong angle. Usually I can tell by the way it "feels" if I'm in a good or poor viewpoint. But not always. Four years ago I wrote a short story called "The Boy Who Cooked." The title character, Benny, was the antagonist, and the viewpoint character was a woman protagonist whose name changed with each of the many versions I wrote. I couldn't sell the story. But I continued writing it, on and off, for four years, always keeping the boy, but frequently changing the characters around him, including the viewpoint character. The total number of pages devoted to that story runs into several hundred, which is some indication of my devotion to a character. But finally I gave up and put the story away.

Meanwhile, I had written and sold a story called, "No Such Thing as a Happy Marriage" (*Redbook*), in which the viewpoint character was a wife and mother named Jenny. Six months after that story was published, my editor, in a letter to me, mentioned Benny, the boy who cooked. Even before I had finished reading the letter, Benny, like Lazarus, rose from the dead. Why couldn't I write a new story for Benny? And why couldn't I surround him with the same cast of characters I had used in "No Such Thing as a Happy Marriage," with Jenny as the viewpoint character? I could, and I did. This time the viewpoint felt right; the voice flowed clearly from a stable position, and I wrote the story in a matter of hours. After four years of roaming through my typewriter, Benny had found his place, and his story, "The Boy Who Cooked," was published in *Redbook*.

The author's attitude toward a character (and his desire to create a similar attitude in the reader) can help determine the angle from which he views him. If the character is obviously sympathetic, the reader will identify. With some characters, however, the reader may feel only a tentative sympathy, until he is shocked into understanding by some revelation which allows him to feel complete sympathy. Sometimes, reader and character start out with a great distance between them. Perhaps their worlds are totally different. The author gradually pulls the reader into the character's world, and the reader ends by feeling sympathy. (I have this experience, as a reader, when I read Jean Genêt, for example.) A difficult relationship for an author to achieve is one in which the reader is forced to identify, perhaps unconsciously, with a character he dislikes. He is left wondering what there was about the story that fascinated him. What he may not realize is that, being human, we all have our share of unattractive qualities, and seeing them in someone else stirs our recognition. Playwright Harold Pinter frequently achieves this kind of relationship.

In my story, "An Uncompromising Girl" (*Redbook*), my aim was for tentative sympathy and eventual complete sympathy. As the author (concealed narrator), I speak in the third person through the focal character. The channels of information between author and reader are a combination of the author's words, thoughts, and perceptions, and the character's words, actions, thoughts, perceptions and feelings. I used the angle of the character attempting to see herself from the outside, but erring in her vision—a position which placed limits on my "knowledge" of the character.

Earlier I spoke of the writer's voice, which I related to his vision of life and which includes his entire personality. Now, to that voice I would add two more voices: the story voice, which is the pace, the music, the tone of the story; and the voice of the viewpoint character, since it is through his eyes that we see everything that happens. Actually, it is impossible to separate all these voices, fused as they are into a creation that has passed through a maturing process in the author's mind and found its way to the page, either in harmony or dissonance. But for the sake of clarity, let us for a moment consider the voice of the viewpoint character.

If a story is told in the first person through a character (and not the author), then that character's voice is ever-present, and the writer, like the method actor, must know the character's every thought, act, feeling and desire. He must know his truth, his conscious and unconscious life, what he wants, or thinks he wants, and the difference between the two. My story "Don't Call Me Darling" (*Redbook*), was written from such a viewpoint. I had to know my character's attitude toward herself as a woman pursuing a career. I had to know how she felt about women's rights in general. And how she felt about friendship and human communication. I had to understand her intellect, her ambitions, her habits, and her insights. When she spoke, she revealed herself as a careful individual, and this voice had to remain consistent throughout the story, even though some of her attitudes were undergoing a change.

When an author knows the details of action and speech in a

197

character, he is in control of his material. He can become more familiar with his character by spending time with him, engaging him in conversation or argument, as if he were a living entity. He may even want to get up from his typewriter to act out a detail, a gesture, or an entire scene, in order to visualize it more clearly in his mind. Creating characters, seeing them come to life, is an exciting experience.

The entire experience of a story, from start to finish—and it may cover a period of several years—is an exciting one, in spite of the hard work, frustration and failures. Not a small portion of that excitement lies in the discoveries that are made, for in any work of creative imagination one looks for insights. What does the story have to say? Does it reinforce a shallow view of life? Or does it open up new insights for the viewpoint character? When I write a story about a character who seems very real to me, am I not at the same time making a discovery about myself? Writing, like acting, is an experiment in living. It is looking at life from another viewpoint. And life can be exciting wherever it is lived, or re-created— on the stage, or on the page.

39

YOU CAN GET THERE FROM HERE

By Eileen Jensen

Writing, like making love, is more fun when you know what you're doing. Editors keep telling me, a working writer, that my short story transitions are good. In looking through my story files to find transitions from my published work to illustrate this article, I was surprised to discover that I was using good transitions ten years ago. I can't brag about it, however, because in the beginning I honestly didn't know what I was doing. What came naturally to the young writer has become conscious craftsmanship. It's a lot more fun now.

What makes a good transition?

A good transition has thrust. It shoves your story forward like a booster rocket tilting a spaceship. Well-timed and carefully triggered, it will put your story into orbit.

Every story has its own pace. Some glide. Others race. A few seem to hop along, grinning. The best transitions are smooth. They do not jar the reader. Transitions, like cosmetics, are most successful when you are unaware of their presence. I believe any intelligent writer can learn to write good, quick, viable transitions. Two things are required: you must pay attention, and you must practice.

For the most part, I use three kinds of transitions in my short stories. I think of them as TIME transitions, ECHO transitions and LEAPFROG transitions.

TIME transitions are the easiest. They also are the most obvious, and you must be careful not to make them dull.

ECHO transitions are more interesting. They link one part of a story to the next part by repeating a certain word or activity or thought on the far side of the transition.

LEAPFROG transitions set up a scene, and skip over it, landing on the next lilypad. This is a tricky transition, but it is lively and interesting and forces your reader to participate in the action.

The TIME transition keeps your reader chronologically oriented. He knows where he is because he has been there before. The story is moving in intervals of time which he understands and relates to. Saturday night means something to everyone. Sunday morning is a different day, indeed. Monday morning? Ouch!

The Time transition becomes art when it is used in a story where time itself (meaning time-passing) is important. Time passes at two levels in such a story. A good example from my own published short stories is "The Loveliest Grapevines in Cleveland" (*Woman's Day*).

This is a story about children growing up in today's migrant culture. I related it through the planting, cultivation, harvest and distillation of one crop of grapes. Time was vital to the story in every way. The family was always moving. It was important to keep track of the ages of the growing children, the number of times the family moved, the length of time it takes a young grapevine to grow and bear fruit, and how long it takes to make wine. Even the passing seasons were important to this particular little story. The children, the grapevines, and the story matured together, going from one transition to the next through time within the story. I planned it that way. The mother in the grapevine story is the star. She's a loving gardener. Susie, the nine-year-old younger daughter, is the narrator. Early on I set the reader to thinking about time:

Last year for Mother's Day, Daddy gave her a riding mower . . .

This mother holds the family together in spite of constant relocation. She does it by cultivating a loving relationship as carefully as she husbands the grapevines. I don't say this in so many words (it's fatal to preach), but I plant the idea in almost every Time transition throughout the story:

When we move to a new house, my mother makes us feel it's home. The first thing she does is plant flowers . . .

I take the time to show the mother doing that. Then—

We've lived in Cleveland for three whole years now. I know Mother cringes at the thought of ever leaving our big old white house on this half-acre . . .

200

And then I flash back, moving the story backwards with a Time transition.

The week we moved in, an old man in the neighborhood brought us a wooden churn as a housewarming gift . . .

And forward—

She planted a willow whip that first year. It's taller than my sister Lissa now. It casts a shade. Buddha could sit under that tree . . .

The mother plants the grapevines.

The next year they didn't look a whole lot better . . .

The mother teaches her girls about life through the example of the vines.

Suddenly, our willow was taller. Buddha could stand under that tree. Our grapevines, three years old now, began to look great . . .

The harvest is near, and the pace quickens. The skilled writer will go to shorter sentences now. Transitions will speed up.

In June we knew we were going to have a crop . . .
In July robins perched on the trellises and eyed the green fruit . . .
In August, the grapes turned from green to bronze to velvety blue . . .
It was the first Wednesday in September, and school started the next week . . .

They make the wine. They wait two months. They bottle it. Eight bottles.

Mother said we would open it for Christmas. Let's see, if we open one bottle a year at Christmas, it will last until I'm eighteen. That's not bad.

Even at the end, you see, I am pushing the reader ahead of time, pointing him into the future.

That may be the most time-oriented story I ever have written. And yet, my files reveal that as far back as October 1959 *McCall's* published my story, "Some Day He'll Come Along," an equally time-conscious tale. In those days I wrote stories in the way some people play the piano—by ear. I knew when it sounded right. Now, so many years later, I can read music—and even compose a bit.

In "Some Day He'll Come Along," I took a romantic girl from the age of twelve through marriage and childbirth at age twenty-seven. She was searching for the one man she would love. The transitions are similar, if somewhat less skilled, than those in the grapevines story.

During her senior year . . .
It began to look as if she'd have to find him in college . . .
The next day he told her he was going into the army after college . . .
After college, her parents sent her abroad . . .
She was twenty-four when she married Howard . . .
Amy worked hard at being Mrs. Howard Garvin . . .
She began to wear maternity clothes . . .
She was twenty-seven when their child was born . . .

Surely any beginning writer can do as much. Or more.

ECHO transitions are the swift ones, extremely valuable in the short-short story. Take "Seasons of the Heart" (*Good Housekeeping*). It is a time-oriented story—but a short one—and transitions must be lightning quick. The narrative is related through gardening metaphors again. (I'm a gardener, and I am sensitive to the parallels between plant life and human existence.) I chose Echo transitions for sheer speed.

This is a story about Meg, a pretty young widow trying to adjust to the untimely death of her husband. When the story opens, Meg is pregnant. She and her husband Tony buy a small apple tree to plant in the backyard of their new house. They plant it while Diana, the disillusioned divorcée next door, watches cynically. Tony boasts—

"My son will play in the shade of this tree."
"If it lives," Diana says.
The tree lived, but Tony died—killed in a speedboat accident.

The echoing word "live" is the trigger to the quick transition. There is life here—going, coming, snuffed out. The transition is accomplished within the space of six words.

Later in the story as Meg struggles to adjust, Diana ridicules the young widow.

202

Meg burst into tears.
It was the last time she cried. In January, she brushed up on her shorthand and took a part-time job.

The Echo in the transition is the word "tears" as related to "cried."
I doubled the effect in that same paragraph when Meg reveals that she is taking

". . . temporary office work. A Skelly girl. It isn't much money, but you meet such interesting typewriters." She also met men, but they were either married or bachelors with dependent mothers, or ex-wives to whom they owed alimony and child support.

The Echo word is "meet." I take her from her first job through a series of men, and do it with one transitional echoing word.
And note that it's also a LEAPFROG transition as well. Meg meets and passes several men within that one transition.
I leapfrog again in the transition in which she accepts a glamorous date with her sophisticated boss who wines and dines her and invites her up to his apartment to see his stamp collection:

"He didn't even have a stamp!" Meg reported indignantly to Diana the next morning.

The transition is both Echo (stamp) and Leapfrog, because we jump over the seduction scene in the man's apartment. The reader knows exactly how that encounter went. We don't need to document it.
Warning: you must not leapfrog any scene which is out of the ordinary and different from the usual encounter. If it's vital, write it! If it's valuable only in passing, leapfrog it.
You can take giant leaps. Imagine this one:

Debbie lay awake all night, thinking of Jim.
Jim lay awake, too—in another woman's arms.

I recall one of my early stories in which I described a lovers' quarrel which broke up an engaged couple. It took place before a dancing party.

They didn't make it to the altar.
They didn't even make it to the dance.

203

By now you should recognize and identify the transitional technique in the quarrel. It's both Echo (didn't make it) and Leapfrog (skip the dance scene).

When you are reading, watch for transitions. Learn to identify them. Be conscious of the writer's craftsmanship. When you begin to notice and recognize what is going on, you will begin to use good transitions in your own writing.

40

STYLE AND THE FICTION WRITER

By Mary Wallace

SOMEONE—I wish I could remember who—once said that he could no more define a gentleman than a terrier could define a rat, but that just as a terrier knows a rat when it sees one, so he knows a gentleman. For most of us, that's how it is with Style.

A veil of mystery surrounds this word; or seems to. Actually only part of the veil is mystery; the rest is misunderstanding, which springs from a tendency to stress the importance of individual style above style in its broader sense. By this imbalance, beginning writers are led to believe they must adopt an individual style; something that will set their writing apart; something extra, like hot fudge topping on the ice cream or mushrooms in the gravy. But individual style—the manner of expression characteristic of a particular writer—though indeed something extra, is not something to be adopted. It develops from the writer's own personality, from every thought and feeling he has ever had, from his whole attitude toward the world about him, and, to some extent, from everything absorbed in years of reading. In short, *it is the writer*. Consequently, there is no need to worry about it, or even to think about it, for it is bound to make its own way to the surface in good time.

On the other hand, there is a very real need to think about style in its broad sense—those features of literary composition which belong to form and expression rather than to the substance of the thought or matter expressed.

That is a dictionary definition, and of course correct as far as it goes. But in the actual writing there can be no such division; form and substance must be one, as inseparable as body and soul. It may be true of a song that "As long as a tune has a right good swing, it doesn't much matter what words you sing," but never make the mistake of thinking that anything comparable can be said of writing—

that as long as the substance is there, any words will do. They won't. The words we use and the way we use them determine the strength or weakness, the brilliance or dullness, of what we write. It is form—*the adaptation of the expression to the idea*—that conveys the substance. A poorly worded thought is not communicated. A poorly presented character does not come alive. A poorly expressed emotion leaves the reader untouched.

But even to think of form as a vehicle is not enough. It is much more than that. It is the means by which the substance is made identifiable. Consider, for a moment, a diamond and a piece of graphite. Both are pure carbon; the difference lies in the internal arrangement of the atoms. Well, words are the atoms of writing; and since we all use (or have available) the same words—all the words in the English language—the difference between good and poor writing must lie in the arrangement of our words. Not entirely, for there are other factors, including the substance itself and the sincerity or insincerity of the writer, but the way in which words are put together is the secret and the only mystery of style.

For help and guidance the beginning fiction writer turns to the short stories or novels of writers successful in those fields. This seems the logical place to turn; and in regard to structure, dialogue, character portrayal, plot development, quite possibly help will be found there. But in regard to style, it is not the best place to turn; first, because of the temptation to imitate, and imitation is a trap; second, because character and story tend to overshadow the actual words used—as they should. I have often been asked what novels by other novelists helped me most. None. I was helped most by the "familiar essayists," from Sir Thomas Browne on up to E.B. White; and I would urge any beginning writer of fiction to make the acquaintance of those masters of style. If those of past centuries seem too far away to be "relevant," then at least read those of the twentieth century, being sure not to overlook Logan Pearsall Smith's *Trivia* and *More Trivia,* two small volumes of which it has been said that "their happy audacity is not more remarkable than the consummate felicity of their expression."

Any approach to style must necessarily be over a roadway solidly paved with the rules of grammar and the principles of composition. But to know the rules, to be able to write sentences that are grammatically correct, is only a first step. The *art* of writing goes beyond the rules into an area where nothing is fixed and absolute; where we must find our way by instinct, by ear, by some subtle awareness of what makes one word or group of words better than another for the expression of what we want to say. Still, since we write in sentences, mastery of the sentence has to be our first goal; and since it is not too much to say that the advantageous or disadvantageous positioning of *one word* can mean the difference between clarity and obscurity, effectiveness and ineffectiveness, to aim at that goal is to set our sights high.

So let's be sure we know just what a sentence is. It is a group of words expressing a *single complete* thought. It must contain, explicitly or implicitly, at least one independent predication. It is a unit, a constituent part of a larger whole, a thread in a pattern, and as such it must pass a double test: how well does it express the thought, and how well does it fit into the pattern?

There is no easy formula to follow. The structure of sentences may vary greatly, and there is no arbitrary limit to their length. In modern writing, simplicity is favored over complexity, and probably it is best—safest, at any rate—to use sentences of moderate length, except when short or long ones are needed for some special purpose.

Very short sentences are useful for emphasis or some other desired effect; but there is a risk, for if the effect is not achieved, a string of short sentences will sound crude or childish. Here is a paragraph from Ernest Hemingway's famous short story, "The Killers":

Outside it was getting dark. The street light came on outside the window. The two men at the counter read the menu. From the other end of the counter Nick Adams watched them. He had been talking to George when they came in.

Well, Hemingway could put it across; but a beginner would be ill advised to write in this manner.

The long sentence, too, has its special uses. If the thought is complex, the sentence may have to be equally so, for there should be no break in the continuity of the thought. For emphasis, for building up a mood, for revealing the way in which a character's mind works, a long sentence can be very effective. But again there is a risk: The effect is lost if the reader becomes lost along the way. Here is one of mine:

207

As in sleep a dream comes, seeming to cover hours, days, even years, yet in truth occupying only the space of a thought as it comes and goes, so in that moment of closing his eyes he had a dream-vision, in which he saw himself standing on the center section of a bridge, of which the part that he had just come over, and the part that he had yet to cross, had been swept away, leaving him stranded, cut off from all the rest of the living world; and all around, as far as the eye could see, was nothing but a desolate gray waste, like the sand-flats and salt-water marshes over which he had driven with Paul one day last winter, on a trip to a coastal town. (*Reason for Gladness,* Funk & Wagnalls)

This is a single thought; division into three or four shorter sentences would therefore be structurally wrong. Beyond that, the length contributes to the dream impression described at the start—the few seconds that seem like years. (Incidentally, with more care, this could have been a better sentence. "Of which" follows too closely upon "in which," and "as far as the eye could see"—a cliché—should have been omitted.)

Then there is the fractional sentence, incomplete in itself but nevertheless expressing a complete thought. This one should be used sparingly, for it must *instantly* suggest the parts needed to make it complete. If it meets that condition, either alone or in its context, then any fraction of a sentence—a subordinate clause, a phrase, even a single word—may stand as a sentence. An extreme example can be found at the start of *Reason for Gladness.* The first sentence, which is also the first paragraph, consists of two words, "Home today." The second sentence—and second paragraph—supplies only one additional detail, "Home today at half-past one." It is not until the third paragraph is reached that the context supplies the missing words needed to make the first two sentences complete. This can scarcely be called "instant," and can be defended only on the grounds that all the familiar connotations of the word "home" come immediately to mind, suggesting any number of complete sentences, though admittedly not "instantly"—"Anne would be going home from the hospital today at half-past one." The purpose was to emphasize "home" and all it connotes. But the writer took great liberty—even greater with the paragraph than with the sentence.

In creative writing, most rules are regarded as flexible, and may—knowingly but never *un*knowingly—be bent or stretched to suit the writer's purpose. The word, the sentence, the paragraph, all have as their primary function the creation of a mood or an impression. They must suggest far more than they actually say, for it is by the power of suggestion that they stimulate the imagination or stir the emotions of the reader.

What is a paragraph? Not merely a break on the page. Like the sentence it is a unit, usually a composite unit, that carries the reader one step forward on a course well laid out by the writer. If it is made up of several sentences, bear in mind that these must be *related* sentences, and that only those details which contribute to one central impression should be included. But there's more to it than that: there's the manner in which the details are arranged. Monotony of construction should be avoided. The sentences that make up a paragraph should vary in length, form, and sound; should be euphonious; and should not start in the same manner or with the same word, unless the writer is purposely using repetition as a means of emphasis.

Repetition is a hazardous device. It can be very dull. It can also be very effective, but only if the writer and the reader hear the same drummer. For better or for worse, in *Blue Meadow* (published by Morrow) I have several paragraphs in which a number of consecutive sentences start with the same word or words. In three or four of these, the repeated word is the name of a character. In another place, I start six sentences intentionally with "She had." Here, in its entirety, is another example of deliberate repetition:

Love was summer sunlight. Love was the fragrance of earth and leaves; the songs of birds; the wind in the trees. Love was a cresting wave, like the sea surf when it rises in an arched wall of green shadow and sunlit foam....

It may be interesting to note that these three sentences, though each begins in the same way, vary in length, and that with the increase in length there is increase in *forward movement,* as comparisons progress from stillness, to sound and motion, to the suggested power of the wave.

Perhaps all this can be called hair-splitting. Perhaps the fine points can be waved aside as nothing more than a bag of tricks. If a writer has a good story to tell, won't the words flow out under their own power and fall naturally into place? Don't count on it. Sometimes words do flow easily, and we all would like to think that when they have flowed easily they have flowed well. Once in a while this is so; but, unhappily, all too often it is not. Never send a manuscript off to an editor until you read and reread it. Revise. Rearrange. And be sure to read it aloud, because the ear will often catch what the eye misses —the unnecessary word, the awkward phrase, the unintended repetition, the pronoun that has lost touch with its antecedent. Examine every sentence for smoothness, coherence, clarity. Keep the reader's comfort in mind. Remember that easy writing usually makes hard reading. Don't be afraid that too much polishing will destroy the spontaneity of what you have written. There is no such thing as too much polishing. The author of *Trivia,* Logan Pearsall Smith, has this to say about it in his Preface:

> "You must beware of thinking too much about Style," said my kindly adviser, "or you will become like those fastidious people who polish and polish until there is nothing left."
> "Then there really are such people?" I asked eagerly. But the well-informed lady could give me no precise information about them.
> I often hear of them in this tantalizing manner, and perhaps one day I shall have the luck to come across them.

And now, to end with a word about endings. Much advice is given about the start of a story, the need to capture the reader's interest with the first line or two. The ending is no less important. A good beginning increases the chances of a story's being read; a good ending, its chances of being remembered. Not knowing when to stop is a common fault; but even if a stop is made at the right point, simply to stop is not enough. There must be an *ending,* something that acts as a fixative.

More than forty years ago I read *The Forsyte Saga.* I still remember the closing line—"He might wish and wish and never get it—the beauty and the loving in the world"—and how sorry it made me feel for Soames. Everything the reader has learned about Soames in the three books of the *Saga* is condensed in that single line. There is nothing remarkable about the words themselves; they are simple and ordinary words. The poignancy is in the way they are put together—yet it seems an entirely simple and ordinary way.

That is the mystery. And that is Style.

41

EXPERIMENTING WITH PERSPECTIVE

By Barbara Rohde

WHENEVER I tell someone I am working on a story and he asks the inevitable, "What's it about?" I find myself pausing before I answer. I can't decide whether to answer in terms of the events of the story ("Well, it's about this family on a summer vacation in Europe, and their little boy who has a stuffed cat he is always losing...") or to answer in terms of its meaning (Well, it's about the relentlessness of time and how people deal with that.")

I suppose I should always give both answers, since what makes a story is the coming together of events and meaning. The reason that similar events can have a multiplicity of meanings is a question of perspective. We learn early in our attempts at fiction that a story is not merely a chronology—this happened and then this happened and then this happened—that the meaning of a story depends upon how these events are seen and understood, first of all by the writer, then by the characters within the story, ultimately by the reader.

If I tell you I am writing a scene involving the death of one of my characters, for example, I have not really told you very much. (Our response to the death of Cordelia in *King Lear* is vastly different from our response to the death of the third corpse in an Agatha Christie mystery or the death of the giant in *Jack and the Beanstalk.*) It is the structure I give to my story that will, I hope, reveal the meaning of that death and determine whether the reader will view it with pity and terror, with deep compassion, with relief, or triumph or dismay or merely with an intellectual curiosity about "whodunit."

Thus the power of any story depends upon two things: upon the nature of the writer's vision (whether he sees certain things with more clarity, with a newness, with a depth or breadth beyond the ordinary) and upon his skill in structuring the story so that the reader will share that vision, will see the events in the same way and thus respond to them as the writer did in the creative impulse that evoked the story.

A number of technical skills are involved in the success of that sharing—the selection of descriptive detail, the ability to write dialogue that enables the reader to hear the characters come alive in dramatic scenes, the sense of how much weight to give to different aspects of the story in order to prepare the reader for the climactic insight, and so on. But one of the more important technical skills that I think writers need constantly to experiment with and think about is the use of "perspective"—the question of where you would like your reader to stand to view the events of the story.

Perspective is a common enough term in art classes, even for the very young. I think I was in sixth grade when I first learned some of the techniques of perspective in drawing. It was like a new toy. I filled page after page with telephone poles disappearing into the distance, cups and plates and glasses seen from various angles of vision, or scenes of city street corners, all the lines of the many-storied buildings converging on the horizon at the edges of my paper.

It was then, I suppose, that I first became dimly aware of the difference between "seeing" and "knowing." I *knew* that the top of the cup was a round circle; yet if I placed the cup on the table, a foot or so in front of me, I *saw* the opening as an elipse. The only way I could make my seeing and my knowing come together was to stand over the cup and look directly into it, but then, if I drew what I saw, no one could recognize it as a cup. It looked more like the beginning of a cartoon profile, the handle/nose jutting jauntily into space.

Nowadays I use this example when one of my more literal-minded friends tries to convince me that fiction is not true. I try to explain that often the only way I can make her see the same truth that I see is to create an image that she can look at and respond to, rather than to present her with some abstraction, a statistic or a measurement, that she would call a "fact."

It was long after the sixth grade that I learned that *perspective* comes from the Latin meaning "to see through." That delighted me, as discovering the origin of a word often delights me, and it also evoked images of ways and instruments of "seeing through"— windows and skylights, microscopes and telescopes, keyholes and peepholes and fissures in walls. I began to recognize perspective as a way of helping the viewer to see more clearly and to see more certainly the reality you hope he will see. It is an instrument of focus.

I had been writing short stories for some time before I began to distinguish the questions of perspective that were involved in what I was doing. I had, of course, heard about "point of view"—those categories of first person, omniscient observer, dramatic objective, stream of consciousness, and so on. But, though textbooks and lectures described various points of view, that didn't help me understand what they were for, didn't make me realize the difference that angle and distance could make in the way events were seen in a story, just as they make a difference in the way images are seen on a sketch pad. The descriptions also seemed to imply that the "point of view" involved was the writer's, though obviously the writer, as creator, is always omniscient. It is the reader's point of view that is at issue. The question is how much the writer wants the reader to see and from what distance and at what time and through whose eyes—where he wants the reader to stand to witness the events of the story. It also seemed to me that discussions of point of view rarely discussed the fact that in fiction there is a temporal as well as a spatial dimension.

Let me explain. When we talk about point of view in fiction, we are first of all recognizing the importance of the place the reader is standing in space to view the events. (Is he inside the mind of one of the characters and what is that mind like? or is he standing godlike above the entire scene, or over to one side, away from the heart of things, emotionally uninvolved, an objective witness?) But it is equally important where the reader stands in terms of time. Are the events of the story occurring as the narrator is telling it? Did they occur in the immediate past? The distant past? What has happened in the interval between the occurrence of the events and the telling of the story? What new knowledge does the narrator or the reader have that will change his perception of the events?

The story of Cinderella becomes a radically different story, if, instead of being told at the time of the wedding ("and so they were married") with a brief nod toward the future ("and they lived happily ever after"), it is told two months after the wedding, when Cinderella has discovered the prince is as much of a tyrant as the stepmother and she has merely exchanged one form of bondage for another; or if it is told seven years after the wedding when Cinderella decides that she married the prince merely to escape an intolerable home life and it is the court musician whom she truly loves; or if it is told sixty years after the wedding, at the end of a long and rich married life, on the occasion of the funeral of the prince. If you add to these temporal variations the infinite number of spatial perspectives (the story told through the eyes of an ugly stepsister we sympathize with, for example), the variety of stories within one story becomes almost endless.

There are two aspects of perspective that seem to me particularly important to consider: the question of "distance" and the question of "multiplicity of vision."

The reader's understanding of and emotional involvement with the events of the story depend to a large extent on how close he is to them. When I taught a class in fiction writing a few years ago, I found one of the commonest errors among beginners to be a failure to bring the reader close enough. Frequently, a story would be written without a single dramatic scene to create immediacy. One always had the sense of looking at the action through the wrong end of a telescope. The reader could not hear what was being said, or see the expressions on the faces, or have an inkling of what went on inside the minds. Even the descriptions of setting were slightly out of focus. The reader could tell he was at a beach. There were sun and sand and water, but he could not see clearly enough to tell whether the beach was on the coast of Maine or the coast of Georgia or the coast of Italy.

On the other hand, much of my own experimentation with perspective grew out of a realization that something about a story wasn't working, and what wasn't working had something to do with the fact that I was having the reader stand *too close* to the center of the story. It is easy when writing about children, as I often do, to sound sentimental. It is easy when writing in the first person, as I often do, to sound rather silly if one is writing of romance or heroism or virtue. Here's an example:

"Whenever a friend of mine nods toward a couple we both know and whispers, 'I wonder what he sees in her,' I secretly rejoice in the certainty that no one has ever wondered that about Paul. It is obvious why Paul loves me. My physical beauty is evident at a glance, and at the inevitable second and third glances as well. And after only five minutes with me, total strangers are struck by my wit and intelligence and by the unusual generosity of my nature. They look at Paul with envy and awe."

I had to experiment with distancing, occasionally by changing from the first person to an objective point of view, more often by telling the story, still in the first person, but through the eyes of a person less directly involved with the events. Often I distance with time. (We allow old people the privilege of telling their tales of valor and love, and do not think them silly, unless they are silly old people.) Sometimes I distance by tone or by the attitude of the narrator toward his part in the story. (One can play the comic hero more easily than the noble one.) Occasionally I risk the closeness by exaggerating the closeness, finding that the reader is able to accept wisdom or beauty in the narrator if the flaws and faults and foibles are also visible.

When I mention multiplicity of vision, I refer to the marvelous fact that writers can have their readers stand in more than one place to view the events. We are familiar with those classic tellings of the same story by different characters, like *Rashomon* or Lawrence Durrell's *Alexandria Quartet*. But even the familiar childhood reminiscence is of this nature; the innocence of the child's perspective is poised against the experience of the adult. My own experimentation with the double voice of the childhood reminiscence led me to write what became my first published story—"Even the Devil Gets Lonesome"—which appeared in *Redbook*. In this story of the relationships of three children in the course of their summer vacation, the events are given immediacy and life by being presented in dramatic scenes—at the moment the child is experiencing them. Yet the reader is aware that the person remembering the story is an adult and thus the reader accepts the more complex structural style, the reflective tone, the adult images and allusions.

Frequently the double voice is itself a factor in the meaning of the story, in the complexity of the way the reader views the events. There is the voice of the child (or of the innocent or inexperienced) saying, "This is what I saw and what I felt," and there is the older voice, the voice of experience and knowledge, adding, "Now I understand why it seemed so important." One of the most skillful and moving examples of the use of this double perspective to convey meaning is Hortense

Calisher's beautiful short story, "The Nightclub in the Woods." The main events of the story take place eighteen years before the telling of the story, but it requires those eighteen years, and the gradual "distance that seeps between people, even while they live and lie together as close as knives," to enable the narrator to understand the meaning of those events.

As writers, I suppose most of the time we are calling to our readers, "Oh, look, look. Come see." But it is not enough to call to them. We have to call them to the particular window, to find the crack in the wall for them, to create the mountain we want them to climb. For a reader to share your knowledge, he must look through the spectacles you hand him. That is what I mean by perspective.

42

MULTIPLY BY TWO

By Doris Betts

In my story-writing classes, I can almost predict the content of a first student story. Paragraph one will describe the morning sky, and establish the weather through ten adjectives and adverbs about the condition of that firmament. In paragraph two, we will see the exterior of some building, then pan like a slow camera through an upstairs window and focus on a ringing alarm clock. A hand will reach from under the covers and turn off the jangle. Note that a *hand* will do this. In amateur stories whole human beings rarely function, but disembodied hands, feet, and eyes swarm in midair like insects.

Now a man will get slowly out of bed, and for several long sentences his left foot and then his right foot will carry him into the bathroom where we will have some mention of the "cool tile." As he examines himself in the mirror, the reader will receive his physical appearance plus his full narrated biography, and while *hands* shave his *face,* will be introduced also to his sad memories and sensitive thoughts. By page four, shaven, he will walk to his bedroom window, examine that familiar sky, and will think one profound page, gradually getting around to some dilemma, which will then be explored by flashback. If he happens to own a dog, things get worse. He will explain that dilemma to Fido in lengthy speeches. Fido will wag his tail sympathetically, and so forth.

When I complain to students that nothing is really happening, they are artistically outraged. "Aha! You want me to write pulp plot stories!" To the contrary, my interest is in the literary story which has descended from Chekhov, Joyce, Mansfield, Hemingway, and Katherine Anne Porter. Here, as in *True Confessions,* a story is about meaningful events. Distinctions of "good" and "bad" applied to literary or slick stories are not very useful. It works better to talk about simple or complex stories, in the same way one describes simple or complex biological organisms. The mockingbird, for example, is simply doing more things with life than the amoeba is able to do.

Once that old bugaboo is out of the way, we can direct attention to the material in this typical amateur beginning for a short story. What is taking place? If the reader closes his eyes to visualize events, he will be able to see no more than a turned-off alarm clock and some short whiskers. The writer's clue may lie in the verbs he has chosen to use. In a static, nothing-happening story, these are usually forms of *to be* (he *was*) or weak verbs in which action is either minimal or boring. (He looked, walked, glanced, put, smiled, frowned, thought, remembered, saw, turned, etc.) A character alone, thinking, is not a visualized event, but only a snapshot of a still-featured man lost in thought, raising his eyebrows occasionally. And unless the character is as complex as Hamlet, the writer had better avoid soliloquies.

This is what led us to the dictum for beginning fiction writers: Multiply by two. Start the story with two people on the scene, or bring in a second character before more than five sentences have elapsed. Yes, this produces at first a great many "There-was-a-knock-on-the-door" stories, but at least we are into the area of conflict and interaction, and subtlety will come.

Anyone interested in writing fiction will benefit by reading a book published in the late twenties but still appropriate, *Aspects of the Novel*, by E. M. Forster. Here, Forster points out that there are only five universal human experiences. All men are born, but this is hearsay experience. We do not remember it ourselves, and doctors and mothers must tell us about it secondhand. All men must die, but we have not experienced this yet and can only anticipate its mystery. The corpse has left us no direct testimony. All men sleep about eight hours a day, but although Freud has given us insight into dreaming, there is a limited amount of fiction spent on the act of sleep itself. All men eat about two more hours a day, but how much time in a novel or story is spent on this activity? It is used for social events, for busy scenes, for revelations about families or small communities. This leaves the writer, Forster said, with the fifth universal activity to which men devote the remaining fourteen hours of every day—relationships with other people. So no wonder the writer is tirelessly preoccupied with relations between human beings, through which he may also portray conflicts with self, society, and perhaps God.

Whether students aspire to writing slick, pulp, or literary fiction, we ask them to write dramatic scenes in which two characters will participate. We ask to know where we are—rapidly—and to have some tension exist between these characters. Perhaps one is angry at the other, or wants something, or is trying to get the better of the other. Their dialogue and activity will carry the story forward through an event and an interaction. If a flashback occurs through the viewpoint of one of these characters, it will be "triggered" by something legitimate in the scene—something done or said. None of this gazing at the stormy sky and remembering a sweet day in May twenty years before.

The word "drama" comes from a Greek root which means "doing." Once two people are in a scene, the verbs will begin to "do" something and we can move to the second dictum of short story writing, "Show me, don't tell me." In fiction, interpretation and mood must be sunk below the surface of events, where they will permeate action like a visible stain. A sentence like "Mary was happy," which explains a state of mind, will be revised to "Mary ran laughing up the stairs." The happiness has become implicit in something Mary did, and we have—as our grandfathers used to say —killed two birds with one stone.

The focus on event, as it sinks meaning inside activity, will inevitably shorten stories and make them more dense and compact. Chekhov said in a letter to his brother, "I can speak briefly on long subjects." Never has there been a better definition of what a short story can do. The well-chosen event is, itself, a comment on life. Someone once said the short story writer would do well to adopt as his motto the one used by the Bank of England: *Never explain, never apologize.*

Having two people in a scene brings up automatically other writing techniques such as point of view. So long as the story is rambling along in the author's tone of voice, the author will assume it is focused and unified. After all, this is the way we are accustomed to hearing stories. Somebody relates what happened and nudges us in the ribs to make certain we get the point.

But questions of choice and perspective appear when two characters exist on the same page. Whose story is it? Which of the two is the more important? On whom will the full effect of these events fall? Through which character should the story be told? If Character A is chosen, Character B may not ramble off into his flashback; was the flashback really essential to the story? Is there a third character? What is his relationship to the first two? Like painters, we must decide on a background and foreground, where we will make our picture more vivid and where we will let the less significant recede. As the story is revised and begins to have shape and direction, the writer has a better basis for asking himself the two chief questions used in revising: Do I need it? Does it work? Even if he has written three pages in which his character is taking a long and thoughtful walk in the woods and remembering his old love affair, he may find that the story does not really begin until the character returns to town again and meets his old love with a baby on her hip.

The main value of insisting that a beginning writer "multiply by two," however, is that this alone will help him define for himself what a short story is. It is not the mental experience of a character. It does not take place within a human skull, and attempts to make it do so will only give the reader claustrophobia. One may not begin with a plot and then manufacture characters to act it out; one may create two characters who—by their own natures—will exude disagreements and plots.

Look back at some of the stories in your drawer which were turned down by magazines. How many of them start with a description of the sky? How many make use of dramatic scenes? (The average published short story has five dramatic scenes, in which something takes place *between* characters.) How many of them contain long passages where your main character is all alone, recalling an event which took place before the story actually began?

Multiply by two. Try rewriting the story so the meaningful event takes place—not in the past—but in the story's "now" time, before the reader's eye, with more than one human being on the scene. Often a good idea can be rescued when two characters act it out, and one character stops thinking-it-out.

43

A CINEMATIC APPROACH TO FICTION WRITING

By James Fetler

OVER THE last few years I've attempted a variety of approaches to fiction writing, some of them prudently conventional and some avowedly experimental. I've struggled with the Blueprint Maneuver, fabricating a network of scenes. I've blocked out plots on a chalkboard the way a football coach sets up a series of intricate plays. I've even resorted to writing stories erected on a platform of Lofty Abstractions and Significant Ideas. Either the platform was rickety and my fiction caved in, leaving me with a Message minus a story, or the platform mysteriously evaporated, leaving me with free-floating episodes. Once I made the mistake of attempting to choreograph a novel as if it were a ballet; my characters refused to follow the dance steps I'd worked out for them.

After years of fumbling and probing, I've become aware of something I knew all along but had never consciously applied to my writing. My first impulse is to *look* at life—I mean that in a literal sense, optically. Since childhood I've had a tendency to perceive the world around me in terms of moving pictures that make curious sounds. The *meanings* behind the pictures, the implications and lessons to be drawn, appear much later in my consciousness. The entries in my journals have been invariably pictorial rather than cerebral. Only recently have I acknowledged the fact that this impulse toward visual concreteness is the characteristic that most accurately defines me, and I must therefore not only accept it but also apply it to my writing.

The results have been gratifying. The approach I am now using gives me maximum creative freedom while demanding at the same time sharp critical judgment and artistic control. Since the pictures I see are invariably in motion, I find it easiest to describe my fiction-writing approach by using the analogy of film making. As I wrote my short-story collection, *Impossible Appetites,* I found myself applying many of the techniques of cinematography.

• *Shoot everything in sight, and then some,* which in literary terms means putting down on paper everything you see and observe. Although *Impossible Appetites* is a very short book, the rough draft came to over 1,000 pages. Once I had established the locale, time frame, and general cast of characters for the book, I tried to write everything that came to mind, just as a cinematographer shoots his raw footage, realizing from the very beginning that most of my writing would eventually have to be scrapped.

I kept thinking of Henry James's advice to "try to be one of the people on whom nothing is lost." So I used my typewriter with abandon, concentrating almost exclusively on physical actions and tangible "props." What I wanted, of course, was as much raw material as possible. Using a lot of paper may seem initially wasteful and is indeed time-consuming. But the method justifies the cost—provided you know what to do with the material you've collected.

• *Examine the raw material for shape and motif.* I've concluded from reviewing my journals that life is not really incoherent. Meaningful patterns surround us, but their meaning becomes apparent, as a rule, only in retrospect.

My procedure in writing *Impossible Appetites* was to keep going back over my material (as a film editor might run the film footage forward and back) until some kind of pattern began to emerge. The stories in this collection are about hunger and thirst, but I wasn't aware of that fact while I was getting my observations onto paper. I had collected a large batch of perceptions, but in the early stages I couldn't see a clear shape or pattern coming out of the mass of raw material.

As I pondered over my thousand-odd pages, I found myself staring harder and harder at the "hunger" passages, and almost intuitively I began bracketing and setting aside the scenes that seemed to carry this motif forward.

For example, my sexually frustrated protagonist grumbles about his wife on their honeymoon: *She was still playing roulette at 3:30 A.M. I was hungry and went to the coffee shop for some terrible scrambled eggs. Styrofoam.*

Similarly, a young man reaches out to a woman who has had a brief fling with him: *In the library that evening, as Pelzner took her hand and held it against his cheek, she arose and said matter-of-factly, "There will be no more," and there wasn't.*

In yet another story, a man who confuses religious zeal and sexual passion returns home after an all-night debauch:

> He returned around noon the next day. He looked ravaged and said he was hungry. As Mother was fixing his bacon and eggs he rapped on the kitchen table and said let's go down on our knees and submit to the King. Mother shut off the gas burner and we knelt as he prayed for our souls.

I felt I was now ready for my next step.

• *Cut and discard ruthlessly.* The more cuts I made, the more clearly I was able to discern the organic structure and internal logic of my work. I tried to eliminate every elaborate figure of speech and every lengthy description, and, like a film-maker, I edited out every redundant explanation and transition that I could spot. I found I could shift easily from scene to scene, provided the missing parts of the story were clear in my mind. The following childhood impressions, for example, are disjointed and yet easy to follow:

> I try to sit quietly next to Franz as Father leans forward in the pulpit and points to the doors at the back of the church: there is something he wants everybody to do. Mother stares straight ahead. The choir sings about the blood of the lamb.
> Suddenly I'm awake, the house dark, rectangles of light on the ceiling. Father is in his nightshirt, pacing, pacing. He will break through the walls. Long after Mother stops crying the pacing goes on.
> The asylum is surrounded by a high wooden wall. Franz has climbed up the telephone pole but won't tell me what's happening inside.

In one of my stories, a writer says: *We must learn to discard. The great thing is to give things away.* Taking my cues from cinematography, I extended this to my segments involving profanity and sex. Since I wanted to generate intensity in my erotic scenes and the episodes depicting emotional stress, I used understatement and suggestiveness. Thus a woman entertaining her lover brings "electrical gadgets" to bed; the rest is left up to the reader's imagination. A couple engages in some kind of "beastliness" that leaves welts on the flesh. No details. I've learned from watching many movies that explicit sex and repeated profanity tend to get tedious very fast.

The same principle applies to depictions of other kinds of emotional intensity. Extreme tension often leaves us tight-lipped and vaguely blank. Thus my protagonist reacts to his bad marriage by noting: *Steady drizzle all morning. I don't know what I'm trying to track down. Sparrow said yesterday that my breath smelled bad.* Elsewhere he responds to his father's unexpected death with almost frozen matter-of-factness:

We followed the ambulance to the hospital in San Mateo and seven hours later the doctor announced he was dead. I asked what it was. He said wait for the autopsy, please.

What I was aiming for was a collection of stories as lean and fast-paced as a Truffaut film, and I knew that meant ruthlessly discarding most of my first draft. In the process, I discovered that the next step was surprisingly easy.

• *Juxtapose and splice.* I was now ready to cut and rearrange my rough draft for the best possible effect. As I reworked the chronology and juxtaposed certain scenes, I kept seeing twin movie screens in my mind. The screen on my left showed grainy black and white "documentary" footage similar to the opening scenes of *Jules and Jim;* the screen on my right was filled with softer images full of color and a melancholy tone. Using both screens, I restructured the manuscript to present to the reader stylistic variations and ironic contrapuntal effects.

I especially wanted to develop a protagonist who had the unfortunate tendency of defining himself through the eyes of the people around him, very much like a person who views himself in the shattered mirrors of some decaying Fun House. I tried to suggest that all too often we try to make sense of our inner hungers by taking false cues from the wrong people and converting them into "truths," to the consternation of all concerned. Only when my protagonist begins to recognize these destructive dependencies is he able to go beyond the shattered mirrors towards genuine inner freedom and strength.

Thus the juxtaposing and splicing became an integral part of the book. As in *Citizen Kane,* the fragmented portraits of the hero collided and broke apart, until a more rounded image emerged, revealing the troubled but searching human being behind all the distortions.

By now I had gone through several drafts of the collection, checking the continuity, studying each page as a cinematographer studies each frame of his film. I wanted something to *happen* on every page, something that would induce the reader to read on. Once again, I found myself thinking of movies. The films we love and remember are exciting to watch. This is as true of *Singin' in the Rain* as it is of *The Maltese Falcon.*

Having said all of this, I must acknowledge that, helpful as formulas may be, the creative process remains enigmatic and gloriously unpredictable. Just like the "happy accident" that catches a film-maker completely off guard, the unexpected confronts the writer precisely when he least expects it. In one of my stories a composer complains: *When you strain for the notes, they don't come; when you finally give up, they slide back in the dead of the night.*

As I was assembling my collection, I found myself maddeningly stuck at one point. I couldn't seem to find the right conclusion for my title story, which sets the theme for the rest of the book. I knew I wanted to say something about human hunger and the universal need to reach out for sustenance, but the "picture" kept eluding me. After a restless night, I happened to pick up my copy of *Oliver Twist.* Almost by accident I glanced at the following passage:

> [Oliver] rose from the table, and advancing to the master, basin and spoon in hand, said, somewhat alarmed at his own temerity:
> "Please, sir, I want some more."
> The master was a fat, healthy man, but he turned very pale. He gazed in stupefied astonishment on the small rebel for some seconds. . . . The assistants were paralyzed with wonder, the boys with fear.

As I put the book down, I started imagining a segment from a film, and I could hear the characters talking. I walked over to the typewriter and sat down and typed out the scene that was unfolding for me:

> More dreams last night. Around 4 A.M. I got up from my cot and went to the alcove to smoke. Julie came out of the bedroom. She looked drawn. I said go back to bed. She said you keep asking for more when there isn't any more. I said I'm not asking for more, go to bed. She said Joe, you are constantly asking for more.

The cinema technique had come to my assistance again. I believe it is an approach that any fiction writer can benefit from.

226

44

CREATING A SERIES CHARACTER

By Robert B. Parker

WHILE I have ventured outside the form upon occasion (*Three weeks in Spring, Wilderness, Love and Glory*), it is the chronicle of a series character named Spenser that puts bread and Promise margarine on the table at my house.

Writing about a protagonist who has appeared before and will appear again presents some specialized problems. For instance, you have to find exposition tricks that will inform people who are reading you for the first time, without boring people who have read all your books in sequence. And, while both the writer and the reader are aware that the hero of a series is very unlikely to die, the hero doesn't know it. One has to be careful to render him as a man no less mortal than the rest of us.

But if there are problems in a series, there are also opportunities. If you create a character in one book that you like (Hawk, for instance, in *Promised Land*), you can use him again. And if you didn't get him right the first time, you have another chance, and another. Moreover, you have the chance to develop your hero over a sequence of books and during a span of real time. Thus Spenser, who first appeared when I was 41, can grow, as I have, in the six years since.

There are, then, a few things that are uncommon about writing a series of novels. But there is much more that is common to the craft. In each instance, series or not, I begin with what Henry James called a "treatment," a brief statement of story and locale and major characters. The treatment is normally about two pages in longhand. Don't be misled. This is the hard part. The treatment may take a month of sitting, several hours each day, thinking (my wife says thinking has always been especially trying for me, but one should pay her little mind. She once described me as looking like a Mississippi state cop). I didn't have to think up the protagonist when I set out on my first novel *(The Godwulf Manuscript)*. Spenser sprang fully conceived from my imagination where he had been lurking since I wrote my age in single figures. Because I don't have to imagine the hero, I always start with the scene, i.e., the place, the circumstances, the people that I can write about, the academic scene, for instance, or the book-tour-talk-show scene.

From the treatment, I develop a chapter outline, still in longhand, that lays out the sequence. It's not very fancy (a chapter might be outlined in a sentence, "Spenser drives to Smithfield and talks with the police chief"), and it partakes of none of those insistent curlicues that you learned in school (if there's an A, there has to be a B, etc.). The whole novel gets outlined in five or six pages. It is primarily for my emotional well-being. It saves me from rolling a piece of white paper into the typewriter and then staring blankly not knowing what to write. The outline is there, Linus; I need only look. Sometimes I don't look at all. The outline to *The Judas Goat* was there beside me on the desk every writing day, and I never so much as glanced at it. Sometimes I follow it closely, sometimes I stop mid-book and re-outline something I haven't been able to get right. But I always know pretty much what the story is when I begin to write it.

Then, the outline completed, I have only to write the book. I'm not being cute. Once the story is conceived, the hard part is over. If you have the ability, then executing the book is merely a matter of sustained (though hardly exhausting) effort. Discipline (though hardly of monastic intensity) is required.

If you have the talent without discipline, you'll have thirty pages of a swell novel in your desk for the rest of your life and you'll publish a couple of good short poems somewhere. If you have the discipline without talent you'll have ten unpublished novels in your closet. There's a third possibility, I suppose. You could have discipline, no talent, and a knack, and be Harold Robbins. Ideally, perhaps, all three would be best. But of one thing I am certain. Writers write, and one is not a writer until one has written.

I set myself a minimum number of pages, as a way to get from beginning, through middle, to end. The number of pages varies with circumstance. I have never set the limit lower than two pages a day, or higher than five. Unless I'm on a roll, I stop when I've written my quota. If there is time left in my writing day, I'll turn to something else, but by writing my quota I have fulfilled my responsibility to the book that day.

Since my typescript tends to equate one-to-one to the printed page, five pages a day will give me a two-hundred-page book in forty days of writing. That sounds mechanical, and it is. It is a large task broken down into many small ones. When I can, I try to follow Hemingway's advice to stop while you're hot so it will be easy to start up next day. But sometimes I'm not hot for weeks on end and then I just do my quota. If you wait to be hot you'll accomplish that thirty-page novel mentioned above.

I am not compulsive about writing. I don't work weekends. I don't work nights. If one of my sons is performing, I go and watch. If my wife will take a trip with me, I'll travel. I don't bring a typewriter. If my novel comes out three days later, or two weeks later, it makes small difference. Writing is my livelihood, not my life. And while I can't conceive of not writing at all, I'm not compelled to do it every day.

On the other hand, I do have to do it regularly. I would assume most writers who succeed in publishing any quantity of work do it regularly.

I have always been more interested in the protagonist than in the plot, which is, I suppose, one reason I write largely in the first person. If you're in doubt, I'd urge you to try first-person narration. It's the natural storytelling mode ("You shoulda seen what happened to me at Hampton Beach last night"), and it helps prevent inflated narrative language. If you tell your story in the first person, it is very handy to invent some people who can help you interpret your hero by offering some objective comment. In *The Great Gatsby,* Fitzgerald took that technique to the extreme by having Gatsby's story told to us by Nick Carraway. It is, of course, part of Gatsby's tragedy that he doesn't understand what happened to him. He couldn't have explained it. Carraway had to.

Spenser talks of himself, but for the parts he can't or won't speak of, Susan Silverman serves. She helps us understand him. She helps him understand himself. Hawk too helps illuminate Spenser. The ways in which Hawk and Spenser are alike, and the ways in which they are not alike, are crucial in imagining Spenser.

An interesting story about dull people may be possible, but I can't think of one. For me, the plot is in large part a frame, a series of occasions in which Spenser is able to demonstrate what he is, to enact himself. But to speak of the two, plot and character, as if they were separable is misleading. "What is character," James said, "but the determination of incident? What is incident but the illustration of character?"

The best books are always about more than the plot anyway. They have echoes and implications. They are informed by a sense of how life is, or ought to be. George Higgins wrote about cops and robbers. But his books are also about the thinness of the line between them, and about the way a man should behave, and about the relationships among men in groups. In *True Confessions,* John Gregory Dunne wrote about a murder investigation. But he also wrote about brothers, and hierarchy and autonomy and Catholicism, and Irish-ness. "The only reason for the existence of the novel," James said, "is that it does attempt to represent life." Aspiring writers should give their days and nights to Henry James (and me).

Writing isn't as hard as writers lead you to think it is, but it does not lend itself to shortcuts. Clichés are shortcuts; avoid them like the plague. But there are other more subtle temptations to cut across the field. I remember a manuscript in which the author used one description for two people, something to the effect that they were both huge and bald and menacing. That's a shortcut. The novelist attempting in some way "to represent life" must recognize that rarely in life are two people identical, even if they are minor characters.

A writer does that not because he's lazy, but because he's impatient. He wants to get on with it. It takes some understanding and some self-control to come to terms with the fact that the careful representation of life *is* getting on with it.

I have sometimes made the remark that I don't think writing very teachable. But if you are going to pursue writing instruction despite that admonition (no one has ever lost money rejecting my advice), be certain that your teacher has done what he/she/it teaches. Many people understand reading, but only writers understand writing. An intelligent reader can often say what's good or bad about a piece of writing, and there are critics who have helped me understand my own work better. But only a writer can tell you how (if it can be told): a writer who publishes; for money. I believe that there are very few good novels that don't get published. In fact I believe there are none.

There are, however, good novels that don't get finished. There is no one right way. Each of us finds a way that works for him. But there is a wrong way. The wrong way is to finish your writing day with no more words on paper than when you began. Writers write.

45

HISTORICAL FICTION, ITS INFINITE VARIETY

By Dee Brown

ALTHOUGH I have published more nonfiction than fiction, my first book was an historical novel, and I have returned to that form on several occasions since. I think the reason for this is that I like to read good historical fiction and am constantly challenged by the formidable obstacles that it presents to authors. Other writers may find the creation of historical fiction easy, but in many ways I have found it to be more difficult than straight documented history.

When an imagined story is complete, however, with the characters true to their time and properly fitted into their setting in the past, there is a certain feeling of triumph that does not always come from the writing of pure history. A serious historian cannot alter the record of the past to achieve a dramatic effect, or move characters and incidents around as he pleases in order to create suspense, or invent dialogue.

In the writing of history, an author may suspect that Mr. A made love to a famed courtesan during an important gathering in Paris at the turn of the century, and that was the reason Mr. A committed an act that changed the course of history. But unless proof can be found in a reliable documented source, such as a letter or diary, the supposition remains only a supposition and cannot be presented as a fact in scholarly history. The incident can be used, however, in detail and with invented conversations, in fiction set in that period and place, and this may be one main reason the historical novel has so strong an appeal for writers as well as for readers.

The first requirement for anyone who aspires to the writing of historical fiction is to be born with, or to acquire, a fondness for a certain period and place in our past. Unless one is genuinely fascinated, for example, by the American Revolution, the Victorian Era, the settlement of Australia, America in the 1920's, the Great Depression, World

War II, or some other definite era, one probably should stay clear of writing historical fiction. Variety of subject matter is infinite, but in order to write believably about any period, one must live vicariously in that period. This means a wide acquaintanceship with the contemporary literature and a constant study of whatever graphic materials are available.

Clothing, furniture, food, tools, houses, interiors, streets, methods of transport—everything that existed in a particular period is essential raw material for a writer of historical fiction. If the era being studied occurred after the invention of photography, a writer is blessed with an abundance of sources for all of the above. I have studied a single photograph by the hour to absorb the atmosphere of a time and place. A strong magnifying glass is always a useful tool for bringing out objects which may be obscure even in a sharp 8×10 print, and occasionally it may be helpful to have sections of a photograph enlarged. For historical periods preceding the invention of photography, one must turn to whatever surviving objects can be found in museums, or to artists and illustrators who depicted scenes of everyday life.

To know how people got about, maps are absolutely essential. City streets, highways, and sometimes railroads, have changed through the years. Place names also vanish or change. Atlases for almost any specific historical period and place have probably been published but may not be in print. Whenever they are available, it is a good idea to obtain them, for they are important items for the historical fiction writer's reference shelf.

Periodicals and newspapers of the past have always been among my favorite hunting grounds for colorful contemporary descriptions, although access to a first-rate library is necessary even in this day of microfilm and other forms of miniaturization of print. Newspapers are especially valuable for gaining proficiency in patterns of language, the metaphors and similes, and a knowledge of popular opinions and concerns of the day. In the nineteenth century—which includes my favorite periods—journalism had not been standardized. Reporters wrote as they pleased, with a great deal of zest and color, and most of the better newspapers employed traveling correspondents who roamed all over the country, describing places and incidents with an originality and verve seldom found even in the best travel pieces of today. In a recent book, for example, I was able to describe one of America's popular watering places, after seeing it through the eyes of a traveling reporter for a Philadelphia newspaper, a neophyte writer named Stephen Crane.

The advertising columns may be even more enlightening than the news columns, for they reveal both the gullibilities and sophistications of an era. Among the many bits of information that can be found in advertisements are current prices of necessities and luxuries, sailing times of ships from different ports, railroad fares and schedules between cities, hotel locations and rates, theatrical and sporting events, miraculous cures which reveal the credulities of the past, bank interest rates, offerings of stocks of dubious value. Nothing can bring home the horror of slavery more effectively than a newspaper ad offering $100 for the return of a runaway slave placed next to an ad offering the same amount for the return of a stray horse. Personals have always been popular in newspapers, and throughout the ages most of them reveal that human beings do not really change; the personals columns prove that there are lonely, romantic, and aspiring people in every period of history. Only the methods of expression change.

To gain access to the private thoughts and attitudes of those who lived in the past, one must turn to autobiographies, diaries, and letters. Diaries are my favorites. Too many autobiographies are written intentionally to present the author's best side to the world, and even those that appear to be quite frank may conceal or omit incidents essential to an historical novel in which that person plays an important role. Letters to intimate friends or close family members usually divulge a great deal more about a person than does an autobiography. And diaries, unless they are written purposely for publication, are most likely to reveal the diarist's innermost thoughts. For historical fiction writers, the richest diaries are those that were meant to be destroyed upon the death of the diarist, yet somehow were preserved.

Numerous diaries and letters appear regularly in the many excellent historical journals now being published everywhere. Most of these periodicals are devoted either to a specific period of history, such as the American Civil War, or to a geographical area—a region, or state, or even a county. Usually the diaries and letters that appear in historical journals have been carefully edited and annotated, offering writers of historical fiction a great deal of information and saving them enormous amounts of time that otherwise would have to be spent in research that has already been done.

Libraries and archives around the world also contain countless collections of unpublished autobiographies, letters, and diaries. Some of these may be made accessible to the public only after the passage of many years, and others may have various restrictions upon use of them. Lists of these pristine sources with locations can be found in a series of catalogues of manuscript collections issued by the Library of Congress. If a writer has the patience to ferret out these buried riches and read numerous pages of difficult handwriting, the ink of which is often faded with time, the entire structure for an historical novel may be found in one of them. Such searching, of course, is comparable to gold mining. Finding a big strike is chancy, even if one knows an era well enough to recognize the gold when it is there.

One of my unproven theories is that the best historical novels—the ones that are likeliest to endure—are those that are set in a period that has acquired approximately half a century, or two generations, of perspective.

Sir Walter Scott, who is generally credited with inventing the historical novel, sometimes went further back than a century before his time, but his most vivid works were those set in eighteenth-century Scotland and the border country. He wrote these early in the 19th century. Two generations after the American Civil War, Margaret Mitchell wrote what is undoubtedly the most popular novel about that turbulent era, *Gone With the Wind*. William Makepeace Thackeray wrote *Vanity Fair* (which Margaret Mitchell used as her model) more than a generation after the events depicted. Tolstoi wrote *War and Peace* half a century after the years covered in his epic novel. Perhaps the reason for this is that authors absorb the folk culture of the generations immediately preceding them, and with the insight gained from their elders, can look back down the receding years and see a past time more clearly than did the people who lived then. If this theory holds true, and it may not, then we should be seeing sometime during the next decade a classic work of fiction set in the period of the Roaring Twenties and the Great Depression.

America's unique contribution to historical fiction is the Western story, usually set somewhere west of the Mississippi River between 1840 and 1890, a fifty-year period that saw a mammoth migration across the Great Plains and the Rockies to the Pacific coast. Almost all "Westerns," therefore, are historical fiction. The era includes explorers, fur trappers, wagon trains, the building of transcontinental railroads, cowboys and cattle drives, Indian wars and cavalrymen, lawmen and gunfighters, land settlement and miners, as well as various other ideal subjects for tales of action and adventure.

The Western story has always been a stepchild of literature, perhaps because the genre began in dime-novel form, flourished during the years of the pulp magazines, and now appears mainly in paperbacks. Only a few writers have successfully broken out of the old formula plots and proved that an historical novel in a Western setting can be a work of literature. Walter van Tilburg Clark's *The Ox-Bow Incident,* A. B. Guthrie, Jr.'s *The Way West,* and Charles Portis' *True Grit* are examples. That Western fiction still has a vast number of readers is evident by the constant reprinting of the works of Zane Grey and Max Brand, both of them long deceased, and the enormous current success of Louis L'Amour and several other writers. Nevertheless, authors who work in this field should know that they are always writing under a handicap of literary prejudice.

The so-called "adult" Western of recent vintage is an attempt to take advantage of our hard-won freedom to include language, explicit violence, and erotic scenes that could not be published only a few years ago. Most of the adult Westerns that I have seen are anachronisms, the authors applying modern folk ways and psychology to a past era. Even though there was a great deal of sexual freedom on the frontier, the age was still Victorian. Brutal gunfights also were rare events, and Indians seldom attacked wagon trains. Although human attitudes and public behavior of that time may now seem hypocritical to us, we must remember that shields were drawn over certain matters, women were treated with great deference, and profanity was seldom used in mixed company.

The true adult Western is one in which the characters are drawn to the dimensions of their time, in which they speak and act as people did on the frontier, in which the story is universal in its appeal. Implied relations between men and women, if skillfully done, can often be much more erotic than explicit description.

In writing historical fiction, too many of us (especially those who love the research) have a tendency to overburden the story with thick coatings of historical details. The details are important, of course, but characters and the story should always be foremost.

236

Another rule that I try to live by is one established by the master, Sir Walter Scott. That is not to violate history, not to force real historical characters who have been brought into the story to do anything they could not have done. As it is, our history is afflicted with too many myths, and writers of historical fiction should take care not to compound the old errors or to create new ones.

46

SUSPENSE WRITING

By Mary Higgins Clark

MY PUBLISHER recently forwarded a letter to me from a man who had just read my suspense novels. It was brief and to the point. The reader also wanted to be a writer and he had a question for me: "About how many words and pages are required to turn out a best seller like your own?"

My immediate response was a smile, but it was quickly followed by a feeling of sadness. I don't think that particular aspiring writer will ever make it. And while his question is almost unbelievably naive, it's not the first time it's been asked.

For some reason, I find it difficult to put down advice in an organized manner. Telling someone how to turn out a marketable suspense novel is rather like dancing with an octopus. Which hand (or tentacle) do you reach for first?

However, I think that by attempting to answer the kinds of questions that pop up in my mail and by explaining how a story evolves for me, I might be able to pass along some useful suggestions.

Therefore, with the understanding between us that this will not be a precise blueprint or an annotated "how to," shall we begin?

Question: "I'm eager to write a mystery, but can't think of a plot. Where do you get your ideas?"

Obviously the plot, like the foundation of a house, is the structure on which all else is built. No matter how glib the writing, how enchanting the characters, if the plot doesn't work, or if it works only because of flagrant coincidence or seven-page explanations at the climax, I believe the book is a failure. But where to get the *idea?* Easy. Pick up your local newspaper. The odds are that on the first page or two it contains news of at least one homicide, an aggravated assault, a bank robbery, a mugging, a jailbreak. There also may be a recap on a criminal trial that merits national attention, an update on a series of unsolved murders, and an item about the child who has been missing six months. In other words, material for a dozen short stories or novels.

Now for your own plot. Select a case, one that for whatever reason sticks in your mind. Begin a file on it. Cut out every newspaper item that refers to it. *Know* that case. If a defendant is indicted, try to attend some of the trial sessions. And then—and here's the key—use that case as a nucleus for your story. You're a fiction writer; invent, go further, say to yourself, "What if?"

Several years ago I decided I wanted to try my hand at a suspense novel. Like everyone else, I was faced with the decision: What shall I write? At that time there was a celebrated case in New York in which a young mother was accused of murdering her two children. She stoutly denied her guilt. Two juries rejected her defense. The case fascinated me. I had five children, and the thought of losing any of them gave me nightmares. The thought of not only losing them but being accused of *murdering* them was beyond comprehension. A voice in my subconscious whispered, "And then suppose it happened again?" *Where Are the Children?* was in gestation. Let me reemphasize my point: *Where Are the Children?* was not based on the actual case. I took two ingredients: the young mother accused of infanticide; the frantic denials of guilt. With these in mind I began to build the story.

In my opinion time and place are essential contributors to a successful suspense novel. I chose to set *Where Are the Children?* on Cape Cod for a number of reasons. The Cape offers privacy. New Englanders and particularly "Capeys" do not intrude. The stranger who rents the big house off-season will not be the subject of idle scrutiny. The Cape has mists and fogs, churning surf, nor'easter storms, weatherbeaten captains' houses perched high on embankments above the sea. All these enhance the atmosphere of terror and gloom.

A Stranger Is Watching has as a principal location the bowels of Grand Central Station. Why? There you find dark, damp tunnels throbbing with the echo of rushing trains and groaning machinery; stray cats; underground people silently flitting by; abandoned storerooms, eerie with accumulated cobwebs and grime. I explored the area and knew it was right. And I loved the possibility of the juxtaposition of kidnap victims bound and gagged near a ticking time bomb while overhead thousands of commuters rush through the terminal.

Like the Greeks, I believe in the containment of time. *Oedipus Rex* starts in the morning with the king observing the problems of his stricken domain. It ends a few hours later with his wife a suicide, himself blinded, his world vanished. The swiftness of the action adds to the shock value.

I believe that if you write a book in which people are kidnapped and the villain plans to execute them at a specific time, the suspense is considerably greater than if the reader is only generally concerned about the victims' welfare. In *Where Are the Children?* the reader knows that the kidnapper is planning to throw the children into the rock-filled surf at high tide, seven P.M. In *A Stranger Is Watching,* the time bomb is set to go off at 11:30 A.M. Hopefully as zero hour approaches the reader is sharing the anxiety of the protagonists.

Question: "When I start to write, all my characters sound alike. What am I doing wrong?" That's another good inquiry and a valid problem. Through trial and error, I evolved something of a system that has helped me. The key phrase is *know your people.* Do a biography of them before you begin to write your story. Where were they born? Where did they go to school? What do they look like? What kind of clothes do they wear? Are they sophisticated, easy-going, observant? Are they married? Do they have children?

Think of someone you know or knew as a child who reminds you of the character you're trying to create. Remember the way that person talked, the expressions he or she used. When I was inventing Lally, the bag lady in *A Stranger Is Watching,* I combined two people from my childhood. One was our cleaning woman, who used to come up the street invariably singing "lalala"; the other the proprietor of a hole-in-the-wall candy store near my grammar school. She was one of the homeliest women I've ever known. The boys in my class always used to make jokes about calling her up for a date. Together the candy store proprietor and "Lala," as we nicknamed our cleaning woman, merged into Lally. But then to get the feeling of authenticity, I haunted Grand Central Station and chatted with real bag ladies. One of them became the prototype for Rosie, the other bag lady in *Stranger.*

There are hundreds of examples of fine books which contradict what I'm about to say, but here it is anyhow. I like to write about *very nice people* who are confronted by the forces of evil and who through their own courage and intelligence work their way through to deliverance. Personally, I'm not comfortable with the non-hero or non-heroine who is basically so bad-tempered or self-serving that in real life I would avoid him or her like the plague. I myself don't get emotional satisfaction out of a book in which the villain is so desperately attractive that I find myself rooting for him to beat the system. My villains are, and probably will continue to be, as evil, as frightening, as quietly vicious as I can dream them up. I know I'm on the right track if I'm writing at night and no one else is home and when the house makes a settling noise, I uneasily start looking over my own shoulder.

Another key element in creating characters is to *orchestrate* them. Within the framework of the plot try to have a variety of people in whom your readers will not only believe but with whom they can identify. Never, never throw away a minor character. Let your reader understand him, know what makes him tick. And make it a cardinal rule that every minor character must move the story forward. Suspense by its very nature suggests an express train or a roller coaster. Once on board, you cannot get off until the ride ends. I am committed to the belief that this kind of speedy action is essential to good suspense writing.

Question: "Do you do much research before you start writing?" Yes. Yes. Yes. And as I am working on the book I continue to research. My book, *The Cradle Will Fall,* is about an obstetrician who experiments on and sometimes murders his pregnant patients. I read everything I could get my hands on about artificial insemination, *in vitro* pregnancies, and fetal transplant experiments. I interviewed and picked the brains of a doctor friend who is a researcher in a pre-natal hospital laboratory. I proposed "what if" questions to obstetrician buddies. Then when the book was completed I gave a Xerox to one obstetrician friend. I was in New York. He was in Minneapolis. I was on a tight deadline: He stayed on the phone with me four hours. I had a list of all medical references in the book, e.g. page 2 top line, page 8 fourth paragraph, etc. Jack reviewed every one of them with me. On some he said, "That's fine." On others, he'd suggest changes. For example, near the climax of the book, a desperate search is going on for the gravely ill heroine. Jack said, "It's an emergency. Two doctors are talking. Don't have Richard say, 'She'll need a transfusion when we find her.' Put it this way, 'We'll hang a bottle of O-negative.' "

The Cradle Will Fall is set in New Jersey. The protagonist, Katie DeMaio, is a young assistant prosecutor. My daughter is an assistant prosecutor in New Jersey. She was my expert in police procedure. She went over every line that referred to the working of the court, the prosecutor's office, trials, witness statements, etc. For example, after a

241

murder scene I had the homicide detective post a sign, CRIME AREA. POSI-TIVELY NO ADMITTANCE. I remembered having seen a sign like that some-where. My daughter said, "No, that's wrong. In a suspicious death, we'd leave a cop guarding the premises until the apartment has been thor-oughly searched." In another chapter, I had the prosecutor televise the interrogation of a witness. She corrected me. "In New York that's being done sometimes, but it's still not legal in New Jersey." The point is that authenticity of detail gives the ring of truth to a book.

Question: "How much rewriting do you do when you're working on a book?"

Plenty. But rewriting is a two-edged sword. I know too many people who've spent months working over the first chapter of the projected novel. That's wrong. Get it down. Bumble through it. Tell the story. Then when you have fifty or one hundred pages typed you've got something to work with. It may be at that point you'll start again from the beginning because the book has a fundamental flaw that has become obvious. I wrote fifty pages of *The Cradle Will Fall.* In that first version Katie DeMaio is the twenty-eight-year-old wife of a prominent judge. She is in a minor automobile accident while he is away, stays overnight in the hospital, and while sedated witnesses a crime.

I soon realized something was wrong. I couldn't get worried about Katie. The reason became obvious. Here she is married to an interesting, handsome man, a Superior Court judge. I just knew that when John DeMaio got home the next day, he'd make very sure that no one would hurt his Katie.

How to solve the problem? John had to go. Instead of the *wife,* Katie became the young *widow* of Judge John DeMaio. Immediately, she is in-finitely more sympathetic—vulnerable and alone in the large secluded house she inherited from him. A great additional plus is that we now have room for a love interest. Doctor Richard Carroll, the provocative medical examiner, is very keen on Katie, and she has been holding him off. The reader, we hope, becomes emotionally involved in the potential romance and worries that Katie is sealing her fate because she does not let Richard know she is scheduled for minor surgery. The doctor who will operate on her is planning to kill her.

So there we have it. As I warned in the beginning I suspect this advice has a disjointed quality. I tend to offer writing hints the way an old

County Sligo cousin shared her recipe for Irish soda bread: "Take a handful of this, a fistful of that, a pinch of whatever . . . . Now taste it, love. Does it need more caraway seeds and raisins?"

Nevertheless if any of this advice helps anyone, I'm glad. There is surely no sweeter satisfaction to the suspense writer than to hear a heavy-eyed friend say accusingly, "You kept me up half the night reading your darn book!"

47

THE ULTIMATE IN HORROR

By J. N. Williamson

Let's plunge straight for the jugular: Is there a fictional genre in which—

1. Book editors welcome and truly consider your novel for purchase;
2. Your imagination and writing skills count for something, even if your name isn't yet established;
3. You have a chance to write three or four publishable novels a year without winding up in a rest home; and,
4. You may find your books printed in such quantities that you have an opportunity to earn worthwhile royalty checks?

The answer: an unqualified *Yes*.

Your question is probably even plainer: *How?* How does a mainstream, science-fiction, romance, mystery, espionage or Western novelist get into horror? Where do ideas come from? How is an occult chiller constructed? How important is the title?

You begin writing horror when you remember what it's like to be terrified. You take all those times you didn't want to be alone, or were afraid to turn out the light, and use them. I'm not necessarily talking about fear of the supernatural. However secure a person's life may be, there are times when he feels threatened or afraid. A good writer puts these emotions to use. Furthermore, publishers know that readers experience fear, too, and enjoy it—in books.

Consider that your own nightmares, psychologists say, are trying to tell you something. But they emerge menacingly, with monstrous images and places beyond the bounds of reality. Instead of figuring them out, why not let your conscious mind use them to plot a way of making other people—readers—believe them for awhile.

That's precisely what I did in writing three of my published novels. But if your sleeping mind isn't cooperating, where do ideas for horror novels come from? Read a few paperbacks to see what's being done in the horror field these days. Better still, learn where your own occult interests lie, and ask yourself the successful writer's most useful question: "What if . . . ?" To help you make a choice, here is the genre broken into smaller categories.

1. FAMILIAR HORRORS. In this type, the trick is to update the tried-and-true: werewolves, vampires, Jekyll/Hyde creatures, man-made monsters. Many new writers of horror novels think this is the direction to pursue, and for you it may be. Several recent books are based on these familiar themes. In my novel *Death-Coach,* I introduced a lady vampire as a minor character, and she was so greatly feared and popular that I've had to write three thrillers about her.

One offshoot of this category may be the *primal fear* group, or Nature-run-rampant. Films concentrate heavily on such themes but not many books do. Among those that have are the rats of James Herbert, the roaches of Gregory A. Douglas's *The Nest,* and George Ernsberger's *Mountain King* snakes.

2. LEGEND AND MYTH. Considering the accessibility of fine nonfiction studies such as those by Colin Wilson, Francis Hitching and Benjamin Walker, I'm surprised this sub-group isn't widely explored. Bram Stoker found *Dracula* when he researched factual enigmas and old beliefs. I know of no novels of horror dealing with dinosaurs' disappearances, or Nessie, the Chimera, Scylla, Atlantis, or Stonehenge, for example—they're yours to use. I have read fine horror fiction utilizing magic, the golem, Amazons, and lunar cycles, and my own novels have been based on mind-creatures such as tulpas, dragons and Titans, the whole fairy kingdom, and Pythagorean mysteries.

3. THE TRUE OCCULT. This field runs the gamut from ghosts to reincarnation, from parapsychology to UFOs and end-of-the-worlders. The lines begin to blur in the hands of skilled writers who, in single novels, may borrow from several categories. Ghost stories are traceable to classical authors, the Bible, even prehistoric campfires, but current haunted house themes give the reader at least one bona fide

haunt. Peter Straub's *Ghost Story* and Anne Rivers Siddons's *House Next Door* stand out; so do Herman Raucher's underrated *Maynard's House*. My own ghost story—*Ghost Mansion*—required a sequel *(Horror Mansion)*. Reincarnation, the theory that people are reborn with new identities, remains rife with possibilities. Parapsychology was nearly deeded to Stephen King by virtue of *Carrie* and *The Dead Zone*, but John Farris *(The Fury)*, Charles Veley *(Children of the Dark)*, Gene Thompson *(Lupe)*, Peter Van Greenway *(Medusa Touch)*, and I *(The Evil One; Premonition)* have also explored ESP and its avenues. End-of-the-world books are likely to edge into other genres, including s-f and spy; most of them are futuristic. They include King's *The Stand*, Jeffrey Campbell's *The Homing*, Arthur Herzog's *IQ 83*, and my *Banished*. Books of terror and suspense also may have an occult flavor deriving from the mind-set of their madmen.

4. CONTEMPORARY HORROR. The two basic topics of modern horror novels are children and religion. There are innumerable chillers involving children, either as monsters or victims. John Saul's immense success is founded on children, and our societal ambivalence is indicated by the fact that such children are often *simultaneously* the attackers and the attacked. Bernard Taylor's *The Godsend* is my favorite. (I used to swear I wouldn't focus on children, yet some of my novels do.)

Finally, it is religion—especially *evil* religion—that created modern interest in horror reading. William Peter Blatty's *The Exorcist* and Ira Levin's *Rosemary's Baby* began a maelstrom of alarums connected with Satanism and the black arts. But why not be original and search for other dark divinities? Finding Hecate, for my *Queen of Hell,* and Demiurge, for *Horror House,* helped me present entirely fresh yet ultimate adversaries, and others are there for you to discover. (Unsung masterpieces: Jere Cunningham's *The Legacy,* Robert McCammon's *Baal.*)

The construction of a horror novel is at once easy and difficult to explain or to achieve. Detective and mystery novels, once divided into categories, lend themselves to elementary analysis completely unfair to many outstanding writers.

Still, there are guidelines that may prove useful when you begin your own occult novel. First, perhaps, perceive which of the subsets I identified fits your fundamental concept. There should be enough "bad seeds" in your idea to grow a truly terrifying, fictitious Kudzu. Decide from the outset to frighten your readers, as often as possible. As you would have to do when writing suspense fiction, decide what your ultimate shock will be. Are you intending to scare by means of *disclosure*—surprising the reader with the next-door-neighbor as the werewolf (or Kudzu), or do we follow the monster's progress as he wipes out the world? If the latter technique is employed, it's often wise to resort to what Stephen King calls the "gross-out": holding the reader by virtue of ever-ascending, repulsive scenes, all leading to that dynamite shocker you've saved for last.

Most readers and writers of the occult know that while the gross-out is a cheap way to maintain interest, it is time-honored and susceptible to a range of ingenuity, matched only—occasionally—in science-fiction. Personally, I've tried not to overdo decapitations or find other choice anatomical parts to maim. But the site of attack is no less important than the *manner* by which the body is ripped, paralyzed, severed, or otherwise disposed of. Bullets and car crashes are for mild, temperate crime tales—not horror.

How absurd that sounds—which underscores the fact that horror novels require the writer to be more persuasive and convincing than most other kinds of novels do. The horror writer must convince the reader that such things are for the moment within the realm of possibility. To some extent this is accomplished with atmosphere. Usually credibility can be achieved by contrasting your horror theme and devices with *identifiable protagonists*—people who live, people for whom a reader can *care*. It's a rule of thumb that the farther-out your plot, the more normal your characters should be. Among others, my principal characters have included teachers, widowed mothers, just-published authors, a lady poet, little girls, and a boy who's flunked out of college.

The majority of occult novels begin with a *prologue*. In it, something perfectly hideous happens to a character who isn't germane to the plot. This establishes an atmosphere of menace, and furnishes the reader with a hint of the nature of the monstrous force that (or who) will threaten the main characters.

The nature of the horror novel makes it almost essential for the writer to offer at least one total scare no later than the third or fourth chapter. Otherwise, the reader loses the sense of curiosity and wonder he felt during the prologue. As a reader, I am offended when at the end of an occult novel I'm neither given a "grabber" nor told, clearly, what has happened. End it!

Using these guidelines, the old questions then surface, among them whether one should work from an outline. When I began writing, my outlines were incredibly detailed, and lengthy; one ran nearly twenty-thousand words. These days, while I always work from one and know precisely where I'm headed, I tend to settle for a six- to ten-page, single-spaced outline in which the major events are already conceived. The usefulness of this stems from my notion that a good horror novel has a rhythm as obvious as a jazz or rock beat. To sustain it, I make every effort to end each chapter climactically—with whatever will make the reader want to turn pages. Because, above all, worthwhile occult novels are both entertaining and thought-provoking, qualities naturally emerging from the combination of an original idea and a persistent subliminal hum of *fear*—fear that the characters know at the start or come to know, even while tangential characters are often victims too ignorant to realize the writer has doomed them; fear that will be transmitted to the reader—and to the editor—to the degree that your characters, while briefly sketched, are recognizable and sympathetic.

Where can a writer find greater opportunity to use his or her imagination than in occult and horror fiction? Nowhere, I believe. Its full, free expression is encouraged by thinking editors who have found, as you will, that fear and horror can bring success to a writer.

48

INSIDE THE MYSTERY NOVEL

By Stanley Ellin

To THE author, plot is one of the most important elements of his mystery novel. To the reader, it is one of the least important.

If that sounds like too glittering a generalization, sit down with pencil and paper, consider any mystery novel that has made an imprint on you, then try to outline its plot in fair detail. I do not exclude even that mystery you read yesterday; in fact, it's the one whose plot may now seem to be most opaque.

What you will have remembered with some clarity is what Alfred Hitchcock has labeled The McGuffin, that element which provides purpose for the events in the story. The plan to blow up the city, the search for the lost heir, the pursuit of a vendetta, the million-dollar jewel heist: these are McGuffins and can be summed up in a line. It is only after they have been developed into a dramatic sequence of events leading to the climactic disposition of the case that they may be properly called plots.

Plot is to the mystery novel what the skeleton is to the human body. It must be there to provide form and dimension to the body, but it is not something we are inclined to take notice of. What we are affected by in our view of the body is its fleshy covering. We assume the skeleton is there, all parts in proper conjunction, but, unless we are medical doctors or representational artists, we don't give it any thought at all.

The relevance of this to the mystery novelist is both obvious and paradoxical: He must provide a plot for his story that makes dramatic sense, but if he achieves this, he will not be judged by it. If, however, he totally fails to construct a sound plot, he will be judged by it in very unkind terms.

Not that plotting requires such perfection that failure to achieve it will put the author on the rack. A good many mysteries have plots that are not all that logical or convincing or fair to the reader and yet they have been highly successful. No one put it better than Nora Charles, in Hammett's *The Thin Man,* who, after husband Nick has explained to her his solution of the mystery, says as the last line in the book: "That may be, but it's all pretty unsatisfactory."

So it was, both mystery and solution, each being helped over hard places by the author's nudging, and it took a mordant, objective self-critic like Hammett to make a joke about that in his curtain line for the tale. But in no way did this flawed plot bear on the public reception of the book, either in published form or movie dramatization, because the vastly talented Hammett provided a covering for his skeleton that glossed over all flaws. He created a compatible marriage between two attractive, clever, and articulate people, plunged them into the intellectual and social high life of New York City, A.D. 1932, and presented them in a narrative style so precise and jazzily rhythmical that it is a pleasure to read, line by line. Nick and Nora became immortal as the epitome of what marriage could be when the partners in it really enjoyed each other's company, out of bed as well as in. Such plot as the story displays simply gives them room for that enjoyment.

Hammett could get away with it. And Raymond Chandler, who sometimes scrambled his plots so wildly that he could barely find his own way through them, could get away with it. And so, at times, could Conan Doyle and Agatha Christie and Rex Stout and others of that distinguished ilk. They earned the right to occasional faulty plotting, one might say, by their sheer skill in potent characterization, vivid ambience, and scenes that so satisfy the reader that he, although now and then aware of a little bump on the rails, still takes pleasure in the trip.

The writer who has not yet earned that license, however, must take heed. For his story he has to provide a goal to be attained and a sequence of events that moves the protagonist, plausibly and with dramatic interest, toward that goal. How narrowly this course is to be charted is up to the writer. One may outline each chapter in detail; another may prefer to jot down several giant steps along the way and then depend on inspiration during the writing to fill in the gaps between. But logic must always prevail, and dramatic interest, and, not to be forgotten, the necessity to play fair with the reader.

That last pretty well defines the most difficult plotting problem for the mystery novelist to solve. In a proper mystery, the author must withhold information from the reader or else there is very little mystery. A mystery written from the omniscient viewpoint, where the private thoughts of

250

every character are exposed, cannot fairly obscure the thoughts of any one of them, and that is bound to give away the works very soon, if only by process of elimination. If the writer does try to get away with this, it will eventually become clear that he is manipulating the reader just to sustain the mystery, and in that lies failure of the work as a whole.

Long ago, to get around this, the Comparatively Close Associate was invented: friend or partner or whatever of the protagonist, close enough to him to share in events, not close enough to know his unspoken thoughts. Thus it wasn't the author who was arbitrarily concealing vital information from the reader, it was the limitations of the Comparatively Close Associate that were responsible. Holmes's Watson is, of course, the prime example of this, and it is worth noting that it is the superb, life-like drawing of Watson in his limitations that makes the device work.

But every literary device grows thin with time and usage; this one grew thin, too, and nowadays there is much more reliance on having the reader identify directly with the protagonist rather than through an intermediary. This may be done through first-person or third-person narrative, first person offering instant empathy with the protagonist but demanding that the author manage always to express himself exactly as the protagonist-narrator logically would; third person freeing the author from this obligation but sacrificing instant empathy in the process.

In either case, the vital elements in putting the story across are the characterization of the protagonist—demonstrated in his pursuit of his goal—and the ambience of the locales through which he moves. These, after the brief gratification of finding out how the mystery is solved, are what the reader takes away with him. And, though the reader himself may not be aware of it, these elements are what will make him look forward to the next book featuring that protagonist. It was not Conan Doyle's plotting that won him his audience; it was Sherlock Holmes and the vivid evocation of Victorian and Edwardian London that did it. The persona of Holmes, larger than life yet wholly convincing and sympathetic, is the magic. The same applies to the following generations of private eyes drawn by such writers as Hammett and Chandler where there was an effort to present a more realistic protagonist. Willy-nilly, Sam Spade and Philip Marlowe became commanding and magnetic presences, and the corrupt world they inhabited, a source of endless fascination.

251

Beyond these presences must be others in any compelling narrative. The characters with whom the protagonist interplays are born out of the need of the story's plot. But once born, they must be given the same intense life as the protagonist. Detailed descriptive writing is a dull instrument in achieving this. Seen from the protagonist's viewpoint, the secondary character reveals himself or herself through speech and action. Handled properly, the secondary character on introduction will reveal the outlines of an identity ready to be developed into a full-fleshed image as the story progresses.

In turn, these lesser characters will, occasionally to the writer's surprise, reveal facets of themselves along the way the novelist had not anticipated. They may then affect the course of the plot, give it twists not considered in the preparation of the story line. All to the good, if the writer remains in command and can properly judge whether to explore these unexpected developments or to reject them.

Finally, in terms of reader appeal, the well-written mystery novel provides an acute and graphic sense of place. The room, the building, the street, the neighborhood, an entire area must be more than a stage setting. True, they must be as relevant to the story as a stage setting is to a play; the difference is that the novelist's presentation of locale and setting must reflect the protagonist's view of them. In this way, the author is given an excellent device for digging that much deeper into his protagonist and providing us with unstated insights into his nature. His sensitivity and powers of observation, perhaps his cynicism, his nose for corruption, his sense of hidden menace—all can be suggested by a view of locale he would reflect.

Any description of place, no matter how nicely worded, that goes beyond what the protagonist might make of it instantly suggests the author's hand at work, and there will be a break in the narrative at that point. The one way of avoiding this pitfall is for the writer to know his protagonist so well that he is fully aware of his capabilities and limitations from the start.

Plot is the skeleton, characterization the flesh, everything else the clothing.

Thus, in the long run, the mystery novel devotee who innocently believes he is drawn to certain authors because of their clever plotting is very much mistaken in this.

It is not a mistake that the author himself can afford to make.

49

START WITH AN ANSWER

By Patricia McGerr

"In my end is my beginning." The motto of Mary Queen of Scots might be adopted by many mystery writers. The classic detective novel opens with the discovery of a corpse and ends with a description and explanation of events that led to the murder. So it makes sense to write, or at least synopsize, the final chapter before you compose the rest of the novel. The same approach can also work for the mystery short story. Starting with a solution, you then go on to create the puzzle. Since *Ellery Queen's Mystery Magazine* gives special encouragement to new writers through its "Department of First Stories," I'll illustrate this back-to-front method with three of my *EQMM* stories.

Inspiration for "The Bloody Moustache" *(EQMM)* came from a picture of the Mona Lisa on which Salvador Dali had drawn his own distinctive moustache. A moustache on a woman's portrait, so my thoughts ran, might make a colorful clue to a perpetrator named Dolly (pronounced like the name of the artist). That solution immediately determined the nature of the story. It would use the "dying message" motif created and developed by Ellery Queen. The basic elements of this form are:

1) a victim who survives just long enough to write or speak a few last words or by some other means identify the killer;

2) several suspects (I like four), all supplied with motives and opportunity to commit the crime;

3) an ambiguous dying message that can be interpreted in ways that apply to each suspect;

4) a plausible reason for the victim's using such an eccentric means to point to his attacker;

5) a finale when all interpretations are proved false except the one intended by the victim.

Using these basic elements, the plot quickly took shape. With a portrait required for the message, the logical locale was an art gallery. I have a series character (Selena Mead) whose husband is an artist, so it was easy to place her at the scene. Since she works for an intelligence agency, the victim became a fellow agent assigned to discover which of four people connected with the gallery were using works of art to send defense secrets out of the country. In many "whodunits," it's necessary to provide each suspect with a different motive, but only one was needed in this case.

The next step was to give all the innocent suspects characteristics that seemed to fit the message and then, one by one, rule them out. This was accomplished in the obligatory final scene in which Selena, her husband and another agent analyzed the possibilities:

A. The gallery's assistant manager had a moustache. ("Too obvious. It would have been easier to write his name than to draw a moustache, but he knew the killer would destroy anything that pointed directly to him.")

B. The owner was an elderly Italian, which is "moustache" in underworld slang. ("He dragged himself past two other pictures to reach the girl. So he was probably pointing to a woman.")

C. One of the two female suspects was a bookkeeper and the pictured girl was holding a book. ("A simple X on the book would have given us that lead. The boy was dying. He wasn't playing an elaborate game of charades. The moustache on the girl's lip has to say something that he couldn't get through to us any other way."

D. With three down, they at last made the connection between Salvador Dali and Mona Lisa's moustache that led to the gallery manager, Dolly Wilson, as the murderer.

With the ending in hand, it remained only to set the stage, flesh out the characters, write the narrative and dialogue, and put it all together in a way that would, I hoped, surprise and entertain the reader.

Another story ("Every Litter Bit Helps," *EQMM*) had a more personal genesis. The description of the main character also applies to me:

She clipped coupons. Not the kind that are attached to Treasury notes or corporation bonds but those that appear in newspapers and magazines to be exchanged for discounts at the supermarket.

One day it occurred to me that the candy bar wrappers I was then collecting might help convict a murderer. This called for a thrifty housewife as protagonist and was definitely not a job for Selena, who does her best sleuthing while dining at the White House or dancing with kings. It would be out of character for her to be concerned with "cents-off" or premium offers. Instead, I remembered a homocide detective (Captain Rogan) who had solved a couple of my earlier murders, and I gave his wife the leading role.

Again the solution dictated the form—a conventional detective story with one victim and four suspects. The captain and his men conducted the routine investigation that uncovered strong motives for the victim's wife, son, partner and employee and proved that none of them had an airtight alibi. But it was the candy wrapper picked up by Sheila Rogan (she needed 40 of them to get a T-shirt) that pinned it on the suspect with a sweet tooth.

Sometimes a story idea will evolve from a place, as was the case with my story, "A Date in Helsinki" *(EQMM)*. A few years ago, a between-planes stopover in Helsinki supplied a new background for Selena. Our stay was too short to see much of the city outside the hotel, and the hotel's most distinctive feature was a gambling casino. So I thumbed through my mental file of foreign intrigue problems to which the roulette wheel could provide the solution. Having bought and quickly lost a half dozen chips by playing my own birthday, I saw how one player might, by the placement of his chips, tell another an important date without any overt contact between them. It took longer, though, to figure out (1) what was to happen on that date to make it important and (2) why, since the two players had to be in the same place at the same time, they were unable to communicate directly.

The first question was relatively easy. I considered and discarded a few ideas (assassination, kidnapping, prisoner escape), then settled on the due date of a shipment of weapons to be used to start a revolution in an unnamed country. But the second was more complex. It's a difficulty that frequently arises in espionage fiction since, if the agents act in a simple straightforward manner, there will be no story. So we have to invent circumstances to make odd behavior credible.

For clarification I wrote myself a memo. "The Problem: A has information to pass to B. They don't know each other. Why use a roulette wheel instead of a more traditional method? Like meeting with passwords? Or a phone call? Or a dead drop? Because roulette lets B get the information without being recognized by A. So while it must be established that it's O.K. for B to see A, keeping B's identity secret has top priority."

A second memo set forth the position of the good guys. "Our side knows B, also knows his schedule, that he will stay at a certain hotel in Helsinki and get the information while there. We do not know A or how the information will be passed."

In writing the story these two memos became dialogue between Selena and her husband:

"You can't follow him into his room," she pointed out. "Have you put a mike there and tapped his phone?"

"No. We're sure the meet will take place in the open. The entire transaction has been hedged with caution to keep the gun runners (A) from identifying the rebels (B). They don't want them to add a blackmail bonus to the selling price."

"But if he uses an assumed name, how could they—oh, I see. If they know his room number, someone can take his picture. But, good heavens, Hugh, they've set themselves an impossible goal. There's no way he can get his answer without risking recognition. Even if he's arranged to exchange a password at night in a dark alley, someone can follow him into the light. Even a dead drop isn't risk free. He can't be sure there won't be someone with a camera waiting for him to pick it up. I don't see how it can be done."

Then later:

"Is anonymity imperative for both sides," she asked Hugh.

"No, only for the rebel leader. The gun runners can hire someone to pass on the date without knowing what it means or who hired him. He can be in the open. Why? You have a theory on how it can be done?"

"Sorry, no. I'm just trying to define the problem. It's not quite so unmanageable if only one of the parties has to stay under cover."

"They had a week to figure out a method. We have to do it in hours." Again he checked his watch.

The last sentence, incidentally, introduces a valuable tool for heightening suspense—a ticking clock. Whenever you can, get a time limit for reaching a solution and make it as short as possible.

The ending that you begin with may lie in an unusual or little known fact. This can be particularly useful in writing a short short (1,000–2,000 words) story. The fact may be drawn from personal experience,

256

something you heard or read, or a field in which you have specialized knowledge. It can come from such widely assorted areas as science, history, languages, the arts, sports, even etiquette. In the Selena series, for instance, knowing that elderly Spanish aristocrats do not kiss the hands of young single women enabled her to unmask an impostor. In another case, she cleared an innocent person charged with murder by showing that the witness suffered from protonopia (inability to see red). Stories like this, I've found, bring an unexpected response from readers, who are pleased to learn something new. It's important, therefore, that the facts you offer be accurate.

Keep in mind too that a good ending is only the beginning, a trigger to start your mental processes. No matter how original, clever or surprising, it will succeed only if affixed to a story with strong characters, a logical plot, and good writing. We can seek our own "dying message" in the last words of Gertrude Stein. When, on her deathbed, she was asked by her companion, "Gertrude, what is the answer?" she replied, "In that case, what is the question?"

50

TEN GUIDELINES FOR SALABLE CONFESSIONS

By Elvira Weaver

THE CONFESSION market is hungry for fresh, good stories, gobbling up approximately one hundred sixty of them every month. It is a "byline-less" market, where a beginner has an excellent chance of breaking in, but you must know the ropes. The following are guidelines I have devised in my four years of selling to this specialized field.

1. Begin with a positive-thinking, likable narrator with one stagger-ing problem. In real life, if one thing goes wrong, everything seems to go wrong, but in confessions, the narrator has only *one* problem. I wrote a story in which the narrator was a young, pretty woman carpen-ter in danger of losing her job because the jealous wives of the other carpenters were making trouble for her. This was her *one* problem.

The heroine was also divorced, had two, preschool children, and was getting no financial help from her ex-husband. That was another problem, so I toned it down by showing that she was *glad* to be out of her bad marriage, and was managing financially, thanks to her well-paying, "man's" job. Carpentry was hard, physical work, so I showed her liking to work outdoors and adjusting to the strenuous labor. Her children were in a reliable preschool nursery during the day, and she was never tired or short-tempered with them at night. I went through my story, line by line, and took out even hinted-at problems. When I had finished, my main character's life wasn't a bowl of cherries, but she was coping with everything except one problem: The wives of the other carpenters wanted to get her fired!

Then I focused on this one problem to make it seem truly staggering. Every thought the narrator had, every action she took, every conversa-tion, centered on that problem. There wasn't a moment that her prob-lem was out of her mind. How was she going to keep her job, when the jealous wives were intent on getting her fired?

2. Have the narrator handle the one problem, inappropriately at first, but satisfactorily by the end of the story. A narrator is never passive. She will handle her problem, and because this is a confession (the narrator confessing something she did wrong), she will at first not handle it successfully, refusing to see that the wives might have a legitimate reason for their jealousy.

3. Keep reader sympathy for the narrator. This is probably the most important rule in confessions. Right off, the narrator has a strike against her because she is not handling her problem well, so you must give her at least three good reasons for doing what she does—one of which should go back to her past.

In this story, the reasons for the woman carpenter's blind refusal to see that the wives had any reason to be jealous were a) She didn't flirt with the male carpenters. Quite the opposite: she has to take their macho wise-cracking. b) She never needed much make-up, and she wore none. She dressed in work jeans and boots, never anything cool and sexy. c) (going back into her past) After her disastrous marriage, she didn't even like men much: she certainly wasn't out to "get" one of her co-workers.

Showing the motivation for the narrator's poor handling of her problem made her sympathetic and likable, but I didn't stop there: I never let the woman do anything else wrong for the rest of the story. To make sure, I went through the story again, line by line, and consciously made the narrator likable. When she spoke, she spoke softly; she was patient and loving with her children, never too tired to read them a story. (It is strictly taboo for mothers in confessions to put their children in front of the television.) In transitions, she baked cookies and was kind to animals. Everything she did was sweet and gentle, and love just dripped off those pages as my hurt and bewildered (not angry and vindictive) protagonist fought to keep her job. All she wanted was to work. She could see no reason for the wives to be jealous of her—until at the climax, when one married man who had been kind to her all through the story innocently put his arms around her to comfort her, and the natural attraction between a man and a woman took over. Then she could see the reason for the wives' jealousy, and resolved it satisfactorily by admitting she was not "one of the boys." This woman carpenter's story was my first sale, bringing a check from *Modern Romances* for $335.00!

4. Keep the story ordinary and believable. Confession readers don't want to read stories about terrible people who have horrible things happen to them. They want to read about normal people like themselves and think, "Heaven forbid, but this awful thing might have happened to me!"

In one story, my distraught protagonist's twelve-year-old daughter had suddenly become secretive and rebellious. The narrator handled the problem wrong by not communicating well with her daughter. At the climax of the story, when she discovered her thin, undeveloped little daughter was being coerced into posing nude for a child pornography magazine, she realized her noncommunicative attitude had kept her daughter from confiding in her. In order to carry off that lurid climax, I made the narrator and her family—even the villain and his family—as pleasant and normal as possible. This story sold—to *True Romance* for $200.00—because the reader could identify with the characters.

Reader identity is very important in confessions. Most readers are from blue-collar backgrounds, so give your protagonist a blue-collar background. Have her live in a small, neat house with a husband who works in a factory or a gas station or has some similar occupation, and give her one or two adorable children. If the narrator works, have her job be nothing too far up the economic ladder—a file clerk, a bank teller, a waitress.

5. Write in the warm, first-person confession style. I used to be embarrassed to buy a confession magazine, but you can't look down on a market when you want to write for it. Study the magazines. You'll find they don't deserve their bad reputation. Most are very moral. Absorb the confession style.

A confession story's heroine is a good person, not holding anything back, as she confides her deepest, darkest secret. The reader expects to know everything about her. Is her sex life good? Is she a good housekeeper and a good wife and mother? (She always is unless this is her story problem.) As she goes about her daily life in transitions, slip in lines showing these things. When the reader is finished with your story, she should feel she knows your narrator more intimately than she knows her own sister.

6. Write the story in scenes. Begin by presenting the problem in the opening scene. Always keep the story moving forward, with as little flashback as possible. Have the main character make a statement, then explain it. Don't have any limbo characters. Tell exactly where each one is.

My roommate, Kathy, looked up from the sofa as I came into the living room. "Are you going out tonight?" she asked.

"Yes," I answered. I raised my chin defiantly. "I'm meeting Tom downtown."

Tom and I always met downtown. We'd have dinner at some romantic, out-of-the-way restaurant, then go to a nearby motel to make love. But it was only a temporary arrangement, until Tom felt able to tell his children about us. It wasn't cheap the way Kathy made it out to be!

"I won't be late," I said, ignoring Kathy's disapproving look as I slipped out the door.

7. Make the writing strong, vivid and emotional. Use two-word descriptive phrases—"small, comfortable" living room; "quiet, reserved" mother-in-law; "sexy, blonde" neighbor. Be specific in your writing— two, little boys instead of two children; old, blue station wagon instead of car; handsome, sexy husband instead of husband.

8. Keep the writing tight. Cut out every character in the story who is not essential to it. If children are necessary, have two, not three. A sympathetic narrator would visit her mother or sister if they lived nearby, so if they're not essential to the story, have them live far away or be dead. Be explicit. Don't make the reader wonder about anything. If family members are dead, make it an ordinary death, but not a car crash or a heart attack. Those are overdone.

9. Write about things you know. My first sales were stories about: 1. a woman carpenter: when my husband started his remodeling business, I was the only help he could afford. 2. a mother-in-law: mine is extremely tidy and well-organized. 3. a teen-ager who searches for her birth mother: my two children are adopted.

Confession facts have to be accurate, and you feel much more confident when you write about things you are familiar with. What you don't know, research in the library. Don't lose valuable credibility with an editor—or your readers.

261

10. Find a fresh angle for every story. There is probably not a plot you can think of that hasn't already been written hundreds of times. A fresh angle is what will make your story stand out and sell.

In one story, my narrator was engaged to a man she had met while he was in the Navy. His family lived on a dairy farm in Wisconsin, and they had invited her to visit for a week so they could meet the "city girl who had stolen Cliff's heart."

My fresh angle was that Cliff's family farm was run by women—a widowed mother and two sisters, one divorced and the other married to a useless alcoholic. My heroine went, eager to assure these valiant women that she wouldn't take Cliff away from the farm after they were married. She would adjust to farm living. (Her overzealousness to please was her wrong handling of the situation.)

The modern, up-to-date farm women accepted the narrator immediately, showed her the dairy operation, and asked her help with the bookkeeping. She admired them tremendously and felt honored to be accepted. Then, in the climax, the truth about the women on the farm is revealed: They hadn't been strong women because of the weak men in their lives; they were strong-minded women who had made their men weak—and the narrator was becoming just like them, impatient with Cliff's gentle ways when that had been what had attracted her to him originally. This different twist made my farm story sell first time out, to *Modern Romances* for $375.00.

Confession editors need good, fresh material. Give them what they want, and you will sell.

51

REGENCY ROMP

BY JOAN AIKEN

FIRST, WHAT is a Regency romance? Second, why choose to write one? Third, how are they written? And, fourth, who reads them?

I shall try to answer these questions.

Nobody can profess a knowledge of the Regency field lacking a degree of familiarity with the novels of Georgette Heyer, who, if she cannot be said to have invented the genre, at least gave the twentieth-century version such a personal touch that "school of Georgette Heyer" will probably remain a defining term for decades to come. But let us first take a look at earlier sources.

Pedantically speaking, many romances published during the reign of the Prince Regent, George IV of England as he ultimately became, constituted the first examples of the genre. Of course, novelists who were alive and writing during this period, between 1811 and 1820 (or 1830 when George IV died), felt free to set their stories in other, or indefinite periods, as novelists always do. However present-day writers attempting a Regency romance usually stay within those dates.

What must, without any doubt, be taken as required reading for would-be Regency writers are the novels of Jane Austen, who constitutes all on her own the third or classic school of Regency fiction. Of course, these works have passed beyond any single classification and are for all time and all readers. But they also give one of the most faithful pictures that we have of Regency society, and I do not believe that any writer aspiring to enter the Regency field can even consider putting paper in typewriter without first making a close study of the Austen novels. The style, settings, details on every page of contemporary habits, speech, thought, morality, finance, reading matter, what was considered acceptable behavior and what was not, make them an essential source of period material. Fanny Burney is almost equally important. I myself, when writing in this genre, refresh myself with frequent dips into their books, so as to keep my ear tuned to contemporary rhythms of speech and flavor of vocabulary. My sister (the novelist Jane Aiken Hodge, a specialist in this period) has gone further and possesses a copy of Samuel Johnson's Dictionary; she checks all doubtful words to make sure that they would have been in use at that time and are not later and anachronistic arrivals. "Upset," for instance, meaning distressed, would be anachronistic—the correct eighteenth-century usage would be "overset."

Needless to say, reading lives of contemporary figures, such as Richard Brinsley Sheridan, Beau Brummel, George IV himself, memoirs and letters of the time, such as those of Byron or Prince Pückler-Muskau, contemporary journals like *The Gentleman's Magazine* and *La Belle Assemblee,* or present-day accounts of the period like T.H. White's *The Age of Scandal,* will all help to fill out the background.

It is certainly due to Georgette Heyer that the Regency novel has such an established place in public popularity at the moment, and since readers' expectations are formed on the model she set, it is worth making a study of some of the forty-odd novels she wrote in this genre. She herself, apparently, looked on them as pure potboilers and greatly preferred her own detective fiction, but there can be no question that she took considerable pains with her Regencies and acquired her facts by much careful period research; rather *too* much, indeed, toward the end of her career. The later novels tend to be an indigestible mass of detail about clothes, food, carriages, fashion, with whole paragraphs of slang. Contrariwise, the early novels, such as *Powder and Patch, The Black Moth, The Masqueraders,* are action-packed, but rather too swashbuckling and full of "tushery" and "quothery" for my taste. In my opinion Heyer's middle period, from *The Convenient Marriage* onward, constitutes her best work. As pure entertainment, for charm, humor, ingenuity of plot, and just the right amount of period detail, I believe these middle novels can hardly be faulted.

The usual theme (like that of Jane Austen) is simple: a rather hard-up, though well-born, heroine falls in love with and in the end marries a well-born, rich hero. Occasionally the heroine has money of her own (as in *Regency Buck, Bath Tangle, A Civil Contract*). Then among her difficulties is that of weeding out the fortune-hunters. There is a fair amount of physical adventure: duels, highwaymen, attempted murder for inheritance, espionage, and smuggling are complications with which resourceful heroines have to deal. The later novels rely more on social comedy—accidental or impulsive deceptions and the consequent misunderstandings arising. An impoverished girl pretends to be rich out of pique at the hero's snubbing her; a rich hero, in order to tease his snobbish relatives, pretends to be poor; a couple pretend to be engaged so that the heroine can escape from her guardian and come to London to husband-hunt. Or there are predicament-plots: A heroine applying for a post as governess arrives at the wrong house and is swiftly married off by the enterprising hero to his dying villainous cousin in order to avoid inheritance problems.

The plots are not far from those of eighteenth-century comedy—Oliver Goldsmith's *She Stoops to Conquer* and Sheridan's *The Rivals*—and a study of that field is not a bad indoctrination for Regency writers. One of Heyer's very best middle-period novels is *Sylvester,* in which the heroine, affronted by the hero's haughty ways (Regency heroes are nearly always haughty, an amalgam of Darcy, from *Pride and Prejudice,* and Rochester, from *Jane Eyre*), satirizes him in an anonymous novel and subsequently falls in love with him. The turns and twists of this plot are embellished with some of Heyer's best comedy characters: an irascible grandmother; a silly, self-indulgent sister-in-law; an empty-headed dandy, Sir Nugent Fotherby, with a splendid line of Regency slang; and a country squire who thinks more of his horses than his daughters.

Some critics have complained that all Heyer's characters speak the same language, but I think this shows the lack of a perceptive ear. The changing dialogue seems to me one of the great pleasures in a Heyer novel. Heroines talk very correctly, with an eighteenth-century elegance of phrase: " 'The most shocking flirt in town, I am persuaded. He does very well for one's entertainment, but the female who receives his advances seriously will be destined, I fear, to sad disappointment.' "

Younger brothers break out in Regency slang: " 'I ain't so high in the instep!' " And dandies like Sir Nugent Fotherby have a line all their own: " 'I was surprised. You might say I was betwattled.' "

It is not always important, in some historical novels, to use period forms of speech, and I do not think one needs to be fanatical about it. It is very much a matter of opinion. If period setting and characters are strong and convincing, then there should be no need for archaisms. A fairly plain, formal speech without modern slang should be sufficient to create an historical atmosphere. But in the Regency novel, I would make an exception to this rule. The language and vocabulary of that epoch—so clear, precise, elegant, agreeable to the ear—is a delight in itself. The language is, for me, one of the chief pleasures and justifications for writing Regency novels: a wish to refresh oneself by using a more gracious style. It is like putting on a long skirt for evening wear: It immediately gives a grace and dignity lacking in everyday usage.

Consider a few of Jane Austen's run-of-the-mill sentences: "I do not dispute his virtues; but I do not like his careless air." "Vanity was the beginning and end of Sir Walter Elliot's character." "She had nothing against her, but her husband, and her conscience." "It was on the wedding day of this beloved friend that Emma first sat in mournful thought of any continuance."

Another reason for writing Regency novels is that the plots are such fun and so civilized. Compared to our novels today, when a plot in itself is a rarity, the plots of Regency novels contain very little violence, no sadism, no psychological perversions, no doom, no disgust; all turns on ingenuity, good humor, and surprise. It is the literary form of the minuet.

Explicit sex does not flutter the pages of a Regency novel. It is understood that offstage the gentlemen have their doxies, light-skirts, charmers, and the like. But the wise heroine, though aware of such peccadilloes in her suitor, turns a blind eye, and is, of course, herself chaste though spirited. Heroines occasionally elope, but seldom get very far. The worst escapade is likely to be the social sin of driving a high-perch phaeton down St. James's.

The great charm of the Regency period lies in the fact that it is just far enough removed from the present day to be picturesque, and yet not so far as to be uncouth. Our eighteenth-century ancestors' habits of diet and dress, their social manners and customs, were not too distant from our own; only far enough to make it interesting that they breakfasted at noon and dined at six, traveled by coach and took tea late in the evening. Lack of telephones and slowness of communication help with the ramifications of plot.

Still another attraction, I believe, is the fact that in this period, the middle classes had hardly made their appearance in fiction; Regency romances must necessarily be about the aristocracy, which in itself makes an irresistible appeal to the snob in the heart of every reader. Lord Orville, Fanny Burney's hero in *Evelina,* is the prototype Regency hero;

266

though Jane Austen's heroes are not titled, they are all connected to aristocratic families; Mr. Darcy's aunt is Lady Catherine, Edmund's father is Sir Thomas, Henry Tilney comes from Northanger Abbey. There is something quite fascinating about the *smallness* of London society at that time; there were only about 180 peers, and aristocratic society, the *ton,* consisted of about two thousand persons, who all more or less knew each other. When Caroline Lamb threatened Byron with a knife at a ball, the story was all over town in no time.

London must have been a charming city during the Regency period—elegant architectural crescents and terraces, their pale stucco unmarked, their symmetry unblemished; huge green parks and gardens surrounding lordly houses all buzzing with intellectual life. Fashion was changing rapidly. In a short period of time, the crinolines and powdered hair of 1775 shifted to the sylph-like Empire line of gowns of the early 1800's. At that time, a lady's whole toilette weighed no more than eight ounces; girls cropped their hair, damped their petticoats to make them cling, and wore silk shoes and satin mortarboards.

Although society persons were given to gambling, boxing, horse-racing, dueling, and heavy drinking, they were also exceedingly well-educated; elegant, erudite, they studied conversation as an art form; gentlemen were judged by their graceful gait and deportment as well as their accents. A chapter in a book on polite manners was devoted to "How to take off your hat and replace it." One would have liked to live in that time; the next best thing is to try and depict it.

Who reads Regency romances? A wide, devoted, and growing market, judging by the regular reprints of the Georgette Heyer novels and her large school of followers. As the "straight" novel wanders farther and farther into offbeat realms, as limits of permissiveness in fictional violence and pornography become wider and wider, as suspense and detective novels lose ground and the market for Gothics becomes saturated, readers who need, from time to time, what might be defined as a safe, cheerful read, a nice book to curl up with in bed before going to sleep, must find themselves turning with relief to the Regency as one of the last sources of real escapist reading, pure, predictable, good-natured pleasure. The Regency is not one of your historic art forms, it is not going to open up new avenues or break down barricades or inaugurate cults. Its virtues are different. It is for fun.

I can remember an occasion twenty years ago when I had an elderly relative coming to stay with me for two weeks. She was in her late seventies, she was stone deaf, almost blind, she suffered from spasms, heartburn, nervous terrors, and a congenital feeling that she was being cheated, with a consequent surly suspicion of everybody's intentions toward her. I was not looking forward to the visit; I did not see how I was going to bear it. On my way to the station I stopped at a second-hand bookshop and happened to pick up a copy of Georgette Heyer's *Regency Buck,* which I had not read. Dipping into it, as I waited for the train, I could see that it was vintage Heyer. The sheer comfort that book gave me, reading a chapter every night during that exhausting visit, is something I still remember with warmth. If any Regency romance *I* write can give anybody such pleasure, however transitory, then I should feel that a complete justification for having taken to the form, which is all that any writer could ask.

52

ON WRITING SCIENCE FICTION

By Ursula K. Le Guin

I LOOK over my typewriter, out the study window, forty miles north to the mountain called "The Lady"—Mount St. Helens. Since the May 18, 1980 eruption and the May 25 ash-fall, people keep saying to me, "You're a science fiction writer—you should write a story about the volcano!" And I can only stare, and whimper, "But—But—"

I could attempt to describe what the eruption looked like from my study window. I could research and write up a history of the volcano. I could tell the true story of the old man who wouldn't leave his home at Spirit Lake (but that's been better done already in a country song). I could write poetry that has the volcano in it somewhere, some day. There's a great deal any writer could write about the eruption, and the ash-fall, and the people involved. But the one thing no writer could make of it, now, is a science fiction story. Science fiction is about what hasn't happened, but might; or what never will happen, but this is what it might be like if it did.

St. Helens happened. The Lady blew. Having seen that pillar of darkness towering seventy thousand feet above my city, I know that the most and best any artist could do with it is to try—and fail—to describe it.

Before May 18, a major eruption of St. Helens was an *idea*. Since then, it's an *event*. Science fiction works with ideas. It is basically an intellectual form of literature—with all the limitations, and all the potentialities, that go with the dominance of intellect.

I hear a polite mutter in my mind's ear: "The woman is nuts. Brainless heroes bashing brawny villains to rescue bronze-bra'd princesses while boring through Hyperspace towards Beta Bunthi, home of the Bug-Eyed Yrogs—this is intellectual?"

Well, no. But it isn't science fiction, either. It's space opera. Let me define my terms. As far as I can make out, "science fiction" and "speculative fiction" are the same thing—and so henceforth I'll call them SF, which nicely includes both. "Fantasy" covers all imaginative fiction, but may be used as a category including all imaginative fiction *except* SF and horror stories. It also includes "science fantasy." As for "space opera," in print or on the screen, it is to SF what "sword and sorcery" is to fantasy: the stuff produced for mass sales. Not steak, not hamburger, just baloney. Mindless, macho, and miserably imitative; but with a thirty-million-dollar budget it can be lots of fun and very pretty.

Space opera not only borrows hardware and gimmicks from SF, but also filches the great imaginative themes, such as space travel, time travel, alien beings, other worlds. But instead of using them as metaphors of the human condition, as SF does, space opera makes them into meaningless decorations. They are not part of the structure of the work, but serve instead to disguise it. You peel off the space suits and the tentacles, and guess what? Howdy, podner! Welcome to Hyperspace, Texas!—And, frankly, I miss the horses.

A real SF story, book, or film is fundamentally different. It starts with an act of the mind, a step from *is* to *if,* a reach of the imagination into the nonexistent. But it is not a leap into the impossible or the absurd. Indeed, SF dreads absurdity and loves logic almost as much as Mr. Spock does. In SF, the risky act of imagination is controlled by the thinking mind, the intellect. And therefore the discipline it accepts most naturally and gracefully is that of science. Real science: a respect for fact, and a sympathy with the patient way science arrives at fact.

Fantasy makes its connection to ordinary-daylight-outside-the-book-cover-reality through the emotions and through ordinary physical perception. (I could go on about that, but this chapter's about SF, not fantasy!)

SF makes its connection with ordinary-day-light-etc.-reality through ideas—principally the evidence of science and the speculations of the thinking mind. In SF, there is a reason for what happens, and it is a rational reason. The events of the story make sense in a cause-and-effect system. No matter how wildly imaginative they are, they don't happen just because the author likes it that way, or thinks it "feels right." Fantasy admits such reasons unknown to Reason. But SF doesn't. In SF, the questions "Why?" and "How?"—asked at any point in the story—should be answerable.

This doesn't mean that an SF story is an educational lecture with some fictional sugar-coating. Anything but! The ideas are the seed, not the tree—the blueprint, not the building. An SF story that hasn't *grown from* its ideas, but just flatly states them, is dull stuff.

A very few SF writers are practicing scientists, in such various fields as psychology, anthropology, biology, astronomy. Most are not. My impression is that the knowledge of science used by most SF writers comes from self-education—reading books and articles on subjects that interest them. (As for myself, the total of my formal training in science is one semester of anthropology and one of geology.) The point is, what's wanted is not a great mass of technical knowledge, but an attitude towards knowledge—an attitude of curiosity, above all. If learning facts and finding how events connect together bores you, then you probably don't read much SF, and certainly wouldn't enjoy writing it.

Let me try to illustrate this apparently paradoxical situation. Let's take a typical crazy SF invention: A five-hundred-foot-tall woman lands on Earth. Now, first of all, does she walk up Main Street, mashing a Honda at every step, and sit down for a rest on the First National Bank building?

In fantasy, she could. In the space opera movie, she does. In SF, she doesn't, because she can't. If she's really a woman just like us only a hundred times taller, she's too heavy to stand up, let alone walk. Crushed by her own weight—the gravitational pull of the Earth—the poor thing is lying there dying of internal injuries. We know that beings of our general type and mass cannot exceed a certain size, under our local conditions. Brontosaurus was at the limit for a land animal, and he wasn't any five hundred feet tall. Even Bill Walton has problems. And we are following Delany's Law. S.R. Delany, a most innovative writer of SF, put it this way: "Science fiction must not contradict *what is known to be known.*" And we know that it is known that solid 500-foot ladies are impractical.

But what if she's a projection of a five-foot Alien who is staying up in her space ship above the Earth until she finds if it's safe to arrive in person? She meant to beam down a five-foot projection, but the beamer got the size wrong. The technology involved—perhaps using holographic images—is not known to be impossible. Or, what if she really is five hundred feet tall, but, since she comes from a giant gas planet like Jupiter, she is made of airy, gauzy stuff, with almost negligible weight and mass? Realizing that she got the size wrong, she compresses herself into the shape of a five-foot woman weighing 3½ pounds, and walks briskly into the First National Bank building, holding her breath. . . . Well, this is

271

getting pretty hard to explain, but I'm not sure that we've contradicted anything that is known to be known. And so long as that rule is kept, SF is perfectly free to invent. It just has to make sure, as it goes along, that it doesn't contradict *itself*. The pieces must hang together.

Figuring out how it hangs together, all the where-why-what-and-whether, is half the fun of SF, for both the reader and the author. There's so much to know about our friend in the First National Bank Building—what life is like for someone as gauzy and compressible as a silk scarf, and what the weather is like on her home planet, and what kind of society her people might have, since they are all very fragile, very agile, and able to change size and shape at will. And what might have brought her here to Earth, and, as a matter of fact, what she's doing in the Bank. Madame, what are you up to in there?

"Prrswit frumbo rigpot thoom," she says into her Vox-Coder, which instantly prints out in English: * I * AM * GATHERING * MATERIAL * FOR * A * SEARINGLY * REALISTIC * STORY * ABOUT * BANK * TELLERS *

Fantasy and SF certainly overlap, but there is a real difference between them, and in general I believe they are best not muddled up together. A fantasy element—something rationally unexplainable—can be very annoying in an SF story, and often looks like what it is: a bit of laziness on the author's part, sloppy or wishful thinking. The reverse mix, SF intruding into fantasy, often occurs in books for young people by authors who are basically distrustful of the power of fantasy, and so try to explain away the whole thing—"But it was really all a dream!" That's a cheat, and the kids know it.

There is one more thing about SF that I feel I have to mention, but don't want to, because it is so undignified. In workshops I call it PSG. PSG stands for Pseudo-Scientific Garbage. It isn't meant as an insult, merely as a description. After all, the truth is that science fiction is not true. It isn't science. It's fiction. Although it starts from a known fact or an educated guess or at least a crazy but plausible hunch, and although it tries loyally not to contradict what is known to be known and not to stumble over its own internal logic—still, the whole thing is made up. And, especially if it's set in the future or on a different world, *all the details* have to be made up. Here's where the PSG comes in, and here's where the gift for SF may shine brightest.

For example: that Vox-Coder our Alien was using. I didn't explain that it's an instant translating machine, voice-activated. I didn't really have to. It's not a big step from the little hand-carried translator-computers we have right now. The Vox-Coder seems not only possible, but probable. Yet, the more you happen to know about language and translation, the less probable it may seem. Here evidence from one science (computer technology) contradicts evidence from another science (linguistic theory), and you have to take your choice. But your choice is warped by the fact that translators are so handy in SF. Without them, all the Aliens have to spend months learning English, or the Terrans have to painfully learn Voobish. So we gave our 3½-pound Alien a ¼-ounce Vox-Coder. And so I call it, with all due respect, a piece of PSG.

All interstellar space ships are PSG.

Much PSG is truly common property in SF. You learn it simply by reading SF. (Anybody who tries to write SF without having read it is wasting his time and ours.) There's a good deal of genuine sharing: the word "FTL," for example, meaning Faster Than Light. Anybody can fly an FTL ship. More often you don't borrow the name—Vox-Coder, phaser, pinlighter, etc.—but take the general idea and deck it out your own way. Of course you also are free to make up any gimmick or device you want or need, and this is fun. Much of the joyful inventiveness, the shock and beauty of SF is in its PSG. I think of Philip K. Dick's fully automated and highly verbose taxicabs, which tend to argue with their customers, sometimes becoming quite emotional. . . . Of Vonda McIntyre's gentle replacement of the hypodermic needle by the serpent's tooth. . . . Of H.G. Wells's lovely, shimmering Time Machine. . . . Of the pleasure I had trying to figure out what it would feel like to be a woman this month and a man next month and both/neither in between. . . . PSG, all of it. *Taxicabs don't talk!* Only if you're perfectly sure of that fact should you write a story about talking taxicabs.

In 1968 I wrote a book, *The Lathe of Heaven* (and in 1979 WNET/TV made a movie of it). At a climactic point of the book, Mount Hood erupts, and then the extinct volcano inside Portland city limits, Mount Tabor, erupts, and the whole Cascade Range goes off—except Mount St. Helens.

Why did I deliberately leave her out, knowing that she was in fact the likeliest to erupt? I can't explain. When I was writing the book I looked at her out the window, the "misty, blue-grey cone" which is in the story but not here in the real world any longer; and she must have whispered to me, "Sshh. Quiet. I have my own plans."

And I'm very glad I got it all wrong. My job's fiction. I'll leave the reality business to the Lady.

273

53

WESTERNS: FICTION'S LAST FRONTIER

By Loren D. Estleman

Country music and Stetsons are in; disco and headbands are out. On walls that once sported Degas and Cezanne originals, prints of round-ups and gunfights by Remington and Russell explode from frames made of weathered barnwood. Can Western novels be far behind in popularity?

As a matter of fact, they're way ahead. In recent years, Western sales, which can always be expected not to descend below a certain level, have risen steadily. Louis L'Amour, author of *Hondo* and heir to the poncho of such late great frontier fictioneers as Zane Grey and Luke Short, has sprung into national prominence after thirty years of writing about sun-parched deserts and whipsaw-lean cowpokes who roll their own, with one leg cocked over their saddle horns. Douglas C. Jones *(The Court-Martial of George Armstrong Custer, Arrest Sitting Bull)* is recognized by many of today's critics as a major force in contemporary literature.

As the author of six novels set in the Old West, I have one word of advice for the writer who wants to get in on the ground floor of this ranch-style renaissance: Authenticity. You may get published if you write of showdowns between Good and Evil at high noon on Main Street, but critical acclaim and sales will elude you. Describe a lawman waiting with a shotgun in a dark alley to blow the head off a feared killer as he walks past, and you'll be applauded for your realistic portrayal of the true Code of the West.

For a century—from the time of Buffalo Bill to John Wayne—popular fiction has built an entire mythology around tall, silent men with fast draws, who conformed to their own noble creed. Wild Bill Hickok, a professional gambler and sometime lawman who claimed a cut of every game in town, and Wyatt Earp, a political hack whose famed gunfight at the OK Corral in Tombstone represents the first recorded example of gang warfare in modern history, have been presented as "heroes" flawed only by their unwillingness to accept thanks for their humanitarian actions.

The result is that the truth about the West hasn't been scratched. A gold mine of characters and plots far more interesting than anything offered by Hollywood awaits the writer sharp enough to recognize them. Where else would one find someone as juicy as lovely Polly Bartlett, who in 1867 poisoned twenty-two men at the inn she and her father ran in Wyoming for what was in their pockets; or Sam Brown, a gunfighter who once demonstrated his mettle by carving out the heart of an innocent drifter in front of a saloon full of witnesses in California?

Matt Dillon never fascinated me as much as John "Liver-Eatin'" Johnson, a gigantic mountain man in Montana who slaughtered Sioux braves for sport, and who is said to have dined on his victims' entrails. I based the character of Bear Anderson in *The High Rocks* on Johnson, and described him as follows:

> He was even bigger than I remembered him. Crouched though he was . . . he was nearly seven feet of solid muscle without an ounce of suet anywhere . . . The eyes beneath the rim of his fur hood were the clear blue of his Scandinavian ancestors, and his features, despite the leathery grain of his complexion, were even and handsome enough to turn the head of a mining camp's most hardened prostitute. His full beard, like his shoulder-length hair, was reddish and streaked with yellow. The only flaw was a jagged patch near the corner of his jaw on the left side where the whiskers grew sparsely over scar tissue—the remnant, I judged, of an old tomahawk wound.

Granted, the parts might prove difficult to cast in Studio City, but the most memorable characters are larger than life. Johnson himself was hardly less impressive.

Similarly, the narrator of that tale, Deputy U.S. Marshal Page Murdock, bears little resemblance to the popular image of the stalwart lawman. He's unscrupulous but likable—which is more than can be said for the type of peace officer represented by Hugh O'Brian on television twenty years ago. Because I'm more comfortable with Murdock than with the conventional Western hero, he's become the star of a series since his introduction in *The High Rocks*.

I departed from the norm in *The Hider*, my very first Western, when

I made buffalo hunter Jack Butterworth a garrulous old man instead of the taciturn Gary Cooper-type that crops up so often in formula yarns. In reality, after weeks on the prairie with only their horses to talk to, back in civilization these loners were more than eager to bend the ear of whoever would listen to them. It's the braggarts history remembers; nobody would even have heard of Pat Garrett or Bat Masterson had they been as reticent about their adventures as Ben Cartwright and the Lone Ranger. Consider Butterworth's recollection:

". . . Onliest time I was ever in bed past six was the day a twelve-pounder slipped its chocks at Antietam and rolled over my left leg. I was back on the field that next morning, and I brung three Yanks to ground afore a ball from a Colt Dragoon snapped my crutch in half and sent me back to the hospital to get my leg reset."

If not for his new friend's lack of humility concerning his past, narrator Jeff Curry would probably not have decided to accompany him on the hunt for the last surviving buffalo.

This is as good a place as any to discuss dialect. Avoid it wherever possible. Butterworth's speech rings of dropped g's and flatted o's, yet neither of these spelling aberrations appears in print. Once you get into phonetic spelling, comprehension suffers, and consistency is hard to maintain. Since there are quite as many rules to bad grammar as there are to good, don't complicate things. An occasional "brung," an "afore" here and there, one "betwixt" to two hundred lines of dialogue, will carry the illusion. Be very sparing with "I reckons" and "much obliuges," as too much use of Western idiom lends itself to caricature.

As might be expected, decades of distortion have obscured much of the truth. When I set out to write *Aces & Eights,* I was faced with the dilemma of whether to present Wild Bill Hickok as a hero or a villain, or something in between. At length I decided not to make the choice. The story, which opens with Hickok's murder, reveals the events of his life as his killer's trial unfolds, with witnesses for both sides presenting wildly conflicting accounts of his character. In the end, it's up to the readers to determine what kind of man he was.

Again, the watchword is authenticity, as in this passage:

The prosecutor half-turned to see United States Marshal Burdick standing thirty paces away, sideways, his long right arm extended at shoulder level, a big Navy Colt growing out of his hand and pointing at the drunk. A big man except when compared with such as the drunk and the bouncer, he still had his checked napkin thrust inside his high starched collar . . . Black-powder smoke swirled about him and a thin stream of plaster was leaking from a hole in the ornate tin ceiling above his head. In a single, fluid motion he had drawn the revolver from beneath his coat, fired a shot in the air, and pulled down on the drunk while the latter was still bringing his own cumbersome weapon into play.

Here, I've reconciled the fast draw of modern fiction with the calm, take-aim-and-fire stance of historical fact, and clothed them in a few words with the dress and architecture of the late Victorian period. Frontier action takes on a third dimension when rooted in contemporary reality.

The Time-Life series on the Old West is the finest guide I can recommend to the beginner in this field. Period photographs and tintypes, many of them never before published, and hundreds of out-of-the-way facts and fascinating anecdotes, open up a whole new world to the reader who thinks he knows everything there is to learn about the era from movies and television. The bibliography of each is an excellent reading list for those who would delve deeper. If these books don't inspire the tyro, Westerns aren't his meat.

But don't get carried away with authenticity at the story's expense. It must be remembered that between 1875 and 1900, there were fewer violent deaths in Dodge City than there were in any major American industrial center last year. The average westerner would have been as shocked to witness a gunfight as would today's urban dweller. Home was a sod hut on the treeless prairie or a tent on a street of soupy mud, entertainment a seat by the coal-oil lamp with Bible in hand. In order to make this life interesting to the reader, some telescoping of the more exciting events of the age is necessary. But then life itself is always in need of editing. Good luck, pardner!

54

THE HISTORICAL FAMILY SAGA

By John Jakes

Novels that can be classified as family sagas cover more than one generation. Hence, there is usually an historical element in them, too. If this element is strong, and crucial to story development, as it is in The Kent Family Chronicles, then the saga becomes at the same time an historical novel. And while an historical novel may include a family as a set of characters, the two forms have enough in common to be discussed as one.

I think historical novels are again popular because we are searching the past for values and a sense of continuity. We are anxious to be reassured that although we have gone through bad times before, we have survived. The past helps us more readily understand and cope with the present. In anxious times like these, the search for insights and reassurance from history is accelerated.

The popularity of family sagas is likewise a product of the times. With so many families disintegrating under economic and social pressures, we like to read about idealized families that manage to survive every kind of harrowing test.

Historical novels and some family sagas appeal to readers of both sexes — something which cannot be said of the so-called historical romances. While a few books of this kind — the impeccably researched novels of Roberta Gellis come to mind — show concern for the inevitable interaction of background and story, in most historical romances, the emphasis is on the amorous adventures of a heroine. The background is superficial; all of the "research" could have been done in the library in two hours. The romance may be easier to write than the saga or straight novel, but the latter will have a much wider audience.

Here are five factors that I have found essential to writing my historical sagas.

278

1.) Do your homework. Historical novels involve the characters in specific historical events, but even if you are not taking that approach, your story can't be fully effective until you completely understand the period in which you're working.

In *The Seekers,* for example, Gilbert Kent and his wife are in conflict at one point because of Gilbert's public stand on the War of 1812 — a stand which brings angry mobs to the Kent home after dark, further heightening the domestic crisis. It would be impossible to set up this kind of story line if you didn't know how most of Boston's citizens felt about the War of 1812. Of course, it's possible to have your characters feuding over the color of the drapes, or how the eggs are cooked, but if you resort to this in historical fiction, you are shortchanging your reader and failing to take full advantage of the form.

Research is also necessary to decorate the stage, clothe the actors, and furnish the background with appropriate properties — everything from reading material to popular foods of the period. This is true unless you are one of those writers (and there are some successful ones) who visualize next to nothing for readers.

It's impossible for me to work that way. To me the texture of a scene comes every bit as much from the quality and intensity of the weather, the physical surroundings, the costumes of the characters, etc., as from what is actually happening in what we might call the foreground. This is even more true of historical fiction, since one of the primary goals of the form is to evoke a bygone era. The Ticonderoga cannon sequence in *The Rebels,* for example, could not exist without descriptions of the sledges, the weather, the terrain, etc.

2.) Let your research help you plot. When I wrote science fiction, I had to invent almost all of the complications encountered by my protagonists. Writing historical fiction is in that sense much easier. Many of the details can and should come from your research. This is one of the compensations for the hours and hours of reading which precede the writing of a saga or historical novel.

In *The Lawless,* Gideon Kent's various troubles during the Chicago fire were derived from factual incidents I noted while researching that part of the story. Once I got Gideon into the fire setting, the rest — the complications and small turns of plot — came easily.

Research also helped me with a major plot turn in *The Titans.* I decided Michael Boyle would become briefly involved with Louis Kent's wife. The question then became, why? Answer: partly from a long-standing unrequited desire, and partly to get back at Louis, because Louis was about to take some action Michael found intolerable but could not prevent.

What could that action be? Research provided a plausible, interesting answer. Like some other Northerners, Louis was planning to profiteer by trading illegally with the South (and would probably extend the War in the process). More specifically, he was going to trade in salt, a commodity the South desperately needed to preserve meat for feeding its armies. Out of a single bit of information there emerged a long sequence in the book, which both added background and forwarded the story.

The historical fiction writer who complains that it's impossible to think of or find strong plot material hasn't been to the library lately.

3.) Memorize your material, then forget it. Today there is strong interest in historical figures and the events and customs of the past. However, anyone writing historical fiction should constantly keep in mind that the background, although important, remains secondary to telling a story.

A couple of years ago I visited my friend and colleague, Andre Norton. We were discussing some difficulties I'd had with communicating exactly what happened during a major Civil War battle used in one of the books. Andre said she had faced a similar problem once and had finally decided the only sensible approach was to view the battle through one character's eyes and forget the parts that character couldn't see. This is exactly the way I resolved the problem of presentation of the battle of First Manassas in *The Titans*. Much valuable research information had to be scrapped for the sake of the story, but it was the only way.

Even so, a surprising thing occurred. Readers told me afterward that they thought the Manassas sequence conveyed a pretty fair sense of how the battle flowed. For that kind of thing to happen, it's necessary to immerse yourself in research material until you could pass a rigorous examination on it (with no notes!) — then forget all that expert knowledge and just write the story.

Do that, and you should find many places where information can be brought to the fore without giving your work a tone of pedantry. At the end of the Manassas sequence in *The Titans*, right before Gideon is shot, he is trying to find his unit, from which he has been cut off. He travels across the battlefield on horseback; the search allowed me to show many of the circumstances of the battle: the frantic retreat by the defeated Federal troops; the terror of people who had earlier driven out from Washington to have a picnic and watch the fighting; even the presence of photographer Matthew Brady (Gideon sees his wagon), etc. Once you know your background material, concentrate on the story, and you will find your subconscious suggesting many excellent places to integrate the material in a natural way.

I regret to say I have no formula to offer for selecting historical events to be included in a given work, or any rules for choosing which details to include when you're writing about historical personages. I pick what interests me, then try to share my enthusiasm by means of dramatic presentation of the material.

Of course I try to choose major or representative events in the period about which I'm writing, but I have never shoved in material merely because I felt it should be there. When I set a scene in *The Rebels* at the first public reading of the Declaration of Independence in Philadelphia, I did so for three reasons. One, it was a moment of immense significance in our country's history — but that reason alone would not have persuaded me to use the setting. I felt it was also a moment of high drama, and, on top of that, it was interesting, chiefly because of the public reaction. The crowd listening that day cheered and applauded all those sections damning George III; they were quiet, even disinterested during the reading of those portions of the Declaration which we have come to consider its immortal passages.

4.) Sex and violence — what do you think? Again and again, readers and beginning writers raise questions about both of these elements. I guess it shows you what really interests people.

While sex and violence are the stuff of drama — hence, popular with storytellers — writers should use them only in ways that are comfortable to them and natural to the story. As soon as sex or violence is shoveled in gratuitously, the work begins to suffer. Any honesty it may have soon disappears in contrivance.

For much the same reason, I suggest you never consciously think of your story's potential for other media while you are writing. If I designed my books with an eye to what they should be in order to maximize the chance of a Hollywood sale, I would never include half of the material I like. *The Americans* includes one section dealing with the Johnstown flood. It could not be put on the screen except at a cost of several millions of dollars. But one of the benefits of being a writer is that it costs me only time, a few sheets of paper, and a typewriter ribbon to stage the sequence as lavishly as Cecil B. De Mille in his heyday.

I never thought any of the Kent Family Chronicles would be filmed; in fact, I thought that because they were historical fiction, they had three strikes against them. Now, several of those novels have been turned into TV mini-series. If your novel sells to another medium, consider it a happy bonus—but don't plan on it. Above all, don't design your fiction with that goal uppermost. If a Hollywood connection is what you want, move to Los Angeles and write films and TV shows instead of novels and stories.

Sex itself is certainly not overrated, but I find it overrated as an ingredient in fiction. Sex will not sell a bad book, nor measurably boost the sales of a good one. Harold Robbins can write steaming sex scenes, but I have always maintained that sex is not the reason for his success. He is a superb storyteller. You may not like the kinds of stories he chooses to tell, but he tells them with great professionalism and flair.

Actually, sex is just one subdivision — one fascinating manifestation — of one of the great, universal, fail-proof elements of all storytelling: Love. And it seems to me that an effective sex scene must have more than mechanics; it must have a *quality* or point of view — terror (as in Amanda's rape in *The Seekers)* or wonder (Jared's encounter with the prostitute in the same book). Any sexual passage, explicit or otherwise, which lacks this sense of context, this reflection of how the characters feel about each other and about the encounter, is gratuitous and unrealistic.

One of the saddest aspects of our age is not that we are frank about sex, but that we have diminished and cheapened it. Taken it out of context, as it were, so that it is mechanical and disassociated from genuine human feeling. The delightful James Bond movies notwithstanding, sex isn't merely an alternative to going bowling on a date. Hemingway, who wrote of the earth moving, understood this far better than lesser writers who purvey trivialized sex.

The Kent Family Chronicles contain quite a few violent passages. They are there first because I enjoy action stories, and so I enjoy writing them. Beyond that, American history is full of violent episodes, which unfortunately are more interesting than day-to-day routine. Also, we have a streak of violence in our national personality. I like to cite the totally senseless Astor Place riot, to which Bart McGill refers at some length when discussing the emerging American temperament in *The Furies.*

At the same time, violent death is a shattering emotional experience for the perpetrators or survivors, and so I make a conscious effort not to trivialize such events, but to give them the impact they have in real life.

Should you include violence in your fiction? Again, if it's not an element with which you're comfortable, avoid it. You can certainly tell a compelling story without it.

If used, violence ought to be germane to the setting and events of the story. In *The Bastard,* there is no violence during the Boston Tea Party sequence because there was, historically, none during that event. However, after the patriots disbanded, that was another matter. British soldiers had watched the destruction of the tea, and some took reprisals. Philip's encounter with the officer he kills springs naturally from events of that night.

Properly handled, violence can be a powerful motivator of character change, just because it has such a stunning effect on the psyche. The horrors of battle change Gideon's ideas of war in *The Titans.* The violence of the Union Pacific construction gangs changes Michael to a pacifist in *The Warriors.* On a list of factors which you can use to reverse completely the course of a character's behavior, love and death stand at the very top.

5.) The "message" is you. I endorse the old maxim about calling Western Union if you want to send a message. As already noted, your first obligation is to tell a good story. Fiction that sets out to preach may turn out to be effective polemics, but it is usually bad fiction. Or at least not very entertaining.

Each book in The Kent Family Chronicles has an underlying theme. By this I mean I have a certain purpose or scope in mind for the book as a whole. The theme of *The Seekers,* for example, is the first stage of America's westward migration, in all of its many variations.

Let us assume that your objective is to tell a story with some underlying theme. You are not setting out to promote a Message ("Bananas should be banned from supermarkets." "Members of the Whig party should be horsewhipped," etc.). Will your work then be gutless and devoid of a viewpoint? Not at all. Any piece of fiction contains many short "messages" — expressions, explicit or implied, of the author's point of view. As you write, you automatically inject yourself and your feelings about love, birth, death, marriage, the battle of the sexes, politics, morality, money, etc., into every line. A novel's real "message" is its reflection of its author's personality, and that message comes in many parts.

I don't believe it's wise to try consciously to inject these messages into your novel, at least not until you have developed a high order of professionalism — like that of a John D. MacDonald — and can skillfully introduce direct commentary about life and American society into the first-person narrative of a Travis McGee. At first, you'd be wiser to let your messages just happen. If the book is a true extension of your personality, as it should be, the process will take care of itself.

The chance to express yourself in this way is one of the rewards of fiction writing. Historical fiction permits you to go that one better: it permits you to comment on the past and, by indirection, the present. The important thing is not to strain to be profound, but to relax and be yourself. I subscribe to a wonderful piece of advice which I read years ago: "Originality does not consist of saying what has never been said before, it consists of saying what you have to say."

55

PUTTING SCIENCE INTO SCIENCE FICTION

By Gregory Benford

PEOPLE don't read science fiction to learn science any more than others read historical novels to study history. There are easier ways to go about it.

Yet the fact remains that "hard" science fiction—the kind based on the physical sciences—remains the core of the field. The reading public persists in thinking of rockets, lasers and aliens as the central subject matter of science fiction (s-f). Writers like Robert A. Heinlein, Isaac Asimov, and Arthur C. Clarke—all classic "hard" s-f figures—now appear on the best-seller lists.

Similarly, most s-f magazines yearn for more stories with a thorough grounding in science. Such work is in short supply at the offices of *Analog, Omni, Isaac Asimov's Science Fiction Magazine, Amazing,* and even the *Magazine of Fantasy & Science Fiction.* Generally, it is easier to sell a short story with high scientific content than one which concentrates, for example, on social changes, or age-old conflicts in a futuristic setting.

The shortage is even more acute for book publishers. One s-f editor told me recently that at least two-thirds of the manuscripts he receives are fantasy, and many of the rest are only nominally science fiction.

Why is this so? Because science is daunting, complex, and hard to work into a story. Few writers have very much scientific training to build on, and the pace of research is so rapid that you can be outdated while you're working out a plot line. Many s-f stories of twenty years ago look antique now. One reason some published hard science fiction isn't very well written is that the editors can't get anything better.

For the enterprising writer, though, this represents a real opportunity. S-f is traditionally open to new talent and new ideas. The trouble with many beginning authors in the last decade was that their "new" idea often was simple doom-crying—tending to see problems rather than to think of their solutions. Stories built on simple recognition of the unforeseen side effects of technology have a sameness about them, a lack of inventiveness that bores readers.

This is an easy trap to fall into. It may be an unconscious choice; the current glut of fantasy novels (often trilogies) often comes from newer writers, who seem to share the anti-science sentiments of the middle 1970s. Of course, powerful yarns have been spun with this angle and will be again—but it is a high-risk avenue to take.

Admittedly, people with a background in science or engineering have an edge in writing hard s-f. But even if your degree is in linguistics or animal husbandry, and you're interested in science, you can use your training. The fundamental requirement, of course, is that you like "hard" s-f in the first place. Trying to write something you have no enthusiasm or "feel" for is a ticket to disaster. If you have read hard s-f for pleasure, and know the basic motifs, you have already served your apprenticeship.

There are several steps that can help you become a journeyman writer of science-based stories or novels. They aren't hard and fast, of course, but I use them every day.

1. *Do your homework.* Everybody laughs when s-f TV shows routinely mistake "solar system" for "galaxy," use light-year as a unit of time, and commit other howlers. Such blunders seem to pass right by the TV audience, but even one can easily cause immediate rejection among s-f editors.

Science is replete with such terminology (or, uncharitably, jargon). If you need it, be sure you consult a reference. I keep my set of the *Britannica* nearby, but more specialized books are invaluable. A brief list from my own shelf:

The Science in S-F, Peter Nicholls, Editor (Knopf). The best place to start. Covers everything, with many references to fictional treatments and nonfiction background.

Cambridge Encyclopedia of Astronomy, Simon Mitton, Editor (Crown). A good overview, technically accurate and well-written.

Isaac Asimov's Biographical Encyclopedia of Science & Technology (Avon). Tidbits of history and science.

The Quest for Extraterrestrial Life, Donald Goldsmith, Editor (University Science Books). A collection of readings with many speculative ideas.

Black Holes and Warped Spacetime, William Kaufmann (Freeman). The best book on the subject.

The Seven Mysteries of Life, Guy Murchie (Houghton Mifflin). Observations on many sciences. You can pick up many "bits of business" here that lend atmosphere to even the driest facts.

The S-F Encyclopedia, Peter Nicholls, Editor (Doubleday). A thorough listing of major treatments of major s-f ideas, plus much else of interest about the field.

This last entry is invaluable for trying out your newborn idea, to see if somebody used it in a famous story from 1938. Not that you can't reuse an idea, but you should know if you are; that affects how you treat it.

Don't pass up any chance to do some background reading, no matter how minor it seems. *Use* your natural curiosity.

I am working on a novel about archaeology, and I recently had a character remark in passing, "The ancients were building elegant domes when *our* ancestors were hunting mastodons." After I'd typed those words, I realized I had no idea when the mastodons disappeared. A few minutes' checking showed that while they had been hunted to extinction in Europe well before the Greeks, they lived on in North America until a few thousand years ago. I then used this fact later in the conversation, adding an insider's detail that an archaeologist might plausibly know, but the casual reader wouldn't.

2. *Organize!* Technical material needs to simmer in your unconscious. Good hard s-f demands not that you parrot material from an encyclopedia, but that you *think* about it. I let my unconscious do most of my idea-making. I even go to the extent of lying in bed each morning, mulling over the science and plot of my current project, seeing if any idea has surfaced in the night.

To keep myself open to fresh notions, I keep my material handy, so that I can review it whenever I want. That means accumulating clippings, photocopies, copious notes—and organizing them into quickly-findable form, using headings like *Starship, Alien Biology,* and *Techtalk.*

I was browsing through this material when it suddenly occurred to me that an opening line in an already-written chapter could have two different meanings. The line was, "When he woke up he was dead." In the novel it meant one thing, but in the near future it could mean the man had his nervous system cut off. Why? How would he regain control?

Within a few minutes, the material I had filed under *Advanced Medical* fell into place. I used the idea for a separate short story, "Lazarus Rising," which sold for $400 to *Isaac Asimov's Science Fiction Magazine.* Then I incorporated some of this new material into the novel I had been working on, finding that this diversion had opened up new possibilities in the original situation! Simon & Schuster published the novel as *Across the Sea of Suns* in 1984.

3. *Counter-punch.* S-f is full of common assumptions that were once inventive but are now mere conventions. Time and again authors invoke faster-than-light travel so their characters can whiz around the galaxy, righting wrongs, with no more than a few weeks spent in travel. This is good for dramatic unity, but *not* using it can be an asset, if it leads you to a new angle. What would an empire be like if ships moved at a hundredth of light speed? How would it keep political unity? What conflicts would arise?

This policy of truly thinking through the ideas in s-f can lead to major projects. Years ago I started thinking about time travel, and asked myself—as a physicist—how scientists would proceed if they discovered a particle that could move backward in time. Would they send a man backward, as their first experiment? Of course not—too expensive, too dangerous.

So I spent years writing a novel called *Timescape,* in which physicists do nothing more dramatic than to try to send mere *messages* backward in time. This was more than enough to generate conflict and suspense, and I profited by not echoing the ideas of a thousand earlier stories. Asking how events might really happen, given the realities of our world, can always turn up unexplored avenues.

4. *Ask the next question.* This well-known motto, invented by Theodore Sturgeon, might well be the most important for any s-f work. New technology and science appear every day in newspapers and on TV. Much of it is obscure, or just another slight improvement of a particular

widget. But some changes can alter the lives of common people, and these are the most fertile fields for anticipating the unseen effects.

The easiest things to anticipate are problems, but this usually leads to downbeat, hopeless stories. There are two ways out.

First, you can go for the really unexpected side-effect. For example, the news coverage of Barney Clark's heroic use of an artificial heart stimulated my imagination. Would the public always applaud such exotic medical technology? What if for $250 million you could buy not merely a replacement heart, but virtual immortality? I wrote a story about a dying man who could not tolerate the sight of a millionaire buying a whole new life. With nothing left to lose, what would this man do? Pessimistic, in a way—but the story, titled "Immortal Night," sold immediately.

The less risky way around the pessimistic-story trap is to see an unexpected *positive* aspect of what looks at first pretty bleak. For example, the Coming of the Computer. Will its ability to save and check information lead to a "surveillance society" where we have no secrets from the government? Think of a way computers can help thwart the police state—and show it in action. So many people fear computers already, such a story could be very popular.

5. *Show the "tip of the iceberg."* The most dreaded beast in hard s-f is the Expository Lump. That's the long paragraph explaining how a new invention works, or what the ecology of a strange planet is like, or some other necessary but intrusive material. You have to explain a lot without slowing down the action.

Suppose your hero is on a low-gravity planet. Don't lecture your reader about it, throwing in the mass and size and atmospheric details of your world. Instead, let your hero notice *in passing* that many kinds of large animals have wings for gliding or flying, that life in trees is more abundant, etc. This one colorful detail allows the reader to fill in much of the background himself.

This can work even better in near-future stories. In my novel *Timescape,* I dealt extensively with a runaway biological disaster. The foreground is concerned with scientists and how they work, but I realized I hadn't shown how advanced knowledge of manipulating the genetic code would affect ordinary life. How could I fill this in without devoting much space to it? My solution was to let a character notice that a road-filling job outside his laboratory was being done by apes. These animals had had their intelligence artificially enhanced until they could follow verbal orders and do manual labor. This, and one or two other quick touches, gave the background color I wanted.

Even if you're weak on science, you don't have to give up the hard s-f story. The most important role of science in s-f is establishing *setting,* and you can do that with reading or travel.

Years ago I sold a short story, but I couldn't put it out of my mind. Slowly I saw that it was the beginning of a novel—but the larger plot had to occur at the Jet Propulsion Laboratory in Pasadena. I didn't know anything about how working space scientists talked or thought. So I used my journalistic connections to find out. I had written articles for *Smithsonian* and *Natural History,* so I cited these credits to line up several visits to J.P.L. There I got to know several space scientists and picked up those little nuggets of detail I later used in *In the Ocean of Night.*

To the s-f reader, the "bits of business" incorporating the atmosphere of hard s-f are often enough to convince him you know what you're talking about. Then he will go along for your ride, to whatever strange and wonderful places you wish to take him.

56

WRITING THE HISTORICAL-ROMANCE ORIGINAL

By Laurie McBain

I RECEIVED a letter the other day from a young woman, an aspiring writer, who wanted some advice about the novel she was working on. Midway through the letter she wrote, " . . . I get really discouraged about my book, and I ask myself why I think that plain old so-and-so can write a romantic novel." In response to that question I think, well, who *do* you have to be to write a novel? If you have a story in you and a basic understanding of the English language, and if you have a certain tenaciousness of mind and spirit, then why not you? Everyone has to begin sometime.

I used to wonder at my own audaciousness in submitting my novel to some unseen, omniscient editor in faraway New York. There were many obstacles that I was blithely unaware of at the time. Perhaps, had I known the odds against getting an unsolicited first novel published, I might never have had the courage to submit my manuscript. However, as I was ignorant of this and I did have a story to tell, I set my insecurities and trepidations aside and decided I had nothing to lose by submitting my novel.

There are indeed high odds against an unsolicited manuscript finding a publisher. In the first place it usually gets assigned to the "slush pile," that awesome stack of no-name manuscripts that will eventually get read by someone, someday. I *did* have two important factors that worked in my favor. The type of novel I was endeavoring to write, the historical romance, was enjoying incredible success with the public. Also, I sent my manuscript to the right publishing house. You may well ask, "How *do* you find the right publisher?" The next time you happen to be in a bookstore, look along the shelves and see what types of books certain publishers are currently producing. You would be wasting your valuable time and effort sending a detective novel to a publishing house that specializes in science fiction. Once you have a feel for which publishing house would be your best bet and you'd like some more information about it, there are several useful market guides that annually update publishers' editorial requirements and list the addresses, names of editors, and whether they want to see a complete manuscript or just an outline and a sample chapter.

I selected my publisher, Avon Books, because they were publishing the type of novel I had written, and also because they were one of the few publishers at that time (1974) to accept unsolicited manuscripts. This was information I learned from one of the guides I consulted. Since I was a novice to the publishing world, without contacts or an agent, this information was invaluable to me.

People often wonder where writers begin, why they choose the subjects that they write about. What might fire up the imagination of one writer might leave another writer cold. History, for me, catches hold of my imagination and ignites a spark that sends it in all directions, but it wasn't until I began reading historical novels that the past truly came alive. Suddenly, I was experiencing history through the eyes of fascinating characters created by magicians who knew about the clothes these people wore, the food they ate, the houses they lived in, the mode of transportation they used and the events that concerned their lives. History was no longer merely a series of dusty dates and long-ago incidents, but a place made up of real people who could love and hate, feel jealousy and happiness, and experience all of the emotions of living.

I became completely enraptured by historical novels and read all I could find. Actually, this reading for pleasure was important training for writing my own novel. I unconsciously learned how other authors handled plots and characters, action and mystery, and absorbed it all. Where the idea for my first novel came from, I don't know. But I did know that once I began to develop my characters and plot, I had made a commitment and had to see it through to the end.

It is difficult to explain exactly how a writer knows how to develop a story. Some might say it is instinct, that it is a natural feeling of knowing what is right or wrong for the novel. That may be true, but only partly. Much of knowing what to do comes from past experience that becomes part of you, and you then use it instinctively.

Once you have the idea for your novel, how do you begin to organize for it? I started out using index cards for my research, but having once dropped over two hundred of them on the floor, I switched to a small, loose-leaf notebook (8 " x 6 ") that is easy to thumb through while searching for the exact piece of information I need. Also, I find it useful sometimes to sketch many of the clothes and pieces of furniture I want to describe. If I have a picture of a dress or hairstyle in front of me, I know what I want to say in describing it. I have an instant image of the way the curls hang, or the way the bustle sits in the back of a gown. One of my notebooks has sections for characters, plot development, specific descriptions, poems, and fashions (i.e., a glossary of clothing materials). Few people today know exactly how cherry-derry, Florentine nankeen, or superfine, common materials of yesterday, look or feel.

You must try to acquaint yourself with every aspect of life in a different era if you are to make your novel believable. I don't think any detail is too small. By using colloquialisms of the period in your dialogue, by describing the fashions and furnishings of the day, by vividly depicting the social mannerisms, you are coloring in the picture you have drawn.

When you write the historical novel, you can build upon the romantic feelings that many people have for the past. Readers are eager to lose themselves in another age and experience the past through the characters and world you create. This intrinsic romanticism is an important advantage for writers of historical novels. At the same time, it can be a disadvantage, for your research must be thorough and accurate. You want the reader to hear the rustle of silk skirts and the pounding of horses' hooves, to smell the aromatic blend of herbs in an Elizabethan herb garden, or to feel the salt spray on the deck of a sailing ship. The mood, made up of detailed descriptions, adds to the mystique and romance of the past, and it must be real for you if it is to be for the reader.

As in the development of any project, you often run across problems that have to be solved before you can proceed. I have found it helpful to work up an outline. I do not let the outline dictate to me, but use it merely as a guide. It lets me see what is coming up and helps me to pace myself. However, I am always ready to make allowances for the changing roles of developing characters and plot twists that sometimes come out of the blue in the course of writing the novel. You must be flexible. For example, when I was writing the first several chapters of my novel, *Tears of Gold,* I realized that my hero wouldn't be making an appearance until the latter part of the third chapter. I felt he should be introduced to the reader sooner, and so I added a prologue. This not only brought the hero into the story earlier, but set up an event concerning the hero and heroine that would have far-reaching effects later in the novel. The reader realizes this and will feel the tension as he anticipates the reckoning.

Another problem I became aware of in the initial stages of *Tears of Gold* was that my heroine needed a maid. Because of the back-fastening dress styles of the period, my heroine, unless assisted, would be spending most of her time struggling in and out of her gowns. That is how the character of Jamie, the feisty little Irishwoman, evolved. Her role grew into a major secondary character, extending beyond my original concept of her role. Through her eyes the reader sees a different perspective of the heroine and her family.

And that brings me to the importance of characters in a novel. You may have a unique plot full of twists and turns, richly detailed research and a devastating denouement, but if your characters aren't fully developed, if they do not seem to live and breathe, you have failed. One of the best ways to catch and hold the attention of readers throughout your novel is to get them involved with your characters. Whether your characters feel anger, love, hate, or joy, they must generate this emotion in the reader.

In *Tears of Gold* I purposely had my heroine seem hard and unfeeling in the beginning. But as the story progressed, so did Mara's personality. I tried to show that she was changing, learning to grow as a person as the novel moved toward its conclusion. In order to engender sympathy and a gradual understanding of the complex nature of Mara, I delved into her background, and also showed a completely different side of her nature in the unselfish love she had for her nephew Paddy.

In the historical romance, the hero and heroine are idealistically conceived. Although they are not perfect—indeed, you would not want them to be—you do have to stay within certain guidelines. The hero and heroine are, after all, the embodiment of romance. They are the man and woman readers will want to identify with, fall in love with, and wish were a part of their own lives. You should not tamper with that dream. That is why it is important to develop a full company of interesting secondary characters. They can border on many extremes, from buffoonery to villainy, and can be painted with a broader stroke of the pen than the hero and heroine. But more than that, these secondary characters help to carry and advance the novel. It is the interaction among all of the characters that makes for a rousing and moving story—one that will be remembered long after the reader turns the last page.

I am a storyteller, and I strive to entertain people. If, when that last page has been turned and the book has been closed, the reader still thinks about the characters and wonders what is happening to them, then I have succeeded. If I have made the reader dream of the past, laugh and cry with my characters, experience suspense and adventure, and ultimately feel satisfied, then I feel I have done my job.

57

"BUT THAT'S IMPOSSIBLE!"

By Bill Pronzini

SUPPOSE A man walks into the sixteenth-floor suite of an attorney one morning, is admitted to the lawyer's private office, and ten minutes later two witnesses hear a gunshot from within. Suppose these witnesses have the presence of mind to lock the only door immediately after the crime, thereby trapping the visitor in that one room. Suppose the police, when they arrive, find the attorney dead of a gunshot wound and the visitor alone with the body. And suppose a subsequent search of the man, of the office, and of the grounds sixteen stories below proves conclusively that no weapon exists anywhere.

You might say, "But that's impossible!"

What if a detective is hired to guard some two hundred expensive presents at a swanky wedding reception? What if the presents have been placed in a room whose windows are all locked and which has been searched by the detective and found to be uninhabited? What if later he is sitting in the hallway, watching the locked (and only) door to the room, when suddenly he hears the sound of glass shattering—and upon breaking down the door he finds one gift box open on the floor, empty of the valuable ring it had contained? And what if he also finds the largest of the windows broken and all the glass shards on the outside lawn, indicating that the window had been smashed *from the inside?*

Again you might say, "But that's impossible!"

In both cases, however, you would be wrong. For in the world of the "impossible crime" story, nothing is impossible. Guns *can* cease to exist inside locked offices after a murder; windows *can* be mysteriously broken under the nose of the keenest detective.

It has been said that Americans love puzzles. The crime puzzle, of which the impossible is the purest form, concerns itself not only with whodunit, but with *how*dunit. It is the puzzle for the connoisseur. Solving crime puzzles provides a good deal of satisfaction for the reader and offers the reassurance of order in a sometimes chaotic world. The more difficult the enigma, the greater the satisfaction in solving it. But the ultimate gratification belongs not to the solvers of the puzzles, but to the writer who, like a magician, can outwit even the most experienced and clever puzzle addict through misdirection, manipulation, and skillful sleight-of-hand.

Does such a prospect appeal to you? If so—if you like puzzles, enjoy reading and writing mystery stories, and have an inventive imagination—you possess the basic tools to write an impossible crime story. With these tools, and with a working knowledge of the form and the observance of a few important rules, you can create your own salable mystery. And your own high-point of satisfaction.

The most important technical requirement, as with any genre or subgenre, is a thorough understanding of what the impossible is and what it should and should not be. Before you attempt to write one of your own, you should read those created by the form's best writers past and present, and become conversant with its history, its classics, and its clichés. The basic impossible story theme is the murder of someone, or the disappearance of someone or something, from a locked room or other closed (or, conversely, wide-open) space. There have been a vast number of variations on this theme, and variations on the variations, since the first locked-room novel, Israel Zangwill's *The Big Bow Mystery,* was published in 1958. (The first locked-room short story, Poe's "Murders in the Rue Morgue," appeared a half-century before that.) What may strike the uninformed writer as a brilliant gimmick or variant may in fact have been used in a book or books fifty years ago—and would bring an instant rejection from knowledgeable editors if reused today.

The Grand Master of the impossible was John Dickson Carr, who wrote dozens of novels and short stories during his 40-year career, nearly all of which make use of one or more ingenious impossibles. His novel, *The Three Coffins,* is notable not only for a pair of masterful crime puzzles, but for its "locked-room lecture"—with an entire chapter (#17) devoted to a study of the ways and means in which a murder may take place, or appear to take place in a locked room.

Each of these basic methods is discussed at length in the chapter, but to whet your interest I'll list them in brief here:

1. The crime is not murder, but a series of coincidences ending in an accident that looks like murder.

297

2. It is murder, but the victim is impelled to kill himself or to die an accidental death.

3. It is murder, by a mechanical device already planted in the room and hidden undetectably in some innocent-looking piece of furniture.

4. It is suicide, which is intended to look like murder.

5. It is a murder which derives its problem from illusion and impersonation.

6. It is a murder which, although committed by somebody outside the room at the time, nevertheless seems to have been committed by somebody who must have been inside.

7. It is a murder depending on an effect exactly the reverse of number 5; that is, the victim is presumed to be dead long before he actually is.

Also discussed in the chapter are ways of gimmicking doors and windows so that they seem to have been locked from the inside. Delivered by Carr's rotund and brilliant detective, Dr. Gideon Fell, the "locked-room lecture" is invaluable to anyone who intends to write an impossible crime story.

A vital nonfiction book is Robert Adey's *Locked Room Murders* —an exhaustive bibliography, complete with plot summaries and historical commentary, of more than 1300 "impossible" novels and short stories appearing throughout the world in the past eighty years. Published in England by a small press (Ferret Fantasy) in 1979, it is available in this country through any metropolitan bookstore specializing in mystery and detective fiction. (It should be noted that this book not only summarizes plots but also provides, in a separate section, summaries of the solutions as well. This section should not be consulted until after you have read the works in question, particularly those of John Dickson Carr, Clayton Rawson, and other experts. Peeking at the answers to puzzles is neither fair nor satisfying, after all, nor is it instructive.)

Once you have become well-versed in the background of the impossible story, and you're ready to begin plotting one of your own, you should keep in mind the following general rules. You *can* sell an impossible if you break one of these rules (I've done so myself), but your chances will be considerably lessened. And you *can't* sell any story that breaks two or more.

Originality. As noted earlier, the number of variations already used is large; to repeat any of them, without offering a unique variation-on-a-variation, is to meet with immediate rejection. Your thorough study of the form will help to eliminate this problem. So will imagination. Remember, *nothing* is impossible in the realm of the impossible. Although the number of used variations is large, the number of unused variations is infinite; you can make your murder, theft, or disappearance as different or amazing or spectacular as you like. The more unusual and baffling it is, the more easily you'll find a home for it in print.

Plausibility. This is an adjunct of originality and just as important. No matter how far-fetched, how unusual, your plot may seem to be *on the surface,* it must have a wholly logical explanation. The gimmick can be improbable—a number of John Dickson Carr's wonderful plots are improbable—but like every one of Carr's plots and devices, it must nonetheless be plausible. The reader must be able to maintain his suspension of disbelief, to say to himself at the denouement, "Yes, that *could* happen."

Do not use such devices as secret panels, trap doors, door bolts turned from outside by means of pliers or string, daggers made of ice, exotic poisons, acrobatic midgets, or trained monkeys. Gimmicks like this were the staple of some detective-story writers in the early 1900s, but by today's standards they are both hackneyed and implausible. If you can't think of a more original explanation for a locked-room murder than a secret panel through which the murderer entered and escaped, you'd better try your hand at a different type of story.

Simplicity. The plot of your story may be as intricate as you care to make it, but the impossible itself—the gimmick, the method behind the mysterious occurrence—should be kept simple. Any contrivance requiring more than a couple of pages or a large amount of technical jargon to explain should be avoided. Most real-life murders are relatively simple affairs; most classic locked-room fictional murders (or disappearances) are relatively simple, too. It is the artistry of the writer, the manipulation of events to create the illusion of complexity, that permits the crime to take on its fantastic qualities.

For this reason, you should shy away from the use of complicated mechanical devices. These strain credibility and require too much explanation. Also avoid the criminal mastermind who invents an ornate and involved contrivance when it would have been much easier for him to commit his crime in a straightforward fashion. It is much more believable to make the culprit an average, if clever, individual with simple criminal motives; to provide himself with an alibi, to conceal something, to take advantage of a given situation, to make it look as though someone else is guilty. It is not necessary, in fact, for the villain to plan an impossible crime; an elementary murder plot can turn into an "impossible" (as Carr demonstrates in his *Three Coffins* lecture), by coincidence or accident.

Fair play. The preponderance of impossibles are detective stories; the puzzles are solved by a detective who follows clues, uses his powers of observation, and arrives at the truth by logical deduction. If your story falls into this category, you must remember to give the reader the same opportunity to solve the enigma that you give your detective. He must be privy to the same clues as the investigator, and you must not withhold any important facts or supply him with deliberate misinformation. Readers don't mind being fooled, but they want to be fooled fair and square.

To illustrate these four rules, as well as the structure of the impossible crime story, I offer the solutions to the two crime puzzles I postulated at the beginning of this article. The premises are those of a pair of my own stories first published, some years apart, in *Ellery Queen's Mystery Magazine*. The first, "Proof of Guilt" (the disappearing gun), came into being as the result of a question I asked myself one morning: "How could someone shoot someone else in a locked room and then get rid of the weapon without himself leaving the room?" The first thing that occurred to me was, "What if he *ate* it?" A facetious and preposterous notion, of course . . . or is it?

Suppose the victim was shot not with an ordinary gun but with a homemade weapon, a sort of zip gun made of several component parts which could, after using, be broken down again into those separate components. Suppose the murderer was a drifter who had worked at a number of odd jobs, but there is a four-year gap in his past that he refuses to discuss. And suppose the police discover an old poster that explains his whereabouts during those four years—an old carnival sideshow poster bearing the words: STEAK AND POTATOES AND APPLE PIE ARE OUR DISH; NUTS, BOLTS, PIECES OF WOOD, BITS OF METAL IS HIS! THE AMAZING MR. GEORGE, THE MAN WITH THE CAST IRON STOMACH.

Now the idea of a gun-eating villain is no longer either facetious or preposterous; improbable, perhaps, but plausible nonetheless. The sideshow poster quoted above is not unveiled until the third-to-last paragraph of the story, and the final line reveals that the murderer had, indeed, eaten the zip gun after the shooting. (This particular impossible is an example of one in which the fair-play rule does not apply. The detective-narrator does not solve the crime until it is too late to do anything about it, and then only by turning up the poster. The emphasis is on the surprise revelation of the gun having been ingested, not on deduction.)

"A Nice Easy Job" was born while I was reading a mystery novel in which a policeman solved a murder by looking at a broken window and observing that there were no glass shards on the floor inside the room, when the culprit claimed that it had been broken from outside. "Whenever you break a window," the detective said, "the glass will always fall in the opposite direction. All these shards are outside; therefore this window was broken from within."

This fact happens to be true—under normal circumstances. But, I asked myself, was there a way to break a window from the outside so that all the shards would fall *toward* the person? And I discovered that there was. A strong man could attach a suction clamp—one of those bar-type gadgets with rubber cups at each end, like the ones used in the film *Topkapi* to lift a heavy glass case—and then lock it down so that the cups are securely suctioned to the glass; by giving the clamp a hard, rocking jerk or two, he could then break the window and have all the shards fall in his direction.

With my basic impossible worked out, I devised the set of circumstances in which a valuable ring would be stolen from a locked room the Nameless Detective was guarding. The thief perpetrated the crime in such a fashion to make it seem that "Nameless" had broken down the door in order to steal the ring itself; by the detective's own testimony, the room containing the wedding presents was empty and nobody, it is subsequently established, could have gotten in or out of the room through the broken window.

By deduction and clue-gathering (this one *is* a formal detective story), Nameless discovers that the ring had been stolen sometime earlier, when he and the culprit and three other men were in the room. What the thief had done was to palm the ring from a small ring box as he was replacing it in the larger gift box. Later, after breaking the window with the suction clamp, he threw a small bogus present in through the opening from outside, knocked the gift box off the table, and thereby created the illusion that it had been dislodged when the ring was stolen.

301

Like most successful impossibles, these two of mine seem obvious when finally explained. It is the structuring of them, remember, the sleight-of-hand, that turns them into puzzles and gives them the appearance of incredibility. And makes them so satisfying, too.

The impossibilities are limitless . . .

58

PLANNING AND PLOTTING THE DETECTIVE STORY

By Catherine Aird

A FULL-LENGTH detective story is made up of individual chapters. This much is obvious. It is the construction and organization of these individual chapters that, in my opinion, merit the attention of anyone writing a first detective story.

It hardly needs saying that the first and last chapters are among the most important in the detective novel—and probably in any story. Starting used to be easier: "Once upon a time. . . ." The old-fashioned storytellers may have had a stereotyped beginning to their tales, but at least the listener knew at once where he was: in the land of make-believe. The storyteller of today, who is writing fiction as opposed to recounting fact, has as one of his first tasks the creation of that make-believe. He hasn't got very long in which to do it, as his tale has to get underway as quickly as possible. Even the first sequence is important.

The modern writer isn't surrounded by a circle of eager listeners, hanging on his every word with no other entertainment in sight, so the fiction writer has to attract and sustain interest against competition a medieval troubador would not have begun to know about. In the writing of detective fiction, this quite often means having the body of the victim on page one. For many readers and writers, this is quite a good place for it to be. It is terribly tempting to establish an elaborate setting first, but this approach has its dangers. Of course the setting has to be established, but if possible, it should be done within the context of the action, rather than before it. I think this is very important.

If the body is not on page one, it certainly must appear no later than the end of chapter one. There are, of course, exceptional circumstances in which this rough-and-ready rule does not apply. There may be one or more missing persons; the plot may not concern bodies at all but, say, forgery or drugs; the whole story may be about fraud, and, if there is a murder, it may be only incidental. As a generalization, though, I think the main problem of the story should be apparent from reading the first chapter, whether it is who kidnapped the heiress, who robbed the bank, or "Who Killed Cock Robin?"

One of the advantages of having the body in chapter one is that the presence of a victim demands action, no matter what the setting is. This action may involve the full and detailed panoply of the police procedural story or a gifted amateur sleuth cooperating with the appropriate authorities. Either way, the activity engendered by the discovery of the body of the victim necessarily carries the reader into the next chapter.

The murderer should appear, in my view, no later than chapter two—or chapter three, if a particularly large amount of background writing is required—but he must, by hook or by crook, so to speak, be there as soon as possible, taking his place in the plot. It is a great temptation to have the murderer play a subordinate role in the story, but this, alas, will not do. This temptation arises because it is technically difficult to write about someone whom you—and you alone as the writer—know to be the murderer. But I cannot stress too strongly the importance of keeping him visible.

Time spent, therefore, in considering the role of the murderer within the story is not wasted. A conscious effort should be made from the very beginning to see that his function in the plot is significant enough so that you can keep him in front of the reader without obvious contrivance. This will also allow his villainy to be made increasingly clear in subtle ways throughout the book. It is obvious to all those who read and write detective fiction that for profound psychological reasons neither victim nor murderer is ever an entirely sympathetic character. Both are going to be lost, so to speak—one at the beginning of the book and one at the end—and by some long and deep-seated convention, the reader does not expect either loss to be too poignant.

By the time you come to chapter three, you may broaden the situation to indicate that *Things Are Not What They Seem*. In fact, in good detective stories they seldom are, and the experienced reader will expect something more. By chapter three or four, the author should be giving a slight twist to the problem outlined in chapter one. This is more subtle than simply presenting a complicated problem at the outset.

There is a school of thought that holds that most of the important

304

clues to the correct solution of the detective mystery should be given in the first three chapters, albeit presented with great subtlety, and that all the clues really necessary should have appeared no later than chapter six, even though they are still well hidden. I try my hardest to subscribe to and follow this theory and can recommend a most useful exercise in connection with it.

Take your first three chapters and underline what you know to be the significant clues. Ask yourself whether—if you *knew* these were the factors that were important—you could solve the problem as outlined in chapter one. If so, then it should also be possible for a really astute reader of the genre to do so, too. Repeat the process when you have written six chapters and consider if an ordinary intelligent reader could have worked out who the murderer was, had he known what was significant as he was reading.

If the answer to both exercises is "No," you should go back and work in more clues. Remember, though, that it does not matter at this stage how well hidden they are; what is important is that they are there. If you haven't written your own first six chapters yet, I suggest that you take a detective story that you personally find satisfying and practice the exercise on it. The wisdom of hindsight will show you where—and how carefully—the author has given you the information that he or she wanted you to have, even though you were unaware of its significance at the time.

It is also important that all the main characters of the story are present no later than chapter three. Bringing them in later than, say, chapter four, smacks of contrivance. If, for example, the plot hinges on the long lost brother turning up from the mysterious East, then a clue to his existence should have been given before this point in the story. (On the subject of characters, a small point, but one that can save some time: Make sure that none of the names of your characters end in the letter s. Apostrophes need especially careful watching.)

Also, before the story advances too far, it is necessary to introduce the particular suspects with whom the detective is concerned. The reason for the popularity of the closed community (the country house, cruise ship, etc.) as a setting soon becomes apparent. Limiting the number of suspects to those characters at the house party or other confined setting is essential and one that devotees of the detective novel will quickly recognize.

Hoard your exciting chapter endings and try to space them so that those chapters finishing on a high note do not come one after the other. Spacing them out is better than having two cliff-hanger chapter endings in succession, followed by four more pedestrian ones. It is axiomatic that every single chapter in a detective story must have some action: Description and dialogue are not enough. Also, I believe that chapters should not exceed 3,500 to 4,000 words, but this decision is up to the individual writer. The ending of a chapter is a good point at which to change the venue of the scene, end a particular sequence of action, or bring in a new clue.

By chapter six some further important action is called for. Theoretically, the ideal is to have some minor excitement or discovery at the end of every third chapter and a more major event after chapters six and twelve. In fact, by chapter twelve you will, I think, feel the necessity for this yourself. It is really quite difficult to stop the plot from closing in on the author about two-thirds of the way through, and it is at this point that there is often a second murder. Real aficionados of the crime story know that it is by no means uncommon to have as the victim a character who, up to this particular point in the story, has been the chief suspect. This has the merit of opening up the story in more ways than one.

This juncture should be one of the two really high peaks in the story, as opposed to the climax which, of course, should be the highest peak of all. Another important point is that the denouement, although it comes of necessity after the climax, should not be anti-climactic. Detective stories, ironic as it may seem, usually do have at least satisfactory, if not happy, endings, and no small part of the readers' satisfaction comes from the knowledge that all—*all*—the loose ends in the plot have been neatly tied.

One factor that can contribute greatly to an effective climax and explanation is the clearing up of any points that can be cleared up in the third chapter from the end, leaving the last two chapters for the climax and, of course, the last part of the chapter for the explanation, a winding up of the action—a confession, a conviction, or what you will. There are always some small points, or perhaps even large red herrings, that can be disposed of effectively before the grand finale, sometimes even adding to its excitement. If you can get them out of the way before the climax and thus reduce the post-revelation explanation, so much the better.

I hope that what I have written does not read too much like a formula, because that is not what it is meant to be. Nor does it detail a pattern that I myself conscientiously follow in every book I write. What it does attempt to do is to save you at least some misplaced effort when you write your first detective story. Be strong-minded enough to ignore all well-meaning advice if you have better ideas. You could be right. But as will be apparent to anyone who has tried his hand at writing one, a detective story seldom springs—like Athena—fully formed from the author's forehead.

59

ELEMENTS OF THE POLICE PROCEDURAL NOVEL

By Rex Burns

Given the development of the writer's sense of which words live and which don't — a development that for me comes as much through reading as through writing — I think the areas most pertinent to a successful police procedural are four: research, setting, plot, and character.

These divisions are, of course, artificial. As in any "recipe," the elements blend and influence each other; and in any art such as cooking or writing, the whole is greater than the sum of its parts. But though each writer must discover for himself this sense of life or wholeness, some of the basic elements contributing to it can be distinguished. Let's begin with research.

The kind of research I favor is quite basic: my main source for information is the daily newspaper. I figure that if a newspaper article about a crime interests me, it will interest other readers. Naturally, the newspaper story must undergo a metamorphosis before it comes out as fiction. For one thing, there are the questions of libel and plagiarism; and, for another, too great a reliance on the facts as reported can cause a story to become quickly dated.

More important is the question of a good yarn — an interesting newspaper article is only a germ, a bud. It provides a sequence of events and an indication of setting for the full-grown fiction. For example, the following paragraph from a UPI newswire release was the nucleus of a chapter of a novel I was working on: "The raids in Cordoba began when a small airplane, circling the city to apparently coordinate the attacks, threw a bomb that exploded without causing injuries near a provincial bank about 11 A.M." In short, a newspaper article can provide a rich source of actual whats, wheres, and whens. The whys and the whos are the novelist's responsibility.

A second good source of information for the police procedural writer is court records. Affidavits, depositions, and transcripts — in addition to the writer's sitting in on court hearings — help provide not only events and incidental tidbits for a story, but also the language of narration. Increasingly, a cop, especially a senior officer such as a detective, must understand the technology of the law. Every technology has it jargon, and this can be found in legal records and in courtrooms.

Both newspaper stories and court records are as valuable for what they leave out as for what they offer. To get some of that which is left out, read the story with the questions "how?" and "why?" in mind. For instance, that favorite phrase of reporters, "police, acting on a tip from an informant . . ." gives rise to such questions as: Which policeman? Who was the informant? What incentive did he have for informing? What kind of communication — telephone, written, conversational? Who believed the informant? Who didn't? How much time passed between the tip and the raid? These and similar questions come up when the novelist begins creating the fictional world which will embody any actual events he chooses to use.

Though the writer's imagination furnishes the answers to such questions as those asked above, that imagination can be stimulated by a third kind of research which I've found to be most beneficial: interviewing. A policeman, like almost everyone else, enjoys talking about his work, and most municipalities have programs for bettering police-community relations. And a writer — despite what his neighbors may think — is a member of the community. In a larger town, check with the department's public information office. Departments in smaller towns tend to be less formal, and I think somewhat less accessible, perhaps because their manpower tends to be insufficient and the training less professional, generating a defensive attitude. The prosecutor's office and the sheriff's office are also worthwhile avenues of approach. For me, this interviewing tends to be quite casual and takes place during a duty watch; there's a lot of time for conversation during eight hours of riding in a patrol car.

Armed with some specific questions derived from reading newspapers and reports, the interviewer can start filling in those blanks found in the documents. The answers don't have to be related to the same cases read about — in fact, I like it better if they aren't. The novelist deals with probability, and patterns of common behavior offer more freedom for the invention of particulars than does the mere reporting of facts, which is where the journalist ends and the novelist begins. Unlike what takes place on most television talk shows, an interviewer-novelist should be a good listener and, speaking for myself, a copious but surreptitious notetaker. It also helps to train your eye for such minutiae as manufacturer's labels, model numbers, organization charts — in short, anything that gives quick specific detail for your story's setting. Interviewing also provides the latest slang and technical jargon.

The manner of introducing those technical terms into the narrative varies. If a character honestly might not know what a particular device or procedure is called, he can simply ask someone in the story. The character and the reader become informed together. I use this device sparingly, since my characters in the Gabe Wager books are generally professional and well-trained. (Moreover, as a reader, I get damned irritated when a story's development is continually interrupted by some idiot who needs everything explained to him.) Another means of introducing technical terms is to use the phrase in normal dialogue and let the descriptive passage carry the explanation: " 'Let me have the Kell-Kit,' said Wager. Sergeant Johnston handed him the small body transmitter. . . ." Or, for variation, the equation may be reversed: " 'Let me have the body transmitter,' said Wager. Sergeant Johnston handed him the small Kell-Kit." I'm not sure if police departments have yet surpassed the federal government in the use of acronyms and arcane initials, but these are an essential part of bureaucratic jargon. It is a rule of thumb in writing first to use the full phrase, then, in the next sentence or two, the more common initials: "Wager turned to his little book of Confidential Informants. The first C. I. was. . . ." No explanatory passage is needed, and the action moves without interruption.

Research, then, is the foundation for the police procedural, and on that foundation are built in setting, plot, and character. Setting is, of course, easiest to create if it's well known to the writer. For the Gabriel Wager stories, that means Denver. Ironically, my editors more than once pointed out that a street which I invented wasn't on their map of Denver, or an odd-numbered address should be on the north rather than south side of a particular avenue. But the familiarity I mean is as much in flavor as in fact, and its manner of presentation is — for me — impressionistic. The single well-chosen detail that captures the flavor of the setting and gives focus and life to an otherwise sketchy scene is part of the economy I associate with the "grittiness" of a police procedural. A gothic, a novel that explores states of mind, or a sci-fi fantasy may call

310

for more sweeping and panoramic descriptions to create a mood or sustain a romance. But I find harmony between a spare style and the realistic police story. Since this descriptive technique tends to emphasize action rather than setting, and since a police procedural is akin to a report — and a report is usually about "what happened" — the emphasis on concrete and concise detail feels right to me.

The concern with what happened brings us to plot. Plot is not just *what* takes place but *why* it takes place. The police procedural may or may not use the mystery as the basis of suspense. If the police do not know who the perpetrator is, then unraveling the mystery becomes the plot — i.e., the gradual revelation of motive and opportunity. But often, in life as well as in fiction, the police do know who the villain is, and the plot centers on gathering enough evidence for a viable court case. The manner of getting this evidence is quite tedious and even dull — questioning fifty or a hundred witnesses, long hours of surveillance, studying accounting records. The problem for the storyteller in the police procedural field becomes one of remaining true to reality without boring the reader. One technique that fits the police procedural is focusing attention on new methods of surveillance or on the ever-changing avenues of legal presentation. Here, research is indispensable. Another device is to give your detective more cases than one. This is by no means unrealistic, but a good story requires that the cases somehow work together toward a single conclusion. That's the old demand of art for unity, a unity seldom apparent in real life.

Another very familiar technique for maintaining interest is the foil — someone who offers byplay for the protagonist. A foil should serve a variety of purposes, all contributing toward the unity of the novel. The character used as a foil — a rookie, for instance — may be a device not only for explaining police procedure, but also for revealing the protagonist's character through his reaction to the foil's activities.

I try to make character as interesting as case. The strongest novels are those with living characters to whom the action is vital, and this holds true for any tale, even a plotless one. But whether it's a who-done-it or a how-to-prove-it, the police story is fundamentally an action story, and in it the development of character should not impede the action. Ideally, character development and action should coincide; but where they do not, I tip the balance in favor of action, possibly because I envision the Gabe Wager series as one long novel of perhaps fifteen volumes, and this view gives me plenty of room to let the character grow.

311

There are several other concrete devices that aid the quick presentation of character without interrupting the action. One device especially useful for creating secondary characters is the "signature" — a distinctive act, speech pattern, or habit of thought that identifies and distinguishes one character from another. This signature may be simple: one secondary figure from *The Alvarez Journal* smokes cigars, another has an old man's rumbling cough, a third speaks administrative jargon. Or, if the character is of more importance to the story, a combination of signatures may be used to flesh him out. At its worst, this device generates cliché characters — the western bad man with his black hat and sneer. At best, the signature makes the character become alive and individualized — the girth, thirst, and cowardice of Falstaff. The problem, of course, is to characterize without caricaturing — unless your aim is satire. The novelist's ability to create real characters can be improved by reading other writers who are very good at it: Shakespeare, Flaubert, Faulkner. Another means is "reading" friends and neighbors: What exactly is it that distinguishes one of your acquaintances from another? Given universal human qualities, what makes one individual different from another?

Minor and secondary characters, while absolutely necessary, do not give life to the action. Rarely can any story, police procedural or other, do without a protagonist. Again, because of the importance of action in police procedurals, the writer is faced with the need for an economical development of his main character. The technique I have chosen for my Gabe Wager series is by no means new: It's the familiar "recording consciousness" of Henry James, the restricted third-person point of view, in which every event and concept in the story is presented from the perspective of a single protagonist. I've found several advantages to this device: The action proceeds and the protagonist's character is revealed at the same time. The reader is faced with the same limitations of knowledge as the protagonist, and thus the element of suspense is heightened. Using third person rather than first person puts distance between the reader and the protagonist and offers another dimension to the story, which helps the reader through those necessary and authentic but often slow stages of a case's development.

This narrative technique also has shortcomings. The author can't give the reader any information that the protagonist does not have, thus leaving little chance for irony or depth. For this point of view to work, the

312

author must also have a total understanding of the protagonist. While it may not be relevant to the story, it is nonetheless necessary if the character's actions are to be consistent.

First-person narration achieves many of the same results but brings an even closer identification between author and character. Think of the popular image of Mickey Spillane, for example. I prefer third person because it enforces objectivity and quite possibly because, unlike Gabe Wager, I'm not a good cop.

Focusing all the action through Wager's perspective, then, contributes to a unity of action and characterization in which action dominates but character development follows quite closely and, I hope, unobtrusively. I try to achieve this by placing a heavy emphasis on dialogue. By its very nature, dialogue is dramatic — the characters are onstage talking rather than being talked about by a narrator. Again, the signature is very important, and I play a little game of trying to see how many lines of dialogue I can put together without having to state who is speaking. The idea is that each character's voice should be distinct enough to indicate the speaker.

I place the police procedural in the category of literary realism. The contemporary, the probable, the routine, determine my choice of a realistic subject. Once I select my subject, the elements of research, setting, plot, and character are indispensable, and, in my Gabe Wager police procedurals, all of these elements must contribute to the action.

60

WRITING THE SUSPENSE-ADVENTURE NOVEL

By Clive Cussler

I HATE to write.

Quite frankly, I see nothing blasphemous in admitting it. There are thousands of writers who find scribbling words on paper a colossal drag. Writing is a damned tough way to make a buck, at least to most people. I seethe internally when I hear or read about those Pollyannas who merrily peck away at their typewriters, whistling while they create, morning, noon and night, tossing off 20,000 words between coffee breaks.

I hate them, too.

On a good day of total effort, beginning at nine o'clock and ending at five (an old routine carried over from my advertising agency days), I'm lucky if I turn out four finished pages or 1,000 words. And then I have to take a long walk, indulge in a martini and take a snooze prior to dinner, before I'm mentally rejuvenated enough to return to the land of the living.

When I finally type THE END to a novel, the clouds part and the sun bursts through, flowers blossom across the land, angels sing along to harp music, and I deflate like an old balloon whose elastic is shot.

Therefore, because writing is so exhausting, to me at any rate, I plan and research each project thoroughly before hitting the proper keys to spell out CHAPTER ONE. My problem is that I can visualize my characters, backgrounds, and events as though I were standing in the middle of the action, so the difficult part is turning all these wonderful sights and sounds into mere words that place the reader amid the action, too.

To me the readers come above all else. I look upon them as guests who have gone out of their way to spend time and expense to indulge in whatever small enjoyment I can provide. My particular genre is suspense-adventure, so in order to get off the mark quickly, I must find a concept that grabs the reader's fancy before he turns past the title page. Within the realm of adventure there are thousands of subjects and tales that have great appeal. One of the trends in fashion at present is for novelists to write fiction based loosely on a non-fiction event. This often revolves around a "what if" principle. For instance, one day I asked myself, what if they raise the *Titanic*? The next question that entered my mind was why? Obviously the cost of salvaging the great liner from two and one-half miles down in the abysmal depths would be enormous. What reason would justify the effort and expense? Out of this pre-examination a plot was born.

Without a concept hook to hang your plot on, you have nothing. The swashbuckler of yesterday who chopped up the moustached villains and did little else but carry the insipid heroine off into the sunset at the finish won't cut the mustard today. The idea of having a blimp bomb the Superbowl as in *Black Sunday* was a good hook for a "what if" adventure. *Airport* and of course *Jaws* are other successful stories that embraced this principle.

More than ever, the reader who shells out for your novel is looking for an escape. It's a fact of life, that if you don't aim your talents at the market, you won't sell. If the reader isn't presold by an author's past reputation, or by word-of-mouth recommendation, or a blitz publicity campaign, he has no other reason to select your masterpiece except for one hell of an intriguing concept.

Assuming that you have the story the world is waiting to devour, you should now turn your energies to the next step in the adventure novel—structure.

Gotcha! I'll bet you thought I was going to say plot or perhaps characterization. Not so. Next to a mind-boggling concept, structure is the most important foundation for a novel. Whether you intend to write it in the first person or the third is elementary. You should take the path that makes you comfortable. First person allows you to probe the hero or heroine's mind in depth; you see only what they see. The third-person narration, on the other hand, gives a wider range of freedom to travel into areas the first person cannot follow. Seeing the action from the central character's eyes limits the writer to what I call the "Formula-A Structure." You travel with the narrator from prologue to epilogue, seeing only what he sees. This is a common practice among new writers because of its basic simplicity.

However, I do not mean to suggest that Formula A is mundane. Hardly. It has been used with great success by writers since man first scratched in the sand. The classical love stories, mysteries and, yes, horror stories, too, have taken advantage of its storytelling smoothness. Formula A also makes for a tight tale that involves the readers as closely in the action as though they were the parrot on Long John Silver's shoulder.

For writers who turn on to intricate plotting and a cast of hundreds, Formula B is the only way to fly. Here the third-person viewpoint throws open the floodgates of creativity, and you can pull the reader through a labyrinth of subplots, "sideplots," and "twistplots." You have the opportunity of setting the scene in a jet over the Arctic in one chapter and suddenly switching to a camel caravan crossing the Sahara in the next.

Leon Uris, Robert Ludlum, and Harry Patterson alias Jack Higgins are all masters of the complex structure. Instead of studying flowery prose and in-depth characterization as most writers are prone to do, you should examine quite closely the organization and precision the authors mentioned above weave throughout their stories. Harold Robbins, for example, used the epilogue as the prologue in *The Adventurers,* and then went on to slip his hero deftly in and out of first- and third-person narration.

Do you intend to utilize the advantages of a prologue to set up future conflicts? Will you need an epilogue to tie the ends together? Have you the guts to combine several plots into one? Have you considered dividing your novel into different parts? This is what we mean by structure.

There are no hard-and-fast rules for structuring the modern adventure novel. In Formula A, you must keep your hero believable and the action moving to keep readers turning the pages. With Formula B, the trick is to keep them second guessing and so involved with who's-doing-what-to-whom they can't put the book down. This is achieved by alternating your characters and their personal conflicts so that in the beginning there seems to be no comprehensible connection. Then as the plot unfolds, they're all irresistibly drawn together into an ever-heightening climax. I call this threading the needle. You've got to sew all your characters into the same pocket and thereby give your reader a satisfying conclusion.

A satisfying conclusion can never be stressed too strongly. How many books have you read that began like gangbusters and then fell to pieces in the end? The sad result is that you forget them damned quickly while a tale that has a smash ending stays with you.

All too often a writer will sit down with a blockbuster concept and barrel through the first half of the story only to fall off a cliff because he had no idea where he was going in the first place. You have to know what you're aiming at in the last chapter and then backtrack and work toward it. That's why planning your structure is so important. Creative blueprinting can't turn a bad book into a good one, but it sure helps.

When it comes to plotting, so much has been written by renowned authorities of mystery and adventure writing, I see no reason simply to repeat most of their well-known rules. I plot as I go. Many novelists write an outline that has almost as many pages as their ultimate book. Others knock out a brief synopsis. Again, do what is comfortable. If you have to plot out every move your characters make, so be it. Just make sure there is a plausible purpose behind their machinations. A good reader can smell a phony plot a block away.

In modern adventure writing, the trend seems to be to sacrifice great gobs of character-probing in favor of fast-paced action. Sad to say, most critics are still hung up on finely tuned character definition. but then critics only concern themselves with how well a book is written. The guy who actually lays down the cash for it is more interested in how well it reads.

Alistair MacLean, perhaps one of the finest adventure writers of the last several decades, favors rapid pace over character psychiatry. His people are sharply defined in their looks and mannerisms and come across very well, without pages of historical background.

The hero in my series is usually described through the eyes of other characters. These observations, usually in small doses, occur only when they appropriately add to a particular scene or action.

They don't make good heroes these days. The anti-hero seems to be currently in vogue, especially in detective and spy novels. But pure adventure is something else again. A Casper Milquetoast just won't do. Men readers want to identify with the shrewd, devil-may-care hero who surmounts every obstacle put up by the opposition and emerges

317

victorious in the end. Likewise, women, in spite of the current hoopla about equality, still secretly yearn for the rugged he-man to sweep them off their feet. If you doubt this last statement, simply take a look at the staggering sales figures of the romantic novels by Rosemary Rogers and several other astute women writers.

In most dramatic genres, the reader likes to identify with the characters and to experience what they see and feel. In adventure, the reader runs along the sidelines, cheering everyone on—a prime reason for your characters to be bigger than life, but still believable. That's what's called walking the tightrope. On one hand, you run the risk of making some characters too ordinary. On the other, you don't dare allow them to become comic book Supermen or Wonderwomen.

If your hero must save the world, at least let him act human while he goes about it. He should still put his pants on one leg at a time, sneeze occasionally, blow his nose, and feel the urge to go to the bathroom. What man can identify with another who does none of these? Same with women. I like my girls to zing in a few four-letter words when they're angry or frustrated. Show me one who doesn't at least say "Damn!" after ramming a painted toenail through a pair of new pantyhose.

There is an old saying in the advertising business: "See what your competitors are doing, then do just the opposite." That's the whole idea of writing a book: You're telling a story no one else has told before.

When I decided to develop a series hero, I looked around the field and studied everyone from Sherlock Holmes to James Bond to Travis McGee. I figured the last thing the adventure arena needed was another private detective, spy or CIA agent. So I created a guy by the name of Dirk Pitt who is the Special Projects Director for NUMA (the National Underwater & Marine Agency). Fortunately, I stumbled onto a good thing. The mysteries that can be expanded upon in and around water are as boundless as the oceans themselves. I might mention that I chose the name Pitt partly because it is one syllable, thus making it easy to say, "Pitt did this, and Pitt did that," etc.

My final suggestion relates to what I said earlier about treating the reader as an honored guest. Every so often I'll stop and ask myself, what would the reader like to see at this particular moment in the story? Then I'll try my best to give it to him. I figure that since my reader paid good money or took the time and trouble to check out my efforts from the library, the least I can do is place his interests above mine.

I don't cotton to writers who engrave on marble what *they* think should be read. My work is geared strictly to provide a few hours of enjoyable escape. I don't believe in imparting personal philosophy, social commentary, or hidden meanings between the lines. Some writers prefer to be called novelists, some storytellers, others spokesmen for the masses.

Me: I'm an entertainer, no more, no less.

61

WRITING PROPOSALS THAT GET BOOK CONTRACTS

By Samm Sinclair Baker

EVERY word of this brief chapter has just one focus: to help you put together a nonfiction book proposal that will get a publishing contract. I've cut every word that doesn't move to that objective.

I emphasize that point immediately, because it's exactly what you must do in shaping your proposal. Concentrate on presenting not why *you* think the book will sell (you're prejudiced), but *facts* to convince the editor and others at the publishing house to approve a contract. Eliminate everything else, no matter how charming or amusing or impressively "literary" you think your beloved words may be.

This may seem obvious, but practically every proposal draft by a beginning or experienced writer (including myself) I've seen has contained extraneous material. Such flab must be chopped out ruthlessly, or you'll lose the editor's attention and the contract opportunity. Eliminate any "look how good I am" and "see how beautifully I write" indulgences. Each word must move forward "why this book will sell."

Does the quality of the book proposal make a buy-or-reject difference? Before I became a co-author and prepared clear, orderly, convincing proposals, four of my books were turned down due primarily to inept, unfocused presentations. Since many other factors are involved in signing a book, a fine presentation doesn't guarantee getting a contract—but it sure helps.

My first two books were mystery novels that I offered as complete manuscripts. It's extremely difficult to sell a fiction book proposal unless you're a best-selling novelist, or unless you present at least three irresistible chapters.

On my nonfiction books, I've re-examined and analyzed the proposals carefully. All of them, from the first presentation I wrote as a beginner, through three blockbuster best sellers and others, follow the same contract-getting structure presented here for the first time anywhere. This is what has worked for me:

1. Book Title and Primary Sales Point(s)
   . . . presented as copy for jacket blurb
2. Market Potential
   . . . why this book will sell effectively
3. Personal Background Assets
   . . . biography, research, experience
4. Essentials, Uniqueness
5. Chapter Contents
   . . . chapter titles, main points in each
6. First Chapter of Book
   . . . preferably two or three finished chapters
7. Special Promotional Power
   . . . quick synopsis of unique features to project in interviews, all-media publicity
8. Cover Letter

I arrived at this structure in presenting my first nonfiction book for the general public—*Miracle Gardening*. I developed this solid sequence not out of the blue but based on hundreds of productive presentations for advertising campaigns during my 20-plus years in advertising agencies. I realized that the format that had been successful in selling ad campaigns amounting to millions of dollars should work in getting a book contract. It did.

Another tip from my Madison Avenue experience: Every word in the ad presentations was honed to convince the people who had to O.K. the campaign. I achieved the transference in my mind of becoming the advertiser reading, not the agency man writing. As you conceive your presentations, learn to channel your viewpoint to become the editor reading rather than the author writing.

1. Book Title and Primary Sales Point

As a beginning writer (as perhaps you are), I concentrated on boiling down the essence of the projected gardening book to one or two statements that would best attract book buyers. Therefore, it would appeal to the editor and publishing staff. My first page stated:

Gardening Book Proposal:

MIRACLE GARDENING

How to grow bigger, brighter flowers, thicker lawns, and huge mouth-watering vegetables, using the amazing new scientific miracle substances and methods.

Plus 1001 Tips
for Today's Gardener.

By Samm Sinclair Baker

That succinct, irresistible appeal to gardeners, who seek always to grow the best, hit home with the editor. She told me later, "Reading that powerful promise to gardeners, I had to continue—instead of stopping at the first page of a proposal as I usually do."

That opening page seems simple, easy to create. Not so. To arrive at those few compelling words, stated as an enticing reward for the reader, took me endless trying and revising. I kept changing titles, sequences, sentences innumerable times over a period of weeks. It still takes prolonged effort, no matter how many proposals I write. The extraordinary application to getting it exactly right is worth it in order to get that thrilling call or letter: "We want your book."

2. Market Potential

I've been told that most book proposals don't cover market potential, but I consider it an important element. To delineate the potential market for the book, I cite facts, not empty superlatives. I keep the data crisp, clear, sound, interesting. In the case of *Miracle Gardening,* I listed figures showing the impressive growth in the number of gardens and gardeners, and accelerating dollar sales of gardening products and supplies. All this grew from extensive research enabling me to quote authoritative statistics and sources—government agencies, trade journals, newspapers, associations.

The editor said, "This material helped me a lot. I was able to present the sales potential of the book factually to the marketing director and others who have to O.K. acceptance. Instead of saying, 'I think there are a lot of people who'll want this book,' your data gave me proof of the potential. You saved me a lot of digging in preparing *my* presentation."

3. Personal Background Assets

Of course it's helpful if you can show a list of successful published books. I couldn't. Instead, I stressed my background in gardening: "At age four, my father gave me some radish seeds. I planted and tended them. When I pulled up my first radish, I rubbed off the soil, bit into it—and it bit me back. I've been bit by the gardening bug ever since. By experience, I know how gardeners think, what they want and need . . ."

I detailed in few words my work on gardening accounts in advertising, how my copy built a mail order nursery from little one-inch ads to full pages in newspapers as a big national advertiser . . . "Sales proved that I know how to write to gardeners." I described my research for the proposed book, contacts with leading agricultural universities, scientists, experts, agricultural agents. Such digging is available in practically every field.

You don't need special magic or miracles in your background. If you haven't thorough knowledge of the subject, either through experience or research or other learning, you probably shouldn't be proposing a book. Of course you have the know-how or can get it—say so, backed by facts that prove your contention.

4. Essentials, Uniqueness, Superiorities

In the case of *Miracle Gardening,* I foresaw that the editor would be asking herself, "Why another gardening book?" So I asked that question in my proposal—and answered by naming specific modern garden aids. I listed fresh information, tips not covered by any other gardening book. I had studied the available books thoroughly, and provided explicit details.

Examples: I told about the new (at that time) water-soluble plant foods, how they had been developed in a noted university laboratory by top scientists, identified by name. I described and included in my presentation photos of tests using radioactive isotopes in specially prepared liquid fertilizer, checked with a Geiger counter. The fascinating tests proved that nutrients went from soil to top of a six-foot-high rose bush in minutes. Yes, I included in the proposal actual plant photos and drawings, charts and graphs—all obtained through research sources, with permissions to reproduce them in my proposed book. Again, proved facts, not self-serving, questionable claims.

Keep in mind that the editor is human, a reader, attracted by eye-catching visual material when available. So are members of the editorial and marketing committee who must approve the contract—all individuals saying "Show me."

The proposal for my book, *Reading Faces,* co-authored with Dr. Leopold Bellak, included a half-dozen photos of celebrities, with lines drawn on the faces according to the Bellak Zone System, the basis for the face-reading method to be taught in the book. I included compact instructions for reading faces.

Furthermore, instead of ignoring any competition, I named and described three other books published in the past ten years about reading faces. Then I explained exactly how our book would be entirely different and markedly superior. That negated any objections about competitive books which might block a contract. Our eventual editor told us, "I was fascinated, tried the Zone System on my own face in the mirror, then ran down the hall to try it on others. Soon the place was in an uproar, with everyone reading someone else's face. Your clear, simple demonstration in the proposal made this an easy sale."

5. Chapter Contents

I include in each presentation a listing of chapter titles, and a compact description of the content of each chapter. Sure, that's a lot of work because you're constructing the framework of the entire book. I consider that necessary because I'm asking a publisher to invest a lot of time and money in editing and producing my book.

Editors understand that proposed chapter titles and sequences are subject to change as you write the book. They can't ask for a contract, however, without clear delineation for the editorial and marketing board of what you're urging them to buy. For instance, in offering my first co-authored book, *Questions and Answers to Your Skin Problems,* I knew it wasn't enough to note one chapter heading as "Allergies." Here's the listing in the actual proposal:

Chapter 4. ALLERGIES AND RELATED PROBLEMS
Allergy Questionnaire. Allergy to Cosmetics. Food Allergy. Allergy to Drugs and Chemicals. Sensitivity to Detergents and Cleansers. Allergy to Various Materials. Allergy to Insect Bites. Miscellaneous Allergy Questions. Hives. Eczema. Poison Ivy.

Chapter listings and explanations convey two essential points to the editor and board: a) The scope of the book and that it will provide detailed information that readers need and want. b) The author knows the subject and will cover each facet fully. Some presentations require more chapter contents detail than others, as in the case of my book, *Your Key to Creative Thinking:*

Chapter 1. HOW THIS BOOK CAN MAKE YOU MORE CREATIVE
What is Creativity?
Proof that You Can Be More Creative.

AVOID-THE-OBVIOUS MENTAL-EXERCISE PUZZLERS

Since each chapter would include Practice Puzzlers of different types, I included some actual Puzzlers, some illustrated. My purpose was two-fold: to demonstrate exactly what a puzzler is, and to intrigue the editor as an individual. The presentation included a dozen actual puzzlers, of 82 planned for the book, such as this sample:

ANALYSIS PUZZLER: THE CASE OF THE MYSTERIOUS LETTER
The postmaster in a small town found this letter addressed with only these three words on the front:

WOOD
JOHN
MASS

What were the right name, city, state for delivery?
(Printed with other answers in back of book:)
ANSWER: The object is to analyze clearly why the three words were placed in that peculiar formation. Why is "JOHN" under "WOOD" and over "MASS."? Obviously:

JOHN UNDERWOOD
ANDOVER, MASS.

When the editor called to offer a contract, she said, "Those sample puzzlers helped sell us the book quickly. I tried them on my family. Their enjoyment clinched it for me." Proof that it pays to be innovative in your presentation. Just be sure that the attention-getting items make a pertinent point.

6. First chapter
The proof of the pudding is in the first chapter of your book. You can talk endlessly about the wonderful book you're *going* to write, but with a beginning writer in particular, the only validation for the publisher is the manuscript itself—one or more chapters. I usually present three chapters.

A would-be author complained to me, "That's an awful lot of work."

325

I agreed, "By the time I've listed chapter titles and contents, and written several chapters, about one-third of my work on the whole book is done. But I don't know whether the book will be worthy until I've done that much work. And if I don't believe in it enough to put in that extensive effort, how can I expect a publisher to have the faith to invest in my book?"

7. Special Promotional Power

Because of my background in business and advertising, I've always believed that it's up to me, along with the publisher, to promote my book. Therefore, I finish each book proposal with a short synopsis of my own special ability to promote the proposed book. I cite unique features which lend themselves to interviews on TV, radio, all media.

Get the evidence across in a few sentences, indicating that you're eager to help sell the book after it's published. Describe any visual material you can offer. You don't have to be an actress or a lecturer. If you have a background in teaching, that's a natural. Or mention speaking exposure as a club officer, active PTA member, salesperson, ability to instruct people verbally in your book subject.

Skip this section if you prefer—it's up to you. I've found it productive to include all the specific plusses embodied in the book project. They've definitely helped me get contracts.

8. The Covering Letter

In my experience, a book proposal must speak for itself—convincingly. No fancy binders. Just double-spaced loose pages, plus any exhibits, in a file folder. If your factual presentation doesn't confirm that your book is worth publishing, a ton of superlatives in a covering letter, or in your proposal, won't help, may turn off the editor. My covering letters are short and simple, for instance:

The proposal herewith for a new nonfiction book, *Reading Faces,* demonstrates its unique content and sales potential. Thank you for your kind attention and consideration. I trust that I may hear from you soon.

How long should a book proposal be? There is no set length. Keep it as short as you possibly can, making sure that every word is useful. Double-check to eliminate anything unnecessary. Include everything essential, holding the editor's attention by including only meaningful content.

This is all-important: You must grab and hook the editor's attention right in the first lines of your proposal. You do that by appealing to the editor's self-interest in finding a book that is a potential profit-maker or will benefit the publisher in specific ways. An example of an opening is the first paragraph of this article. I rewrote it repeatedly until I arrived at words that I believed would capture your self-interest and keep you reading.

Give the same essential attention and effort to the opening of the first paragraph of the first chapter of your book—which will be part of your presentation. I reworked again and again the opening lines of *The Complete Scarsdale Medical Diet* before submitting the proposal. It proved worthwhile—all part of formulating a blockbuster best seller. I compressed a long opening chapter to these few sentences (written in the person of the doctor):

I, personally, explain the Scarsdale Medical Diet's phenomenal popularity in two words: *"It works."* A slim, trim lady said to me recently, "Your diet is beautifully simple, and the results are simply beautiful." I just say, "It works."

After that grabber, do you think that an editor, or an overweight person, could stop reading?

The basic presentation structure I've set down here has worked repeatedly for me, and for others I've helped. My way is not the only way. If it doesn't suit your personal views, then do it your way, of course. You're an individual with your own ideas, your own focus, your own right to be yourself.

If your presentation is rejected, check it carefully again. If it appears right, submit it elsewhere. Even a superb presentation may be turned down by a particular publisher for reasons over which you have no control—such as not wanting *any* book on that subject. I kept resubmitting and writing, then sold some of my nonfiction books from complete manuscripts.

62

WHEN YOU NEED A NONFICTION IDEA

By Max Gunther

"WHERE do you get all your ideas?" This question has been thrown at me often in two decades of free-lance nonfiction writing, but until recently I wasn't very good at answering it. I could only mumble, "Oh, ideas just pop into my head. Who knows where an idea comes from?"

Today I think I have some more specific and satisfactory answers to offer. After finishing my fourteenth book some months ago, I decided to let my typewriter cool for a month or so. One thing I hoped to do in this restful time, if I could, was analyze the operation of my own brain and maybe organize it better. I asked myself: Where have your best ideas come from? If you want a hot book or article idea next year or in the next several years, where will you start looking?

I went back through my files to 1956, the year I sold my first free-lance effort to the old *Saturday Evening Post,* and tried to reconstruct the births and maturings of my favorite ideas. I couldn't remember every idea's beginning, but many came back to me with startling clarity. Whenever memory allowed, I jotted down what I was doing at the time the idea came to me, what the source was, what state of alertness or curiosity made me think, "Aha! Idea!" I've now put together a short list of rules that I will impose on myself when I next need an idea. Instead of waiting for ideas to come from nowhere, a nonfiction writer should:

1. *Talk to people.* Go out of your way to find them. Go to parties even though you hate parties. Go to school board meetings. Join bridge clubs. Sell greeting cards door-to-door. Talk to people who sit next to you on trains and planes, in diners, on park benches. Do anything that will get you into communication with other men and women.

Solitude is useful sometimes during the actual writing process, but as a means of generating ideas, it seems valueless. I honestly can't recall a single good idea that ever came to me while I was simply sitting or ambling around alone, staring into space.

Some of my most profitable ideas have sprung from conversations with other people. A remark by an acoustical engineer led to an article on the science of sound, which I sold to *Playboy*. A rambling talk with a television sales executive sowed the seed of a three-part *TV Guide* report on TV's problems with sex. A fellow I met casually started me on a mental journey that ended as *Instant Millionaires,* a Playboy Press book.

2. *Read newspapers hungrily.* Radio and TV news reports aren't nearly detailed enough. Only a newspaper can give you the depth, the background, the odd sidelights that can trigger a salable idea. A non-fiction writer should read at least one good, solid metropolitan paper every day, from front page to back, including obituaries and shipping news, and other material that might seem to be of only narrow interest.

A *New York Times* obit of an industrial inventor led me to the first article I ever sold to *True,* back in 1958. Over the next twelve years I was to sell well over a hundred more pieces to *True*—and, needless to say, I still read obits. Similarly, I plow through the *Times*'s food-and-fashion page and its national weather column every day, though neither section contains much that interests me personally. In the fashion section one day, I read an offhand reference that blossomed into a *Ladies' Home Journal* story on runaway wives, and an equally casual remark in the weather column became a *True* piece on scientific attempts to control weather.

3. *Read magazines* — not just those that attract you personally or those you hope to write for, but also the unfamiliar ones, the obscure ones, the ones that operate beyond your normal range of interests. By buying or scrounging an unfamiliar magazine and finding out what its editors and writers are thinking about these days, you can trigger fresh thoughts in your own head.

I don't normally read magazines that deal with money and investment, but one day on an airplane I borrowed a Wall Street trade journal from the fellow sitting next to me. Its letters-to-the-editor column contained a humorous note about a goofy new way to predict what the stock market will do, and a month later I sold *Playboy* a piece on oddball market-playing techniques. Similarly, I'm not a coin collector, but a magazine devoted to the hobby once gave me an idea for an article about gold, which I sold to *True.*

4. *Never scorn an idea because it is "publicity."* Nearly every big and medium-sized company, college, hospital and government agency has a publicity chief, usually called the news director or public relations director. This man's or woman's job is to get the organization favorably mentioned in the press. It is considered chic in some writers' circles to sneer at publicity people, on the ground that everything they say is self-serving. This attitude seems fairly dumb to me. Publicity may be self-serving, but it can also be interesting.

If you are an idea-hunting nonfiction writer, you should get to know the publicists in companies and institutions near you. They will gladly mail you news of their organizations and work. Listen to them with care; they may provide you with an idea for an article or a book.

A publicity man working for Johnson Wax, makers also of an insect repellent, gave me the idea for a *Travel & Leisure* story on mosquitoes. A college publicity woman planted the seed of a *Playboy* piece on the annual national campus manhunt in which businesses try to grab the brightest graduates. These publicists dealt with me because they hoped to get the product or college mentioned in print (which, in fact, happened). If I had refused to listen to them, I would have lost two sound ideas, not to mention two pleasantly hefty checks.

5. *Browse in books that aren't meant for browsing.* Spend an hour or two thumbing through some fact book like *The World Almanac* or an encyclopedia yearbook. Those columns of dry facts and figures look pretty dull to most people, but not to a writer hunting ideas. In these volumes you will find a wealth of information, greatly condensed, on what people are doing and thinking in the world today. Any of those statistics could sow the seed of an article or even book idea. An equally useful kind of browsing can be done in the yellow pages of any city phone book. The thousands of products and services

that are offered for sale there tell much about our society and its problems and dreams.

Leafing through a fact book in the library one morning, I was captivated by an odd little set of statistics dealing with highway accidents. According to these figures, there are more accidents on an average Saturday than on any weekday. This peculiar fact simmered in my head for a long time and finally led me to write a book. *The Weekenders,* published by Lippincott, studied what Americans do on weekends and why.

Many of my ideas have come from phone books. Thumbing through the yellow pages once in the mid-1960s, I saw a pest-control company's ad. This item became a *True* article on the centuries-long war of man against rat. About ten years later, in 1974, a rodenticide ad in another phone book made me think it was time to take a fresh look at the same subject. This new piece sold to *Today's Health.*

6. *Mine your own experiences.* You have done and are doing many things in your life that may seem dull and routinely familiar to you, but these same things may be interesting, even fascinating, to other people who aren't living with them every day. Your problem: if something seems mundane to you, how do you alert yourself to the possibility that the world might want to read about it?

We get back to what I said before about talking to everybody in sight. Your primary purpose in all these conversations is to be a listener, but a secondary purpose is to test other people's reactions to what is in your head. If you find people asking alert, interested questions about something you've said or done, ask yourself whether you've stumbled onto a potential nonfiction idea.

I lived with a good idea for fifteen years, never seeing it, until somebody else pointed it out to me. The somebody else was my wife. I had spent much of my spare time in those fifteen years trying to build a squirrel-proof bird feeder that really worked. One evening, after my umpteenth design had proved a failure, my wife and I spent an entertaining hour recalling all the other failures. Suddenly she said, "Why don't you preserve all this for posterity? Write an article about it!" She was right, of course. The thought had never occurred to me because squirrels and bird feeders had become too familiar to me, too much a part of my daily life. I sold the story, along with some pen-and-ink sketches, to *Travel & Leisure.*

Another salable idea, an article on office romances, stayed undiscovered by me in the same way for a long time, until a conversation with another person woke me up. For years a good friend of mine, a married man, had been carrying on a love affair with an unmarried woman in his office. The situation was giving him a lot of pain, and once in a while he would tell me about his feelings of guilt and helplessness. At a cocktail party one weekend, talking with a woman who had been involved in a similar experience, I tried to explain some theories about emotional bonds between men and women who work together. She looked at me archly and said, "You're writing an article about this, aren't you?" I hadn't been, but I knew instantly that I should have been. *Good Housekeeping* bought it.

63

WRITING THE PERSON-CENTERED MAGAZINE ARTICLE

By Crescent Dragonwagon

"I can teach anyone," says Crescent Dragonwagon, leaning back in her office chair, "how to write the kinds of magazine articles that readers will read and editors will buy." The oddly named young woman, bundled up in three or four sweaters on a cold January day, is the author of more than ten books for children and adults, as well as numerous magazine articles for publications, ranging from Cosmopolitan, McCall's *and* Seventeen, *to regional magazines like* Los Angeles Magazine, Arkansan, *and* Atlanta. *Pushing back from the kitchen table that serves as a desk in her comfortable office, Dragonwagon rises to place another log on the stack already burning in the fireplace. "Article writing is not that difficult," she says thoughtfully, sipping from a pottery mug that will be refilled with coffee ("my work drug") several times during our conversation. "Even when I interview my subjects I can feel a good story shaping up, I can feel which quotes are going to be usable where."*

But hasn't she been writing for many years? "Fifteen," she says. "Fifteen professionally, forever unprofessionally. But I still use the same basic techniques that I started with; I've just practiced them enough so they've become automatic by now." As if in agreement, the large calico cat that lies beside the fire bursts suddenly into loud purrs.

If I were not myself Crescent Dragonwagon, but another writer interviewing Crescent Dragonwagon on how to write magazine articles, this piece might not only have begun as above, it would have carried through in the same vein. That vein, as far as technique goes, is simply this: *Get to the idea(s) through the person (people) involved.* In this case, the idea would be "How to write magazine articles," and the person would be Crescent Dragonwagon, just as, in a recent article I did, the idea was "How to find and recognize southern antiques," and the person was Deanne Levisson, a passionate collector and dealer in southern antiques. Our imaginary author would have taken you, the reader, through an explanation of why Crescent Dragonwagon believes that "the person in the article is always important," that "the writer has to know the person to be able to reveal the person to the reader," and that "revelation of the person is best done through dialogue, anecdotes, and brief description." By the end of the article, you would not only have learned something about magazine writing, you would have learned something about Crescent Dragonwagon: what she had for lunch, what pictures hang in her office, how she looks and dresses and sounds and gestures.

But what does what I had for lunch have to do with how I write magazine articles? If writing magazine articles is the point of our imaginary piece, why would our fictitious author deviate from that point?

Because our fictitious author—let's call her a she—wants to get you to *read her article*. And she knows that to do that she has to get you hooked, interested, involved, which can be most easily accomplished through the revelation of a real, live, perhaps slightly eccentric person. Now you may be wildly fascinated by how to write articles. But the average Jane or Joe is not. Take it as a general rule: Virtually *all* highly readable magazine articles are "human interest." Because we're human, human beings interest us, and the writer who writes for general-interest magazines must know and use this simple fact. You know the way a particular, very ill child will grab public attention through media exposure: the seven unsuccessful operations for the rare blood disease, the loving parents now $250,000 in debt, the father laid off for spending too much time away from his job, the baffled specialists, the small brave child fighting for life despite the odds? If, in the light of such a story in the papers, on the radio, on television, donations of blood are requested, you can bet that *thousands* of pints of blood will be received, far more than the individual child could possibly use. Yet how many of these generous donors give blood as a matter of course for general use in stocking blood banks, although this also helps people in need? But *those* people are anonymous, unknown. Only when the emotions are involved through the description of a particular child's case, a case described by the media in wrenching, painful, personal detail, do most people feel moved enough to take action and give blood.

334

Writers ask people to take action: to become readers by paying attention, engaging their minds, turning pages, blocking out distraction. To get a reader to take action, the writer must move and involve, and with rare exceptions, the best way is through the specific person who can humanize your story best, or *a* specific person, or people, whom you choose. If you want to write about the critically low shortage of reserves of blood in blood banks, it's up to you to go out and *find* that child who's suffering because of that shortage. Write about how the blood shortage affects her and her family. Then move to the general issue, from and through the specifics of one person.

How do you *find* the person behind the story? First, every writer should have antennae out at all times, and naturally each writer will gravitate toward particular types of articles. For example, on a personal level I am deeply concerned about nuclear proliferation and its dangers (for, I feel, on this issue rests all other matters, even magazine-article writing, since magazine pieces are neither read nor written by extinct species). Yet, as a writer, I know that "nuclear proliferation" per se is too large and abstract an issue for a writer like me (non-technical, general interest, non-scientific) to take on. At a barely conscious level, I had my radar out for *my* kind of nuclear story—as I have my radar going for my kind of story on anything that interests, troubles, moves, or amuses me. When I heard an Arkansas housewife address a group of church and garden club members in a town of 1,200 about how close the world is to nuclear holocaust; when, on that perfectly ordinary sunny morning in mid-America where the coffee was steaming and the plates of cookies waiting for post-meeting munching; when, on that morning, I looked around and saw tears in the eyes of most of the women in that room, I was not so blinded by my own tears that I failed to recognize that I had found "my" nuclear story. Titled "I Couldn't Just Sit Around and Wring My Hands," my profile of this housewife, Betty Bumpers, appeared in *McCall's*.

Another personal interest, holistic health, led me to do a column called Body/Mind for *Arkansan,* a regional magazine. In looking for a person to place "behind" the overdone topic of stress, I found an engaging, articulate doctor, who had himself suffered from stress-related illness. In profiling him, I made the topic of stress fresh and interesting for readers.

At other times, I simply happen onto interesting events, places, that demand an article, though they do not reflect my personal concerns. Almost invariably the person or people "behind" such stories are self-evident. I stopped at Banta's Apple Orchard and Pie Shop in Alpena, Arkansas, every time I drove from Little Rock to my then-home, Eureka Springs. Banta's was a natural for *Arkansan,* and Frieda and Ralph Banta were naturally the people I angled it through. When, on another occasion, I randomly selected MPG Car Rentals out of the Los Angeles phone book because I wanted to lease a small car (which their ad promised) and I learned I was MPG's *first customer,* again, a magazine nonfiction piece was natural. When I learned that MPG's founder Jules Lederer was not only the founder of Budget Rent-a-Car but also the advice columnist Ann Landers's former husband, an article (through Jules) was inevitable. That piece—entitled "Dear Ann Landers: I Want to Rent a Car with High MPG"—appeared in *Los Angeles Magazine.*

Having found the person behind the story, how do you reveal him or her to the reader? First, you spend time with him or her. How to conduct a good interview is a whole other article, but, basically, you draw your subject out, you listen, you do not try to impress with your erudite wisdom but ask basic, even *dumb* questions. You want responses in *their own* words. And frequently, *frequently,* you say, "Could you give me a specific example?" or "Do you remember anything in particular from that period?" For it is through specificity more than anything else that the person becomes alive.

Specificity means getting your subject's syntax down; specificity means being precise. An article without specificity is as bland as tapioca pudding without sugar, salt, and vanilla. A tapioca-bland example: "Business was slow in the early days of Banta's Orchard." A hundred times more flavorful: " 'Back in our first years,' recalls Frieda Banta, 'we really thought we'd set the world a-fire if we sold two pies in a day.' " Rarely should an author say something in his or her own voice if the subject has said it with passion, vehemence, humor, or regional syntax. Quote rather than state whenever possible.

Specificity also means using anecdotes, small stories within a story, preferably told at least in part in the first person by the person you've selected to be "behind" the story. Consider the lead of the stress article referred to earlier:

Dr. Ken Goss, professor and Chairman of the Department of Family and Community Medicine at University of Arkansas for Medical Sciences, likes to use this example with his students: "Say that three patients come into the emergency room, each with a simple, one-inch, uncomplicated skin laceration, a surface wound. The first cut himself in his workshop; he was whittling and the knife slipped. The second was attacked by his spouse. And the third was a suicide attempt. Same physical problem. Do you treat the three of them the same way?"

Here's the Betty Bumpers article lead:

In the early summer of 1981, Betty Bumpers, wife of Arkansas Senator Dale Bumpers, was driving back home from Washington, D.C., when her 19-year-old daughter Brooke asked a question. "Mother, if we—this country—had a nuclear disaster, and our family somehow managed to survive it, where would we all meet afterwards?"

Occasionally you will hear a great anecdote that doesn't really fit the chronology of your nonfiction piece as a lead. If it's good enough, use it anyway; then flash back or move forward from the time of the anecdote. How do you know if an anecdote is worth the extra trouble and skill it will take to double back chronologically? Well, when you were interviewing your subject, did you laugh or smile when you heard that little story? Did you say, "Ah, ah," or lean forward in your chair, or exclaim, "You're kidding! *Really?*" If *you* were interested, your reader will be, too.

Even when you must use your own voice, try to intersperse it with quotes from your subject, and—unless you are a well-known writer whose opinions people have some reason to be interested in—*use your voice in sensuous, precise description, rather than analytically.* By this I mean, describe *briefly* what you see, taste, hear, touch, smell; since the reader is possessed of sense organs, this is the way to put him or her right there. If done right, this adds great immediacy to a piece. From "Low Calories and High Cuisine," the profile of Chef Paul Bash, this second paragraph sets the scene:

. . . Wine is being measured, steel gray stoves and ovens are heating, sauces are being whisked, lettuces rinsed, onions sauteed in butter. Delectable and somehow clean, ungreasy cooking odors permeate the air. A huge roast, tied with string, lies in state, raw and ready, waiting to be seasoned and baked. In the pastry kitchen, sugar is being measured by the quart, chocolate melted, cream whipped, for today's Brandy Alexander Pie.

In articles about writing for magazines, I've noticed that while the lead is frequently mentioned, the end of a piece often gets short shrift. The vast majority of good articles, though not all of them, are in some way circular. The last paragraph or sentence in some way connects with the lead or sums up the entire article. In a piece about garden club members learning to do political lobbying on environmental issues, for instance, I began with the following:

"Everyone has this image of garden club members as little old ladies in tennis shoes," says Verna Brimm, 63, conservative chairman of the DeKalb Federation of Garden Clubs in Georgia. "Well, we are, we are! But that doesn't mean we aren't aware of the large environmental issues that affect all of us, such as clean air and safe disposal of nuclear waste. We *are* aware . . . and we care, intensely."

I ended with the following:

"Many women love our planet, and love is one resource that will be exhausted only if we forget to use it. Well, we won't forget. We women can move mountains! When we do our best, angels can do no better." She smiles delicately. "Yes, we're pushing back the horizons of those little old ladies in tennis shoes!"

"Some call this method of article writing 'semifictional,'" says Dragonwagon, by now warm enough to have shed several of her layers. "And it's true that many of the techniques I use—direct quotes, anecdotes, brief sensuous description, having the ending circle back to the beginning—are also techniques used in writing fiction; certainly I use them in my novels. But 'semi-fiction' is misleading, since articles of this type, when well done, are far more realistic, more factual in the way they present information, than the more abstract, impersonal, fact-on-fact kind, which are rarely even published any more. Life does not proceed abstractly; everything we get involved in, even the most abstract issues, we get at through people somewhere down the line. I'd call this style, perhaps, 'naturalistic,' except, of course, the writer works for this sense of naturalness."

Once again Dragonwagon rises, fills her coffee cup for the third time, and kneels by the fire. She turns an intense face, lit on one side by the flames (for it is now growing dark outside the office) and strokes the cat. "I hope that gives you enough for your article," she says. "I've got to get back to my own work now." The cat, as if she's heard this before, yawns deeply.

338

64

SO, YOU WANT TO BE SYNDICATED?

By Ann Ferrar

Jack Anderson. Abigail Van Buren. Jimmy Breslin. Erma Bombeck. Rex Reed. Ann Landers. Chances are that some of these by-lines appear in your local newspaper—and in mine.

These syndicated columnists are free lancers with steady markets and regular checks in their mailboxes.

Almost anyone can become syndicated—just as almost anyone can grow up to be President. The syndicated market may be as hard to crack as a set of brass knuckles, but people *do* break in.

Who ever heard of Martin Sloane before his "Supermarket Shopper" column appeared in papers across the country only a few years ago? Sloane, a former real estate lawyer, was burdened with the task of food shopping when his wife had to visit an ill relative. Overwhelmed by the confusing array of refund offers, Sloane grouped his coupons into categories. He saved so much money through organization that he abandoned his law practice and founded a refunding magazine for consumers.

David Hendin, editorial director of United Feature Syndicate, was looking for a refunding column. Sloane approached Hendin, and within six months the syndicate's sales force sold the column to some four hundred newspapers. Sloane receives thousands of letters each month from readers. He's had a book published and a radio program, both as a result of the column.

Sloane's story is proof that you don't have to be a Pulitzer Prize-winning writer to be a syndicated columnist. All you need is a hot idea with national appeal, one that's strikingly original enough to grab editors, but not so off-the-wall that it makes them doubtful of its salability.

If this sounds like a "Catch-22" situation, you're absolutely right. Newspaper editors are generally a conservative lot and, according to

339

Hendin, they don't like to risk a new feature unless everyone else is buying it.

"In today's economy," he says, "the chances of getting a column (or comic strip or puzzle) into 200 newspapers are not good, and a syndicate isn't likely to keep a feature that makes mediocre sales. We get thousands of submissions each year, but if we introduce four new comics and two or three new text features a year, that's a lot."

What kind of material do syndicates need? Everything that the average paper needs: news and topical items, human interest features, personality profiles, entertainment, humor, travel, fillers, practical how-to's and advice, cartoons, puzzles.

The larger syndicates usually avoid esoteric material—there is little room for poetry, mood pieces, or fiction in such a commercially oriented market. There are hundreds of smaller syndicates, though, that handle columns on a wide range of specialized subjects—sewing, rock music, religion, women, gardening, minority interests, automobiles, travel, humor. Some even distribute business-related items to trade magazines.

If you're not already a newspaper addict, become one. Read as many papers as your library has on file—both large-city and small-town papers. Notice what recurring columns they use and look for informational voids.

Martin Sloane's "Supermarket Shopper" column fills a gap. He doesn't give recipes or discuss the dangers of food preservatives, since this information can be found elsewhere. His angle—making sense of the maze of refund offers—zeroes in on a major need in these inflationary times: getting bargains at the supermarket.

If you seriously want to write a continuing column (or create a puzzle or comic strip), choose a topic you know and love—something you'd feel comfortable specializing in and writing about week after week after week. Ask yourself if you'd be able to deliver your column consistently on deadline. (You can't keep a hundred papers waiting.) Could you continue to come up with original ideas? What happens if you become bored with your chosen topic? Would your writing turn stale?

Even if you satisfy yourself on these questions, don't expect to breeze into a syndicate office and walk out with a contract if you have no credentials at all. The best route is to get yourself established in a

340

local newspaper first. There's no stronger argument than tearsheets of your published work to convince wary syndicate editors that other papers might be interested in your writing, too. If you're pitching a continuing column, submit five or six samples so editors can judge how well you sustain your topic. Needless to say, a national syndicate won't touch local or regional subject matter. And don't bother submitting political commentary, medical or psychological advice unless you have a substantial background in these areas.

There are basically five ways to get syndicated:

(1) *The larger syndicates* (United Feature Syndicate, King Features Syndicate, Universal Press Syndicate, and Field Newspaper Syndicate are a few) distribute mostly continuing columns, comic strips, and puzzles, on a contract basis. They usually split the profits 50-50 with the creator, though some companies give big-name writers a larger percentage. The pay per column depends on the number of papers that buy your work. An unknown columnist may earn as little as a few dollars per column in the beginning. Unless you're a big-name writer or your idea really takes off, you will never get rich in syndication.

In exchange for splitting the profits, the syndicate handles all the selling and promotion of your material. Though you'll only be earning half, chances are your work will appear in a far greater number of papers than you could reach on your own, so the 50-50 split is worth it.

The large syndicates often buy all the rights to your column, cartoon, or puzzle, which means that if you decide to change syndicates, they can hire someone else to continue your original creation.

If you can't sell your idea to a large syndicate, try the smaller ones. But be aware that smaller operations don't have the facilities to promote your column that the big ones do.

(2) *Feature services* (such as Newspaper Enterprise Association) distribute columns, puzzles, and comics in "packages." You will usually receive a fixed rate per column, on contract. The rate may not depend on the number of papers that use your work; unknown writers should expect to start quite low.

(3) *Self-syndication*—a last resort if you cannot break in any other way—is an arduous task, not for the weak-willed. You have to be a

341

crackerjack salesperson, because you'll be doing all the selling and promotion. There's a lot of "busy work" and expense involved—making photocopies, stuffing envelopes, mailing samples and negotiating individual contracts with each newspaper, all of which can take considerable time away from your creative endeavors.

Milton Rockmore left an established syndicate in order to distribute his column, "View from the Top," on his own. He felt the legwork involved in going solo was worth the trouble because he didn't have to split his profits with anyone.

"The syndicate's salesman may represent thirty or forty columnists," he says. "They'll push the big names, but they may not reach into their sample bag to pull you out. Beyond the initial promotion needed to launch a new column, a big syndicate may not continue to promote you." But, he adds, "if you can't take rejection, forget self-syndication."

Rockmore kept at it for 11 years, building a clientele of about sixty newspapers. But success took its toll when he started a second column, "How to Make Extra Money." It caught on so well that Rockmore had to drop "View from the Top" and turn distribution of "How to Make Extra Money" over to the Register and Tribune Syndicate in Des Moines, Iowa. "Self-syndication is an 18-hour-a-day job," he admits. "I simply needed more time to do other things."

Robert Yoakum, a self-syndicator who writes a three-times-a-week topical humor column, left the Los Angeles Times Syndicate after a disagreement over the editing of his column. (Depending on who you are and how good your writing is, you might be able to negotiate a "no-editing" clause in your contract.

Yoakum advises against self-syndicating now, since costs are sky-high and many papers demand camera-ready or "scanner" copy. Certain IBM and Sperry-Remington typewriters, used with special typewriter elements, can produce copy that can be fed or "scanned" into a newspaper's electronic editing system via AP or UPI wires. This necessitates having a video display terminal installed in your home and linked to one of the wire systems—quite a costly project.

"The newspaper industry is in a transition phase," says Yoakum. "If Mark Twain were writing a column now, nobody would buy it unless it came in on the computer. . . . This is hurtful to small operators and will probably cut down on diversity."

(4) There is also a market for one-shot features (as opposed to continuing columns) and article series at some syndicates and news services, such as Independent News Alliance and Los Angeles Times Syndicate. It's exactly the same as free-lancing for magazines, except that the writer's individual feature (or series) would appear in newspapers across the country. You're paid a fixed rate for individual pieces, on a free-lance basis; no contract is involved.

(5) Many syndicates are on the lookout for good books that can be excerpted or serialized in newspapers. The syndicate editors do the actual excerpting; the author and/or publisher approve the final draft. How-to books, biographies of famous persons, and contemporary lifestyle books are among those most commonly excerpted. The publisher or agent might bring the book to the attention of the syndicate and try to get it excerpted or serialized.

Is trying to break into syndication worth the effort? According to Robert Yoakum, "It's an exhilarating experience if you succeed." Martin Sloane puts it even more enthusiastically: "It's inspiring to write a syndicated column, because of all the mail you get. I've had letters from people who've said my column has helped them save so much money that they couldn't feed their family any other way. When I get responses like that, it's worth it, even if I have to stay up till three in the morning to get the column out."

Begin by consulting the reference shelves in your public library. *The Writer* and *The Writer's Handbook* list a selected number of syndicates and give a complete picture of the type of material syndicates use.

Working Press of the Nation has a comprehensive list of syndicates, along with the names of their writers and cartoonists and the names of their columns and comic strips. This information is indispensable for informing you what *not* to submit. (If a particular syndicate already distributes "Travel Whirl," don't send it travel material.)

Syndicated Columnists, a book by Richard Weiner available at some libraries, tells who creates what for whom.

Editor & Publisher Syndicate Directory, Editor and Publisher Yearbook, and *The Literary Market Place* list the names and addresses of just about every syndicate outlet under the sun.

If you'd like to try self-syndication, check *Ayer Directory of Publications, Editor and Publisher Yearbook,* and *The Literary Market Place* for newspaper chains and individual daily and weekly papers throughout the country.

65

ARTICLE OUTLINES BRING SALES

By William E. Miles

"Put it before them briefly so they will read it, clearly so they will appreciate it, picturesquely so they will remember it and, above all, accurately so they will be guided by its light."

Give Joseph Pulitzer a prize for this nearly century-old advice to reporters! Although the publisher of the New York *World* was referring to newspaper stories, his remarks are just as applicable today to magazine article outlines. Brevity, clarity, color, accuracy—that's the gift-wrapping of the package you are inviting an editor to open when you submit an outline of a subject you hope will spark his interest in your article.

An outline should be kept as short as possible, preferably one page single-spaced. Sometimes, of course, the subject demands more detailed explanation—but try not to let it exceed two pages. Within this framework, fill it with enough colorful facts and figures to catch the editor's eye and indicate the authenticity of the material.

Typed on a separate page or pages, the outline should be accompanied by a brief covering letter and sufficient return postage. A sample covering letter might read like this: "Would you be interested in taking a speculative look at a 2,000-word article on the order of the attached outline? My articles have been published in . . ." (naming some of the magazines you have sold to or listing whatever other qualifications you may have). Then, paper-clipped to the covering letter, the outline itself. For example:

Pranks for the Memory

Practical jokes are probably so-called because they are practically never a joke to the victim—who often winds up on something funny as a crutch. Even Mark Twain, an inveterate practical joker much of his life, confessed in his later years that he "held the practical joker in limitless contempt."

The late Bennett Cerf, another humorist who held practical jokers "in low esteem," once waxed particularly indignant over the dirty trick perpetrated on a Chicago bridegroom. After passing out at a bachelor party, he awakened to find his right arm in a cast. His fun-loving friends told him he had broken it in a brandy-inspired brawl—forcing him to spend his entire honeymoon with a perfectly good arm in a painfully tight cast.

Such practical jokers, according to Cerf, are "under no circumstances to be confused with humorists." But American history, dating back to pre-Revolutionary War days, is filled with hundreds of other examples of more harmless exercises in hilarity that don't deserve the harshness of his critical verdict.

One of the earliest of these was conceived by General Israel Putnam, a hero of the French and Indian War, after being challenged to a duel by a British army officer. Putnam selected as his choice of weapons two powder kegs into which he bored holes and inserted slow fuses. When the fuses burned down to an inch of the kegs, the British officer beat a hasty retreat—from barrels filled with onions!

But some practical jokes turn out to be really practical—as in the case of a "green" engineer at the General Electric plant who was assigned by old-timers as a prank the "impossible" job of frosting light bulbs on the inside. Marvin Pipkin not only found a way but, at the same time, devised a method of strengthening the bulbs so they would last much longer—cutting the cost to consumers in half!

An article of mine, based on this outline, appeared in *Elks Magazine*.

If this makes the outline approach to article sales sound easy, it isn't. An outline is only the bare bones of an article and no skeleton key guaranteed to unlock all editorial doors. For every idea that clicks, you may receive a dozen or more rejections. And sometimes the article itself is rejected after the outline has received a speculative O.K. For one reason or another, the article may just not live up to its billing.

But whether it does or not, outlines are not only attention-getters, but time-savers. A complete article can take a month or so to research and write and another month or so languishing in editorial offices awaiting a decison. An outline, on the other hand, requires only cursory research—enough to establish an intriguing lead and some supporting information. Only after the "go-ahead" (if you get it) do you need to start researching the subject in depth.

Editors also answer queries far more rapidly than they return articles—so even a rejection has its bright side. If the query is turned down, you've saved yourself unnecessary work in more ways than one. When outlines are returned, as they usually are, there's no retyping involved (except for another covering letter), if you decide to try elsewhere.

Another important aspect of an outline is that an editor, who likes the general idea, may have some suggestions of his own as to how he'd like it

346

handled. An article I sold to *The Lion* is a good example of this. My original idea was to take a swipe at juries because of the way they were influenced by clever lawyers (and sometimes their own ignorance) into returning strange, far-out verdicts. I had no solutions to the problems in mind when I submitted the following outline to the editor:

THE TROUBLE WITH JURIES

FBI statistics show that 90 out of every 100 murderers are arrested, 50 receive some sort of punishment, and two are sentenced to death. This means that almost half of all accused killers are acquitted after their mandatory trials by jury in cases of first degree murder—presumably the guilty as well as the innocent.

This assumption was borne out by an investigation of the jury system in Pennsylvania which disclosed some juries had reached their verdicts by drawing straws or flipping coins. Other jurors were found to have rushed through their deliberations in order to get to a dance or a lodge meeting on time.

Although Thomas Jefferson described juries as "the best of all safeguards for the person, the property and the reputation of every individual," many legal experts regard them as outmoded relics in this modern age. Trial by jury stems from trial by oath in which the accused, swearing to his innocence, was supported by twelve "oath-helpers," or compurgators, who attested to their belief in his statements. This "jury of peers" was intimately acquainted with the defendant and the circumstances of the alleged crime. But in our day, as Dr. Joseph Catton points out, an attempt is made to select persons who know *nothing* about the offense. "There are those who believe," he adds wryly, "that today's jurors know nothing about anything."

Other criminologists contend that a modern jury is generally made up of persons unfamiliar with the law who often miss the significance of technical rulings by the judge. Even in cases where court rulings are simple and understandable, the jury sometimes ignores them. There is one actual case on record in which members of the jury, disregarding the evidence and the judge's charge, all knelt in prayer—and came up with a verdict!

The editor replied: "I'd be happy to consider your article 'The Trouble with Juries' with one important condition. I'd like to see the piece conclude with some constructive recommendations from authorities on how the jury system could be improved and/or replaced by better systems."

Further research incorporated his suggestions into the article whose whole thrust was changed, including the lead, when it appeared in *The Lion* under the new title, "Of Juries and Judgments."

The lead (aside from the idea) is probably the most important part of an outline, because it's the first thing to attract an editor's eye. One good means of accomplishing this is to tie it to a particular city or state even though the actual subject matter may range far afield. Here's an outline with just such a lead that resulted in a sale to the *Chicago Tribune Magazine:*

Chicago's long history of accomplishments includes the honor of being the first city to introduce what some engineering experts have called one of the ten most complex and ingenious inventions of the past hundred years. Back in 1893 it put the "zip" in the zipper when a sample of the original slide fastener was placed on display at Chicago's Columbian Exposition for use by the Fair's hootchie-kootchie dancer, Little Egypt, as a rapid skirt-release.

But it was the zipper, not the stripper, that caught the eye of a visitor to the Fair—Colonel Louis Walker of Meadville, Pa.—and he hired the inventor, Whitcomb L. Judson, to improve his original patent on a "locker or unlocker for automatically engaging or disengaging an entire series of clasps by a single continuous movement."

After years of experimentation, the device was finally perfected in 1913 and, four years later, a Brooklyn tailor made the fastener famous by attaching it to money belts which he sold to sailors at the Brooklyn Navy Yard. The Navy itself was soon using the fastener on flying suits. And during the depression, a dress company tried out the novelty as a sales booster—taking the industry by storm. Soon the zipper's long story of "ups and downs" was over. Its slide to success had begun!

Leads come in all shapes and sizes and there are dozens of other ways of writing that all-important first paragraph whose purpose is to sell a particular editor on a particular idea. For instance, the "striking statement" lead:

Lightning, the silent partner of thunder, has frightened more people—and killed fewer—than any other common danger. In fact, your chances of being killed by a lightning bolt are one in a million.

The editor liked this outline lead well enough to keep it intact when my article "Striking Down Lightning Myths" was published in *Wheels Afield*.

Another editorial eye-opener is the "news peg" approach—tying the article to a current happening or upcoming event—or the "anniversary angle" like this outline lead for my article "Meters By The Mile" that appeared in *The Rotarian* more years ago than I care to remember:

Ten years ago last October 1,500 parking meters went on trial in New York City. They were immediately found guilty by protesting motorists who charged that they interfered with their constitutional privileges of life, liberty and the pursuit of free parking space . . .

But why go on? The point is that, varied as they were, all of these leads had one thing in common—an ability to grab the editor's attention and keep him reading. From these examples, you can see that I like to write a lead (and sometimes an ending) that will be used more or less "as is" in the finished article if the outline receives an editorial O.K.

This gives the editor a good idea of what to expect—not only of the subject but of the style in which it will be written. For an outline must persuade the editor that you not only have a good idea, but possess the ability to handle it well.

66

THE MARKET FOR TRADE JOURNAL ARTICLES

By Dana K. Cassell

ARE you looking for a market area that welcomes the newcomer, that is insatiable in its demand for articles, columns, and photos, that numbers in the thousands of existing publications? There is such a market—the trade journal field.

To give you an idea of the size of the trade journal market, the Standard Rate & Data Service volume of consumer magazines *and* farm publications numbers approximately 700 pages, while its companion volume of business publications is over 1,500 pages.

And because many trade journals operate with small staffs, they depend on free-lance writers for much of their material. In the years I've been writing for trade journals, I've noticed that the majority of editors handle their own correspondence and send personal replies to queries and manuscript submissions. This is especially encouraging to the newcomer.

Trade journals are magazines aimed at people in a particular type of business (*Drug Topics* for drugstore owners, *Southern Motor Cargo* for trucking companies); or at people engaged in a particular profession/job area within a company (*Visual Merchandising* for store designers and display managers, *Employee Relations Bulletin* for personnel managers).

When you study market listings, you'll find that trade journals use virtually every type of material, from how-to and humor, to interviews and personal experience—and everything in between. But the two most needed types of articles—and the easiest entree for the newcomer to the field—are business profiles and how-to articles.

Trade journal readers are interested in finding out how to make more money, save more money, sell more products, cut expenses, or solve a business problem. Technically, the business profile (sometimes referred to as a "case history") qualifies as a how-to, because it tells how a particular business or a specific person did something to make more money, save more money, etc.

Don't worry if *you* don't know how to do all these things. In truth, most professional business writers have little or no background in many of the areas they write about. What they do is locate the people who *do* know, "pick their brains," then put what they've learned down on paper in an interesting and informative article.

Although you don't need an M.B.A. degree to write for the trade journal field, you do need a pro-business attitude. If you begrudge every nickel in profits that business owners make, you'd better stay away from trade journal writing. You will never be able to tell readers convincingly how to realize even more profits without having your disdain show through. A good trade journal writer finds business fascinating and gets excited whenever he or she uncovers a new or different way to market a product, display merchandise, or improve productivity.

What you also need is the ability to write tightly and concisely. There is no room in a trade journal article for flowery phrases that do not impart any real information. The business owners and managers who read trade journal articles don't have much time to read magazines, they want to get to the meat of the article immediately and absorb the information within a few minutes.

If you want to attract the attention of an editor, both your queries and your completed manuscripts should get right to the point, and say what you have to say. Most trade journal articles run between 1,500 and 2,000 words; many are closer to 1,000 words.

This is not to say that business writing has to be dull or mundane. In fact, the process of tightening your writing will probably tend to improve it. You'll find yourself using more powerful verbs instead of adjectives and adverbs; more precise nouns rather than words of explanation.

The quickest route to publication in this field is to come up with a good idea, query the editor, then research and write the article.

You'll find ideas for trade journal articles in the same places you find ideas for any other type of article: newspapers, magazines, seminars, watching, listening, past experience, etc. One business writer stated that he can easily make $300 to $400 by just walking through a shopping center, making notes, and writing articles on the business operations he finds going on there.

What you should look for are different and/or successful methods of advertising, displaying merchandise, hiring/training employees, communicating to employees or customers, merchandising, building repeat customers, protecting profit, and increasing profit and efficiency. Here are three examples of ideas I picked up from three different sources.

1. *Newspapers.* A short (8 column inches) UPI article in a local newspaper about policemen who had been turned loose in a department store with orders to shoplift everything they could. The experiment was to alert local retailers to how easy it is to get away with extensive shoplifting. The three officers made off with $459.00 worth of merchandise, including an outboard motor.

I immediately recognized a trade journal article idea here on how to stop shoplifters, which I eventually sold in various different forms, for a total of over $1,500.

2. *Magazines.* Skimming through a sample copy of a trade journal, I came across a filler item which stated that the Small Business Administration had released the results of a survey on why customers stop patronizing a particular store or business. One statistic, that 68 per cent leave because of the attitude of indifference by an employee, prompted the article, "Coping with Employee Indifference."

3. *Personal observation.* While talking to the husband-wife owners of a local craft store, I discovered that when they had bought the store four years earlier, it had been half its size, resulting in a jumbled mess of merchandise. By doubling the store area, they were able to organize their displays, widen aisles to aid the handicapped in wheelchairs, and install a play area for infants and toddlers to use while mothers shopped. The reorganization of displays had reduced their shoplifting losses! Here was information of interest to other craft store owners. It appeared in *Profitable Craft Merchandising* as a store profile stressing interior display arrangement and store expansion vs. relocating.

Each of these article ideas was sold as the result of a query letter. A good query letter will immediately interest the editor so that he wants to hear more. The need to hook the editor is as important as hooking the reader in the article itself. For this reason, 90 per cent of my opening paragraphs in query letters will end up being the lead paragraphs in the articles themselves.

Here's the actual query letter that I sent to *Modern Jeweler,* to sell them on my idea of a piece on shoplifting:

Editor
Modern Jeweler
7950 College Blvd.
Shawnee Mission, KS 66201

Dear Editor:

Three policemen dressed in plain clothes were recently turned loose in a Titusville, Florida, department store with orders to shoplift everything they could get their hands on, preferably the most expensive items. The local police chief saw it as a scheme to alert stores in the area to how easy it is to get away with extensive shoplifting.

In a total of one hour's work spread over two days, they made off with $459 worth of merchandise including an outboard motor, bowling ball, sleeping bags, coffee maker, and several men's shirts. None of the men was challenged as they plundered the store.

This experiment only accented the shoplifting statistics nationwide. Approximately $12,000,000 worth of merchandise is shoplifted from retail stores each selling day. And some of the items hit hardest are jewelry and watches due to their resale value and desire by lower income groups. The cost to store owners has reached such proportions that it has been recognized as a contributing factor in some bankruptcies.

With this in mind, I am currently preparing an article tentatively titled, "How to Stop Shoplifters." My sources include law enforcement officials, retail store managers, and crime prevention studies. I believe the information will be invaluable to readers of *Modern Jeweler.*

With your permission, I would like to submit the completed article to you on speculation. If you desire additional information, I can provide an expanded outline; and any helpful comments you may have will be appreciated. I could deliver a completed manuscript in approximately one month. Interested?

Cordially,
DANA K. CASSELL

Research methods and approaches

1. My first step in the shoplifting piece was to write to the U.S. Department of Commerce for a listing of their available publications, from which I was able to obtain all kinds of statistics and background information on shoplifting. Since government publications are not copyrighted, the material was free to use in return for crediting its source.

If I had stopped here—even though I had plenty of material for an article—it probably would not have sold because it would have been too dry. What editors and readers want are quotes and anecdotes to liven up the piece. So I telephoned a number of jewelers to ask them about their shoplifting experiences and how they combatted the problem. These quotes helped focus the article and made it of more specific interest to readers.

There followed a few more phone calls to area police officers and private security companies for their expert opinion on how retailers can cut down on shoplifting losses. A couple of them came across with some interesting and pertinent anecdotes.

2. For the article on why customers leave companies, I relied almost completely on phone interviews with craft retailers around the country. I looked up their numbers in the Yellow Pages (you can find telephone books from all areas of the country at your library or telephone company business office), then called and asked for the owner or manager. When I had him or her on the line, I stated my name, that I was a free-lance writer doing an article for *Profitable Craft Merchandising,* and asked them a few questions relating to steps they took to eliminate employee apathy.

To their answer I added additional tips and suggestions on the subject found in a booklet published by the Small Business Administration. The SBA is an excellent source of business information, available free or at a nominal cost. Contact your regional office for a list.

3. The profile on the couple who enlarged their store necessitated on-location research. I made an appointment with the owners and went to see them. For the next hour, I talked to them about the changes they had made and why, and noted the results of those changes. Store profiles also require photos to illustrate points made in the article, so I took a roll of 35-mm exposures on Tri-X b/w film.

Writing a trade journal article isn't much different from doing any other type of article. You still have to catch the reader's attention in the opening paragraphs, state your premise, use your research (statistics, quotes and anecdotes) to prove that premise, include as much helpful how-to information as possible, and then bring it all to a satisfactory conclusion.

Trade journals pay from 1¢ a word to $500 per article, though most pay about $100. The shorter length and crisper style will allow you to complete two to three business articles in the same time you would spend producing one long article for the general consumer market, which would pay $250 to $300.

Since many different types of businesses have the same problems but read different trade publications, you can often reuse your basic research material with changes in focus and slant. It is not unusual for a good solid trade journal idea to earn between $1,000 to $2,000 from sales of various pieces using different slants.

The trade journal market can bring the writer a good return for time and effort put into it, and the sheer numbers of publications plus the cooperation of its editors, make it an excellent target for the free-lance article writer.

67

GETTING IMPOSSIBLE-TO-GET INTERVIEWS

By Dennis E. Hensley

DOLLY PARTON, Charles Kuralt, Jeanne Wolf, Emmylou Harris, Andy Griffith, Harry Mark Petrakis, Joyce DeWitt—I can hardly count the number of interviews I conducted last year. I do interviewing almost exclusively. The personality profile sells quickly and for good money. Besides, it's a fascinating specialty.

The trouble is, a lot of other good writers do interviews, too. It's a wide-open market. For steady sales, I've had to be the first reporter to interview a person about a new topic (which isn't as *easy* as you may think), or I've had to get interviews with people who are supposedly impossible to talk with (which isn't as *hard* as you may think).

Of the hundreds of interviews I've conducted in the last ten years, four particular ones stand out as personal achievements in my writing career. These four interviews were rated impossible to get, but I managed to get them anyway.

I interviewed then U.N. Ambassador Andrew Young after the White House put its 1978 gag order on him following his *Paris Match* interview. I interviewed Dr. Ralph Honzik, who had been the campus physician at Kent State on the day of the National Guard shootings, even though for career protection and ethical reasons he had refused to be interviewed by James A. Michener when Michener was researching his book on the Kent State ordeal.

Ed McMahon, a surprisingly jealous guardian of his privacy and a man always on the go, was also the subject of one of my interviews, as were Walter and Charlotte Baldwin, the mother- and father-in-law of the Rev. Jim Jones of Guyana, despite the fact that they had been advised by the FBI and their family attorney to talk to no one.

What gave me the edge in each case? Why was I successful when other interviewers had failed? Actually, there isn't one simple answer, but rather a combination of five different factors.

1) *Luck.* Yes, there are such things as blind fate and luck, but they are no good to you unless you are ready to take advantage of them. That was my situation with Dr. Ralph Honzik.

At a dinner sponsored by a social club, Dr. Honzik was seated across from me. He had left Kent State the year after the shootings and had become a campus physician at Ball State University in Muncie, Indiana, where I was working as a reporter for the *Muncie Star.* He had kept a low profile for three years, but I just happened to catch him in a talkative mood. After identifying myself as a reporter, I asked him if I could pose a few questions for a newspaper interview, and he said yes.

Since I never go anywhere without two ballpoint pens and a pocket notebook, I was able to take notes. You should get into the same habit. If possible, put a short list of basic interview questions on the back page for quick reference, too.

The questions I begin with ask things like this: What is a typical day like at your job? What are your short- and long-range career objectives? What are your strengths and weaknesses? What previous jobs have you had and how did you choose your current occupation? What sorts of books and magazines do you read? What are your hobbies? What part does your family play in your life? What sort of educational background do you have?

Once you've used these stock questions to get your subject relaxed and talking, you then can begin to ask more direct questions designed just for that individual, i.e. "How did you first learn that some of the Kent State students had been shot?"

Always be ready. You never know when you'll be seated next to a politician on a plane or find a famous actor thumbing through a book or magazine in your local bookstore. Take advantage of luck.

2) *Persistence and availability.* The adage, if at first you don't succeed, is still valid. And it's especially true when it comes to getting interview appointments. When you are rebuffed, you must continue to call or write. Show your subject that you are serious about wanting to talk to him or her.

Furthermore, you must always make yourself available and adaptable to the subject's personal circumstances and schedule. After many rebuffs, I finally landed an interview with Ed McMahon.

I phoned the publicity director of the event at which McMahon was appearing and told her that I was a free-lance writer wanting to interview

Ed McMahon. She told me that she had no authority to schedule interviews and that I would have to talk to McMahon's manager or local sponsor. I had already gone that route and had been given the brush-off, so I asked her if she knew where McMahon was staying. She did and told me the name of the motel.

By waiting half a day in the lobby and then riding in the back seat of a car that was taking him to the airport, I was able to interview Ed McMahon without interrupting his schedule. Even as I was asking him questions, McMahon was eating a sandwich and studying a speech. It was awkward, but at least I got the interview, and that's what counted.

The unusual circumstances of the McMahon interview also emphasize the need to be fully prepared in advance. It's wise to use a cassette tape recorder when interviewing. You should check its batteries, microphone, and tapes to be sure everything is functioning. Your cassettes should be 60-90 minutes long so that you won't have to stop your interview more than once to flip over the tape.

Be sure to ask your subject for permission to tape the interview. Most people won't mind. However, if your subject is bothered by the running tape recorder, ease his or her mind by saying, "I use this recorder to help guarantee accuracy, but if you want to say anything off the record just tell me, and I'll click it off for a moment." Usually, the subject gets so involved in responding to your questions, he or she soon forgets about the recorder (especially if you set the mike in one spot and leave it alone). However, should your subject be adamant about not wanting a recorder on, give in and instead ask permission to take notes. Whenever in doubt about something, say, "Now let me get this straight: You said . . . " and then have him or her confirm what you've written.

Some of your subjects may ask to read your interview or article before you submit it for publication. This can be both a good and bad idea. If the person wishes only to double-check dates, figures, direct quotes and the spelling of names, such a reading can be very helpful.

However, random additional editings by people can sometimes ruin your manuscript's sales potential. If given a chance to edit final copy, some people will cross out your references to their "graying hair" or "furrowed brow" or they will add anecdotes about their children or pets. It can be disastrous.

Each interviewer must decide whether or not to allow the subject of the interview final-draft approval. Personally, I view myself as a better judge than my subjects of how copy should be written. My practice, therefore, is to tell the subject right away that I do not give final-draft-approval privileges to my interview subjects. Other interviewers disagree with me on this and view final-draft approval as a common courtesy. It's for you to decide.

To protect yourself legally from possible suits and avoid later rebuttals, however, you should do three things: (1) if possible, record your entire interview as evidence of what you were told; (2) ask, on tape, for permission to interview your subject and record his or her affirmative response; and (3) explain, on tape, that you will be recording the entire interview and have your subject say, "Yes, I understand that my responses are being recorded for possible subsequent publication."

One interviewer I know goes so far as to type out an "Interview Permission Form" which states that on a specified date the subject granted permission for said writer to interview him or her. Both the subject and a witness sign it. This is a rather heavy-handed option that might inhibit your subject and spoil any chance for a relaxed conversation.

You should also prepare by having plenty of questions written out—to help you not only stimulate your memory but also overcome the inevitable dry-throat syndrome that can develop when you are suddenly face to face with a famous person.

My first major interview was with Johnny Cash. Cash was coming to our town, and I convinced an area newspaper editor that if he would get me a press pass, I would get him a good interview. I was fine until I walked up to Cash's hulking six-foot-plus frame and looked into his face. Then I went blank. Here was a superstar, a legend. And who was I? No one.

Fortunately, Johnny Cash was as friendly as he was famous, and we got through the interview successfully. But that's not always the case, so to feel confident, be professional and rely on your prepared questions.

In addition, you should take notes as your subject is talking. The tape recorder preserves the conversation, but you will also need to give descriptive details with the dialogue. Since few magazines today use the straight Q. & A. format of transcribed dialogue, note how the subject is dressed, any hand motions he makes, how he sits or stands or moves, how his hair or moustache or beard looks, the tone of his voice, the timbre of his laugh, facial expressions, mannerisms, and physical actions that will help give the reader a visual picture of him.

Even in a crowded room, such as a party or a convention, your interview will be basically one on one. That means you have the responsibility to describe everything about it. Cram as much information-gathering as you can into your limited amount of time.

3) *Leverage.* Many times the person you are trying to interview will sidestep you, ignore your calls, and refuse to acknowledge your letters. That's the time to involve a third party, a person with leverage over the person you want to interview. That could be the person's boss or sponsor or agent or public-relations director or partner. Whoever it is, get to him or her and explain honestly why you feel you should have a chance to conduct the interview.

Procedures that can aid you in this process include offering the reluctant subject some guarantees, such as an advance look at some of your questions before you arrive for the interview, or some benefits—the good publicity the subject will gain for his or her career. Your subject will not expect to be paid for sitting for the interview, and you should not offer any payment.

Should it ever mean the difference between getting an interview or not getting one, promise that you won't ask questions about sensitive topics. (For years Jerry Lewis would grant interviews only if questions about Dean Martin were not asked.) Also, point out that the interview might benefit the subject by giving him or her a chance to tell the "other side" of a controversial story.

4) *Secondary topics.* Some subjects will refuse to be interviewed because they do not know what to expect. They don't know you personally, they have no idea what questions you will be asking, and they may not be familiar with the publication in which the interview is to appear. To overcome these fears, stay away from your primary topic of concern and instead talk about a secondary matter, but something you know is of tremendous interest to the subject.

There is nothing fraudulent in this. After all, nothing can stop the person from suddenly starting to say, "No comment," or from showing you to the door. Most often, however, what happens is that the subject discovers that you are easy to talk to and that your only interests are listening and reporting accurately what he or she says.

360

In an interview with a bank president, for example, you can start off with a secondary subject, such as his hobby of rare-coin collecting, and eventually ease him into your primary topic of what is being done to capture a team of counterfeiters who recently hoodwinked two of his bank's tellers.

That was my approach with Andrew Young. When he appeared as a guest speaker at the college I work for, his aide announced that no press conferences or interviews would be allowed. I approached the aide privately and asked if I could get a few quotes from the Ambassador regarding his prior visits to our campus (going back 24 years to when he came to visit one of our students, Jean Childs, whom he later married). The aide arranged for me to see the Ambassador right after breakfast the next morning. We hit it off well, and I spent more than an hour with Mr. Young and his assistant, talking about many subjects. This led to a two-page spread in the *Indianapolis Star Magazine* later that month. Newspaper Sunday supplements, by the way, are excellent markets for personality profiles.

Parenthetically, I might add that it benefits you if you keep posted on personalities coming to your area colleges, business clubs, civic theaters, and the like. In order to get good interviews, you have to be aware of where the best prospects for interviews are going to be.

5) *Non-professional contacts.* Sometimes interviews can be set up only after you approach several people who can lead you to friends or relatives of your target subject. At times, a whole chain of people is involved. For example, if you have a friend who has a brother who has a roommate who has a cousin who once dated Steve Martin, having successive meetings with these people may be your only way of getting to interview Martin himself.

Unlike sponsors or managers, these people have no leverage over the person you want to interview. They cannot schedule or order an interview. But they can at least put you in touch with your subject.

This is how I was able to interview Mr. and Mrs. Baldwin. After their daughter, Marceline, and their son-in-law, the Rev. Jim Jones, had drawn global focus because of the Jonestown, Guyana, massacre, the Baldwins withdrew into their home (in the small town of Richmond, Indiana) and refused to talk to anyone. For ten days reporters from TV networks, radio stations, and the print media congregated on the Baldwins' front yard, waiting for a public statement. It never came. At length, the FBI and local police dispersed the crowd. I then made *my* move.

Some months before the Guyana tragedy, I had taught a workshop one weekend at Indiana University East in Richmond. I still had the names and addresses of my students. These people were my only contacts in that town. I began to call them one by one to see if any knew the Baldwins or knew of someone who did.

After seven dead-end calls, I reached a former student whose husband had a boss who had a girlfriend who was the next-door neighbor of another daughter of the Baldwins. It took me more than two weeks to get myself introduced to each person in that chain, but I finally accomplished it. The Baldwins' daughter ultimately arranged for my former student and me to talk with her parents for ninety minutes at their home. To this day, I'm still generating articles based on that one in-depth interview.

When you are ready to sell your profile, review your notes, and pick out the two or three main points of interest. Write a query letter describing your subject in general and two or three areas of main interest. Decide upon the most likely markets for your profile and send off query letters.

You may wish to try the Sunday supplements in your state, if your subject is known only statewide. Or you may want to focus on women's magazines or retirees' publications or other specialized publications closely allied to your interviewee's career. But the point is, don't write your profile until you get a go-ahead from an editor. You'll save time, money and labor by writing it the first time as near to that editor's requirements as you can.

Make your query letter interesting, readable and intriguing. Emphasize to the editor that you have conducted an interview which was supposedly impossible to get. Stress the exclusive nature of your submission. Remember, the more difficult-to-get the interview seems to be, the more impact it will have upon the editor.

So, my suggestion to free-lance writers who have been considering trying the personality profile is to try all five of my tactics to land a real scoop: an impossible-to-get interview!

By the way, does anyone happen to know the name of Bette Midler's dentist or butcher?

68

BEATING THE ODDS IN THE CARD GAME

BY EDWARD J. HOHMAN

WITH fifteen years in the business of free-lance greeting card writing, I have often felt like a gambler at heart. Rejections and slow periods are a natural part of the business, but you can improve your chances by sharpening your skills, getting all the inside information you can, and showing your cards in the most receptive places.

Whether your ambition is to write Humorous, Studio, Conventional, Sensitivity or Religious material, the opportunities are there. Editors are always looking for fresh, new ideas; meeting their requirements and making sales will depend on how well you are prepared. While many of you know the ground rules, others, new to the field, may neglect to include some of these basic elements of salable greeting card verse.

Check your greeting card material to be sure you are following these guidelines:

1) The card should have a "me-to-you" message. In humorous and studio cards, don't just come up with a gag; you must work the gag into an appropriate greeting.
2) Your message should be clear, uncluttered, and easily understood by card buyers.
3) If you use rhymed verse, check the meter or "beat." When writing prose, remember that brevity is often best. Don't ramble on. Prune and edit your material; submit your very best.
4) Type your material on 3 × 5-inch or 4 × 6-inch cards. Number each submission and be sure you put your name and address on the back. Need I remind you to keep duplicates, and record where you send each batch and when? These are all MUSTS, if you are to compete and survive in this competitive field.

If your interests lie in the creation of humorous and studio material, you've picked the best-paying categories. At this writing, studio ideas can bring as much as $80 each from major publishers. Humorous verse and ideas may be lower, but they still top conventional verse, which runs from $1.00 to $3.00 per line.

Humorous and studio ideas may come thick and fast when you are on a "creative roll." I've had the good fortune to sell four out of seven studio card ideas, created during a one-hour writing session. It won't happen every time, and you're bound to come up with some "duds," but it's nice to know the possibility exists.

You can help speed the process of coming up with studio and humorous material by organizing and using a clipping file of humorous drawings, cartoons and photos, anything that helps "set the scene." The majority of my sales of humorous card ideas have come from going through my files.

On one occasion, a picture of a mother kangaroo with a little one in her pouch caught my eye. I clipped the picture and pasted it on the front of a studio-shaped card. Outside, I lettered the words: ANOTHER BIRTHDAY? On the inside, I simply put the phrase: HANG IN THERE, BABY! Best Wishes! The idea brought a $40 check.

Another studio card sale, that brought me $25, began with a picture of a little girl on a swing. The cover caption read: SINCE IT'S YOUR BIRTHDAY, I'M SENDING YOU A COUPLE OF GIRLS WHO ARE REAL "SWINGERS" . . . . Inside, I had pasted photocopies of two little girls swinging and simply lettered "Happy Birthday" beneath them.

Originality is of vital importance in the creation of greeting card ideas. The editor of Amberley Greeting Card Company reports that he gets at least ten cards a week that mention calling the fire department to put out all the candles on a birthday cake!

The first thing to enter your mind when you're creating a humorous card isn't likely to be unique. Keeping a close watch on what is being published can prevent your duplicating existing cards.

As you look over the variety of humorous cards on the racks, you'll notice that many of them have more than one or two illustrations. Having this in mind during your creative sessions will help you envision your humorous verse in finished form and will help you write more salable material. My own sales of humorous card verse picked up tremendously when I began to allow enough space beween the lines of my typed submissions for appropriate illustrations.

Here's an example of an eight-line verse which was submitted in this manner:

I'm sure no Fortune Teller
Crystal balls just aren't for me
Reading palms is one more thing
That's not quite my cup of tea
If there is something in the cards,
I guess I'd miss that too . . .
But I'm REALLY GREAT ON BIRTHDAYS . . .
I predict the BEST for YOU!
Have a Happy One!

In submitting the preceding verse to Sangamon Company, I had even included some suggestions for artwork, which I felt would be appropriate. This isn't a necessity, but it can't hurt unless you get too involved or suggest complex illustrations. Use good judgment. The same advice goes for the submission of dummy cards or mock-ups. If you have art ability and an idea that really "needs to be seen to be appreciated," go to it.

I've had the good fortune to work on assignment from time to time. Getting an order by phone for a particular greeting card message and working up several variations for approval always manages to start my creative juices flowing. A seven-page Juvenile Birthday "Coloring Book" was a rush assignment not too long ago. One of three verses I submitted involved a Rabbit "Magician" and his animal friends. Sangamon purchased the card verse that read:

A COLORING BOOK FOR YOUR BIRTHDAY

This Bunny works magic,
He's really quite tricky
'Cause out comes a cake,
Topped with icing that's sticky!

A wave of his wand,
And look what appears . . .
An elephant friend,
With long flapping ears!

A few magic words
Prove he's really a smarty,
'Cause out of a trunk
Come more friends for your Party!

365

So here they all are
With a wish that's for you.
And the fun's just begun . . .
They need coloring, too!
HAPPY BIRTHDAY!

You can readily see that one has to "think young" to create greeting card verse for the little folks. It takes a clever combination of verse and art to put such ideas together successfully.

To many writers, creating conventional and religious verse will not have the same appeal as humorous and studio material, but I have found it a refreshing change. Here is an example of one of my conventional Christmas verses, which was purchased by Warner Press:

TO THE ONE I LOVE AT CHRISTMAS

There's more to special days like this
Than sometimes meets the eye,
There's more than just a shopping list
Of gifts that one must buy.

There's more than just a Christmas tree
And bows of holly, too,
For none of these would mean a thing
If I couldn't be with you!
MERRY CHRISTMAS!

Revising verse you have on hand can prove to be very rewarding. I've had dozens of sales result from the submission of material that was rewritten. Changing the wording, the focus, the sending situation, or the rhyme scheme can perk up rejected verses or messages and make them more acceptable to editors. Here's an example of a General Male Birthday verse that was revised to fill the need for a "Dad's" Birthday card. The original (unsold) verse read:

ON YOUR BIRTHDAY

It's not just a fine occasion
We pause to celebrate,
You're one fine guy,
And that is why
We hope it turns out great!
HAPPY BIRTHDAY!

366

The revised verse for "Dad" read:

IT'S YOUR BIRTHDAY, DAD!

It's a very special birthday
We pause to celebrate,
You're one fine Dad,
And I'm sure glad
To wish you one that's great!
HAPPY BIRTHDAY!

Not much of a change, you say? But when the need for a specific card arises and the publisher asks you to fill that need, you have an advantage when you have material available to submit, with some revisions and rewriting.

To make your way successfully as a free lancer, you must keep abreast of publishers' needs as well as the trends in current greeting cards on display at local outlets.

By consulting market listings in *The Writer's Handbook,* you can make sure you keep up to date on new information as it becomes available. The National Association of Greeting Card Publishers issues an informative pamphlet that offers suggestions and includes a list of member publishers. You may receive a copy by writing to them at 600 Pennsylvania Avenue, S.E., Washington, DC 20003; be sure to enclose a stamped self-addressed envelope.

Don't hesitate to resubmit material to publishers who may not have been receptive some years ago. Remember, editors change, times change, and perhaps your writing has changed to meet their current needs. At the present time, there is a company interested in over a dozen of my ideas. They had always liked my work, but my previous submissions were sent at the wrong time. Had I not kept after them, the present opportunity might not have developed.

Keeping to a definite writing schedule and refusing to let rejection slips get you down are two "musts" you must follow if you expect to succeed as a greeting card writer. If you have basic writing ability, a flair for verse or prose, and an understanding of and interest in greeting cards, you owe it to yourself to give this challenging field your maximum effort. The demand is there, and the rewards are most satisfying.

367

69

GETTING STARTED IN BOOK REVIEWING

By Lynne Sharon Schwartz

I LIKE to think of a new book as a mysterious geological treasure, a rock never before handled. The delighted discoverer's first, most natural response is, What have we here? I hold the rock in the palm of my hand to examine it: what are its colors, its contours, its special beauty (or ugliness)? Is it like others I've seen, enough like them, even, to fit into a generic category? Is it more or less beautiful than those of its kind? Or is it, though it bears a surface family resemblance, distinguished by intriguing, individual markings?

The "what have we here" approach will yield a reviewer fruitful results. Every book deserves this careful attention; every one is unique— though some uniquely bad—and demands to be judged for its intrinsic, living qualities. The opposite approach might be labeled "negative criticism." The negative critic appraises a book on the basis of what it has failed to accomplish, with the failings usually derived from the critic's own notion of how he or she would have handled the subject. Not only unfair but misleading, too. For a critic's job is to leave aside his own musings and try temporarily to share the author's view. What has the author set out to do? is the crucial question. (If you believe, however, that what the author has set out to do is not worth doing, better pass up that book. It deserves a fighting chance, and you as critic deserve a more worthwhile application of your talents.)

Now, it is far easier to be explicit about the goals of nonfiction than of fiction. When I reviewed a biography of Margaret Sanger, it was not difficult to decide whether or not the book gave an accurate, coherent, inclusive account of Sanger's life. (The larger question of how well it does so, compared to other efforts, is more complex.) Again, in *Visions of Glory,* Barbara Grizzuti Harrison set out to detail the history of the Jehovah's Witnesses and of her experiences among them. I became convinced of her thoroughness and accuracy and said so in my review. But it is far harder to be unequivocal about fiction, since fiction at its best does not set out to prove or to do anything. To say that *Anna Karenina* "shows" what happens to an upper class nineteenth-century Russian woman who commits adultery would be literary blasphemy. Fiction is the working out of an inner vision; it is impossible to "judge" anyone's vision, and quite a delicate matter to evaluate its metamorphosis into words.

Still, books must be brought to the attention of readers, and a paid reviewer has certain obligations to an audience which sound exceedingly obvious yet are too often ignored. First, to tell the reader specifically what is in the book: to return to the rock analogy, describe its size, shape, color, texture and distinctive marks; the category it belongs to, its antecedents, its relative standing among others of its kind. If nonfiction, the premises on which it is based and the conclusions it reaches, the major issues and points raised along the way, the extent to which they are covered. If it is fiction, the themes, the areas and vicissitudes of life the author is preoccupied with. Plot summaries, as we all remember from school, should be minimal. But a dash of the reporter's standard questions—where, what, when, how, and why—will prove helpful. Above all, a discussion of the nature and interaction of the characters as they grow from the novel's inception through its development and close, is essential.

Secondly, an evaluation of style. Books, our fact-oriented age tends to forget, are made of words, in the best instances deftly laced together to create a texture that mirrors or complements its subject. Everyone, in the privacy of his brain, spins theories and fantasies. Only a writer labors to put the theories or fantasies into words. It is precisely for this labor with words, as much as for the quality of the content, that a book should be assessed. What is the flavor of the author's special idiom? Does the style aid or hinder the emergence of the themes? An even larger question, does the use of words enhance or detract from the richness and capacity of our common inherited language?

Finally—and here is what frightens many new reviewers—a personal judgment. In book reviewing, as in so much else, there is no way out of accountability for one's views. Certainly, don't review a book unless you have the courage and authority to state your convictions honestly. But once you do, don't shrink from the truth, pleasant or not; it is, after all, what the editor hired you for. (On the other hand, beware of using the seductive power of print for airing private grievances; if a book inspires you to invective or sarcasm for dubious personal reasons, better pass it up. Again, both you and the book deserve better handling.)

Since books are composed of words, ideally an astute, literate reviewer should be able to handle a book on any subject, and indeed some national magazines have successfully assigned books to critics outside the field. Practically speaking, however, as a beginning reviewer, you should get to know as thoroughly as possible the field you choose to work in.

When I started reviewing, I felt competent to write about current fiction because I was, after all, primarily a writer of fiction, besides having read it all my life and having taught literature at Hunter College. Nonetheless, with my first efforts I overprepared — not a bad thing to do, as it turned out. I made sure I was familiar with an author's earlier books so I could see the latest one in the context of a body of work. Naturally this meant more crammed reading and time spent in relation to money earned than was comfortable, but I felt I owed this to the author and my readers. I still do. (Anyone reading this is surely aware that reviewing is not one of life's more lucrative occupations.) Often, especially in brief reviews, hardly more than a sentence or two referring to the earlier works found its way into my final draft, yet I felt that the background knowledge improved my review and gave it a justified tone of authority.

I had trepidations for some time, though, about reviewing nonfiction. What could I claim to know about real facts in the real world? Nevertheless, intrigued by the advance publicity, I asked to review Ellen Moers' *Literary Women* for *The Nation*. Faced with the book's wealth of data, presented by someone who had evidently read every word penned by a woman over the past 200 years, I felt incompetent. Yet, as I read the book, not only did great forgotten chunks of my early studies return to me, but I found whatever else I needed to know on its pages. In my review, besides giving the usual information, I turned my attention partly to the controversy the book had engendered by its considering women authors apart from men, a controversy on which I had very definite and educated opinions.

Encouraged by that venture into nonfiction, I requested of *Ms. Magazine* Ann Cornelisen's *Women of the Shadows,* about the lives of Southern Italian peasant women. Here I worried that my ignorance of agricultural economy, of the difficulties of industrialization, and such, would hamper me. However, I had read other books on the region, and had lived in Italy and traveled through the areas Cornelisen wrote about. I hoped that this firsthand knowledge would stand me in good stead, and I believe it did. But I would hesitate to review a similar book on the lives of peasant women in Turkey or Morocco, places I know nothing about.

In brief, know your subject by study or by firsthand experience, or both. Then if, as occasionally will happen, you are given a book you feel overwhelmed by, stick to what you know and perceive, avoid grandiose generalities, and in the end, trust your instincts. Above all, don't attempt to sound authoritative when there is no basis for authority. I remember how pleased I was, as a beginner, to be offered a book by *The Chicago Tribune Book World,* but how distressed on opening the desired package to find a novel of World War II, filled with details of military strategy, sabotage, fortifications — subjects I knew nothing about and disliked besides. I turned to page one with a sense of duty. In the book itself, I found all I needed to know about strategy, and found in addition, to my pleasant surprise, that like all good novels, *Kramer's War,* by Derek Robinson, was about human beings working out their complex, connected destinies in a situation of great stress. I was able not only to review it but to enjoy it as well. Needless to say, I avoided undue discussion of strategy, fortifications, or deployment of troops.

The above remarks apply once you have the book in hand, but the novice reviewer is probably wondering, How do you get the books assigned? Timing is of the essence. Since newspapers' Sunday sections are prepared weeks ahead and magazines often months ahead, you need to know what titles are coming out well in advance of publication date. *Publishers Weekly,* the invaluable trade magazine, lists forthcoming books, as does *Library Journal.* From their brief and pithy descriptions you can find which books are suitable for you.

Getting the first assignment is difficult, yet a newcomer's prospects are not totally bleak. It's best to try your local papers or weeklies first, even if it means working for no pay temporarily—not advisable as a long-term habit, but worth the initial sacrifice. Send the editor a sample review, your best effort of course, with the names of several forthcoming books you'd like to try, and a few persuasive lines telling why you are especially qualified to review them. Don't be daunted if the first tries fail. The erosion technique—wearing down a solid, recalcitrant object by a light, steady trickle—has been known to work. Certainly competition is stiff, but if editors discover someone with a dash of originality, a capacity for felicitous use of language, a strong sense of organization and a willingness to work doggedly at improving, they will generally succumb. They also, incidentally, will be grateful for a readable, correctly spelled and punctuated manuscript, submitted on time.

Once you have established yourself locally you might try larger markets, sending around tear sheets of previous work. By all means follow up any leads from friends or colleagues. When book review editors send out the word that they're looking for new writers, they usually mean it.

It's extremely important to be aware of the tastes, readership, slants, if any, space limitations, and general tone of the magazine you're writing for. Your chances of impressing *The National Review* with an iconoclastic critique of capitalism are about as great as getting a laudatory review of Richard Nixon's memoirs into *The Village Voice*. In a realistic way, try to suit your review to the publication. If this requires too great a dislocation of your own values, better to try elsewhere. I have found it possible to write for varied periodicals without doing damage to my fundamental opinions about a book. When reviewing *Women of the Shadows* for *Ms.*, I stressed its feminist aspects more than I would have, say, for *The Nation,* where I might have dwelt more on the inequities inherent in the system of land tenure. Both themes were vital and important—the choice was a matter of emphasis, bearing in mind the concerns of prospective readers.

Once you are in the hard-earned position of writing fairly freely for a number of places (that is, once editors have come to trust you), you will find that magazines vary greatly in the way they handle review copy. Very few editors print every word as written. Some, like Emile Capouya, former Literary Editor of *The Nation,* make changes so small, subtle and apt that I, for one, never noticed them at first, only felt vaguely that my review was better than I thought. Others ask for extensive changes, either for style and coherence, or because of space limitations. In any case, it helps to be cooperative with editors, whose experience is usually vast and long. (Unless, of course, their requests involve distorting your opinions for extraneous reasons, which is unacceptable and happens, at least to my knowledge, thankfully seldom.)

Now, suppose you have won the coveted assignment and have the book in hand. How to proceed? The reading is often the hardest part of the job, very different from reading for pleasure. One reads at first with the unsettling sense of needing to remember everything, much like studying for an exam. This compulsion passes, but you do unquestionably owe the book and your audience an attentive reading. Authors frequently complain that their critics seem not to have read the book, or to have read some other book. There is no way of telling whether this is true, but at least new reviewers can avoid the imputation.

I usually read a book twice, once slowly, occasionally marking passages along the way, and the second time quickly, to get a sense of overall shape, flow, and pattern. One soon learns to read with pen in hand—but stopping for real notes fragments the experience of first reading. Note-taking during the second reading is more effective. Both readings are invariably accompanied by familiar conflicts which one learns to take in stride. If I am enjoying the book too much, I worry about losing objectivity, not paying enough attention to how the author achieves his or her effects and simply luxuriating in them. On the other hand, if I dislike the book, I make enormous efforts not to become resentful of my task and thus dislike it more than warranted. I try to look for good points that any one of my innumerable small prejudices may prevent me from noticing. In either case, it is hardly relaxing.

After the two readings I write down my general impressions with illustrations from the book, and organize them under several inclusive headings, which gives me a loose outline. I then proceed with the best intentions of working from this outline, but habitually write the piece straight on, barely glancing at the notes until later, to see that I've covered everything and to locate appropriate examples. It might be suspected that the extra reading, note-taking and outlining are wasted effort. Yet in the end it seems that the intense preparation is somehow needed for the rather swift, "thoughtless" writing process. Also, the outline exists as security in case I run dry halfway through. I don't presume that this method of total immersion, a valiant semblance of scholarly organization, and then an abandoned dash to the finish line can work for anyone else. I do offer it to demonstrate the devious, cumbersome and idiosyncratic ways that reviews get written.

Next come the patient correcting, revising, cutting and moving of parts, drudgery to be sure, but performed with the immense relief of knowing that the thing *exists*, in need only of tinkering. Always, when the review is typed in final form and on its way to the mailbox, I get wild flashes of insight informing me my work is all wrong: I should have kept in what I cut out and cut out what I kept in. These hand-on-the-mailbox insights are an inevitable part of the writing process and should be totally disregarded. (It may help to keep the finished review for a few days to give it a last check before mailing.)

There are, in addition, a few outside impediments to straight thinking that a novice reviewer should be aware of. One is an author's reputation. Depending on the murky depths of a reviewer's secret nature, he or she may be tempted to encourage or to attack new writers (regardless of the merit of the work), or to sustain or stab the reputation of well-known writers (also regardless of merit). To these temptations, the adage "Know thyself" is the best antidote; better still, "Guard against thyself or don't review the book at all." Reviewing books by friends or acquaintances—a common if doubtful practice—requires similar restraint or total abstinence.

Other reviews and publishers' blurbs are powerful obstacles as well. But while the first can be summarily dealt with (never read them till your own review is safely in the mail), advertising, jacket copy, or those ingratiating notes from the publicity staff telling how wonderful the book is, are less easy to avoid. What publicity people say should be regarded as a skillful pass in a complex ball game. The serious danger enters if the uninitiated reviewer's expectations are raised. "Smith's new novel relentlessly plumbs the depths of A, with brilliant insights into B, so that his style is reminiscent of C and D, though paradoxically echoing the uniqueness of E." Smith's book may in fact be a fine one, but a neophyte reviewer diligently in search of A, B, and C is sure to be disappointed, as well as blinded to the book's true worth.

The final questions that keep reviewers tossing in bed at night are, Have I praised a book that everyone will see immediately is idiotic? and Have I panned a masterpiece? The first is more easily dispensed with. It is unlikely that a competent reviewer, after years of reading, will fail to spot awful work. Moreover, it is probably more honorable to err on the side of generosity. But not to recognize genius is to be dull indeed, is it not? I had this experience reviewing a recent novel by a moderately well-known writer. I had read excerpts in a magazine and liked them, but after finishing the whole novel I realized it set enormous goals and failed to achieve them. The book turned out to be the focus of a good advertising campaign; other reviews appeared and were for the most part favorable. I considered retiring. First, though, I went back to the book dispassionately, my review already in print. It was still unsuccessful, and I was glad to have said so.

For one learns, after much time and ink and struggle, that there are no absolute standards of accomplishment, especially today when traditional and experimental modes rightfully flourish side by side. Reviewers' opinions will vary as much as readers'; the difference is that reviewers are expected to have the skill to articulate clearly what they think and why they think it. That is the most, in all conscience, that one can do, and it is no small task. Once it is done, let the reader be left to his own devices.

70

REFERENCES REQUIRED

By William M. Wiecek

How OFTEN in your writing have you been stumped for a fact about America's past? Whether you are writing fiction or nonfiction, you sometimes need to find or verify historical data, either to keep your piece accurate or to get your narrative moving. When did General William Tecumseh Sherman's troops capture Atlanta in the March to the Sea? What do we know about the life of Thomas Jefferson's wife, Martha Wayles Skelton Jefferson? Where—or, for that matter, what—was the Natchez Trace? Who tried to assassinate President Harry Truman in 1950, and why? You can find answers to these and numberless other questions about American life in some twenty or so reference books commonly used by historians and others who work with the American past.

When you have an historical question, sometimes the quickest way to the answer lies in ordinary reference materials used by all writers. *The New York Times* and its index will guide you to journalistic accounts of America's history back to the Civil War. The *World Almanac* and the *Information Please Almanac* sometimes give you just that little fragment of information you are looking for. The *Readers' Guide to Periodical Literature,* that old standby that we have all used since our high-school days, leads you to articles written in the twentieth century about your topics. And of course the *Encyclopedia Britannica* and *Encyclopedia Americana* are . . . well, encyclopedic.

But there are times when you need more specialized data, or information packaged in some more usable format than you can find in newspapers, almanacs, magazine articles, and encyclopedias. Where do you turn? The historian's working reference materials more likely than not can help you out.

You might begin with a comprehensive guide to all of American history: the eight-volume *Dictionary of American History* (1976). A dictionary only in the sense that its entries are in alphabetical order, the *DAH* is a collection of articles on all important subjects and persons in American history. You would go to it, for example, if you were wondering why Thomas Jefferson achieved the Louisiana Purchase, or wanted a brief narrative of the events leading up to the firing on Fort Sumter. Thomas Cochran and Wayne Andrews have edited an earlier edition of the *DAH* down into a one-volume desk reference, the *Concise Dictionary of American History* (1962). A comparable one-volume compendium of events, ideas, persons, and places in the American past is Thomas H. Johnson's *Oxford Companion to American History* (1966), which is somewhat more up-to-date than the *CDAH,* and is especially good in the fields of cultural and social history.

But the premier desk reference guide, the volume that most historians would choose if they had to pick just one book-companion for their stay on a desert island, would be Richard B. Morris's *Encyclopedia of American History* (1976). Half this indispensable book is a tightly chronological narrative of the American past; the rest is a topical summary of different subjects: five hundred biographical sketches, plus sections on immigration, constitutional history, agricultural development, commerce and industry, science and technology, medicine, finance and banking, labor, religion, education, literature, media, fine arts, and music. Who and what were the Ashcan School of American painters? When did the moldboard plow come into general use? During what period did most East European Jews immigrate to America? These are the sorts of questions you bring to the *Encyclopedia.*

Writers of fiction and nonfiction usually have biographical queries, seeking either facts about real historical figures or suggestions about patterns for a fictional character's circumstances or behavior. In American history, they can find a wealth of biographical references, beginning with the eleven-volume *Dictionary of American Biography* (1964), brought up to date by *Supplements* that cover the period to 1955. I know from my own experience as a contributor to the *DAB* how much research goes into those little biographies and how meticulously the editors work over contributions to assure high standards of accuracy and literary grace. Like the *DAH,* its sibling, the *DAB* has a one-volume compendium called, naturally enough, the *Concise Dictionary of American Biography* (1977). The *CDAB* is the second volume I reach for when I have a question; it and the *Encyclopedia of American History* together should cover most simple queries about the American past. The *DAB* does not include persons living at the time of its compilation; neither does the five-volume *Who Was Who in America,* one of the Marquis Company's *Who's Who* series. A valuable specialized biographical guide is *Notable American Women, 1607–1950* (1971), highly regarded among historians for its scholarly standards. It has been updated by *Notable American Women: The Modern Period* (1980).

Suppose you want to find the exact wording of lines from Lincoln's Second Inaugural ("With malice toward none, with charity for all. . . .")? The documentary collection for you is Henry Steele Commager's *Documents of American History* (1973), a compilation of the most important primary sources of our past. Here you will find such documents as the Mayflower Compact, Robert E. Lee's farewell to his army after Appomattox, and John F. Kennedy's 1963 American University address. The editor has judiciously excerpted the documents, eliminating irrelevant verbiage but unerringly including any important quotation you might be seeking. If you have a pithy aphorism rattling around in your head, and you want to find who said it, or what its exact words were (for example, P.T. Barnum's "There's a sucker born every minute"), your best bet is that great reference classic, *Bartlett's Familiar Quotations.* Bartlett's is made doubly useful by its index of authors, and by a remarkably thorough index of key words (like "sucker," "born," and "minute"). And if the words of your quote puzzle you after you have looked them up, you can check two excellent dictionaries of political terms, oddly enough compiled by men at opposite ends of the political spectrum: William L. Safire's *New Language of Politics* (1972) and Eugene McCarthy's *The Crescent Dictionary of American Politics* (1968). Both are limited to political jargon and Safire's is the more extensive and chatty. They do a lot more than tell you what a political term like "Mugwump" means and how it was coined: there is a lot of history in their entries.

Sometimes you need a pictorial depiction of a place or an event. Atlases are a good place to start. If you haven't looked at one lately, you'll be pleasantly surprised to find that they are now much more than the traditional collection of maps and a gazetteer (dictionary of place names). The best one-volume atlas is the *American Heritage Pictorial Atlas of United States History* (1966), crammed full of imaginative and suggestive information, drawings, graphs, and tables. Its "Portfolios" contain bird's-eye drawings of such things as mid-nineteenth century cities and selected battles of the War for American Independence and the Civil War. If you are writing a period piece set in antebellum New Orleans or St. Louis, or if you have wondered about the lay of the land for Pickett's charge at the battle of Gettysburg, the splendid illustrations in this atlas will draw your imagination into the scene. If your concerns are exclusively military, the *West Point Atlas of American Wars* (1959) is a good resource. Finally, the old classic, Charles O. Paullin's *Atlas of the Historical Geography of the United States* (1932), which crowned the sub-field of historical geography, remains valuable more than a half-century after its publication.

If you need statistical data, the one-volume *Historical Statistics of the United States, Colonial Times to 1970* (1975) is excellent. Do you need to know the average life expectancy of black females in the 1920s? How many immigrants entered the United States from Russia before the First World War? These are the kinds of questions you take to the *Historical Statistics*.

These reference aids are likely to answer any routine question you have about American history, but sometimes you will have a hard, specific, and obscure question beyond their scope. (What was the weather like as Lincoln delivered the Gettysburg Address? What exactly did a soldier of the Continental Line wear for a uniform at Yorktown? What were common gold-mining techniques at the time of the Klondike strike?) Here you must resort to a bibliographic guide to get you to the kind of book that will provide an answer. Fortunately, American history is blessed with some excellent bibliographies. The most commonly used is the third edition (1974) of the *Harvard Guide to American History,* in two volumes. But, as is true with *Webster's Unabridged Dictionary,* professionals still find its predecessor, the second edition (same title) useful if not preferable. Helen J. Poulton compiled a helpful *Historian's Handbook* (1972) that is not limited to American history; it covers all areas of the world. Jacques Barzun and Henry Graff, *The Modern Researcher* (third edition, 1977), is a beautifully-written guide to research in all fields, but with a strong emphasis on history. It also includes brief bibliographic information. It and the introductory chapters to the *Harvard Guide* contain fine discussions of the arts of writing, and belong in your personal writer's library next to Fowler and Strunk and White. Finally, if your query takes you really far afield into esoterica, you will need the bibliographic assistance of the reference librarian's bible, *Guide to Reference Books* (ninth edition, 1976) and its 1980 supplement, published under the auspices of the American Library Association. This is the essential bibliographic tool, leading you to virtually any reference book you are likely to need.

Let me conclude this list with a mention of two general reference tools that are not specifically historical, but that are so irradiated with history that no personal reference collection should be without them. The *New Columbia Encyclopedia* (1975), inexpensive but massive, contains excellent entries on numerous historical subjects. The longer entries have brief bibliographies of their topics, leading you to further sources of information. As a non-scientist, I find the *Columbia Encyclopedia* particularly useful for specific queries I have about scientific, engineering, and technical subjects, including those having an historical slant (such as: What was Sir Ernest Rutherford's original conception of the model of an atom? Why was Antoine Lavoisier, France's greatest chemist of his time, guillotined during the Terror?). The other essential reference handbook is the *American Heritage Dictionary of the English Language,* the most usable of the modern desk dictionaries.

When you use these reference materials, don't short-change yourself by resorting to them only to verify facts and data, or just to answer specific queries. If you let them, they will prove to be wonderful springboards to your writer's imagination. By all means, go into them to get a quick and accurate answer to a question, but go in the same spirit that you enter the library stacks: in a browsing frame of mind. You will be rewarded with the experience of a writer's serendipity. For example, I turned to my desk copy of the *Concise Dictionary of American Biography* one day to check someone's vital dates, stumbled across the entry for Samuel Isaac Schereschewsky, and thereby met a fascinating figure. Born into a Jewish family in Lithuania, he immigrated to the United States as a young man, converted to the Episcopal faith, was ordained, and ended his distinguished career as the Episcopal bishop of Shanghai. Fluent in many languages, he translated the

Bible and the Prayer Book into Chinese. What a life! What incredible materials for a character! Or consider the dramatic opportunities revealed to you in the brief sketch of David Terry's life in the *CDAB:* migrating to California in the year of the Gold Rush, 1849, Terry became a judge of the California Supreme Court and eventually its Chief Justice. He resigned, killed a man in a duel, left the Golden State to serve in the army of the Confederacy, was one of the Confederate self-exiles in Mexico, returned to California, married a woman whose past set gossips' tongues wagging, lost out in some litigation presided over by his former colleague, United States Supreme Court Justice Stephen J. Field, and was killed by Field's bodyguard on a train when he seemed to be threatening the jurist. What materials for a play, a novel, a biography!

Used with insistent curiosity and an open mind, the reference materials of American history can lead any writer to the incredible riches of our past, an inexhaustible mine of materials for fiction and nonfiction.

71

FREE-LANCING FOR CITY MAGAZINES

By Don Kubit

WHILE free-lancing in itself is a tough enough way to earn a living, making a go of it in economically depressed Detroit nowadays practically qualifies me for a spot, next to the snail darter, on the endangered species list. I just have to believe that if I can survive as a free-lance writer, as I have for years, in a city in which cutbacks and layoffs are daily headlines, I must be doing something right.

I have managed to keep my head above water by writing primarily for *Monthly Detroit*, the area's city magazine, and over the past several years I have had by-lines in the majority of issues—and, more important, got paid. While some may feel that this makes me a regional writer, that geographical chauvinism is precisely why I am able to support myself as a writer.

Detroit is my hometown, so I have both a sense of its history and a participant's feel for what is currently going on around town. Talk to any editor of any city magazine across the country and he'll tell you that that sort of "insider's" knowledge is one of the keys to breaking into print in city magazines.

The growth of city magazines over the past decade has provided local free-lance writers with a rare opportunity. Almost every city magazine *depends* on free lancers to supplement their relatively small in-house writing staff and, consequently, the editors are often more willing to take the time and effort to encourage and develop beginning writers. And, since they are basically competing with Sunday newspaper supplements for local talent, their pay scales tend to be somewhat higher.

From *Boston* to *Los Angeles, Cleveland* to *Corpus Christi*, city magazines share a basic philosophy—to provide the middle-to-upper income, better-educated class of readers, with articles revolving around the "quality of life" in their specific area. Who better to know (and write) about that measure of livability than a person who resides there?

From my own experiences and discussions with a half dozen city magazine editors, I have discovered that the kinds of articles they are looking for fall into designated categories. I have dubbed them the Four Urban P's: PROBLEMS, PERSONALITIES, PLEASURES and PERCEPTIONS. Any one or any combination usually results in a sure-fire "strike."

For the most part, issue-oriented pieces are written by a city magazine's staff writers who have the contacts and facilities to explore crime, drugs, rising politicians, and massive downtown development projects. I would advise free lancers to concentrate more on issues and events within their own communities, e.g., small entrepreneurs; ethnic neighborhoods; the rehabilitation of old houses and movie theaters; the impact of a suburban shopping mall on a town's main street merchants; local political races. There are satellite topics, but every city magazine, regardless of its location or region, has a metropolitan area readership. Residents of one borough or suburb are naturally curious about the goings-on crosstown, because some day they may face similar problems.

Some beginning writers disregard potential article ideas on the grounds that "the local newspapers have already covered that." If it is a major issue, no doubt they have, but city magazine writers have to go beyond the obvious to find an overlooked angle. A few years ago, one of the most over-reported stories in these parts was a battle over a proposed road expansion in the Detroit suburb of Troy. Hardly a heart-wrenching issue, but the local weeklies and the two major dailies in Detroit covered this point-counterpoint situation as if it were a Papal visit. However, in their deadline rush to report all the brickbats, they failed to look at the total picture. With one phone call, I learned that opposition to the planned road-widening started because building the proposed right of way meant cutting down a 50-year-old copper beech.

A second phone call uncovered the fact that a simple driveway separated the offices of the two main antagonists—Minoru Yamasaki, a world-renowned architect fond of quoting Henry David Thoreau, who wanted to turn the road into a pedestrian plaza, vs. city manager Frank Gerstenecker, a cost-efficient type who had the facts and figures to show that the road should become an eight-lane highway. My article, "A Tree Grows in Troy," portrayed a classic confrontation of divergent personalities and philosophies.

I suggested that my piece be published in the monthly issue coinciding with the final zoning commission hearing on the road project. Although the hearing received only a one-sentence mention in my article, it was an important news peg that made an otherwise tired, old topic more timely.

Personifying a lifeless cement-and-mortar problem leads us to the second mainstay of city magazine articles—local personalities. People like to read about their neighbors, and almost every city magazine editor would admit that at least part of his function is to serve as a sort of provincial version of *People* magazine. The possibilities for local profiles are nearly endless, with media celebrities at the top of the list— the face behind the voice of a popular disc jockey, the life beyond the anchor of a TV newsman.

Sports personality features are another favorite category, and instead of writing about the highly-publicized All-Star pitcher or All-American tailback, a free lancer would be wise to seek out the little-known center who only snaps for punts and field goals; the lesser-known souvenir concessionaire at baseball games; or the unknown driver of the Zamboni machine, which resurfaces the ice between periods at a hockey game. Don't overlook amateur athletes—young, Olympic-minded gymnasts, a senior citizen softball team, pool hustlers, bowlers, country club caddies, an up-and-coming boxer who works out in a local gym.

Don't forget about people who once lived in your area and went on to fame and fortune elsewhere. Detroit is not exactly considered a breeding ground for celebrities, but its notable list of alumni include Robin "Mork" Williams, Pam "Mindy" Dawber, the Motown sound originator, Berry Gordy, Jr., and his superstar pupil Diana Ross, Gilda Radner, Lily Tomlin, Joyce Carol Oates, and Soupy Sales. The nostalgic reminiscences of ex-residents frequently equal guaranteed sales for city magazine free lancers. There is also what I refer to as the Who-Feeds-the-Ducks? group—a motley collection of potentially interesting profiles, from museum guards to homicide detectives, community volunteers to cabbies, registered nannies to card-carrying witches. I once met a family attorney whose culinary hobby eventually led him to start his own commercial taco factory; the owner of a sports paraphernalia store who was the original proponent of the Super Bowl XVI staged in Pontiac, Michigan. I wrote his story for *Monthly Detroit,* and during Super Bowl week, it gained national attention.

An essential role of every city magazine is to keep its readers informed of what's happening on the social scene. Each month, there is an extensive registry of planned entertainment events for the metropolitan area and an accompanying "restaurant guide."

These tabulations are usually handled by an assigned "listings" staffer, but periodically, this function is expanded into what is called a "service piece"—a ratings game featuring the *best of* this and the *most of* that. These articles generally fall into three categories: 1) food—the juiciest steak, the cheesiest cheesecake, the tangiest chili, etc.; 2) entertainment—the friendliest singles bars, the loudest punk rock havens, the classiest jazz clubs, etc.; and 3) travel—getaways, hideaways and weekend breakaways.

Since all of these classifications are highly subjective, a free-lance writer should not feel that he or she has to be a qualified expert on any given subject in order to write about it. One man's favorite pizza is another man's ersatz Frisbee. If you have an interest and are willing to do the research, your biggest obstacle is defending your choices.

You might even think of a more offbeat approach: ranking roads according to potholes; a list of the most popular books borrowed from local libraries; an inventory of the biggest shoe sizes, submarine sandwiches, salad bars, etc., in your town. The funnier, the more clever and, sometimes, the tackier, the better.

City magazine editors are most receptive to shorter pieces (around 1,000 words) on music, the arts, and local history. If you enjoy and/or know of a struggling painter, a promising sculptor, a talented but overlooked dance company, write about it. Culture sells to a cultured audience.

Whether you live in the city or in the suburbs, it's your town. If you have an interest in something—from politics to potholes—exploit it.

Maybe all you have is an opinion, a personal experience you share with friends and neighbors. Expand it, explore it, write it, and you could well have a marketable article. Every city magazine offers a back-of-the-book final page, a space for an 800- to 1,000-word personal essay presented less for the subject per se than how that view is expressed.

Most city magazines offer free "writer's guidelines." Send for them. They give you a more precise idea of what the publication is looking for and provide an excellent way to make a first contact with an editor.

When you get ready to compose a query letter, be aware of three factors:

1) Never, absolutely never, send carbon copies. If you don't want a form letter response, don't send out a form letter request. Tailor *your* city magazine idea to *your* city magazine editor. It is essential for you to keep abreast of what the magazine has already published. Not only does this allow for possible follow-up pieces, but even a great article idea will be rejected if your subject happens to be on the cover of the issue currently or recently on the newsstands.

2) Be specific. In addition to explaining what your article is about, mention whom you intend to interview, approximate length, the point of view you plan to take, and, as briefly as possible, spell out any credentials you have to qualify you to do the piece. But, don't oversell the article. If you have an interesting idea about local governmental shenanigans, don't try to pass it off as the next Watergate scoop and yourself as the next Woodward or Bernstein.

3) The writing style of the query letter should be the style you will use in the proposed article. In fact, the first paragraph of your query can be the proposed lead of your piece. City magazines are looking for writers. Introduce yourself with your words. First impressions count.

Finally, here are some of my golden rules for free-lancing for city magazines:

* Be thorough—read and analyze all forms of printed material, from the wedding announcements through the classifieds of daily and weekly newspapers, advertising flyers, newsletters, signs in store windows . . . and become a conscientious producer of story ideas.

* Be curious—if something or someone caught your attention, it's a good bet that your neighbors' interest was also piqued . . . find out what it means.

* Be available—stop by the offices of your city magazine. In addition to looking through their stack of other city magazines for story ideas that would also apply to your town, get to know the staff. And let

them get to know you. There have been many times when I pitched an idea that an editor rejected, but he had a notion of his own, needed a free lancer, and one happened to be sitting right in front of him.

* Be disciplined—clean, accurate copy is a must; meeting deadlines is a given.

* Believe in yourself—the only way to approach free-lancing is not to sell yourself short.

72

STARTING YOUR ARTICLE RIGHT: SIX STEPS

By Omer Henry

Have you ever wished you knew why an editor returned one of your articles? Have you doubted that he had a valid reason for doing so?

It's possible, even probable, that editors, being human, make errors. It's more likely, however, that for every wrong decision by an editor, he's right on target a hundred times. Otherwise, he'd soon be out of a job. It is also likely that most often the reason he sent your article back is that you didn't start it right.

Starting an article right involves six simple steps. If you are a new writer, one who sells occasionally, or even one with an impressive track record, you'll find these six elements valuable.

First, the subject. You need to know what topics the magazine to which you intend to submit your article generally publishes. You'll get this information by reading the market lists and news of new magazines and their requirements in *The Writer* and *The Writer's Handbook,* and by studying the magazine itself.

Writer's guidelines are another excellent source of a magazine's needs and requirements. These will be sent on request, but be sure to enclose a self-addressed stamped envelope. Here's an idea of what you can expect from that source:

Face-to-Face, published by the United Methodist Church, P.O. Box 801, Nashville, TN 37202, reports it is for readers aged 15 to 18 inclusively. Its purpose is "To speak to young persons' concerns about their faith, their purpose in life, their personal relationships, goals, and feelings. . . . Articles and features to 1800 words with photographs are used on subjects of major interest and concern to high school young people. These include dating, marriage, home and family life, school extracurricular activities, vocations, and so forth."

Signature, 880 Third Avenue, New York, NY 10022, is much more detailed in its editorial guidelines: "Travel pieces are upbeat, aimed at the sophisticated traveler, and include both foreign and domestic subjects. We reach beyond the strictly 'destination' approach, seeking stories with an interesting premise or news peg: Monte Carlo becomes 'Americanized'; Tibet opens to travelers; Britain's green thumb; the 'eatingest' town in France; Hemingway's Venice."

Armed with such information I find it difficult to understand how one can fail to select a suitable subject for the magazine he has in mind.

Once you have chosen a suitable subject, you are off to a good start. You've passed milestone number one. But that is all. No editor ever bought an article simply because it was on the right subject.

What comes next? Let me illustrate: Not long go I learned of a deaf mute who was running his own business and doing well. Since I knew that *Grit* often publishes articles dealing with the handicapped, I felt that this deaf man might be a suitable subject for that publication. Therefore, in step two, I conducted my preliminary research. My objective was to get facts upon which to build a query—a strong sales letter—to the editor of *Grit.*

From the friend who had given me the original information about the deaf man, John Yeh, I obtained the article in which Yeh's story first appeared in a local weekly newspaper. In it, I found that Yeh had emigrated with his parents from Taiwan to the United States when he was twelve. He had learned to read English by virtually memorizing the Chinese-English dictionary. Because he could find no work, even after he earned a master's degree from the University of Maryland, he and his three brothers decided to open their own business. This background information gave me element three—an idea.

It is not enough for a query to include only a suitable subject: If an editor is going to consider it seriously, the query tells how the writer proposes to handle the subject and what the theme of the article is. That must be important. My idea for the article about Yeh was to show that a deaf person, if he prepares himself, can become a highly successful businessman.

Now I was ready for step four—writing the query. It is difficult to overemphasize the importance of a query. Usually, it is your introduction to an editor. It tells him whether you have done your homework, whether you know a good idea when you see it, whether you can write in an entertaining and forceful manner, whether you are careful with facts.

Something needs to be said about multiple queries. Writers like to use multiple queries because they are time-savers. But some editors will not give you an assignment based on a query if they know it has gone to other publications. Although multiple queries are more acceptable today than they were a decade ago, the new writer will do well to avoid using them.

Any query must make clear what you have to offer. It should be brief. I almost never send out a query that is more than one page long, and often it is far less than that. Here is the query I sent to *Grit* about John Yeh:

John Yeh knew from bitter experience how difficult it is for a deaf person, no matter how well qualified, to obtain work. This, he felt, was wrong. If one were capable of performing the required duties, he should be given an opportunity to do so.

Yeh set out to aid at least a few hearing impaired people to improve their quality of life by obtaining jobs. With the aid of a loan from the Small Business Administration, Yeh and his three brothers opened Integrated Microcomputer Services, Inc., a computer systems services and software development firm.

That was three years ago. Today IMS utilizes 8,300 square feet of office space, employs 80 individuals, about twenty percent of whom are college educated but deaf. Sixty percent of the personnel can communicate with sign language.

In fiscal 1982, IMS revenues amounted to $2.8 million. Projected 1983 revenues are $8.5 million. Thus it is clear that even though Yeh is deaf, he has not only found suitable employment for himself and his brothers, but has also opened the door to at least a few individuals with hearing impairment.

Grit readers would find this story entertaining, informative, and highly inspirational. I'd like to do it for you. Are you interested in it?

That query brought a "go ahead" from *Grit*. However, when I query an editor for whom I have not worked, I give him a brief statement of my journalistic pedigree, i.e.:

Credentials:
Author: *Writing and Selling Magazine Articles* (The Writer, Inc.)
Editor: Field Editor for *Fuel Oil News,* the leading journal in its field.
Contributor: Here I name a few magazines for which I've written—publications comparable to the one I'm trying to reach. Then I add, "and for more than a hundred national newspapers and magazines."

In the Yeh story, my next step—number five of the six elements—was to research the article. By telephone I arranged to interview John Yeh. Since he is deaf, his secretary acted as interpreter. I prepared a list of questions designed to elicit the information I'd need in writing the article I had offered to write. Here is that list:

1. I have your name as John Yeh. Is that correct?
2. Where were you born? When?
3. When did you come to America? Why? Who came with you?
4. Where did you establish your home?
5. Where in U.S. did you first attend school?
6. How did you manage to communicate?
7. What did you study? Why?
8. Did you go to college? Where? Why?
9. What did you study in college? Why?
10. Did you do graduate work? Where? What did you study?
11. Are you married? What is your spouse's name?
12. What was your first job in U.S.?
13. What was your next employment?
14. Why did you found IMS? When? Where did you get the money?
15. What services does IMS offer?
16. How many employees does IMS have? How many are handicapped?
17. How do the hearing employees communicate with the deaf?
18. How well do the handicapped employees perform?
19. What is your position with the firm? Who owns it?
20. What is the firm's objective?
21. How good is business?
22. What comments would you like to make?

Mr. Yeh gave me a bulky file filled with information about IMS and a news release reporting that the Maryland Department of Economic & Community Development Advisory Commission had awarded IMS the 1982 Bill Pate Award for outstanding contributions to Maryland's economy.

Then came the picture-taking session—item six of the necessary steps in starting an article right. I think it is a mistake to believe that only a professionally trained photographer can take pictures suitable for illustrating a magazine article. I have had no formal training in photography, yet I do the photographs for nearly all of my articles. I frequently do color shots that are used on magazine covers.

Even if you must take a course in photography in order to produce suitable photos, it is time and money well spent. Photographs are often more important than the text in selling an article. Frequently, editors ask to see my pictures before they give me a go-ahead for an article. And pictures pay exceptionally well. You're really missing a bet if you fail to furnish photographs with your article.

If you feel you can't make the pictures yourself, perhaps you have a friend who will cooperate with you in doing the job. If not, ask the subject if he has photographs you may use in illustrating the article.

When you are doing a piece about a company, the chances are it will be glad to give you a good supply of photographs. Recently, I visited Disney World at Orlando, Florida. From the Public Relations office, I obtained a generous supply of literature and pictures that I plan to use when I write an article on the subject.

A few years ago, when I was doing a travel piece about the famous Stone Mountain Park at Atlanta, Georgia, the state Tourist Office furnished me with excellent photos and transparencies, which I used to illustrate the article for *The Washington Times*.

When I had taken all the six steps in preparing to write the Yeh article, I returned to my study and transcribed the interview. I found I had an abundance of material—including many direct quotations—for my article. Since I had started the project right, actually writing the piece was a simple matter. When I finished it, I mailed it to *Grit* and shortly afterward received a check.

In over half a centry of free lancing, I've learned that if I offer editors an article that is built as I have outlined here, it is likely to sell. You can do the same.

73

HUMOR IS PUBLISHABLE

By Richard Armour

Two of the hardest forms of writing to publish these days are poetry and fiction. But that doesn't disturb me the slightest, because I don't write either kind. Oh, I wrote some serious, even morbid, poetry when I was in high school. However, I got that out of my system, along with whatever was causing my acne, and never again wrote poetry in the manner of Ezra Pound, T.S. Eliot, or even Edgar A. Guest.

As for fiction, I once wrote a short story. In one of my rare flashes of wisdom, I tore it up. Not at once, of course, but after it came back from sixteen magazines, each time with a printed rejection slip and no encouragement whatsoever.

I admire writers of poetry and fiction. I think they write two of the highest forms of literary art and creativity. So I am sorry if this is a difficult time for publishing their work. I hope there is a change of taste, or whatever is necessary, and that poets and writers of short stories and novels will have their editors knocking at their doors or writing them begging letters: "Please send us something—anything."

But my bent, and with the passing years I am growing more bent than ever, is humor—humor which takes the form of light verse rather than poetry and light nonfiction rather than fiction. The way my mind works, or plays, is indicated by the fact that when I typed the word "difficult" in the paragraph above, it first came out "fiddicult." The word "fiddicult" so entranced me that I found it difficult, or fiddicult, to go on.

If you study the market lists in an inclusive and reliable reference work, such as *The Writer's Handbook,* you will encounter time after time such discouraging comments as "Most articles staff written," "Currently overstocked," "No fiction," "No poetry," "No unsolicited manuscripts considered," and "Query." But you will also find, if you look hard enough, "Humor," "Humorous pieces, 1,000 to 2,000

393

words," "Humorous or human-interest articles," "Satire, sophisticated humor," "Light treatment, lively, enjoyable style," and so on.

Or study the magazines themselves, as I do. Often I find a magazine
that uses humor occasionally, in prose or verse, yet makes no mention
of it in the brief description in a market list. Many times, over the
years, I have come upon a magazine that seemed to me to need
humor, but perhaps its editor was not aware that it did. I have tried
prose or verse humor on such a magazine and occasionally have
broken in, sometimes making the market my own. Thus I had a half
page in a medical journal every month for twenty-three years.

So the markets for humor exist. They take more ferreting out than
they did when I started to write almost fifty years ago. In those days I
was writing for several magazines that no longer exist, such as *Liberty*
and *Look,* and others that (I think mistakenly) have given up the humor
that once livened their pages.

Now we come to the heart of the matter: writing humor that will
sell. I should like to be methodical about this, perhaps even a little
pedagogical, and so shall list the points I have in mind. Or rather, the
points I *had* in mind, because they are out of my mind, as I myself
am often thought to be. (In fact, the most wide-ranging of my books
of prose humor, selected from my writings in sixteen magazines, is
entitled precisely that: *Out of My Mind.*)

1. It is as hard to make readers laugh as it is to make them cry. In
other words, humor of marketable caliber is no easy literary form.
Humor in verse (i.e. light verse), for instance, is more than a matter
of writing something that rhymes. At its best, it is more rational, if
not more intellectual, than much of today's serious poetry, and it is
far more concerned with both the correctness and the tricks of technique. Rarely has successful, publishable light verse been written as
free verse—without rhyme or meter. Don Marquis is one of the few
who managed it. And rarely has it been published when it featured
purposely bad meter and outrageous rhymes. Ogden Nash was a
genius at parodying poetry and contriving original, unexpected rhymes
—rhymes a serious poet would never use. But it would be risky to try
to follow in Nash's nimble footsteps.

There is a reason for emphasis on technique in light verse. The
serious poet has lofty thoughts and evocative imagery (metaphors,
similes, personification, etc.). Lacking these, the light verse writer

substitutes the various techniques of meter and rhyme, often trying to surprise.

2. If you wish to write publishable humor in the form of light verse, you must do a little homework, and domework. Read, study, and analyze the works of the best published writers, past and present, of humorous writing. Go back to the work of such as Samuel Hoffenstein, Arthur Guiterman, F.P.A. (Franklin Pierce Adams), Dorothy Parker, Morris Bishop, David McCord, Ogden Nash, Margaret Fishback, and Phyllis McGinley. Phyllis McGinley, by the way, was the only light verse writer to win the Pulitzer Prize, in 1961, though by that time she had become what I would call a writer of light poetry.

3. Prose humor can take the form of either fiction or nonfiction. A short story can be light, even funny. It may even be wild, zany. But it may be merely playful, or have touches that give comic relief to what would otherwise be a serious piece. Humorous or light prose can go beyond the feature or magazine short story to the novel or even to the stage—or screen. There is always the wonderful possibility that a humorous piece can be the basis of a Broadway hit or a film with a major comic star like Woody Allen. You can dream, can't you? I hope you can, because that is one of the things that keeps a writer writing.

4. One further advantage of writing humor in prose is that it can be almost any length, whereas light verse must be kept short (usually four to twelve lines). A good marketable length for prose humor is around 1,200 words, but certain publications use humor pieces that run to about 3,000 words. Thus, a piece of prose humor can be more than a filler. It can be a feature article that will be listed in the table of contents. This gives the writer more of a showcase than a humorous poem and may lead to bigger, if not better, things.

5. But let me come back to earth, or to the more immediately possible, in the marketing of humor. Since, as I have indicated, I am not a writer of fiction, I make use of humor in nonfiction. I do this in two ways: (1) I put a light touch into what might have been a serious article on some such subject as education, the family (and divorce), politics, inflation, aging, travel—just about anything. Or (2) I toy with some personal yet universal bit of trivia, such as plastic plants, paperclips, losing my glasses case, wire coat hangers, or my neighbor's leaves that suddenly became mine.

I have placed more-or-less humorous articles in the first category in *The Christian Science Monitor, The New York Times, Parents, Woman's Day,* the in-flight magazines of several airlines, and so on. I have found even more takers of the second type of short humorous articles, including "The Phoenix Nest" (formerly in the *Saturday Review* but now syndicated by the Associated Press), *Los Angeles* and other regional magazines, and *The Saturday Evening Post.*

6. For me, humor in book form has proved one of the most marketable types of writing. This includes humor in books for children. (Let me say that I think the sense of humor, like the imagination, is livelier in children than in most adults.) A book of humor, if original, timely, and highly polished (though the signs of effort should not show), is almost as publishable as a how-to book. And there is always the possibility of doing a humorous how-to book, which would bring you double rewards.

Despite what many say, humor is not dead. Maybe sick humor is, after getting more and more sickening, and that's all right with me. I try to write healthy humor, perhaps because I have a healthy respect for humor, and when I have written it I try to find a market for it. Usually, but not always, I do. I have to hunt harder than I once did, but I am a determined hunter. Perhaps I need a bird dog, or a word dog.

The world needs humor today and, fortunately, some editors are aware of this. All you have to do to get your humor published is to write publishable humor, and then find the right place for it. It is as simple as that. As a matter of fact, I once wrote, and published, an article on the so-called funny bone. What is funny about the funny bone is that there is nothing funny about it.

74

POETRY'S SLANT VISION

By Josephine Jacobsen

POETRY IS the most honored and least read form of literature. Many intelligent and highly literate readers haven't read a poem since leaving college. The most common complaint is, "I'm just not up to poetry. I honestly don't feel that I understand it." Usually added: "I wish I did."

The same person will attribute this impenetrability to the difficulties of modern poetry, saying or implying that if only poets wrote like Tennyson or Wordsworth, the complainer would be an avid reader. But both the speaker and the spoken-to know that this is doubtful, to put it kindly.

Why then does poetry hold, as it does, a place of such respect in the minds of its non-readers? I think it is because there is a deep feeling, conscious or not, that if it can be reached, there is in poetry some sort of truth, of illumination, of pleasure, some quintessentially *different* quality that exists nowhere else. And those who know poetry, as readers or as writers, know, too, that this is nothing less than the truth. William Carlos Williams said it once and for all, bluntly: "You have no other language for it than the poem."

Among the greatest rewards a poet can have is one of those letters that arrive from an unknown reader, saying that some particular poem has penetrated to an area nothing else has reached—has released an emotion or a comprehension which the reader has never been able to express, to put into language—that magic which enables us to understand what we mean.

How it does this, like anything to do with true art, is partly a mystery; but its comprehensible part is made up of a number of strengths. One of these strengths is its ability to overcome an initial hazard: its own medium. While the painter, the sculptor, the musician, work in a medium that is not pinned down by any dictionary, or assumed to be within reach of anyone over the age of two, the poet has to work in one that is everyone's property; the medium in which advertisements are composed, news is relayed, orders are given, the thousand details of daily life are expressed.

Form and vocabulary are the poet's basic tools. The qualities he wants in his work—strength, concision, penetration, memorability—all must come through these. There is the classic argument, which never will be resolved, between established and free forms, between those who feel that both rhyme and rhythm are more dangers than aids, and those who see them as part of the very marrow of the poem. It seems to me a bootless, though occasionally pleasurable, contention. The approach of the individual poet is deeply built into his poetic genes. Never can he successfully write against his own grain, to please reader, editor, or even himself. There is a quality that makes all poetry a whole, but it will never be a right-or-wrong choice of concept. The poet will find in his own work changes (or else he should stop writing), but they will be organic, not imposed. The fact that my own work has moved from an originally lyric, usually rhymed, somewhat head-long form, subsequently to one looser, more superficially informal and explorative; and then, at the moment, to one highly compressed, in which the aim is an explosion tightly contained, certainly doesn't point this development out as the necessarily desirable path.

As in politics, or for that matter in anything else, the extremes rarely listen to one another. Those who cling to rhyme and scansion, to inherited forms, often won't admit that there are always perils, and have their own danger of dullness and monotony, and the lack of living invention; and those who totally equate originality with the bizarre, rather than the discovered connection, are determined not to admit the profound need for rhythm, for some form of varied repetition, however subtle, which is an essence of poetry. The enduring response to nursery rhymes, to street games, simply cannot be denied. Can anyone argue that "I, said the fly/With my little eye/I saw him die . . ." or "One, two, button my shoe/Three, four, shut the door" survive because of their intellectual content? But then, before one can turn around, this is being used for an argument that poetry can thump along like a street band.

Beginning poets—and for that matter, all others—need constantly to be aware of reverse options, and possibilities, and above all to beware of that modishness that is the enemy of poetry—the ear cocked constantly to the critical or editorial reaction, instead of being ruled by the response to the individual poem's necessity. Each poem *has* its own necessity. Every poet has experienced the false start, the realization that somehow the poem is being forced into a form—or even more dangerously—a tone, that is not its own.

But before all the decisions on form, comes the matter of language—this particular poem's language. Nothing is more dangerous to a poem than the idea that poems are composed in a special language, that "poetic words" are of its essence. Such words are far more useful to prose, which controls and incorporates them, though they are dangerous enough there. It is the way words are used and the relationships between them that turns them into poetry. It is the connections they make, the sounds by which they respond to each other, the surprises of their possibilities, that make for the quality of poetry. That surprise, which is one of the essential ingredients of poetry, comes in part from the sudden transformation of a word—a revelation of its meaning, what it can say, here, now. There is an oblique quality in poetry that has nothing to do with obscurity or preciousness, with anything that lacks the particular truth. To be chary of poets' dicta, I would quote only one other—Emily Dickinson's "Tell all the truth/but tell it slant." The elaborate, the self-conscious, is hostile to poetry. Everyone who has dealt with masses of the poetry of beginners knows that its most common fault is a lack of original imagination clothed in purportedly "poetic" language.

"Poetry is. . . ," "Beauty is . . ." are sentences never to be completed. "One of the things poetry is . . ." is, on the other hand, an endlessly fascinating and often valuable attempt.

An experienced poet is rarely in need of advice other than that he must give himself. A beginning poet, however talented, is a different matter. We constantly use the expression "beginner," but it is a very tricky one. There is the beginner in the common sense of the term, one who has little experience in wrestling with his art. But the question of "beginning" is vital to all poets. One of the innumerable pitfalls in the writing of poetry is self-repetition; the danger that, having discovered that there is a kind of poem one can accomplish successfully, one will linger in that tried territory, putting a bit of extra polish, of extra ingenuity, on a poem which breaks no new ground, shows no sign of the discoveries that life forces upon us. Such work, however expert, has about it something sad, and limited. The worst part of this is that the poet, conscious that his poems of this year, in their vision, are identical to those of earlier years, often is driven to substitute linguistic shock and wrenched syntax for poetic growth. One needs to repeat that growth with its altered vision, is organic, not imposed. Of course this is frightening, but whoever said that the writing of poetry was an unintimidating occupation?

On one of the early space-flights, the astronauts took along, among other forms of life, a spider, to see how the problem of weightlessness would affect *her* occupation. The spider, at first baffled, after repeated attempts finally managed a new method of constructing its troublesome web—and to a poet that was one of the exciting results of the flight. I wrote a poem about that, and it ended, "You frighten me very much. Am I to understand then/that there is no end, absolutely no end, to beginning?" Every poem is a web constructed by that spider.

The necessity to discard or modify concepts and methods is often a painful one, and the immediate results often discouraging. But like the spider web, one of the things a poem does is to demand a different, a hitherto unperceived connection. The theme, the subject matter, will have been used a thousand times; but the poem will make a surprising but valid connection, will see things by its own instinct. In the reader, it will require a leap of recognition; but the honest truth must be there to be recognized. Nothing sows distrust and distaste more quickly than the reader's realization that what seemed originally a new and marvelous flower, turns out to be, on closer inspection, rootless and artificial—whether made of cheap paper or silk. That distrust expands from the poem to the poet. No cliché can be more flattening.

Another of poetry's primary demands is that of particularity. No quality is more vital. Generalization is poison to the poem. And it is generalities that especially beset the beginner. In the excitement and optimism of that moment in which the possibility of that poem occurs, there is an attempt to conquer a giant theme. The poem will be ambitious, but vague. It will talk about "beauty" "love" "evil" without one flash of intimate, particular revelation. I remember struggling to read with an open mind a submitted poem of which the title was "Life." I really knew that the problem was probably a beginner's necessity to explain somehow that the impulse driving him to write the poem had

400

significance and universality. The poem can bring us to the universals of "beauty" "evil" "death" "love" only through the most focused concentration on the particular.

Keats writes of joy. But joy is a figure, *whose hand is ever at his lips/ bidding adieu.*

The poor poet is caught between the demands of the particular, and the necessity that the particular should relate to some aspect of the universal.

The second most common cause for disaster for the tyro poet is the unconscious belief that because something has happened to him for the first time, it is of interest to the reader. His excitement, his revelation, is a preparation, not a product. A disaster, a joy, a perception, will go into the human experience, which is the raw material for poetry; but, untransformed, *unprocessed,* so to speak, it can tell us nothing that moves us. *There is no other language for it but the poem.* Poetry has no purpose; but its happiest side-effect is the unknown reader who writes, "That is what I have known and never been able to express . . ."; "that has given me, in language, the relief of recognition"; "that has allowed me to communicate with myself."

Poems such as William Carlos Williams's "Asphodel That Greeny Flower," or Auden's "Lay Your Sleeping Head, My Love," or Yeats's "Sailing to Byzantium," rise to their accomplishment by the indispensable qualities of strong emotion under technical discipline, used so that the reader instantly feels that there is "no other language for it but the poem." And of course at the core, there is always that X, never totally subject to analysis, but always unarguable.

Obviously, the language of poetry alters with time—it develops, incorporates, discards—especially discards. While certain words and phrases remain alive and untarnished in their own context—those of the Elizabethan lyrics, for example—they would seem artificial and even ridiculous in the context of contemporary life, the only material from which we can make our own poetry. Constantly, new influences, especially those of our inescapable daily history, enter our work, bringing with them their own vocabularies. But any word that leaps out at the reader, claiming attention beyond its service to the poem, will be fully as destructive as the prostrate cliché. Poor poet, walking his narrow line between opposed dangers: the danger of producing guess-what-happened-to-me-last-night verse, on the one hand, or the artificiality of something disconnected from his own emotional experience, on the other; between a flat lack of originality, and a wrenched and effortful invention; between a plodding rhythm and assured rhyme, and a secret invasion by prose; between the fatal generalization, and true poem's universality.

And the strange thing is that, in the process of writing the poem, it is dangerous for the poet to be conscious of any of these perils. Thinking about what the poem must *not* be, is fatal. That is criticism; that comes later. Like the centipede, which questioned as to its method of locomotion, never moved again, the poet, considering the *how* of what he is doing as he does it, is lost. Better a hundred blunders, a hundred discarded poems. Like the athlete, the poet cannot stop in mid-career, to analyze the poetic motion. All that has been learned, been experienced, will go into his poem. But, reading it over at once, then again days later, the poet has vanished, and a cold and demanding eye is fixed on each word of each line.

It is possible to argue that good poetry is becoming more difficult to write. We have lost many common assumptions; changes hurtle forward at a previously inconceivable speed, giant problems of total destruction, of transformations of life, surround us. But it is also possible—and I think true—to say that never has poetry been such a necessity, never have we needed that momentary order and peace brought by the poem, as we do right now. Auden said that poetry changes nothing; the event will go forward just as though the poem did not exist. But it does change something—us. Through the slant vision of poetry we learn new truth, and for that truth we have indeed no other language.

75

EVERYONE WANTS TO BE PUBLISHED, BUT...

BY JOHN CIARDI

AT A RECENT writers' conference I sat in on a last-day session billed as "Getting Published." Getting published was, clearly, everyone's enthusiasm. The hope of getting published will certainly do as one reason for writing. It need not be the only, nor even the best, reason for writing. Yet that hope is always there.

Emily Dickinson found reasons for writing that were at least remote from publication. Yet even she had it in mind. She seems to have known that what she wrote was ahead of its time, but she also seemed to know that its time would come. If Thomas H. Johnson's biography of her is a sound guide, and I believe it is, she spent her last ten years writing her "letters to the future." The letters, to be sure, were addressed to specific friends; yet they were equally addressed *through* her friends to her future readers. As Hindemith spent ten years composing his quartets and then ten more creating the terms by which they were to be assessed critically, so Emily spent ten years writing her poems (1776 of them, if I recall the right number), and then ten more years stating the terms for their reception.

Even she, then, had an audience (which is to say, publication) in mind. Nor do I imply that the desire to publish is an ignoble motive. Every writer wants to see himself in print. No writer, to my knowledge, has ever been offended when his published offerings were well received. The desire to publish becomes ignoble only when it moves a writer to hack and hurry the work in order to get it into print.

Poetry, of course, is relatively free of commercial motive. Every generation has its Edgar Guest. Ours, I suppose, is Rod McKuen. These are writers whose remouthing of sentiments catches some tawdry emotional impulse in commercial quantities. Yet such writers—or so I have long suspected—must come to believe seriously in the inanities they write. I doubt that they have sold out to the dollar sign: more tragically, they have sold out to themselves.

Such writers aside, it is hard to imagine that anyone would think to bribe a poet to write a bad poem. It would follow then (all temptation to cheat being out of the equation) that the only reason for writing a poem is to write it as well as one possibly can. Having so written it, one would naturally like to see it published.

I was, accordingly, in sympathy with the conference members—but I was also torn. For I had just spent days reading a stack of the manuscripts these people had submitted, and I had found nothing that seemed worthy of publication. I sat by, thinking that session on getting published was an exercise in swimming in a mirage. I even suspected a few of those present of drowning in their mirages.

Then one of the hard-case pros on the conference staff delivered a statistic. "You want to get published?" he said. "Fine. Look at the magazines. What are they publishing? The answer is, roughly, 98 percent nonfiction and not quite half of one percent poetry. Yet of the manuscripts submitted at this conference, seventy-six are poetry and only two are nonfiction." He paused. "Now you tell me," he said, "where are you going to get published?"

The hard case, as it happened, was a successful nonfiction writer for the large-circulation magazines; he had dismissed from consideration the literary quarterlies that do publish poetry, sometimes without payment, but sometimes with an "honorarium." To the quarterlies, I would certainly add our two excellent poetry tabloids, *The American Poetry Review* and *Poetry Now.*

For poetry does get published, though not on terms that would be attractive to the big-circulation pros. Poets *qua* poets do not run into serious income tax problems. So be it. If a little is all one asks, then a little is enough. I have never known of anyone who turned to poetry in the expectation of becoming rich by it. Were I to impersonate the hard-case pro at that conference, I could argue that a writer writes as an alcoholic drinks—which is to say, compulsively, and for its own sake. An alcoholic expects no special recognition for being helpless in his compulsion: Why should a poet expect money and recognition for his compulsion?

The fact is that the good poets do generally find their rewards and recognitions. Ego being what it is (and the poet's ego more so), any given poet may think his true merit has been slighted. For myself, whatever I have managed to make of my writing (and it has been a love affair, not a sales campaign), I have always felt that my own satisfaction (or at least the flickering hope of it) was a total payment. Whatever else came has always struck me as a marvelous bonus. And there have been bonuses—grants, prizes, even a small, slow rain of checks. How could I fail to rejoice in that overflow of good? I wish it to every writer, and wish him my sense of joy in it.

But there is more to it. The hard case's manuscript count stayed with me. Can seventy-six poets and two nonfiction writers be called a writers' conference? He hadn't mentioned fiction, and I never learned how many fiction manuscripts had been turned in. But why, I asked myself, would seventy-six turn to poetry and only two to nonfiction? All writing is writing; all of it is part of one motion. I have enjoyed trying different sorts of writing. This present piece, for example, is nonfiction. It is part of the same exploration that poems take me on.

I asked myself the question, but I know I already had the answer —at least part of it—from the poems I had read and criticized. The poems had been bad, and I had fumbled, as one must, at trying to say why I thought they were bad. I wished on that last day that the conference were just starting and that I had ahead of me another chance to identify the badness of the poems. But perish that thought: I was emotionally exhausted.

Yet on that last day the reason so few of the conference members had turned to nonfiction seemed clear to me. Even to attempt nonfiction a writer must take the trouble of acquiring some body of information. The poems I had read lacked anything that could be called a body of information. The writers seemed to have assumed that their own excited ignorance was a sufficient qualification for the writing of poetry.

I wanted to go back and say to my conferees, "Your poems care nothing about the fact!" Isn't that another way of saying they were conceived in ignorance? Not one of the poets I read had even tried to connect fact A to fact B in a way to make an emotional experience of the connection. The writing lacked *thingness* and a lover's knowledge of thing.

Consider these lines by Stanley Kunitz (the italics are mine):

> Winter that *coils* in the thickets now,
> Will *glide* from the fields, the *swinging* rain
> Be *knotted* with flowers. On every bough
> A bird will *meditate* again.

405

The diction, the rhyming, the rhythmic flow and sustainment are effortless, but how knowledgeably things fall into place! Winter *coils* in the thickets because that snow that lies in shade is the last to melt, thinning down to scrolls of white by the last thaw. Winter will then *glide* from the fields—and what better (continuous, smooth) motion for the run-off of the last melt? The *swinging* rain (what word could better evoke our sense of April showers?) will then be *knotted* (as if) with flowers while birds (as if) *meditate* on every bough. The rain, of course, will not literally be knotted with flowers, nor will birds, literally, meditate. Yet what seems to be a scientific inaccuracy is of the central power of metaphor. Metaphor may, in fact, be conceived as an exactly felt error.

Metaphor is supposed to state the unknown in terms of the known. It is supposed to say X equals Y. Yet when we say "John is a lion," we do not think of John with a mane, with four clawed paws, nor with a pompon tipped tail. We extract from "lion" the emotional equivalent we need and let the rest go. The real metaphoric formula is X does-and-does-not-equal Y. Kunitz understands this formula. His knowledge of it is part of his qualification as a master poet.

There is more. More than can be parsed here. But note how the italicized words *hearken* to one another, each later term being summoned (by some knowledge and precision in the poet) by what went before. The italicized words form what I will dare to call a chord sequence by a composer who has mastered musical theory.

The passage, that is to say, is empowered by a body of knowledge of which I could find no trace in the poets I had been reading at the conference. My poets had been on some sort of trip. Their one message was "I feel! I feel!" Starting with that self-assertive impulse (and *thing* be damned), they then let every free association into the poem. They were too ignorant even to attempt a principle of selection.

I do not imply that I know what any given poem's principle of selection ought to be. To find the principle that serves best and to apply it in a way to enchant the reader is the art and knowledge of the poet. Everything in a good poem must be *chosen* into it. Even the accidents. How else could it be when one stroke of the pen will slash a thing out forever? All that has not been slashed out, it follows, is chosen in.

Ignorance, as nearly as I could say it (too late), was what had really stifled the poems I had read. The writers had not cared enough to learn their own art and use their eyes.

They will, I suppose, get published. Some of them somewhere. But have they earned the right to publication? I ask the question not to answer it. It is every writer's question to ask for himself.

76

CREATING TELEVISION STORIES AND CHARACTERS

By Stewart Bronfeld

CREATING stories and the characters in them is what script writing is really all about. The rest — the technology, the business, the timing and the luck—are also found in a thousand other activities of life. But when, in the matrix of a blank page, a story starts to emerge which never before existed, and characters are born and develop who never lived before that moment, something very special is happening. It is part craft, part art and (there's no other word) part magic.

The magic of the creative process remains basically mysterious, like any other kind of birth. The art is a product of the artist's personality and thus differs with each person. But the craft is based on experience, common sense and professional techniques and *can* be learned and practiced.

Principles and rules and fashions of playcraft change but one bedrock truth remains constant: *the basis of effective drama is conflict.* Learn this and you learn a lot. Sophocles knew it. Shakespeare knew it. And the writer of the script for that popular TV series you saw last Tuesday knew it. The conflict of man against man, man against woman, man against nature, man against himself—the clang of two opposing forces coming against each other makes for drama. The conflict may be Big and Important—the numberless masses tearing down the mighty regime of the Czar in *Dr. Zhivago*. Or it may be small and wistful—a fat, homely butcher and a plain neighborhood girl making a clumsy grab at a chance for love in *Marty*.

Consider one of the most successful motion pictures of all time, *Gone With the Wind.* Along with her skill for recreating a colorful time and place and sheer storytelling art, Margaret Mitchell built her story with such effective dramatic conflicts that both the book and the movie are still very much alive (and making money) today. While the Civil

War itself was not directly one of the conflicts (for conflict implies two opposing forces and the North almost never appears in her work), it served as a suitable backdrop for the interplays of strong dramatic conflicts with which the author fashioned her story and characters:

The Old South versus the emerging reality of a new and different world.

Rhett Butler, who could have any woman he wanted—*except* the one he wanted most.

Scarlett O'Hara, beautiful enough to attract any man *she* wanted—except the one she wanted most.

Ashley Wilkes, torn between wanting Scarlett and needing Melanie.

These characters, with their frustrations and longings, could have become no more than soap opera figures—just as *Macbeth* could have become no more than a murder melodrama. The difference, in both cases, was that the authors had the gift of imparting life to their characters and meaning to their conflicts. Thus audiences *cared;* they still do.

Examine any good story and you will discover the conflict that motivates the main character(s) and moves the plot along. One of Somerset Maugham's most enduring stories is *Of Human Bondage,* whose very title highlights the conflict of the young surgeon fighting against his imprisoning love for a worthless girl. But just as enduring, if not as deep, are Laura Lee Hope's children's books about the Bobbsey Twins, each of which gets the kids into some conflict which, happily, is resolved in the final pages.

Sometimes if you look carefully you find the same basic conflict in widely different stories. In *Tom Sawyer,* it is wanting to be good to a loved one (Aunt Polly) versus the pull of adventure with wilder companions. The same conflict (in a dog instead of a boy) is the basis for the drama in *The Call of the Wild.* And, in essence, nearly the same conflict is at the heart of the story of the opera *Carmen.*

The knowledge that conflict makes for drama is a nuts-and-bolts tool which writers can use—especially when they sit at their writing desk caught up in a conflict of their own, namely, "I've got a rough idea of a plot but I don't know what to do with it." First, *think of the plot in terms of the conflict or conflicts involved.* If you cannot identify any, you probably do not have the basis for a very strong story idea. This in itself is an accomplishment, for it can save hours of work, reams of paper and pangs of disappointment later.

409

What contributes drama to the plot is not the conflict itself, but rather what the character does and how he or she does it in response to that conflict. People are naturally more interested in people than they are in circumstances. What engages their attention is not so much the adventure as the adventurer, not the danger so much as how the people react to what is menacing them, not the surprise ending, but how the characters in the story are affected by, and respond to, the surprise.

This simple but fundamental fact that people are primarily interested in people is the basis for another important tool of scriptcraft: *characterization,* the development in a character of specific personality traits. Examine most successful movies and television series and you will find they often have one thing in common: a well-drawn central character (or characters) whose personality traits are clearly defined. These traits may be good ones or bad ones, but they are distinctive. Early in a movie, over the weeks in a TV series, these characteristics become familiar to the viewer. They add a dimension of depth and reality to the character. Another (and perhaps paramount) reason for the enduring success of *Gone With the Wind* is the author's skillful use of characterization; Rhett Butler and Scarlett O'Hara were so vividly conceived and depicted that millions of readers and viewers have found it impossible to believe they are not real people.

On television, the mortality rate of new programs is appalling. Not many new shows survive a season's journey through the ratings mine field. Half-hour comedies are especially popular with viewers, and so smoke pours out the stacks of the Hollywood fun factories day and night as they churn out an endless assembly line of new shows, in which "wacky" characters do "wacky" things—and get "wacky" ratings and disappear. Sometimes, before they expire, they are desperately switched from one time slot to another, scrambling around the network's program schedule like escaped hamsters.

Why do so few of them take root and prosper? The answer, I think, is that they are sitcoms, or situation comedies—which means their emphasis is on ever-zanier "situations," with the people in them seldom developed beyond the cartoon character stage. But there *are* half-hour comedies that become popular successes with longtime runs and high ratings. While they also may be called sitcoms in the trade, these shows might be more accurately called "charcoms," for their humor

410

comes not from artificially contrived "situations," but from artfully created characterization.

Among them was one of the most successful television series of all time, *The Mary Tyler Moore Show*, which ended only because the star grew tired of the weekly grind. The program immediately became a top success on the rerun circuit and established something of a record for the price paid for syndication rights. The secret of the show's success was clearly the effective characterization established by the original creators and skillfully followed by all the subsequent script writers. The funny situations almost always resulted from, or were related to, the regular cast's character traits, which were familiar to every viewer. Proof of the power of good characterization is the fact that no less than three of the show's characters were spun off into successful series of their own: Rhoda, Phyllis and Lou Grant.

What makes this kind of "charcom" so successful is also what makes many dramatic series attain great popularity while their competition regularly arrives and departs. This includes action-adventure shows. *Kojak*, for example, was a tremendous hit, and still is, in its syndication afterlife. But *Kojak* was never really about cops-and-robbers and drug busts; it was primarily about Lieutenant Theo Kojak.

Therefore, whether you are writing a script for a television series, a single original teleplay or a movie, a prime factor to consider is the importance of character creation. Even when you feel your plot is the paramount consideration in a particular script, your characters should never be mere puppets manipulated to suit it. It does not always take a full-scale portrait to make a character come alive; sometimes a few well drawn strokes can do it.

The best and strongest plots, however, are those that evolve naturally, even inevitably, out of the characterization. These stories have more impact, because they are more believable. There is good reason for this. In the lives of most of us, very few important things happen for totally external reasons; what happens to us is often the result of what we do—and what we do is often the result of what we are. That is true of you and me and your potential viewers. If it is also true of your characters in what you make happen to them, they will be perceived not as concoctions, but as living characters with a dimension of depth and reality. Thus your story will not merely gain the attention of the audience; it will make some impact upon them. There's a difference; it means they will *care* about what they are watching. And, as producers, directors and story editors well know, when an audience feels an involvement, it shows in the ratings and at the box office.

Let us see an example of plot developing out of characterization. Jane is a timid young woman, terrified of asserting herself, due in large part to her overbearing mother. She is constantly driven to gain her mother's approval, seldom succeeding. A situation arises at work wherein problems are causing the company's management to consider going out of business. Jane, who has a keen and analytic mind, has diagnosed the problems and feels she has a solution that may save the company. The frantic meetings of the managers behind closed doors are getting louder each day.

Conflict: Jane's desire to offer her solution, thus possibly becoming a heroine, getting her reward and making her mother proud of her—versus her inability to push herself into the councils of upper management and possibly be rebuffed and humiliated. It's not *Hamlet,* but it is the basis for an interesting human drama with which the audience can identify.

The point is that the characterization I created for Jane does not function merely as a kind of outer garment she wears as she makes her way through the plot; the plot evolves directly out of her characterization. If I changed the kind of person Jane is, my plot would no longer work. The two—characterization and plot—are welded together.

Some writers may have an intuitive ability to create a fully defined character as they go along; however, it cannot hurt (and will always help) to write a detailed sketch or profile of any major character first. Creatively, the more you "know" about a character the more you contribute to his or her reality in the script. Practically, facets of the character's personality will often strongly suggest plot ideas. (When one of my characters is especially well defined, I occasionally become aware that he or she is really writing the scene, while I follow along at the typewriter, interested and even curious to find out what will happen next.)

However, writers do vary in both their skill and their inclination for characterization. For some writers, formulating a plot is paramount, and the people caught up in the action are merely vehicles to advance the story line. Obviously, if a plot is compelling enough, viewers will

412

be interested in what is happening even though they are not particularly interested in those to whom it happens. Many movies and television series attest to this. While I believe a more memorable story will evolve out of characterization, I would much rather see a script with an intriguing plot moving at a well-orchestrated pace even though with cardboard characters, than one with vividly sketched characters whose personalities are fascinating, but *nothing really happens*.

There is a test the script writer should apply to his or her work as it proceeds to be sure that there is a consistent plausibility to the characters and the plot. The test is *motivation*. Motivation makes the difference between actions seeming real or staged. People are not robots; they generally do what they do for a reason. Sensible people act from sensible reasons and fools act from foolish reasons. The writer looks at each action of the main characters and asks, "Would this particular person do this, in this particular circumstance?"

The movies of the thirties and forties, mostly ground out by writers on a weekly salary, were often written as fast as they were typed, and frequently had no time to bother with motivation. Now they live on mainly at 2:30 A.M. on television and there is a reliable way to identify them in the TV listings: the word *decides*. "An heiress decides to run off with her gardener . . ." "A millionaire decides to take a slum kid into his household . . ." Whenever you see the word *decides* in a movie listing, you know that the only motivation involved is that it was Thursday and the script was due in the producer's office by Friday. When you look over your script after a cooling-off period, try to be objective enough to note whether your character "decides" to do something just because, solely for plot purposes, you want him to. If he does, if proper motivation is lacking, it is a sign that the scene (or possibly a larger segment of the script) requires rethinking and rewriting.

There is another element in any kind of story, one not so susceptible to definite guidelines. I refer to *theme*. Writers generally are writers because they have an inclination (or perhaps an impulsion) to communicate. But the reason any individual writes any particular story must vary, not only with each writer but with each story he or she writes. We all have different interests, different outlooks on life and different matters we consider important; if these motivate us when we sit down to do our communicating—our writing—our work will reflect a theme.

413

In a story, plot is what happens. Theme is the larger framework of meaning in which it happens. Larger stories have larger themes, and lesser stories have lesser themes. In the powerfully written and expansively produced *The Godfather,* the theme was that evil is self-consuming. In a program I saw last night in a half-hour comedy series, the theme was the importance of good friends later in life.

Do not confuse a theme with a "message." The writer should not be trying to make a commentary on his or her theme, only to *air* it. Reflection on the meaning should rest with the viewer.

Do all writers have themes for their stories? The answer is, not all the time (and not always consciously). But a theme is an asset to any literary work. First, it elevates the story because there is some central meaning to it all. Then, it assures a better, more unified construction to the script, for it provides a general reference point to guide the direction of the plot and the development of the characters.

Herman Melville wrote, "To produce a mighty book, you must choose a mighty theme." You will find, however, that when it happens, it is more as though the mighty theme chose *you.*

77

HOW TO SELL YOUR TELEVISION SCRIPT

By Richard A. Blum

MARKETING a television script requires strategy, determination, and a realistic understanding of the industry. The marketplace is extremely competitive, and even the best projects written by established professionals might end up on the shelf. Still, an *excellent* original script—submitted to the right person at the right time—might suddenly break through all barriers. The key word is *excellent*. It makes no sense to submit a script unless you feel that it is in the most polished form (even then it will be subject to rewrites), and that it represents the highest calibre of your creative potential. One might think producers are inclined to see the masterpiece lurking behind a rough draft script. More likely, they'll focus on the weaknesses, compare it to top submissions, and generalize about the writer's talents. So, if you feel uncertain about the professional quality of a work, hold off submitting it. Your next work might show you off to better advantage.

Since unsolicited scripts tend to be lost or "misplaced" by production companies, it's a good idea to have a sufficient number of copies. The *minimum* number you will need is three—one for your files, one for submission, and one for inevitable rewrites. More realistically, you'll probably want additional copies for two or three producers, an agent or two, and your own reserve file for unanticipated submissions. Incidentally, fancy covers and title designs are totally unnecessary. Three inexpensive paper fasteners can be punched through the left hand margins of the manuscript. Scripts are usually photocopied to avoid the smudged look of carbons.

The Writers Guild

The Writers Guild of America protects writer's rights, and establishes minimum acceptable arrangements for fees, royalties, credits, and so on. You are eligible to join the Guild as soon as you sell your first project to a signatory company (one who has signed an agreement with the Guild). A copy of your contract is automatically filed and you will then be invited to join the membership. Before you sell the next project, you *have* to be a member of the Guild; otherwise, no signatory company can hire you.

The one-time membership fee is $500. In addition, 1% of yearly earnings as a writer (or $10 quarterly if you earn less than $1,000 as a writer).

Any writer can register a story, treatment, series format, or script with the Writers Guild of America. The service was set up to help writers establish the completion dates of their work. It doesn't confer statutory rights, but it does supply evidence of authorship which is effective for ten years (and is renewable after that). If you want to register a project, send one copy along with the appropriate fee ($10 nonmembers; $4 members) to: Writers Guild of America West, Inc., Registration Service, 8955 Beverly Blvd., Los Angeles, CA 90048. (Writers Guild of America East, Inc., 555 West 57th Street, New York, NY 10019, a separate corporation, is part of this national organization.)

You can also register dramatic or literary material with the U.S. Copyright Office—but most television writers rely on the Writers Guild. The Copyright Office is mainly used for book manuscripts, plays, music or lyrics, which the Writers Guild will not register. For appropriate copyright forms (covering dramatic compositions), write to: Register of Copyrights, Library of Congress, Washington, D.C. 20559.

The release form or waiver

If you have an agent, there is no need to bother with release forms. But if you're going to submit a project without an agent, you'll have to send to the producer or the production company for a release form—or waiver—in advance. (Addresses of selected production companies are listed at the end of this chapter.) Most production companies will return your manuscript without it. The waiver states that you won't sue the production company and that the company has no obligations to you. That may seem unduly harsh, but consider the fact that millions of dollars are spent on fighting plagiarism suits, and that hundreds of ideas are being developed simultaneously and coincidentally by writers, studios, and networks.

The waiver is a form of self-protection for the producer who wants to avoid unwarranted legal action. But it also establishes a clear line of communication between the writer and producer. So rest assured, if legal action is warranted, it can be taken.

The cover letter

When you prepare to send out your project, draft a cover letter that is addressed to a *person* at the studio, network, or production company. If you don't know who is in charge of program development, look it up in the trade papers, or telephone the studio receptionist. If she says, "Mr. So-and-So handles new projects," ask her to *spell* "Mr. So-and-So." That courtesy minimizes the chance of embarrassment, and maximizes the chance that the project will wind up at the right office.

The letter you write should sound professional. There's no need to offer apologies for being an unsold writer, or to suggest that the next draft will be ten times better than this one. If a cover letter starts off with apologies, what incentive is there to read the project?

Here's the tone a cover letter might have:

Dear_____
 I've just completed a mini-series called FORTUNES, based on the book by Marian Sherry. I've negotiated all TV and film rights to the property, which is a dramatic adventure series about a family caught in the California Gold Rush. I think you'll find the project suitable for the mini-series genre. It's highly visual in production values and offers unusual opportunities for casting.
 I look forward to your reaction. Thank you for your cooperation.
Sincerely,

The letter doesn't say I'm an unsold writer in the midwest or that Marian Sherry is my sister-in-law who let me have the rights for a handshake. Nor does it take the opposite route, aggressively asserting that it is the best project the studio will ever read. There's no need for such pretentions. The cover letter sets the stage in a simple and dignified manner. The project will have to speak for itself.

Submitting a script

Independent producers represent the widest span of marketing potential for the free-lance writer. If one producer turns down an idea, there are many others who might still find it fresh and interesting. However, the smaller independent producer is not likely to have the financial resources to compete with the development monies available at the network or studio.

Production companies do have that bargaining power. The distinction between smaller independents and larger production companies is their relative financial stability and current competitive strength on the airwaves. Production companies form and dissolve according to the seasonal marketing trends and network purchases. The more successful production companies have become mini-studios in their own right, with a great number of programs on the air and in development. Some of the more recognizable entities are Q.M. Productions (Quinn Martin), M.T.M. Enterprises (Mary Tyler Moore), T.A.T. Communications (Norman Lear), and Lorimar Productions (Lee Rich).

The major motion picture studios are in keen competition with production companies. Only six major film studios have aggressive and viable television divisions: Columbia Pictures—TV; Paramount Pictures—TV; Metro-Goldwyn-Mayer (M.G.M.)—TV; 20th Century-Fox—TV; Universal—TV; and Warner Brothers—TV. (Addresses at the end of this chapter.) They represent highly fertile ground for program development; strong deals can be negotiated by agents for the right project.

At the top of the submission ladder is the network oligarchy: ABC, CBS, NBC. Once a project is submitted at this level, there's no turning back. If a project is "passed" (*i.e.,* turned down), it's too late to straddle down the ladder to independent producers. *Their* goal is to bring it back up to the networks (who in turn must sell to the sponsors).

The closer the project comes to the network, the more limited the number of buyers. As the submission moves up the ladder, it faces stiffer competition and fewer alternatives. So you see that the marketplace is highly competitive, although not totally impenetrable. Your submission strategy will depend on knowing the marketplace trends and organizing a campaign to reach the most appropriate people and places.

There's no better way to stay on top of marketing and personnel changes than reading the trade papers—*Daily Variety* (1400 N. Cahuenga Blvd., Hollywood, CA 90028) and the *Hollywood Reporter* (6715 Sunset Blvd., Hollywood, CA 90028). The trades reflect the daily pulse of the entertainment industry on the West Coast. Moreover, each paper offers a weekly compilation of production activities ("TV Production Chart," "Films in Production," etc.), which lists companies, addresses, phone numbers, and producers for shows in work. A careful scrutiny of those lists will provide helpful clues to the interests and current activities of independent producers, production companies, and studios.

One of the most comprehensive marketing sources is *The Scriptwriters' Marketplace,* a quarterly publication of the *Hollywood Reporter,* which identifies key contacts at major studios and production companies in the current TV season.

A similar resource is the "Television Market List" published regularly in the *Writers Guild of America Newsletter.* It lists all current shows in production or pre-production, and identifies the story consultant or submission contact for each show. As in *The Scriptwriters' Marketplace,* it states whether or not a show is "open" for submissions, and whom to contact for assignments. A careful reading of these and other publications, such as *Ross Reports Television* (150 Fifth Avenue, New York, NY 10011), a monthly magazine that lists new television programs and their producers, can help bring you closer to making knowledgeable and practical decisions about marketing your own projects and scripts.

In the network marketplace, you have a choice of submitting a script to a great number of places at the same time or sending it selectively to a few individuals. The specific strategy depends on the needs of the marketplace at the time. You should determine which producers and production companies are particularly interested in the type of project you have developed.

Options, contacts, and pay scales

If a producer is interested in a project he or she will propose a *deal, i.e.,* the basic terms for a contract. If you have no agent, now is the time to get one. *Any* agent will gladly close the deal for the standard 10% commission. An attorney would be equally effective, or if you have an appropriate background, you might want to close the deal yourself. The need for counsel depends on the complexity of the proposed deal, and the counter-proposals you wish to present.

On the basis of your discussions, a *Deal Memo* is drawn up which outlines the basic points of agreement—who owns what, for how long, for how much, with what credits, royalties, rights, and so on. The deal memo is binding, although certain points may be modified if both parties initial it. The *Contract* is based on the terms of the deal memo and is the formal legal document. If you're dealing with a producer who is a signatory to the Writers Guild (most established producers are), the contract will adhere to the terms of the Minimum Basic Agreement (M.B.A.) negotiated by the Writers Guild of America.

A producer can either option your work, purchase it outright, or assign you to write new material. If the property is *optioned,* the producer pays for the right to shop it around (which means the project can be submitted by the producer to a third party, e.g., the network). During the option period, you can't submit the project to anyone else. Typically, option money is relatively small; perhaps $1,500 or $2,500 for a six-month period. But the writer will be paid an additional sum of money if the producer elicits interest and moves the project forward. If the producer fails to exercise the option (*i.e.,* if the option expires), the rights revert back to the writer.

A *Step Deal* is the most common form of agreement between producers and free-lance writers. It sets forth fees and commitments for story and teleplay in several phases. The first step is at the *story* stage. When the writer turns in a treatment, the producer pays for it—at least 30% of the total agreed upon compensation—but the producer does not have to assign that writer to do the script. If the writer *is* retained, the producer exercises the *first draft* option. When that draft of the script is turned in, the writer receives a minimum of 40% of the total agreed upon compensation. Now the producer has the final option—putting the writer to work on the *final draft*. Once that script is received, the writer is entitled to the balance of payment. The *Step Deal* is a form of protection for the producer who can respond to the quality of content, the inviolability of delivery dates, and the acceptability of the project to the networks. It also guarantees the writer that his or her work will be paid for, whether there is a cut-off or a go-ahead on the project.

How to get an agent

A good agent is one with a respectable track record, a prestigious list of clients, and a reputation for fairness in the industry. There is no magical list of good agents, although the Writers Guild does publish a list of agents who are franchised by the Guild. (Send $1.00 to Writers

Guild West, *Attn: Agency List,* 8955 Beverly Blvd., Los Angeles, CA 90048.) Names and addresses of literary and dramatic agents appear in *Literary Market Place* (Bowker), available in most libraries. A list of agents can also be obtained by sending a stamped, self-addressed envelope to Society of Authors' Representatives, P.O. Box 650, New York, NY 10113.

If you have no agent representing you, it's difficult to get projects considered by major producers. One of the best ways is to submit your work to an agent who already represents a friend, a professor, a long-lost uncle in the industry. If you are recommended by someone known to the agency, it makes you less of an unknown commodity. If you have no contact, make a list of possible agents for your project, and prioritize them in your submission status file. You might send the project to one top agency for consideration, or to a select number of agencies at the same time.

A brief cover letter might introduce you as a free lancer looking for representation on a specific project. If you don't get a response within six to eight weeks, you can follow up with a phone call or letter, and submit the project to the next agent on your list. Don't be discouraged if you get no response at first; just keep the project active in the field. If the script or presentation is good enough, you might eventually wind up with some positive and encouraging response from the agency.

If an agent is interested in your work, he or she will ask to represent it in the marketplace. If the work sells, the agent is entitled to 10% commission for closing the deal. If the work elicits interest but no sale, you have at least widened your contacts considerably for the next project.

The larger agencies offer an umbrella of power and prestige, but that elusive status is seriously undermined by the sheer size of the agency itself. Many clients inevitably feel lost in an overcrowded stable, and newcomers can hardly break into that race. In contrast, a smaller literary agency provides more personalized service, and is more open to the work of new talent. If you're going to seek representation, the smaller agency is the likely place to go. But don't be fooled by the label "small." Many of these agencies are exceptionally strong and have deliberately limited their client roster to the cream of the crop. In fact, many smaller agents have defected from executive positions at the major agencies. So you'll have to convince them you're the greatest writer since Shakespeare came on the scene—and that your works are even more salable.

How do you prove that you have the talent to be a star talent? It's all in the writing. If your projects look professional, creative, and stylistically effective, you're on the right track. Indeed, you can call yourself a writer. If the artistic content is also marketable and you back it up with determination and know-how, you might just become a *selling* writer.

And that is the "bottom line" for success in the television industry.

Networks, Studios and Production Companies

(Note: New submissions should be addressed to the Head of Program Development.)

NETWORKS

ABC-TV
2040 Ave. of the Stars
Century City, CA 90067
or, 1330 Ave. of the Americas
New York, NY 10019

CBS-TV
7800 Beverly Blvd.
Los Angeles, CA 90036
or, 51 West 52nd St.
New York, NY 10019

NBC-TV
3000 W. Alameda
Burbank, CA 91523
or, 30 Rockefeller Plaza
New York, NY 10020

MAJOR STUDIOS

Columbia Pictures-TV
3000 Colgems Sq.
Burbank, CA 91505

MGM-TV
10202 W. Washington Blvd.
Culver City, CA 90230

Paramount Pictures-TV
5451 Marathon St.
Los Angeles, CA 90038

20th Century Fox-TV
10201 W. Pico Blvd.
Los Angeles, CA 90064

Universal Studios-TV
100 Universal City Plaza
Universal City, CA 91608

Warner Bros. TV
4000 Warner Blvd.
Burbank, CA 91505

SELECTED INDEPENDENT
PRODUCTION COMPANIES

Lorimar Productions
3970 Overland Ave.
Culver City, CA 90230

M.T.M. Enterprises
4024 Radford Ave.
Studio City, CA 91604

QM Productions
1041 North Formosa Ave.
Los Angeles, CA 90046

T.A.T. Communications/Tandem
Productions
5752 Sunset Blvd.
Los Angeles, CA 90028

78

BEFORE THE FINAL CURTAIN

By Jean Raymond Maljean

AFTER TYPING FINAL CURTAIN on that play manuscript, you may have had an inkling that the word FINAL was premature.

What actually has come to an end is your solitary command over this property. Now you'll wrangle with the director, alternately winning and losing battles over sweeping changes in the original script. Actors and actresses will press you, via the director, to alter their lines, business, and characterization.

The conflict will not be confined to your plot. Amidst all these creative minds, you have a hassle on your hands. A good thing, too. It may be your baby, but it takes teamwork to deliver it into the world. Through tedious rehearsals you'll cut, change, and add scenes all the way until opening night. Assuming your play was optioned by a successful producer or organization, you'll be sitting in the theater as hundreds of ticket holders arrive, each a survivor of bumper-to-bumper driving through heavy traffic, having suffered an exorbitant price for dinner, baby sitter, and parking. What kind of evening's entertainment have you prepared to reward their faith in the work of a new playwright?

Do you know what they want?

Do they know?

Audiences are not certain about that. The critics who will also be on hand can articulate what reaction the audience feels in the reviews the next day—not that all critics are infallible, but they do make a study of theatrical successes and failures.

Over the years I have compiled the following checklist, after observing what critics like and dislike about the plays they have reviewed. You should test your script against each item before the critics have a chance to do so.

And until you do, hold that FINAL CURTAIN.

• Who is your protagonist? The story may follow the lives of many but, to prevent diffusion, the audience must identify with one central character.

• Does the audience know a great deal about this person? Do they care what happens to him or her? If not, what's all the fuss about?

• Is your central character's conflict against another person? The environment? Him- or herself? A play without conflict is not a play, and the conflict will be between you and your audience.

• Endow the antagonist with redeeming virtues. No bad guys, please. Allow the player to feel justified in portraying the role with conviction. One playwright's antagonist could be another playwright's protagonist.

• Does your protagonist change as a result of the struggle? Or does he "just come to think of things in a new light" and decide to change his mind? Or hers? People don't just "change their minds" in plays, any more than they do in real life. People change when conflict turns them inside out and wrenches them away from their former pattern of living. If this is one of your writing faults, change your mind.

• Have you written a play or a manuscript? Is it something you can visualize, moving, changing shape—or is it simply a printed page to be read? I've composed a limerick to illustrate:

A playwright who used language purely
Placed semicolons and commas securely.
He wrote for the page
But not for the stage
So his audience left prematurely.

• What does your protagonist want? If he doesn't want something with all of his heart and soul and mind and body and every fiber of his being, he is an excessively boring person.

• Is your story about people or about plot? Start with people. They'll find lots of plots and help you work them out. Try to avoid average people. Average people are boring to audiences, even to average audiences. You may press your ear against the wall to eavesdrop on "average" neighbors who are fighting, but you won't plunk down $20 for a theater ticket to watch it. Try to create salty, contradictory, lovable, hateable, strong-willed individuals.

• Emotions. Have you made the audience cry, laugh, fume with rage, shiver with fright, tingle with nostalgia, etc.? Put your audience through the wringer. It's what they want.

• Is there enough action onstage to keep the audience's attention riveted on the development? Nothing wastes an evening in the theater like two lovers talking to each other endlessly without action. Too many plays are just chit-chat.

• Does the plot build? Is there rising action throughout?

• Is it real action or just "business"? You're not going to get away with a static play by having your actors hammering and sawing and jumping around, entering and exiting frequently, or making them move furniture all over the stage.

• And don't use the ploy of moving the plot forward by phone conversations. These are deadly! Audiences tire of this device and are also irritated by a play that is broken into many small scenes. Sometimes this works, but usually it keeps the audience from losing themselves in the story.

• If it's suspense you're after, you must build ever-increasing fear by fueling the plot with more and more new dangers, even if nothing horrible happens until the end. Recently, I read a play that will certainly be panned if it is ever produced. A killer is loose. Two men with shotguns wait for him to appear. They wait and wait and wait—and so does the audience. Waiting is not suspense. Waiting is waiting, and that is sleep inducing.

• If any action happens offstage, can it be brought onstage? The audience doesn't want to hear about it, they want to see! A distinction between action and movement must be made here. When a director reads your play, he retains important happenings but crosses out all stage directions such as, "crosses to stage right, sits on chair," etc. Don't usurp the director's blocking privileges.

• Is your exposition exciting? Some believe that it's not possible to make exposition entertaining, but it can be done with a few more months' work. In the old days, plays opened with two servants swinging feather dusters as they spoke to each other about what had taken place before the play started. Unfortunately, there are still some remnants of

426

feather-dusting in plays by neophytes. A good hint: Chop off the first 6 pages of your script and watch the exposition improve. Free of verbal fat, the action will get off to a fast start. You may easily restore any essential lines that have thus been displaced. Another hint: Finish the play, then go back and rewrite the exposition when you've come to understand what you're trying to do.

• Have you finished all of your exposition by the end of Act I? By Act II, you should have nothing but rising action headed straight for the denouement.

• Do you know how to divide the two acts? An audience has more patience in the beginning, so make Act I long and Act II short. But, whatever you do, be sure to end Act I with a cliff-hanger so that everyone will show up again after intermission.

• Don't preach or explain too much. Don't insult the intelligence of your audience.

• Are your characters entirely different from one another? If any two are similar, fire one of them. Orchestration is the key. You must also remember that the producer who reads your play must pay a salary for each player that you "hire" by writing him or her into your script.

• Is the vocabulary and speech pattern of each character distinctive? Eavesdrop on authentic conversations. Take notes on how people talk to one another.

• Will the audience learn about your characters by what they do, through their actions and reactions? (No one should have to explain himself.) Show, do not tell!

• Did you create personas so exciting and powerful that an actor or actress would want to use a scene from your play as an audition piece? Consider the player. He or she is sick to death of picking up parts that mouth some pet philosophy of the playwright. He wants to portray someone who is good and bad, who has human frailties and virtues. Try to take a part in a play reading as a performer, and you'll soon realize how disappointing it can be to take the part of a wooden dummy. Think like an actor or actress when you write. Cast yourself in some of your own roles and walk around reading aloud. Plays are for acting.

427

• Did you keep your lines short, or do you have actors spouting two or three sentences in each line? Except for some unusual plays, most lines should resemble ping-pong volleys with occasional paragraphs of greater length to vary the rhythm.

• Did you make the mistake of repeating something to be certain the audience will remember? Cut repeats: even stupid people keep track of an exciting story.

• Does each line move the play forward? If not, cut the line and save it for another play, so it won't be a total loss.

• Have you cut your play down to the bone? No, you haven't. Go right back and cut out all those lukewarm lines. Then when it's lean, make another major cutting. Slash away. You do it in your garden; why not with something as important as a play? After you make the cuts, see how it flows. An otherwise perfect script could be totally ruined by excessive length—125 pages could deal the death blow.

• Have you prepared the way for major action by planting seeds? Don't just drop something on the audience. They want to guess ahead. Let them be part of the experience. If your protagonist drives a sword through someone in Act II, that instrument should have been introduced in Act I in some minor way. Also, the entrance of each character should be prepared for.

• Does your play break new ground? If it covers an idea that is not new, is it presented in a new or unique way? Also, re-examine your script to make sure you haven't rewritten one of the great classics all over again. Once was enough. (This is the most common fault. Check it out again.)

• Can you summarize the premise of your play in one sentence? If not, the play may be attempting to say more than is possible within the framework. That will cause diffusion and confusion. The premise of a play is usually a statement like "Pride goeth before a fall," "Love is blind," or "Greed can bring about destruction." Keeping it in mind will assure unity throughout. Anything that does not lead to your premise should be pruned away from the script.

428

• Did you use lots of four-letter obscenities because it's chic? They don't shock anymore. When the fad disappears, and it will, your play will be dated. And never use current jargon, if you want your play to enjoy a long life.

I originally compiled this list to remind myself of the faults most often cited by critics, but I keep forgetting them. In fact, I wrote the first draft of this article on the backs of pages of my plays that were rejected for such infractions.

79

Rx FOR COMEDY

By Neil Simon

THE idea of a prescription for comedy is obviously ridiculous. What works for one playwright rarely works for another, and even the fact that a certain approach succeeded for a writer before does not mean that it will surely produce an amusing play for that same scribe a second time. The knowledge of this grisly reality gives me a healthy insecurity, which I consider a great asset. Insecurity encourages a writer to be open to criticism by competent professionals; it allows him to face up to the need to revise or rewrite. Of course, *everybody* cheerily tells a playwright how to repair his script and it takes cool courage and wondrous manners to endure the amateurs' well-meant advice. In Boston during the tryout of *The Odd Couple,* I had been up till four o'clock in the morning rewriting the third act—for the fifth time. Exhausted, I finally fell asleep on my typewriter. At seven A.M. a dentist from Salem, Mass., phoned to tell me how *he* would fix the third act. I thanked him and promised myself I would call him at five the next morning to tell him how I would fix his bridgework.

I happen to like rewriting, a good deal of which is often necessary after one sees how a scene actually "plays" on stage in rehearsal or tryout. Each chance to fix, polish and tighten is a glorious reprieve— something I never had in the urgent world of weekly television. I suppose the greatest problem the writer in the theater has is to face "those ferocious critics." My problem is even greater. I write my own critics' reviews as I'm writing my play. I place Walter Kerr just behind my right shoulder holding in his hand a big stick—with rusty nails. If I get verbose or careless or stretch for jokes, Mr. Kerr lets me have it right across the knuckles.

This article originally appeared in *Playbill* Magazine, January 1966. Reprinted courtesy of Playbill, Inc.

The jokes are a special hazard. In the first of 112 versions of *Come Blow Your Horn,* the opening five minutes of the play were crammed with good jokes—in fact, some of the best I had ever written—and the scene was terrible. The audience, knowing nothing of the characters or the situation, could not have cared less. Now I know enough to start with the characters. Where do they come from? In the case of *The Odd Couple,* from a party I attended in California. All the men there were divorced, all their dates were their new girl friends. Most of these men were sharing apartments with other divorced men because alimony payments forced them to save money. In *Barefoot* and *Come Blow Your Horn,* at least one or two characters in each play resembled, perhaps in speech patterns, mannerisms or personal outlook, someone I've actually known.

Looking back at what and how I write, I seem to begin a play with two people of completely opposite nature and temperament, put them in an intolerable situation, and let the sparks fly. The extra ingredient, and very important, is that they must both emphatically believe that their way of life is the right one. Then it's the playwright's job to support *both* those beliefs. As for form, I prefer my comedies in three acts. When I start, I write extensive notes for the first act, a sketchy outline for the second and nothing for the third. I'm rather curious myself as to what will happen in the third act. Sometimes I don't find out for certain until a week before we open on Broadway.

If there is anything remotely resembling a key to comedy in theater, I'd guess that it is for the writer, director and actors to apply one simple rule. Never treat it as a comedy. The actors and characters must treat their predicament as though their lives depended on it. Not an easy achievement, I admit. Play it too seriously and the laughs are gone. Play just the comedy and ditto. In casting, my preference is not to go with the "established comic" but with a good actor who understands comedy. Walter Matthau, Robert Redford and Mildred Natwick are among the best.

One question I'm asked quite often is if I consider myself funny. I suppose I apply my own personal humor to life in the same manner as I would in a play. I need a situation. Put me around a table with real funny men like Buddy Hackett or Jonathan Winters or Mel

Brooks and I fade like a shrinking violet. No fast repartee for me. I shine trapped in an elevator with six people and a German Shepherd licking my ear.

To me, the first ten minutes of a comedy are critical. The writer must (1) set up the rules and the situation, (2) catch the audience almost immediately. Once the rules are announced, farce, satire, straight comedy or whatever game you're playing, the audience will believe you so long as you stick to those rules and that game. I believe in starting the conflict in the opening minutes (e.g., the poker game in *Odd Couple*) and to be as theatrically arresting as possible. The idea of opening on an empty stage in *Barefoot* intrigued me. Then I begin with some new event in the life of our hero, something that has never happened to him before.

My writing routines are actually rather prosaic. No midnight oil burns in my lamp. I type in an office or at home, and put in a ten to five day with a short lunch break. I may do a complete draft of a play, use it as an outline and then set to work on a more finished version. I like to get into the writing quickly to "hear how the characters speak," for once I hear the speech patterns it is easier going. I ought to point out that my insecurity is such that even as I'm writing one play, I'm beginning to think ahead to the next. So if this one doesn't quite pan out, well. . . .

Once a play goes into rehearsal, my "normal" routine ceases and the midnight oil begins to burn. There seems to be less time for social obligations, children and—horror of horrors—the Giants' football games.

Do I need quiet when I'm working? It depends. If there are no problems in the script, they could be digging the new subway under my typewriter. But one day recently my two little girls were on the other side of the house playing jacks. And as the ball bounced softly on the thick rug, I ran from the study screaming at my wife, "Can't you keep those kids quiet?"

She looked at me with knowing affection and pity.

"I'm sorry the scene's not going well, Doc," she answered with ancient female wisdom.

If there's anything I can't stand, it's a smart aleck wife—who happens to be right.

80

WRITING POETRY FOR CHILDREN

By Myra Cohn Livingston

I NEVER intended to write poetry for children. It was a complete accident, and even today I marvel that it happened at all. I was eighteen, in college, and writing what I considered far more important—poetry about love! My instructor at Sarah Lawrence College, Katherine Liddell, had given us an assignment; we were to use alliteration and onomatopoeia. I turned in some verses. "These," she said to me in her converted closet-conference room, reeking with the odor of Sano cigarettes, "would be wonderful for children. Send them to *Story Parade*" (a magazine for boys and girls published by Simon & Schuster). I grudgingly followed her instructions—the accompanying letter, the self-addressed stamped envelope. Several weeks later the envelope came back. I threw it onto a pile of papers and three weeks later became so angry with Miss Liddell's folly, that I ripped it open to confront her with her error. I caught my breath. The editor had carefully clipped three of the poems, and there was a letter accepting these for publication.

It took me eleven years for my first book, *Whispers and Other Poems,* written when I was a freshman, to be accepted for publication by the same editor, Margaret K. McElderry, who had seen the manuscript when I was in college and encouraged me to continue writing. I know now that during the war years few new books were published, and certainly poetry for children was far down on the list of desired manuscripts. In those days, I read *The Writer* religiously, hoping to find someone who would want my work, and collected a sheaf of rejection slips.

But I did not write and never have consciously written *for* children. I cannot understand why the world appeared to me from the start as through the eyes of a child—of my own childhood—or why, even today, most of the poetry I write comes out that way. The only clue I

433

have is that, even as an anthologist, I am drawn to (or write) those poems that speak to the subjects, emotions, and thoughts of children in a diction they understand.

My own poems have often been called "deceptively simple"; the first review of *Whispers* scathingly accused me of writing about "simple, everyday things," as though this were some sort of evil. Perhaps this is because many adults forget that to the child, these very things are what pique his curiosity, engage his attention. As the poet-in-residence for our school district, in my visits to schools and libraries throughout this country, and in teaching courses for teachers at U.C.L.A. Extension, I note that today's child is very different, in many respects, from the child I was, or that my children are, but that many things remain eternal. Children may know more facts, be more worldly wise, but the curiosity, wonder and fresh way of looking, the joys and pains and doubts, seem just as they always were.

I would like to suggest that anyone who wishes to write poetry that children might enjoy face up to a few basics about this vocation. The climate today is far more receptive to poetry than it was a number of years ago when the English—Walter de la Mare, Robert Louis Stevenson, and A. A. Milne—dominated the field. America has given us Elizabeth Madox Roberts, David McCord and Harry Behn, to mention but a few—and there are many exciting middle-aged and young poets publishing today whose work is excellent. We no longer have to take second place to the English, but we do have to recognize that poetry is still somewhat of a stepchild in juvenile literature. Children, themselves, are more apt to read a story in a picture book than to read poetry, for most adults and teachers feel uncomfortable about presenting it. Even Mother Goose is not as well known as once she was. And poetry demands an involvement of the emotions, whether it be laughter or wonder or a more serious way of viewing the world.

The crisis we seem to face now is the mistaken notion that *anyone* can write a poem. The Poets-in-the-Schools program, in many areas, has too often, in my opinion, fostered undisciplined writing, that which John Ciardi has called "a spillage of raw emotion." Any word or series of words written down are called "poems." This, as I see it, is a great disservice to the children who are falsely praised, but it also applies to older aspiring poets. Many of the high school and college students have had no real discipline. Metrical feet, scansion, forms are unknown. Of course, we do not want didactic, sing-song verse, the moralizing of a Henley's "Invictus" or the elusive fairies of Rose Fyleman. What we do need is true poetry that takes into account the interests and yearnings of the young and leads them toward a process of humanization.

In offering suggestions to the person who wishes to write such poetry, I would ask that he ask himself if anything of the child remains in him—a way of looking, tasting, smelling, touching, thinking; if he is in touch with the contemporary child and his way of viewing the world, if he is truly comfortable with children. I would also suggest that he make the commitment to learn the basics of writing in disciplined forms and meters. One cannot, for example, attempt a limerick without knowing how to use the iambus and anapest correctly, nor even free verse without knowing why it *is* free verse.

Another, and perhaps more elusive point, is that the writer understand and believe that poetry for children is not second-best; there is a tendency on the part of many to feel that a so-called children's poet is one who has failed in writing adult poetry, or that it is "easy" to do. The poet who writes for children exclusively is a sort of second-class citizen.

Although I have spent almost twenty years sharing with young people poetry ranging from Mother Goose to T.S. Eliot, it is difficult to give any definite answer as to what sort of poetry children like best. We know through experience that levity is always high on the list, and humor is important, for it counters the view of poems as soul-building messages in high-flown diction. But many a child prefers the more serious. The more a young person is exposed to poetry, the more refined is his taste in this, as in all arts. I would hope that any writer aspiring to publish poetry would not write for what he thinks is the juvenile market, but rather concentrate on his own strengths. The word-play of David McCord is something that comes naturally to his art; curiosity and a love for nature are intrinsic to Harry Behn's work; and Elizabeth Madox Roberts wrote about experiences of her own as a child.

My own poetry has gone through a series of changes. Trained in the traditional rhyme/meter school, I have at times broken away to free verse, knowing that the force of what I wished to say had to dictate the form. Yet I do not feel I could have made this break without a sure knowledge of the disciplines, taught to me by Robert Fitzgerald and Horace Gregory. I know that there are many who would take issue with me, who feel that anything one wishes to put down, if arranged in a certain order, is a poem.

This change may best be shown by contrasting my first published poem, "Whispers," to later work:

> Whispers
>   tickle through your ear
>   telling things you like to hear.
>
> Whispers
>   are as soft as skin
>   letting little words curl in.
>
> Whispers
>   come so they can blow
>   secrets others never know.

Most of my verse in *Whispers, Wide Awake, Old Mrs. Twindlytart* and *The Moon and a Star* was written in traditional forms. But in *A Crazy Flight* (published in 1969), what I wanted to say suddenly refused to be confined by rhyme. The need to use repetition and a freer form of expression asserted itself in a poem that also picked up some current speech patterns of the children I was then teaching:

THE SUN IS STUCK

> The sun is stuck.
> I mean, it won't move.
> I mean, it's hot, man, and we need a red-hot
>   poker to pry it loose,
> Give it a good shove and roll it across the sky
> And make it go down
> So we can be cool,
> Man.

Yet, *The Malibu,* my poem inspired by the moon landing and America's concerns with litter, combined both the rhyming couplet and some elements of free verse:

Hey moonface,
man-in-the-moonface,

do you like the way
we left your place?

can you stand the view
of footprints on you?

is it fun to stare
at the flags up there?

did you notice ours
with the stripes and stars?

does it warm you to know
we love you so?

moonface,
man-in-the-moonface,

thanks a heap for the rocks.

In *The Way Things Are,* the meter follows a child's pattern with a different rhyme pattern, in "Growing: For Louis."

It's tough being short.

Of course your father tells you not to worry,
But everyone else is giant, and you're just the
way you were.
And this stupid guy says, "Hey shorty, where'd
you get the long pants?"
Or some smart beanpole asks how it feels to
be so close to the ants?
And the school nurse says to tell her again how
tall you are when you've already told her.
Oh, my mother says there's really no hurry
And I'll grow soon enough.

But it's tough being short.

(I wonder if Napoleon got the same old stuff?)

But the rhymed couplet creeps up again and again in *4-Way Stop* (published in 1976):

Ocean at Night

Mother Wave sings soft to sleep
the fish and seaweed of the deep

black ocean, and with quiet hands
pats to peace her tired sands,

her kelp and driftwood; fills her shoals
with gleaming tides, and gently pulls

across her bed the pale moonlight.
And this is night. And this is night.

Throughout these later books are outcroppings of free verse with which I am still experimenting, but there is an inherent pull that constantly draws me back to the containment of fixed forms. I have finally begun to tackle the haiku and cinquain, most demanding in their use of words:

Even in summer
bees have to work in their orange
and black striped sweaters.

Like any other poet, I feel that the most important factor in my poetry writing is not that I set out to write in any given form, but that I must find the right form for the subject matter. For this is when —and only when—the poem "comes right" for me.

What is right for me is not so for everybody. There are no surefire methods, although I do believe that one must know the basics and rules before breaking them. Even children need these rules, for without them, they flounder and grow dissatisfied with what they are doing. What we all have in common is that we are still learning, and, I hope, growing and changing.

81

LIGHT VERSE: QUESTIONS AND ANSWERS

By Richard Armour

Light verse is a minor art or craft, but there is a good deal of art and craft to it. In fact there is often more technique involved in light verse than in serious poetry. Phyllis McGinley once said that light verse is (or should be) less emotional and more rational than poetry, though I think she won the Pulitzer Prize not so much for light verse as for what I would call light poetry. At any rate I agree with her that light verse is not to be taken too lightly by the writer. Quite aside from talent, and a special way with words and ideas, one must know the fundamentals, and more than the fundamentals, of versification: meter, rhyme, and all the rest.

The best modern light verse writers, such as Phyllis McGinley, Ogden Nash, David McCord, Morris Bishop, Arthur Guiterman, Samuel Hoffenstein, Dorothy Parker, Margaret Fishback, and Ethel Jacobson, have also been poets or mock poets. Having read and absorbed the writings of poets and light verse writers who went before them (and light verse is as old as Chaucer), they sharpened their skills and eventually developed styles of their own.

Some of these poets are still with us and still writing, but not quite so much and not quite so lightly. It is about time for a whole new generation. Magazine markets are fewer and book publishers more wary, but there is still a substantial readership for light verse if it is original and skillful and has something to say. I thought it might be helpful to give some basic pointers and to put them in question and answer form. These, at any rate, are the questions I am most often asked and the answers I most often give:

Q. *What is the difference between light verse and poetry?*

A. Light verse is a kind of poetry. It is poetry written in the spirit of play. Since it may not have the high thoughts or the imagery of poetry, it makes up for lack of these by emphasis on technique. The first requirement of a light verse writer is sure command of meter and rhyme. But along with technique, as in any writing, there must be something new to say, or a new way of saying something old.

Q. *What are the best subjects for light verse?*

A. Since you are writing for people, you should write about what people are most interested in. And people are most interested in people. In other words, the best subjects are those that have to do with the foibles of the human race, such as the relations of man to wife and of parents to children; the effort to get along with one's neighbors and one's colleagues and one's boss (unless one *is* the boss); the struggle with waistline and hairline; bank accounts, charge accounts, and no accounts; hosts and guests; passing fads in food and clothing and cars and sports; buying a house or building a house or running a house or being run by a house; vacations and travel and luggage and tips; pets; youth and age and the in-between adolescent; illness and doctors and remedies and recuperation and exercise; automation and the computerized society in relation to the bewildered individual; people who are meddlesome or pompous or stupid or inconsistent— in short, all aspects of the human comedy. Here is an example of a piece of light verse on a subject of universal interest:

> MONEY
> Workers earn it,
> Spendthrifts burn it,
> Bankers lend it,
> Women spend it,
> Forgers fake it,
> Taxes take it,
> Dying leave it,
> Heirs receive it,
> Thrifty save it,
> Misers crave it,
> Robbers seize it,
> Rich increase it,
> Gamblers lose it . . .
> I could use it.

440

Q. *Where does one look for ideas?*

A. You not only look but listen. You keep your ears open as well as your eyes. Sometimes a chance phrase or a cliché will trigger a piece of verse. In addition to looking at and listening to people, you read, read, read. You read books and magazines and newspapers. Now and then, if you are on the alert, an idea will pop up. Newspapers, especially, are mirrors reflecting the absurdities of mankind—and womankind. Light verse should concern subjects that concern people. It should strike common chords, be human, be universal.

Q. *What is the best length for a piece of light verse?*

A. Brevity is a requisite of all forms of humor. Recently a critic writing in *Esquire* made the wise observation: "Humor is like guerrilla warfare. Success depends on traveling light . . . striking unexpectedly . . . and getting away fast." This applies especially to light verse, which is a condensed, almost telegraphic, form of humor—verse being more compressed than prose anyhow. Light verse is briefer today than it was in the more leisurely nineteenth century, and less intricate than in those days of the ballade and the villanelle. Usually it runs from two lines to eight or ten or twelve. Only rarely to sixteen or more. That is, if you want to sell it. By the way, this is the shortest piece I ever sold (to the *Saturday Review*):

> MAID'S DAY OUT
> Thurs.
> Hers.

Q. *What are the best verse forms to use?*

A. Simple iambic and anapestic meter, rather short lines (trimeter or tetrameter), couplets and quatrains. If you don't know what these are, go to your local library and get Clement Wood's *Poets' Handbook* or look at the back part of Clement Wood's *The Complete Rhyming Dictionary*. You can't expect to enter a highly competitive field, in which technique plays such a large part, without knowing the fundamentals of versification.

Light verse should be technically correct in rhymes and meters, and, if possible, not only correct but fresh and original. I have mentioned short lines. You may also use the longer pentameter (five stress) line, which has been the most popular form in English poetry ever since Chaucer, but it usually leads to somewhat more serious treatment, and the rhymes (much more important in light verse than in serious poetry) are a bit far apart.

Q. *Are there any other suggestions for writing salable light verse?*

A. It should, usually, have an element of surprise or some sort of clincher at the end. (See "Money" quoted above.) But it should not rely too much on the last line, in that case spoken of slightingly as "terminal humor." Good light verse should be amusing all the way through, with maybe something a little special at the close. And it should be given the additional help of a good title—one that is original and appropriate.

Q. *How do you find markets for light verse?*

A. You can look at the market lists that appear from time to time in issues of *The Writer* (or write in for the back issue containing light verse markets). But you should also examine the magazines themselves, to see whether they are using light verse and, if so, what type. I take a good many magazines, but in addition I spend many hours on my haunches at newsstands, checking the magazines I don't take. (Forgive me, managers of drug stores and supermarkets. I still buy enough from you.)

As for knowing markets—submitting light verse to the right place at the right time—this is as important today as ever. It is perhaps more important now than it was thirty years ago, because the markets are fewer and the competition is keener. But, again, when I started out I knew my markets, *The Saturday Evening Post* and *The New Yorker*, as a long-time reader of both.

Markets change and you have to keep up with them. *The Saturday Evening Post* still uses light verse on the "Post Scripts" page, but there are few poems scattered through the back pages of the magazine. And *The New Yorker* uses less verse, and such verse as it uses is less light than in what I think of as the Good Old Days, when Harold Ross was editor.

442

Today, in addition to the "Post Scripts" page, there is "Light Housekeeping" in *Good Housekeeping,* and "Parting Shots" in *The American Legion Magazine.* In addition to these well-edited pages, where you have to fight off a multitude of free-lancers, there are other more specialized magazines like *Gourmet* and *Golf* that occasionally use light verse. You will find more of these in market lists or discover them for yourself by reading the magazines.

Q. *How do you submit light verse?*

A. Type it, double-spaced, one poem to a page, with your name and return address in the upper corner (it makes no difference whether left or right) of the page. Submit one to three poems at a time. You may be able to get in four, along with a stamped self-addressed envelope, for the same postage, if the paper is not heavier than sixteen-pound weight, a good weight for all manuscripts. No letter is necessary or desirable. What could you say? Editors have enough to read anyhow. Another thing—there is no need to say anything about protecting your manuscript. Editors are honest and the U.S. mails are safe. If something is bought, what is usually bought is first North American serial rights, which means the first run in a North American newspaper or magazine.

Q. *Do you need an agent?*

A. An agent might be helpful, but most agents won't bother with light verse. And most don't know the markets as well as you will know them if you study the magazines as I have suggested. It's a do-it-yourself field.

Q. *When do you do your writing?*

A. Whenever I get a chance, which isn't often enough. I long ago gave up "waiting for an inspiration"—else I would still be waiting. I also gave up trying to set aside regular hours for writing, though I would do this if I could. Since I have several other time-consuming activities, I write when I can. But my conscience or compulsion or whatever it is weighs so heavily on me that I feel frustrated and remorseful if I do not write a little something—prose or verse—each day, seven days a week. (I am writing this on a Sunday morning—

443

after having gone to church.) Some days I write for ten minutes; some days I write for ten hours. One advantage of light verse is that it can be written during short periods. With a schedule such as mine, I am glad I am not a novelist.

Q. *Do you still get things back?*

A. Yes, indeed. I use returned verses as scratch paper on which to write new verses. My method with editors is erosion. After a while, I wear them down. But it takes patience and postage. The difference between the professional and the amateur, in this business, is that the professional becomes discouraged less easily.

Q. *Do you get printed rejection slips or letters?*

A. Both. And sometimes I get neither—just the poem back, in the return envelope, which is really very sensible. I think rejection slips are a waste of paper. If I get a poem back, I know, without any printed explanation, that it has been rejected. Of course I am grateful for a letter, or even a brief note. One editor with whom I dealt for many years used to grade my poems, as if I were a student in Freshman Composition. Though he might buy a poem that he graded "B minus" or even "C plus," only once did he ever give me an "A." It was for this piece, which is included in my collection, *Nights With Armour:*

THE LOVE LIFE (AND DEATH) OF A MOOSE

Up in Newfoundland some 20 moose, mistaking Diesel train horns for mating calls, have been lured to death on the tracks.—*News item.*

> Imagine this beast of the frozen Northeast
> With its annual amorous craze on,
> Seduced by the toot of a choo-choo en route
> Into making a fatal liaison.
>
> Conceive of its sighs as it straddles the ties,
> Unaware of the killer it's dating.
> The honk of the train has gone straight to its brain,
> And its mind is completely on mating.
>
> Appalling? Of course, but just think how much worse
> It would be, and no words shall we weasel,

> Should an engine tear loose from its tracks when a moose
> Makes what sounds like the call of a Diesel.

This, by the way, is a pretty good example of playfulness, zany point of view, exaggeration, out-of-the-ordinary rhyming, and fancy footwork (with metrical feet)—some of the ingredients of light verse.

Q. *Of the light verse you have written, what is your own personal favorite?*

A. This is almost impossible to answer. Sometimes, in a depressed mood (that is, daily), I like nothing I have ever written. Other times I run onto something I wrote years ago, and had forgotten, and wonder that I had ever written anything so good. This, instead of making me happy, depresses me further, because it convinces me that I am on the downgrade and shall never do so well again. But usually I like best whatever I have written most recently. This goes not only for my light verse but for my books. Perhaps I can dodge the question by quoting a piece of light verse that seems to be a favorite of others and is fairly typical.

MY MATTRESS AND I
Night after night, for years on end,
My mattress has been my closest friend.

My mattress and I are cozy and pally;
There are hills on the sides—I sleep in the valley.

It clearly reveals the shape I'm in:
Where I'm thin it's thick, where it's thick I'm thin.

Its contours reflect the first and the last of me.
It's very nearly a plaster cast of me.

I miss my mattress when I am gone;
It's one thing I've made an impression on.

This is about all there is to it. Everything depends on your sense of humor, your original way of looking at things (including yourself), your handling of rhyme and meter and words, and your ability to be critical of what you write and to compare it honestly with what is being published.

Now I have to get back to work, because light verse, no matter

445

how easy it looks (and it should be made to look easy) is work, hard work. And when a piece of light verse comes off right—when it is original in concept, and funny, and nicely turned—the light verse writer gets, in his way, as much of a feeling of accomplishment, even creativeness, as a serious poet.

82

POETIC DEVICES

By William Packard

THERE is a good story about Walter Johnson, who had one of the most natural fast balls in the history of baseball. No one knows how "The Big Train" developed such speed on the mound, but there it was. From his first year of pitching in the majors, 1907, for Washington, Walter Johnson hurtled the ball like a flash of lightning across the plate. And as often as not, the opposing batter would be left watching empty air, as the catcher gloved the ball.

Well, the story goes that after a few seasons, almost all the opposing batters knew exactly what to expect from Walter Johnson—his famous fast ball. And even though the pitch was just as difficult to hit as ever, still, it can be a very dangerous thing for any pitcher to become that predictable. And besides, there were also some fears on the Washington bench that if he kept on hurtling only that famous fast ball over the plate, in a few more seasons Walter Johnson might burn his arm out entirely.

So, Walter Johnson set out to learn how to throw a curve ball. Now, one can just imagine the difficulty of doing this: here is a great pitcher in his mid-career in the major leagues, and he is trying to learn an entirely new pitch. One can imagine all the painful self-consciousness of the beginner, as Johnson tried to train his arm into some totally new reflexes—a new way of fingering the ball, a new arc of the elbow as he went into the wind-up, a new release of the wrist, and a completely new follow-through for the body.

But after awhile, the story goes, the curve ball became as natural for Walter Johnson as the famous fast-ball pitch, and as a consequence, Johnson became even more difficult to hit.

When Walter Johnson retired in 1927, he held the record for total strike-outs in a lifetime career (3409), and he held the record for total pitching of shut-out games in a lifetime career (110)—records which have never been equaled in baseball. And Walter Johnson is second only to the mighty Cy Young for total games won in a lifetime career.

Any artist can identify with this story about Walter Johnson. The determination to persist in one's art or craft is a characteristic of a great artist and a great athlete. But one also realizes that this practice of one's craft is almost always painstakingly difficult, and usually entails periods of extreme self-consciousness, as one trains oneself into a pattern of totally new reflexes. It is what Robert Frost called "the pleasure of taking pains."

The odd thing is that this practice and mastery of a craft is sometimes seen as an infringement on one's own natural gifts. Poets will sometimes comment that they do not want to be bothered with all that stuff about metrics and assonance and craft, because it doesn't come "naturally." Of course it doesn't come naturally, if one hasn't worked to make it natural. But once one's craft becomes second nature, it is not an infringement on one's natural gifts—if anything, it is an enlargement of them, and an enhancement and a reinforcement of one's own intuitive talents.

In almost all the other arts, an artist has to learn the techniques of his craft as a matter of course.

The painter takes delight in exploring the possibilities of his palette, and perhaps he may even move through periods which are dominated by different color tones, such as viridian or Prussian blue or ochre. He will also be concerned, as a matter of course, with various textural considerations such as brushing and pigmentation and the surface virtue of his work.

The composer who wants to write orchestra music has to begin by learning how to score in the musical notation system—and he will play with the meaning of whole notes, half notes, quarter notes, eighth notes, and the significance of such tempo designations as *lento, andante, adagio,* and *prestissimo.* He will also want to explore the different possibilities of the instruments of the orchestra, to discover the totality of tone he wants to achieve in his own work.

Even so—I have heard student poets complain that they don't want to be held back by a lot of technical considerations in the craft of poetry.

That raises a very interesting question: Why do poets seem to resist learning the practice and mastery of their own craft? Why do they

448

protest that technique *per se* is an infringement on their own intuitive gifts, and a destructive self-consciousness that inhibits their natural and magical genius?

I think a part of the answer to these questions may lie in our own modern Romantic era of poetry, where poets as diverse as Walt Whitman and Dylan Thomas and Allen Ginsberg seem to achieve their best effects with little or no technical effort. Like Athena, the poem seems to spring full blown out of the forehead of Zeus, and that is a large part of its charm for us. Whitman pretends he is just "talking" to us, in the "Song of Myself." So does Dylan Thomas in "Fern Hill" and "Poem in October." So does Allen Ginsberg in "Howl" and "Kaddish."

But of course when we think about it, we realize it is no such thing. And we realize also, in admiration, that any poet who is so skillful in concealing his art from us may be achieving one of the highest technical feats of all.

What are the technical skills of poetry, that all poets have worked at who wanted to achieve the practice and mastery of their craft?

We could begin by saying that poetry itself is language which is used in a specific way to convey a specific effect. And the specific ways that language can be used are expressed through all of the various poetic devices. In "The ABC of Reading," Ezra Pound summarized these devices and divided them into three categories—phonopoeia (sight), melopoeia (sound), and logopoeia (voice).

SIGHT

The image is the heart and soul of poetry. In our own psychic lives, we dream in images, although there may be words superimposed onto these images. In our social communication, we indicate complete understanding of something when we say, "I get the picture"— indicating that imagistic understanding is the most basic and primal of all communications. In some languages, like Chinese and Japanese, words began as pictures, or ideograms, which embodied the image representation of what the word was indicating.

It is not accidental that our earliest record of human civilization is in the form of pure pictures—images of bison in the paleolithic caves at Altamira in Northern Spain, from the Magdalenian culture, some 16,000 years B.C. And there are other records of stone statues as pure

449

images of horses and deer and mammoths, in Czechoslovakia, from as far back as 30,000 years B.C.

Aristotle wrote in the "Poetics" that metaphor—the conjunction of one image with another image—is the soul of poetry, and is the surest sign of genius. He also said it was the one thing that could not be taught, since the genius for metaphor was unaccountable, being the ability to see similarities in dissimilar things.

Following are the principal poetic devices which use image, or the picture aspect of poetry:

image—a simple picture, a mental representation. "That which presents an intellectual and emotional complex in an instant of time." (Pound)

metaphor—a direct comparison. "A mighty fortress is our God." An equation, or an equivalence: A = B. "It is the east and Juliet is the sun."

simile—an indirect comparison, using "like" or "as." "Why, man, he doth bestride the narrow world/Like a Colossus..." "My love's like a red, red rose."

figure—an image and an idea. "Ship of state." "A sea of troubles." "This bud of love."

conceit—an extended figure, as in some metaphysical poetry of John Donne, or in the following lines of Shakespeare's Juliet:

Sweet, good-night!
This bud of love, by summer's ripening breath,
May prove a beauteous flower when next we meet...

SOUND

Rhythm has its source and origin in our own bloodstream pulse. At a normal pace, the heart beats at a casual iambic beat. But when it is excited, it may trip and skip rhythm through extended anapests or hard dactyls or firm trochees. It may even pound with a relentless spondee beat.

In dance, rhythm is accented by a drumbeat, in parades, by the cadence of marching feet, and in the night air, by churchbell tolling.

These simple rhythms may be taken as figures of the other rhythms of the universe—the tidal ebb and flow, the rising and setting of the sun, the female menstrual cycles, the four seasons of the year.

Rhythm is notated as metrics, but may also be seen in such poetic devices as rhyme and assonance and alliteration. Following are the poetic devices for sound:

assonance—rhyme of vowel sounds. "O that this too too solid flesh would melt..."

alliteration—repetition of consonants. "We might have met them dareful, beard to beard, And beat them backward home."

rhyme—the sense of resonance that comes when a word echoes the sound of another word—in end rhyme, internal rhyme, perfect rhyme, slant or imperfect rhyme, masculine rhyme, or feminine rhyme.

metrics—the simplest notation system for scansion of rhythm. The most commonly used metrics in English are:

iamb ($\smile\prime$)
trochee ($\prime\smile$)
anapest ($\smile\smile\prime$)
dactyl ($\prime\smile\smile$)
spondee ($\prime\prime$)

VOICE

Voice is the sum total of cognitive content of the words in a poem. Voice can also be seen as the signature of the poet on his poem—his own unmistakable way of saying something. "Only Yeats could have said it that way," one feels, in reading a line like:

That is no country for old men...

Similarly, Frost was able to endow his poems with a "voice" in lines like:

Something there is that doesn't love a wall...

Following are the poetic devices for voice:

denotation—literal, dictionary meaning of a word.

connotation—indirect or associative meaning of a word. "Mother" means one thing denotatively, but may have a host of other connotative associations.

personification—humanizing an object.

diction—word choice, the peculiar combination of words used in any given poem.

syntax—the peculiar arrangement of words in their sentence structures.

rhetoric—"Any adornment or inflation of speech which is not done for a particular effect but for a general impressiveness..." (Eliot)

persona—a mask, an assumed voice, a speaker pretending to be someone other than who he really is.

451

So far these are only words on a page, like diagrams in a baseball book showing you how to throw a curve ball. The only way there can be any real learning of any of these devices is to do endless exercises in notebooks, trying to master the craft of assonance, of diction shifts, of persona effects, of successful conceits, of metrical variations.

Any practice of these craft devices may lead one into a period of extreme self-consciousness, as one explores totally new reflexes of language. But one can trust that with enough practice they can become "second nature," and an enhancement and reinforcement of one's own intuitive talents as a poet.

83

GUIDELINES FOR
THE BEGINNING PLAYWRIGHT

By Louis E. Catron

YEARS OF teaching playwriting probably have been more educational for me than for my students. Several hundred young playwrights have taken one or more of my classes since I first started teaching at the College of William and Mary in 1966, and they have taught me that writing a play can be simplified—maybe not made "easy," but certainly "easier"—if certain boundaries are imposed.

We began experimenting with guidelines because so many playwrights were expending too much creative energy chasing nonproductive fireflies. We found that these limitations help playwrights over difficult hurdles. More, they are highly important for the overall learning process.

To be sure, for some writers the very idea of imposed limits appears to be a contradiction in significant terms. How, they ask, can I do creative writing if you fence me in?

Their objections have merit. Limitations often inhibit the creative mind, and many creative people expend a great deal of effort seeking clever ways of circumventing the rules. Certainly I've had students react to the guidelines with the fervor of a bull to a red flag and we've had to arm wrestle about the rules.

Nonetheless, imposition of limitations is a way of life in all creative arts. Theatre is no exception. As a play director, for example, I have found that one key portion of my job is establishing parameters of character for actors, holding these walls tightly in place during rehearsals, and encouraging the performers to create depth within those limitations.

We're talking about the contrast between the casual and sloppy meandering of a Mississippi River versus a tightly confined Colorado. The former changes directions so often that it confuses even experienced riverboat captains, but the latter is held so tightly in direction that it cuts the Grand Canyon. Discipline is essential for the creation of beauty.

The beginning playwright is encouraged to accept the following guidelines to write his or her first play. Later plays can be more free. Indeed, deliberately breaking selected guidelines later will help you better understand the nature of dramatic writing. For now, however, let these guidelines help you in your initial steps toward learning the art and craft of playwriting.

1. *Start with a one-act play.* A full-length play isn't merely three times longer and therefore only three times more difficult. And that a one-act is simpler doesn't mean it is insignificant. The one-act play can be exciting and vibrantly alive, as has been shown by plays such as *No Exit* (Sartre), *Zoo Story* (Albee), *The Maids* (Genet), *the Dumb Waiter* (Pinter) and *The Madness of Lady Bright* (Wilson).

Starting with the one-act lets the writer begin with a canvas that is easily seen at a glance, instead of a mural that covers such a huge space perception doesn't grasp it all.

The one-act typically has only a few characters, is an examination of a single dramatic incident, and runs about half an hour in length. It usually stays within one time frame and one place. Because there are fewer complexities, you'll be able to focus more upon the actual writing, and you'll have less concern about a number of stage problems which come with full-length plays.

2. *Write about something you care about.* Writing manuals usually tell the beginner to write "about what you know best." I think that can lead a beginner to think in terms of daily, mundane events. Better, I believe, is for the beginner to *care;* if the playwright is involved with the subject, that interest will pull an audience along.

3. *Conflict is essential to drama.* Quibble me no quibbles about plays which may not have conflict. For *your* first play, there should be conflict. Drama is the art of the showdown. Force must be opposed by force, person (or group) by person (or group), desire by desire.

If there's no conflict, the dramatic qualities are lost. The result may still hold the stage, but the odds against it are increased. More important, even if the one-act has no conflict and yet holds the stage, the playwright hasn't learned that all-significant lesson about showing conflict. You'll want to know that when you write more.

4. *Let there be emotion.* People *care,* in your first play, I hope; people feel strongly, whether it is love or hate, happiness or despair. If you are able to get them emotional, your characters more than likely are going to be active and going somewhere. The audience will care more about emotional people than those dull-eyed, unfeeling dramatic deadbeats.

5. *Stay within the "realistic" mode.* Realism deals with contemporary people, the sort who might live next door, in their contemporary activities, and with selective use of ordinary speech. It avoids the aside and the soliloquy. It is quite comfortable inside the traditional box set. Realism is selective, and sometimes critical, in its presentation of objective facts.

Realism is the familiar mode you've seen most often: it dominates television, and only a handful of movies break away from realism. No doubt you've also seen it on stage more than any other mode. Because you know it best, your first play will be easier to write if you stay in realism. Expressionism, absurdism, symbolism, epic: avoid these for your first experience with playwriting.

(Examples of realism would be full-length plays like *Ghosts* or *A Doll's House,* both by Ibsen, or one-acts like *Ile* and other sea plays by O'Neill. More recent plays tend to be eclectic—primarily but not totally realistic, like the full-length *Death of a Salesman,* by Arthur Miller, or the one-act *Gnadiges Fraulein* by Tennessee Williams.)

6. *Limit the number of characters.* Too many characters and you may lose some: they'll be on stage but saying and doing nothing, so you'll send them off to make dinner or fix the car while you focus on the remaining characters you like better. Consider eliminating those who are dead.

Strenuously avoid "utilitarian" characters—those people who make minor announcements (in older drawing-room plays they say little more than, "Dinner is served"), or deliver packages or messages (Western Union's delivery boy, remember, is as much a relic as the butler). Such characters tend to be flat and no fun for playwright, performer or audience.

Some utilitarians are confidants, on stage to serve as ears so the protagonist will be able to speak inner thoughts without resorting to the soliloquy. The confidant in this sort of case turns out to be about as vital as a wooden listening post.

Confidants, by the way, are easily recognized: their faces are covered with a huge question mark. They seem to be asking questions eternally, without any apparent interest in question or answer. The playwright uses the confidant to get to the answer. If such a person is necessary, let the character be more than a pair of ears.

Just how many characters should be in the play?

Three is a good number for the first play. The triangle is always helpful; three characters allow development of good action and conflict and variety. More, and there's the risk of excess baggage; less, and the characters may quickly become thin and tired.

7. *Keep them all on stage as long as you can.* All too often I've seen plays developing potentially exciting situations, only to be deflated by the exit of a prime character. The audience will feel let down—promised excitement evaporated through the swinging door.

A flurry of activity with entrances and exits is deceptive. There may be a feeling of action but in truth there's only movement of people at the door. The more such business, often the less the drama: in class we begin to comment jokingly about wanting a percentage of the turnstile concession.

The beginning writer needs to learn to keep all characters alive and actively contributing to the play's action. So, then, you need to try to keep them all on stage as long as you possibly can. If you have a character who keeps running out, perhaps he ought to be eliminated.

You needn't invent a supernatural force to keep them in the same room, by the way, although I've seen my student writers come up with fascinating hostage or kidnap situations and locked doors in order to justify keeping everyone present. All of that is clever, but all you need is action that involves all the characters.

8. *No breaks: no scene shifts, no time lapses.* Just as some playwrights have people leaving when stage action is growing, so also are there authors who cut from the forthcoming explosion with a pause to shift scenery or to indicate a passage of time. There is a break in the action and that always is disappointing. Such lapses are all too often barriers to the play's communication with the audience.

If you have in mind a play that takes place first in an apartment, then in a grocery store, then in a subway, you have let the motion pictures overly influence your theatrical concept. It just won't wash, not in a one-act stage play; with so many sets and breaks producers will shy away from your script. (Yes, yes, you can cite this or that exception, but we're talking about a beginner's first play, not a script by someone with an established reputation.)

Reduce the locales to the *one* place where the essential action occurs, and forget the travelogue. So also with the jumps in time: find the *single* prime moment for these events to take place.

Later you can jump freely in time and space, as Miller does so magnificently in *After the Fall.* Your first play, however, needs your concentrated attention on action, not on inventive devices for jumping around through time and space.

9. *Aim for a thirty-minute play.* One-act plays are delightfully free of the restrictions placed upon full lengths, and can run from only a few minutes to well over an hour. The freedom is heady stuff for a beginning writer.

Aim for around half an hour. Less than that and you probably only sketched the characters and action; much longer, and you might exhaust your initial energies (and your audience!). Your goal, of course, is to be sure you achieve adequate amplification; too many beginners start with a play only eight or ten minutes long, and it seems full of holes. Your *concept* should be one that demands around half an hour to be shown.

10. *Start the plot as soon as you can.* Let the exposition, foreshadowing, mood and character follow the beginning of the plot (the point of attack). Get into the action quickly, and let the other elements follow.

11. *Remember the advantage of the protagonist-antagonist structure.* Our era of the anti-hero apparently has removed the protagonist from the stage. Too bad. The protagonist is a very handy character indeed, and the protagonist-antagonist structure automatically brings conflict which, you recall, is essential for drama.

The protagonist is the "good guy," the one with whom we sympathize and/or empathize, the central character of the play. A better definition: *The one whose conscious will is driving to get a goal.* The antagonist stands firmly in the way. Both should be equal forces at the beginning of

457

the play: if one is obviously stronger, the conflict is over quickly and so should the play be.

(If you do not fully understand the personality of a true protagonist, look at Cyrano in Hooker's translation of Edmond Rostand's *Cyrano de Bergerac*. Cyrano is so strongly a conscious will moving actively that it takes several antagonists to balance him.)

12. *Keep speeches short.* Long speeches often grow boring. Sometimes they are didactic; the playwright delivering The Play's Message. Always they drag the tempo. But the worst sin of a long speech is that it means the playwright is thinking just of that one character and all the others are lying about dead.

Short speeches—quick exchanges between characters—on the other hand keep all of them alive and make the play appear to be more crisp and more vital. The play will increase in pace and you'll automatically feel a need to increase the complications.

How long is "short"? Let the dialogue carry but one idea per speech. Or, to give you another answer, let your ear "listen" to the other characters while one is talking, and see who wants to interrupt. A third answer: try to keep the speeches under, say, some twenty words.

One grants the effectiveness of the "Jerry and the Dog" speech in Albee's *Zoo Story*. It makes a nice exception to this guideline. But there are very few such examples, and there are many more examples of plays where the dialogue is rich and effective because the playwright disciplined the talky characters.

13. *Complications are the plot's heartbeat.* John wants Mary. Mary says fine. Her family likes the idea. Her dog likes John. His parrot likes Mary and the dog. So John and Mary get married. They have their 2.8 kids, two cars, a dishwasher, and they remember anniversaries. Happiness.

Interesting? Not very. Dramatic? Hardly.

John wants Mary. Mary is reluctant, wondering if John simply is in love with love. John is angry at the charge. Mary apologizes. John shows full romanticism. Mary worries again. Mary's grandmother advises Mary to take John to see what love really is by visiting Mary's older sis who everyone knows is happy in marriage. Mary and John visit. Sis and her husband Mike are having a violent fight; mental cruelty; damning accusations. Sis gets John to help her and he unwillingly does; Mike pulls John to his side; Mary yells at John for causing trouble.

That's the first ten minutes.

I think you'll grant it has more potential than the first sketch. *Complications* keep it vital, moving, alive. *A play depends upon conflict for its dramatic effect, and complications are the active subdivision of the basic conflict.*

So, then: the traditional baker's dozen—thirteen guidelines which will help you with your first play. They will help you avoid pitfalls which have lamed so many playwrights, and they will give you a basic learning experience which will help you with future plays.

84

THE EXPERIENCE OF THE POEM

By Ann Stanford

ONE may think of the ingredients of a good poem as an experience and a fresh perception of that experience. The experience need not be original or new, but the perception should be. Think of Gerard Manley Hopkins' delight in spring, a feeling old as humanity, couched in the freshest of images:

> Nothing is so beautiful as spring—
>> When weeds, in wheels, shoot long and lovely and lush;
>> Thrush's eggs look little low heavens, and thrush
> Through the echoing timber does so rinse and wring
> The ear, it strikes like lightnings to hear him sing;
>> The glassy peartree leaves and blooms, they brush
>> The descending blue; that blue is all in a rush
> With richness; the racing lambs too have fair their fling.

Hopkins' language is vital because his feeling about spring is intense and his own. He has taken the familiar ingredients of a poem about spring and made them into a new vision.

A contemporary example of a poem drawn from everyday experience is May Swenson's "Water Picture,"* which describes the reflection of objects in a pond; it begins:

> In the pond in the park
> all things are doubled:
> Long buildings hang and
> wriggle gently. Chimneys
> are bent legs bouncing
> on clouds below. A flag
> wags like a fishhook
> down there in the sky.

---

* From *To Mix with Time*. Charles Scribner's Sons. Copyright © 1963, by May Swenson.

460

The arched stone bridge
is an eye, with underlid
in the water. In its lens
dip crinkled heads with hats
that don't fall off. Dogs go by,
barking on their backs.
A baby, taken to feed the
ducks, dangles upside-down
a pink balloon for a buoy.

Seen in detail from a new angle, an ordinary experience becomes extraordinary and the substance of poetry. The fresh perception makes the old experience unique.

And the perception is conveyed through language. The words and combinations we choose must be carefully screened to see that they are not the old stereotypes through which we blind ourselves to the world. In his poems, e. e. cummings tore words apart and put the parts back into new combinations so that his language might reveal a new view of the world. Most of us will not follow his way, but we need to be sure we see what we see as it is, not as we think it is. There is a tree before you. What kind of leaves does it have? Are they alternating on the stem? Do they resemble plumes? Are they flat on the air like lily-pads in the water? Hopkins' journal frequently takes account of such phenomena:

Elm leaves:—they shine much in the sun—bright green when near from underneath but higher up they look olive: their shapelessness in the flat is from their being made . . . to be dimpled and dog's eared: their leaf-growth is in this point more rudimentary than that of oak, ash, beech, etc that the leaves lie in long rows and do not subdivide or have central knots but tooth or cog their woody twigs.

Such careful looking, such precision in visual perception, is a first step in writing poetry. If you cannot see what a tree looks like, it will be hard to tell anyone what a feeling feels like. Because in poetry we are dependent on the concrete manifestations of the world to use as symbols of our feelings and our experiences. This is especially true in lyric poetry. But apt suggestive details give credibility to narrative poems and character sketches as well. A good exercise in poetry is to record exactly what you see before you with no large statements about what is there. Simply describe it as if you are seeing it for the first time. An artist practices by carrying a sketch pad and drawing

461

wherever he may be. In the same way, the result of the poet's sketch may not be a poem, but the practice will help develop a technique for handling a more complex subject when it does appear. Here is an example, a description of a shell done as an exercise:

Being which is the size of my palm
almost and fits the upcurled fingers
flat-cupped the thirty-four fingers
end in points set close together
like the prongs of a comb
sea-combing straining the waters
they are printed on your back
brown waves cutting light sand
waves—merging inward
lighter and lighter and closer
whirling
into the self-turned center
of yourself.

Just as there are two kinds of perception—what is seen and what is experienced—there are two kinds of possibilities for exact or innovative language. And there are chances also for trite or easy observation on both levels.

A poem will not always die of a single cliché; indeed, a common observation can even be used for a deliberate artistic purpose. Only someone who has really mastered his craft, however, should dare to use a phrase which borders on the trite. Dylan Thomas sometimes uses old phrases but remakes them by small changes, so that they emerge as live word combinations like "once below a time." But I can think of no poetic situation in which a "rippling stream" or "glassy pond" can add anything but tedium. Worse than the cliché at the literal or visual level, is the cliché at the experiential level, the large abstract concept such as:

Life, like time, moves onward.

The large concept gives the reader a stereotyped experience. Perhaps this is why some very bad poetry appeals to a number of undiscriminating readers: it repeats the stereotype of experience they have in their own minds and gives them nothing new to test it by. A good poem should jolt the reader into a new awareness of his feeling or his sensual apprehension of the world. One of the great mistakes is to make a poem too large and simple.

Poetry is an art which proceeds in a roundabout fashion. Its language is not chosen for directness of communication, for the passing on of facts, like "the plane arrives at five," or "today it is raining," although either of these facts could be a part of a poem. The truth that poetry attempts to communicate is reached by more devious means. Many of the devices thought of as being in the special province of poetry are devices of indirection: the metaphor or symbol, which involves saying one thing and meaning another; paradox, the welding of opposites into a single concept; connotations beyond the direct meaning of a word or phrase, and so on. When we think of the way things are in the world, we find that poetry is not the only area in which the immediate fact is disguised, distorted, or concealed. Poetry does this in order to reach a more complex truth. Other situations involve indirection for other reasons. Purpose determines the directness of statement. Take the guest telling his hostess he enjoyed the party. Did he really? But in saying this he is expressing some other feeling beyond the immediate situation. He may be expressing sympathy or long affection or any number of emotions rather than measuring the quality of his enjoyment of the moment. Take advertising, which often tries to pass along not so much a fact as a feeling about something. Take the art of the magician—the better the more deceiving. For the poet to speak too glibly may be to oversimplify his experience. The poet must constantly ask himself: "Is this the way it really felt? Is this the whole experience? Am I overlooking or suppressing part of it?"

As I write this, a living example has appeared before my eyes. I am looking at the tree just outside the window. If I should give you my visual experience at this moment, I should have to include a lizard that has climbed twenty feet up the trunk and is now looking at me. In my stereotyped picture of trees, birds sometimes come to rest, but not lizards. In my stereotype of the loss of a friend through death, there is sorrow, not anger. But I have felt anger at the death of a friend, and there is a lizard in this tree. The real includes these disparate elements. The poet must think of what he has really experienced. He gives certain real details, certain suggestions. The reader combines these into the experience intended by the poet, the real message of the poem, and so participates in its creation.

The poet uses three types of ingredients in his poem: at the first

463

level is what can be immediately caught by the senses—by sight, by hearing, tasting, feeling, smelling. I call this the literal level: the poet describes what is literally there. This poem of my own is written almost entirely at this level:

THE BLACKBERRY THICKET *

I stand here in the ditch, my feet on a rock in the water,
Head-deep in a coppice of thorns,
Picking wild blackberries,
Watching the juice-dark rivulet run
Over my fingers, marking the lines and the whorls,
Remembering stains—
The blue of mulberry on the tongue
Brown fingers after walnut husking,
And the green smudge of grass—
The earnest part
Of heat and orchards and sweet springing places.
Here I am printed with the earth
Always and always the earth ground into the fingers,
And the arm scratched in thickets of spiders.
Over the marshy water the cicada rustles,
A runner snaps sharp into place.
The dry leaves are a presence,
A companion that follows up under the trees of the orchard
Repeating my footsteps. I stop to listen.
Surely not alone
I stand in this quiet in the shadow
Under a roof of bees.

The sights and sounds caught by immediate sensation are described; the memories are of the same immediate quality. Even the ending of the poem is a literal description, although the reader may find there, if he likes, connotations that go beyond the literal.

Much of modern American poetry is written at this level. If not total poems as here, at least sections of poems. Most readers of modern poetry, many editors, look for this literal quality. Here, as I said earlier, the poet must look carefully and sensitively and report exactly. Notice, next time you read a poem, how much of it contains this literal looking and what details the poet has chosen to give the appearance of reality. Even an imagined experience should have some of this literal quality.

The next level of poetry is the metaphoric, in which one thing is compared with another. The conventional poetic devices of simile, metaphor, symbol are part of this level. Comparison often mingles with the literal. In Elizabeth Bishop's well-known poem "The Fish," * exact description is aided by comparison:

> I looked into his eyes
> which were far larger than mine
> but shallower, and yellowed,
> the irises backed and packed
> with tarnished tinfoil
> seen through the lenses
> of old scratched isinglass.

The juxtaposing of two things that are not wholly alike but that are alike in some way is one of the ways that poetry creates a new view of the world. Comparisons or analogies can be used thus as part of description, or they can make a total poem. They can be either one-way or two-way comparisons. For example, the fish's eye can be said to resemble isinglass, but isinglass does not remind one of a fish's eye. It is not always necessary or desirable that the comparisons work both ways. Another example, Shakespeare's comparison of true love to a "star to every wandering bark," is effective even though within the poem he is not also comparing a star that guides to love. He is defining love in terms of a star, but not a star in terms of love.

However, often the poet uses a two-way analogy. The doubleness of the analogy is especially effective where the whole poem is in the form of comparison. Here is a poem of mine which satirizes the work of committees.

THE COMMITTEE †
by Ann Stanford

Black and serious, they are dropping down one by one to the top of the walnut
    tree.
It is spring and the bare branches are right for a conversation.
The sap has not risen yet, but those branches will always be bare
Up there, crooked with ebbed life lost now, like a legal argument.
They shift a bit as they settle into place.

---

* From *Poems: North and South*. Houghton Mifflin Company. Copyright © 1955, by Elizabeth Bishop.
† © 1967 The New Yorker Magazine, Inc.

Once in a while one says something, but the answer is always the same;
The question is, too—it is all *caw* and *caw*.
Do they think they are hidden by the green leaves partway up the branches?
Do they like it up there cocking their heads in the fresh morning?
One by one, they fly off as if to other appointments.
Whatever they did, it must be done all over again.

Here, what is said about the crows can be applied to a committee, but it is also true of crows, at least the ones I have observed in my neighborhood. This, then, is a two-way analogy.

There is another level at which poets sometimes work: the level of statement. Much of Wordsworth's poetry is statement, as:

> This spiritual Love acts not nor can exist
> Without Imagination, which, in truth,
> Is but another name for absolute power
> And clearest insight, amplitude of mind,
> And Reason in her most exalted mood.

This is a hard and dangerous level for most poets. Much poetry, especially amateur poetry, constantly attempts statement without backing it up with the literal or analogic or comparative level. The poem which merely states, except in the hands of a master, falls flat because it does not prove anything to the reader. He is not drawn into the background of the statement. He is merely told. If his own experience backs up the statement, he may like the poem, but he likes it only because of his experience, not because of what the poem has done for him.

Masters of poetry, on the other hand, sometimes make one large statement and spend the rest of the poem illustrating or proving it. Hopkins does this with the statement "Nothing is so beautiful as spring—"; May Swenson does it in a more specific way in "Water Picture." William Carlos Williams in "To Waken an Old Lady" defines old age by describing a flock of birds in winter. His only reference to age at all is the first line, "Old age is." Without the first line to suggest the definition, the poem could be simply a nature description. Emily Dickinson often makes an abstract idea come to life by defining it in visual terms:

> Presentiment is that long shadow on the lawn
> Indicative that suns go down;

466

The notice to the startled grass
That darkness is about to pass.

It would be a rare poem which could exist on one of these levels—
that of literal description, that of metaphor, or that of statement—
alone. Poems usually combine these in varying proportions. There
are dangers to the poetry, besides triteness, at all levels. Flatness,
dullness, and poor selection of details menace literal description.
Metaphor is endangered by irrelevance; a metaphor which does not
contribute in tone or feeling may turn the reader away from the
poem as a whole. Statement is most dangerous, for it must be proved.

A poem which succeeds may also have a fourth level—the transcendental level, where the connotations of the poem extend on beyond the limits of the poem. But the transcendental may hardly be
striven for. We only recognize it when it shimmers in the exceptional
poem.

Meanwhile the poet works at what he can. He looks for the whole
significance of the experience. He renders it—even more, he understands it—through language built around his own view. His new seeing is what will make the experience of the poem worth telling once
more.

85

MESSAGES BELONG IN TELEGRAMS

By Connie C. Epstein

Sam Goldwyn, driving force of Metro-Goldwyn-Mayer, once said, "If you want to send a message, send a telegram." Although he is not usually thought of as a source of good advice for children's authors, his remark is one the aspiring writer for the young would do well to take to heart. Message writing is usually bad writing, and children's books appear to be especially vulnerable to it. In fact, it may be the reason children's writing is often considered a lesser art.

Katherine Paterson, a Newbery Medal winner, expressed her feelings about message writing very cogently: When an interviewer asked her, "What are you trying to do when you write for children?," he was clearly disappointed when she answered that she was simply trying to write as good a story as she possibly could. She concluded, "He seemed to share the view of many intelligent, well-educated, well-meaning people that while adult literature may aim to be art, the object of children's books is to whip the little rascals into shape."

What is message writing? After all, every writer has a point of view, and without it a book is boringly bland. My definition is that the message writer believes in one or more universal truths that hold for everyone, whatever the circumstances. The artistic writer, on the other hand, is interested in people as individuals, the way each behaves and why. She or he describes them as clearly as possible and then trusts the reader to draw the appropriate conclusions from the actions of the characters.

All kinds of messages have shown up in children's books ever since children's writing was first considered a form of its own. At first, proper manner, good habits, and virtuous behavior were a prime concern. Today's writers continue to worry about virtuous behavior, but the problems have changed. Instead of thumb-sucking, stories deal

468

now with the terrors of drug addiction. Or writers may feel they should instill proper attitudes toward social problems such as racism, sexism, and ageism.

Some of the early children's cautionary tales seem startling, to say the least, in this day and age. There is the famous *Struwwelpeter (Slovenly Peter)* by Heinrich Hoffman, published in Germany in 1845. It was considered a great advance in the development of children's books, for it used the technique of comic exaggeration, a largely missing ingredient until then. Still, to cure Little Suck-a-Thumb of his bad habit, the tailor cuts off his thumb with his shears. The illustration shows the blood dripping down, and the caption reads, "That made little Conrad yell."

I learned good table manners from a book that had dropped the violence but retained both the preaching and the humor. Certainly it pulled no punches when it advised on right and wrong. This Manual of Manners for Polite Infants was titled *Goops and How to Be Them* by Frank Gelett Burgess, first published in 1900, a collection of verses about a strange subculture of bald, round-headed beings. The opening poem read:

> The Goops they lick their fingers,
> And the Goops they lick their knives;
> They spill their broth on the tablecloth—
> Oh, they lead disgusting lives!
> The Goops they talk while eating,
> And loud and fast they chew;
> And that is why I'm glad that I
> Am not a Goop—are you?

We recited these lines in a chorus whenever any one of the three children in our family made a slip at the dinner table and, strangely, thought they were funny rather than irritating. Perhaps the silliness was a relief in contrast to the parental lecture. Anyway, the priggishness didn't offend us and apparently doesn't offend children today, for I find to my surprise that the book is still in print.

Humor, in fact, has saved many a morality tale. One that I was most closely connected with was *The Chocolate Touch* by Patrick Skene Catling, a modern variation on the legend of King Midas (Morrow). In it, everything the hero touches turns to chocolate, and it preaches the evils of greed unabashedly, but a number of the effects are really very funny. In retrospect, I think it was more popular with children than with critics, so much so that Morrow brought out a new reillustrated edition with considerable success.

Judging from the manuscripts submitted to children's book editors, I would say that the temptation to pass along a constructive message to children continues unabated. Everyone who cares about young people these days worries about the problems of addiction to alcohol and drugs. This topic turns up constantly. Sometimes the concern takes such precedence over characterization that we get dialogue like the following:

> "If Sandy hadn't messed with drugs, she'd still be alive. . . ."
> "Well, it won't ever happen to me," Tommy answered.
> "I'm sure Sandy thought it would never happen to her."
> "I guess you're right. After all, a lot of famous people have overdosed—Janis Joplin, Jimmy Hendrix."

I can't believe that any two teen-agers ever talked to each other this way, and I doubt that any other reader would be convinced, either. Unfortunately, drug addiction is not solved so simply, and this whole story loses credibility because the writer has clearly put the message before characters and plot, a reverse of writing priorities.

Because this writer has taken his message so seriously, the reader cannot take him seriously—certainly not as an author. Adult writing-in-progress rarely suffers from the disease of wishful thinking in quite so virulent a form, with the possible exception of religious work, in which the message is truly the medium. To master their craft, children's fiction writers must constantly guard against wishful thinking and not play their characters false, or they always will be considered lesser artists.

Some people are surprised that a topic as unpleasant as drug addiction appears in juvenile writing at all, but the extent of this modern plague has pretty well settled the question. Regrettably, it is part of the scene for teen-agers in most large urban areas. More to the point is the artistry with which the subject is handled. When believable characters and plot are created, the problem falls into perspective.

The danger is the "single-issue novel," narrated in first person so that it is limited to the scope of one, sometimes immature, sensibility. All too often, the characters in such a story are defined entirely in terms of their attitude toward the problem—in this case addiction. It is their

470

only topic of conversation and the sole motive for their actions. If characters and plot are given proper priority, however, then the problem is only one part of the whole, and the story is probably not considered a problem novel at all.

The present-day problem novel seems to me simply the latest form of message writing. Even now when we smile about the Goops of the past, children's fiction is still afflicted with obvious messages.

Manuscripts written for little children usually do not get entangled with complicated social problems, but they sometimes try even more earnestly to instruct in good behavior. In one manuscript I saw last year entitled *The Little Ice Cream Truck Who Hated Snowballs,* a personalized truck explained to a group of children the dangers of throwing things at moving vehicles. Perhaps this concept would work visually as an animated television commercial for Good Humor sticks, but between covers it seems a thinly disguised tract.

Another recent example carried the title *Aunti-Pollution and the Bubble-Gum Mess.* Aunti-Pollution was a turtle who stepped on a wad of gum and needed the help of all her animal friends to make her clean again. Pollution is of crucial importance today, but presenting it in terms of do's and don'ts for the young runs the risk of turning them off with a lecture or, at the least, of making them always uncertain exactly how the word *anti* is spelled.

When messages dominate a story, all the characters are likely to be stick figures, but one type suffers especially: the villain. Adventure tales desperately need a good, credible villain to make them work properly, yet all too often the writer wants to shield child readers from evil and cannot bring himself to describe wrong-doing with conviction or, for that matter, with understanding. In fact, the villain in this kind of story may be more important to its success than the hero, and you should be sure to develop him or her with just as much or even more care.

Of course, citing examples of what not to do is much easier than offering advice on good technique. Recently the children's writer Beverly Cleary had the following to say about messages:

There are those who feel that a children's book must *teach* a child. I am not one of them. Children prefer to learn what is implicit in a story, to discover what they need to know. As a child I was tired of being taught when there was so much room for improvement in adults.

471

These remarks were made in acceptance of an award for her story, *Ramona and Her Mother,* in which Mrs. Cleary did reluctantly allow there was a message. She didn't know it was there until she had finished the book (which is a good thing to remember: let the characters grow naturally and the moral will emerge of itself), and then the message turned out to be for adults, not for children at all. Ramona learns at last that though she has done exasperating things like squeezing out an entire tube of toothpaste, her mother does love her. So Mrs. Cleary concluded, "If there are any adults in the audience who feel that a book for children *must* have a moral, here it is: Children need to be told in words that their parents love them."

In other words, the child's point of view should be paramount. Try to imagine how the *child* in your dramatic situation would feel, and relate adult reactions to this feeling. If you are truly seeing the world through the eyes of children, you can hardly send them a message about it at the same time. Perhaps the biggest challenge for the children's writer is the leap in point of view that must always take place. From memory, instinct, and observation, the writer is always re-creating another, slightly different sensibility. The adult writer is frequently able to take the far easier course of writing from his or her personal reactions and perspective.

Children's writing is said to have come of age in the United States since World War II, for in that period it came to be recognized as a distinct area of publishing with formal standards of its own. Those who care agree that children deserve the finest writing and resent the notion that it is in any way a lesser art. But until we remember to use Western Union, not children's books, for our messages, I suspect they won't be completely accepted in the mainstream. Sam Goldwyn was a smart man, and we should listen to him.

472

86

SCIENCE FICTION FOR YOUNG READERS

By Douglas Hill

THE DISTINGUISHED American poet, novelist and science fiction writer Thomas M. Disch once rather sourly remarked that "all science fiction is children's fiction." His tongue may have been in his cheek, but he was reflecting a fairly general view that there is still something slightly disreputable about SF (which is the proper abbreviation, not "scifi"). Hence, there must be something slightly peculiar, if not immature, about those who persist in reading it into adulthood.

Nonetheless, a great many of us do persist, maintaining and usually enlarging that addiction that we first acquired when we were around 12 or 13. For that matter, the vast majority of SF *writers,* including me, started out as young fans, or addicts.

When I began writing SF for young readers—after some ten years and nearly 20 books of adult nonfiction—I felt it had to be a simple enough process. I could clearly remember what I liked reading when I was 12 or 13, so I set out to write along those lines.

And though it did not by any means turn out to be quite as simple as that, the basic premise was accurate: Children who develop an interest in SF do not leap directly from Marvel Comics to the luminous riches of novels by Ursula K. Le Guin. They progress through SF by stages— and the early stages are, without a doubt, children's fiction.

When I began writing science fiction books for children (my first, *Galactic Warlord,* was published in 1979 in England), I went straight into space adventure. There are plenty of other options within the incredible breadth of SF—the future on Earth, time travel, alternative universes, alternative pasts or futures, contacts with extraterrestrials (cuddly or otherwise). But as a kid I had liked reading about adventures on other worlds; I'd had an idea for an interplanetary hero with a particular problem and purpose; and I was encouraged by the fact that television and films were creating a huge audience for space adventure, even in 1977 B.S.W. (Before *Star Wars*).

So out into the galaxy I went, with my hero, the Last Legionary, and a cast of rather more than thousands. And I found—because this was my first crack at any kind of longer fiction, let alone children's fiction— that I had to learn a great many ground rules, mostly the hard way. Some of them may seem fairly obvious to experienced professionals, but they may help to clarify the thinking and planning of anyone contemplating a similar lift-off into SF.

The ground rules fall into two categories, with a certain amount of overlap. I had to learn about writing *adventure* fiction, for children today; and I had to learn about writing more or less specialized *genre* fiction.

The adventure element seemed paramount at first, mainly because I have never written anything like it. I had stumbled, probably by instinct, onto the first main prerequisite, a clearly defined and fairly fundamental "good *vs.* evil" plot—otherwise defined as a good guy against a number of bad guys. No matter how many subplots or temporary diversions you want to weave in, that central plot must always be clearly defined and visible, a broad, straight and well signposted freeway with a discernible goal in view.

So, too, the characters must be clearly defined and distinguishable— but that is made easier in SF, where aliens and mutants with weird names and weirder shapes can easily be distinguished from a very human hero. In the same way, space adventure readily provides the unusual or exotic settings on other worlds that can lend tone and atmosphere, heighten the sense of excitement or menace, and add integrated little plot twists.

Of course, adventure fiction requires you to place the emphasis on drama and suspense and action, rather than on subtle interplay of character or delicate tapestries of descriptive prose. These days, if you interrupt the progress of the story with too many pages of descriptive writing, a young reader is likely to toss the book aside and watch TV. So you keep description to a minimum, sometimes just a few spare sentences to prime a young reader's imagination, and let him take it from there.

Pace is the key word: You start off with a "hook," an attention-getting bit of action or excitement, and then you keep it moving—even accelerating as you approach the climax.

474

Naturally, there will be lulls, brief transitional passages when the characters talk among themselves, or travel from one place to another, or in other ways slow down for a short while and perhaps let the reader's pulse rate settle. But even in these lulls, there are valuable chances to underline the "what will happen next?" suspense—as well as useful possibilities for character development, comic relief, scenery changing, signposting time shifts and plot twists, and so on.

At such times the usefulness of giving the hero a companion, a sidekick, is especially clear. Hero and friend can converse, and so can not only expand the characterization and make a tension-easing joke or two, but can also clarify the narrative—reminding the reader where the story is, where it's likely to go next, and where it must go ultimately (that "discernible goal" of the overall plot). It's for this reason, among others, that the Lone Ranger has Tonto, Batman has Robin, and my hero has a sardonic winged alien chum named Glr.

I could go on and on about what I've learned in the course of writing adventure fiction, but the best writers make their own rules, and break them, and get away with it. "Rules" is probably the wrong word, with its overtones of restraint and contrivance—which can be fatal to a high-tension, fast-moving adventure story if it means forcing the narrative into directions where it doesn't want, naturally, organically, to go.

For instance—I always make fairly substantial synopses of my books at the start, partly for my own use and partly because the publishers need them as a basis for commissioning the work. But more often than not the book will break away from the synopsis at many integral points, because as the characters take on a life of their own within the plot framework, they also begin to assume some control—showing the writer better ways to move smoothly through the transitions, to develop the story and tie up the loose ends in a natural and unlabored way.

Still, that initial synopsis or outline is crucial, if you want to prevent too much meandering away from the main plot line and allocate the action to various chapters in the proper proportion. My books for children tend to be about 35,000 words long, and the chapters are also necessarily short—averaging about 2,000 words each, tailored to the attention span of a youngster of the 1980s. Also, many of the chapters end with something akin to a cliffhanger, something that slightly raises the voltage of suspense and makes the reader want to hurry on. And I'm simply not adept enough to parcel out the drama and action in the right chapter proportions as I go along, while at the same time trying to handle all the other elements.

I need a synopsis, or plan, to keep me on line—as, I think, most writers do. I also need to put a book through several revised versions, usually five or six. But a plan is not sacred: you control it, not the other way around, and you can alter or abandon it whenever a better idea or pattern comes into your mind.

As for the writing of *genre* fiction, in my case science fiction, I can again offer general hints from my experience, without insisting that they are hard-and-fast rules or restraints.

The fact that much science fiction takes place in the future and/or on alien planets can seem to mean that in dreaming up a story, nothing is *impossible*. The future offers a nearly infinite scope for change and development of the human condition; and alien worlds offer a literally infinite universe of possibilities. So it would seem that you can really let your imagination off the leash, in SF. But in fact that freedom only goes so far.

The watchword here is credibility. If you want to invent an alien race, or to depict humanity as developing in some wildly unusual genetic way, you have to keep it *believable*—within its own imaginative context. As a very simple example, suppose you want your future human beings to be winged. You can't just attach angelic pinions to people as they are now, and get on with your story. Human beings would have to have changed and evolved in other ways—with alterations to bone structure and musculature, with social and cultural changes (flying people wouldn't live in one-story bungalows), and so on.

The SF imagination can be brought back to earth, so to speak, with this need to achieve credibility. You also need to avoid too much complexity, because again you don't want to halt the progress of the story for pages and pages of description and explanation. And you don't want to introduce your strange aliens or mutations, or fantastic technological devices, merely for their *own* sake, just to be clever or to add extra exotic texture. They should play a functional role in the plot (unless they are only glimpsed in passing, very briefly, as part of the otherworldly background).

Also, you needn't be over-conscious of the generic term "science fiction," which is something of a misnomer. Young readers don't want essays on the future of astrophysics or biochemistry with a light sugar coating of dramatic action. They want a good absorbing story, though SF often does, broadly, confront important issues having to do with man's uneasy relationship with science and the general "future shock" of a high-tech society. But not even adult readers of SF, on the whole, like to be overwhelmed by science or handed a thinly disguised sociological treatise. Science fiction is just a special form of imaginative fiction, and the emphasis is on the fiction.

But at the same time you can introduce a few touches of science and technology as part of the exotic (but credible) background. Children will happily accept brief allusions to advanced forms of spacecraft, or futuristic machines, and you merely need to include a phrase or two of explanation where the meaning isn't already clear from context. And then it can help if the writer has at least a smattering of up-to-date scientific awareness, if only to avoid "howlers"—like populating the bleak barrenness of Mars or Venus with civilized, intelligent beings, or indeed any kind of life at all. Never forget that scientific and technological "progress" is high-speed, and accelerating. When I began reading SF as a young reader, space shuttles and holograms and micro-chips were still science fiction.

Even more important may be the need to have an adequate awareness of the genre in all its forms. Many young readers may prefer to dip into SF only now and then, but many more are hard-core fans, or addicts. And, as I said earlier, nearly every SF *writer* I know of began in the same way, as a juvenile fan. SF is a genre that breeds addicts—a merry, ingroup world of fan magazines and conventions and specialized, cultish expertise. It's not easy to wander in from the outside and write an SF story that is believable and effective and that doesn't unknowingly make use of some already overused device or terminology. You need to be aware of the competition—not just other SF books, not just films and TV, but also the comics, the video games, the fantasy board games, the toys . . .

It can be daunting, but children today are immersed in it, and so you must be, too, or else you're likely to start a story about a little green alien marooned on Earth—or about a space-traveling hero named Luke Skywalker. I came close enough to a version of the latter, in 1977, when I was planning to name my hero "Kyle Wandor." But then there was a British TV series called *1990* with a hero named Kyle; and an

American fantasy writer produced a series featuring a hero named Wandor. So my Last Legionary is now known as "Keill Randor," and he seems quite happy about it.

There are, of course, advantages for the writer in the present bombardment by SF. Addicts of SF generally tend to be collectors, which means that they like to own all the work of a writer they like. It also means that they are quite happy with the series format—trilogies, quartets and so on—though of course each book should be as self-contained as possible, like the episodes of a TV series (as opposed to a serial).

A principal advantage in the current abundance of TV and film SF lies in the impetus it gives young people to read books. That may seem a contradiction, but consider—SF is imaginative fiction, and the imagination flourishes best when it has room to operate. TV and films provide *everything,* in full color, leaving hardly any room for imaginative children to dream about what the strange planet and its eerie alien beings might look like, because the visuals give them so much detail. But an SF book, sketching its descriptions with a few swift and telling strokes, leaves enormous scope for the readers to go on dreaming, to add the fine detail and extra exotic flourishes.

If reading adventure space fiction can lead some children into reading other kinds of SF (and more books generally), the writer can feel gratified. Children may well see not only that the SF they enjoy at the movies or on TV has its counterparts in book form, but that the written word can offer more exciting, positive, lasting pleasures.

87

CLUES TO THE JUVENILE MYSTERY

By Joan Lowery Nixon

When I see the words 'mystery,' 'secret,' or 'ghost' in the title of a book for children," a librarian once told me, "I automatically order five copies, because I know the books will be read so eagerly they will soon be in shreds."

And when I announced to my family that I thought I'd switch from writing for adults to writing for children, one of my young daughters immediately said, "If you're going to write for children, you have to write a book, and it has to be a mystery!"

What are the magic ingredients of a mystery novel for the eight-to-twelve age group that draw young readers to it? What does a writer need to include in his story so that his readers won't be able to put the book down until they have come to the last page?

In a mystery story the idea is often the starting point. Sometimes this idea can come from a magazine article or news item. I once read an article about artifacts being smuggled out of Mexico that led to research on the subject and eventually to a juvenile mystery novel.

Sometimes the idea can come from experience. When we moved to Corpus Christi, Texas, we found ourselves in the middle of a hurricane. The eye of the storm missed our city, but the force of the rain, wind, and waves caused tremendous damage. The area had been evacuated, but I wondered what someone would have done who couldn't leave—who, for some reason, had been left behind in the confusion. The beach houses could not withstand the force of the storm, or stay intact, but what if high on the hill there stood a stone "castle," strong enough to survive the storm and to shelter its occupants? And what if this castle were known to have as its only occupant a ghost? Out of these questons came my book *The Mystery of Hurricane Castle*.

A study of the New Orleans French Quarter, with its legends of pirate treasure and its modern day fortune-tellers, grew into a mystery novel; and the idea of someone trapped on a cruise ship, or unwilling to leave when the "all ashore" is sounded for guests, because he thinks he has just overheard the plans for a murder, developed into *The Mystery of the Secret Stowaway.*

A mystery novel should give the reader an interesting background that will expand the child's horizons. Phyllis A. Whitney, in her excellent mystery novels for children, has taken her readers to many exciting and unusual foreign settings. But even the author who cannot travel can make a small town on the coast of Maine, or a truck stop in the middle of the Arizona desert, colorful and interesting to the child for whom this too is a new experience.

Deciding upon the main character is the next step in developing the mystery novel. It is his story. He (or she) will have to solve the mystery, and he will go about it in his own individual way.

It is important to make the main characters well-rounded, interesting and actively alive. The children who read the novel will want to identify closely with them and eagerly follow their adventures to the last page. They should have a minor fault or two—something with which children feel familiar. Maybe the boy's in trouble because he can't seem to remember to keep his room tidy, or perhaps the girl's impatient and plunges into things without thinking.

The main character preferably should be twelve or thirteen years old—at the top of this age group. Eight-year-olds will read about older children, but older children do not want to identify with younger children. Plots featuring boys and stories with girls as main characters are equally popular.

Once an editor told me, "Most of the mysteries I get take place during the summer vacation. I'd like to see one in which the main character was going to school." So in *The Mysterious Red Tape Gang,* I placed my main character right in the middle of the school year. His problem with turning in homework on time gave him a character flaw and added some humor to the story.

A little light humor can be a good ingredient in a mystery novel. I learned this lesson when I was writing my first mystery. I read chapters to my children, and my fifth-grade daughter would sometimes say, "It's scary for too long. Put in something funny." What she was telling me, in essence, was to break the mood of suspense occasionally. The author can't, and shouldn't, sustain tension in the story from beginning to end. It should have peaks of suspense and valleys—breathing space, one might say, and natural humor is a good ingredient to use for this purpose.

In order to make the main character more of a "real person," I think it's good to give him a personal problem to handle along with the mystery to solve. For example, in one story I let my character's fear of a neighborhood bully turn to compassion and a tentative attempt at friendship as he began to realize what made this boy behave like a bully. In another, I matched two girls as friends—one who thinks her younger brothers and sisters are a burden, and the other an only child who lives in an adult world. Each girl learns from the other, and each learns to appreciate her own family life.

The story must be told from the main character's viewpoint only, although if there are two characters traveling this mysterious road together—friends, brothers, or sisters—the viewpoint can include them both. You are telling the story through your main character's eyes, and it's important not to have anything happen of which he or she isn't aware. She may see an obvious clue and overlook it, thinking it's not important; or he may sidetrack his efforts, and thereby come closer to danger, thinking something is important that is not; but in either case, it is that main character's story alone and the author of the juvenile mystery must keep this in mind.

As to clues, children love the puzzle in a mystery. They love to find obvious clues which the main character seems to miss. They love to search for clues which the main character has discovered, but the readers haven't figured out. Both types of clues are needed in a mystery, but the hidden clues shouldn't be too well hidden. After the solution of the mystery is reached, at the end of the story, the reader should think, "Of course! I remember that! I should have known it all along!"

Sub-mysteries, which are complications, unexpected scary situations, or new questions raised, should be used throughout the story. They all tie into the main mystery, although some of them can be solved along the way. Each chapter, through action and suspense, moves the mystery closer to its solution, and each chapter should end with something tense or a little frightening—a cliff-hanger ending—so that the reader cannot stop at the end of the chapter, but must read on to see what happens. An example is this chapter ending for *The Mysterious Red Tape Gang:*

Linda Jean grabbed my arm and squeezed so tightly that the pressure of her fingers was painful. "Mike," she whispered, "those men might hurt my father!"

The same thought had occurred to me. I wanted to answer her; but my mouth was dry, and I tried to swallow.

Mr. Hartwell's face looked awful. He was like a trapped animal.

"Mike!" Linda Jean whispered. "You've got to do something!"

Children read for pleasure, not for all the reasons for which adults read—because the book is a best seller, or because one received it as a Christmas present. If a child doesn't like a book, after the first page or two, he puts it down and looks for something else to read.

Therefore, the story should immediately introduce the main character, lead into the mystery as soon as possible, and grab the reader. In the opening paragraphs of *The Mysterious Red Tape Gang,* I set the scene, established the mood of the story, introduced my main character, told something about the other characters who would be important, and gave the first hint of mystery to come:

My father gets excited when he reads the newspaper at the breakfast table. Sometimes a story makes him mad, and he reads it out loud to my mother. And all the time he reads, he keeps pounding his fist on the table.

Once, when his fist was thumping up and down, my little brother, Terry, carefully slid the butter dish over next to my father just to see what would happen. Terry had to clean up the mess, but he said it was worth it.

Sometimes my father reads a story to me, because he says a twelve-year-old boy ought to be aware of what could happen if he fell in with bad companions.

At first I tried to tell him that Jimmy and Tommy Scardino and Leroy Parker weren't bad companions, but I found out it was just better to keep quiet and listen.

"Michael," he said one morning, "listen to this! The crime rate in Los Angeles is rising again! People are being mugged, cars being stolen. A lot of it is being done by kids! Watch out, Michael!"

I nodded. What I had planned to do after school was work on the clubhouse we were building behind our garage, along with Tommy and Jimmy and Leroy. None of us wanted to steal cars. In the first place, it's a crime, and in the second place, we can't drive.

The mystery novel should have plenty of action. The old-fashioned mental detection type of story, with lots of conversation and little action, is out of date even with adult readers. With children it's doubly important to include a great deal of action and excitement in mystery stories.

However, dialogue is important, too. Dialogue not only breaks up a page and makes the story look more inviting in print, but it draws the reader into the story in a way narrative description cannot do. A careful mix of dialogue with lots of action usually results in a fast-paced, suspenseful story.

The ending of a mystery novel is important to the writer, because it's one of the first things he must think about in planning his book. After he has mentally worked out the idea of the mystery, who his main character will be, and how the story will begin, he should decide how it will end. Once this is established, the middle will fit into place, with the clues planted and the direction of the action set. I find it helpful to make an outline, chapter by chapter, so vital clues and important bits of planted information won't be omitted.

A good mystery should always be logical, and the ending should be satisfying. It should never depend on coincidence. The main character must solve the mystery. If it's necessary to bring in adults to help out—such as the police or someone who could give advice—it must be the decision of the main character to do so.

The ending of a mystery novel should satisfy the reader, because it should present an exciting climax. The solution of the mystery should contain all the answers, so a drawn-out explanation of who-did-what-and-why isn't needed. Throughout the story the reader must be given reference points he can remember—well-planted clues. Just a page or two should be used to end the story and tie up all the loose ends concerning the main character's relationship with others in the book.

Stories for the reader of eight to twelve shouldn't be gory or horrifying: characters can be captured or threatened, but description should be kept within the bounds of good sense. The occult can be used in stories for this age, and can be left unexplained, if the author wishes, as the witchcraft in Scott Corbett's *Here Lies the Body*. At the author's whim, ghosts can be explained, or left forever to haunt future generations.

As for the title: Writers should remember the key words for which librarians look and make their titles mysterious or frightening. Some child who wants the pleasure of following a character through a scary adventure will reach for that book.

Mysteries for the readers of grades one to three, who are learning to read, have become increasingly popular with editors. These are "light" mystery novels—not as involved, and not as frightening as mystery novels for older brothers and sisters. The mystery tends to be more of a puzzle to solve than a threatening situation to investigate.

These stories are designed for 42 or 43 pages in a 48-page book. On each page, there are from one to eight lines, with six to eight words to a line. The vocabulary is not controlled, but is kept within the boundaries of common sense as to words a very young reader could read and understand.

As in the mystery for the eight-to-twelve-year-olds, the story opens with action and interest, and immediately introduces the main character. Within the limited number of words, the characters and the stories cannot be written with as much depth; but along with the mystery, the main character's relationship with others can still be shown. The plot should include a surprise kept from the reader, which sustains the suspense.

In *The Secret Box Mystery,* no one can guess what Michael John has brought to school in a box for his science project, even when it gets loose in the room. In *The Mysterious Prowler,* someone leaves a nose print on Jonathan's window, bicycle tracks across his muddy yard, and calls on the phone but won't speak; and Jonathan sets out to discover who the prowler is.

As in the eight-to-twelve novel, the solution of the mystery in books for beginning readers is in the hands of the main character, although he or she is allowed to have a little more help from friends.

88

WRITING NONFICTION FOR YOUNG PEOPLE

By Karen O'Connor

Young people are fascinated by facts, intrigued by real-life stories, and often motivated to action after reading about a man or woman's exciting experiences. Ask any librarian, and you will find out what the most popular subjects are: horses, dinosaurs, science, sports, pets, hobbies, careers, space travel, biographies, disasters, the super-natural—the list could go on and on.

Many new writers overlook or avoid the rich and rewarding field of juvenile nonfiction. Some feel they need to be experts in a given field to be able to write about it. Others assume that writing for children means writing only stories. Still others think it's difficult to find suitable ideas for nonfiction articles or books for young people, and the result is that they never even explore the possibilities.

In my experience, however, the juvenile nonfiction market is one of the most exciting fields open to today's free-lance writer. Nearly every one of my books and articles has come from personal experiences I've had as a mother, teacher, Camp Fire leader, volunteer librarian, language arts consultant, and college instructor. Your life offers the same variety of experience, perhaps even more so.

Honing an idea

When a particular idea or subject or experience flags my attention, I look at it from every angle. I analyze it, process it, and study it until I reach that exhilarating point of discovery when a stray fact or statistic suddenly "connects" with something I've experienced and can relate to.

Rudolph Flesch suggests that writers draw upon all of their ideas, experiences, and memories, then "move them about until you feel the click, the electric spark, the sensation of 'That's it!'" This seems to be the element that makes writing nonfiction as creative as writing fiction, fantasy or poetry.

Specifically, *where* does one locate sound ideas, and *when* they do appear *how* does a writer know which ones to go with and which to discard? Each item on the following list is a proven source of exciting and marketable nonfiction ideas, and you, too, can discover gold in your own backyard or that of your neighbor.

Look closely at your past and present activities, education, interests. If you are a parent or have worked as a teacher, scout leader, coach, or salesperson, you've probably had dozens of experiences with young people—and have taken them for granted. If so, take a second—or a third—look.

My first book for the middle-grade reader, *How to Make Money* (Watts), came from my daughter's successful neighborhood business: putting on birthday parties, doing light housekeeping, plant and pet sitting, and running errands.

I wrote a tennis dictionary with help from my tennis-playing son; my youngest daughter's love of horses led to my first career book, *Working with Horses* (Dodd, Mead); and my fascination with zoos and how they run resulted in my career book, *Maybe You Belong in a Zoo* (also Dodd, Mead). If I had ignored my own interests and intuition, none of these books would have been written.

Outside sources

What you haven't experienced personally, you can discover through reading—books, magazines, newspapers, brochures, anything—watching television, attending a lecture or watching a play or movie. These were just some of the sources I used to help shape my ideas for books on the new astronauts, natural disasters in recent times, and a biography of women writers. I combed journals, newspaper articles, and earlier biographies for background information; watched related television specials; and corresponded with agencies and people who had some connection with the subjects I was writing about and could furnish me with pertinent information.

When I'm looking for a new and marketable nonfiction idea, I approach my daily reading and viewing in a purposeful way, rather than simply browsing and hoping. It really works to do this. For example, a "Dear Abby" letter, an article in the *Christian Science Monitor,* and a report in the *San Diego Union* all contributed to my latest project on animal rights. I set out to find related material, and I did.

Talk to authorities in your particular field of interest. Their expertise adds credibility to any book or article. Even though you might be able to find the same information in a library, your writing will feel more authentic when you quote an expert on your subject.

When planning my book on zoo careers, I called the public relations director at the San Diego Zoo. She set up twenty interviews for me with a variety of employees at the zoo—from the chief cook to the head curator. I couldn't have learned what I needed to know without her and the working staff, who actually do the day-to-day work in the zoo.

For a book on special effects in films, I interviewed several behind-the-scenes experts at Disney, Paramount, and Universal studios. My book would not have been as interesting or accurate without their professional assistance, which provided authentic, factual information.

You don't have to be the most polished interviewer to land a good interview. Simply approach busy people with enthusiasm, friendliness, and professionalism. This means planning your questions ahead so that you have a blueprint to follow and will make the most of the time you have. Set a specific time limit for the interview, convenient for both of you. If you get nervous, just think of yourself having a relaxed conversation with a friend over coffee. That always works for me.

In general, people love to talk about what they know, offer advice, and see their names in print. Without exception, I've found those in every field of work and with every kind of background and experience willing to contribute to a book for young people. To me, interviewing is one of the easiest and most enjoyable ways to strengthen nonfiction writing skills, whether the writer is a newcomer to the field or a veteran.

The people close to you—family, friends, co-workers, neighbors—often provide the richest and most unexpected resources. Friends and acquaintances are eager to talk once you get them started. Tell them what you have in mind, and they are often likely to have an idea to contribute or a friend in the business who can help you. Listen to them carefully. You don't have to use everything you hear or follow every lead. That's where the writer's ability to select and discard plays an important role. Keep only what you need and want for your project.

Moving young people from the vast outer world of facts into the

487

satisfying inner world of creative information is one of the most exciting possibilities available to a nonfiction writer. And the ideas, opportunities, and experiences we need to bring this about are everywhere, if we are alert to them.

Your particular idea, your unique presentation, your special vision and angle may provide the bridge that takes a eager young person from idle curiosity to independent thinking and a new interest.

89

WRITING FOR THE TEEN-AGE MARKET

By Gloria D. Miklowitz

RECENTLY, at a dinner party, a man sitting next to me said, when he learned I was writing a teen-age novel about a rape victim, "How are you qualified to write on that subject? And why are you doing it, for the money?"

When I got over my first reaction of surprise, I answered him. (A lot of people would like to ask me that question, but are embarrassed to.)

First, as to qualifications. You don't have to be a rape victim to understand how he or she might feel, I said. I've written about a black male on drugs, about a teen-age runaway, and about an unwed mother. I'm neither black nor male, never ran away, and my children are my husband's. But, certain emotions are universal, and these are the emotions I draw from. What does it feel like to be tempted by something very badly, and to fight the temptation? If you ever felt that, then you know how my black teen-ager felt when tempted by drugs again, a temptation he wants to yield to, but doesn't.

What is it like to feel anger? I've been angry. Everyone has. You just remember that feeling when you write a scene in which the character feels anger.

Haven't you ever been afraid? I asked the man at the table. When I write about my rape victim, I'm writing about her fear, after being raped, of walking down a street, of being in a crowd where she might see her attacker again.

Have you never felt insecure? I asked the man. I have. When I wrote my book about a young paramedic student who lacks confidence, I understood that feeling, because I have lacked confidence.

Now, as to the second question, do I do it for money? To that I answered No, and Yes. First, No. I write about teen problems because they concern me. I want to say something to troubled teen-agers that

489

may help them deal with their problems. I want to say something that may stop another teen-ager on the brink of making a terrible mistake, from taking that wrong step. I have a message, in other words, not a moral to be yelled out in print, but a message, nevertheless.

In my novel *Turning Off,* for example, I say in effect: If you find work that interests you and makes you respect yourself, you won't get into trouble.

In *A Time to Hurt, A Time to Heal,* a story about a 15-year-old whose problems result from her parents' divorce, I say, You must be responsible for your own behavior.

In *Runaway,* a novel about a 15-year-old girl placed in a home for delinquents because she has run away once too often, I say: You can't run away from yourself; the solution to your problems is only within you.

And in *Unwed Mother,* a story of another 15-year-old girl who has a baby out of wedlock and keeps it for a time, I say many things, such as: If you are going to be sexually active, take precautions. But mostly, I say: Love is thinking of the loved one's needs, as well as your own.

My rape book has another message: Life has its dangers; be aware of them.

Now, on the question of money. Does this come into my thinking before I write a book? Yes, of course. I don't think I'd tackle a book I didn't think had a chance of selling. I'm in the business of writing to sell. Still, when I believe in a book and think it has a good story problem and a good theme, the chances are high that it *will* sell.

What are the elements of a teen-age novel today? Well, to begin with, you are writing for the 12-to-15-year old, in seventh to ninth grade. These books are generally about 40,000 words long, or about 150-175 manuscript pages. We're talking about fifteen to twenty chapters of about 2,000 words each. We're talking about three scenes per chapter, or forty-five to sixty scenes in a book. Those are the statistics.

Since writing is a business, let's talk money. If your book sells to a hardcover house, you'll probably get from $1,500 up as an advance, depending on your subject and name. If the book goes to paperback, also, there'll be more. Three of my books were original paperbacks with Tempo Books, an imprint of Grosset and Dunlap. They are now put out by Grosset and Dunlap in hardcover editions for libraries. I get a full 10% royalty on the retail price on hardcover sales because the same publisher brings out both editions. If Tempo had sold the hardcover rights to another publisher, I'd receive only half the royalties.

Now, to the "how to's." Let's start with the idea. I'll use, as an example, how I went about researching and writing my *Runaway* book.

The idea to do a book on a home for delinquent girls was suggested by a friend. She was a volunteer at such a home in Pasadena. "Why don't you write about these girls' problems?" she asked.

My first step was to call the director and ask if I might interview him about the home and the problems the girls had. "What's a typical girl like here? What's her background? Her problems? How do you deal with these problems?" are the kind of questions I asked, while my trusty tape recorder whirred away. The director responded, but in abstract terms—nothing really specific. When I asked permission to interview some of the girls and some of the counselors, he absolutely refused. Invasion of privacy.... I went home, transcribed my notes, and figured that was that.

A couple of months later, the *Los Angeles Times* did a series on the terrible conditions at Juvenile Hall, a detention facility for delinquent teens, held there until their court hearings. The *Times* also did a series on runaways. My interest revived. One day, I phoned the Hollywood police station (where many runaways are brought) and arranged to interview a police officer who deals with these young people. The interview helped me understand police procedure and gave me a profile of the kids themselves.

Next step was to bone up on the subject. I went to the library and read every magazine article on runaways written during the previous two years. I learned where they ran to, the facilities for helping these children, why they ran, and so on. The more I read, the more interested and concerned I became. Finally, I called Juvenile Hall and was given a guided tour by the PR people. I saw the schoolrooms, the buildings and cells, the holding room, and learned about their daily schedules. I returned another day to attend hearings where children and parents faced the judge, and where the judge decided what was to be done with the child.

491

I came home from these visits eager to get to the typewriter, and quickly wrote the first two chapters of my book. The book opens in Juvenile Hall. I could describe the room Vicki was in, because I had seen it. I knew what classes she might have attended, and took her down the halls to the courtroom, where, by the end of chapter two the judge decrees that she will be placed in Lavender Lane Cottage, and warns she had better shape up or next stop for her will be Sybil Brand, a hardcore prison.

Now, I was stuck. What goes on in Lavender Lane Cottage, I had to know. I started phoning around to all the homes in the Los Angeles area where delinquent teen-agers were placed. To four calls, the answer was No; it would invade the girls' privacy. But on the fifth call, I hit a possible. Vista del Mar's director said he'd at least "talk" to me, and "see." I went down to Vista and showed the director several of my books and told him what I hoped to achieve. Finally he said, "O.K. You can have dinner with the girls in Cottage B. But you are not to ask them any direct questions about themselves."

A foot in the door. I was delighted. I went to the cottage the next evening as uptight as a spy in the enemy camp. The housemother introduced me, and I told the girls why I had come, what I hoped to learn from them. The girls were polite, but unrevealing. During dinner they talked freely—about washing their hair, the latest movie they had seen, but of nothing that showed me how they felt or thought.

After dinner, two of the girls asked if I'd be willing to read their poetry. I went into their room, read the poetry, and commented on it. Then I said, "Will you do me a favor now? Will you listen to these two chapters of my book and tell me what *you* think?"

I read them the chapters, and from that moment on, I was their friend. They identified with my character completely, saying, "That's just how it was for me in Juvie! That's just how I felt!" And they opened up to me then, telling me all the things I needed to know.

Again and again, I returned to visit, taking along new chapters as they were written, and asking more questions. I interviewed their housemother, their social workers, and their counselors. I went to a local high school and spoke with the school counselor about the special problems the teachers had with these girls. As an example, quite in passing, the high school counselor remarked that often a runaway, because she has attended school so irregularly, among other reasons, has a very poor self-image. When she returns to school, she's likely to link up with the problem kids at school, the drug users and troublemakers. I used this truth in my book.

When my main character, Vicki, first comes to the home, all she wants is to run away again. At school, she becomes involved with a boy who can only hurt her further. By the end of the book, through a nursing course she takes at school which gives her a sense of worth, she gains enough self-esteem to consider a relationship with a much nicer young man.

This, then, explains how a middle-aged woman like me, whose children have already moved on to college, can remain in touch with the teen-ager with problems.

In working on my present book, I've used much the same method of gathering information. I read all I could find about rape, its victims and their problems. Last year, I joined a rape hot line so I could understand the problems of the rape victim better, and perhaps gain firsthand contact with some. Through the hot line, and through police vice squad contacts, I've interviewed in-depth three victims, and would like to speak with even more so I can incorporate in my one character the universal problems and emotions.

Before I begin work on a book, I have two things firmly in mind. One, the story problem. This can always be put into the form of a question. In *Runaway,* it was: Will Vicki finally find a better way to deal with her life than running away? In my present book, the question is: Will Andrea be able to absorb the trauma she has experienced and face life with confidence again?

The second thing I need to know is the theme, the message I'm sending the reader. I've already mentioned the themes of several of my books. Sometimes, to be sure I don't stray from my story question and theme, I type them up and scotch tape them to the top of my typewriter.

Unlike some writers who can plan ahead, chapter by chapter, what they will do, I have only the vaguest notion of what will happen next. I do know the beginning, and I have a fair idea of how I'll develop the end, but what happens in between doesn't come to me until I'm at the typewriter and the characters take me where they're going. It's agony when the characters seem to be asleep, and you want them to wake up and *do* something, *say* something, *think* something. But, when they do wake up and take over your subconscious, it's magic, because the words just flow out through your fingers to the type-writer, and when you read them back, you can't imagine where they came from.

Finally, each chapter, like a single brick in a wall, builds a little more of the story, until the book is done and the wall is neatly in place, each brick complementing the one beside it, creating an effect of unity, grace, and—one hopes—beauty.

Now, how will you sell it? Some time before the book is done, when I'm sure I can pull all the strands together, I query. My query tells the editor the book's title, length, and audience, the story question and theme, and gives an enticing summary of its contents. I enclose a self-addressed stamped post card on which I type the name of the publisher to whom I sent the query, and list two choices: "I'd love to see your book," or "Thanks, but no. Maybe next time." One publisher crossed out the word "love" and made it "like." He wrote, "Maybe I'll change it to love after reading it." If you do not receive a response to your query within three weeks, query another publisher. My experience has been that the "yes" answers come within about two weeks. Editors not interested in a manuscript of mine often take up to two months to respond.

When you get a yes on a query, ship off the book manuscript addressed to the editor who requested it, marking your envelope, *Manuscript Requested,* so it by-passes all the sub-editors and goes direct to the editor who asked to see it. Then, get busy on another book. If it doesn't sell to the first publisher, try the next and the next. Don't be discouraged, and don't let a rejection, even a nasty one, destroy you. Maybe the editor had a fight with her husband that day, or maybe she had missed her analyst that week, or maybe her job was shaky and she was taking it out on you.

Finally, I encourage all of you who really care about young people and who have something to say to them to write for that market. It's a big market and growing, especially for paperback originals. And there's room in it for all of us.

90

WRITING FOR YOUNG CHILDREN

By Charlotte Zolotow

CHILDREN's book writing includes fiction for children from picture books on up to the young adults, non-fiction—biography, autobiography and factual books—and of course poetry. In short, it includes every category of adult writing that exists, and everything that is true of distinctive writing for adults is also true of fine literature for children.

But there is in writing for children an additional skill required. It is easier to address our peers than those who are different from ourselves. And children are different from adults because they live on a more intense level. Whatever is true of adults is true of children, only more so. They laugh, they cry, they love, they hate, they give, they take as adults do—only more so. And this is what makes writing for children different from writing for adults.

One must first of all, over and above everything, take children seriously and take writing children's books seriously. Over and over I have met people who feel that writing for children is a first step to doing "something really good." A fairly successful, but undistinguished author of many children's books said to me one night, "Some day I'm going to do something really good. I'm going to write a novel or a play."

What this gentleman's abilities as an adult writer will be, I don't know. His children's books, however, lack something. There is nothing in them that would make a child put one down and say, "What else has this person written?" (A question children have asked many times after first reading a book by Ruth Krauss, Maurice Sendak, Else H. Minarik, Laura Ingalls Wilder, Margaret Wise Brown, E. B. White, Marie Hall Ets, E. Nesbit, P. L. Travers, Beatrix Potter— the great writers of children's literature.)

This remark of his made me understand why. *He doesn't respect what he is doing.* If he ever gets to his serious play or novel, it won't be that he came via children's books, but that he finally did take seriously what he was doing. I don't think writers of this sort should be writing for children at all. Children's books are an art in themselves and must be taken seriously. Anyone who regards them simply as a step along the way to "real" writing is in the wrong field.

I should make clear here that when I use the word *seriously* I don't mean *pompously.* I don't mean that every word is holy or that it should be heavy-handed. Some of the most delightful humor in books today is in the books for children. Some of the wildest kind of nonsense is there, too. But the writers are saying something seriously in their humor and in their nonsense—something that is real to them and meaningful to them—and they are saying it the best way they can without writing down to an audience whose keenness and perception they must completely respect.

There is a popular misconception about children's books that exists even among literate people. And it exists most particularly in the area of the picture book. A television writer once told me, "I never read my children what's in a picture book. I make up my own story to go with the pictures." He was quite pleased with himself—had no idea of the absurdity his smug assumption "that anyone can write a children's book" contained. He didn't realize that though his stories might amuse his own kids, delighted with the sound of his voice, the expression of his face, and the feeling of well-being his spending time with them gave them, a *published* story must be a finished, well-rounded work of art. In cold print, a story has to be good. The wandering, sketchy bedtime stories we tell our children have to be formed and shaped and sharpened before they can be printed, illustrated, bound in a book to be read over and over again to thousands of children who are strangers to the author's face and voice.

Some of my own books have indeed come out of stories I originally told my children, but years later, and after much thought, much reforming, reshaping, pruning, and in a voice or style that was a writer's, not a mother's. There is an immense difference.

In some picture books there are just a few words on a page. Certain immortal lyrics are four lines long. A sonnet has only fourteen lines. But the brevity doesn't mean they are "easy" to write. There is a special gift to making something good with a few words. The ability to conjure up a great deal just from the sound of a word and its relation to the other words in the sentence, the gift of evocation and denotation, is not only special to the poet but to children themselves. To say that he has had a good time at school that morning, a child may simply tell you, "The teacher wore a purple skirt." The recipient of this confidence would have to be close enough to the particular child to know that purple is her favorite color; that summing up a whole morning's events by that color is equivalent to having an adult say, "excellent wine"; that, in fact, in this child's vocabulary "purple" is a value judgment and the sign of a happy morning. And since children themselves so often use this oblique, connotative language, the writer who is fortunate enough to have retained his own childlike vision can speak to them in this special poetic shorthand that evokes worlds in a word.

A picture book writer must have this gift of using words carefully, of identifying with, understanding, projecting himself into the child's world. He must know and feel what they know and feel with some of the freshness of their senses, not his experienced adult ones. He must know what children care about a given situation. This is usually quite different from what an adult in a similar situation is thinking, wanting, seeing, tasting, feeling; and sympathy and empathy (and memory) are necessary, not condescension, not smugness, not superiority, not serious observation from an adult point of view.

And while the brevity of a picture book makes the author's use of words particularly selective, the rest of what I've said applies not only to picture books but to books going up in age group to the young adults. It is a question of experiencing at that particular level how the small or "middle-aged" child feels.

The best children's book writers are those who look at the world around them with a childlike vision—not childish, which is an adult acting like a child—but with that innocent, open vision of the world that belongs to the various stages of growing up, a clearer, more immediate, more specific, more honest, less judging vision than the adult one.

Children come fresher, with less cant, less hypocrisy, less guilt, to the world around them than even the most honest adults are apt to. Children smell good and bad things without inhibition. They taste, they hear, they see, they feel with all their senses and not so much interfering intellect as the adult, who will label things by applied standards, preconceived standards of good or bad—a good smell or a bad smell, a good taste or a bad taste. Children are realists of the first order. They have fewer preconceived ideas than adults. To them, flowers may smell bad. Manure may smell good. They have no fixed judgments yet. Most things are still happening to them for the first time. The first time water comes from a faucet, heat from a radiator, snow falls, the *real* itself is *magic*.

Because of this, children are open to belief in fantasy—fairies can exist if snow can fall, magic can happen if there are cold and heat, moon and stars and sun. Nothing is routine yet. They live more immediate lives than adults, not so much of yesterday or tomorrow. They are open to the moment completely. They respond to every detail around them completely. (That is why they are so often tiring to be with.)

I remember once the poet, Edwin Honig, came to visit us. He had never met our daughter Ellen, who was then four. They liked each other immediately. And when she offered to show him the house, he left his drink on the front porch and went off into the house with her. When I came in a few minutes later, he was holding her in his arms, and she was pointing into the living room.

"That is the fireplace where we have fires in winter.

That is the rubber plant where one leaf died.

That is the radio where we had the tube fixed.

That is the best chair but our dog sits in it." She might have invited him to see if he could smell the dog in the chair if I hadn't come in.

"You know," Honig said to me, "she's living everything here for me."

A poet could understand this. And in this sense that is what everyone who writes for children must be.

Always remember that the field of children's books is exciting and specialized. It is full of pitfalls that adult writing is free from, not the least of which is that a child's point of view is so different from that of an adult—more different at three than at six, and more so at six than at nine. And even when the child and adult reaction is identical—at any age level—in being hurt, in wanting, in hating, in loving, it is more intense. Adults are like a body of water that has been dammed up, or channeled. Children haven't these constrictions yet on their emotions. They abandon themselves to emotion, and therefore everything from a cake crumb to an oak tree means more to them.

If you are to write for children, you must be absolutely honest with yourself and with them. Willa Cather once advised a young writer never to hold back on any idea or phrase when it fitted something he was writing, in the hope of using it later in something better. Never hold back on what fits the book you are writing for children either. Remember how you felt about things when you were a child; remember, remember that adults might laugh and say, "tomorrow he'll forget," but right then, at the moment, the child feels and believes in his pain or his joy with his whole being.

A famous children's book editor once said, "Young people can and will accept the very best truly creative people will give them." And in a *New Yorker* article about Maurice Sendak, one of the finest children's book artists and writers today, it was stated, "Too many of us . . . keep forgetting that children are new and we are not. But somehow Maurice has retained a direct line to his own childhood."

This is what anyone who wants to write for children must do.

91

STORYTELLING: THE OLDEST AND NEWEST ART

By Jane Yolen

SOME time ago I received one of those wonderful letters from a young reader, the kind that are always signed mysteriously "Your fiend." This one had an opening that was an eye-opener. It read:

Dear Miss Yolen:
I was going to write to Enid Blyton or Mark Twain, but I hear they are dead so I am writing to you...

Of course I answered immediately—just in case. After all, I did not want that poor child to think that all the storytellers were dead. Because that was what the three of us—Enid Blyton, Mark Twain, and Miss Yolen—had in common. Not style. Not sense. Not subject. Not "message or moral." The link was clear in the child's mind just as it was in mine. Blyton, Twain, and Yolen. We were all storytellers.

Nowadays most of the storytellers *are* dead. Instead, we are overloaded with moralists and preachers disguised as tale tellers. Our medium has become a message.

So I want to talk to you today about the art of and the heart of storytelling; about tales that begin, go somewhere, and then end in a satisfying manner. Those are the tales that contain their own inner truth that no amount of moralizing can copy. The Chinese, the *New York Times* reported in 1968, were recruiting "an army of proletarian storytellers" who were ordered to fan out into the countryside and "disseminate the thoughts of Chairman Mao." They told the kind of stories that end: "As a result, the evil wind of planting-more-watermelons-for-profit was checked." These tales waste no time in getting their message across. But they are sorry excuses for stories. As Isaac Bashevis Singer has said: "In art, truth that is boring is not true."

Storytelling may be the oldest art. The mother to her child, the hunter to his peers, the survivor to his rescuers, the priestess to her followers, the seer to his petitioners. They did not just report, *they told a tale.* And the better the tale was told, the more it was believed. And the more it was believed, the truer it became. It spoke to the listener because it spoke not just to the ears but to the heart as well.

These same stories speak to us still. And without the story, would the tale's wisdom survive?

The invention of print changed the storyteller's art, gave it visual form. Since we humans are slow learners, it took a while to learn that the eye and ear are different listeners. It took a while to learn the limits and the limitlessness of two kinds of tellers—the author and the illustrator—in tandem. And it has taken us five centuries, dating from Gutenberg, to throw away the tale at last.

Children, the last audience for the storytellers who once entertained all ages, are finding it hard to read the new stories. Their literature today is full of realism without reality, diatribes without delight, information without incantation, and warning without wisdom or wit. And so the children—and the adults they grow into—are no longer reading at all. The disturbing figure I heard only last month is that 48% of the American people read no book at all in the past five years.

And so I dare. I dare to tell tales in the manner of the old story-tellers. I do not simply retell the old tales. I make up my own. I converse with mermaids and monsters and men who can fly, and I teach children to do the same. It is the only kind of teaching I allow in my tales.

What of these stories? There is a form. First, a story has a beginning, an opening, an incipit. Sometimes I will use the old magical words "Once upon a time." Sometimes I vary it to please my own ear:

Once many years ago in a country far to the East....

There was once a plain but goodhearted girl....

In ancient Greece, where the spirits of beautiful women were said to dwell in trees....

Once on the far side of yesterday....

In the time before time, the Rainbow Rider lives....

Once upon a maritime, when the world was filled with wishes the way the sea is filled with fishes....

501

But always a story begins at the beginning. That is surely a simple thing to remember. Yet my husband begins reading any book he picks up in the middle and, if he likes it, he will continue on. He says it does not matter where he begins, with modern books—and he is right. If stories and books no longer start at the beginning, why should the reader? And if, as Joyce Cary says, "... reading is a creative art subject to the same rules, the same limitations, as the imaginative process...," then a story that begins in the middle and meanders around and ends still in the middle encourages that kind of reading.

Now I am not saying that a story has to move sequentially in time to have a beginning. One does not have to start with the birth of the hero or heroine to start the story at the beginning. Still, there must be a reason, a discernible reason, for starting a tale somewhere and not just the teller's whim. The person who invented the words "poetic license" should have his revoked.

What of the story's middle? First it should not be filled with middle-age spread. But also, it should not be so tight as to disappear. Do you remember the nursery rhyme:

> I'll tell you a story
> About Jack O'Nory,
> And now my tale's begun.
> I'll tell you another
> Of Jack and his brother,
> And now my tale is done.

Where is the middle of that story? It should be the place in the tale that elicits one question from the reader—*what then?* The middle is the place that leads the reader inevitably on to the end.

Is that not a simple task? I run a number of writers' groups and conferences, and all persuasions of writers have passed through. There are the naive novices who think that children's books must be easier to write because they are shorter and the audience less discriminating. There are the passable writers, almost-pros who have had a story or two published in religious magazines and are ready to tackle a talking animal tale or—worse—a talking prune story where inanimate objects converse on a variety of uninteresting subjects. And there are the truly professional writers whose combined publications make a reasonable backlist for any publishing company. And they all have trouble with the middles of stories.

502

The problem is one of caring. Too few writers today care enough about storytelling. If they should happen in the throes of "inspiration" to come upon a beginning and an ending, then they simply link the two together, a tenuous lifeline holding two climbers onto a mountain.

Of course the middle *is* the mountain. It is the most important part of the book, the tale, the story. It is where everything important occurs. Perhaps that is why so few people do it well.

What of the end? Ecclesiastes says: "Better is the end of a thing than the beginning thereof." An overstatement perhaps. But if the end is not *just* right, and is not filled with both inevitability and surprise, then it is a bad ending.

Adults are quite willing to forgive bad endings. I saw only recently a review of an adult book that said, in essence, the ending is silly, unconvincing, and weak, but the book is definitely worth reading. Children will not forgive a weak ending. They demand a rounding off, and they are very vocal in this demand. I remember reading a story of mine in manuscript to my daughter, then age seven. It was a tale about three animals—a sow, a mare, and a cow—who, tired of men and their fences, decided to live together. When I finished reading, with great feeling and taking the dialogue in special voices, I looked up at my audience of one. She looked back with her big brown eyes.

"Is that all?" she asked.

"Well, that's all in this story," I said, quickly adding "Would you like another?"

She tried again. "Is that all that happens?"

"Well, they just...I mean they...yes, that's all."

She drew in a deep breath. "That *can't* be all," she said.

"Why?" I asked, defeated.

"Because if that's all, it's not a story."

And she was right. I have not yet worked out a good ending for that story, though I am still trying. G.K. Chesterton noted this about fairy tale endings, which are sometimes bloodier than an *adult* can handle. He wrote: "Children know themselves innocent and demand justice. We fear ourselves guilty and ask for mercy."

But lots of stories can still have a beginning, a middle, and an end and not be right. If they are missing that "inner truth," they are nothing. A tale, even a small children's tale filled with delight, is still saying something. The best stories are, in Isak Dinesen's words, "a statement of our existence." Without meaning, without metaphor, without reaching out to touch the human emotion, a story is a pitiable thing; a few rags upon a stick masquerading as life.

I believe this last with all my heart. For storytelling is not only our oldest art, it is our oldest form of religion as well; our oldest way of casting out demons and summoning angels. Storytelling is our oldest form of remembering; remembering the promises we have made to one another and to our various gods, and the promises given in return; of recording our human-felt emotions and desires and taboos.

The story is, quite simply, an essential part of our humanness.

92

WRITING THE PICTURE BOOK STORY

By Mary Calhoun

You want to write for children. Picture books. You tell stories to your children or the neighbor's children, and they just love your stories. *And this is good.* If you're telling stories, you already have the first qualification for writing picture books: You are a storyteller. The person who can spin a yarn is the golden one who will fascinate the four-to-eight-year-olds.

Then why aren't the publishers snapping up your stories and publishing them in beautiful four-color editions? Just what I wanted to know when I first started writing down the stories I'd told my boys. Rejection notes from editors commented:

"Too slight."

"Not original."

"We've used this theme several times."

"Too old for the age group."

I can't tell you all the reasons editors reject picture book scripts—such as "might encourage kids to make mess in the kitchen," "might encourage kids to try this and kill themselves." You'll just have to experience some of the rejections yourself. However, these are the general heart of why picture books are rejected:

"Not enough body and plot."

"Idea not big enough."

"Not ready to be a book."

"Things happen to the hero rather than he making things happen."

"Action too passive."

"Basic situation not convincing."

And over and over, "Too slight."

Sound familiar? Use the rejection list to check your stories—my compliments. The thing is, there's a lot more to writing for children than reeling off a story.

Now about picture books.

First, definitions: A picture book is one with pictures and a story to be read to or by a child between the ages of three and eight. (Publishers usually say four-eight, but many a "mature" three-year-old can enjoy having a picture book read aloud to him.)

Of course, there are other picture books for young children. For the two- and three-year-old there are the counting books, the ABC books, the "see-the-cat" books. There are picture books with a very slim text line, books conceived by the artists mainly for the sake of the art work. (No, you don't have to supply the artist for your story; the editor will do that.) There are the "idea" books: non-fiction—exploring "what is night?", "what is time?"—and such books as *A Hole Is to Dig* and *Mud Pies and Other Recipes*, charming ramblings on an idea, but not stories.

Here let's concern ourselves with the traditional picture book, one with a story from which the artist gains his inspiration for the pictures.

What goes into a picture book story?

As I see it, the elements are four: idea, story movement, style and awareness of audience.

First of all, the *idea*. Without a good idea, the writer is dead. Most often, I'd guess, a picture book script is rejected because the idea isn't good enough. What's a good idea? Make your own definition; I suppose each writer and editor does. I'd say, though, that basically the hero is vivid, the basic situation and the things that happen in the story are fascinating to a child. And generally there is a theme, some truth you believe, such as "you can master fear." Not a moral tacked onto the story, but the essence of the story, the hero and events acting out the theme.

How do you come by good ideas? Perhaps in the long run only heaven can help you, but it seems to me that primary is rapport with children—and a strong memory of your own childhood feelings and reactions.

"Tell me a story" many times a day keeps the old idea-mill grinding. Many of my picture book and magazine stories grew directly from contact with my children.

One day I hugged Greg, saying, "You're an old sweet patootie doll." "What's a patootie doll?" asked Greg, so I launched on a spur-of-the-moment tale. The theme was (I discovered after I'd written down the story) "know who you are and be glad for it." *The Sweet Patootie Doll* was first published in *Humpty Dumpty's Magazine* and later became my first published picture book.

A magazine story, "Cat's Whiskers", came into being because Greg was always climbing into things and getting stuck—in buckets, under the porch, even in the washing machine. I coupled this with the idea that cats use their whiskers to measure whether they can get through openings; in the story the boy sticks broomstraws on his face for whiskers, and the story goes on.

However, here was a story idea too slight for a picture book. Not enough happened, really, and there was no real theme in the sense of a universal truth.

This brings us to a point valuable to beginning writers: If your story is rejected by book editors, try it on the children's magazines. The magazines have high standards, too, of course, but they can be your training ground and means of being published while you learn. It was my lucky day when a book editor said, "Not ready to be a book. Have you thought of sending it to a magazine?" My story, "Lone Elizabeth," went through many rewritings, but finally was published in *Humpty Dumpty's Magazine*. "Bumbershoot Wind" was termed "too slight" by a book editor but appeared in *Child Life*.

Actually, all of the elements of a story are tied into the idea, but let's go on to consider them in detail.

Story movement. I choose to call it this, rather than plot, for this suggests just what a story for children must do: move. Children like a story that trots right along, with no prolonged station-stops for cute conversation or description. Keep asking yourself (as the child does), "What happened next?"

In picture books there needs to be enough change of action or scenery to afford the artist a chance to make different pictures. Some stories are very good for telling aloud, but when you look at them on paper, you see that the scene hasn't changed much.

A book editor pointed this out for me on my "Sammy and the Something Machine." In this fantasy, Sammy makes a machine out of which come in turn mice, monkeys, mudpies, pirates and hot dogs. (It grew from my Mike's chant at play, "I'm making, I'm making!") This story went down on paper perfectly well in *Humpty*

Dumpty's Magazine, where there are fewer illustrations than in a picture book. But the scene doesn't change; there's that machine, over and over, turning out different things.

When your story is moving along vigorously, the scene changes will follow naturally—*if* the idea is storybook material. If the story moves but there's not much possibility for picture change (better let the book editors decide this), it may still be a fine story for some magazine.

Style. Of course, your style will be your own, and only you can develop it through writing and trying out and thinking about it and forgetting about it as you plunge ahead in the heat of telling a story.

The story content to some extent will indicate the style, that is, choice of words, length and rhythm of sentences. The story may hop joyously, laugh along, move dreamily, or march matter-of-factly. For study, you might read aloud folk tales and attune your ears to varieties in cadence: the robust, boisterous swing of a western folk tale; the rolling, measured mysticism of an Indian folk tale; the straightforward modern "shaggy dog" story; the drawling wry humor of the southern Negro folk tale.

If you already are telling stories to children, you're on your way to developing your style. However, "telling" on paper is slightly different from telling aloud, where the *effect* is achieved by a few judiciously chosen words and the swing of sentences.

I've had some success with one approach to the written story, and I've seen examples of it in other picture books. I call it "vividry." To me it's more vivid and succinct to say that than "vivid effect," and this explains what "vividry" is: words chosen with economy for their punch. For example, in a certain book I choose to say "little mummy mice." "Mummified mice" might be more proper, but to me it sounds textbookish. "Mummy mice" rolls off the tongue and seems a more direct idea-tickler for the child.

In college journalism courses, our bible was Rudolf Flesch's *The Art of Plain Talk.* From it we learned the value, in newspaper writing, of using sentences of short or varied length; strong verbs; short, strong nouns and many personal pronouns. Flesch might have been writing a style book for children's picture books.

We all know the delight in finding "the exact word" for a spot in a story. Never is this more effective than in children's books. Magazines for children generally have word-length requirements. Try putting a full-bodied story into 800 to 1,000 words. Every word counts. Writing for the magazines can be excellent training in choosing words and cutting out the lifeless ones.

I'm not saying, however, that big words have no place in a picture book script. Writing "controlled vocabulary" books for the young is a specialized art, and those books are used mostly by teachers and parents to stimulate a child's desire to read. Several book publishers now put out series of "easy-to-read" books. If you are interested in this field, read some of the books and query the editors on requirements. In the general picture book, though, I think children like to come upon an occasional delightfully new and big word. Haven't you seen a four-year-old trotting around, happily rolling out "unconditionally" or some other mouthful he's just heard? It's the *idea* of the story that the writer suits to the age group, not every given word in the story.

And this brings us to *awareness of audience*. I've mentioned rapport with children. If you're around them you know what they're thinking and wishing, what their problems are. And you'll know if a story idea is too old for the three-to-eight-year-olds or just plain wouldn't interest them.

With a small child underfoot or in tow, you see the details of the world that fascinate him: how a spot of sunlight moves on the floor; a cat's relationship with his tail (I used this one in "Tabbycat's Telltale Tail"); or the child's own shadow. (I haven't been able to make a good story of this; maybe you can.)

A child will watch a hummingbird moth at work in a petunia bed and report wisely, "He only goes to the red ones. White petunia must not taste good."

All of this, *plus awareness of the child's emotions, plus turning your mind back to remember how it was with you as a child,* tells you what to put into a picture book.

And then there's the other way to be aware of your audience: reading, reading all the good books and stories written for that age. Then you begin to see what has pleased children. You get the feel of what is suitable for that age group. You also see what has already been done, so that your own ideas can be fresh, not trite. You read "The Three Pigs," and the books about the Melops and you say to yourself, "Very well, but a story about a pig has never been told just in *this* way," and you start off on your own particular pig story. As you read (perhaps to a child to catch his reactions, too), you may begin to draw your conclusions of what is good in children's literature, what is slightly sickening, how the stories are put together, what has worked.

It has interested me, for instance, to notice how many of the traditional stories are built on what I call a "core of three." Three brothers, three mistakes, three attempts at a solution. "The Three Pigs" makes me wonder if the composer weren't slyly trying to see just how many times he could use three. Three pigs, three encounters with men carrying building materials, three houses visited by the wolf, "chinny-chin-chin," etc. In so many of the stories, the use of three attempts to solve the problem is effective in building intensity to the climax.

So there you have it: idea, story movement, style and awareness of audience. Study them, use them in your rewrites, let them sink into your subconscious.

And then don't worry about techniques as you tell the story. For the first, last and most important thing is: you must *like* the story! You're having a ball telling it. Right at this moment, it's the most wonderful story ever told to man or child.

That, finally, is what gives the story sparkle and makes editors say, "This will make a wonderful picture book!"

93

MAGIC, CRAFT, AND THE MAKING OF CHILDREN'S BOOKS

By Nancy Willard

I GREW up in a house full of books. And once, during a long illness when I was nearly nine years old, I set out to read all of them. What stopped me almost immediately were the books that the previous owner of the house had bought to fill his empty shelves so that he should appear at least as well educated as his neighbors. Among his stately volumes of Dickens and Swift was a Victorian novel dealing with pregnancy in which that word was not once mentioned, and a treatise on the human body written for the young, which claimed that each of my bodily functions was governed by a magic dwarf. On the bottom shelf stood several dozen etiquette books. The chapters on servants included the correct liveries for your groom, your coachman, your butler, your page, your parlor maid, your nursemaid, your lady's maid, and your chamber maid. To me these books were as exotic as the descriptions of court life in "The Sleeping Beauty" or "Cinderella."

Among the discoveries I made in this haphazard course of study was *Alice's Adventures in Wonderland,* number two in a set of ten books that had "Children's Classics" stamped on the bindings. How, I thought, could any book given the adult seal of approval be entertaining? But the pictures in *Alice* were attractive, and I read the book. Indeed, I read it twice. Then I looked at the other nine volumes in the set. They included *Gulliver's Travels, The Arabian Nights, The Odyssey, The Iliad, The Pilgrim's Progress, Kidnapped,* and *Huckleberry Finn.* Many of these were the same books I had run across in the "grown-up" library downstairs. Today I am not surprised. For years children have appropriated books intended for adults, and adults have appropriated books intended for children.

As a writer of children's books, I have asked myself what qualities give the best books for children this broad appeal. Thinking back over the books I read with as much pleasure now as I did when I was eight or nine,

I realize that my favorite writers never limited their vocabulary because they were writing for children. A writer's vocabulary is part of his style. His favorite words, however peculiar, become our favorite words. If a child wants to know what happened next, he is not going to be put off by an unfamiliar vocabulary.

But I notice, too, that the best writers for children use simple words because simple language is the most effective. I once heard John Gardner tell a group of students to go through the dictionary and make a list of all the simple words they knew but didn't commonly use. I tried it and didn't even finish the A's. I already had more words than I could use in a lifetime.

The question of what makes a book appeal to both adults and children goes well beyond vocabulary, however. I want to look at that question, using fantasy rather than realistic fiction. I grew up aware of two ways of looking at the world that are opposed to each other and yet can exist side by side in the same person. One is the scientific view. The other is the magic view. Most of us grow up and put magic away with our other childish things. But I think we can all remember a time when magic was as real to us as science, and the things we couldn't see were as important as the things we could. I call this belief in the power of the invisible, the magic view of life. And I believe that all small children and some adults hold this view together with the scientific one. I also believe that the great books for children come from those writers who hold both.

I have recently seen how the magic view shapes our understanding of the most common events. Over a period of several years I kept a notebook in our kitchen in which I jotted down the questions my son, now eight, asked me. Many could be answered with facts, that is, with a scientific or historical answer. Did the Pharaohs brush their teeth? Who was the first person to use a fork? Who invented the pretzel?

There is a book in our public library that answers such questions, and it is so popular that I am lucky if I can find it on the shelf once in six months. It is called *Stone Soup,* by Maria Leach, and it is the history of common things. There you will find the name of the woman who first introduced the fork to England. And if you turn to another book, *The Book of Firsts,* by Patrick Robertson, you will find that the Chinese claim to have invented the first toothbrush in 1498, and that pretzels were invented in the thirteenth century by a monk who gave them as a reward to children for learning their prayers. In the shape of the pretzel, a sharp eye can discern the shape of the children's folded hands, which all goes to show that there are a good many stories in the world that need not be made up but only found out. Cats, dogs, flowers, seashells, presidents, wars, knives, eyeglasses, shoes—everything in the world has a history, and to a child, for whom these things are new, every history is worth telling.

But there is another kind of question children ask that comes not from a scientific or historic interest in things but from a magic view of them. Some of the questions I jotted down speak for themselves:

> When a mouse falls on its knees, does it hurt?
> Can I eat a star?
> If I stand on my head, will the sleep in my eye roll up into my head?
> If I drop my tooth in the telephone, will it go through the wires and bite someone's ear?
> How soft can loud be and still be loud?
> Am I growing all the time? Even when I'm walking?
> Do moths eat the wool off lambs?
> Where does time go? Into the air?
> Do caterpillars play like children? Do butterflies make a noise?
> Could we Xerox the moon?
> Am I in my life? Are you in yours?
> What happens if I open a clock and touch the ticky part?

These questions arise from a belief that practically everything in the universe is alive. Out of this belief the best fantasy is written. And fantasy need not be an escape from the problems of the "real world." You won't find a better collection of stories about murder, poverty, child abuse and abandonment than Grimms' fairy tales. But nothing could be further from the "problem books" now being published on these subjects. A "problem book" is first cousin to those jokes that the traveling patent medicine man would tell when he wanted to collect a crowd. He'd start out telling you a good story and end up trying to sell you something. And once you saw the ulterior motive, you felt cheated. The only problems the storyteller should worry about are narrative ones. How do I start my story? How do I keep my reader interested? How do I end my story?

As a child I loved Grimms' fairy tales, not because they instructed me or enlarged my understanding, but because they kept me on the edge of my chair. The authors never forgot their audience — the children, who want to be entertained and would just as soon go out and climb a tree as

513

listen to you. It's no accident that some of the most popular children's books began as stories told to real children. *Alice's Adventures in Wonderland* was started by Lewis Carroll during a boating expedition for the amusement of the three young daughters of a friend. The first draft of *The Tale of Peter Rabbit* is to be found in a letter to Noel Moore, the son of the young woman who had been Beatrix Potter's own governess.

But I believe that in both these cases the child was primarily the catalyst that got the stories going. What Maurice Sendak says about the source of his own work holds true for all makers of children's books. For Sendak, the child for whom he writes is the part of himself that still believes in magic. The child is the imagination at its freest; the adult is the disciplined craftsman who shapes the imagination into a book.

In the end, what really makes a book beloved both by children and adults is the quality of the writing itself. When I reread the books I loved as a child, I notice the scenes that stayed with me, and I find that it was the writing, not the action, that fixed them in mind. Here is the opening paragraph of a scene from *Mary Poppins,* one of my favorite stories:

"Perhaps she won't be there," said Michael.
"Yes, she will," said Jane. "She's always there for ever and ever."

What this beginning gives you is a situation that only the rest of the story can resolve. It opens with an argument, a sure-fire way of getting your reader's attention. Further the dialogue puts you into the middle of an ongoing conversation, so that you feel the action has already started.

It is one of the paradoxes of writing for children that the more fantastic the events you describe, the more you must convince your reader that you are not making anything up. To borrow an image from Marianne Moore, if you make up imaginary gardens, you must put real toads in them. Beatrix Potter claimed that she never made anything up. I did not realize the truth of this until I visited her house and recognized the chimneys, cupboards, lanes, barnyards, and pastures of her own farm as the very places I had come to love in her books. The writers of the greatest fantasies for children could not have written as convincingly of other worlds without a thorough knowledge of this one: of human nature, of science, of history, of life.

Anything made to last is not made quickly. You are writing for the child who will pick up your book a hundred years from now and for the child who may read it tomorrow. A friend of mine, Lore Segal, once told me the effect of *The Iliad* on her son when he was a child. She had read up to the chapter in which the Greeks enter Troy, concealed in the wooden horse. The revelation of what this meant for the Trojans came to the boy as he was riding with his mother on a bus, in the middle of Manhattan. The Trojans were doomed. The child suddenly burst into tears. What a compliment to Homer! In the twentieth century, on a bus in the middle of Manhattan, a child was weeping for the lost Trojans. A classic is a book that makes you weep or laugh more than twenty centuries after it was written. What writer could possibly ask for more?

94

WHAT EVERY WRITER NEEDS TO KNOW ABOUT LITERARY AGENTS

By Ellen Levine

Q. *At what stage in their careers should writers look for an agent— or will a good agent find them?*

A. Most agents prefer to begin a working relationship with a writer when there is a book-length work to market, rather than articles or short stories. Some agents prefer writers who already have publication credits, perhaps magazine publication of shorter work. However, a writer who has never published before, but who is offering a book which deals with a unique or popular topic may also have an excellent chance of securing an agent. Quite a number of agents are actively looking for new writers, and they comb the little magazines for talented writers of fiction. They also read general interest and specialty magazines for articles on interesting subjects, since they might contain the seeds for books. Some agents visit writers conferences and workshops with the express purpose of discovering talented authors who might be interested in representation.

Q. *How does a writer go about looking for a legitimate agent?*

A. Writers can obtain lists of agent members from two professional organizations—The Society of Authors' Representatives (SAR) or The Independent Literary Agents Association (ILAA)— by writing to these organizations at (for SAR) P.O. Box 650, Old Chelsea Station, New York, NY 10113 and (for ILAA) 21 W. 26th St., New York, NY 10010. Writers can also obtain a more complete list of agents by checking the "Agents" section of *Literary Market Place* (LMP), available from R. R. Bowker, 205 E. 42nd St., New York, NY 10017, or as a reference work at the local library. Finally, the Authors Guild at 234 W. 44th St., New York, NY 10036 will supply a list of agents.

Q. *How important is it for an agent to be a member of SAR or ILAA?*

A. It is not essential for a good agent to belong to either organization, but membership is very helpful and adds credibility and professionalism to the agency. These organizations schedule meetings to discuss issues and problems common to the industry and their members work together to solve them. Expertise is often shared; panels and seminars are regularly scheduled, often including key publishing personnel. There are also certain codes of professional ethics, which members of each group subscribe to. This, of course, is to the writer's advantage.

Q. *Do literary agents specialize in particular types of material—novels, plays, nonfiction books, short stories, television scripts? Are there some categories that agents could not profitably handle that could better be marketed by the authors?*

A. Most of the agents' listings in LMP specify which kind of material the agency handles. A few agencies do have certain areas of specialization such as screenplays, or children's books, as well as more general fiction and nonfiction.

Q. *Should a writer query an agent (or several agents) before sending him or her his manuscript(s)?*

A. It is acceptable for a writer to query more than one agent before sending material, but it should be made clear to the agent that the writer is contacting several agents at one time. It is even more important for the writer to clarify whether he plans to make multiple submissions of a manuscript. Most agents prefer to consider material on an exclusive basis for a reasonable period of time, approximately four to eight weeks.

Q. *What do agents look for before accepting a writer as a client?*

A. An agent usually takes on a new client based on his or her enthusiasm for that writer's work and a belief that it will ultimately be marketable.

Q. *Once an agent has agreed to take a writer on as a client, what further involvement can the agent expect and legitimately ask of the writer?*

517

A. It may take longer to place the work of a new author, and the client should be patient in the process. If the writer has made contact with a specific editor or knows that there is interest in the work from a specific publisher, he or she should inform the agent. The writer should feel free to continue contacts with book editors with whom he or she has worked, and to discuss ideas with magazine editors.

Q. *Do most agents today ask for proposals, outlines, synopses, etc., of a book-length work before taking on the job of reading and trying to market the whole book? Do agents ever prepare this type of material, or is that solely the author's function?*

A. This varies among agents. A popular procedure for consideration of material from a prospective client is the request of an outline or proposal and the first 50 or 100 pages. If the book is complete, some agents might request the completed manuscript. It is common practice to submit a nonfiction work on the basis of one or more chapters and a synopsis or outline. The extent of the sample material needed is often based on the writer's previous credentials. It is generally the author's job to prepare the outline and the agent's to prepare the submission letter or the "pitch."

Q. *When, if ever, are multiple queries or submissions allowable, acceptable, desirable? By agent or by author?*

A. If an author is working without an agent, multiple submissions to publishers are acceptable only if the author informs the publisher that the book is being submitted on that basis. However, this can sometimes backfire since those publishers who will read unsolicited manuscripts may not care to waste the staff's reading time on a manuscript that is on simultaneous submission to five other publishers. Multiple queries with one-at-a-time submissions upon receipt of a favorable reply are probably more effective for a relatively new author. However, if a writer has a nonfiction project that is obviously very desirable or timely (an inside story, a current political issue), it is of course expedient to proceed with a multiple submission. This should be done carefully, informing all the participants of the deadline, ground rules, and so on. Agents must judge each project individually and decide on the appropriate procedure. If more than one publisher has expressed an interest in a specific writer or project, a multiple submission is not only appropriate, it is fair and in the author's best interest if there are competitive offers. If a book is very commercial, an auction may well be the result of a multiple submission. If other factors, such as a guaranteed print order or publicity plans are important, a multiple submission without the necessity of taking the highest bid may bring the best results. If an agent routinely makes multiple submissions of all properties, credibility may be lost. If this practice is reserved for the projects which warrant it, the procedure is more effective. It is usually not appropriate to send out multiple copies of a promising first novel. It may be for the inside story of last week's Congressional investigation.

Q. *What business arrangements should a writer make with an agent? Are contracts common to cover the relationship between author and agent? How binding should this be and for what period of time?*

A. Author-agent business arrangements vary among agencies. Some agents will discuss commission, expenses, and methods of operation with their authors, and this informal verbal agreement is acceptable to both parties. Others will write letters confirming these arrangements. Several agencies require contracts defining every detail of the business arrangements, and others require formal, but less extensive contracts. Written agreements often contain a notification of termination clause by either party with a period varying from 30 days to a full year. A few of the agency agreements require that the agency continue to control the subsidiary rights to a book even after the author and agent have parted. Most agents include what is known as an "agency clause" in each book contract the author signs, which provides for the agency to receive payments for the author due on that book for the complete life of the contract, whether or not the author or agent has severed the general agency agreement. In a few cases this clause will contain the provision mentioned above (compulsory representation of the author's retained subsidiary rights). It is important for a writer to discuss these and all aspects of the agency's representation at the beginning of the relationship. In addition to understanding clearly commission rates and expenses he or she will be required to pay, a writer might want to discuss such matters as expectations for consultation on marketing, choice of publishers, the number of submissions to be made, frequency of contact with agent, and so on. *Poets and Writers, Inc.* at 201 West

519

54th Street, New York, NY 10019 has published a helpful handbook entitled *Literary Agents: A Writer's Guide* ($5.95), which addresses these issues. Commissions vary among agents. The range is often between 10% and 20%. Some agencies may vary the commission for different rights, charging 10% or 15% for domestic sales and 15% or 20% for foreign sales. Certain agencies have different rates for different authors, depending upon the length of time the author has been with the agency, the size of the publishing advance, or the amount of editorial and preparatory work the agent must do before marketing the book. Some agents work more extensively in an editorial capacity than others and may make detailed suggestions and ask for revisions before marketing a work.

Q. *Can a writer express a preference to the agent concerning the particular publishing house or kind of house he would prefer for his book?*
A. Writers should share with their agents any preferences or ideas they may have about their work, including which publishers would be most appealing, and in which format they envision their books. However, writers should not be dismayed if their agents feel in some cases that a particular preference may be unrealistic or inappropriate.

Q. *How much of the business side of publishing does the writer need to deal with, once he is in the hands of a competent agent?*
A. An agent acts as a writer's business representative for his publishing affairs. Most agents do not act as a writer's overall financial manager, and if an author begins to earn a substantial income, he or she may be well-advised to consult with a C.P.A. and/or tax attorney. The prudent writer, while entrusting his business affairs to his or her agent, will want to stay informed about these matters.

Q. *How much "reporting" can a writer legitimately expect from the agent who has agreed to handle his work?*
A. This would depend on the agent's individual style and the writer's need and preference. Many agents keep clients informed about the progress of submissions by sending copies of rejection letters; others do not, and will give the writer a summary periodically. A writer

should be kept informed of all important events and conversations with editors and co-agents about his or her work; for instance, a favorable *Publishers Weekly* review that has come in, a substantial delay in publication, a paperback auction date that has been set. On the other hand, writers should not expect daily contact with an agent as an established routine.

Q. *What involvement, if any, should a writer have in the contract that the agent makes with a publisher? Does he have the right, responsibility to question the terms, change them, insist on higher royalty rates, advertising, etc., or is this left entirely to the agent, along with the sale of substantial rights?*

A. It is the agent's responsibility to consult with the author before accepting any of the basic terms of an offer such as the advance, royalties, subsidiary rights, and territories granted. If the author has any particular reasonable requests which he or she would like to include in the contract, such as approval or consultation on the jacket design, it is the author's responsibility to let the agent know before the start of negotiations. The choice of an agent should imply the author's trust and confidence in the agent's expertise in negotiating the contract and securing the best possible financial and legal terms for the author. Authors should read contracts carefully and ask questions about any provisions, if necessary. However, it is not reasonable for an author to ask for changes in every clause or expect provisions that are extremely difficult to obtain, particularly for authors who have not had best sellers. For instance, advertising guarantees in contracts are not common for new authors. If the author has chosen a skillful agent, he or she should have confidence in the agent's explanation of what is or is not feasible in a contract with a particular publisher.

Q. *If an agent feels that he cannot place a manuscript and the author feels that it is marketable, or, at least, worthy of publication, can the author try to sell it on his own?*

A. If this happens on occasion and the agent has no objection, the author should feel free to try after discussing what he or she plans to do. The agent will want to be informed so that no prior obligation, such as an option requirement, is breached. If the author's agent repeatedly feels that the author's manuscripts cannot be placed, perhaps it is time for the author and agent to re-examine their relationship and discuss a change.

Q. *What services, other than the marketing of the manuscripts, negotiating the terms of their publishing contracts and related business arrangements may authors reasonably expect from their agents?*

A. In addition to marketing manuscripts, agents often help authors in formulating book ideas, passing along book ideas from editors when appropriate, and making introductions to appropriate editors if the author is between projects and free of contract obligations. Agents also follow up on various details of the publication process, such as production schedules, publicity, promotion, suggestions of other writers who might offer a quote for the jacket. The agent should also disseminate reviews, quotes, and information on subsidiary rights sales such as reprint and book club sales. Agents also examine royalty statements and, when necessary, obtain corrected statements.

Authors should not expect an agent to act as a secretary, travel agent, or bank. On the other hand, it is inevitable that a more personal bond may often form in the author/agent relationship, and in certain cases, agents do become involved to varying extents in friendships with their clients. In fact, hand-holding, "mothering" and counseling are not unfamiliar to many agents in dealing with certain authors. This is really a function of the agent's personality and often a conscious decision about how personally involved with his or her clients that particular agent wishes to be. A client should not expect that agent to solve his or her personal problems routinely.

Q. *How would you sum up the major role the agent plays in selling an author's work?*

A. If a manuscript is marketable, a good agent can short-circuit the random process of submissions by knowledge of the market, publishers, and the tastes and personalities of specific editors. However, an agent cannot place unsalable work. An agent can also be effective in the choice of marketing strategy for a particular work—should the book be sold as a trade paperback? Is a "hard-soft" deal best for the project? Would the author best be served by an auction, or would select individual submissions with editorial meetings be best?

95

THE 10% SOLUTION

By Anita Diamant

Each time that I have had the privilege of talking to a group of writers, the consensus seems to be that it is harder today to find a good agent than a publisher. True? Well, legitimate agents work on a 10% commission basis, and of the manuscripts submitted to an agent by new writers only a very small percentage will prove to have sales potential. The agent will have spent time and energy in appraising these materials with no certainty of any income. After all, 10% of nothing doesn't really help to pay the rent!

But does this mean that in the field of book publishing, a new writer, or even a once-published writer, must attempt to sell a work himself? Not necessarily. There is no question about the fact that an agent can be enormously helpful to both an experienced and a new writer, depending upon the kinds of personalities involved and the type of relationship that can be established. While an agent is primarily the writer's business representative, it would be most unusual if a personal relationship between them did not come into being. I like to feel that my writers are not only my clients but also my friends, based upon our mutual interest and respect for each other.

It is important, however, for the writer to understand the function of a literary agent — what to expect from the agent and what a literary agent either can or cannot be asked to do. I feel that I can help my clients, not just by selling what they write, but also by advising them about the potential markets for the work they are planning and assisting them in smoothing out problems of plot and treatment in their manuscripts. Writers may expect agents to be so experienced that the advice they give their clients would be invaluable. But it is unrealistic for a writer to expect the agent to act as a publicity director, to handle bookstore sales, to act as a banker, or to offer psychiatric advice.

How can a writer obtain the services of a suitable agent? Although our agency is not eager to take on any number of unpublished writers, we do read and answer every letter of inquiry sent to us. It is extremely helpful for a prospective client to tell us something about his or her work, background, and why he or she feels he has a salable work in progress. We are frequently tempted to ask for sample chapters and an outline of the proposed book, and in many instances, we have found salable manuscripts in this way. The cliché, "Write, don't telephone," applies here, because our office time is taken up largely with numerous telephone calls from our clients, publishers, and editors, and we simply cannot take additional time to answer telephone queries from new writers.

When my assistant was asked what literary agents really do, he answered simply, "They talk on the telephone and go out to lunch." And while this may seem simplistic, frankly this kind of activity takes up much of our time. Lunches are important, for this is when agents meet editors and publishers to discuss projects. It is so much easier to sell a book on a personal, eyeball-to-eyeball basis, and any good agent can, through the dramatic presentation of an idea, create enormous interest on the part of an editor. (Of course, there are times when a writer does not fulfill that excitement in the presentation of the material!)

You are probably aware of the fact that legitimate literary agents do not advertise for writers, any more than legitimate publishers advertise for book properties. Then how does one go about finding an agent? The best way, of course, is through recommendation. If a writer has a friend who has had a book published, he can ask this person for the name of his agent. He then may write a letter to the agent, mentioning the recommen-

Agents are listed in *Literary Market Place*, published by R. R. Bowker Company, and the Society of Authors' Representatives (P.O. Box 650, Old Chelsea Sta., New York, NY 10113) also publishes a list of members, which will be sent if a stamped, self-addressed envelope is enclosed. In addition, a newer group of agents, the Independent Literary Agents Association (21 W. 26th St., New York, NY 10010) will send a list of members to those enclosing a stamped return envelope. Any agent listed in these three sources would be knowledgeable and reputable and would have a grasp of the markets and the requirements of various publishers today.

There are times when a new writer may be able to start on his own, and in the case of specialized books, such as books on crafts, juveniles and certainly academic subjects, a writer may find it relatively easy to make a direct contact and sell a manuscript. Many publishing houses, however, will not read manuscripts that come "over the transom," and consequently, if at all possible, a writer should attempt to find an agent. Also, there are some editors who find it difficult to deal directly with a writer and prefer to talk to an agent about business matters. (We have even had to shift a successful author from one large publishing house to another because of an unfortunate relationship between the writer and the editors at the first house.) The agent should always negotiate for the client and should run interference between editor and writer, when necessary.

When a writer complains — and not always unreasonably — about the lack of promotion and publicity for his book and the fact that it cannot be found in major bookstores, the agent takes up the complaint with the publisher. Acting as the intermediary, the agent, who is most apt to know when the complaint is justified, either telephones or makes a personal call on the publisher to straighten out the problem.

The agent frequently assumes the role of arbiter between two writers working together, since many collaborations, I find, begin happily and end disastrously.

An agent is most important to a writer in reading and working out the details of a book publisher's contract. While there are standard clauses that can rarely be changed in any publishing contract, still, the agent is more likely than the writer to know the customs and mores of the business and will be able to determine just what is negotiable and what will have to remain intact. At a writers' conference at which I was a speaker, I found that many writers were curious about the comparable benefits of using a lawyer against those of using a literary agent. There are many attorneys who specialize in literary properties and who can be extremely helpful in advising their clients about specific clauses in a contract. But the average lawyer has had little experience in this highly specialized form of legal document and may "make waves" that may not be beneficial to the writer's interests. On one occasion I sold a book manuscript to a major publisher for a new client who in turn had her lawyer read the contract. He made changes in minor clauses that worked against the author's interests!

525

In negotiating contracts, agents make every effort to retain subsidiary rights, such as first serial excerpt, foreign rights, television, motion picture, and so on, for these in many cases bring the authors larger sums than the initial book publication. But agents are aware that in the case of new writers, publishers will not yield on the usual 50-50 split in the proceeds from the sale of paperback or book-club rights. Also, many of the clauses that refer to the author's liability are difficult to alter, and here again, agents know just how far they can go in requesting changes in the contract.

Apart from benefiting from the agent's know-how in negotiating contracts, a writer also benefits from the agent's knowledge of the kind of publisher to whom a particular work should be submitted, and the form in which the material is most likely to be sold. For example, when I read a novel manuscript, I must determine at once whether it would be best to submit it for hardcover publication, or whether it should go directly to a paperback publisher. There is, of course, a difference: Though many books on the hardcover best-seller list are similar in style to paperbacks, a book must be fast-moving and filled with incident to appeal to the paperback audience. Also, I have to make the same kind of decision in deciding where to submit a nonfiction book idea for what we term the "oversize paperback," instead of a standard rack-size. The oversize paperback is a new and very profitable market today, and it has opened up many possibilities for nonfiction writers.

The work of literary agents has become so specialized that they have to decide not only which publisher would be best for a manuscript, but also which editor would offer a relationship that might be most *simpatico* for the author. If possible, I like to have my client and the editor meet at the very outset, so that they can work together without having any misunderstandings later on. This, of course, works most effectively when the contract for a book is signed before the book is completed.

At times, the agent is also faced with the important decision of whether to auction a manuscript or just to offer it on a multiple-submission basis. It should be stressed that auctions and multiple submissions are techniques that can be used *only* by agents, not by writers themselves. These are techniques by which we try to get a quick response from a publisher. In the case of a multiple submission, we send out several copies of the proposal or manuscript simultaneously to various publishers. But the whole purpose of this lies in telling each publishing house that a multiple submission is being made: Each house understands that it is in competition for the property offered. The same procedure is followed with an auction, but in this case the agent informs the publishers that there is a "floor" — a minimum advance that the author will find acceptable. Each house is then given a brief period to make an offer over the "floor." Although such auctions have received wide publicity recently, these are highly competitive techniques and should be used only very rarely — and then only by professionals.

This is another instance in which an agent's experience in professional matters is useful in making decisions for the benefit of the author. And that is why it is so important for a writer in selecting an agent to feel that he or she can place complete trust in the judgment of such a representative. Agents can make mistakes, of course, but they are likely to make fewer if they are dealing from knowledge and experience.

An agent receives a 10% commission on all domestic sales of manuscripts, including all rights, such as sales to magazines, television, syndicates, films, cassettes, and so on. However, in the case of British sales, we charge 15%, and on other foreign sales, a 20% commission. The increased commissions are charged because we all have representatives abroad who in turn have to be compensated for their work.

Is it worth 10% of a writer's income to have an agent? I am prejudiced, of course, but I sincerely think so. After all, an agent's function does not cease when a writer becomes established, witness the fact that such top authors as Irving Wallace, Arthur Hailey, Harold Robbins, and Erica Jong are all represented by agents. And I feel certain that all these successful writers would agree that they are more than reimbursed by the "10% solution."

96

SUCCESSFUL COLLABORATION
When Two Pens Are Better Than One

BY LEONARD FELDER

IN RECENT years, the best-seller lists regularly include a number of books co-authored by relatively unknown collaborators. Millions of readers can tell you that Irving Howe wrote *World of Our Father*. Only a few perceptive individuals remember that Howe's best seller was co-written "with the assistance of Kenneth Libo." Former Los Angeles District Attorney Vincent Bugliosi has sold millions of copies of his suspense novels and nonfiction books, including *Helter Skelter* and *Shadow of Cain*. Below Bugliosi's name on each book you will find either "with Curt Gentry" or "with Ken Hurwitz."

A ghostwriter is someone who essentially does 100% of the writing for a non-writer's book; a collaborator is a partner who works in tandem with a celebrity author, and each contributes equally to the ideas, outlines, drafts and revisions of their joint effort. A collaborator is paid a percentage of the publisher's advance and royalties in return for being a writing partner. Ghostwriters usually receive the entire advance in order to write the book, but after publication receive a smaller percentage of royalties than the collaborators.

Another major difference between collaborators and ghostwriters lies in the cover credit given to the various forms of co-authorship. Collaborators almost always receive acknowledgment as a "with" or an "and" on the covers of their books. While occasionally a ghostwriter will receive credit in the form of an "as told to," the vast majority of ghostwriters are never publicly acknowledged.

While each partnership has its own unique genesis, there are some easy-to-follow steps that have worked for many co-authors in finding a celebrity partner. These include:

—Let your friends and relatives know that you are interested in finding a well-known partner who needs a co-author. The more widespread your network of connections, the more likely you will hear about an author in need of assistance.

—Give your card to the lecturers, public figures and celebrities you meet at seminars, book signing events, conventions, and public gatherings.

—When you write something of quality either for an academic or commercial publication, send a copy and a personal note to well-known individuals who might benefit from your work. Be sure to mention that you are interested in their comments and suggestions.

—Just as editors keep an eye out for anyone who is noteworthy, so can you look for and establish correspondence with individuals you respect and admire. One way to start is to stay in contact with celebrities and experts you have interviewed for free-lance articles or academic assignments.

—When you think you have a commercially viable book idea that might be of interest to someone famous, write to that person to suggest a collaboration, in most cases through his or her agent, manager, publicist, or personal assistant. If your idea has merit and your timing is right, you will eventually reach your prospective partner.

—Eventually you may become one of the collaboration specialists publishers call upon whenever they need a co-author or ghostwriter for a major book project. You might also use your track record as a co-author to obtain a publishing contract on your own book project.

There are many reasons for becoming a collaborator, among them the following:

—By getting paid for your writing and meeting the high standards of your partner and your publisher, you will improve your craft and grow as a professional writer.

—15–50% of a celebrity author's lucrative advance and royalties is a lot more than 100% of the small advance you might obtain if you are lucky enough to get a publishing contract on your own.

—Instead of facing rejection slips, you will be able to build your career and establish publishing contacts. Most co-authors eventually write their own books.

—Celebrities and qualified experts can be a rewarding challenge to work with on a one-to-one basis.

—While your celebrity partner is conversing with talk show hosts from Cleveland to Calcutta, you can be working on your next project.

Writing as a collaborator carries with it some specific challenges rarely found in other forms of writing. For instance, you may find that many book projects require a first-person narration that is more intimate and direct than the "we" which is actually the case. Even if some of the ideas are your own, you may have to write them in the "I" voice of your celebrity partner in order to avoid confusing the reader.

Sometimes there will be conflicts in which your partner wants to edit out passages or ideas you would like to keep. While you can argue all you want, if your partner insists "I can't say that," or "No one will ever believe that came from me," you will have to accommodate his or her wishes without sacrificing the quality of the writing. Considerations of "mine" and "yours" should be put aside while you engage in the revising and editing of your manuscript. In most cases, your partner will welcome and respect your suggestions to improve the readability of the book. The more you can bring out the best in your partner, the more successful the project.

The rule of thumb for co-authorship fees is anything but clear-cut. On the first book I co-authored, I was more than happy to receive 15% of the advance and royalties. (Once again, 15% of something is better than 100% of nothing.) In most cases, you should expect to receive anywhere from 25%–50% of the advance and royalties, including royalties from paperback editions, book clubs, foreign rights and other related income.

If your writing partner is not very well known, you might consider accepting a flat fee and forgetting about the never-to-be-seen royalties. For instance, if your dentist asks you to collaborate on his memoirs *Of Caps and Crowns* and you know the worldwide demand for his book will never exceed 50 copies, ask for a flat fee of between $15–30 per hour. If your writing partner is a relative unknown who has the potential for a commercially successful book, an up-front fee of $75–300 per day plus a 25%–50% share of royalties is standard.

Among the most financially successful collaboration authors are Samm Sinclair Baker and Mickey Herskowitz, whose combined book sales are in excess of 10 million copies. Baker has collaborated on more than 28 self-help books, including The Scarsdale Diet and The Stillman Diet. Herskowitz has been a "with" on the celebrity biographies of Gene Autry, George Blanda, Howard Cosell, Walter Cunningham, Leon Jaworski, Jimmy the Greek, Dan Rather and Bob Uecker.

Even if you and your writing partner are "the best of friends," it is essential that you have a written agreement on your respective shares of the book and the way your names will be listed on the book's cover. Under no circumstances should you as a collaborator let your name be omitted from the cover or title page. Unless your name appears in both places, it will not be included on the library catalogue card or in *Books in Print*. In order to build your writing career and reputation, you will need to spell out in advance in your agreement that your name must appear on the title page and cover or jacket, even if it is in smaller type.

In the written agreement with your partner, be sure to specify when your job ends. For instance, most co-authors specify that they will write a first draft and one complete rewrite. If an additional rewrite is needed, you as the co-author can agree to write it for an additional fee or let a ghostwriter finish the book without changing your cover credit or royalty percentage.

In addition, there are times when you want your agreement to extend to income received long after the book is written. For instance, you will want to specify that you will receive a percentage of movie, television, sequel books, merchandising and any other related subsidiary rights that result from your joint project. As an example, if you wrote a political novel in collaboration with a public figure, you would be entitled to any film, sequel novels, syndicated articles or commercial ventures that use the same characters or ideas as your book. If you think your negotiation with your partner will be complex or that the stakes are lucrative, it is helpful to consult an attorney who understands entertainment and publishing contracts.

97

QUERIES FOR *LADIES' HOME JOURNAL*

By Sondra Forsyth Enos
Executive Editor, *Ladies' Home Journal*

I TEND TO SAVE the week's queries until late Friday afternoon, when the phones cease ringing and the production editors have stopped inundating my desk with galleys marked "Rush! Proof immediately!" And each time I open the blue folder that holds a new batch of mail, I experience the same rush of excitement. Maybe, just maybe, in this stack of fifty or one hundred passed on to me by the first readers, there will be a jewel of a proposal—gracefully written, peppered with fresh insights, and scrupulously substantiated. Sometimes, I find a letter like that. And I am overjoyed. Nothing pleases me more than to "discover" a fledgling writer or meet an established scribe who hasn't yet contributed to *Ladies' Home Journal*. True, we have a stable of cherished writers who work for us regularly, but we're eager to add to the list. And, yes, we do buy articles from absolute unknowns, if their writing meets our standards. (In fact, I once found a writer in the reader mail! Hers was the wittiest crank letter I'd ever read, so I urged her to submit a query, which she did. I bought the resulting piece, and she has gone on to sell both fiction and non-fiction to several national publications.)

All right. So now you know that sending query letters to *LHJ* is not an exercise in futility. While we receive thousands a year, we do read every one—and we're rooting for you. What you need to know now is how to compose a stand-out—a query that will move the first readers to judge it worth my time, and one that will then cause me to give you a go-ahead "on spec," and perhaps even make a definite assignment.

First off, let me tell you about our readers, so you'll know how to slant your ideas. We appeal to a mass audience, young and old alike, in urban, suburban and rural areas as well as small towns. That's a tall order, but you'll have an easier time focusing your query if you think about our "average" reader. She's 42 years old, married, has at least a high school education but more likely two or more years of college, is the mother of two or three children, and she probably works (often part-time) but doesn't think of her job as a career. She's involved in her community and thinks of herself as responsible, thrifty, tasteful and intelligent. She trusts *Ladies' Home Journal* to bring her useful, accurate information and uplifting entertainment. But for all her worthy qualities, she's also young at heart and well-informed about the events of today's world. After all, this decade's forty-year-old came of age during the turbulent, activist sixties and seventies, and whether or not she's traded her blue jeans for dress-for-success suits or forsaken picket lines to be a full-time homemaker, she is still vibrant, active, attractive, thoughtful and independent. To satisfy her, you've got to respect her and give her the kind of information-packed, clear, compelling writing we consider our hallmark at *LHJ*.

Naturally, we like to offer her a good mix of nonfiction each month, so I'll share with you the categories we try to use in every issue:

1) *Ladies' Home Journalism.* By this I mean hard-hitting, newsy articles, backed by statistics and expert quotes, and rounded out with authentic case histories. Examples of this sort of piece in recent issues are: "Innocence for Sale," by Rita Rooney (April 1983), "Old Before Her Time," by Katherine Barrett (August 1983), "Teenagers and Alcohol: Holiday Hazard, Year-round Tragedy," by David Koningsberg, Beth Weinhouse and Joan Wechsler (December 1983) and "Rape: The Battle of the Sexes Turns Violent," by Rita Rooney (September 1983). If you take a look at these stories, you'll see that they often combine reportage with service (addresses to write to, phone numbers, and so on).

2) *"Ordeal" articles.* These are moving accounts, either in the first person or as-told-to, of triumph over tragedy. I see the genre as both informational and inspirational. Hence, we try to include a service box whenever possible, so that people with a similar problem can get help. Two of my favorites have been "The Long Journey Home," by Barbara Gervais Street (February 1983), and "Journal From an Upstairs Bedroom," by Paula Parson as told to Jane Marks (March 1983).

533

3) *Emotional articles*. This category includes pieces on marriage, the extended family, personal emotions such as insecurity and envy, and sexuality. Because these topics are evergreens, superb writing is more important here than anywhere else. I think of the pieces as special treats for the reader—a refreshing break from concern about responsibility to others. The tone should be warm yet authoritative, and above all, encouraging. If you're not an "expert," you'll need authority quotes, and case histories usually help to bring the article to life. (Warning: This genre is harder to pull off than it sounds.) For good examples of this category see "How to Make Love to Each Other," by Alexandra Penney (January 1983), "The Can't Live With Him/Can't Live Without Him Marriage," by Sally Platkin Koslow (April 1983), "Those Crazy Little Fears," by Diane Elvenstar, Ph.D. (October 1983), "Family Flirtations," by Yvonne Dunleavy (December, 1983) and "The New Kind of Office Affair," by Carol Ann Pearce (October 1983).

4) *A Woman Today*. This is a reader-written column, but professional writers are welcome to contribute. These articles differ from "ordeals" in that the issues are more universal and concern all aspects of women's lives, the joys as well as the sorrows. We look for moving first-person pieces, either serious ("I Had a Heart Attack," by Mary Rae Altherr, R.N., February 1983; "Why Didn't Anyone Teach Me to Say No?" by Anna Barnes, August 1983; "I Was Accused of Child Abuse," by Peggy Daugherty, November 1983), or light ("Mommies Can't Get Sick," by Bonnie West, May 1983). Also we sometimes use men's articles in this space, particularly those that address the problems of men *vis à vis* today's "new woman." A good example is "Kiss Daddy Goodbye," by Peter McCabe (June 1983).

5) *Surprises*. The most exciting query is the one that convinces us to forgo the "formula" and print something we might not have thought of ourselves. These are rare, but memorable. Two classic examples (both came in over the transom!) are "The Diet that Changed Our Lives," by Susan Moskowitz (October 1981), and "Reflections on my Golden Wedding Anniversary," by Elma Chickering, in the How America Lives column (February 1982). Clearly, humor falls into this category.

There you have it. Oh, yes—decorating, food, fashion, beauty, childcare, animal care, medical pieces, money, "Can This Marriage Be Saved" and celebrity profiles are either staff-written or assigned to contributing editors. But that still leaves a lot for you to do for us. I hope you'll be inspired to sit down and write a proposal that shows me you have style and smarts, plus a sense of what the 80's *Journal* woman can't resist reading. Some Friday afternoon, your sparkling query (neatly typed with a clean ribbon, of course, and free of coffee stains) might catch my eye. That would be just as much of a thrill for me as it would be for you.

98

HOW TO WRITE AN ARTICLE LEAD

By Don McKinney
Managing Editor, *McCall's*

"SHE is sitting alone in the crumb-strewn kitchen, clutching a yellow coffee cup in her quivering hands and thinking of ways to kill her husband."

As article leads go, that is right in there with " 'Take your hand off my knee,' cried the duchess," the all-time cliché example of a success-ful way of catching the reader's attention. I have no idea where the duchess' amatory experience was published, if anywhere, but the quote I opened with was the first paragraph of an article by Maxine Rock which appeared in *Atlanta Weekly*. She sent it to us, along with some queries, to show us the kind of work she could do. It certainly caught our attention, and she is now working on an assignment for us.

There is, of course, no ideal lead. There is probably not even an ideal lead for any particular article, although, as an editor, I think I know the best way to begin each piece I edit, and it's not always the way the writer did it. But I have started with this example because it seemed an arresting way to begin, and also because I wanted to emphasize the importance of the lead, not only to catch the eye of your eventual reader, but to spark the interest of the editor you hope will publish it.

How can you figure out what your lead ought to be? The best advice I can offer here is: When in doubt, begin at the beginning. I don't, of course, mean the beginning of time, or the beginning of a person's life, but the beginning of the main thrust of the narrative. We ran an article recently about a mother who had been reunited, after fifteen years, with a son she had not seen since he was two years old. The article did not begin with the father's abduction of the boy, because that was not what the piece was about; it began with his grandmother's discovery of a newspaper article that she thought might reveal where the boy could be found. From there on, the article almost wrote itself, as it led us into the narrative, flashed back to explain who these people were and what had happened to them in the past, and then continued on describing the events as they unfolded.

Another article we published, this one a series of flying saucer sightings in a small town in New Hampshire, began this way:

> For Bob Giglio, a reporter for Hillsboro's weekly newspaper, *The Messenger*, and for the county's various police departments, it began on July 6, 1977. His life has not been the same since.

How can you argue with that for a lead? It pulls you right in, promising you that something pretty spectacular is going to happen here, and you'd better stay with us while we tell you about it. Just the mood you want your reader to be in.

All narratives, of course, do not begin on a moment of high drama. The story of a treasure hunt, for instance, might well start at the moment the divers on the sunken ship spotted the coral-encrusted box that is supposed to contain the gold. Without revealing what was in the box, the writer might then flash back in time to the main characters of his article learning of the treasure's existence, and determining to find it. The article could then continue on in sequence, leading back to the dramatic moment with which he began and then telling what happened next.

I started by talking about narratives because they're the easiest to write, and are always in demand. They are among our most popular features, and we never have enough of them on hand. And, if the writer has a good article idea to begin with, and can tell it simply and directly without a lot of "writing," it's almost foolproof.

The problem is a little more difficult when you're writing an essay about human behavior. One example might be the real meaning behind what people say, the "hidden messages" that may be concealed within our most innocuous comments to one another. Claire Safran, who has been a successful magazine writer and editor for many years, began this way:

> "Frankly, my dear, I don't give a damn."
> With those parting words, the most famous exit line in movie history, Rhett Butler turns his broad back and walks out the door. Scarlett O'Hara, red-eyed

but forever gorgeous, watches him go and decides that she will "think about it tomorrow."

Every marriage has its share of angry-walking-out-the-door scenes, and the way these scenes turn out often depends on the words we use. What is one partner saying? What is the other one hearing?

Claire has caught our attention with a familiar line, which has impact because we don't expect it and wonder how it ties into the article she's writing. In the next paragraph, she tells us what she is up to, and by now we are, or ought to be, hooked. We have all wondered just what a friend or lover is really saying, what they really want, and perhaps this article will help us decode these hidden thoughts. This is another ever-popular form of article—one that tells you something about yourself, and about the people you care most about. It is a staple of women's magazines, but appears in one form or another in most other magazines as well.

Almost all magazines also use profiles, a word used to describe articles about some prominent personality, which got their name from the label *The New Yorker* began putting on them back in 1925. The profile can be a simple interview or an in-depth biography, but however ambitious it may be it's a good idea to introduce the personality as quickly as possible. A veteran magazine writer from California named Joe Bell did a joint profile of Joanne Woodward and Paul Newman for us a few years ago which began like this:

"You know," said Joanne Woodward, "you've never once asked me what it's like to live with Paul Newman." True, I said, and not because I had forgotten. She thought that over a moment, then said pensively: "I went through a period where I felt if one more person asked me what it was like to live with Paul Newman, I was going to leave him. Or just open up and let everybody know what he's *really* like—he has skinny legs, and all that. Why doesn't somebody ever ask him what it's like to live with *me*?"

That works well for a number of reasons. It brings them both on stage in the first paragraph, it gives us the idea that Joanne Woodward is not entirely happy with a career spent largely in her husband's shadow, and it promises something that will be lively and candid and a good bit more revealing than your usual movie star puff piece.

Natalie Gittelson's problem was to introduce us to Lucie Arnaz, who, despite her considerable stage, movie and TV success, is still thought of by many as "I Love Lucy's" little girl. And, as this highly

538

talented writer makes clear at once, that connection has been made too often for Lucie, and her feelings about it are going to provide much of the tension that will make this article interesting:

> From the moment Lucie Arnaz throws open the front door of her big, sprawling, comfortable apartment on New York's Central Park West, she lets you know—in the nicest way, but unmistakably—that being known as Lucille Ball's daughter is not her idea of heaven. "Since I've been able to talk, that's all anybody has ever asked me: 'What's it like to be the daughter of Lucille Ball?'" says this tall, beautiful wife and mother, whose tousled dark curls have begun to show the first fine strands of gray.

We have met our heroine and know what she looks like; we also know one of the main things that is bugging her. And we want to know what she might have to say next.

Another approach is needed when the person to be profiled is not a current celebrity whose name is instantly recognizable. In that case, you are going to have to start off by telling the reader why he or she should be interested—what there is about this person that makes him or her worth reading about. One of my favorite writers, W. C. Heinz, was given the assignment many years ago of writing an article about a prizefighter named Bummy Davis, a man who was already dead when Bill Heinz began to write, and who had not been a dominant figure in the fighting game when he was alive. Bill began like this:

> It's a funny thing about people. People will hate a guy all his life for what he is, but the minute he dies for it, they make him out a hero, and they go around saying that maybe he wasn't such a bad guy after all because he sure was willing to go the distance for whatever he believed or whatever he was. That's the way it was with Bummy Davis.

This is certainly not a conventional lead, and it's written in a deliberately colloquial way that's meant to capture the flavor of the subject, and right away we're intrigued. Bummy Davis may not have been a champion, but this is not your standard fan magazine story of a hero; the writer is up to something interesting here, and we want to find out what it is.

Let me leave profiles now and move on to just two more types of article—the medical or health piece and the humorous essay. The medical article is another one in which you must get right to the point, establishing your theme and relating its subject to the reader. In magazines like *McCall's*—in fact, in all but the more technical or specialized magazines—the reader is going to want to know just how this information is going to affect his or her life. So the first paragraph or two are going not only to have to tell us what this is about, but also to find a way to bring it home to the reader. Carol Kahn did this very effectively in an article about what scientists are finding out about why people age:

> In our youth-conscious society, most of us jog, diet, dye our hair, cream our faces and do everything we can to prolong that coveted state of being, youth. Fortunately, there is a body of science called gerontology that is busy finding out exactly what is necessary to prolong not only youth but good health and the length of our lives. Fortunately, too, there are things we can do right now to help do just that.

In a humorous article, the first thing you have to do is set a mood. You probably won't want or be able to start off with a laugh, but you had better begin by getting across the flavor of the material, whether it is to be a light look at married life or an off-the-wall satire or shaggy dog story. I think Prudence Mackintosh, a marvelously gifted and attractive Texan, did a particularly good job of that in an article we adapted from her delightful book *Thundering Sneakers:*

> I was never a particularly feminine child. I bit my fingernails, stepped on my untied sash and was assigned the role of Cheeta, the chimp, when my older brother and his gang played Tarzan of the Apes. Being a brunette in a hot climate, I still can't keep myself together the way cool blondes seem to do. But now that I live in a house with three young sons, a husband and a tomcat, I'm trying harder. The need for the feminine influence is so painfully obvious around here; and it was clear that mine was inadequate the morning that Jack, my ten-year-old, asked, "Mom, have you ever had jock itch?"

Erma Bombeck, of course, is the all-time champion at starting a smile working at the corners of your mouth before you've gotten beyond the first sentence or two. Here's the way she started off a *McCall's* piece a few years back:

> I've always worried a lot, and frankly I'm good at it. I worry about introducing people and going blank when I get to my mother. I worry about a shortage of ball bearings and about a snake coming up through my kitchen drain. I worry about the world ending at midnight and getting stuck with three hours on a 24-hour cold capsule. I worry about getting into the *Guinness Book of World Records* under "Pregnancy: Oldest Recorded Birth." I worry about what the dog thinks when he sees me coming out of the shower. . . .

540

But we can't all be Erma Bombeck, even though, unfortunately, an awful lot of us try. But we can learn from her techniques, even if we don't copy her style. It seems effortless, and perhaps it is, but the strain always shows when another writer tries to copy it.

To go back to what I said earlier, there is no one perfect lead. And if you sit there staring at the blank page until you find it, you may never write another word. If you're lucky, of course, the right lead may come unbidden to your mind, as naturally as writing your byline. If not, just start writing and hope you will run across it as you go. When you have finished, sit back and ask yourself a couple of questions. Why am I telling the reader this? What is the single most interesting or surprising aspect of my story? What is going to capture readers' attention, make them stop here and not flip the page? What will persuade them to turn away from the TV set and spend some time with me?

And always remember: don't overpromise. Nothing angers a reader (or an editor) more than an article that promises more than it delivers. Somebody had better have a hand on the duchess' knee, and he had better mean business.

99

WRITING QUERIES THAT SELL

By Stephen Whitty
Assistant to the Senior Editor, *Cosmopolitan*

LAST Friday, I did something I have to do about once a month. I loaded up two shopping bags with unsolicited manuscripts—essays, articles, and short stories—filled another bag with rejection slips, note paper, envelopes and stamps (some writers still forget to enclose SASE's) and headed for the train. Home, I made a big pot of coffee, tried to find a comfortable place on the couch, and settled down to read.

Six hours later, I'd gone through a hundred and forty manuscripts—four teetering stacks of envelopes. I'd found three pieces to pass along, and counted that as a victory.

What was wrong with the other hundred and thirty-seven manuscripts? Some were badly written, to be sure—poorly spelled, amateurishly scrawled on loose-leaf paper. But many were perfectly competent, professional pieces of work. They just weren't right for *Cosmopolitan*. And because of the volume of mail I have to go through, all I had time to do was to return the manuscripts with standard rejection slips.

If these writers had queried first, many of them would have realized the articles wouldn't work for us—and they would have saved themselves not only postage, but the lost four to six weeks their manuscripts spent in transit. A good, specific query letter—and it doesn't have to be more than a few sentences—can help you pinpoint a market, test an editor's interest, line up an assignment. A query letter is an invaluable tool, but many writers are still not sure how to use it.

The surest way to type yourself as an amateur in the eyes of an editor is with a badly done query, or one that asks all the wrong questions. How can he risk assigning a 3000-word piece if you have trouble with a brief letter? Queries should sparkle, or at the very least, be clear, professional, and direct, and quickly outline the article you'd like to write.

Queries are *not* supposed to ask for writers' guidelines or the magazine's rate of payment. Nothing is more annoying than a first-time writer informing you that he is "selling First North American periodical rights only," or that she "expects payment of $1000, plus necessary expenses." Rights and expenses are details the editor will negotiate with you (or your agent, if you have one), not something that you insist on at the start. Only a known, published author can get away with this sort of behavior. Don't write, either, that "any reasonable offer will be accepted." This only makes you seem desperate.

Money, I think, is best left out of queries. It's a little premature, anyway, to start talking about fees—you're not sure yet if the magazine's even interested in seeing your piece on speculation. It is a good idea, though, to write the magazine before you query and ask for their writers' guidelines, enclosing an SASE. The form letter you'll get in reply will tell you all you need to know about minimum rates of payment, length of articles, and names of appropriate department heads.

Finally, don't begin your query with "Has your magazine ever run an article on. . . ? " or apologize "I'm not sure this is the sort of thing you do, but . . ." Do your homework. Before you even think of querying a magazine with an article, go out and buy a couple of issues—at least three. Study them. Many writers tell me, "I've read your publication since I was 14." That doesn't mean a thing—there's a great difference between reading a magazine while you're stretched out on your couch with a box of chocolates, and examining it as a professional. Look at the table of contents. Try to break the articles down into categories. What sort of piece is the magazine most interested in? Whom are the articles aimed at? Pinpoint your market. *Cosmopolitan* will not buy the same sort of story that *Ladies' Home Journal* buys. *Playboy* runs entirely different fiction from *Penthouse*. Do your research. Once you're sure of the magazine's style, and needs, you're ready to query.

Queries can run anywhere from three sentences to four pages long. Most of the ones I see are no more than a page long—usually more than enough. Let's assume, then, you're writing a one-page, three-paragraph query.

1. *Tell me what you're going to say—enticingly:* If I'm looking at 140

pieces of mail, and your query letter on broken homes begins, "In the article which I am proposing to write, I plan to deal with the growing trend toward single-parent families, and the resultant effects on . . ." I'm not going to read much further. On the other hand, a letter on the same subject beginning, "One out of every two marriages ends in divorce. And many of these separations splinter a family—one parent here, another there, the children buffeted back and forth on weekends" will hook me. The first writer might have done wonderful research on the children of broken homes, but he hasn't made the article sound interesting.

Here's an example from the mail: "There's an innovation in the age-old mating game, and it really works: Video-dating. These relationship shops have migrated eastward from California since the first one opened in Los Angeles five years ago. I've been doing delightfully personal research for the past two years and can fill your readers in on a most unique shopping spree they can try themselves." In three more paragraphs, the writer described some of her experiences and her proposed treatment of the subject. We were interested enough after requesting the piece on speculation to make it an assignment. Later, we bought it, and promptly assigned her another—at a much better price. If that first query letter hadn't been so intriguing—if she'd deluged me with statistics, for example—it wouldn't have happened.

Here's another, different example: "This is a story filled with the shame of maternal neglect caught on the pyre of unexpressed love and devotion. Compensatory acceptance of a degrading situation brings them to the edge of the pit from which few can escape—only greater love and strength can overcome the slide to stygian eternity." Apart from being awkwardly studded with Thesaurus-sized words, this is maddeningly unclear—exactly what is the author proposing? (Farther on, she admits that this is a short story—fiction, poetry, humor and cartoons aren't things that are queried effectively. Better just to send in the piece.)

That first paragraph of a query has to hook the editor and establish your topic in just a few sentences. Look at the leads to newspaper features for guidance, or imagine your first paragraph as the beginning of your finished article. Grab my attention—but don't confuse me with too many complex statistics at first, or sloppy and obtuse metaphors.

544

2. *Say it again—and describe your approach:* You've hooked the editor in the first paragraph. Now you have to reel him in. Explain why your story is different from the thirty others he's seen that year on divorce (or camping out, or computers). Will you be interviewing people in the business? Celebrities? A prime selling point for the video-dating article was that the author had gone through the experience herself and used this paragraph to mention some of her adventures. Will you be doing your article as a first-person account? Another writer sold an article on ineffective psychotherapy—a familiar topic—by explaining she wanted to do her piece as a quiz, "Should You Shed Your Shrink?" Have you decided on an unusual slant? Don't deluge me with facts, or try to convince me with chest-thumping ("My article will be the first complete guide . . ."), but if you've found an interesting angle, let me know about it.

3. *Now sell yourself:* Finally, you have to convince me to want *you* to write it. This is the hardest part for many writers—even professionals who've sold often—because you are, on a very personal level, hawking yourself. The best thing to tell me, of course, is that you've published articles before—frequently—and enclose Xeroxes of the clips. Don't lie. Editors don't usually take your word alone—they'll ask to see clips if you say you have them—and if you've claimed to have "regularly published in *The Times*" and this turns out to be two letters to the editor, they're not likely to want to have anything to do with you.

If you haven't published before, though, it's not necessary to advertise it. "This will be my first article," some honest authors confess, and editors groan. If you have some experience in the area—you're writing about hospitals and you're an R.N.; or you're reporting on rape and you've worked in counseling centers—now's the time to let me know. Magazines do really want to encourage first-time writers. Don't tell me you have a B.A. in Creative Writing or are a graduate of Wellesley— there are plenty of Wellesley graduates around who can't write, and lots of worthless Creative Writing degrees.

Finally, sign off with something graceful and quiet—"I look forward to speaking with you about this" is fine. Avoid high-pressure closings such as "This is a timely article that *must* be published soon to be

545

effective" or the threatening "I'll be calling you in a few days to speak with you further." Sign your name, make sure your address is on the letter and the self-addressed, stamped envelope, drop it in the mail, and try to forget about it. Don't call the magazine every week to see what the editor has decided. She'll get in touch with you. Put the entire letter and proposal out of your mind—and start working on the next.

Here are some common mistakes that immediately mar an otherwise excellent query and stamp you as an amateur. Don't make them!

• *Don't write on "cute" or "borrowed" stationery.* Professional writers don't write on paper with little mushrooms, or "Freelance Writer" and a quill pen stamped across the top of the page. Neither should you. A query letter is a business proposition—it should look like one. And unless you work for a newspaper, or magazine, don't write me on company stationery. It looks odd to be getting a query from the general salesman for Akron Rubber. Plain white paper and envelopes are best.

• *Don't address it to "the editors."* Most magazines—the reclusive *New Yorker* being an exception—will gladly tell you who reads article proposals. Call or write for writers' guidelines and get a specific name. Don't think that if you address your query to the Editor-in-Chief he or she will be the first to read it; it will probably be read by an assistant. But if you just address it to "The Editors," or worse—just care of the magazine—your letter will sit around the mailroom until some kindly editorial assistant decides to adopt it. Don't mark it "Personal" or "Confidential."

• *Don't address it to the wrong person.* Check the magazine's masthead or guidelines for the name of the editor in charge of the appropriate department. Double-check the most recent issue just before you mail. Staffs change, and you'll want your letter to go directly to the right person. Yesterday, I received a short story addressed to a fiction editor who hasn't been on the staff for five years. Deduction: the writer doesn't read the magazine—and got her information from a five- or six-year-old source book. Make sure your information is up-to-date. And don't misspell the editor's name.

• *Don't try to intimidate the editor.* If you are sending out multiple queries, you probably should tell the editor as a professional courtesy—but don't use this as an excuse to boast that "This proposal is being offering to all the country's major magazines" or threaten that

"An early response is *essential* in acquiring this piece." Truly professional writers don't have to bully, and don't try to. Tell the truth quietly.

• *Don't send a query that looks like a form letter.* Type a new letter for each editor you query and send the original. If possible, mention the name of the magazine in the body of the letter. Address your query to a specific person; *don't* simply insert a name into an impersonal form letter. Query letters should be professional but personal, businesslike but inviting.

• *Don't send in a letter full of misspellings.* "I would like to eksplore the workins of the Democradic party" read one query. I didn't have to read much more to make a decision. Everybody makes typos—just make sure you clean yours up before you send out the letter. If you can't spell, no editor will assume you can write.

100

MANUSCRIPT PREPARATION
AND SUBMISSION

By Joyce T. Smith

A MANUSCRIPT submitted for publication competes with hundreds of others which cross the editor's desk. It follows that the manuscript which is professional in appearance, easy to read, and is free of careless mistakes is more likely to receive better attention than those which do not meet these requirements. The rules of manuscript preparation are simple, but the writer who wishes to have his manuscript considered seriously by editors should follow them carefully. For the most part, the mechanical requirements for manuscripts are the same for all publishing houses and magazines. Publications which have special style requirements will usually send such information on request.

The basic and most important rule of manuscript preparation is: *The manuscript must be typed, double-spaced, on standard 8½ × 11 white paper, on one side of the page only.* Handwritten manuscripts, however legible, are not welcome.

TYPING

Whether a writer types his manuscripts on a manual or electric typewriter, or works on a word processor, he should be sure that the type face is clear and clean. (Some of the unusual type faces now available on typewriters, while suitable for personal use, tend to become illegible on manuscripts.) The type should be clean, and the ribbon (black) should be in good condition, producing clear, legible type. Margins of one inch to an inch and a half should be left on both sides and at the top and bottom of the page.

Writers with word processors should not use dot-matrix printers for manuscripts submitted to editors, because the type is so hard to read. Only the daisy-wheel printer produces clear, readable, typewriter-like type, so this is the obvious choice for writers.

Manuscripts should be typed on good white bond paper (8½ × 11). Weights of 14 lbs., 16 lbs., or even 20 lbs. for short manuscripts, are acceptable. Avoid too thin a paper (onionskin, for example) or a very heavy weight (such as parchment), which are difficult to handle and to read. Remember, too, that paper especially treated for easy erasing is also easily smudged. For making carbon copies, inexpensive "second sheet" paper is available. But whatever paper is used, a writer should always make and keep a carbon copy of every manuscript, since occasionally a manuscript is lost. Copies made by Xerox or similar duplicating processes should not be submitted to an editor, though a writer may make such copies of the original for his own use.

The name and address of the author should be typed in the upper left- or right-hand corner of the first manuscript page. About one-third down the page, the title is typed in capital letters, followed a line or two below by the author's name. Leave a three-line space and begin the text.

Pages should be numbered consecutively in the upper right- or left-hand corner, followed by the author's surname or the title of the manuscript in full or abbreviated form. This helps identify a page that may become separated from the whole manuscript. The first page does not have to be numbered.

Although not essential, the approximate number of words in the manuscript may be typed in the corner of the first page opposite the author's name and address. The figure should be *only approximate*, and may be estimated to the nearest round number by multiplying the average number of words in a line by the average number of lines on a page, and then by multiplying that answer by the number of manuscript pages.

After the manuscript has been typed, the author should read it over carefully, not only for sense and factual errors, but also for typing, spelling, and grammatical errors. If a page has only one or two errors, the corrections may be made neatly in ink by crossing out the whole word and writing it correctly in the space immediately above. Or an omitted word or short phrase may be inserted in the space above, with a slant line or caret to indicate the exact place for the insertion. If lengthy insertions are necessary, the entire page (or sometimes several pages) should be retyped.

Since editors assume factual accuracy as well as correct spelling, punctuation, capitalization, and word usage, a final check of these "mechanics" of writing is essential before you send out your manuscript. Here are a few check points:

Enclose all direct quotations in quotation marks. Quotations within quoted material are indicated by single quotes. All quoted material must appear exactly as originally printed. Whether you are quoting the Bible, Shakespeare, a few lines from a poem that you remember (song lyrics, however brief, *always* require permission for quotation), recheck these before you send your manuscript out; do not rely on your memory.

When quoting material of more than three lines, indent the passage quoted, omit quotation marks except to indicate quoted dialogue, and type it single space. (If you wish to quote copyright material of more than a few words, it is advisable to obtain permission of the copyright owner.)

Dialogue is enclosed in quotation marks, with the words of each new speaker beginning a new paragraph.

Italics to indicate emphasis should be used sparingly for maximum effect, but there are some "rules" for italicizing. Book and play titles names of magazines and newspapers, and foreign words are generally italicized. (Titles of short stories, essays, poems, and other parts of books or longer works are enclosed in quotation marks.)

The pages of short manuscripts should be fastened with a paper clip. Do not pin, tie, bind, or staple the pages together in any other way. The pages of a book manuscript should be left loose and mailed in a box.

Book manuscripts

Follow general rules for manuscript preparation, and also include a title page (not required for short manuscripts) on which the title is typed in capital letters about half-way down the page. On the line immediately below type the word "By" and your name. The entire manuscript should be numbered consecutively from the first page to the last. (Do not number the pages of the individual chapters separately.) Begin each new chapter on a new page, typing the chapter number and chapter title (if any) about three inches from the top. Leave two or three spaces and then proceed with the text.

Sometimes the question of illustrations arises, especially in writing children's books. Most publishers assign artists after the manuscript is accepted. If the author has collaborated with an artist, then, of course, the text and sample illustrations may be submitted together. Similarly, if the author is also the artist, it is not advisable to submit *complete,* original illustrations, unless the publishers request you to do so.

SHORT ITEMS

Type poetry double-spaced, leaving three or four spaces between stanzas. Begin each new poem—no matter what its length—on a separate page, putting your name and address at the top right of each.

Fillers are also typed double-spaced, one to a page, with your name and address on each, and for fact fillers the source should be indicated. Because of the volume of manuscripts received, many magazines do not acknowledge or return fillers, but the author may assume that if he has not heard in three months, he may offer it for sale again.

Greeting card publishers sometimes have special specifications for the submission of verses or ideas, i.e., ideas should be submitted on 3 × 5 cards, one idea to a card, etc. Requirements for art work also vary greatly, and prospective contributors should check directly with the companies and should study manuscript market lists.

FOOTNOTES

Research publications and other scholarly works may require footnotes and bibliographies, and in typing these manuscripts, writers should follow standard accepted forms as given in the widely accepted reference manual, *A Manual of Style* (University of Chicago Press).

If the manuscript requires footnotes, type these in the body of the manuscript, immediately after the line to which the note refers, using a raised number or a symbol such as an asterisk in the text and correspondingly at the beginning of the footnote. Footnotes more than one line long should be typed single-space and set off from the text by a rule above and below it.

QUERY LETTERS

Before you submit a complete nonfiction manuscript—either article or book length—it is advisable to send a brief query letter to the editor describing the proposed article or book. The letter should also include information about the author's special qualifications for dealing with the particular subject, and for a book-length manuscript, an outline of the book and a sample chapter may be included. Otherwise, no covering letter is necessary when submitting a manuscript, though the writer may include a brief note simply indicating that the manuscript is submitted for possible publication. No amount of self-praise will bring about a sale if the manuscript is unsuitable, nor will the absence of a letter discourage an editor from accepting it. If you are submitting a manuscript following a positive response to your query letter, you may indicate this fact in a brief note accompanying it. For book manuscripts, a letter is often sent separately, stating that the manuscript has been mailed under separate cover.

REPORTS ON MANUSCRIPTS

Monthly or weekly magazines, as well as large publishing houses, may take several weeks—and often longer—to read and report on manuscripts. For bi-monthlies, quarterlies, some literary magazines, and small publishing houses with limited editorial staffs, two or more months may elapse before reports are made to authors.

If you have had no report on a manuscript after a reasonable time —six to eight weeks for a large company—you may write a brief, courteous letter inquiring about the status of your manuscript.

To save time and postage—and to approach the business of marketing manuscripts in a professional way—it is essential for free-lance writers to study editorial requirements of various publications as described in market lists and by examining the publications themselves. Read several issues of any magazine to which you may wish to submit material. Familiarize yourself with the types of books published by various publishers by browsing in a library or bookshop, and by watching their advertising.

It is common practice to submit a manuscript to only one publisher at a time. Although this may seem unfair and time-consuming, it is the only way to avoid the difficulties that may arise if, for example, two editors wish to buy the same manuscript. Although the practice of sending the same query to more than one publisher at a time used to be frowned upon by editors, it has gained widespread acceptance today.

When submitting a manuscript, address it to the editor by name, if you know it, or to the editor of the particular part of the magazine—Fiction Editor, Articles Editor, Features Editor, etc., also by name, if possible, otherwise by title. The same is true for book publishers: Address your manuscript to the editor in charge of the particular division for which your book is suited: Juvenile Editor, Religious Editor, etc.

RIGHTS

As a rule, a writer submitting a manuscript to a magazine should not stipulate on his manuscript or in an accompanying letter what rights he is offering. Although most magazines buy only "First North American Serial Rights," with the author retaining all other rights, some publications buy *all* rights as a matter of policy. It is therefore best for the writer to discuss with the editor at the time of acceptance what rights the magazine is interested in.

First North American serial rights means that a magazine is buying the exclusive right to publish the material for the first time and only once. Purchase of *second serial rights* gives the magazine the right to reprint the material once after its original publication—twice in all. Some magazines buy *all periodical rights,* that is, the exclusive right to print and reprint the material here and abroad in magazine form. Generally, magazines buy only periodical rights, and all further rights—for television, motion pictures, book use, etc., belong to the author.

PART IV

WHERE TO SELL

Free-lance writers should be encouraged by the number of new and varied markets that are included in this year's edition of THE WRITER'S HAND-BOOK, as well as by updated earlier listings. There has definitely been a shift over the years in the kinds of magazines that offer the best opportunities for free lancers: At one time, the best way for beginners to break into print was by way of the "pulps" (magazines publishing detective and mystery stories, science fiction, westerns, etc.), but today the most attractive (and highest paying) markets are for specialized articles: City and regional magazines, in-flight and travel magazines, business publications and specialized magazines covering such fields as health, computers, science, consumer issues, agriculture, etc.

Certainly, every writer has a special interest, expertise, or hobby—whether it's gardening, hang-gliding, bird watching, horses, cats, chess or astrology—and there's at least one publication devoted to every one of these areas. Such interests and activities can generate dozens of articles, if a different angle is used for each magazine and the writer keeps the audience and editorial content in mind. One nonfiction field that has opened up considerably in the last decade is the market for science and computer writing, with attractive science magazines cropping up in increasing numbers on newsstands across the country. All of these magazines try to attract a general audience through readable, jargon-free articles on such subjects as computer technology, energy, astronomy and medicine, and are natural markets for writers with any scientific or technical knowledge.

It is important for writers to keep in mind how receptive the short article markets are, because the paying markets for short fiction are limited (although some of the general-interest and women's magazines do publish good stories by beginners and pros alike). We highly recommend that beginning fiction writers look into the small literary and college publications, which are always interested in the work of talented writers. They usually pay in copies only, but publication in the literary journals, many of them prestigious, can lead to recognition by editors of larger-circulation magazines, who often look there for new talent.

The market for poetry continues to be tight, with non-paying markets outnumbering paying markets many times over; but it is usually much easier for the beginning poet to get established and build up a list of publishing credits, if he submits material to the literary journals.

In the field of drama, community, regional and civic theaters and college dramatic groups offer the best chance for the new playwright to see his work "come alive" on the stage. Indeed, aspiring playwrights who can get their work produced by any of these theaters have taken an important step toward breaking into the competitive dramatic field—many of today's well known playwrights received their first recognition in the regional theaters. In addition to producing plays and giving dramatic readings of new works, many theaters also offer excellent grants, fellowships, and outright cash payments.

Though a representative list of television shows is included in this section of the HANDBOOK, writers should be aware of the fact that this market is inaccessible without an agent, and most writers break into it only after careful study of the medium, and a long apprenticeship.

In book publishing, the increased costs of production have forced most publishers to cut back drastically on the number of titles they bring out, and this, of course, means a dramatic reduction in the opportunities for writers. Still, there is good reason for beginners to be optimistic, since dozens of first novels are published every year, as are nonfiction books by beginners with knowledge in a particular field—careers, popular psychology, household hints, cooking, and woodworking, for instance. Writers who combine talent with persistence and determination may very well see their books in print.

There is one area of book publishing—the romance novel field—that has experienced such huge growth in the past few years that novelists with all levels of experience have an excellent chance for publication (often of several titles a year). Millions of readers are devouring romances, contemporary and historical, for teen-agers, young adults and older readers, and paperback houses continue to create new imprints to satisfy their readers' interests and needs. The most encouraging aspect of this field is that most romance editors welcome unsolicited manuscripts (in contrast to most hardcover book publishers, who ask for queries with outlines and sample chapters). "Tip sheets," or guidelines, are generally available from most romance publishers, and writers are urged to study these carefully, and to read several romance novels published by a particular company before submitting any material. A special listing of romance novel publishers, with brief descriptions of their needs, is included in the HANDBOOK's market section.

All information in these lists concerning the needs and requirements of magazines, book publishing companies, and theaters comes directly from the editors, publishers, and directors, but writers should realize that editors move and addresses change, as do requirements. No published listing can give as clear a picture of editorial needs and tastes as a careful study of several issues of a magazine, and writers should go to their local library to look at back issues of any publication to which they'd like to submit material, or write directly to the editor for a sample copy (often free or available at small cost).

ARTICLE MARKETS

The magazines in this list are in the market for free-lance articles of many types. The list is divided into the following categories: general magazines; publications devoted to sports and fitness, conservation, outdoors, travel, cars, etc.; magazines that emphasize women's interests, lifestyles, and gardening; city and regional magazines; business and trade magazines; house magazines and company publications; and specialized magazines.

Only the largest trade and business publications that are interested in free-lance material are listed. Writers who are able to write articles in a particular technical or business field can find the names of thousands more in *Ayer Directory of Publications,* available in most libraries. Periodicals in a wide variety of specialized areas are listed. The *Directory,* which contains an index according to classification, does not list editorial requirements, and writers should query these magazines before submitting manuscripts.

Juvenile article markets are listed under *Juvenile, Teen-Age and Young Adult Magazines.* Markets for male-oriented or adult articles, true detective stories, etc., are listed under *The Popular Market.* Religious magazines appear under *Religious and Denominational Publications;* and markets for literary articles and essays can be found under *College, Literary and Little Magazines.*

GENERAL MAGAZINES

AFRICA REPORT—833 U.N. Pl., New York, NY 10017. Margaret A. Novicki, Ed. Well-researched articles by specialists, 1,000 to 4,000 words, with photos, on current African affairs. Pays $150 to $250, on publication.

ALCOHOLISM/THE NATIONAL MAGAZINE—1004 N. 105th St., Seattle, WA 98133. Articles on all areas of alcoholism: treatment, education, prevention and recovery. Pays 7¢ to 10¢ a word, on publicaton.

AMERICAN HERITAGE—10 Rockefeller Pl., New York, NY 10020. Byron Dobell, Ed. Articles, 750 to 5,000 words, on historic background of American life and culture. No fiction. Pays from $300 to $1,500, acceptance. Queries only.

AMERICAN HISTORY ILLUSTRATED—2245 Kohn Rd., P.O. Box 8200, Harrisburg, PA 17105. Articles, 2,000 to 3,500 words, soundly researched. Style should be popular, not scholarly. Pays $300 to $500, on acceptance. Query.

THE AMERICAN LEGION MAGAZINE—Box 1055, Indianapolis, IN 46206. Daniel S. Wheeler, Asst. Pub./Ed. Articles, about 2,000 words, on current world affairs, American history, and subjects of contemporary interest. No fiction or exposés. Pays $100 to $1,000, on acceptance. Query.

THE AMERICAN SCHOLAR—1811 Q St., N.W., Washington, DC 20009. Joseph Epstein, Ed. Non-technical articles and essays, 3,500 to 4,000 words, on current affairs, the American cultural scene, politics, arts, religion and science. Pays $350, on acceptance.

AMERICANA—29 W. 38th St., New York, NY 10018. Michael Durham, Ed. Articles, 1,000 to 2,000 words, with historical slant: restoration, crafts, food, collecting, travel, etc. Pays $350 to $500, on acceptance. Query.

AMERICAS—OAS, Administration Bldg., 19th and Constitution Ave., Washington, DC 20006. A. R. Williams, Man. Ed. Features, to 2,500 words, on life in Latin America and the Caribbean. Wide focus: anthropology, the arts, travel, technology, etc. No political material. Query. Pays from $200, on publication.

ANIMAL KINGDOM—New York Zoological Society, Bronx, NY 10460. Eugene J. Walter, Jr., Ed.-in-Chief. Articles, 1,000 to 2,500 words, with photos, on natural history, ecology and animal behavior, preferably based on original scientific research. No articles on pets. Pays $250 to $750, on acceptance.

ANIMALS—MSPCA, 350 S. Huntington Ave., Boston, MA 02130. Susan Burns, Ed. Journal of the Massachusetts Society for the Prevention of Cruelty to Animals. Articles, to 3,000 words, on animals. Photos. Pays $50 to $75, on acceptance. Query.

ARMY MAGAZINE—2425 Wilson Blvd., Arlington, VA 22201. L. James Binder, Ed.-in-Chief. Features, to 5,000 words, on military subjects. Essays, humor, news reports, first-person anecdotes. Pays 8¢ to 12¢ a word, $5 to $25 for anecdotes, on publication.

THE ATLANTIC—8 Arlington St., Boston, MA 02116. William Whitworth, Ed. In-depth articles on public issues, politics, social sciences, education, business, literature, and the arts, with emphasis on information rather than opinion. Ideal length: 3,000 to 6,000 words, though short pieces (1,000 to 2,000 words) are also welcome. Pays $1,500 to $7,000, on acceptance.

BETTER HOMES AND GARDENS—1716 Locust St., Des Moines, IA 50336. David Jordan, Ed. Articles, to 2,000 words, on home and family entertainment, money management, health, travel, pets, and cars. Pays top rates, on acceptance. Query.

BRITISH HERITAGE—P.O. Box 8200, Harrisburg, PA 17105. Well-researched articles, 1,000 to 3,000 words, blending travel with British history and culture (including the Empire and Commonwealth countries) for readers knowledgeable about Britain. Pays $60 to $80 per 1,000 words, on acceptance. Query. Send SASE for guidelines.

CALIFORNIA HIGHWAY PATROLMAN—2030 V. St., Sacramento, CA 95818. Carol Perri, Ed. Articles, with photos, on transportation safety, California history, travel, topical, general items, etc. Photos. Pays 2½¢ a word, extra for black and white photos, on publication.

CAPPER'S WEEKLY—616 Jefferson St., Topeka, KS 66607. Dorothy Harvey, Ed. Articles, 300 to 500 words: human-interest, personal experience for women's section, historical. Pays varying rates, on publication.

CAT FANCY—P.O. Box 6050, Mission Viejo, CA 92690. Linda Lewis, Ed. Articles, from 1,500 to 3,000 words, on cat care, health, grooming, etc. Pays 3¢ to 5¢ a word, on publication.

CATS—P.O. Box 37, Port Orange, FL 32029. Address Eds. Articles, 1,000 to 2,000 words, with illustrations or photos, on cats: unusual anecdotes, medical pieces, humor, articles on cats in art, literature or science. Pays 5¢ a word, extra for illustrations, on publication. Replies in 8 weeks.

CHATELAINE—Maclean Hunter Bldg., 777 Bay St., Toronto, Ont., Canada M5W 1A7. Mildred Istona, Ed. Articles, 3,000 words, for Canadian women, on current issues, personalities, medicine, psychology, etc. Pays $750 for personal-experience pieces, from $1,000 for articles, on acceptance.

CHICAGO TRIBUNE MAGAZINE—See Sunday.

THE CHRISTIAN SCIENCE MONITOR—One Norway St., Boston, MA 02115. Katherine Fanning, Ed. Articles on travel, education, food and lifestyle; interviews; literary essays, to 800 words, for Home Forum; guest columns, to 800 words, for editorial page. Pays varying rates, on acceptance.

COLUMBIA—Box 1670, New Haven, CT 06507. Elmer Von Feldt, Ed. Journal of Knights of Columbus. Illustrated articles, 3,000 words, on science, history, sports, current events, religion, education and art. Humorous pieces, to 1,000 words. Pays $200 to $600, on acceptance.

COMMENTARY—165 E. 56th St., New York, NY 10022. Norman Podhoretz, Ed. Articles, 5,000 to 7,000 words, on contemporary issues, Jewish affairs, social sciences, community life, religious thought, cultural activities. Pays about 10¢ a word, on publication.

COMMONWEAL—232 Madison Ave., New York, NY 10016. Peter Steinfels, Ed. Catholic. Articles, to 3,000 words, on political, social, religious and literary subjects. Pays 2¢ a word, on acceptance.

CONSUMERS DIGEST—5705 N. Lincoln Ave., Chicago, IL 60659. Frank L. Bowers, Ed. Articles, 500 to 3,000 words, on subjects of interest to consumers: products and services, automobiles, travel, health, fitness, consumer legal affairs, family investments and financial management. Photos. Pays from 20¢ a word, extra for photos, on publication. Buys all rights. Query with resumé and samples of writing.

COSMOPOLITAN—224 W. 57th St., New York, NY 10019. Helen Gurley Brown, Ed. Guy Flatley, Man. Ed. Articles, to 4,000 words, and features, to 2,500 words, on issues affecting young career women. Pays $1,500 to $2,000 for full-length articles, less for features, on acceptance. Query.

COUNTRY JOURNAL—Box 870, Manchester Center, VT 05255. Thomas H. Rawls, Man. Ed. Articles, 2,500 to 3,000 words, for country and small-town residents; practical, informative pieces on contemporary rural life. Pays about $500, on acceptance. Query.

COUNTRY LIVING—224 W. 57th St., New York, NY 10019. Mary Roby, Man. Ed. Short articles on houses decorated in the country style, country crafts, antiques, and lifestyles. Photos. Pays $200 to $300, on acceptance.

THE CRISIS—NAACP, 186 Remsen St., Brooklyn, NY 11201. Maybelle Ward, Ed. Dir. Articles, to 1,500 words, on civil rights, problems and achievements of blacks and other minorities. Pays in copies.

DALLAS LIFE—*The Dallas Morning News,* Communications Center, Dallas, TX 75265. Melissa East, Ed. Well-researched articles and profiles, 750 to 2,000 words, with photos, on contemporary issues, personalities, or subjects of strictly Dallas-related interest; short humor features, also Dallas-related, 500 to 750 words. Pays 10¢ and up a word, on acceptance. Query.

DAWN—628 N. Eutaw, Baltimore, MD 21201. Bob Matthews, Exec. Ed. Illustrated feature articles, 1,500 words, on subjects of interest to black families. Pays $100, on publication. Query.

DIVERSION MAGAZINE—60 E. 42nd St., Suite 2424, New York, NY 10165. Stephen N. Birnbaum, Ed. Dir. Articles, 1,200 to 3,000 words, on travel, sports, hobbies, entertainment, food, etc., for physicians. Photos. Pays from $350, on publication. Query; no unsolicited manuscripts.

DOG FANCY—P.O. Box 6050, Mission Viejo, CA 92690. Linda Lewis, Ed. Articles, 1,500 to 3,000 words, on dog care, health, grooming, etc. Photos. Pays 3¢ to 5¢ a word, on publication.

DYNAMIC YEARS—215 Long Beach Blvd., Long Beach, CA 90802. Lorena F. Farrell, Exec. Ed. General-interest features, 1,000 to 3,000 words, and column items, 350 words, with emphasis on fitness and diet, retirement planning, personal finance and investment, health, lifestyles and celebrities, sports, professional life and advancement, the world of work, second and third careers, etc., all geared to the 45 to 65 age group. Photos. Pays $150 to $350 for column pieces, $500 to $2,000 for features, extra for photos, on acceptance. Query.

EARLY AMERICAN LIFE—Box 8200, Harrisburg, PA 17105. Frances Carnahan, Ed. Illustrated articles, 1,000 to 3,000 words, on early American life: arts, crafts, furnishings, architecture; travel features about historic sites and country inns. Pays $50 to $400, on acceptance. Query.

EASY LIVING—1999 Shepard Rd., St. Paul, MN 55116. Peggy Brown Black, Ed. Articles, 1,000 to 1,800 words, for customers of financial institutions, on personal finance, lifestyle, consumerism, money, and some foreign travel. Pays $250 to $600, on acceptance. Query.

EBONY—820 S. Michigan Ave., Chicago, IL 60605. Herbert Nipson, Exec. Ed. Articles, with photos, on blacks: achievements, civil rights, etc. Pays from $150, on publication. Query.

THE ELKS MAGAZINE—425 W. Diversey Pkwy., Chicago, IL 60614. Herbert Gates, Man. Ed. Articles, 3,000 words, on business, sports, and topics of current interest for non-urban audience with above-average income. Informative or humorous pieces, to 2,500 words. Pays $150 to $500 for articles, on acceptance. Query.

ENVIRONMENT—4000 Albemarle St., N.W., Washington, DC 20016. Jane Scully, Man. Ed. Articles, 2,500 to 6,500 words, on environmental, scientific and technological policy and decision-making issues. Pays $75 to $300, on publication. Query.

EQUINOX—7 Queen Victoria Rd., Camden East, Ont., Canada K0K 1J0. Frank Edwards, Exec. Ed. Articles, 4,000 to 8,000 words, on geography, biology, astronomy, sciences, the arts, industry, and adventure. Department pieces, 500 to 750 words, for "Nexus" (science and medicine) and "Habitat" (man-made and natural environment). Pays $1,250 to $2,000 for features, $250 to $350 for short pieces, on acceptance.

ESQUIRE—2 Park Ave., New York, NY 10016. Gene Stone, Sr. Ed. Articles, 250 to 7,000 words, for intelligent adult audience. Pays $250 to $1,500, on acceptance. Query.

FACT: THE MONEY MANAGEMENT MAGAZINE—711 Third Ave., New York, NY 10017. Daniel M. Kehrer, Ed.-in-Chief. Carefully researched articles on personal money management and investing, 1,500 to 2,000 words. Pieces, 1,200 to 1,800 words, for departments: bonds, funds, real estate, insurance, stocks, etc. Pays from $200 to $500, on acceptance.

FAMILY CIRCLE—488 Madison Ave., New York, NY 10022. Margaret Jaworski, Articles Ed. Articles, to 2,500 words, on child care, consumer affairs, changing lifestyles, health and fitness, jobs, money management, food, travel, gardening; true-life dramas. Query required. Pays on acceptance.

560

THE FAMILY HANDYMAN—1999 Shepard Rd., St. Paul, MN 55116. Semi-technical articles, to 1,000 words, with photos, on do-it-yourself home improvement, maintenance, and repair, plus how-to features on projects around the home. Pays varying rates, on acceptance.

FAMILY WEEKLY—1515 Broadway, New York, NY 10036. Tom Plate, Ed., Kate White, Exec. Ed., Tim Mulligan, Man. Ed. Short, lively articles on prominent individuals, health, medicine, money management and family advice. Pays from $200, on acceptance. Query.

FATE—Clark Publishing Co., 500 Hyacinth Pl., Highland Park, IL 60035. Mary M. Fuller, Ed. Documented articles, to 3,000 words, on strange happenings. First-person accounts, to 300 words, of true psychic or unexplained experiences. Pays from 5¢ a word for articles, $10 for short pieces, on publication.

FIREHOUSE—515 Madison Ave., New York, NY 10022. Dennis Smith, Ed.-in-Chief. Articles, 500 to 2,000 words, on trends in firefighting equipment and practice and lifestyles of firefighters. Profiles. On-the-scene accounts of fires. Pays $100 to $200, on publication. Query.

FORD TIMES—Rm. 765, P.O. Box 1899, Dearborn, MI 48121-1899. Arnold S. Hirsch, Ed. Articles, to 1,500 words, on contemporary American life and trends, travel, outdoor activities. Profiles of personalities, well-known and not. Pays to $700, on acceptance. Query.

FOREIGN POLICY JOURNAL—11 Dupont Circle, N.W., Suite 900, Washington, DC 20036. Charles William Maynes, Ed. Articles, 3,000 to 5,000 words, on international affairs. Honorarium, on publication. Query.

FOREIGN SERVICE JOURNAL—2101 E. St. N.W., Washington, DC 20037. Stephen R. Dujack, Ed. Articles on American diplomacy, foreign affairs and subjects of interest to Americans representing U.S. abroad. Pays 2¢ to 10¢ a word, on publication. Query.

FORUM, THE INTERNATIONAL JOURNAL OF HUMAN RELATIONS—1965 Broadway, New York, NY 10023-5965. Articles, 2,500 words, on sex. Pays $400 to $800. Send manuscript or two-page proposal.

THE FREEMAN—Foundation for Economic Education, Irvington-on-Hudson, NY 10533. Paul L. Poirot, Ed. Articles, to 3,000 words, on economic, political and moral implications of private property, voluntary exchange, and individual choice. Pays 5¢ a word, on publication.

FRIENDLY EXCHANGE—1999 Shepard Rd., St. Paul, MN 55116. Adele Malott, Ed. Articles, 1,000 to 2,500 words, for traditional, home-owning families, on domestic travel, gardening, home decorating, personal finance, sports and the outdoors, consumer interests, etc. with Western U.S. tie-in. Pays $300 to $700 for features. Departments are generated exclusively by reader mail. Pays on acceptance. Query.

FRIENDS—30400 Van Dyke, Warren, MI 48093. Tom Morrisey, Features Ed. Active lifestyle articles and upbeat subjects for owners of Chevrolet cars and trucks. Photos (4 color trans.). Pays from $400, on acceptance.

GAMBLING TIMES—1018 N. Cole Ave., Hollywood, CA 90038. Len Miller, Ed. Gambling-related articles, 1,000 to 6,000 words. Pays $100 to $150, on publication.

GAMES—515 Madison Ave., New York, NY 10022. Jacqueline Damian, Ed. Short articles on unusual games and original games and puzzles. Pays varying rates, on publication. Query.

GENTLEMEN'S QUARTERLY (GQ)—350 Madison Ave., New York, NY 10017. Philip Smith, Man. Ed. Sophisticated features for men, about 2,500 words, on grooming, personal finance, health, travel, lifestyles. Pays $300 to $400, on publication. Query with outline required.

GEO MAGAZINE—Two Grand Central Tower, 140 East 45th St., New York, NY 10017. Kevin Buckley, Man. Ed. Articles 3,000 to 5,000 words, with photos, on natural history, anthropology, art, architecture, travel, exotic places and adventure. Pays about $2,500, on acceptance. Query.

GLAMOUR—350 Madison Ave., New York, NY 10017. Ruth Whitney, Ed.-in-Chief; Rona Cherry, Exec. Ed. Articles on careers, health, psychology, interpersonal relationships, etc.; editorial approach is "how-to" for women, 18 to 35. Fashion and beauty material staff-written. Pays from $900 for 1,500- to 2,000-word articles, from $1,200 for longer pieces, on acceptance.

GLOBE—2112 S. Congress Ave., West Palm Beach, FL 33406. Robert Taylor, News Editor. Factual articles, 500 to 1,000 words, with photos: exposés, celebrity interviews, consumer and human-interest pieces. Pays from $50 to $1,500.

GOOD HOUSEKEEPING—959 Eighth Ave., New York, NY 10019. Joan Thursh, Articles Ed. In-depth articles and features, 1,200 to 5,000 words, on controversial problems, topical social issues; dramatic personal narratives about unusual experiences of average families; sharply-angled pieces about celebrities; research reports on news of interest to women, for "Better Way." Pays top rates, on acceptance.

GOOD READING—Litchfield, IL 62056. Articles, 500 to 1,000 words, with B/W photos, on current, factual subjects of general interest; business; personal experiences which reveal success in human relationships. Pays $10 to $100.

GOODLIFE—Suite D-110, 1401 West Paces Ferry Rd., Atlanta, GA 30327. Gene Gabriel-Moore, Exec. Ed. Articles on travel, fashion, food, automobiles, wine, home design, for affluent audience. Pays top rates within 30 days of acceptance. Very limited free-lance market.

GOURMET—560 Lexington Ave., New York, NY 10022. Gail Zweigenthal, Man. Ed. Articles, 2,500 to 3,000 words, on food, travel, good living, for sophisticated audience. Pays good rates, on acceptance.

GRIT—208 W. Third St., Williamsport, PA 17701. Joanne Decker, Assignment Ed. Articles, to 500 words, on religion, communities, jobs, recreation, families and coping. Pays 12¢ a word, extra for photos, on acceptance.

HARPER'S MAGAZINE—2 Park Ave., New York, NY 10016. Unsolicited articles and queries welcome. Considers fiction submitted through an agent only.

HISTORIC PRESERVATION—1785 Massachusetts Ave., N.W., Washington, DC 20036. Thomas J. Colin, Ed. Articles from published writers, 1,500 to 4,000 words, on historic preservation, maritime preservation and people involved in preservation. High-quality photos. Pays $300 to $850, extra for photos, on acceptance. Query required.

HORSE ILLUSTRATED—P.O. Box 4030, San Clemente, CA 92672. Linda Lewis, Ed. Articles, 1,500 to 3,000 words, on all aspects of owning and caring for horses. Photos. Pays 3¢ to 5¢ a word, on publication.

HORTICULTURE—755 Boylston St., Boston, MA 02116. Steven Krauss, Man. Ed. Authoritative, well-written articles, 1,500 to 3,000 words, on all aspects of gardening and horticulture. Pays competitive rates. Query.

HOUSE & GARDEN—350 Madison Ave., New York, NY 10017. Louis O. Gropp, Ed.-in-Chief. Shelley Wanger, Articles Ed. Articles on decorating, architecture, gardens, the arts. Query. Rarely buys unsolicited manuscripts.

HOUSE BEAUTIFUL—1700 Broadway, New York, NY 10019. Carol Cooper Garey, Sr. Ed./Copy. Service articles related to the home. Pieces on beauty, travel and gardening mostly staff-written. Pays varying rates, on acceptance. Send for writer's guidelines. Query with detailed outline and SASE.

INFANTRY—P.O. Box 2005, Fort Benning, GA 31905. Articles, 2,000 to 5,000 words, on military organization, equipment, tactics, foreign armies, etc., for U.S. infantry personnel. Pays varying rates, on publication; no payment made to U.S. Government employees. Query.

INQUIRER MAGAZINE—*Philadelphia Inquirer,* Broad and Callowhill Sts., Philadelphia, PA 19101. David Boldt, Ed. Local-interest features, 500 to 7,000 words. Profiles of national figures in politics, entertainment, etc. Pays varying rates, on publication. Query.

INQUIRY—1320 G. St. S.E., Washington, DC 20003. Doug Bandow, Ed. Libertarian monthly. Articles to 5,000 words, on civil liberties, economics, foreign policy and current political developments. Columns, 1,000 to 2,500 words, on law, politics, education, economics, and media. Pays 10¢ a word, on publication. Free sample copy. Query preferred.

INTRO—3518 Cahuenga Blvd., W., Los Angeles, CA 90068. Lori Kimball, Ed. Articles, 1,500 to 4,000 words, on contemporary living trends. Features, 1,500 to 2,500 words, on travel, finance, health, and psychology. Sophisticated and/or humorous fiction. Pays varying rates. Query.

THE JOURNAL OF FRESHWATER—Box 90, 2500 Shadywood Rd., Navarre, MN 55392. Articles on issues and solutions relating to the freshwater environment, for lay readers. Pays $150 to $300, on publication. Query.

THE KIWANIS MAGAZINE—3636 Woodview Trace, Indianapolis, IN 46268. Scott B. Pemberton, Exec. Ed. Articles, 1,500 to 2,500 words, on home, family, career and community concerns of business and professional men. No travel pieces, interviews, profiles. Pays $250 to $750, on acceptance. Query.

LADIES' HOME JOURNAL—3 Park Ave., New York, NY 10016. Articles on contemporary subjects of interest to women. Personal experience and regional pieces. Queries only (with SASE) to Exec. Eds. Jan Goodwin or Sondra Forsyth Enos. Fiction and poetry through literary agents only. Not responsible for unsolicited manuscripts.

LADY'S CIRCLE—23 W. 26th St., New York, NY 10010. Mary Terzella, Ed. Articles, 2,000 to 3,000 words, with photos, on how-to crafts, hobbies, women in home-based businesses, "do-gooders," child care, home management, saving time and money, and people overcoming handicaps. Pays to $125, extra for photos, on publication. Query with outline.

LAUGH FACTORY—400 S. Beverly Dr., #214, Beverly Hills, CA 90212. Jamie Masada, Pub. Humorous articles, 600 to 3,000 words; pictures with captions, single jokes, and cartoons. Pays negotiable rates, on publication.

LEATHERNECK—Box 1775, Quantico, VA 22134. Ronald D. Lyons, Ed. Articles, to 3,000 words, with photos, on U.S. Marines. Pays $50 to $75 per printed page, on acceptance. Query.

THE LION—300 22nd St., Oak Brook, IL 60570. Robert Kleinfelder, Senior Ed. Official publication of Lions Clubs International. Articles, 800 to 2,000 words, and photo essays, on Club activities. Pays from $50 to $400, including photos, on acceptance. Query.

LISTEN MAGAZINE—6830 Laurel St. N.W., Washington, DC 20012. Francis A. Soper, Ed. Articles, 500 to 1,500 words, on problems of alcohol and drug abuse, for teenagers; personality profiles. Photos. Pays 5¢ to 7¢ a word, extra for photos, on acceptance. Query. Guidelines available.

LIVING SINGLE—40 S. Third St., Columbus, OH 43215. Timely and topical features, 700 to 3,000 words, on the quality and improvement of all aspects of single life. Pays competitive rates for articles, on acceptance.

THE LOOKOUT—Seamen's Church Institute, 15 State St., New York, NY 10004. Carlyle Windley, Ed. Factual articles on the sea. Features, 200 to 1,500 words, on the merchant marines, sea oddities, etc. Photos. Pays $25 to $100, on publication.

McCALL'S—230 Park Ave., New York, NY 10169. Robert Stein, Ed. Interesting, unusual and topical first person essays, narratives, reports on health, home management, social trends relating to women of all ages, 1,000 to 3,000 words. Humor. Human interest stories. Job column. Pieces for VIP-ZIP and regional sections; consumer, travel, crafts. Essays, 1,000 words, for "Back Talk," a forum for airing fresh and often controversial views on all subjects. Pays top rates, on acceptance.

MADEMOISELLE—350 Madison Ave., New York, NY 10017. Kate White, Articles Ed. Articles, 1,200 to 2,500 words, on subjects of interest to literate young women. Pays from $350, on acceptance. Query.

MAINSTREAM AMERICA—2714 W. Vernon Ave., Los Angeles, CA 90008. Henry M. Miller, Ed. Articles, 500 to 3,000 words, on successful people, as well as historical pieces that will inspire and motivate, for Black audience. Pays 6¢ to 8¢ a word, on publication.

MARRIAGE & FAMILY LIVING—St. Meinrad, IN 47577. Kass Dotterweich, Man. Ed. Articles, to 2,000 words, on husband-wife and parent-child relationships. Pays 7¢ a word, on acceptance. Query.

MD MAGAZINE—30 E. 60th St., New York, NY 10022. A. J. Vogl, Ed. Articles, 750 to 2,500 words, for practicing physicians, on the arts, history, other aspects of culture. Fresh angle required. Pays from $200 to $700, on acceptance. Query.

METROPOLITAN HOME—750 Third Ave., New York, NY 10017. Service and informational articles for metropolitan dwellers in apartments, houses, co-ops, lofts, and condominiums, on real estate, equity, wine and spirits, collecting, etc. Pays varying rates. Query.

MIDSTREAM: A MONTHLY JEWISH REVIEW—515 Park Ave., New York, NY 10022. Joel Carmichael, Ed. Articles; reviews. Pays 5¢ a word, on publication.

MILITARY REVIEW—U.S. Army Command and General Staff College, Fort Leavenworth, KS 66027. Col. John D. Bloom, Ed.-in-Chief. Articles, 2,500 to 4,000 words, on tactics, national defense, military history and any military subject of current interest and importance. Pays $25 to $100, on publication.

MODERN MATURITY—215 Long Beach Blvd., Long Beach, CA 90801. Ian Ledgerwood, Ed. Service articles on living, food, health, employment, travel, and leisure activities, for persons over 50 years. Nostalgia, inspirational articles, personality pieces, Americana, to 2,000 words. Photos. Pays $150 to $3,000, extra for photos, on acceptance.

MOMENT—462 Boylston St., Boston, MA 02116. Carol Kur, Man. Ed. Sophisticated articles, 2,000 to 4,000 words, on Jewish political, social, literary, and religious issues. Pays from $100, on publication. Query.

MONEY—Time-Life Bldg., New York, NY 10020. Marshall Loeb, Ed. Articles on personal finance: how to earn more money, invest more profitably, spend more intelligently and more pleasurably, save more prudently, and enhance your career. Pays on acceptance and publication. Query.

THE MOTHER EARTH NEWS—105 Stoney Mt. Rd., Hendersonville, NC 28791. Roselyn Edwards, Submissions Ed. Articles on alternative life styles, for rural and urban readers: home improvements, how-to's, indoor and outdoor gardening, family pastimes, etc. Also, self-help, health, food-related, ecology, energy and consumerism pieces. Profiles. Photos. Pays varying rates, on acceptance. Send for writer's guidelines.

MOTHER JONES—1663 Mission St., San Francisco, CA 94103. Deirdre English, Ed. Investigative articles, political essays, cultural analyses. Pays $750 to $1,000, after acceptance. Query.

MS.—119 W. 40th St., New York, NY 10018. Address Manuscript Ed. Articles relating to women's roles and changing lifestyles; general interest, how-to, self-help, profiles, reviews, etc. Fiction. Pays varying rates, on acceptance.

MUSEUM MAGAZINE—720 White Plains Road, Scarsdale, NY 10583. Sharon AvRutick, Man. Ed. Articles, 750 to 2,500 words, on museums and related subjects: science, art, natural history, history, etc., for museum-goers. Photos. Pays $150 to $750, on acceptance. Query first. No recent report.

THE NATION—72 Fifth Ave., New York, NY 10011. Victor Navasky, Ed. Articles, 2,000 to 2,500 words, on current issues. Pays about 2¢ a word up to $150, on publication. Query.

NATIONAL ENQUIRER—Lantana, FL 33464. Articles, of any length, for mass audience: topical news, the occult, how-to, scientific discoveries, human drama, adventure, personalities. Photos. Pays from $325. Query; no unsolicited manuscripts accepted.

NATIONAL GEOGRAPHIC—17th and M Sts. N.W., Washington, DC 20036. Wilbur E. Garrett, Ed. First-person articles, 6,000 words maximum, on travel, exploration, mountaineering, seafaring, archaeological discoveries, natural history, industries, commodities, science, occupations, living patterns. Photos. Pays to $8,000, extra for photos, on acceptance. Query required. No unsolicited manuscripts.

NATIONAL GUARD—One Mass. Ave. N.W., Washington, DC 20001. Reid K. Beveridge, Ed. Articles, 2,000 to 4,000 words, with photos, of interest to National Guard members. Pays $200 to $500, on publication.

NATIONAL SCENE MAGAZINE—L. H. Stanton Publications, 22 E. 41st, New York, NY 10017. Claude Reed, Jr., Ed. Profiles and news pieces, 750 to 1,500 words, for Black audience. Pays $100 to $300, on publication. Queries are preferred.

THE NATIONAL SUPERMARKET SHOPPER—P.O. Box 500, Franklin Sq., NY 11010. Lee Shore, Man. Ed. Articles, 1,500 to 2,500 words, on consumer issues and smart shopping, with emphasis on food purchases and household activities. Fiction, to 2,500 words, with supermarket orientation. Pieces on innovations in supermarkets, shopping techniques, new products, legislation and government regulations concerning supermarkets, food, etc. Pays 5¢ a word, on publication.

NATURAL HISTORY—American Museum of Natural History, Central Park West at 79th St., New York, NY 10024. Alan Ternes, Ed.-in-Chief. Informative articles, to 3,500 words, by experts, on anthropology and natural sciences. Pays $750, on acceptance. Query.

NEW AGE—342 Western Ave., Brighton, MA 02135. Articles, for readers interested in self-development and awareness, on natural foods, holistic health, education, disarmament, etc. Pays from 10¢ a word, on publication. Query.

NEW REALITIES—680 Beach St., San Francisco, CA 94109. James Bolen, Ed. Articles on holistic health, personal growth, parapsychology, alternative lifestyles, new spirituality. Pays to $150, on publication. Query.

NEW WOMAN—205 Lexington Ave., New York, NY 10016. Pat Miller, Editor/Publisher. "The most important thing for writers is to read the magazine to become familiar with our needs before querying." Articles on new lifestyles. Features on financial advice, legal advice, careers, marriage, relationships, surviving divorce, diets and health. Pays varying rates, on publication. Query.

NEW YORK—755 Second Ave., New York, NY 10017. Edward Kosner, Ed. Laurie Jones, Man. Ed. Feature articles of interest to New Yorkers. Pays from $350 to $3,000, on acceptance. Query required; not responsible for unsolicited material.

THE NEW YORK TIMES MAGAZINE—229 W. 43rd St., New York, NY 10036. Address Articles Ed. Timely articles, approximately 4,000 words, on new items, forthcoming events, trends, culture, entertainment, etc. Pays $350 to $500 for short pieces, $1,000 to $2,500 for major articles, on acceptance. Query.

THE NEW YORKER—25 W. 43rd St., New York, NY 10036. Address The Editors. Factual and biographical articles, for "Profiles," "Reporter at Large," "That Was New York," "Annals of Crime," "Onward and Upward with the Arts," etc. Pays good rates, on acceptance. Query.

NUCLEAR TIMES—298 Fifth Ave., New York, NY 10001. David Corn, Assoc. Ed. Terse, timely news articles, to 1,500 words, on the nuclear disarmament movement, the arms race, nuclear weapons and nuclear war. Pays 12¢ a word, on publication.

OCEANS—Fort Mason Center, Bldg. E., San Francisco, CA 94123. Keith K. Howell, Ed. Articles, to 5,000 words, with photos, on marine life, oceanography, marine art, undersea exploration, seaports, conservation, fishing, diving, and boating. Pays $100 per printed page, on publication. Query. Guidelines available.

OFF DUTY—3303 Harbor Blvd , Suite C-2, Costa Mesa, CA 92626. Informative, entertaining and useful articles, 900 to 1,800 words, for military service personnel and their dependents, on making the most of off duty time and getting the most out of service life: military living, travel, personal finance, sports, cars and motorcycles, military people, American trends, etc. Pays 13¢

to 16¢ a word, on acceptance. European and Pacific editions also. Guidelines available. Query.

OMNI—1965 Broadway, New York, NY 10023-5965. Dick Teresi, Ex. Ed. Articles, 2,500 to 3,000 words, on scientific aspects of the future: space colonies, cloning, machine intelligence, ESP, origin of life, future arts, lifestyles, etc. Pays $800 to $2,000, less for short features, on acceptance. Query.

ON CAMPUS—Inter-Collegiate Press, Inc., 6105 Travis Lane, P.O. Box 10, Shawnee Mission, KS 66201. Ellen Parker, Ed. Annual. Articles, 1,000 to 3,500 words, for college freshmen—how-to, travel, humor, book reviews, interviews, profiles, etc. Pays $30 to $400, on acceptance. Queries are preferred.

OPTIMIST MAGAZINE—4494 Lindell Blvd., St. Louis, MO 63108. Dennis R. Osterwisch, Ed. Articles, to 1,500 words, on general-interest topics of interest to members of civic-service clubs. Pays from $100, on acceptance. Query.

ORGANIC GARDENING—33 E. Minor St., Emmaus, PA 18049. M. C. Goldman, Exec. Ed. Articles, to 2,500 words, for organic gardeners: raising fruits or vegetables, greenhouse/indoor growing, herbs, natural pest control, nutrition, foods, building soil, new developments in plant breeding, etc. Photos. Pays $250 to $750, extra for photos, on acceptance. Query.

PARADE—750 Third Ave., New York, NY 10017. Fran Carpentier, Articles Ed. National Sunday newspaper supplement. Factual and authoritative articles, 1,000 to 1,500 words, on subjects of national interest: sports, health, education, consumer and environmental issues, science, the family, etc. Profiles of well-known personalities and service pieces. No fiction, poetry, games or puzzles. Photos with captions. Pays from $1,000. Query. SASE required.

PENTHOUSE—1965 Broadway, New York, NY 10023-5965. Claudia Valentino, Man. Ed. Peter Bloch, Exec. Ed. General-interest or controversial articles, to 5,000 words. Pays from 20¢ a word, on acceptance.

PEOPLE IN ACTION—1720 Washington Blvd., Ogden, UT 84404. Caroll McKanna Halley, Ed. Personality profiles about people overcoming, enjoying, helping others, 800 to 1,200 words; occasional humorous pieces, 500 words. Pays 15¢ a word, $35 for color photos, on acceptance. Query or send manuscript with photos (no black & white). Celebrity Chief feature, 400 to 600 words, must include recipe; need not be celebrity.

PLAYBOY—919 N. Michigan Ave., Chicago, IL 60611. James Morgan, Articles Ed. Sophisticated articles, 4,000 to 6,000 words, of interest to urban men. Humor; satire. Pays to $3,000, on acceptance. Query.

PLAYGIRL—3420 Ocean Park Blvd., Suite 3000, Santa Monica, CA 90405. Vanda Krefft, Sen. Ed. Feature articles, 2,500 to 3,000 words, for contemporary women, age 20 to 35. Celebrity interviews, 3,000 to 4,000 words. Pays negotiable rates. Query with published clips.

PRESENT TENSE—165 E. 56th St., New York, NY 10022. Murray Polner, Ed. Serious reportage and personal journalism, 2,000 to 3,000 words, with photos, on developments concerning Jews worldwide; profiles of Jewish life. Pays $100 to $250, on acceptance. Query.

PREVUE—P.O. Box 974, Reading, PA 19603. J. Steranko, Ed. Lively articles on films and filmmakers; entertainment features and celebrity interviews. Length: 4 to 25 pages. Pays varying rates, on acceptance. Query with published clips.

567

PRIME TIMES—Suite 120, 2802 International Ln., Madison, WI 53704. Ana Maria Guzman, Assoc. Ed. Articles, 500 to 2,500 words, for over-50 or retired credit union people. Departments, 400 to 500 words. Pays to $750, on acceptance, for first rights, on publication for second rights. Query.

PRIVILEGE—3906 Church St., Mount Laurel, NJ 08054. Monique Whitaker, Ed. Quarterly publication for bank credit card holders association. Articles on consumer topics and travel pieces. Photos. Query first. Pays 20¢ a word, on publication.

THE PROGRESSIVE—409 E. Main St., Madison, WI 53703. Erwin Knoll, Ed. Articles, 1,000 to 3,500 words, on political, social problems. Light features. Pays $75 to $300, on publication.

PSYCHOLOGY TODAY—1200 17th St. N.W., Washington, DC 20036. Address Manuscripts Ed. Most articles assigned to researchers in the social sciences. Query.

PUBLIC CITIZEN MAGAZINE—P.O. Box 19404, Washington, DC 20036. Quarterly. David Bollier, Ed. Investigative reports and articles of timely political interest, 500 to 1,500 words, for members of Public Citizen Organization: consumer rights, health and safety, environmental protection, safe energy, tax reform and government and corporate accountability. Photos, illustrations. Pays to $50.

READER'S DIGEST—Pleasantville, NY 10570. Kenneth O. Gilmore, Ed.-in-Chief. Unsolicited manuscripts will be returned unread. General interest articles already in print. Will consider well-developed, written queries also. Address the Editors.

RECOVERY!—2100 N. 105th St., Seattle, WA 98133. Christina Johnston, Ed. Articles on meeting the challenges of recovery, to 3,000 words, for alcoholic/substance abusers. First-person pieces, 1,200 to 1,400 words, on how problems of recovery were solved. Fillers, humor, jokes, puzzles, 250 to 400 words. Pays $15 to $25 for fillers, and about 10¢ a word for articles, after publication.

REDBOOK—224 W. 57th St., New York, NY 10019. Annette Capone, Ed.-in-Chief. Susan Edmiston, Articles Ed. Articles, 1,000 to 3,500 words, on subjects related to relationships, sex, current issues, marriage, the family, and finances. Pays from $750, on acceptance. Query.

THE RETIRED OFFICER MAGAZINE—201 N. Washington St., Alexandria, VA 22314. Address Manuscript Ed. Articles, preferably with photos, 1,000 to 2,500 words, of interest to military retirees. Current affairs, contemporary military history and humor, and pieces on travel, hobbies, and second-career job opportunities. Pays to $400, extra for photos, on acceptance. Query preferred. Send for writers guidelines.

ROLL CALL: THE NEWSPAPER OF CAPITOL HILL—201 Mass. Ave. N.E., Washington, DC 20002. Sidney Yudain, Ed. Factual, breezy articles with political or Congressional angle: Congressional historical and human-interest subjects, political lore, etc. Political satire and humor. Pays modest rates, on publication.

ROLLING STONE—745 Fifth Ave., New York, NY 10151. Magazine of modern American culture, politics, and art. No fiction. Query; "rarely accepts free-lance material."

THE ROTARIAN—1600 Ridge Ave., Evanston, IL 60201. Willmon L. White, Ed. Articles, 1,200 to 2,000 words, on international social and economic issues, business and management, human relationships, travel, sports, environment, science and technology; humor. Pays good rates, on acceptance. Query.

THE SATURDAY EVENING POST—1100 Waterway Blvd., Indianapolis, IN 46202. Ted Kreiter, Senior Ed. Articles, 2,500 to 3,000 words, on education, medicine, the arts, science, politics. Articles on sports, home repairs (with photos). Photo essays. Pays varying rates, on publication. Query with outline.

SATURDAY REVIEW—214 Mass. Ave., N.E., Suite 460, Washington, DC 20002. Frank Gannon, Ed. Articles, 1,000 to 3,000 words, on literature and the arts—film, theater, music, dance, photography, television, etc. Pays on publication. Query with outline.

SAVVY—111 Eighth Ave., New York, NY 10011. Wendy Reid Crisp, Ed. Service articles and business features for women executives. Writers must be familiar with the magazine before submitting material. Pays $300 to $1,500, on publication. Query.

SELF—350 Madison Ave., New York, NY 10017. Phyllis Starr Wilson, Ed. Articles for women of all ages, with strong how-to slant, on self-development. Pays from $750, on acceptance. Query.

SHOW-BOOK WEEK—*Chicago Sun-Times,* 401 N. Wabash Ave., Chicago, IL 60611. Steven S. Duke, Ed. Articles, profiles and interviews, to 1,000 words, relating to fine arts or lively arts. Pays $75 to $100, on publication. Query.

SIGNATURE—641 Lexington Ave., New York, NY 10022. Horace Sutton, Ed. Magazine of the Diners Club and Citicorp. Articles, 1,500 to 2,500 words, on travel, sports, entertainment, wine, spirits and gastronomy for well-traveled, upper-class readers. Pays $600 to $2,000, on acceptance. Query.

SMALL WORLD—Volkswagen of America, Troy, MI 48099. Ed Rabinowitz, Ed. Articles, 600 to 1,500 words, for Volkswagen owners; profiles of well-known personalities; inspirational or human-interest pieces; travel; humor. Photos. Pays $100 per printed page, on acceptance. Query. Guidelines on request.

SMITHSONIAN—900 Jefferson Dr., Washington, DC 20560. Marlane A. Liddell, Articles Ed. Articles on history, art, natural history, physical science, etc. Query with SASE.

SOAP OPERA DIGEST—254 W. 31st St., New York, NY 10001. Meredith R. Brown, Ed. Features, to 1,500 words, for people interested in daytime and nighttime soaps. Pays from $200 on acceptance. Query.

SOUTHERN EXPOSURE—P.O. Box 531, Durham, NC 27702. Michael Yellin, Ed. Investigative articles, in-depth reports and essays, 500 to 4,000 words, exploring civil rights and Black politics, nuclear power and utility reform, labor education and organizing, land use, and Southern women. Also uses short stories, 500 to 3,000 words, poetry and fillers. Pays from $50 to $250, on publication.

SPORTS ILLUSTRATED—Time/Life Bldg., New York, NY 10020. Myra Gelband, Articles Ed. Pieces, 1,000 to 2,000 words, on sports-related topics, with a regional tie-in. Limited free-lance market. Pays $500 to $1,000, on acceptance. Guidelines available. Query.

THE SPOTLIGHT—300 Independence Ave., S.E., Washington, DC 20003. Vincent J. Ryan, Man. Ed. Articles covering national and world polit-

569

ical affairs of type not appearing in the Establishment press. Pays on publication. Query required.

THE STAR—P.O. Box 2003, Tarrytown, NY 10591. Topical articles, 50 to 800 words, on human-interest subjects, show business, lifestyles, the sciences, etc., for family audience. Pays varying rates.

SUCCESS—342 Madison Ave., New York, NY 10175. Scott DeGarmo, Ed.-in-Chief. Profiles of successful individuals, executives; entrepreneurs; psychology, behavior, and motivation articles, 500 to 3,500 words. Columns on personal finance and health. Pays from $250, on acceptance. Query.

SUNDAY(formerly *Chicago Tribune Magazine*)—435 N. Michigan, Chicago, IL 60611. John Twohey, Ed. General-interest articles, to 3,000 words. Pays on publication. Query.

THE TIMES MAGAZINE—Army Times Publishing Co., Springfield, VA 22159-0200. Marianne Lester, Ed. Articles, to 3,000 words, on current military life. Photos. Pays $50 to $300, on publication.

TOASTMASTER—Box 10400, Santa Ana, CA 92711. Tamara Nunn, Ed. How-to articles, 1,000 to 3,000 words, for members of Toastmasters International, stressing communications, leadership, self-development, specific examples and illustrations. Pays $25 to $125, on acceptance. Query.

TOWN AND COUNTRY—1700 Broadway, New York, NY 10019. Kathryn Livington, Exec. Ed. Considers one-page proposals for articles only. Rarely buys unsolicited manuscripts.

TROPIC—*The Miami Herald,* One Herald Plaza, Miami, FL 33101. Kevin Hall, Ed. Essays and articles on current trends and issues, light or heavy, 1,000 to 4,000 words, for sophisticated audience. Pays $400 to $1,000, on publication. Query.

TV GUIDE—Radnor, PA 19088. Andrew Mills, Ass't Man. Ed. Short, light, brightly-written pieces about humorous or offbeat angles of television. Pays on acceptance. Query.

US—215 Lexington Ave., New York, NY 10016. Richard Sanders, Art. Ed. Non-entertainment features, human-interest stories, 1,200 to 1,500 words, with emphasis on dramatic, controversial or trendy. Pays $500, on publication. Query, with published clips.

VFW MAGAZINE—Broadway at 34th, Kansas City, MO 64111. Magazine for Veterans of Foreign Wars and their families. James K. Anderson, Ed. Articles, 1000 words, on current issues, solutions to everyday problems, personalities, sports, etc. How-to and historical pieces. Photos. Pays 5¢ to 10¢ a word, extra for photos, on acceptance.

VILLAGE VOICE—842 Broadway, New York, NY 10003. David Schneiderman, Ed.-in-Chief. Articles, 500 to 2,000 words, on current or controversial topics. Pays $75 to $350, on acceptance. Query.

VOGUE—350 Madison Ave., New York, NY 10017. Amy Gross, Features Ed. Articles, to 1,500 words, on women, entertainment and the arts, travel, medicine and health. General features, fiction. Rarely buys unsolicited manuscripts. Pays good rates, on acceptance.

WASHINGTON DOSSIER—3301 New Mexico Ave., NW, Washington, DC 20016. Don Oldenburg, Ed. Features with a Washington, D.C. slant. Sophisticated investigative pieces, personality profiles, service articles, etc., 1,000 to 2,500 words. Pays 10¢ to 20¢ a word, on acceptance. Query.

THE WASHINGTON MONTHLY—1711 Connecticut Ave., N.W., Washington, DC 20009. Charles Peters, Ed. Investigative articles, 1,500 to 5,000 words, on politics, government and the political culture. Pays 10¢ a word, on publication. Query.

WEEKDAY—20 N. Wacker Dr., Chicago, IL 60606. Informative articles, 200 to 1,000 words, on solutions to everyday problems: consumer affairs, legal and community issues, real estate, etc. Pays $20 to $50, on acceptance.

WEEKLY WORLD NEWS—600 S. East Coast Ave., Lantana, FL 33462. Joe West, Ed. Human-interest news pieces, about 500 to 1,000 words, involving human adventure, unusual situations, and off-beat stories from foreign countries. Pays $125 to $500, on publication.

WESTERN & EASTERN TREASURES—P.O. Box Z, Arcata, CA 95521. Rosemary Anderson, Man. Ed. Illustrated articles to 1,500 words, on treasure-hunting, rocks, and gems. Pays 2¢ a word, extra for photos, on publication.

WESTWAYS—Box 2890, Terminal Annex, Los Angeles, CA 90051. Mary Ann Cravens, Man. Ed. Articles, 1,000 to 1,500 words, and photo essays, on western U.S., Canada, and Mexico: history, contemporary living, travel, personalities, etc. Photos. Pays from 20¢ a word, extra for photos, 30 days before publication. Query.

WISCONSIN—*The Milwaukee Journal,* 333 W. State St., Milwaukee, WI 53201. Beth Slocum, Ed. Trend stories, essays, humor, personal-experience pieces, profiles, 500 to 2,000 words. Pays $100 to $500, after publication.

WOMAN'S DAY—1515 Broadway, New York, NY 10036. Rebecca Greer, Articles Ed. Articles, 500 to 3,500 words, on subjects of interest to women: marriage, education, family health, child rearing, money management, interpersonal relationships, changing lifestyles, etc. Dramatic first-person narratives about women who have experienced medical miracles or other triumphs. "Reflections": short, provocative personal essays, 1,000 to 1,500 words, humorous or serious, dealing with concerns of interest and relevance to women. Pays $2,000 for essays, top rates for articles, on acceptance.

WOMAN'S WORLD—177 N. Dean St., Englewood, NJ 07631. Janel Bladow, Articles Ed. Articles, 800 to 2,500 words, of interest to middle-income women between the ages of 18 and 60, on love, romance, careers, medicine, health, psychology, sex, travel, dramatic stories of adventure or crisis. Pays $300 to $1,000, on acceptance. Query.

WOODMEN OF THE WORLD MAGAZINE—1700 Farnam St., Omaha, NE 68102. Leland A. Larson, Ed. Articles on history, travel, sports, do-it-yourself projects, science, etc. Photos. Pays 5¢ a word, extra for photos, on acceptance.

WORKING WOMAN—342 Madison Ave., New York, NY 10173. Anne Mollegen Smith, Ed. Articles, 1,000 to 2,500 words, on business and personal aspects of working women's lives. Pays from $400, on acceptance.

YANKEE—Dublin, NH 03444. Judson D. Hale, Ed. Articles, to 3,000 words, with New England angle. Photos. Pays $100 to $700 (average $450 to $550), on acceptance.

LIFESTYLE, WOMEN'S AND GARDENING MAGAZINES

ALLIED PUBLICATIONS—P.O. Drawer 189, Palm Beach, FL 33480. Connie Dorval-Bernal, Ed. Articles, to 800 words, on business and technical careers, insurance, management, foreign travel, fashion, beauty and hairstyling. Photos; cartoons. Pays 5¢ per printed word, extra for photos and cartoons, on publication. Query.

AMERICAN BABY—575 Lexington Ave., New York, NY 10022. Judith Nolte, Ed. Articles, about 1,500 words, for new or expectant parents; pieces on child care. No poetry. Pays on acceptance.

THE AMERICAN ROSE MAGAZINE—P.O. Box 30,000, Shreveport, LA 71130. Harold S. Goldstein, Ed. Articles on home rose gardens: varieties, products, etc. Pays in copies.

AMERICANA—29 W. 38th St., New York, NY 10018. Michael Durham, Ed. Articles 1,000 to 2,000 words, with historical slant: restoration, crafts, food, antiques, travel, etc. Pays $350 to $500, on acceptance. Query.

BABY TALK—185 Madison Ave., New York, NY 10016. Patricia Irons, Ed. Articles, 1,500 to 3,000 words, by mother or father, on babies, baby care, etc. Pays varying rates, on acceptance. SASE required.

BEAUTY DIGEST—126 Fifth Ave., New York, NY 10011. Diane Robbens, Ed. Reprints of book and magazine pieces, 2,500 to 3,500 words, on beauty, health, exercise, self-help, for women. Pays varying rates, on publication.

BEST BUYS MAGAZINE—150 Fifth Ave., New York, NY 10011. Carol J. Richards, Ed. Articles, 950 to 1,700 words, that help consumers get the most value for their money. Pays $50 per published page, on publication. No manuscripts will be returned.

BETTER HOMES AND GARDENS—1716 Locust St., Des Moines, IA 50336. Doris Eby, Ed. Dir. Articles, to 2,000 words, on home and family entertainment, money management, health, travel, pets, and cars. Pays top rates, on acceptance. Query.

BON APPETIT—5900 Wilshire Blvd., Los Angeles, CA 90036. Barbara Varnum, Articles Ed. Articles on fine cooking, cooking classes, and kitchens. Query, with samples of published work. Pays varying rates, on acceptance.

BRIDE'S—350 Madison Ave., New York, NY 10017. Address Copy and Features Dept. Articles, 1,000 to 3,000 words, for engaged couples or newlyweds, on communication, sex, housing, finances, careers, health, babies, religion, in-laws, the marriage relationship. Pays $300 to $600, on acceptance.

CAPPER'S WEEKLY—616 Jefferson St., Topeka, KS 66607. Dorothy Harvey, Ed. Articles, 300 to 500 words: human interest, personal experience, historical. Poetry, to 15 lines, on nature, home, family. Novel-length fiction for serialization. Letters on women's interests, recipes, hints, for "Heart of the Home." Jokes. Children's section. Pays varying rates, on publication.

CHATELAINE—Maclean Hunter Bldg., 777 Bay St., Toronto, Ont., Canada M5W 1A7. Mildred Istona, Ed. Fiction, 3,000 words, on relationships, family and social themes. Articles, 3,000 words, on controversial subjects and personalities of interest to Canadian women. Pays $750 for personal-experience pieces, from $1,000 for articles and fiction, on acceptance.

CHRISTIAN HOME—Box 189, 1908 Grand Ave., Nashville, TN 37202. David Bradley, Ed. Articles on parenting, marriage and devotional life, 1,000 to 1,500 words, for couples and families. Pays 3½¢ to 4½¢ a word, on acceptance.

THE CHRISTIAN SCIENCE MONITOR—One Norway St., Boston, MA 02115. Katherine Fanning, Ed. Marilyn Gardner, Ed., Living/Children's pages.

Phyllis Hanes, Food Ed. Articles on lifestyle trends, women's rights, family, parenting, consumerism, fashion, and food. Pays varying rates, on acceptance.

COMPLETE WOMAN—1165 N. Clark, Chicago, IL 60610. Attn. Cheryl Jeska, Assoc. Ed. Articles, 500 to 1,500 words, with practical advice for women, on careers, health, personal relationships, etc. Inspirational profiles of successful women. Pays varying rates, on publication.

COSMOPOLITAN—224 W. 57th St., New York, NY 10019. Helen Gurley Brown, Ed. Guy Flatley, Man. Ed. Roberta Ashley, Exec. Ed. Betty Nichols Kelly, Fiction and Books Ed. Articles, to 4,000 words, and features, to 2,500 words, on issues affecting young career women. Fiction on male-female relationships: short shorts, 1,500 to 3,000 words; short stories, 4,000 to 6,000 words; mystery and other novels; condensed books, 30,000 words. Pays from $1,500 for full-length articles, $650 to $1,000 for short stories, $300 to $600 for short shorts, on acceptance.

COUNTRY LIVING—224 W. 57th St., New York, NY 10019. Rachel Newman, Ed. Short articles and photographic stories, on decorating houses in the country style, country crafts, antiques, and lifestyle. Articles pay $200 to $300, on acceptance.

CREATIVE IDEAS FOR LIVING (formerly *Decorating and Craft Ideas*)—P.O. Box 2522, Birmingham, AL 35201. Katherine Pearson, Ed. Feature articles, 700 to 1,000 words, on good-quality creative projects, decorating, and personality pieces for the "Life in Crafts" department. Pays from $350, after acceptance. Query.

DECORATING AND CRAFT IDEAS—See *Creative Ideas for Living.*

ESSENCE—1500 Broadway, New York, NY 10036. Susan L. Taylor, Ed.-in-Chief. Provocative articles, 1,500 to 3,000 words, about black women in America today: self-help and how-to pieces; celebrity profiles. Short items, 500 to 750 words, on work and health. Fiction, 1,500 to 3,000 words. No unsolicited poetry. Pays varying rates, on acceptance. Query for articles.

THE EXECUTIVE FEMALE—120 E. 56th St., Suite 1440, New York, NY 10022. Susan Strecker, Man. Ed. Features, 6 to 12 pages, on investment, money-savers, career advancement, etc., for executive women. Articles, 6 to 8 pages, for "More Money," "Horizons," "Profiles," and "Entrepreneur's Corner." Pays varying rates, on publication. Limited freelance market.

FAMILY CIRCLE—488 Madison Ave., New York, NY 10022. Gay Bryant, Ed.-in-Chief. Margaret Jaworski, Articles Ed. Jamie Raab, Fiction Ed. Nicole Gregory, Books and Nonfiction Ed. Eleanore Lewis, Poetry Ed. Articles, to 2,500 words, on home and money management, marriage, family, child-rearing, consumer affairs, social and political issues, health and fitness, food, gardening, travel, humor, etc. Query required. Family-oriented short fiction, to 2,500 words, that involves real-life situations, and has an interesting, fanciful, or philosophical viewpoint. Short shorts, 2 pages. Poetry, nostalgic and seasonal verse, to 20 lines. Pays good rates, on acceptance. Enclose SASE with all material submitted.

THE FAMILY FOOD GARDEN—464 Commonwealth Ave., Boston, MA 02215. Robert Fibkins, Ed. Practical articles, with photos, on home gardening, garden living, and cooking.

THE FAMILY HANDYMAN—1999 Shepard Rd., St. Paul, MN 55116. Semi-technical articles, to 1,000 words, with photos, on do-it-yourself home improvement, maintenance and repair, plus how-to features on projects around the home. Pays varying rates, on acceptance.

FAMILY JOURNAL—P.O. Box 6024, Columbia, MO 65205. Kathleen Horrigan, Submissions Ed. Practical and anecdotal articles on parenting, from pregnancy through age 8. Pays negotiable rates. Send for guidelines.

FAMILY WEEKLY—1515 Broadway, New York, NY 10036. Thomas Plate, Editor. Kate White, Exec. Ed. Tim Mulligan, Man. Ed. Short, lively articles on prominent individuals, health, medicine, money management and family advice. Pays $200 to $500, on acceptance. Query.

FARM & RANCH LIVING—5400 S. 60th St., Greendale, WI 53129. Bob Ottum, Man. Ed. Articles, 2,000 words, on rural people and situations; nostalgia pieces, profiles of interesting farms and farmers, ranches and ranchers. Poetry. Pays $15 to $400, on acceptance and on publication.

FARM WOMAN NEWS—P.O. Box 643, Milwaukee, WI 53201. Ruth C. Benedict, Man. Ed. Personal-experience, humor, service-oriented articles, and how-to features, to 1,000 words, of interest to farm and ranch women. Pays $40 to $250, on publication.

FARMSTEAD MAGAZINE—Box 111, Freedom, ME 04941. Lynn Ann Ascrizzi, Sen. Ed. Articles, 700 to 4,000 words, on organic home gardening, farming methods for small farms, livestock and marketing for the small farmer, self-reliant lifestyles, and homestyle recipes. Pays 5¢ a word, on publication. Query preferred.

FEELING GREAT—45 W. 34th St., New York, NY 10001. Jane Collins, Assoc. Ed. Articles, 800 words or 1,500 to 2,000 words, on health, fitness, diet, psychology, beauty, fashion, and women's issues. "We like our articles to have an upbeat, positive flavor, but we do not shrink from difficult problems and issues." Pays 25¢ a word, on acceptance. Magazine is associated with the Elaine Powers health and fitness organization.

FLARE—777 Bay St., Toronto, Ont., Canada M5W 1A7. Jane Hess, Assoc. Ed. Service articles, 1,500 to 3,000 words, on health, careers, relationships, and contemporary problems, for Canadian women aged 18 to 34. Profiles, 750 to 1,500 words, of up-and-coming Canadians. Pays on acceptance. Query.

FLOWER AND GARDEN MAGAZINE—4251 Pennsylvania, Kansas City, MO 64111. Rachel Snyder, Ed.-in-Chief. How-to articles, to 1,200 words, with photos, on indoor and outdoor home gardening. Pays 7¢ a word, on acceptance. Query preferred.

FRIENDLY EXCHANGE—1999 Shepard Rd., St. Paul, MN 55116. Adele Malott, Ed. Features, 1,000 to 2,500 words, for young traditional family members between ages 19 and 39 living in the western half of the U.S. Subjects include sports, outdoors, domestic travel, family activities, heritage, culture, consumer information, personal finance. How-to's on decorating and gardening. Must have western tie-in. No poetry, fiction, cartoons. Photos. Pays $300 to $700, extra for photos. Query preferred. Send for writer's guidelines and sample copy.

GARDEN—The Garden Society, Botanical Garden, Bronx, NY 10458. Ann Botshon, Ed. Articles, 500 to 2,500 words, on botany, horticulture, ecology, agriculture. Photos. Pays to $300, on publication. Query.

GARDENS FOR ALL NEWS—180 Flynn Ave., Burlington, VT 05401.

574

Ruth W. Page, Ed. How-to articles on food gardens and orchards, general-interest pieces for gardeners, 300 to 3,000 words. Pays $15 to $300, extra for photos, on acceptance. Query preferred.

GLAMOUR—350 Madison Ave., New York, NY 10017. Ruth Whitney, Ed.-in-Chief. Barbara Coffey, Man. Ed. Rona Cherry, Exec. Ed. Janet Chan, Articles Ed. How-to articles, from 1,500 words, on careers, health, psychology, interpersonal relationships, etc., for women aged 18 to 35. Fashion and beauty pieces staff-written. Pays from $1,000.

GOOD HOUSEKEEPING—959 Eighth Ave., New York, NY 10019. Joan Thursh, Articles Ed. Naome Lewis, Fiction Ed. In-depth articles and features on controversial problems, topical social issues; dramatic personal narratives with unusual experiences of average families; sharply-angled pieces about celebrities, 1,200 to 5,000 words. Ideas on subjects of practical interest to women for "Better Way." Short stories, 2,000 to 5,000 words, with strong identification for women, by published writers and "beginners with demonstrable talent." Pays top rates, on acceptance.

GROWING CHILD/GROWING PARENT—22 N. Second St., Lafayette, IN 47902. Nancy Kleckner, Ed. Articles to 1,500 words on subjects of interest to parents of children under 6, with emphasis on infant and toddler years. No first-time birth experiences, no poetry. How-to and information articles preferred. Pays 15¢ a word, on acceptance. Send SASE for writers' guidelines. Query.

THE HERB QUARTERLY—Box 275, Newfane, VT 05345. Articles from 1,500 words, on herbs: practical uses, cultivation, gourmet cooking, landscaping, herb tradition, unique garden designs, profiles of herb garden experts, practical how-to's for the herb businessperson. Include garden design when possible. Pays on publication. Send for writers' guidelines.

HOME MAGAZINE—140 E. 45th St., New York, NY 10017. Olivia Buehl, Ed. Articles of interest to homeowners: remodeling, decorating, how-to, project ideas and instructions, taxes, insurance, conservation and solar energy. Pays varying rates, on acceptance. Query, with 50- to 200-word summary.

THE HOMEOWNER—149 Fifth Ave., New York, NY 10010. Jim Liston, Ed. Articles, 500 to 1,500 words, with photos, on do-it-yourself home improvement and remodeling projects. Pays $100 to $150 per printed page, on acceptance. Query.

HORTICULTURE—755 Boylston St., Boston, MA 02116. Steven Krauss, Man. Ed. Authoritative, well-written articles, 1,500 to 3,000 words, on all aspects of gardening and horticulture. Pays competitive rates. Query first.

HOUSE & GARDEN—350 Madison Ave., New York, NY 10017. Louis O. Gropp, Ed.-in-Chief. Denise Otis, Martin Filler, Co-Eds. Articles on decorating, architecture, gardening, the arts. Query; rarely buys unsolicited manuscripts.

HOUSE BEAUTIFUL—1700 Broadway, New York, NY 10019. Carol Cooper Garey, Senior Copy Ed. Service articles related to the home. Pieces on beauty, travel and gardening mostly staff-written. Pays varying rates, on acceptance. Send for writer's guidelines. Query with detailed outline. SASE required.

HOUSTON HOME & GARDEN—5615 Kirby, Suite 600, P.O. Box 25386, Houston, TX 77265. Joetta Moulden, Ed. Articles on interior design, regional gardening, cooking, household repairs, etc. Pays $2.50 per column inch, on publication. Limited freelance market. Query.

LADIES' HOME JOURNAL—3 Park Ave., New York, NY 10016. Myrna Blyth, Ed. Articles of interest to women. Send queries with outlines to Jan Goodwin, Sandra Forsyth Enos, Ex. Eds. Fiction and poetry accepted through literary agents only. Books, fiction, poetry editor: Constance Leisure.

LADYCOM—1732 Wisconsin Ave., N.W., Washington, DC 20007. Sheila Gibbons, Ed. Articles, 800 to 2,000 words for military wives in the U.S. and overseas, on lifestyles; pieces on issues of interest to military families; fiction. Pays $75 to $500, after acceptance. Query.

LADY'S CIRCLE—23 W. 26th St., New York, NY 10010. Rose Marshall, Ed. Articles, 2,000 to 3,000 words, with photos, on "how-to" needlework and crafts, hobbies, "do-gooders," child care, home management, diet, women's health issues, women with home businesses, and people overcoming handicaps. Fiction, to 2,000 words, Pays $125, extra for photos, on publication. Query with outline.

LIVING SINGLE—40 S. Third St., Columbus, OH 43215. Jim O'Connor, Senior Ed. Timely, topical and well-researched features, 700 to 3,000 words, on the improvement of all aspects of single life. No humor, poetry or first-person material. Pays competitive rates, on acceptance.

LUTHERAN WOMEN—2900 Queen Ln., Philadelphia, PA 19129. Terry Schutz, Ed. Articles, with photos, on subjects of interest to Christian women. No recipes, homemaking hints. Fiction, 1,000 to 2,000 words, on personal growth and change. Short poems. Pays to $50 for articles, $35 to $40 for fiction, on publication.

McCALL'S—230 Park Ave., New York, NY 10169. Robert Stein, Ed. Articles, 1,000 to 3,000 words, on current issues, human interest, family relationships. Short stories, to 3,000 words, on contemporary themes, for intelligent women. Short shorts, 2,000 words. Pays top rates, on acceptance.

MADEMOISELLE—350 Madison Ave., New York, NY 10017. Kate White, Articles Ed. Eileen Schnurr, Fiction Ed. Articles, 1,200 to 2,500 words. Fiction, 2,500 to 4,000 words, for young women. Pays from $350 for articles, from $1,000 for fiction, on acceptance.

MANHATTAN COOPERATOR—23 Leonard St., 3rd Floor, New York, NY 10013. Victoria A. Chesler, Ed.-in-Chief. Articles, 750 to 1,000 words, on subjects related to co-op and condo ownership—from taxation, new legislation, management and maintenance, to interior design, weekend diversions, travel, food and wine. Pays $50 to $175.

METROPOLITAN HOME—750 Third Ave., New York, NY 10017. Charla A. Lawhon, Asst. Man. Ed. "We use articles for the following departments: Collecting (subjects should relate to home design—collectibles that can be used); Real Estate and Equity (news in mortgages, home financing, other home-oriented money matters); Object Lessons (our 'buymanship' column. In the past, we've covered how to buy whirlpools, what to look for when buying a telephone, how to find the perfect restaurant stove); Wine and Spirits. Article lengths vary from 800 to 1,500 words, and payment (made on acceptance) is commensurate with the length and subject of the article. Query first."

MODERN BRIDE—One Park Ave., New York, NY 10016. Mary Ann Cavlin, Man. Ed. Articles, from 1,500 words, for bride and groom, on wedding planning, financial planning, juggling career and home, etc. Pays on acceptance.

THE MOTHER EARTH NEWS—105 Stoney Mountain Rd., Hendersonville, NC 28791. Bruce Woods, Ed. Articles on alternative lifestyles for rural and urban readers: home improvements, new ideas in cost- and energy-efficient housing, how-to's, indoor and outdoor gardening, crafts and projects, innovative self-employment and supplementary income enterprises, etc. Also self-help, health, food-related, ecology, energy, and consumerism pieces; profiles. Pays from $100 per published page, on acceptance. Query first; address Roselyn Edwards, Submissions Ed.

MS. MAGAZINE—119 W. 40th St., New York, NY 10018. Address Manuscript Editor, specify fiction, nonfiction, or poetry. Articles relating to women's roles and changing lifestyles, general interest, self-help, how-to, profiles; fiction. Pays varying rates; on acceptance. Query. Accepts very little free-lance material.

NEW AGE—342 Western Ave., Brighton, MA 02135. Articles, for readers interested in self-development and awareness, on natural foods, holistic health, education, disarmament, etc. Fiction, 1,200 to 4,000 words. Poetry. Pays from 10¢ a word, on publication. Query preferred.

NEW BODY—888 Seventh Ave., New York, NY 10106. Judy Jones, Ed. Lively, readable, service-oriented articles, 1,000 to 2,000 words, by writers with background in health field: exercise, nutrition, and diet pieces for men and women aged 18 to 35. Pays $250 to $500, on publication. Query preferred.

THE NEW CLEVELAND WOMAN JOURNAL—106 E. Bridge St., Cleveland, OH 44017. Linda Kinsey, Ed. Articles, 1,200 words, "geared to the upwardly mobile woman. We want fresh material with an emphasis on Cleveland—not the old, tired subjects of 'how to dress for success' and how to manage a two-income family." Pays $2.50 per column inch, on publication.

NEW WOMAN—205 Lexington Ave., New York, NY 10016. Pat Miller, Editor/Publisher. "The most important thing for writers is to read the magazine to become familiar with our needs before querying. Articles on new lifestyles. Features on financial advice, legal advice, careers, marriage, relationships, surviving divorce, diets and health. Pays varying rates, on publication. Query.

1001 HOME IDEAS—3 Park Ave., New York, NY 10016. Anne Anderson, Ed.-in-Chief. General-interest articles, 500 to 2,000 words, on home decorating, furnishings, antiques and collectibles, remodeling, gardening. How-to and problem-solving decorating pieces. Pays varying rates, on acceptance. Query.

ORGANIC GARDENING—33 E. Minor St., Emmaus, PA 18049. M. C. Goldman, Exec. Ed. Articles, to 2,500 words, for organic gardeners: building soil, growing food plants, new developments in horticulture, plant breeding, etc. Pieces on energy conservation and health, for "Organic Living," on food preparation, storage, and equipment, for "Gardeners' Kitchen." Photos. Pays to $750, extra for photos, on acceptance. Query.

PARENTS—685 Third Ave., New York, NY 10017. Elizabeth Crow, Ed.-in-Chief. Articles, 2,000 to 3,000 words, on growth and development of infants, children, teens; family; women's issues; community; current research. Informal style with quotes from experts. Pays from $300, on acceptance. Query.

PLAYGIRL—3420 Ocean Park Blvd., Santa Monica, CA 90405. Vanda Krefft, Articles Ed. In-depth articles, 2,500 to 3,000 words, for contemporary women. Fiction, 1,000 to 3,000 words. Humor; satire. Payment negotiable. Query.

REDBOOK—224 W. 57th St., New York, NY 10019. Annette Capone, Ed.-in-Chief. Kathy Sagan, Fiction Ed. Susan Edmiston, Articles Ed. Fiction and articles for young women. Pays from $1,000 for short stories; $850 for short shorts, 1,400 to 1,600 words. Pays $750 for personal-experience pieces, 1,000 to 2,000 words, on solving problems in marriage, family life, or community, for "Young Mother's Story." SASE required. Query for articles and fiction over 12,000 words.

SAVVY—111 Eighth Ave., New York, NY 10011. Wendy Reid Crisp, Ed. Service articles for women executives, 500 to 3,000 words, on business politics, finance, entrepreneurs. Pays $300 to $1,500, on publication. Query.

SELF—350 Madison Ave., New York, NY 10017. Phyllis Starr Wilson, Ed. Articles for women of all ages, with strong how-to slant, on self-development. Pays from $750, on acceptance. Query.

SLIMMER—3420 Ocean Park Blvd., Santa Monica, CA 90405. Angela Hynes, Ed. Articles, 2,500 to 3,000 words, and columns, 1,000 words, on beauty, skin care, diet, exercise, fashion, and sports, for women aged 18 to 35. Pays $300 to $350 for features, $100 for columns, 30 days after acceptance. Query.

SOMA—1201 E. Atlantic Blvd., Pompano Beach, FL 33060. Judy Goldstein, Ed. Nutritionally-oriented articles for women aged 35 to 50, on beauty, sex, preventative aging, and diet. Also sensational topics of interest to women. Pays $200 to $400, thirty days after acceptance. Query with published clips.

SUNDAY WOMAN—235 E. 45th St., New York, NY 10017. Merry Clark, Ed. Articles, 1,500 to 2,000 words, for women: celebrities, health, topical issues, families, lifestyles, relationships, money management, careers, women entrepreneurs, success stories of women in business. Pays from $150 to $500, $50 for reprints, on acceptance. Query.

TODAY'S CHRISTIAN PARENT—8121 Hamilton Ave., Cincinnati, OH 45231. Mildred Mast, Ed. Informative, inspirational or humorous articles, 600 to 1,200 words, on application of Christian principles in marriage, child-rearing, pleasures and problems of parenting, and adult family relationships. Timely articles on relevant issues, from a Christian perspective. Pays varying rates, on acceptance. SASE required.

TOWN & COUNTRY—1700 Broadway, New York, NY 10019. Arnold Ehrlich, Ed. Dir. Limited free-lance market; considers one-page proposals for articles only.

VIRTUE—P.O. Box 850, Sisters, OR 97759. Lee Zanon, Ed. Articles, 1,000 to 1,500 words, on the family, marriage, self-esteem, working mothers, food, decorating; profiles of Christian women. Fiction. Pays 7¢ per word, on publication.

VOGUE—350 Madison Ave., New York, NY 10017. Amy Gross, Features Ed. Articles, to 1,500 words, on women, entertainment and the arts, travel, medicine and health. Fiction, 500 to 4,000 words. Sometimes buys unsolicited manuscripts. Pays good rates, on acceptance.

WEIGHT WATCHERS MAGAZINE—360 Lexington Ave., New York, NY 10017. Linda Konner, Ed.-in-Chief. Psychological pieces, 1,200 to 1,500 words, on weight control, health and nutrition, and inspirational success stories. (Send success stories to Trisha Thompson, Assoc. Ed.) Pays from $250, after acceptance.

WOMAN—1115 Broadway, New York, NY 10010. Sherry Amatenstein, Ed. Personal-experience pieces, 1,000 to 2,000 words, for single women who want to better their relationships, careers or lifestyles. Short interviews with successful women for "Woman in the News," and "Bravo Woman." Pays $25 to $125, on acceptance. Query.

WOMAN'S DAY—1515 Broadway, New York, NY 10036. Rebecca Greer, Articles Ed. Eileen Herbert Jordan, Fiction Ed. Serious, human-interest or humorous articles, to 3,500 words, on marriage, child-rearing, health, relationships, money management, leisure activities, etc. Provocative personal essays, 1,000 to 5,000 words, humorous or serious, for "Reflections." Quality short stories. Pays top rates, on acceptance. Query for articles.

WOMAN'S WORLD—P. O. Box 6700, Englewood, NJ 07631. Janel Bladow, Articles Ed. Elinor Nauen, Fiction Ed. Articles, 800 to 2,500 words, of interest to middle-income women aged 18 to 60, on love, romance, careers, medicine, health, psychology, sex, travel, etc. Fast-moving short stories, 4,500 to 5,000 words, with light romantic theme. Mini-mysteries, 1,500 to 1,700 words, with "whodunit" or "howdunit" theme. No science fiction, fantasy, or historical romance. Pays $300 to $1,000 for articles; $1,000 for short stories, $500 for mini-mysteries, on acceptance.

WOMEN IN BUSINESS—9100 Ward Parkway, Box 8728, Kansas City, MO 64114. Sharon K. Tiley, Ed. American Business Women's Assn. Features, 1,000 to 1,500 words, for working women between 35 and 55 years. No profiles. Pays on acceptance. Written query preferred.

WOMEN'S CIRCLE—Box 428, Seabrook, NH 03874. Marjorie Pearl, Ed. Articles on crafts, hobbies, money-saving projects and other subjects of interest to homemakers. Pays varying rates, on acceptance.

WOMEN'S CIRCLE HOME COOKING—Box 1952, Brooksville, FL 33512. Barbara Hall Pedersen, Ed. Food-related articles, to 1,200 words; humorous fiction, to 400 words. Pays to 5¢ a word, on publication.

WOMEN'S SPORTS AND FITNESS—310 Town and Country Village, Palo Alto, CA 94301. Amy Rennert, Ed. How-to's, profiles, and sports reports, 500 to 2,500 words, for the active woman. Health, fitness, and sports pieces. Photos. Pays from $25, on publication.

THE WORKBASKET—4251 Pennsylvania, Kansas City, MO 64111. Roma Jean Rice, Ed. Instructions and models for original knit, crochet, and tat items. How-to's on crafts and gardening, 400 to 1,200 words, with photos. Pays 7¢ a word for articles, extra for photos, on acceptance; negotiable rates for instructional items.

WORKBENCH—4251 Pennsylvania, Kansas City, MO 64111. Jay W. Hedden, Ed. Illustrated how-to-articles on home improvement and do-it-yourself projects, with detailed instructions, energy conservation and alternatives, manufactured housing. Pays from $125 per printed page, on acceptance. Send SASE for writers' guidelines.

WORKING MOTHER—230 Park Ave., New York, NY 10169. Vivian Cadden, Ed. Well-thought-out articles, 1,500 to 2,000 words, for working mothers; child care, home management, the work world, single mothers, etc. Pays around $500, on acceptance. Query, with detailed outline.

WORKING WOMAN—342 Madison Ave., New York, NY 10173. Jacqueline Giambanco, Ex. Ed. "We're focusing more and more on the business/professional woman, and run articles on all aspects of management and finance. Other subjects we're interested in: computers, corporate fashion, business travel and the office. We also run profiles of successful businesswomen and small businesses, as well as pieces on unusual lifestyles of working women, and some leisure topics. No poetry, fiction, or humorous pieces. Query first." Pays from $400, on acceptance, for 1,000- to 2,500-word articles.

YOUR HOME MAGAZINE—P.O. Box 2315, Ogden, UT 84404. Peggie Bingham, Ed. Upbeat articles, 800 to 1,000 words, with color transparencies, for renters and homeowners, on renovating, decorating, remodeling; garden/patio/outdoor articles; short home/garden humor pieces. Bridal section needs bridal etiquette, traditions, fashion, beginning entertaining, etc. Pays 15¢ a word, $35 for color photos, on acceptance. Query with SASE.

SPORTS, FITNESS, RECREATION, AUTOMOTIVE, CONSERVATION, AND OUTDOOR MAGAZINES

AAA WORLD—1999 Shepard Rd., St. Paul, MN 55116. Dick Schaaf, Ed. Auto safety, driving and general travel pieces, 750 to 1,500 words. Pays $300 to $600, on acceptance. Query preferred.

AERO—P.O. Box 6050, Mission Viejo, CA 92690. Dennis Shattuck, Ed. Factual articles, 1,000 to 4,000 words with photos, on subjects relating to aircraft ownership, use, and piloting. Pays $75 to $250, on publication. Query.

THE AMATEUR BOXER—P.O. Box 249, Cobalt, CT 06414. Bob Taylor, Ed. Articles on amateur boxing. Fillers. Photos. Pays $10 to $40, extra for photos, on publication. Query preferred.

THE AMERICAN FIELD—222 W. Adams St., Chicago, IL 60606. William F. Brown, Ed. Yarns about hunting trips, bird-shooting; articles to 1,500 words, on dogs and field trials, emphasizing conservation of game resources. Pays varying rates, on acceptance.

AMERICAN FORESTS—1319 18th St., N.W., Washington, DC 20036. Bill Rooney, Ed. Well-documented articles, to 2,000 words, with photos, on outdoors, stressing recreational and commercial use of forests. Photos. Pays on acceptance.

AMERICAN HANDGUNNER—Suite 200, 591 Camino de la Reina, San Diego, CA 92108. Cameron Hopkins, Ed. Semi-technical articles on shooting sports, gun repair and alteration, handgun matches and tournaments, for lay readers. Pays $100 to $500, on publication. Query.

AMERICAN HUNTER—1600 Rhode Island Ave. N.W., Washington, DC 20036. Mike Hanback, Man. Ed. Articles, 1,400 to 2,000 words, on hunting. Photos. Pays on acceptance.

AMERICAN MOTORCYCLIST—American Motorcyclist Assn., Box 141, Westerville, OH 43081. Greg Harrison, Ed. Articles and fiction, to 3,000 words, on motorcycling: news coverage, personalities, tours. Photos. Pays varying rates, on publication. Query.

THE AMERICAN RIFLEMAN—1600 Rhode Island Ave., N.W., Washington, D.C. 20036. Bill Parkerson, Ed. Factual articles on use and enjoyment of sporting firearms. Pays on acceptance.

ARCHERY WORLD—11812 Wayzata Blvd., Suite 100, Minnetonka, MN 55343. Richard Sapp, Ed. Articles, 1,000 to 2,000 words, on all aspects of bowhunting and target archery, with photos. Pays from $100, extra for photos, on publication.

THE ATLANTIC SALMON JOURNAL—1435 St. Alexandre, Suite 1030, Montreal, Quebec, Canada H3A 2G4. Joanne Eidinger. Material related to Atlantic salmon—conservation, ecology, politics, etc. Fiction (1,500 words), articles, (1,500 to 3,000 words), and short fillers and poetry (50 to 100 words). Pays $100 to $450, on publication.

BACKPACKER MAGAZINE—One Park Ave., New York, NY 10016. John A. Delves, Ed. Articles, 250 to 3,000 words, on backpacking, technique, kayaking/canoeing, mountaineering, alpine/nordic skiing, health, natural science. Photos. Pays varying rates. Query.

THE BACKSTRETCH—19363 James Couzens Hwy., Detroit, MI 48235. Ruth LeGrove, Man. Ed. United Thoroughbred Trainers of America. Feature articles, with photos, on persons involved with thoroughbred horses. Pays after publication.

BASEBALL ILLUSTRATED—*See Hockey Illustrated.*

BASKETBALL ANNUAL—*See Hockey Illustrated.*

BASSMASTER MAGAZINE— B.A.S.S. Publications, P.O. Box 17900, Montgomery, AL 36141. Bob Cobb, Ed. Articles, 1,700 to 2,100 words, with photos, on freshwater black bass and striped bass. "Short Casts" pieces, 400 to 800 words, on news, views, and items of interest. Pays $100 to $350, on acceptance. Query.

BAY & DELTA YACHTSMAN—2019 Clement Ave., Alameda, CA 94501. Dave Preston, Man. Ed. Humorous features, satire and cruising stories. Must have Northern California tie-in. Photos and illustrations. Pays varying rates.

BC OUTDOORS—#202, 1132 Hamilton St., Vancouver, B.C., Canada V6B 2S2. Henry L. Frew, Ed. Articles, to 1,500 words, on fishing, hunting, conservation and all forms of non-competitive outdoor recreation in British Columbia, Alberta, and Yukon. Photos. Pays from 10¢ to 15¢ a word, extra for photos, on acceptance.

BICYCLING—33 E. Minor St., Emmaus, PA 18049. James C. McCullagh, Ed. Articles, 500 to 2,500 words, on recreational riding, commuting, equipment, and touring, for serious cyclists. Photos; humor. Pays $25 to $400, on publication. Query. Guidelines available.

BIKEREPORT—P.O. Box 8308, Missoula, MT 59807. Daniel D'Ambrosio, Ed. Accounts of bicycle tours in the U.S., personal–experience pieces, interviews, humor, and news shorts, 800 to 1,500 words. Pays $25 to $65 per published page. Query.

BILLIARDS DIGEST—875 N. Michigan Ave., Chicago, IL 60611. Michael Panozzo, Ed. Trade and consumer articles, 1,200 to 2,000 words with photos, on billiards. Pays $100 to $150, on publication.

BIRD WATCHER'S DIGEST—P.O. Box 110, Marietta, OH 45750. Mary B. Bowers, Ed. Articles, 600 to 2,500 words, for bird watchers: first-person accounts; how-to's; pieces on endangered species; profiles. Poetry, cartoons, fillers. Pays to $50 for articles, $25 for reprints, $5 for fillers, $10 for cartoons, $10 for poetry, on publication.

BOATING—One Park Ave., New York, NY 10016. Roy Attaway, Ed. Illustrated articles, 1,000 to 2,000 words, on power boating. Pays good rates, on acceptance. Query.

BOW & ARROW—Box HH, 34249 Camino Capistrano, Capistrano Beach, CA 92624. Jack Lewis, Ed. Articles, 1,200 to 2,500 words, with photos, on bowhunting, field and target archery; profiles and technical pieces. Pays $50 to $200, on acceptance. Same address and requirements for *Gun World*.

BOWHUNTER MAGAZINE—3150 Mallard Cove La., Fort Wayne, IN 46804. M. R. James, Ed. Adventure and how-to-articles, 500 to 5,000 words, on bow and arrow hunting. Photos. Pays $25 to $250 and up, on acceptance.

BOWLERS JOURNAL—875 N. Michigan Ave., Chicago, IL 60611. Mort Luby, Ed. Trade and consumer articles, 1,200 to 2,000 words, with photos, on bowling. Pays $75 to $200, on acceptance.

BOWLING—5301 S. 76th St., Greendale, WI 53129. Rory Gillespie, Ed. Articles, to 1,500 words, on amateur league and tournament bowling. Profiles. Pays varying rates, on publication.

CAR AND DRIVER—2002 Hogback Rd., Ann Arbor, MI 48104. David E. Davis, Jr., Ed. Articles, to 2,500 words, for enthusiasts, on car manufacturers, new developments in cars, etc. Pays to $1,500, on acceptance.

CAR CRAFT—8490 Sunset Blvd., Los Angeles, CA 90069. Jeff Smith, Ed. Articles and photofeatures on unusual street machines, drag cars, racing events; technical pieces; action photos. Pays from $150 per page, on publication.

CASCADES EAST—716 N.E. 4th St., P.O. Box 5784, Bend, OR 97708. Geoff Hill, Ed./Publisher. Articles, 1,000 to 2,000 words, on outdoor activities (fishing, hunting, backpacking, rafting, skiing, snowmobiling, etc.), history, and scenic tours in Cascades region of Oregon. Photos. Pays 3¢ to 7¢ a word, extra for photos, on publication.

CHESAPEAKE BAY MAGAZINE—1819 Bay Ridge Ave., Annapolis, MD 21403. Betty Rigoli, Ed. Technical and how-to articles, to 1,500 words, on boating, fishing, conservation, in Chesapeake Bay. Photos. Pays $65 to $85, extra for cover photos, on publication.

CITY SPORTS MONTHLY—P.O. Box 3693, San Francisco, CA 94119. Maggie Cloherty, Ed. Articles, 1,700 to 3,000 words, for active Californians. Pays $175 to $325, on publication. Query.

CONNECTICUT RIDING—*See Northeast Riding.*

CORVETTE FEVER—Box 55532, Ft. Washington, MD 20744. Pat Stivers, Ed. Articles, 500 to 2,500 words, on Corvette repairs, swap meets, and personalities. Corvette-related fiction, about 700 lines, and fillers. Photos. Pays 10¢ a word, on publication.

CRUISING WORLD—524 Thames St., Newport, RI 02840. George Day, Ed. Articles on sailing, 1,000 to 3,000 words: technical and personal narratives. No fiction, poetry, or logbook transcripts. 35mm slides. Pays $100 to $1,000, on acceptance. Query.

CYCLE MAGAZINE—780-A Lakefield Rd., Westlake Village, CA 91361. Allyn Fleming, Man. Ed. Articles, 6 to 20 manuscript pages, on motorcycle races, history, touring, technical pieces; profiles. Photos. Pays on publication. Query.

CYCLE WORLD—1499 Monrovia Ave., Newport Beach, CA 92663. Paul Dean, Ed. Technical and feature articles, 1,500 to 2,500 words, for motorcycle enthusiasts. Photos. Pays $100 to $200 per page, on publication. Query.

CYCLING U.S.A.—P.O. Box 1069, Nevada City, CA 95959. Jim McFadden, Ed. Articles and features on bicycle racing. Pays up to $150 for 850 words, extra for photos, on publication. Query for special assignments.

CYCLIST—20916 Higgins Ct., Torrance, CA 90501. John Francis, Ed. Articles on all aspects of bicycling: touring, travel and equipment, and fiction, 1,000 to 2,000 words; fillers; profiles. Pays to 50¢ a word, on acceptance.

THE DIVER—P.O. Box 249, Cobalt, CT 06414. Bob Taylor, Ed. Articles on technique, training tips, for coaches, officials, divers. Photos. Pays $15 to $20, extra for photos, $3 to $5 for cartoons, on publication.

DIVER MAGAZINE—#210, 1807 Maritime Mews, Granville Island, Vancouver, B.C., Canada V6H 3W7. Neil McDaniel, Ed. Articles, 1,000 to 2,000 words, on aquatic life, diving equipment, technology, dive sites, diving medicine, underwater photography, commercial and scientific diving. Fiction; humor. Photos. Pays $2.50 per column inch, extra for photos, on publication. Query.

EASTERN BASKETBALL—Eastern Basketball Publications, West Hempstead, NY 11552. Rita Napolitano, Man. Ed. Articles on college and high school basketball in the Northeast. Pays $70, on publication. Query.

FIELD & STREAM—1515 Broadway, New York, NY 10036. Duncan Barnes, Ed. Articles, 2,000 to 3,000 words, with photos, on hunting, fishing, camping, conservation. Fillers, 350 to 900 words, for "How It's Done." Cartoons. Pays from $500 for articles with photos, $250 to $350 for fillers, $100 for cartoons, on acceptance. Query on articles.

FISHING WORLD—51 Atlantic Ave., Floral Park, NY 11001. Keith Gardner, Ed. Features, to 2,500 words, with photos, on fishing sites, technique, equipment. Pays $300 for major features, $25 to $100 for shorter articles. Query preferred.

THE FLORIDA HORSE—P.O. Box 2106, Ocala, FL 32678. F. J. Audette, Publisher. Articles, 1,500 words, on Florida thoroughbred breeding and racing. Pays $100 to $150, on publication.

FLY FISHERMAN—Box 8200, Harrisburg, PA 17105. John Randolph, Ed. Articles, to 3,000 words, on how to and where to fly fish. Fillers, to 100 words. Pays from $35 to $400, on acceptance. Query.

FLYING MAGAZINE—One Park Ave., New York, NY 10016. Richard Collins, Ed. Articles, 1,500 words, on personal flying experiences. Pays varying rates, on acceptance. Study issues of magazine before submitting. SASE required.

FOUR WHEELER—21216 Vanowen, Canoga Park, CA 91303. Dianne Jacob, Exec. Ed. Adventurous articles, technical pieces, related to four wheeling. Coverage of four-wheel drive events. Photos must accompany articles. Pays varying rates, on publication.

FUR-FISH-GAME—2878 E. Main St., Columbus, OH 43209. Ken Dunwoody, Ed. Illustrated articles, 800 to 2,500 words, preferably with how-to angle, on hunting, fishing, trapping, camping or other outdoor topics. Some humorous or where-to articles. Pays $40 to $200, on acceptance.

GAME AND FISH PUBLICATIONS—P.O. Box 741, Marietta, GA 30061. Publishes outdoors magazines for nine states. Articles, 2,000 to 2,500 words, on hunting and fishing. How-to's and adventure pieces. Profiles of successful hunters and fishermen. No hiking, canoeing, camping, or backpacking pieces. Pays $150 for state specific articles, $250 for general articles, on publication.

GOAL—600 3rd Ave., 27th fl., New York, NY 10016. Player profiles and trend stories, 1,500 to 2,000 words, for hockey fans with knowledge of game and the players, by writers with understanding of the sport. Pays $100 to $200, on publication. Query.

GOLF DIGEST—495 Westport Ave., Norwalk, CT 06856. Jack McDermott, Ed. Instructional articles, tournament reports, and features on players, to 2,500 words. Fiction, 1,000 to 4,000 words. Poetry, fillers, humor, photos. Pays varying rates, on acceptance. Query preferred.

GOLF JOURNAL—Golf House, Far Hills, NJ 07931. Robert Sommers, Ed. U.S. Golf Assn. Articles on golf personalities, history, travel. Humor. Photos. Pays varying rates, on publication.

GOLF MAGAZINE—380 Madison Ave., New York, NY 10017. George Peper, Ed. Articles of 1,500 words, with photos, on golf. Shorts, to 500 words. Pays $500 to $1,000 for articles, $75 to $300 for shorts, on publication.

GUN DIGEST AND HANDLOADER'S DIGEST—Suite 315, One Northfield Plaza, Northfield, IL 60093. Ken Warner, Ed. Well-researched articles to 5,000 words, on guns and shooting, equipment, etc. Photos. Pays from 10¢ a word, on acceptance. Query.

GUN DOG—P.O. Box 68, Adel, IA 50003. David G. Meisner, Pub. Features, 1,000 to 2,500 words, with photos, on bird hunting: how-to's, where-to's, dog training, canine medicine, breeding strategy. Fiction. Humor. Fillers. Pays $25 to $75 for fillers and short articles, $100 to $300 for features, on acceptance.

GUN WORLD—*See Bow & Arrow.*

GUNS & AMMO—8490 Sunset Blvd., Los Angeles, CA 90069. Howard French, Ed. Technical and general articles, 1,500 to 3,000 words, on guns, ammunition, and target shooting. Photos, fillers. Pays from $150, on acceptance.

HANDBALL—930 N. Benton Ave., Tucson, AZ 85711. Vern Roberts, Ed. Articles, 1,000 to 2,000 words, on handball and handball players. Photos; fillers, 30 to 40 words. No payment.

HANG GLIDING—U.S. Hang Gliding Assn., P.O. Box 66306, Los Angeles, CA 90066. Gilbert Dodgen, Ed. Articles and fiction, 2 to 3 pages, on hang gliding. Pays to $50, on publication. Query preferred.

HOCKEY ILLUSTRATED—355 Lexington Ave., New York, NY 10017. Stephen Ciacciarelli, Thomas Walsh, Eds. Articles, 2,500 words, on hockey players, teams. Pays $125, on publication. Query. Same address and requirements for *Baseball Illustrated, Wrestling World, Pro Basketball Illustrated, Pro Football Illustrated,* and *Basketball Annual* (college).

584

HORSE & RIDER—Box 555, 41919 Moreno Rd., Temecula, CA 92390. Ray Rich, Ed. Articles, 500 to 3,000 words, with photos, on Western and English riding and general horse care: training, feeding, grooming, etc. Pays varying rates, before publication. Buys all rights.

HORSEMAN—5314 Bingle Rd., Houston, TX 77092. Linda Blake, Ed. Articles, to 2,500 words, with photos, primarily on western horsemanship. Pays from 7¢ a word, extra for photos, on publication. Query.

HORSEMEN'S YANKEE PEDLAR—785 Southbridge St., Auburn, MA 01501. Nancy L. Khoury, Pub. News and feature-length articles, about horses and horsemen in the Northeast. Photos. Pays $2 per published inch, on publication. Query.

HORSEPLAY—Box 545, Gaithersburg, MD 20877. Cordelia Doucet, Ed. Articles, to 3,000 words, on eventing, show jumping, horse shows, dressage, and fox hunting, for horse enthusiasts. Pays 9¢ a word, after publication.

HOT BIKE—2145 W. La Palma, Anaheim, CA 92801. Paul Garson, Ed. Technical articles, 4,000 words, on motorcycles. Event coverage on high performance street and track motorcycles, with emphasis on Harley-Davidsons. Pays $50 to $100 per printed page, on publication.

HOT ROD—8490 Sunset Blvd., Los Angeles, CA 90069. Leonard Emanuelson, Ed. How-to pieces and articles, 500 to 5,000 words, on auto mechanics, hot rods, track and drag racing. Photo-features on custom or performance-modified cars. Pays to $150 per page, on publication.

INSIDE RUNNING—9514 Bristlebrook Dr., Houston, TX 77083. Joanne Schmidt, Ed. Articles on running in Texas; fiction. Photos. Pays $25 to $75, extra for photos, on acceptance.

KEEPIN' TRACK OF VETTES—P.O. Box 48, Spring Valley, NY 10977. Shelli Finkel, Ed. Articles of any length, with photos, relating to Corvettes. Pays $25 to $200, on publication.

KNAPSACK—American Youth Hostels, 1332 I St., N.W., Suite 800, Washington, DC 20005. Dave Gilbert, Ed. Articles, 800 to 1,200 words, on hosteling in U.S. and abroad, and on outdoor activities and issues of interest to hostelers. No payment for unsolicited manuscripts.

MICHIGAN OUT-OF-DOORS—P.O. Box 30235, Lansing, MI 48909. Kenneth S. Lowe, Ed. Features, 1,500 to 2,500 words, on hunting, fishing, camping and conservation in Michigan. Photos. Pays $50 to $150, on acceptance.

MID-WEST OUTDOORS—111 Shore Dr., Hinsdale, IL 60521. Gene Laulunen, Ed. Articles, 1,500 words, with photos, on where, when and how to fish in the Midwest. Fillers, 200 to 500 words. Pays $15 to $35, on publication.

THE MINOR PRO FOOTBALL NEWS—135 Prospect, Elmhurst, IL 60126. Ronald J. Real, Pub. Minor Pro Football Assn. Lively feature articles, 500 to 2,000 words, with photos, about minor-league football teams. Pays from $15, on publication.

THE MORGAN HORSE—Box 1, Westmoreland, NY 13490. Articles, 500 to 3,500 words, on equestrian and Morgan topics. Pays $25 to $300 for article with photos. Query.

MOTOR TREND—8490 Sunset Blvd., Los Angeles, CA 90069. Tony Swan, Ed. Articles, 250 to 2,000 words, on autos, racing, events; how-to pieces, profiles; photos. Pays $62 per manuscript page, on acceptance. Query.

MOTORHOME MAGAZINE—29901 Agoura Rd., Agoura, CA 91301. Bill Estes, Ed. Barbara Leonard, Man. Ed. Articles, to 2,000 words, with color slides, on motorhomes; travel and how-to pieces. Pays to $350, on acceptance.

NATIONAL PARKS MAGAZINE—1701 18th St., N.W., Washington, DC 20009. Michele Strutin, Ed. Articles, 1,000 to 2,000 words, on natural history, wildlife, outdoors activities, travel and conservation as they relate to national parks: illustrated features on the natural, historic and cultural resources of the National Park System. Pieces about legislation and other issues and events related to the parks. Pays $75 to $200, on acceptance. Query. Send for guidelines.

NATIONAL RACQUETBALL—4350 DiPaolo Center, Dearlove Rd., Glenview, IL 60025. Chuck Leve, Ed. Articles, 1,000 to 1,500 words, on health and conditioning. How-to's. Profiles. Fiction. Material must relate to racquetball. Pays $25 to $150, on publication.

NATIONAL WILDLIFE AND INTERNATIONAL WILDLIFE—1412 16th St., N.W., Washington, DC 20036. Mark Wexler, Man. Ed., *National Wildlife.* Jon Fisher, Man. Ed., *International Wildlife.* Articles, 1,000 to 2,500 words, on wildlife, conservation, environment; outdoor how-to pieces. Photos. Pays market rates, on acceptance. Query.

NAUTICAL QUARTERLY—373 Park Ave. South, Tenth Floor, New York, NY 10016. Joseph Gribbins, Ed. In-depth articles, 3,000 to 7,000 words, about boats and boating, U.S. and foreign. Pays $500 to $1,000, on acceptance. Query.

NORTHEAST OUTDOORS—P.O. Box 2180, Waterbury, CT 06722-2180. Howard Fielding, Ed. Articles, 500 to 2,500 words, preferably with B/W photos, on camping in Northeast U.S.: recommended private campgrounds, camp cookery, recreational vehicle hints. Stress how-to, where-to. Cartoons. Pays to $80, on publication. Send for guidelines.

NORTHEAST RIDING—209 Whitney St., Hartford, CT 06105. Paul Essenfeld, Ed./Pub. Motorcycle-related articles, 500 to 1,000 words, for motorcyclists in the Northeast, who ride for recreation and commuting. Pays negotiable rates, on publication.

OCEAN REALM—2333 Brickell Ave., Miami, FL 33129. Patricia Reilly, Ed. Articles, 1,200 to 1,800 words, on scuba diving and ocean science and technology. Department pieces: adventure; technology/medicine; instruction; photography and marine life. Photos. Short items, 100 to 500 words, for "FYI": up-to-date news items of interest to the diving community. Pays $100 per published page, $5 for FYI, on publication.

OFFSHORE—981 Chestnut St., Newton, MA 02164. Herbert Glick, Ed. Articles, 1,000 to 3,000 words, on boats, people and places along the New England coast. Photos. Pays from $2.50 per column inch, on acceptance.

ON TRACK—17165 Newhope St., "M", Fountain Valley, CA 92708. Steve Nickless, Edit. Dir. Features and race reports, 500 to 2,500 words. Pays $3 per column inch, on publication. Query first.

OUTDOOR AMERICA—1701 N. Ft. Myer Dr., Suite 1100, Arlington, VA 22209. Quarterly publication of the Izaak Walton League of America. Articles, 1,500 to 2,000 words, on natural resource conservation issues and outdoor recreation. Pays from 10¢ a word for major features, on publication. Query Articles Ed. with published clippings.

586

OUTDOOR LIFE—380 Madison Ave., New York, NY 10017. Clare Conley, Ed. Articles on hunting, fishing and related subjects. Pays top rates, on acceptance. Query.

OUTSIDE—Continental Bank Building, 1165 N. Clark, Chicago, IL 60610. High-quality articles, with photos, on sports, nature, wilderness travel, adventure, etc. Pays varying rates. Query.

PENNSYLVANIA ANGLER—Pennsylvania Fish Commission, P.O. Box 1673, Harrisburg, PA 17105-1673. Address Editor. Articles, 250 to 2,500 words, with photos, on freshwater fishing, boating in Pennsylvania. Pays $50 to $200 on acceptance. Must send SASE with all material. Query.

PENNSYLVANIA GAME NEWS—Game Commission, Harrisburg, PA 17120. Bob Bell, Ed. Articles, to 2,500 words, with photos, on outdoor subjects, except fishing and boating. Photos. Pays from 5¢ a word, extra for photos, on acceptance.

PERFORMANCE HORSEMAN—Gum Tree Corner, Unionville, PA 19375. Miranda Lorraine, Articles Ed. Factual how-to pieces for the serious western rider, on training: pulling shoes, improving riding skills, etc. Pays from $200, on publication. Query.

PICKUPS & MINI-TRUCKS—8490 Sunset Blvd., Los Angeles, CA 90069. John J. Jelinek, Ed. How-to and feature articles on pickups and vans for the street. Pays $75 per printed page, on publication. Writers' guidelines available with self-addressed, stamped envelope.

POPULAR SCIENCE—380 Madison Ave., New York, NY 10017. Herbert Shuldiner, Exec. Ed. Factual articles, 300 to 2,000 words, with photos and illustrations, on new products for home, car, boat, or outdoor activities. Pays varying rates, on acceptance. Query.

POWDER MAGAZINE—P.O. Box 1028, Dana Point, CA 92629. Pat Cochran, Man. Ed. Articles, 100 to 2,500 words, for advanced and expert downhill and cross-country skiers: equipment, environmental issues, new trends and techniques. Profiles; features on ski areas. Photos. Pays 15¢ to 20¢ a word, extra for photos, on publication. Query first.

POWERBOAT—15917 Strathern St., Van Nuys, CA 91406. Mark Spencer, Ed. Articles, to 1,500 words, with photos, for powerboat owners, on outstanding achievements, water-skiing, competitions; nontechnical how-to pieces. Pays about $200, on publication. Query.

PRACTICAL HORSEMAN—Gum Tree Corner, Unionville, PA 19375. Miranda D. Lorraine, Articles Ed. How-to articles on English riding, training, and horse care. Pays on publication. Query.

PRIVATE PILOT—P.O. Box 6050, Mission Viejo, CA 92690. Dennis Shattuck, Ed. True-experience pieces and technically-based aviation articles, 1,000 to 4,000 words, for aviation enthusiasts. Photos. Pays $75 to $250, on publication. Query.

PRO BASKETBALL ILLUSTRATED—See *Hockey Illustrated.*

PRO FOOTBALL ILLUSTRATED—See *Hockey Illustrated.*

ROAD RIDER MAGAZINE—P.O. Box 6050, Mission Viejo, CA 92690. Bob Carpenter, Ed. Articles, to 1,500 words, with photos or illustrations, on motorcycle touring. Cartoons. Pays from $100, on publication.

THE RUNNER—1 Park Ave., New York, NY 10016. Marc Bloom, Ed.

Features, 3,000 to 4,000 words, and columns, 900 to 1,500 words, for runners. Pays varying rates, on acceptance.

SAIL—34 Commercial Wharf, Boston, MA 02110. Keith Taylor, Ed. Articles, 1,500 to 3,000 words, with photos, on sailboats, equipment, racing, and cruising. How-to's on navigation, sail trim, etc. Pays $75 to $800 on publication. Writer's guidelines sent on request.

SAILBOARD NEWS—P.O. Box 159, Two S. Park Pl., Fair Haven, VT 05743. Mark Gabriel, Ed. Interviews, articles, and how-to pieces on boardsailing and the boardsailing industry. Photos. Pays from $25, on publication.

SAILING—125 E. Main St., Port Washington, WI 53074. William F. Schanen, III, Ed. Features, 700 to 1,500 words, with photos, on cruising and racing; first-person accounts; profiles of boats and regattas. Query for technical or how-to pieces. Pays varying rates, on publication. Writer's guidelines sent on request.

SAILORS' GAZETTE—5580 4th St., N., St. Petersburg, FL 33703. Alice N. Eachus, Ed. Articles 500 to 2,000 words, with photos, on Southeastern sailing. Emphasis on cruising and how-to's. Pays to 6¢ a word, extra for photos, on publication.

SALMON TROUT STEELHEADER—P.O. Box 02112, Portland, OR 97202. Frank W. Amato, Ed. Factual articles, 750 to 2,500 words, with photos, on salmon, trout and steelhead fishing in Western states, Midwest and East coast. Pays to $200, on publication.

SCORE, CANADA'S GOLF MAGAZINE—287 MacPherson Ave., Toronto, Ont., Canada M4V 1A4. Articles, to 3,000 words, on travel, golf equipment, and golf history. Personality profiles. Fillers, 50 to 100 words. Pays $25 for fillers, $150 to $400 for features, on assignment and publication.

SHOTGUN SPORTS—P.O. Box 340, Lake Havasu City, AZ 86403. Frank Kodl, Ed. Articles with photos, on trap and skeet shooting and hunting with shotguns. Pays $25 to $200, on publication.

SIERRA—530 Bush St., San Francisco, CA 94108. James Keough, Ed. Articles, 1,000 to 2,500 words, on environmental, conservation topics, hiking, backpacking, skiing, rafting, and cycling. Books reviews; Children's Dept.; photos. Pays from $200, extra for photos, on acceptance. Query.

SKI MAGAZINE—380 Madison Ave., New York, NY 10017. Dick Needham, Ed. Articles, 1,300 to 2,000 words, on skiing. Pays $100 to $300, on acceptance. Query.

SKI RACING—Two Bentley Ave., Poultney, VT 05764. Don A. Metivier, Pub./Ed. Interviews, articles, and how-to pieces on national and international alpine and nordic ski competitions. Photos. Pays from $1 per column inch, on publication.

SKIING—One Park Ave., New York, NY 10016. Alfred H. Greenberg, Ed. Personal adventures on skis, from 2,500 words (no first-time-on-skis stories); profiles and interviews, 50 to 300 words. Pays $150 to $300 per printed page, on acceptance.

SKIN DIVER MAGAZINE—8490 Sunset Blvd., Los Angeles, CA 90069. Bonnie J. Cardone, Exec. Ed. Illustrated articles, 500 to 2,000 words, on scuba diving activities, equipment and dive sites. Pays $50 per page, on publication.

SKYDIVING—P.O. Box 189, Deltona, FL 32728. Michael Truffer, Ed.

588

Timely news articles, 300 to 800 words, relating to sport and military parachuting. Fillers. Photos. Pays $25 to $200, extra for photos, on publication.

SMALL WORLD—Volkswagen of America, Inc., Troy, MI 48099. Ed Rabinowitz, Ed. General-interest features, to 1,500 words, relating to Volkswagen cars and their owners. Color slides. Pays $100 per printed page on acceptance. Query first.

SNOWMOBILE—11812 Wayzata Blvd., Suite 100, Minnetonka, MN 55343. C. J. Ramstad, Ed. Articles, 700 to 2,000 words, with color photos, related to snowmobiling: races and rallies, trail rides, personalities, travel. How-to's; humor; cartoons. Pays to $450, on publication. Query.

SNOWMOBILE WEST—P.O. Box 981, Idaho Falls, ID 83402. Steve Janes, Ed. Articles, 1.200 words, with photos, on snowmobiling in the western states. Pays to $100, on publication.

SOCCER AMERICA MAGAZINE—P.O. Box 23704, Oakland, CA 94623. Lynn Berling–Manuel, Ed. Articles, to 1,000 words, on soccer: news, profiles, coaching tips. Pays $25 to $100 for features, within 60 days of publication. Query.

SOUTH CAROLINA WILDLIFE—P.O. Box 167, Columbia, SC 29202. John E. Davis, Ed. Articles, 1,000 to 3,000 words, with regional outdoors focus; conservation, natural history and wildlife, recreation. Profiles, how-to's. Pays from 10¢ a word, on acceptance.

SPORT MAGAZINE—119 W. 40th St., New York, NY 10018. Neil Cohen, Man. Ed. Query before submitting material.

THE SPORTING NEWS—P.O. Box 56, 1212 N. Lindbergh Blvd., St. Louis, MO 63132. Dick Kaegel, Ed.-in-Chief. Articles, 1,000 to 1,500 words, on baseball, football, basketball, hockey, and other sports. Pays $150 to $750, on publication.

SPORTS AFIELD—250 W. 55th St., New York, NY 10019. Tom Paugh, Ed. Articles, 2,000 words, with quality photos, on hunting, fishing, natural history, personal experiences, new hunting/fishing spots. How-to pieces; humor; fiction. Pays top rates, on acceptance.

SPORTS AFIELD SPECIALS—250 W. 55th St., New York, NY 10019. Well-written, informative fishing and hunting articles, 2,000 to 2,500 words, with photos, with primary focus on how-to techniques: include lively anecdotes, and good sidebars, charts or graphs. Pays to $450 for features, on acceptance. Query.

SPORTS CAR GRAPHIC—8490 Sunset Bolvd., Los Angeles, CA 90069. John Hanson, Ed. Articles, 500 to 1,000 words, on modified sports cars; technical how-to pieces. Pays to $500, on acceptance. Guidelines available.

SPORTS ILLUSTRATED—Rockefeller Center, New York, NY 10020. Myra Gelband, Articles Ed. Articles, 1,500 to 5,000 words, on sports personalities, issues, trends, and events. Offbeat features, to 1,500 words. Pays from $1,000 for articles, $500 to $1,000 for shorter features, on acceptance.

SPORTSCAPE—1318 Beacon St., Brookline, MA 02146. Mark Onigman, Man. Ed. Articles, 2,000 to 3,500 words, primarily on participant sports in New England. Sport-related fiction, 2,000 to 3,000 words. Pays $200, on acceptance.

SPUR MAGAZINE—P.O. Box 85, Middleburg, VA 22117. Address Ed. Dept. Articles, 300 to 5,000 words, on Thoroughbred racing and breeding.

Profiles of people and farms. Historical and nostalgia pieces. Pays $50 to $250, on publication. Query.

STOCK CAR RACING—P.O. Box 715, Ipswich, MA 01938. Dick Berggren, Ed. Articles, to 6,000 words, on stock-car drivers, races, and vehicles. Photos. Pays to $350, on publication.

SURFER MAGAZINE—Box 1028, Dana Point, CA 92629. Steve Pezman, Pub. Paul Holmes, Ed. Articles, 500 to 5,000 words, on surfing, surfers, etc. Photos. Pays 10¢ to 15¢ a word, $10 to $600, for photos, on publication.

SURFING—P.O. Box 3010, San Clemente, CA 92672. David Gilovich, Ed. Chris Carter, Assoc. Ed. First-person travel articles, 1,500 to 2,000 words, on surfing locations; knowledge of sport essential. Pays varying rates, on publication. Query.

TENNIS—495 Westport Ave., P.O. Box 5350, Norwalk, CT 06856. Shepherd Campbell, Ed. Instructional articles, features, profiles of tennis stars, 500 to 2,000 words, Fillers; humor. Photos. Pays from $100 to $500, from $50 for fillers and humor, on publication. Query.

TENNIS, U.S.A.—1515 Broadway, New York, NY 10036. Cindy Schmerler, Man. Ed. Articles, 250 to 1,500 words, on local and sectional tennis personalities and news events. Pays $25 to $250, on acceptance. Query; uses very little free-lance material.

TENNIS WEEK—6 E. 39th St., New York, NY 10016. Eugene L. Scott, Pub. Linda C. Pentz, Ed. In-depth, researched articles, from 1,000 words, on current issues and personalities in the game. Pays $75 to $150, on publication. Query.

THREE WHEELING—Box 2260, Costa Mesa, CA 92628. Bruce Simurda, Ed. Articles, 1,000 to 1,500 words, relating to three– and four–wheel, all-terrain vehicles. Pays $60 per printed page, on publication. Query.

TOTAL FITNESS—15115 S. 76 E. Ave., Bixby, OK 74008. Anne Thomas, Man. Ed. Articles, 1,500 to 3,500 words, for casual fitness buffs and athletes, on diet, health, fitness, nutrition and exercise. How-to's. Photos. Pays 10¢ a word, on acceptance.

TRAILER BOATS—16427 S. Avalon, P.O. Box 2307, Gardena, CA 90248. Jim Youngs, Ed. Factual articles, 500 to 2,000 words, on boat, trailer of tow vehicle maintenance and operation, skiing, fishing, cruising. Fillers; humor. Pays 7¢ to 10¢ a word, on publication. Query.

TRAILER LIFE—29901 Agoura Rd., Agoura, CA 91301. Bill Estes, Ed. Articles, to 2,500 words, with photos, on trailering, truck campers, motorhomes, hobbies and RV lifestyle. How-to pieces. Pays to $400, on acceptance. Send for guidelines.

TURF AND SPORT DIGEST—511–13 Oakland Ave., Baltimore, MD 21212. Allen L. Mitzel, Jr., Ed. Articles, 1,500 to 4,000 words, on national turf personalities, racing nostalgia, and handicapping. Pays $75 to $200, on publication. Query.

ULTRASPORT—11 Beacon St., Boston, MA 02108. Chris Bergonzi, Ed. Articles, on athletic endeavors which are out of the mainstream; profiles and descriptive pieces, to 3,000 words; athletics-related fiction, to 3,500 words; humor, to 1,500 words. Pays $800, on acceptance. Query.

VELO-NEWS—Box 1257, Brattleboro, VT 05301. Barbara George, Ed. Articles, 500 to 2,000 words, on bicycle racing. Photos. Pays $1.75 per column inch, extra for photos, on publication. Query.

WASHINGTON FISHING HOLES—P.O. Box 499, Snohomish, WA 98290. Address Terry W. Sheely. Detailed articles, with specific maps, 800 to 1,500 words, on fishing holes in Washington. Local Washington fishing how-to's. Photos. Pays on publication. Query.

WASHINGTON WILDLIFE—c/o Washington State Game Dept., 600 N. Capitol Way, Olympia, WA 98504. Wayne Van Zwoll, Ed. Articles, 300 to 2,500 words, on fish and wildlife management and related recreational or environmental topics. Fillers, to 150 words. Photos. Pays in copies. Query.

WATER SKIER—P.O. Box 191, Winter Haven, FL 33882. Duke Cullimore, Ed. Offbeat articles and photo essays on waterskiing. Pays varying rates, on acceptance.

THE WESTERN BOATMAN—16427 S. Avalon, P.O. Box 2307, Gardena, CA 90248. Ralph Poole, Ed. Articles, to 1,500 words, for boating enthusiasts from Alaska to Mexico, on subjects from waterskiing and salmon fishing to race boats and schooners. Pays 10¢ a word, on publication. Query preferred.

THE WESTERN HORSEMAN—P.O. Box 7980, Colorado Springs, CO 80933. Chan Bergen, Ed. Articles, around 1,500 words, with photos, on care and training of horses. Pays from $150, on acceptance.

WESTERN OUTDOORS—3197 E. Airport Loop, Costa Mesa, CA 92626. Timely, factual articles, 1,500 to 1,800 words, of interest to western sportsmen. Pays $200 to $300, on acceptance. Query.

WESTERN SALTWATER FISHERMAN—6200 Yarrow Dr., Carlsbad, CA 92008. Carl Calvert, Ed. How-to and where-to articles, 1,500 words, for the serious salt water angler of the West Coast, from Alaska to the South Pacific: new products, fishing techniques, profiles. Photos. 1,200 to 1,500 words. Pays $50 to $300 on acceptance. Query first.

WESTERN SPORTSMAN—P.O. Box 737, Regina, Sask., Canada S4P 3A8. Red Wilkinson, Ed. Articles, to 2,500 words, on outdoor experiences in Alberta and Saskatchewan; how-to pieces. Photos. Pays $75 to $225, on publication.

WIND SURF—24581 Del Prado, Dana Point, CA 92629. Drew Kampion, Ed. Articles on all aspects of windsurfing. Pays 10¢ to 25¢ a word, on publication.

WINDRIDER—P. O. Box 2456, Winter Park, FL 32790. Nancy K. Crowell, Ed. Features, instructional pieces, and tips, by experienced boardsailors. Fast action photos. Pays $50 to $75 for tips, $100 to $200 for features, extra for photos, after publication. Query first.

THE WOMAN BOWLER—5301 S. 76th St., Greendale, WI 53129. Paula McMartin, Ed. Profiles, interviews, and news articles, to 1,000 words, for women bowlers. Pays varying rates, on acceptance. Query with outline.

WOMEN'S SPORTS AND FITNESS—310 Town and Country Village, Palo Alto, CA 94301. Amy Rennert, Ed. How-to's, profiles, and sports reports, 500 to 2,500 words, for active women. Health, fitness, and sports pieces. Photos. Pays from $25, on publication.

WRESTLING WORLD—See *Hockey Illustrated.*

YACHT RACING & CRUISING—23 Leroy Ave., P.O. Box 1700, Darien, CT 06820. John Burnham, Exec. Ed. Articles, 8 to 10 typed pages, on sailboat racing and equipment, regatta reports, cruising techniques. Photos. Pays $150 per published page, on publication. Query.

YACHTING—P.O. Box 1200, 5 River Rd., Cos Cob, CT 06807. Deborah Meisels, Assistant Ed. Articles, 2,000 words, on recreational power and sail boating. How-to and personal-experience pieces. Photos. Pays $250 to $450, on acceptance.

TRAVEL AND INFLIGHT MAGAZINES

AAA WORLD—1999 Shepard Rd., St. Paul, MN 55116. Dick Schaaf, Ed. Auto safety and general domestic travel pieces, 900 to 1,300 words, and other topics of interest to AAA members. Pays $300 to $600, on acceptance. Query preferred.

ACCENT—Box 2315, 1720 Washington Blvd., Ogden, UT 84404. Peggie Bingham, Ed. Articles, 500 to 1,200 words, on interesting places, ways to travel, famous travelers, money-saving tips. How-to's; humor. Color photos. Pays 15¢ a word, $35 for photos, on acceptance. Query preferred.

AIRFAIR INTERLINE MAGAZINE—25 W. 39th St., New York, NY 10018. Gayle Guynup, Ed. Travel articles, 1,000 to 2,500 words, with photos, on shopping, sightseeing, dining, for airline employees. Prices, discount information, and addresses must be included. Pays $75, after publication.

ALASKAFEST—Suite 503, 1932 First Avenue, Seattle, WA 98101. Ed Reading, Ed. Alaska Airlines' inflight magazine. Articles 800 to 2,500 words, on general-interest subjects, adventure travel, and business, with West Coast or Alaska focus. Travel articles should be about the *experience* of traveling. Absolutely no "destination" pieces with details about hotels and transportation. Photos. Pays from $100, extra for photos, within two weeks after publication.

AMERICAN WAY—Box 61616, Dallas/Fort Worth Airport, TX 75261. Walter A. Damtoft, Ed. American Airlines' in-flight magazine. Features, 1,500 to 1,750 words, on health, business, the arts, etc.; profiles of people and places. Photos. Pays $100 for shorts, from $300 for full-length pieces, on acceptance. Query Articles Editor, Mail Drop, 3D08. No recent report.

CHEVRON USA—P.O. Box 6227, San Jose, CA 95150. Mark Williams, Ed. Quarterly. Articles, 800 to 1,600 words, on travel and leisure activities in the United States. Travel anecdotes, 50 to 250 words. Color slides. Pays about 25¢ a word for articles, $25 for anecdotes, on acceptance; extra for slides on publication. Send for free sample copy and guidelines.

CHICAGO TRIBUNE—Travel Section, 435 N. Michigan Ave., Chicago, IL 60611. Harriet Choice, Exec. Travel Ed. Travel articles, 1,000 to 3,500 words, with photos. Pays $85 to $300, extra for photos, on publication.

CONTINENTAL (formerly *EXTRA*)—East/West Network, 5900 Wilshire Blvd., Suite 800, Los Angeles, CA 90036. John Johns, Edit. Dir., Joan Yee, Travel Ed. Continental Airlines' in-flight magazine. Uses mostly free-lance material. Query. Same address for *Ozark,* Pacific Southwest *PSA Magazine,* Republic's *Republic Scene.*

DIESEL MOTORIST—Diesel Automobile Assn., Box 335, Fort Lee, NJ 07024. Query Editor. Articles, to 1,500 words, on travel, bargains, economy, energy, news, new products, investments, "place reports," "insider reports," etc., related to diesel cars. Photos. Pays $25 to $150, on publication. Query, with story outline and SASE.

DISCOVERY—Allstate Motor Club, Allstate Plaza, F3, Northbrook, IL 60062. Mary Kelly Selover, Ed. Articles, 1,000 to 2,500 words, with photos, on travel. Pieces on auto-related and regional subjects. Pays $500 to $1,000, on acceptance. Queries required.

EASY LIVING—1999 Shephard Rd., St. Paul, MN 55116. Peggy Brown Black, Ed. Quarterly financial and general lifestyle magazine, with one travel article, 1,200 to 1,800 words, per issue. Photos. Pays $250 to $600, extra for photos, on acceptance.

ENDLESS VACATION—P.O. Box 80260, Indianapolis, IN 46280. Address M. Kathryn Hannon. Bimonthly read by vacation timeshare owners. Articles, 1,000 to 5,000 words, and short features, 800 to 1,200 words, on such travel and vacation-related subjects as sports and recreational activities, cultural attractions, health and fitness, food. Pays from $300, on acceptance. Query with clips and outline.

EXTRA—See *Continental*.

FORD TIMES—Ford Motor Co., Room 765, P.O. Box 1899, The American Rd., Dearborn, MI 48121. Arnold S. Hirsch, Ed. Articles to 1,800 words, on current subjects, profiles, places of interest, travel, humor, outdoors. Main focus is on North America but some international. Pays from $450, on acceptance. Query with SASE.

FREQUENT FLYER—888 Seventh Ave., New York, NY 10019. Coleman Lollar, Ed. Articles, 1,000 to 3,000 words, on all aspects of frequent business travel, and on general-interest subjects, for sophisticated, affluent audience. No "personal-experience" pieces. Pays $100 to $500, on acceptance. Query preferred.

FRONTIER—Inflight Publishing Co., P.O. Box 1002, 4100 S. Parker Rd., Aurora, CO 80014. Capt. C. A. Stevens, Ed. Frontier Airlines' in-flight magazine. Entertaining articles, 1,500 words, on travel, business, lifestyles, sports, and entertainment, general interest subjects, and inspirational articles. Short pieces, 300 to 1,000 words. Pays to $350, extra for photos, on publication. Query preferred.

INFLIGHT—P.O. Box 2315, Ogden, UT 84404. Wayne DeWald, Ed. Articles, for male, business-oriented audience, on travel, sports, business. Personality profiles; humor. Photos. Feature length: 1,500 to 2,000 words. Shorts: 300 to 600 words. Pays 15¢ a word, $35 for color photos, on acceptance. Query.

INTERNATIONAL LIVING—2201 St. Paul St., Baltimore, MD 21218. Elizabeth Philip, Ed. Newsletter. Short pieces and features, 200 to 1,000 words, with useful information on living abroad, investing overseas, and unusual travel bargains. Pays to $150, on acceptance.

MICHIGAN LIVING—Automobile Club of Michigan, 17000 Executive Plaza Dr., Dearborn, MI 48126. Len Barnes, Ed. Informative travel articles, 500 to 1,500 words, on U.S., Canadian tourist attractions and recreational opportunities; special interest in Michigan. Photos. Pays $100 to $300, extra for photos, on acceptance.

THE MIDWEST MOTORIST—12901 N. Forty Drive, St. Louis, MO 63141. Tom Sitek, Man. Ed. Articles, 1,000 to 1,500 words, with photos, on travel, transportation and consumerism. Pays $50 to $200, on acceptance or publication.

NATIONAL GEOGRAPHIC—17th and M Sts., N.W., Washington, D.C. 20036. Wilbur E. Garrett, Ed. Publishes first-person articles on human geography, exploration, natural history, archaeology, and science. Half staff written; half by recognized authorities and published authors. Does not review manuscripts. Query Suggestions Editor.

NATIONAL MOTORIST—One Market Plaza, Suite 300, San Francisco, CA 94105. Jane Offers, Ed. Illustrated articles, 500 or 1,100 words, for California motorists, on motoring in the West, car care, roads, personalities, places, etc. Photos. Pays from 10¢ a word, extra for photos, on acceptance.

THE NEW YORK TIMES—229 W. 43rd St., New York, NY 10036. Michael J. Leahy, Travel Ed. Considers queries only; include writer's background, description of proposed article. No unsolicited manuscripts or photos. Pays on acceptance.

NORTHWEST ORIENT—34 E. 51 St., New York, NY 10022. Northwest Orient's in-flight magazine. Features, 2,000 to 3,000 words, on travel, business, lifestyles, sports, and entertainment. Columns, 1,000 words, on science, travel, and finance. Profiles. Pays from $700 for articles, from $450 for columns, on acceptance.

OFF DUTY MAGAZINE—3303 Harbor Blvd., Suite C-2, Costa Mesa, CA 92626. Bruce Thorstad, U.S. Ed. Travel articles, 1,800 to 2,000 words, for active duty military Americans (aged 20 to 40) and their families, on U.S. regions or cities. Military angle preferable. Pieces with focus on an event or activity, with sidebars telling how-to and where-to. Photos. Pays from 10¢ a word, extra for photos, on acceptance. Query. Send for guidelines. European and Pacific editions. Foreign travel articles for military Americans and their families stationed abroad.

OHIO MOTORIST—P.O. Box 6150, Cleveland, OH 44101. F. Jerome Turk, Ed. Articles, 1,500 to 2,500 words, with photos, on domestic (preferably in Ohio) and foreign travel, automotive subjects. Pays $100 to $300, on acceptance.

OZARK—See *Continental.*

PACE—338 N. Elm St., Greensboro, NC 27401. Leslie Daisy, Man. Ed. Articles of interest to business travelers; economic reports, job "how-to's," and workplace related subjects. Payment varies, on publication.

PSA MAGAZINE—See *Continental.*

THE REGISTER—P.O. Box 11626, 625 N. Grand Ave., Santa Ana, CA 92711. Laura Bly, Travel Ed. Articles, 600 to 2,500 words, with photos, on unique travel destinations and consumer topics. Require "nuts and bolts" sidebar with hotel costs, airfare, etc. Pays from $50, extra for photos, on publication.

REPUBLIC SCENE—See *Continental.*

SIGNATURE MAGAZINE—641 Lexington Ave., New York, NY 10022. Barbara Coats, Articles Ed. Articles on travel in U.S. and abroad; service features on leisure and entertainment topics: food, wine, sports, the arts, etc. Pays good rates, on acceptance. Query.

SKY—12955 Biscayne Blvd., North Miami, FL 33181. Lidia de Leon, Ed. Delta Air Lines' in-flight magazine. Articles on business, lifestyle, high tech, sports, the arts, etc. Color slides. Pays varying rates, on publication. Query.

SMALL WORLD—Volkswagen of America, Inc., Troy, MI 48099. Ed Rabinowitz, Ed. Travel articles on unique places, to 1,500 words, with color photos, relating to Volkswagens. Pays $100 per printed page, on acceptance. Query.

TRANSITIONS—18 Hulst Rd., Amherst, MA 01002. Kathleen A. Bemben, Asst. Ed. Articles, to 1,500 words, with B/W photos, for long-stay travelers abroad: work, study, travel. Include practical, first-hand information: travel deals, work and study opportunities, etc. No destination pieces. Pays on publication. Send SASE for guidelines.

TRAVEL AGE WEST—582 Market St., San Francisco, CA 94104. Don Langley, Man. Ed. Articles, 800 to 1,000 words, with photos, on any aspect of travel useful to travel agents, including names, addresses, prices, etc.; news or trend angle preferred. Pays $1.50 per column inch, after publication.

TRAVEL & LEISURE—1120 Ave. of the Americas, New York, NY 10036. Pamela Fiori, Ed.-in-Chief. Articles, 1,000 to 2,500 words, on destinations and leisuretime activities. Regional pieces for regional editions. Pays $600 to $2,500, on acceptance. Query; articles on assignment.

TRAVEL HOLIDAY—Travel Bldg., Floral Park, NY 11001. Scott Shane, Ed. Informative, lively features, 1,800 to 2,000 words, on foreign and domestic travel to well-known or little-known places; featurettes, 800 to 1,000 words, on special-interest subjects: museums, shopping, smaller cities or islands, special aspects of a destination. Pays from $250 for featurettes, $400 for features, on acceptance. Query with published clips.

TRAVEL SMART FOR BUSINESS—Dobbs Ferry, NY 10522. H. J. Teison, Ed. Articles, 200 to 1,000 words, for company executives and business travel managers, on lowering travel costs and increasing travel convenience. Pays on publication.

TRIP & TOUR—P.O. Drawer 189, Palm Beach, FL 33480. Distributed by travel agents nationwide, to their customers who are planning trips. Articles, 800 words, on foreign and domestic travel. Pays 5¢ a word (maximum payment $40), on publication.

UNITED MAGAZINE—East/West Network, 34 E. 51st St., New York, NY 10022. David Breul, Ed. United Airlines' in-flight magazine. Profiles of unusual Americans. Travel pieces on United destinations. Interviews. Pays varying rates, 60 days after acceptance. Query.

USAIR—34 E. 51st St., New York, NY 10022. Richard Busch, Ed. In-flight magazine of USAir. Articles, 1,500 to 3,000 words, on travel, business, sports, entertainment, food, health, and other general interest topics. No downbeat or extremely controversial subjects. Pays $350 to $800, on acceptance. Query.

VISTA/USA—Box 161, Convent Station, NJ 07961. Exxon Travel Club. Patrick Sarver, Ed. Travel articles, 2,000 words, on North America, Hawaii, Mexico and the Caribbean. Pieces, 300 words, for "Places of Interest," on unusual places to visit in North America. Pays from $600 for articles, $100 for column pieces, on acceptance. Query with writing sample. Limited free-lance market.

YANKEE MAGAZINE'S TRAVEL GUIDE TO NEW ENGLAND—Main St., Dublin, NH 03444. Sharon Smith, Ed. Articles, 500 to 2,000 words, on unusual activities, restaurants, places to visit in New England, for tourists. Photos. Pays $50 to $300, on acceptance. Query with outline and writing samples.

CITY AND REGIONAL MAGAZINES

ADIRONDACK LIFE—420 E. Genesee St., Syracuse, NY 13202. Laurie J. Storey, Ed. Articles, 2,000 to 3,000 words, with photos, on New York's North Country outdoors and recreational activities, history, natural history and wildlife. Pays $100 to $350, on publication. Query.

ALASKA—Box 4-EEE, Anchorage, AK 99509. Tom Gresham, Ed. Articles, 1,500 words, on life in Alaska and northwestern Canada. Pays on acceptance. Write for guidelines.

ALOHA, THE MAGAZINE OF HAWAII—828 Fort St. Mall, Honolulu, HI 96813. Rita Gormley, Ed. Articles, 2,000 to 3,000 words, fiction, to 4,000 words, poetry, on Hawaii and its ethnic groups. Photos. Pays 10¢ a word, extra for photos, $25 per poem, on publication. Query.

AMERICAN WEST—3033 N. Campbell Ave., Tucson, AZ 85719. Mae Reid-Bills, Man. Ed. Well-researched articles, 1,000 to 3,000 words, written in a lively style, with good illustrations, on Western history and Western traditions. Pays from $200, on acceptance. Query.

ARIZONA—The Arizona *Republic,* Box 1950, Phoenix, AZ 85001. Paul Schatt, Ed. Articles, 500 to 3,000 words, on people and issues of interest to Arizona readers. Humor, cartoons. Photos. Pays $40 to $400, before publication.

ARIZONA HIGHWAYS—2039 W. Lewis Ave., Phoenix, AZ 85009. Richard G. Stahl, Man. Ed. Professional, well-researched, lively articles, 2,000 words, related to Arizona: contemporary events, history, outdoor adventures, and travel. Photos. Pays 20¢ to 30¢ a word, extra for photos, on acceptance. Send for writers' guidelines.

ARKANSAS TIMES—Box 34010, Little Rock, AR 72203. Bob Lancaster, Ed. Articles, to 6,000 words, on Arkansas history, Arkansas people, travel, politics. All articles *must* have strong AR orientation. Fiction, to 6,000 words. Some poetry. Pays $50 to $300, on acceptance.

ATLANTA—6285 Barfield Rd., Atlanta, GA 30328. Neil Shister, Ed. Articles, 2,500 words, on Atlanta subjects or personalities. Pays $600 to $1,000, on publication. Query.

THE ATLANTIC ADVOCATE—P.O. Box 3370, Gleaner Bldg., Prospect St., Fredericton, N.B., Canada E3B 5A2. Harold P. Wood, Ed. Well-researched articles on Atlantic Canada and general-interest subjects; fiction, to 1,500 words. Pays to 8¢ a word, on publication.

ATLANTIC CITY MAGAZINE—1637 Atlantic Ave., Atlantic City, NJ 08401. Mary Johnson, Ed. Articles, 500 to 5,000 words, on Atlantic City and Southern New Jersey: casinos, business, personalities, environment, local color, crime. Pays $50 to $500, on publication. Query.

AUGUSTA SPECTATOR—P.O. Box 3168, Augusta, GA 30904. Faith Bertsche, Pub. Historical articles and features on travel or food that tie in to Georgia and South Carolina. Fiction, to 2,000 words. Poetry; submit to Barri

Armitage. Pays to $25 for articles, in copies for poetry, on publication. Query for articles.

AUSTIN—Box 1967, Austin, TX 78767. Hal Susskind, Ed. Articles, 800 to 1,500 words, on Austin. Photos; cartoons. Pays varying rates, on publication. Query.

AVENUE—145 E. 57th St., New York, NY 10022. Michael Shnayerson, Ed. Articles, 2,000 to 2,500 words, for Upper East Side New Yorkers, and residents of affluent suburbs around the country. Profiles of Upper East Siders in business and the arts, food, fashion. Fiction. Pays $400 to $500, on publication. Query.

AVENUE M—100 E. Walton, #36A, Chicago, IL 60611. Art Desmond, Ed. Articles, 500 to 1,000 words, on lifestyles, finance, and travel, for residents of Near North area of Chicago. Profiles. Pays $25 to $50, on publication. Query preferred.

BALTIMORE MAGAZINE—Suite 800, 26 S. Calvert St., Baltimore, MD 21202. Stan Heuisler, Ed. Articles, 200 to 5,000 words, on metropolitan area: investigative reporting, personality profiles, consumer and service pieces. Photos. Pays varying rates, on publication. Query.

BIG VALLEY—16161 Roscoe Blvd., Suite 201, Sepulveda, CA 91343. Linda Roberts, Ed. Articles, 500 to 3,000 words, on celebrities, issues, newsmakers, education, health, fashion, sports, entertainment, dining, etc., in California's San Fernando Valley. Pays $100 to $500, within 6 weeks of acceptance.

THE BOSTON GLOBE MAGAZINE—*Boston Globe,* Boston, MA 02107. Michael Larkin, Ed. Articles, 2,500 to 5,000 words, on general-interest topics—historical, nostalgic, humorous, arts and science, medicine, etc. Profiles and interviews (not Q&A). No travelogues or personal essays. Regional tie-in not necessary, but a news peg is important. Also uses novel excerpts, ethnic or humorous. Pays $500 to $1,000, on publication. Enclose clips and SASE.

BOSTON MAGAZINE—300 Massachusetts Ave., Boston, MA 02115. Donald Forst, Ed. Informative, entertaining features, 1,000 to 4,000 words, on Boston area personalities, institutions and phenomena. Pays $250 to $1,200, on publication. Query Charles Matthews, Articles Ed., or Kate Broughton, Service Features Ed.

CALIFORNIA—P.O. Box 69990, Los Angeles, CA 90069. Katherine Pandora, Ass't. Ed. Features, 3,000 to 6,000 words, with California focus, on politics, business, environmental issues, ethnic diversity, sports. Service pieces; profiles; well-researched investigative articles. Pays $1,250 to $2,500 for features, $350 to $750 for shorter articles and columns, $100 for pieces (to 250 words) for "Reporter" section, $100 to $150 for "People" section, on acceptance. Query.

CALIFORNIA LIVING—110 Fifth St., San Francisco, CA 94103. Hal Silverman, Ed. Sunday supplement to *San Francisco Examiner.* Articles, 1,500 to 2,500 words, on lifestyles, leisure activities, business, history, jobs, people, etc., in the San Francisco area. Photos. Pays $175 to $250.

CAPE COD LIFE—872 Main St., Osterville, MA 02655. Brian F. Shortsleeve, Ed. Articles, 2,000 to 2,500 words, on current events, business, history, nature and gardening, art, real estate, architecture and housing—anything that pertains to life on the Cape and Islands. Regional tie-in "absolutely necessary." Pays $3.00 per published column inch, on publication. Query.

CAPITOL, THE COLUMBUS DISPATCH SUNDAY MAGAZINE—Columbus, OH 43216. Articles, to 5,000 words, preferably related to Ohio. Photos. Pays negotiable rates, extra for photos, after publication.

CENTRAL FLORIDA—P.O. Box 7727, Orlando, FL 32854. Rowland Stiteler, Ed. Articles on a wide variety of topics; must deal in some way with Central Florida. Pays 5¢ to 10¢ a word, on publication. Query.

CHARLOTTE MAGAZINE—P.O. Box 221269, Charlotte, NC 28222. Melinda Meschter, Ed. Articles, 2,500 words, on local and regional personalities, consumer interest, finance, law, home and garden, arts, travel, lifestyles, and business. Pays $40 to $250, 30 days after publication.

THE CHARLOTTE OBSERVER AND THE CHARLOTTE NEWS—Box 32188, Charlotte, NC 28232. Cynthia Struby, Features Ed. Newspaper features, travel articles, 500 to 1,000 words, for audience in Western NC and SC. Pays $25 to $75, on publication.

CHESAPEAKE BAY MAGAZINE—1819 Bay Ridge Ave., Suite 200, Annapolis, MD 21403. Betty D. Rigoli, Ed. Technical, how-to and personal-experience articles, to 1,500 words, on boating, fishing, and conservation, in Chesapeake Bay. Photos. Pays $65 to $85, extra for color slides, on publication.

CHICAGO—303 E. Wacker Dr., Chicago, IL 60601. John Fink, Ed. Articles and fiction, 1,000 to 5,000 words, related to Chicago. Pays varying rates, on acceptance. Query.

CHICAGO HISTORY—Clark St. at North Ave., Chicago, IL 60614. Timothy C. Jacobson, Ed. Articles, to 4,500 words, on urban political, social and cultural history. Pays to $250, on publication. Query.

CHICAGO TRIBUNE MAGAZINE—See *Sunday.*

CINCINNATI MAGAZINE—617 Vine St., Suite 900, Cincinnati, OH 45202. Laura Pulfer, Ed./Pub. Articles, 1,000 to 3,000 words, on Cincinnati people and issues. Pays $75 to $100 for 1,000 words, on acceptance. Query with writing sample. Buys all rights.

COASTAL JOURNAL—Box 84, Lanesville Sta., Gloucester, MA 01930. Randy Greenfield, Ed. Articles, 2,500 words, on the New England coast, past, present and future trends, current events, personalities and nautical history. Fiction, same length. Fillers. Photos. Pays $100 to $150, on publication.

COLORADO BUSINESS—2500 Curtis St., Suite 200, P.O. Box 5400-TA, Denver, CO 80217. Sharon Almirall, Ed. Articles, 1,500 words, on banking, real estate, transportation, manufacturing, etc., in the Rocky Mountain region. Pays 10¢ a word, on publication. Query.

COLORADO HOMES & LIFESTYLES—Suite 154, 2550 31st St., Denver, CO 80216. Mary McCall, Man. Ed. Articles on homes, lifestyles, fine food, and gardening in Colorado. Essays, on topics relating to Colorado. Pays to 20¢ a word, on publication. Query preferred.

COLORADO MONTHLY MAGAZINE—P.O. Box 22542, Denver, CO 80222. Peter & Eileen Wigginton, Eds. Articles, 500 to 2,000 words, on the arts in the Denver metro area. Fiction, 900 to 2,000 words. Pays 5¢ to 10¢ a word, on publication.

COLORADO SPORTS MONTHLY—P.O. Box 6253, Colorado Springs, CO 80934. Robert J. Erdmann, Ed. Articles, 1,500 to 2,000 words, on individual participatory sports—running, skiing, bicycling, physical fitness, etc.—as they relate to the people, events and areas of Colorado. Pays varying rates, on publication.

COLUMBUS DISPATCH SUNDAY MAGAZINE—See *Capitol.*

COMMONWEALTH, THE MAGAZINE OF VIRGINIA—121 College Pl., Norfolk, VA 23510. Deborah Marquardt, Ed. Sophisticated articles, 1,500 to 3,000 words, with Virginia focus. Short pieces on current events and trends. Pays 10¢ a word. Query.

CONNECTICUT—636 Kings Hwy., Fairfield, CT 06430. Albert E. Labouchere, Ed.-in-Chief. Articles, 1,500 to 2,500 words, on Connecticut topics and issues, people, and style, etc. Pays $100 to $600, on publication.

CORPORATE MONTHLY—105 Chestnut St., Philadelphia, PA 19106. Thomas Bubeck, Ed. Articles, 1,500 to 2,000 words, for business executives in the Philadelphia/Delaware Valley area. Pays varying rates, on publication. Queries required.

COUNTRY MAGAZINE—P.O. Box 246, Alexandria, VA 22313. Philip Hayward, Ed. Articles, 2,000 words, related to life in the Mid-Atlantic region: travel, outdoor sports, gardening, antiques, history, architecture, environment, etc. Fiction. Short poetry. Photos. Pays $3.50 per column inch, extra for photos, on publication. Query preferred. Include SASE.

D—3988 N. Central Expressway, Dallas, TX 75204. Lee Cullum, Ed. In-depth investigative pieces on current trends and problems, personality profiles, and general-interest articles on the arts, travel, fashion, and business, for upper-class residents of Dallas. Pays $350 to $500 for departments, $800 to $2,000 for features. Query.

DALLAS—1507 Pacific Ave., Dallas, TX 75201. D. Ann Shiffler, Ed. Articles, 1,000 words, on local businesses, business people, and self-help topics for managers. Pays $100, on acceptance.

DALLAS LIFE—*The Dallas Morning News,* Communications Center, Dallas, TX 75265. Betty Cook, Ed. Well-researched articles and profiles, 750 to 2,000 words, on contemporary issues, personalities, or subjects of strictly Dallas-related interest. Short Dallas-oriented humor features, 500 to 750 words. Pays from 25¢ a word, on acceptance. Query required.

DENVER LIVING—5757 Alpha Rd., Suite 400, Dallas, TX 75240. Tina Stacy, Publications Dir. Articles, 200 to 2,000 words, on local events and national and regional housing topics: interior decorating, home security, building trends, energy efficiency, etc. Reviews. Pays 10¢ a word, on acceptance. Query.

THE DES MOINES SUNDAY REGISTER PICTURE—*Des Moines Register and Tribune,* 715 Locust St., Des Moines, IA 50304. John Karras, Ed. Features and profiles, to 1,000 words, with photos, with Iowa angle. Pays on publication. Limited freelance market.

DETROIT MAGAZINE—*Detroit Free Press,* 321 W. Lafayette Blvd., Detroit, MI 48231. Articles, to 3,000 words, with a Detroit-area or Michigan focus, on issues, lifestyles, business. Personality profiles; service pieces. Pays $50 to $250.

DOWN EAST—Camden, ME 04843. Davis Thomas, Ed. Articles, 1,500 to 2,500 words, on all aspects of life in Maine. Photos. Pays to 10¢ a word, extra for photos, on acceptance. Query.

ENQUIRER MAGAZINE—*The Cincinnati Enquirer,* 617 Vine St., Cincinnati, OH 45201. Mary B. McDonald, Ed. Articles, 1,000 to 2,700 words: profiles, personal-experience essays, investigative pieces on business, sports, psychology, science, religion, life styles and entertainment. Humor, and some fiction. Pays $85 to $250, on publication. Query.

ERIE & CHAUTAUQUA MAGAZINE—Charles H. Strong Bldg., 1250 Tower La., Erie, PA 16505. Feature articles, to 2,500 words, on issues of interest to upscale readers in the Erie and Chautauqua counties. Investigative pieces. Personality profiles, to 1,500 words. Humor, satire, 750 words. Pays $35 per published page, on publication. Query preferred, with writing samples. Buys all rights. Guidelines available.

ESSEX LIFE—1 Blackburn Dr., P.O. Box 6, Riverdale, Gloucester, MA 01930. General-interest articles, 2,000 to 4,000 words, for residents of Boston's North Shore and Essex County. Fiction. Pays 10¢ a word, on publication. Query with samples of published work for nonfiction.

FLORIDA—*The Orlando Sentinel,* 633 N. Orange Ave., Orlando, FL 32802. Mitch Gerber, Ed. Articles of varying lengths relating to Florida. Pays from $150, on publication.

FLORIDA GULF COAST LIVING—1211 N. Westshore Blvd., Suite 809, Tampa, FL 33607. Milana Petty, Ed. Articles, 750 to 1,200 words, for the active home buyer on the Gulf Coast: home-related articles, moving tips, financing, etc. Pays 7¢ to 10¢ a word, on acceptance. Query preferred.

FLORIDA KEYS MAGAZINE—Box 818, 6187, O/S Hwy., Marathon, FL 33040. Address David Ethridge. Articles, 1,000 to 4,000 words, on the Florida Keys: history, environment, natural history, profiles, etc. Fiction. Fillers, humor. Photos. Pays varying rates, on publication. Query preferred.

FLORIDA TREND—Box 611, St. Petersburg, FL 33731. Richard Edmonds, Ed. Articles, to 2,000 words, on Florida business and businesspersons. Photos. Query.

THE GEORGETOWNER—P.O. Box 3528, Washington, DC 20007. Articles, 3 to 4 typewritten, double-spaced pages, on subjects of interest to residents of Georgetown. Fiction, same length. Poetry. Pays $1.75 per column inch, on publication.

GOLD COAST LIFE MAGAZINE—730 N.E. 44th St., Ft. Lauderdale, FL 33334. B. Austin Moran, Ed. Articles, from 1,000 words, on life styles of southeastern Florida. Pays $50 to $200, on publication.

GULFSHORE LIFE—3620 Tamiami Trail N., Naples, FL 33940. Molly J. Burns, Ed. Articles, 950 to 3,500 words, on personalities, travel, sports, business, investment, humor, nature, in southwestern Florida. Pays $50 to $300. Query.

HIGH COUNTRY NEWS—Box V, Paonia, CO 81428. Ed Marston, Man. Ed. Articles, 500 to 2,000 words, on environmental and natural resource topics related to the Rocky Mountain region. Photos. Pays 3¢ to 6¢ a word, extra for photos, on publication. Query.

HOUSTON CITY—1800 W. Loop South, Suite 1450, Houston, TX 77027. Don Robertson, Exec. Ed. In-depth articles, 500 to 3,000 words, examining society and politics in Houston. Profiles; exposés; consumer pieces. Occasional fiction. Query preferred. Pays varying rates, on publication.

HOUSTON LIVING—Suite 450, 5444 Westheimer, Houston, TX 77056. Cathy R. Lassiter, Ed. Articles, 800 to 1,500 words, for persons in the market to buy a new home, or condominium, or renting until they purchase a home, on interior decorating, home security, apartment living, home improvement, energy efficiency, landscaping. Pays 10¢ to 20¢ a word, on acceptance. Query.

HUDSON VALLEY MAGAZINE—Box 425, Woodstock, NY 12498. Joanne Michaels, Ed.-in-Chief. Regional interest articles, 1,000 to 1,500 words. Photos. Pays 3¢ a word, on publication. Query preferred.

ILLINOIS ENTERTAINER—Box 356, Mount Prospect, IL 60056. Guy Arnston, Ed. Articles, 500 to 1,500 words, on entertainment and leisure time activities in the greater Chicago area. Personality profiles; interviews; reviews. Photos. Pays 3¢ to 5¢ a word, on publication. Query preferred.

ILLINOIS TIMES—Box 3524, Springfield, IL 62708. Harold Henderson, Man. Ed. Articles, 1,000 to 2,500 words, on the "people, places, things and activities" of Illinois outside the Chicago metropolitan area. All material should have a specific Illinois tie-in. Pays 4¢ a word, on publication. Query.

INDIANAPOLIS MAGAZINE—363 N. Illinois St., Indianapolis, IN 46204. Pegg Kennedy, Ed. Feature articles, 500 to 5,000 words, on regional topics. Columns: travel, business, personal finance, health, leisure, fine arts, personalities, calendar shorts. No fiction. Pays $50 to $250, extra for photos, on publication. Query.

INLAND SHORES—Box 86, Hartland, WI 53029. Articles, with good color photos, 500 to 2,000 words, on places, events, history, culture, sports, holiday events, etc., in the Great Lakes region. Pays 5¢ a word, extra for photos, on publication.

INQUIRER MAGAZINE—*Philadelphia Inquirer,* 400 N. Broad St., Philadelphia, PA 19101. David R. Boldt, Ed. Articles, 1,500 to 2,000 words, and 3,000 to 7,000 words, on politics, science, arts and culture, business, life styles and entertainment, sports, health, beauty, psychology, education, religion, home and garden, and humor. Short pieces, 200 to 800 words, for "Our Town" department. Pays varying rates. Query preferred.

THE IOWAN—214 9th St., Des Moines, IA 50309. Charles W. Roberts, Ed. Articles, 1,000 to 3,000 words, preferably with photos, on wide variety of topics, including business, arts, history, profiles, etc. Must have Iowa angle. Pays $100 to $400, on publication. Query.

ISLAND LIFE—P.O. Box X, Sanibel Island, FL 33957. Joan Hooper, Ed. Articles, 500 to 1,200 words, with good color photos, on unique or historical places, wildlife, architecture, on barrier islands off Florida's Gulf Coast. Pays 5¢ a word, including photos, on publication. SASE necessary.

KANSAS!—Kansas Dept. of Economic Development, 503 Kansas Ave., 6th Flr., Topeka, KS 66603. Andrea Glenn, Ed. Articles, with color slides, on people and places, events, history, and industry in Kansas. Pays varying rates, extra for photos, on publication.

LANSING—300 S. Washington Sq., Lansing, MI 48933. Anthony A. Petrella, Ed. Articles, 2,000 to 3,000 words, on lifestyles, history, the arts, politics, energy, etc., in Lansing area. Profiles. Pays $50 to $100, on publication.

LONG ISLAND HERITAGE—29 Continental Pl., Glen Cove, NY 11542. Tim O'Brien, Ed. Articles, 500 to 700 words, on the history and crafts of Long Island. Angle on specific artist or area of collecting antiques helpful. Non-regional pieces on collecting, architecture and art. Photos. Pays to $25, on acceptance. Query preferred.

LONG ISLAND'S NIGHTLIFE MAGAZINE—1770 Deer Park Ave., Deer Park, NY 11729. Bill Ervolino, Ed. Articles, 1,000 to 2,500 words, on entertainment, leisure, personalities. Photos. Pays $50 to $200, on publication. Query preferred.

LOS ANGELES BUSINESS JOURNAL—3727 W. Sixth St., Los Angeles, CA 90020. David Yochum, Ed. Feature articles on specific industries in the five-county Los Angeles area, stressing the how-to. Pays per column inch. Query.

LOS ANGELES MAGAZINE—1888 Century Park E., Los Angeles, CA 90067. Lew Harris, Exec. Ed. Articles, to 3,000 words, of interest to sophisticated, affluent southern Californians, preferably with local focus on a life style topic. Pays from 10¢ a word, on publication. Query.

LOS ANGELES READER—8471 Melrose Ave., Los Angeles, CA 90069. James Vowell, Ed. Articles, 1,500 to 4,000 words, on subjects relating to the Los Angeles/Southern California area; special emphasis on entertainment and the arts. Some fiction. Pays $100 to $300, on publication. Query preferred.

LOUISVILLE—One Riverfront Plaza, Louisville, KY 40202. Betty Lou Amster, Ed. Articles, 1,000 to 2,000 words, on community problems and local business success stories, for business leaders of Louisville area. Photos. Pays from $50, on acceptance. Query; articles on assignment only. Limited freelance market.

MAGAZINE OF THE MIDLANDS—*Omaha World-Herald*, World-Herald Square, Omaha, NE 68102. Hollis Limprecht, Ed. Articles, 500 to 2,300 words, on regional-interest subjects. Humor; photos. Pays $25 to $100, on publication.

MAINELIFE—Box 111, Freedom, ME 04941. George Frangoulis, Ed. Articles, 1,000 to 2,500 words, on home and garden, history, arts and culture, Maine people and business, travel, energy and environment, wildlife. Photos. Pays $50 per page, on publication.

MARYLAND—Dept. of Economic and Community Development, 45 Calvert St., Annapolis, MD 21401. Bonnie Jo Ayers, Ed. Articles, 450 to 1,800 words, on Maryland subjects. Pays varying rates, on acceptance. Query preferred. Guidelines available.

MEMPHIS—460 Tennessee St., Memphis, TN 38101. Kenneth Neill, Ed. Articles, 2,000 to 4,000 words, on a wide range of topics—politics, business, sports, art, fashion, education, medicine, etc. All material must relate in some way to Memphis. Pays $100 to $400, on publication. Queries preferred.

METROPOLITAN DETROIT—422 W. Congress, Detroit, MI 48226. Kirk Cheyfitz, Ed. Articles, 50 to 3,000 words, on subjects related to the Detroit region and Michigan. "Most out-of-state writers have only the slimmest chance of being published, and we discourage their queries." Pays 10¢ to 30¢ a word, on publication. Queries required.

MIAMI/SOUTH FLORIDA MAGAZINE (formerly *Miami*)—P.O. Box 140008, Coral Gables, FL 33114. Erica Rauzin, Ed. Features, 1,500 to 3,000 words, department pieces, 900 to 1,500 words, with strong South Florida focus: personalities, home and garden, humor, trends, life style, etc. No travel pieces or poems. Short, bright items for "Big Orange" section. Send SASE. Pays $50 to $600, on publication.

602

MICHIANA—*South Bend Tribune,* 225 W. Colfax Ave., South Bend, IN 46626. Bill Sonneborn, Ed. Articles, 300 to 3,000 words, on people, places and events in northern Indiana and southern Michigan. Also uses travel articles and profiles of celebrities. Pays $50 to $125, on publication. "Good illustrations often 'sell' a piece to us." Query first.

MICHIGAN LIVING—17000 Executive Plaza Dr., Dearborn, MI 48126. Len Barnes, Ed. Travel articles, 500 to 1,500 words, on tourist attractions and recreational opportunities in Michigan: places to go, things to do, costs, etc. Color photos. Pays $100 to $350, extra for photos, on acceptance.

MICHIGAN: THE MAGAZINE OF THE DETROIT NEWS—Evening News Assn., 615 W. Lafayette Blvd., Detroit, MI 48231. Susan Slobojan, Ed. Clifford A. Ridley, Asst. Man. Ed. Articles, from 750 words, on business, politics, arts and culture, science, sports and education, etc., with a Michigan slant. Cover articles, to 3,000 words. Personal-experience essays and investigative articles. Some fiction. Pays $75 to $400, on publication. Query preferred.

MID-WEST OUTDOORS—111 Shore Dr., Hinsdale, IL 60521. Gene Laulunen, Ed. Articles, 1,500 words, with photos, on where, when and how to fish. Fillers, humor, 200 to 500 words. Pays $15 to $35, on publication.

MILWAUKEE—828 Broadway, Milwaukee, WI 53202. Charles Sykes, Ed. Profiles, investigative articles, historical pieces, 3,000 to 4,000 words; all material must have local tie-in. Pays $300 to $500, on publication. Query.

MISSOURI LIFE—1205 University Ave., Suite 500, Columbia, MO 65201. Douglas Carr, Ed. Articles, 500 to 3,000 words, with photos, on Missouri: history, commerce, culture, people. Photo essays. Pays $50 to $200, on publication. No recent report. Query.

MONTANA MAGAZINE—Box 5630, Helena, MT 59604. Carolyn Cunningham, Ed. Articles, with photos, about Montana history, recreation, conservation, events. How-to's. No personal-experience pieces. Pays varying rates, on publication. Query.

MONTHLY DETROIT—1123 First National Bldg. Detroit, MI 48226. Frank Kuznik, Ed. Articles, 500 to 5,000 words, on Detroit people, issues, lifestyles, businesses. Pays negotiable rates, on publication. Query.

MPLS. ST. PAUL—12 S. 6th St., Ste. 1030, Minneapolis, MN 55402. Marla J. Kinney, Man. Ed. In-depth articles, features, profiles and service pieces, 300 to 3,000 words, with Minneapolis-St. Paul focus. Photo essays. Pays to $500. Query with outline and writing samples.

NEVADA—Capital Complex, Carson City, NV 89710. David Moore, Man. Ed. Articles, 500 to 1,500 words, on Nevada: its history, people, recreation, travel, places and entertainment. Pays $50 to $300, on publication.

THE NEVADAN—*The Las Vegas Review-Journal,* Box 70, Las Vegas, NV 89125. A. D. Hopkins, Ed. Articles, with B/W photos, about 2,000 words, on history in Nevada, Southwest Utah, Northeast Arizona, and Death Valley area of California. Photos. Pays $60, extra for photos, on publication. Query preferred.

NEW BEDFORD—5 S. Sixth St., New Bedford, MA 02740. Dee Giles Forsythe, Ed. Articles, 1,500 to 3,000 words, fiction, to 4,000 words, and poetry, related to the southeastern Massachusetts and Rhode Island area. Special interest in "historical aspects with some current update, on the positive scale, of our region and city." Pays $50 to $150, on publication.

NEW ENGLAND MONTHLY—P.O. Box 446, Haydenville, MA 01039. Daniel Okrent, Ed. Full-length articles, 2,500 to 5,000 words, on politics, business, sports, the arts, nature, etc. in the six New England states. Also uses "shorts" (400 to 1,000 words) and department pieces (800 to 1,000 words). Pays from $100 to $1,350, depending on the length of the piece, on acceptance. Query first for articles.

NEW HAMPSHIRE PROFILES—109 N. Main Street, Concord, NH 03301. David W. Minnis, Ed. Articles, 500 to 2,000 words, on New Hampshire people, travel, sports issues, events, and lifestyles. Pays $100 to $300, on publication. Query.

NEW JERSEY LIVING—830 Raymond Rd., R.D. 4, Princeton, NJ 08540. Marie C. Turi, Asst. Pub. Articles, to 3,000 words, on topics of general interest—business, travel, arts and leisure, fashion, health and fitness, etc. Material must have a tie-in to New Jersey. Pays $50, on publication.

NEW JERSEY MONTHLY—7 Dumont Pl., Morristown, NJ 07960. Richard Szathmary, Man. Ed. Features, 3,000 to 4,000 words, and department pieces, 1,000 to 1,500 words, on general-interest subjects, personalities, issues, and events relating to New Jersey. Essays, 1,000 to 1,500 words, about New Jerseyana. Pays $150 to $1,000, on publication. Query preferred.

NEW MEXICO MAGAZINE—Bataan Memorial Bldg., Santa Fe, NM 87503. Richard Sandoval, Ed. Articles, 250 to 2,000 words, on New Mexico subjects. Pays about 10¢ a word, on publication.

NEW ORLEANS MAGAZINE—Box 26815, New Orleans, LA 70186. Linda Matys, Ed. Articles, 3 to 15 triple-spaced pages, on New Orleans area people and issues. Photos. Pays $50 to $300, extra for photos, on acceptance. Query.

NEW YORK—755 Second Ave., New York, NY 10017. Ed Kosner, Ed. Laurie Jones, Man. Ed. Feature articles on New York City subjects. Payment negotiated and on acceptance. Query.

NEW YORK ALIVE—152 Washington Ave., Albany, NY 12210. Mary Grates Stoll, Ed. Articles aimed at developing knowledge of and appreciation for New York State. Features, 3,000 words maximum, on business, lifestyle, education, history and the arts. Department pieces for regular columns, including "Great Escapes" (travel ideas) and "Expressly New York" (unusual places, products or events in New York). Pays $250 to $300 for features, $50 to $100 for departments. Query preferred.

NORTH DAKOTA HORIZONS—P.O. Box 2467, Fargo, ND 58107. Sheldon Green, Ed. Articles, 3,000 words, on North Dakota history, current events, economy, trends that will affect North Dakotans, etc. Photos. Pays $75 to $300, on publication. Query.

NORTHEAST MAGAZINE—*The Hartford Courant,* 179 Allyn St., Hartford, CT 06103. Larry Bloom, Ed. Articles and short stories, to 5,000 words, with Connecticut tie-in; personal essays, about 1,000 words. Pays $300 to $1,000, on acceptance.

NORTHWEST—1320 S.W. Broadway, Portland, OR 97201. Sunday magazine of *The Sunday Oregonian.* Jack R. Hart, Ed. Articles, to 3,000 words, on Pacific Northwest issues and personalities: regional travel, science and business, outdoor recreation, and lifestyle trends. Personal essays. Local angle essential. Pays $75 to $800. Query first.

OHIO MAGAZINE—40 S. Third St., Columbus, OH 43215. Ellen Stein, Man. Ed. Articles and columns on Ohio personalities, lifestyle, issues, events. Photo features. Shorts on news, people, events and activities. Pays $200 to $850, $15 to $75 for shorts, on publication. Query.

OKLAHOMA TODAY—215 N.E. 28th St., P.O. Box 53384, Oklahoma City, OK 73152. Sue Carter, Ed. Articles, to 1,500 words, on travel and recreation in Oklahoma. Pays 15¢ a word, on acceptance.

ORANGE COAST—18200 W. McDermott St., Irvine, CA 92714. Address Andrea Holm or Janet Eastman. Articles on various topics, with an Orange County tie-in, 3,000 to 6,000 words. Pays $100 to $150, on acceptance.

ORLANDO MAGAZINE—P.O. Box 2207, Orlando, FL 32802. Carole De-Pinto, Man. Ed. Profiles, articles on growth and development in central Florida, business, travel, health and the arts, 1,000 to 1,500 words. Orlando/Central Florida tie-in recommended. Pays $25 to $100, extra for photos, on acceptance.

PD—*St. Louis Post-Dispatcher*, 900 N. Tucker Blvd., St. Louis, MO 63101. Jeff Meyers, Ed. How-to pieces, profiles, personal-experience pieces and investigative articles, 3,000 to 4,000 words: politics, science, life styles and entertainment, psychology, etc. Humor. Pays $125 to $250, on publication. No unsolicited manuscripts. Query.

PENNSYLVANIA MAGAZINE—Box 576, Camp Hill, PA 17011. Albert E. Hilliday, Ed. General-interest features with a Pennsylvania tie-in. No pieces on the Amish, Philadelphia, Pittsburgh, or politics. Pays varying rates, usually on acceptance. Query preferred.

PHILADELPHIA—1500 Walnut St., Philadelphia, PA 19102. Ben Yagoda, Articles Ed. Articles, 1,000 to 5,000 words, for sophisticated audience, relating to Philadelphia area. No fiction. Pays from $150, on publication. Query.

PHILADELPHIA INQUIRER TODAY MAGAZINE—P.O. Box 8263, Philadelphia, PA 19101. David R. Boldt, Ed. Articles, 500 to 7,000 words, mainly by local writers. Pays varying rates, on publication. Query.

PHILADELPHIA STYLE—2019 Chancellor St., Philadelphia, PA 19103. Published for the Philadelphia Convention and Visitor's Bureau. Andrea Diehl, Ed. Articles, 500 to 750 words, on travel, leisure, and entertainment. Pays $10, on publication.

PHOENIX BUSINESS JOURNAL—1817 N. 3rd St., Suite 100, Phoenix, AZ 85004. Tom Kuhn, Ed. Articles on leading and innovative businesses and business people in the Phoenix area. Photos. Pays $2.50 to $3 per column inch, extra for photos, on publication.

PHOENIX MAGAZINE—4707 N. 12th St., Phoenix, AZ 85014. Jeff Burger, Ed. Articles, 1,000 to 3,000 words, on topics of special interest to Phoenix-area residents. Pays $75 to $150 for features, extra for photos, on publication. Query.

PITTSBURGH—4802 Fifth Ave., Pittsburgh, PA 15213. Martin Schultz, Ed. Articles, 850 to 3,000 words, with western Pennsylvania slant. 3- to 4-month lead time. Pays on publication.

PITTSBURGH PREVIEW—4551 Forbes Ave., Pittsburgh, PA 15213. Kimberly Flaherty, Ed. Business-oriented articles for women in the Pittsburgh four-county area. Pays $25 to $200, on publication.

RURAL MISSOURI—2722 E. McCarty St., Jefferson City, MO 65101. Steven Glensky, Man. Ed. Articles, 500 to 3,000 words, on nostalgia, history and people, with rural slant. Pays $30 to $200, on acceptance.

SACRAMENTO MAGAZINE—P.O. Box 2424, Sacramento, CA 95811. Query Man. Ed. Issue-oriented and investigative articles, and profiles and service pieces, 1,500 to 3,000 words. Department pieces, 850 to 1,750 words, on politics, dining out, arts, etc. Pieces, 75 to 350 words, for "City Lights," on interesting people, news items. Pays from $150 for features, on acceptance. Buys all rights.

SAN ANTONIO MAGAZINE—Chamber of Commerce, P.O. Box 1628, San Antonio, TX 78296. Alice Costello, Ed. Articles on San Antonio area. Pays $75 to $300, on publication. Query.

SAN DIEGO MAGAZINE—3254 Rosecrans St., P.O. Box 85409, San Diego, CA 92138. Thomas Shess, Jr., Exec. Ed. Articles, 2,000 to 3,000 words, on local personalities, political figures, life styles, business, history, etc., relating to San Diego area. Photos. Pays $150 to $500, on publication.

SAN DIEGO READER—P.O. Box 80803, San Diego, CA 92138. Jim Mullin, Ed. Articles, 2,500 to 10,000 words, on the general San Diego region. Pieces on travel or national topics will not be considered. Pays $250 to $750, on publication. Query required.

SAN FRANCISCO—950 Battery St., San Francisco, CA 94111. Virginia Butterfield, Ed. General-interest articles, 1,000 to 3,000 words, relating to the San Francisco Bay area. Pays from $100, 30 days after publication. Query.

SEATTLE WEEKLY—1931 Second Ave., Seattle, WA 98101. David Brewster, Ed. Articles, 700 to 4,000 words, on arts, politics, food, business, sports and books with local and regional emphasis. Pays $75 to $800, after publication. Queries preferred.

SHENANDOAH/VIRGINIA TOWN & COUNTRY—See *The Virginian.*

SHREVEPORT—Box 20074, Shreveport, LA 71120. Mary L. Baldwin, Ed. Articles, 1,500 to 2,500 words, on interesting events, activities, and people in the Arkansas-Louisiana-Texas area. Pays $75 to $150, on acceptance. Queries preferred.

SOUTH CAROLINA WILDLIFE—P.O. Box 167, Columbia, SC 29202. John Davis, Ed. Articles, 1,000 to 3,000 words, with regional outdoors focus: conservation, natural history and wildlife, recreation. Profiles, how-to's. Pays 10¢ a word, extra for photos, on acceptance.

SOUTH FLORIDA LIVING—700 W. Hillsboro Blvd., Bldg. 3, Ste. 102, Deerfield Beach, FL 33441. Cynthia M. Marusarz, Man. Ed. Articles on developments in the housing industry, home improvements, security, decorating, energy efficiency, etc.; advice on finding, buying, and maintaining a home or condominium in South Florida. Pays 10¢ a word, on acceptance. Query.

THE STATE: DOWN HOME IN NORTH CAROLINA—Box 2169, Raleigh, NC 27602. Bill Wright, Ed. Features, 500 to 1,500 words, on North Carolina subjects. Pays $10 to $50, on acceptance.

SUBURBIA TODAY—Gannett Newspapers, 1 Gannett Dr., White Plains, NY 10604. Neil S. Martin, Ed. Articles on trends and the environment; profiles of people in the Westchester, Rockland and Putnam counties of New York State. Pays $100 to $300, on publication. Query preferred.

SUNDAY (formerly *Chicago Tribune Magazine*)—*Chicago Tribune,* 435 N. Michigan, Chicago, IL 60611. John Twohey, Ed. Articles, 2,000 to 3,000 words, on politics, arts, health, travel, food, fashions, and home furnishings, for Chicago and Midwestern readers. Pays from $200, on acceptance. Query.

SUNDAY—*The Pittsburgh Press,* 34 Blvd. of the Allies, Pittsburgh, PA 15230. Ed Wintermantel, Ed. Well-written, well-organized, in-depth articles of local or regional interest, 1,000 to 3,000 words, on issues, trends or personalities. No fiction, hobbies, how-to's or 'timely events' pieces. Pays $100 to $400, extra for photos, on publication. Query.

SUNDAY MAGAZINE—*Providence Sunday Journal,* 75 Fountain St., Providence, RI 02902. Jack Major, Ed. Profiles, personal-experience pieces, 1,000 to 1,500 words. Pays $100 to $200, on publication.

SUNSET MAGAZINE—Menlo Park, CA 94025. William Marken, Ed. Western regional. Queries considered but not encouraged.

SUNSHINE MAGAZINE—*News/Sun-Sentinel,* P.O. Box 14430, 101 N. New River Dr. E., Fort Lauderdale, FL 33302. John Parkyn, Ed. Articles, 1,000 to 4,000 words, on all subjects relevant to the interests of South Floridians. Pays 15¢ to 25¢ a word, up to $750, on acceptance.

TALLAHASSEE MAGAZINE—P.O. Box 12848, Tallahassee, FL 32317. William L. Needham, Ed. Personality profiles and articles, 600 to 1,000 words, on local history, arts, politics, etc., relating to northern Florida. Pays 10¢ a word, extra for photos, on publication.

TAMPA BAY MONTHLY—2502 Rocky Point Rd., Suite 295, Tampa, FL 33607. Heidi Swanson, Man. Ed. Life style features, profiles, articles of regional interest, 2,500 to 6,000 words. Shorts, 300 to 1,200 words. Pays $125 to $600 for articles, within thirty days of publication.

TEXAS HIGHWAYS—11th and Brazos, Austin, TX 78701. Frank Lively, Ed. Articles, 200 to 1,800 words, on scenic, recreational, historical and cultural topics—all related to Texas. Pays $150 to $500, on acceptance. Queries required.

TEXAS MONTHLY—P.O. Box 1569, Austin, TX 78767. Sarah Whitson, Man. Ed. Most articles staff-written. Query.

TEXAS WEEKLY——*The Pasadena* (TX) *Citizen,* P.O. Box 6192, Pasadena, TX 77506. Dick Nichols, Ed. Articles, 1,000 to 2,000 words, with a Texas tie-in; particularly interested in Gulf Coast-related pieces. Pays $100, on publication.

THIRD COAST—P.O. Box 592, Austin, TX 78767. Miriam Davison, Man. Ed. Articles, 500 to 4,000 words, on news and entertainment, politics and the arts; personality profiles, with regional tie-in to Austin area. Pays varying rates, on publication. Query preferred.

TOLEDO MAGAZINE—*The Blade,* Toledo, OH 43660. Sue Stankey, Ed. Articles, to 4,000 words, on Toledo area personalities, news, etc. Photos. Pays $50 to $500, on publication. Query.

TORONTO LIFE—59 Front St. E., Toronto, Ont., Canada M5E 1B3. Marq de Villiers, Ed. Articles, 1,000 to 4,500 words, on Toronto. Pays $400 to $1,500, on acceptance. Query.

TROPIC—*The Miami Herald,* One Herald Plaza, Miami, FL 33101. Kevin Hall, Ed. General-interest articles, 1,500 to 3,000 words, for South Florida readers. Pays $300 to $600, on acceptance.

607

TULSA—P.O. Box 1620, Tulsa, OK 74101. Lynn Rollins Price, Man. Ed. Factual business-oriented and human interest articles of local interest, 1,000 to 2,500 words. Pays $75 to $175, on publication. Query.

TWIN CITIES READER—100 N. 7th St., Minneapolis, MN 55403. Deborah L. Hopp, Ed.-in-Chief. Articles, 3 to 10 printed pages, on cultural phenomena, city politics, and general-interest subjects, for local readers aged 25 to 44. Pays to $1.75 per inch, on publication.

ULTRA—2000 Bering Dr., Suite 200, Houston, TX 77057. David Bertugli, Ed. Upbeat, sophisticated features and shorts, on "luxurious" living in Texas: fashion, fine arts, travel, sports, real estate, finance, personalities, etc. Pays varying rates, on acceptance. Query.

UPSTATE MAGAZINE—*Sunday Democrat and Chronicle,* 55 Exchange St., Rochester, NY 14614. Mary Rita Kurycki, Ed. Local or regionally-related articles. Pays $60 to $325, on publication.

UTAH HOLIDAY—419 E. First St., Salt Lake City, UT 84111. Annette S. Rogers, Man. Ed. Articles, 1,000 to 5,000 words, that provide provocative, informative insights into the state, its people and local affairs. Columns, from 1,000 to 1,500 words; "Front Page" opinion pieces, 500 to 2,000 words; fiction, 1,000 to 3,000 words; poetry, to 65 lines. Pays $60 to $500 for nonfiction; $60 to $200 for fiction; $25 to $50 for poetry, on publication. Query.

VERMONT LIFE—61 Elm St., Montpelier, VT 05602. Nancy P. Graff, Acting Ed. Articles, 1,500 to 3,000 words, about Vermont subjects only. Photos. Pays 20¢ a word, extra for photos. Query required.

THE VIRGINIAN (formerly *Shenandoah/Virginia Town & Country*)—P.O. Box 8, New Hope, VA 24469. Hunter S. Pierce, IV, Ed. Dir. Articles, 2,000 words, relating to Virginia, West Virginia and Maryland: folklore, local history, country living, home and garden, outdoor sports, personal experience and adventure pieces. Profiles. No poetry or fiction. Pays varying rates, on publication. Query.

WASHINGTON—13029 Northup Way N.E., Suite 1, Bellevue, WA 98005. Kenneth Gouldthorpe, Ed. Articles on business, arts, politics, history, people, places and ideas related to Washington state. Pays varying rates, on publication.

WASHINGTON DOSSIER—3301 New Mexico Ave., N.W., Washington, DC 20016. Don Oldenburg, Senior Ed. Features, 1,000 to 2,500 words, with a Washington DC connection or angle—personality pieces, investigative articles, service pieces, etc. Readers are sophisticated, so manuscripts must reflect "an insider's savvy." Pays 10¢ to 20¢ a word, within 30 days of acceptance.

WASHINGTON POST MAGAZINE—*The Washington Post,* 1150 15th St., NW, Washington, DC 20071. Stephen L. Petranek, Man. Ed. Personal-experience essays, profiles and general-interest pieces, to 4,000 words, on business, arts and culture, politics, science, sports, psychology, education, children, relationships, behavior, etc. Pays from $100, after acceptance. Query.

THE WASHINGTONIAN—1828 L. St. N.W., Suite 200, Washington, DC 20036. John Limpert, Ed. Helpful, informative, interesting articles, 1,000 to 4,000 words, on Washington-related topics. Pays 20¢ a word, on publication. Query.

WEST FLORIDA LIFE—1487 Second St., Suite C, Sarasota, FL 33577. Pam Daniel, Ed. Articles with a strong regional focus on leisure, sports, cuisine, travel, business, arts and people, 1,000 to 2,000 words. Pays $75 to $150, on publication.

WEST MICHIGAN MAGAZINE—7 Ionia S.W., Grand Rapids, MI 49503. Dotti Clune, Ed. Articles, to 1,500 words, on western Michigan. Query.

WESTERN MASSACHUSETTS MAGAZINE—P.O. Box 76, Northampton, MA 01061–0076. Michael R. Evans, Man. Ed. Articles and fiction, 500 to 3,500 words, on Western Massachusetts subjects. Shorter pieces, 50 to 200 words, on interesting Western Massachusetts information. Pays $20 to $150, on acceptance. Query.

WESTERN PEOPLE—P.O. Box 2500, Saskatoon, Sask., Canada S7K 2C4. Mary Gilchrist, Man. Editor. Articles, to 2,000 words, with photos, for Western Canadians: current events, history, personalities. Short fiction and poetry. Pays from $20 to $175, extra for photos, on acceptance.

WESTERN SPORTSMAN—P.O. Box 737, Regina, Sask., Canada S4P 3A8. Red Wilkinson, Ed. Informative articles, to 2,500 words, on outdoor experiences in Alberta and Saskatchewan. How-to's, humor, cartoons. Photos. Pays $40 to $225, on publication.

WESTWAYS—Box 2890, Terminal Annex, Los Angeles, CA 90051. Mary Ann Cravens, Man. Ed. Articles, 1,000 to 1,500 words, on western U.S., Canada, and Mexico: travel, history, culture, personalities. Photos. Pays from 20¢ a word, extra for photos. Query.

WISCONSIN MAGAZINE—*Milwaukee Journal,* Newspapers, Inc. Box 661, Milwaukee, WI 53201. Beth Slocum, Ed. Articles, 500 to 3,000 words, on business, politics, arts, science, personal finance, psychology, entertainment, health, etc. Personal-experience essays and investigative articles. Pays $200 to $500, on publication. Query.

WISCONSIN TRAILS—P.O. Box 5650, Madison, WI 53705. Susan Pigorsch, Man. Ed. Articles, 1,500 to 3,000 words, on history, nostalgia, outdoor adventure, life styles, food, travel—all tied in to Wisconsin. Also, profiles of artists and craftspeople, short fillers. "We need exceptional photos for most articles, before we will accept them." Pays $50 to $250, half on acceptance, half on publication. Query first.

WORCESTER MAGAZINE—P.O. Box 1000, Worcester, MA 01614. Michael C. Bingham, Man. Ed. Articles, to 1,500 words, on arts and entertainment, fashion, education and occasional other subjects for supplements. Must have some Worcester County angle. Pays $1 to $1.50 per column inch, on publication. Query required; no unsolicited manuscripts.

YANKEE—Dublin, NH 03444. Judson D. Hale, Ed. Articles and fiction, about 2,500 words, on New England and residents. Pays about $500 for features, $750 for fiction, on acceptance.

YANKEE MAGAZINE'S TRAVEL GUIDE TO NEW ENGLAND—Main St., Dublin, NH 03444. Sharon Smith, Ed. Articles, 500 to 2,000 words, on unusual activities, restaurants, places to visit in New England, for tourists. Photos. Pays $50 to $300, on acceptance. Query with outline and writing samples.

TRADE JOURNALS AND BUSINESS MAGAZINES

ABA BANKING JOURNAL—345 Hudson St., New York, NY 10014. Bill Streeter, Ed. American Bankers Assn. Articles, to 2,000 words, on marketing trends, improving practices in commercial bank management. Pays varying rates, on acceptance and on publication. Query.

ADVERTISING WORLD—150 Fifth Ave., New York, NY 10011. Edith Cudlipp, Ed. Articles, from 1,000 to 2,000 words, on international advertising. Pays on publication. Query.

ALTERNATIVE ENERGY RETAILER—P.O. Box 2180, Waterbury, CT 06722. John Florian, Ed. Feature articles, 2,000 words, for retailers of alternative energy products—wood, coal and fireplace products and services. Interviews with successful retailers, stressing the how-to. B/W photos. Pays $200, extra for photos, on publication. Query first.

AMERICAN BANKER—One State Street Plaza, New York, NY 10004. William Zimmerman, Ed. Articles, 1,000 to 3,000 words, on banking and finance-related topics. Pays varying rates, on publication. Query preferred.

AMERICAN BAR ASSOCIATION JOURNAL—750 N. Lake Shore Dr., Chicago, IL 60611. Laurence Bodine, Assoc. Ed. Practical articles, to 3,000 words, to help lawyers in small general practice firms. Humor, 750 words. Pays from $100, $25 for short humor, on acceptance. Query.

AMERICAN BICYCLIST AND MOTORCYCLIST—80 Eighth Ave., New York, NY 10011. Stan Gottlieb, Ed. Articles, 1,500 to 2,800 words, on sales and repair practices of successful bicycle and moped dealers. Photos. Pays from 5¢ a word, extra for photos, on publication. Query.

AMERICAN CLAY EXCHANGE—P.O. Box 2674, La Mesa, CA 92041. Susan M. Cox, Ed. Thoroughly-researched articles to 1,000 words, for collectors and dealers of American-made pottery, with emphasis on antiques and collectibles. Pays $5 for fillers, from $100 for features, on publication.

AMERICAN COIN-OP—500 N. Dearborn, Chicago, IL 60610. Ben Russell, Ed. Articles, to 2,500 words, with photos, on successful coin-operated laundries and drycleaners: promotion, equipment, maintenance, etc. Pays from 6¢ a word, extra for photos, on publication. Query. Send for guidelines.

AMERICAN DEMOGRAPHICS—P.O. Box 68, Ithaca, NY 14850. Bryant Robey, Ed. Articles, 1,500 to 3,000 words, on aspects of demographics, for strategists in industry, government, and education. Pays $100 to $300, on publication. Query.

AMERICAN FARRIERS JOURNAL—P.O. Box L, Harvard, MA 01451. Fran Garvan, Ed. Articles, 800 to 5,000 words, on horse handling, tools, anatomy, etc. Pays $50 per published page, on publication. Query.

AMERICAN LAUNDRY DIGEST—500 N. Dearborn, Chicago, IL 60610. Larry Ebert, Ed. Articles, 300 to 2,500 words, on operation of hospital and hotel laundries, linen supply plants, etc. Photos. Pays from 5¢ per word, extra for photos, before publication. Query.

AMERICAN PAINTING CONTRACTOR—2911 Washington Ave., St. Louis, MO 63103. Rich Hirsch, Ed. Technical articles, to 2,500 words, with photos, on industrial maintenance painting and management of painting business, for contractors and architects.

ANTIQUES DEALER—1115 Clifton Ave., Clifton, NJ 07013. Nancy Adams, Ed. Articles, 1,500 words, on national and international trends and news in antiques business. Features by authorities in specific fields. Fillers, 750 words. B/W photos. Pays on publication. Query.

THE APOTHECARY—895 Cherry St., Petaluma, CA 94952. Susan Keller, Man. Ed. Articles, 2,000 to 4,000 words, for pharmacists, on management and marketing techniques, and computer topics. Pays $250, on acceptance. Query. SASE required.

ARCHITECTURAL METALS—221 N. La Salle St., Chicago, IL 60601. James Mruk, Ed. Articles, 1,000 to 2,500 words, on how to design, construct, erect and maintain architectural metal products. Photos, illustrations. Pays varying rates, on publication. Query.

ARCHITECTURE—1735 New York Ave., NW, Washington, DC 20006. Donald Canty, Ed. Articles, to 3,000 words, on architecture and urban design; book reviews. Pays $100 to $500, extra for photos. Query required.

AREA DEVELOPMENT MAGAZINE—525 Northern Blvd., Great Neck, NY 11021. Tom Bergeron, Ed. Articles for top executives of manufacturing companies, on industrial and office facility planning. Pay $30 per manuscript page. Query.

ART BUSINESS NEWS—2135 Summer St., P.O. Box 3837, Stamford, CT 06905. Vicki Wray, Ed. Articles, 1,000 words, for art dealers and framers, on trends and events of national importance to the art industry, and relevant business subjects. Pays $75, on publication. Query preferred.

ART MATERIAL TRADE NEWS—6255 Barfield Rd., Atlanta, GA 30328. Nancy Celani, Ed. Articles, from 800 words, for dealers, wholesalers, and manufacturers of artist materials. Fillers. Pays 10¢ a word, on publication. Query.

AUTOMOTIVE EXECUTIVE—8400 Westpark Dr., McLean, VA 22102. Noreen S. Welle, Man. Ed. National Automobile Dealers Assn. Articles, 750 to 2,500 words, on management of automobile and heavy-duty truck dealerships and general business and automotive issues. Photos. Pays on acceptance. Query.

BARRISTER—American Bar Assn., 1155 E., 60th St., Chicago, IL 60637. Anthony Monahan, Ed. Articles, to 3,500 words on legal and social affairs, for lawyers. Pays $200 to $500, on acceptance.

BARRON'S—22 Cortlandt St., New York, NY 10007. Alan Abelson, Ed. National-interest articles, 1,200 to 2,500 words, on business and finance. Pays from $500, oon publication. Query.

BEER WHOLESALER—75 S.E. Fourth Ave., Delray Beach, FL 33444. Kenneth Breslauer, Ed. Articles, 8 to 10 typed pages, on business topics of interest to beer and wine wholesalers; as well as profiles of beer distributors. Pays about $120, on publication.

BETTER BUSINESS—235 East 42nd St., New York, NY 10017. John F. Robinson, Pub. Articles, 10 to 12 double-spaced pages, for the small business/ minority business markets, on finance, international trade, technology, etc. Pays on publication. Query.

BETTER COMMUNICATION—175 Washington Valley Rd., Warrenton, NJ 07060. Blixy Taetzsch, Acquisitions Ed. Practical how-to articles, on all aspects of business communication: motivating, persuading, informing, through oral and written communication with employees, co-workers, bosses, clients and customers. Pays $15 to $85, on acceptance. Send SASE for guidelines and sample.

BLACK ENTERPRISE—130 Fifth Ave., New York, NY 10011. Earl G. Graves, Ed. Articles on money, management, careers, political issues, entrepreneurship and lifestyles for black professionals. Profiles. Pays on acceptance. Query.

BOATING INDUSTRY (Incorporating *Marine Business*)—850 Third Ave., New York, NY 10022. Olga Badillo, Ed. Articles, 1,000 to 1,500 words, on marine management, manufacturing and selling, for boat dealers. Photos. Pays 4¢ to 5¢ a word, extra for photos, on publication. Query first.

THE BOSTON BUSINESS JOURNAL—393 D. St., Boston, MA 02210. Nancy P. McMillan, Ed. Articles, 500 to 1,200 words, with emphasis on local markets, its people, companies, economy: features, news, commentary. Pays $50 to $150, on publication.

BROADCAST ENGINEERING—P.O. Box 12901, 9221 Quivira Rd., Overland Park, KS 66212. Bill Rhodes, Ed. Articles, 1,000 to 2,800 words, on engineering and production in commercial AM and FM, educational radio and TV. Items on shortcuts and equipment modification for "Station-to-Station." Pays $75 to $150, $10 to $25 for shorts, on acceptance. Query.

BUILDER—Hanley-Wood, Inc., National Housing Center, 15th & M Sts., N.W., Washington, DC 20005. Frank Anton, Ed. Articles, to 1,500 words, on trends and news in home building: design, marketing, new products, etc. Pays negotiable rates, on acceptance.

BUSINESS AND COMMERCIAL AVIATION—Hangar C-1, Westchester Co. Airport, White Plains, NY 10604. John W. Olcott, Ed. Articles, 2,500 words, with photos, for pilots, on use of private aircraft for business transportation. Pays $100 to $500, on acceptance. Query.

BUSINESS ATLANTA—16255 Barfield Rd., Atlanta, GA 30328. Susan E. Hasty, Man. Ed. Articles, 1,000 to 4,500 words, with Atlanta or "deep South" business angle, strong marketing slant that will be useful to top Atlanta executives and business people. Pays $300 to $800, on publication. Query with clippings.

BUSINESS MARKETING (formerly *Industrial Marketing*)—220 E. 42nd St., New York, NY 10017. Bob Donath, Ed. Articles on selling, advertising, and promoting products and services, for marketing executives. Pays competitive rates, on publication. Query only; not responsible for unsolicited material.

THE BUSINESS TIMES—544 Tolland St., E. Hartford, CT 06108. Deborah Hallberg, Man. Ed. Articles on new products, successful companies, business topics, for Connecticut executives. Pays $1 per column inch, on publication. Query.

BUSINESS VIEW OF SOUTHWEST FLORIDA—P.O. Box 1546, Naples, FL 33939. Mark Brown, Ed. Innovative articles and columns, 750 to 1,500 words, on business, economics, finance; profiles of business leaders; pieces on new trends in technology and advances in management techniques. Real estate and banking trends. Pays $75 to $200, on publication. Query.

CALIFORNIA BUSINESS—4221 Wilshire Blvd., Suite 400, Los Angeles, CA 90010. Michael Harris, Ed. Articles, 1,200 to 1,500 words, on business and econometric issues in California. Pays varying rates, on acceptance. Query.

THE CALIFORNIA HIGHWAY PATROLMAN—2030 V St., Sacramento, CA 95818. Carol Perri, Ed. Articles, 500 to 3,500 words, on traffic safety, recreational vehicle use, travel, consumerism, historic California. Photos. Pays 2½¢ per word, extra for photos, on publication.

CALIFORNIA HORSE REVIEW—Box 646, N. Highlands, CA 95660. Jackie Hester, Ed. Articles, 1,500 to 3,000 words, for professional horsemen, on breeding, training; how-to. Fiction, 1,500 to 2,500 words, on horses, West. Pays $50 to $125, on publication. Query preferred.

CALIFORNIA LAWYER—555 Franklin St., San Francisco, CA 94102. Jonathan R. Maslow, Ed. Articles, 2,500 to 3,000 words, for attorneys in California, on legal subjects (or the legal aspects of a given political or social issue); how-to's on improving techniques in law practice. Pays $250 to $500, on acceptance. Query.

CAMPGROUND MANAGEMENT—500 Hyacinth Pl., Highland Park, IL 60035. Mike Byrnes, Ed. Detailed articles, 500 to 2,000 words, on managing recreational vehicle campgrounds. Photos. Pays $50 to $200, after publication.

CASHFLOW—1807 Glenview, Glenview, IL 60025. Vince DiPaolo, Ed. Articles, 1,500 to 2,500 words, for treasury managers in public and private institutions: cash management; investments; domestic and international financing; developments in law, economics, and tax. Fillers, to 1,000 words. Pays $7.00 per inch, on publication. Query.

CERAMIC SCOPE—3632 Ashworth N., Seattle, WA 98103. Michael Scott, Ed. Articles, 1,000 to 2,000 words, on retail or wholesale business operations of hobby ceramic studios. Photos. Pays 5¢ a word, extra for photos, on acceptance. Query.

CHEMICAL WEEK—1221 Ave. of the Americas, New York, NY 10020. John Campbell, Ed.-in-Chief. News pieces, to 200 words, on chemical business. Pays $10 per column inch, on acceptance. Query.

CHINA, GLASS & TABLEWARE—P.O. Box 2147, Clifton, NJ 07015. Sue Grisham, Ed. Case histories and interviews, 1,500 to 2,500 words, with photos, on merchandising of china and glassware. Pays $45 per page, on publication. Query.

CHRISTIAN BOOKSELLER—396 E. St. Charles Rd., Wheaton, IL 60188. Karen M. Ball, Ed. Articles, with photos, on all phases of Christian bookstore operation, and all levels of library services operation (church, school, college, seminary, etc.): ideas, news reports, store profiles, industry analyses, audiovisual and music merchandising how-to. Pays $10 to $100, on publication. Query. Send SASE for writer's guidelines.

CLEANING MANAGEMENT—17911-C Sky Park Blvd., Irvine, CA 92714. E. Daniel Harris, Jr., Pub. Articles, 1,000 to 1,500 words, on managing efficient cleaning and maintenance operations. Photos. Pays 10¢ a word, extra for photos, on publication.

COLLEGE STORE EXECUTIVE—P.O. Box 1500, Westbury, NY 11590. Marcy Kornreich, Ed. Articles, 1,000 words, for college store industry only; news; profiles. No general business or how-to articles. Photos. Pays $2 a column inch, extra for photos, on acceptance. Query.

COLORADO BUSINESS—2500 Curtis St., Suite 200, P.O. Box 5400-TA, Denver, CO 80217. Sharon Almirall, Ed. Articles, 1,500 to 2,000 words, on banking, real estate, transportation, manufacturing, etc., in the Rocky Mountain region. Pays 10¢ a word, on publication. Query.

COMMERCIAL CARRIER JOURNAL—Chilton Way, Radnor, PA 19089. Jerry Standley, Ed. Factual articles on private fleets and for-hire trucking operations. Pays from $50, on acceptance. Query.

COMPUTER DECISIONS MAGAZINE—10 Mulholland Dr., Hasbrouck Hgt., NJ 07604. Mel Mandell, Ed. Articles, 800 to 4,000 words, on generic uses of computer systems. Pays $30 to $100 per printed page, on acceptance. Query.

COMPUTER GRAPHICS WORLD—1714 Stockton St., San Francisco, CA 94133. Charles Barrett, Man. Ed. Articles, 1,000 to 5,000 words, on computer graphics technology and its applications. Photos. Pays $50 per page, on publication. Query.

CONCRETE INTERNATIONAL: DESIGN AND CONSTRUCTION—Box 19150, 22400 W. Seven Mile Rd., Detroit, MI 48219. Robert E. Wilde, Ed. Articles, 6 to 15 double-spaced pages, on concrete construction and design, with drawings and photos. Pays varying rates, on publication. Query.

CONTACTS—Box 407, North Chatham, NY 12132. Joseph Strack, Ed. Articles, 300 to 1,500 words, on management of dental laboratories, lab techniques, and equipment. Pays 4¢ to 5¢ a word, on acceptance.

CONVENIENCE STORE NEWS—254 W. 31st St., New York, NY 10001. Barbara J. Bagley, Ed. and Assoc. Pub. Features and news items, 500 to 750 words, for convenience store owners, operators, and suppliers. Photos, with captions. Pays $3 per column inch, extra for photos, on publication. Query.

COOKING FOR PROFIT—P.O. Box 267, Fond du Lac, WI 54935. Karen M. Boehme, Ed. Practical how-to articles on food preparation, profiles, case studies, management, 1,000 words. Pays $200 to $300, on publication.

CRAIN'S CHICAGO BUSINESS—740 Rush St., Chicago, IL 60611. Dan Miller, Ed. Business articles about the Midwest exclusively. Pays $9 per column inch, on acceptance.

D & B REPORTS—299 Park Ave., New York, NY 10171. Patricia W. Hamilton, Ed. Articles, 2,000 to 3,000 words, for top management of smaller businesses; government regulations, export opportunities, employee relations; how-to's on cash management, sales, productivity, etc. Pays on acceptance. Query.

DAIRY HERD MANAGEMENT—P.O. Box 67, Minneapolis, MN 55440. Sheila Widmer Vikla, Ed. Articles, 500 to 2,000 words, with photos, on techniques and equipment used in well-managed large and medium dairy operations. Pays $100 to $200, on acceptance. Query.

DEALERSCOPE (formerly *Home Entertainment Marketing*)—115 Second Ave., Waltham, MA 02154. J. M. Barry, Ed. Articles, 750 to 3,000 words, for dealers, distributors, and manufacturers of audio, video, personal computers, satellite TV, etc., on marketing and finance. Profiles; news items. Pays varying rates, on publication. Query first, with samples.

DENTAL ECONOMICS—P.O. Box 3408, Tulsa, OK 74101. Dick Hale, Ed. Articles, 1,200 to 3,500 words, on business side of dental practice, patient and staff communication, personal investments, etc. Pays $100 to $250, on acceptance.

DOMESTIC ENGINEERING—135 Addison St., Elmhurst, IL 60126. Stephen J. Shafer, Ed. Articles, to 3,000 words, on plumbing, heating, air conditioning, and process piping. Photos. Pays $20 to $35 per printed page, on publication.

DRAPERIES & WINDOW COVERINGS—P.O. Box 13079, North Palm Beach, FL 33408. John A. Clark, Ed. Articles, 1,000 to 2,000 words, for retailers, wholesalers, designers and manufacturers of draperies and window coverings. Profiles, with photos, of successful businesses in the industry. Pays $150 to $250, after acceptance. Query.

DRUG TOPICS—680 Kinderkamack Rd., Oradell, NJ 07649. Valentine A. Cardinale, Ed. News items, 500 words, with photos, on drug retailers and associations. Merchandising features, 1,000 to 1,500 words. Pays $25 to $50 for news, $50 to $350 for features, on acceptance. Query for features.

DUN'S BUSINESS MONTH—875 Third Ave., New York, NY 10022. Arlene Hershman, Ed. Articles, 1,500 to 2,500 words, on trends in corporation management, the economy, finance, and company performance. Pays from $500, on acceptance.

EARNSHAW'S INFANTS & CHILDREN'S REVIEW—393 Seventh Ave., New York, NY 10001. Pat Van Olinda, Ed. Articles on designers, manufacturers, retail promotions, and statistics for children's wear industry. Pays $50 to $150, on publication. Query.

EE'S ELECTRONICS DISTRIBUTOR—707 Westchester Ave., White Plains, NY 10604. Edward J. Walter, Ed-in-Chief. News items for distributors of electronic parts and equipment. Pays $2 per column inch, on publication. Query.

ELECTRICAL CONTRACTOR—7315 Wisconsin Ave., Bethesda, MD 20814. Larry C. Osius, Ed. Articles, 1,000 to 1,500 words, with photos, on construction or management techniques for electrical contractors. Pays $80 per printed page, before publication. Query.

ELECTRONICS WEST—2250 N. 16th St., Suite 105, Phoenix, AZ 85006. Walter J. Schuch, Ed. Articles, 1,000 to 3,000 words, on the electronics industry in the southwest: technological innovations and advances, management techniques, profiles of successful companies, etc. Pays 10¢ a word, on acceptance. Query preferred.

ENTREE—633 Third Ave., New York, NY 10017. Geri Brin, Ed. Articles, 100 to 2,500 words, on trends and people in the retail gourmet food and gourmet housewares industry. Pays $20 to $400, on publication. Query.

ENTREPRENEUR—2311 Pontius Ave., Los Angeles, CA 90064. How-to's, 1,500 to 2,500 words, for independent business owners, on running a business: advertising, merchandise, employees, etc. Fillers; columns, 100 to 500 words. Pays 15¢ a word, from $100 for features, $25 for columns, on acceptance. Query.

EXECUTIVE REVIEW—See *Publications, Ltd.*

EXPORT MAGAZINE—386 Park Ave. South, New York, NY 10016. Robert Weingarten, Ed. Articles, 1,000 to 1,500 words, on the export business in foreign countries. Profiles of agents and distributors. Pays $300 to $350, with photos, on acceptance. Query preferred.

FARM BUILDING NEWS—260 Regency Court, Waukesha, WI 53816. Frank Lessiter, Ed. Articles, 500 to 2,000 words, for rural contractors of farm buildings, grain systems, confinement equipment and non-farm rural structures. Pays $50 to $175, on publication. Query.

FARM JOURNAL—230 W. Washington Sq., Philadelphia, PA 19105. Practical business articles on growing crops and producing livestock. Pays $50 to $500, on acceptance. Query required.

FASHION ACCESSORIES MAGAZINE—22 S. Smith St., Norwalk, CT 06855. Reenie Brown, Ed. Dir. Articles, with photos, for handbag and accessory buyers, on store displays, retail promotions; profiles of designers and manufacturers. Pays $75 to $100 for short articles, from $100 to $250 for features, on publication. Query.

FENCE INDUSTRY—6255 Barfield Rd., Atlanta, GA 30328. Bill Coker, Ed./Assoc. Pub. Articles on fence industry; interviews with dealer-erectors; on-the-job pieces. Photos. Pays 10¢ a word, extra for photos, on publication. Query.

FIREHOUSE—515 Madison Ave., New York, NY 10022. John Peige, Exec. Ed. Articles, 500 to 3,000 words, on major fires, trends in equipment, lifestyles of firefighters. Profiles, how-to's. Pays $100 to $300, on publication. Query.

THE FISH BOAT—P.O. Box 2400, Covington, LA 70434. William A. Sarratt, Ed. Articles on commercial fishing, promotion and merchandising of seafood. Short items on commercial fishing and boats. Pays varying rates, on acceptance. Query.

FLORIST—29200 Northwestern Hwy., P.O. Box 2227, Southfield, MI 48037. Susan Nicholas, Man. Ed. Articles, to 2,000 words, with photos, on retail florist business improvement. Photos. Pays 8¢ a word, extra for photos.

FOOD MANAGEMENT—747 Third Ave., New York, NY 10017. Donna Boss, Ed. Articles, on foodservice in healthcare, schools, colleges, prisons, business and industry. Trends and how-to pieces, with management tie-in. Pays to $350. Query.

THE FOREMAN'S LETTER—24 Rope Ferry Rd., Waterford, CT 06386. Carl Thunberg, Ed. Interviews, with photos, with top-notch supervisors and foremen. Pays 8¢ to 12¢ a word, extra for photos, on acceptance.

GIFTS & DECORATIVE ACCESSORIES—51 Madison Ave., New York, NY 10010. Phyllis Sweed, Co-Pub./Ed. Articles, 1,500 to 3,000 words, with photos, on promotions, displays, design features of quality retail shops for gifts, stationery, greeting cards. Color photos. Pays to $150, extra for photos, on publication.

GLASS DIGEST—310 Madison Ave., New York, NY 10017. Oscar S. Glasberg, Ed. Articles, 1,200 to 1,500 words, on building projects and glass/metal dealers, distributors, storefront and glazing contractors. Pays varying rates, on publication.

GOLF SHOP OPERATIONS—495 Westport Ave., Norwalk, CT 06856. Nick Romano, Ed. Articles, 200 to 800 words, with photos, on successful golf shop operations; new ideas for merchandising, display, bookkeeping. Short pieces on golf professionals. Pays $175 to $225, on publication. Query with outline.

THE GOURMET RETAILER—1545 N.E. 123rd St., North Miami, FL 33161. Michael Keighley, Ed. Articles, 2,500 to 3,000 words, for retailers, on products and trends, merchandising, and sales promotion. Pays 5¢ a word, on publication.

GRAPHIC ARTS MONTHLY—875 Third Ave., New York, NY 10022. Roger Ynostroza, Ed. Technical articles, 1,500 to 2,000 words, on printing industry. No profiles. Pays 6¢ to 10¢ a word, on publication. Query.

GREENHOUSE MANAGER—P.O. Box 1868, Fort Worth, TX 76101. Jerry Circelli, Man. Ed. Articles, 2,000 words, of interest to professional greenhouse growers. Pays $100 to $300, on publication. Query required.

HARDWARE AGE—Chilton Way, Radnor, PA 19089. Wendy Ampolsk, Man. Ed. Articles on merchandising methods in hardware outlets. Photos. Pays on acceptance.

HARDWARE MERCHANDISER—7300 N. Cicero Ave., Chicago, IL 60646. J. W. Stapleton, Ed. Articles, to 1,000 words, with photos, on merchandising in hardware and discount stores. Pays varying rates, on acceptance.

HARVARD BUSINESS REVIEW—Harvard Graduate School of Business Administration, Soldiers Field Rd., Boston, MA 02163. Query Editors on new ideas about business management, of interest to senior executives. Pays negotiable rates, on publication.

HEALTH FOODS BUSINESS—567 Morris Ave., Elizabeth, NJ 07208. Alan Richman, Ed. Articles, 1,500 words, with photos, on managing health-food stores: security, health, cosmetics, advertising. Pays on publication. Query.

HEATING/PIPING/AIR CONDITIONING—2 Illinois Cntr., Chicago, IL 60601. Robert T. Korte, Ed. Articles, to 5,000 words, on heating, piping and air-conditioning systems in industrial plants and large buildings; engineering information. Pays $40 per printed page, on publication. Query.

HISPANIC BUSINESS—P.O. Box 6757, Santa Barbara, CA 93160. Jesus Chavarria, Ed./Pub. Features, 2,000 words, on Hispanic business and professional life in the U.S., for Hispanic businesspeople. Articles on culture, education, demographics and career planning. Shorter pieces, 850 words. Pays $250 for features, $75 for shorter pieces, on publication.

HOME ENTERTAINMENT MARKETING—See *Dealerscope.*

HOME FASHIONS TEXTILES—633 Third Ave., New York, NY 10017. Mary Connors, Ed. In-depth features on fashion trends and management; profiles; reports of new products. Photos. Pays varying rates, on acceptance. Query preferred.

HOSPITALS—211 E. Chicago Ave., Suite 700, Chicago, IL 60611. Frank Sabatino, Man. Ed. Articles, 1,000 to 2,000 words, for hospital administrators. Pays varying rates, on acceptance. Query.

HOTELS AND RESTAURANTS INTERNATIONAL—P.O. Box 5080, Des Plaines, IL 60018. Madelin M. Schneider, Ed. Short pieces, 500 words, on tourism and hotel management. Pays varying rates, on acceptance.

HOUSTON BUSINESS JOURNAL—5314 Bingle Rd., Houston, TX 77092. Articles, 1,000 to 1,500 words, on business news in Houston area. Photos. Pays from $3 per column inch, extra for photos, on publication.

ICP SOFTWARE BUSINESS REVIEW—9000 Keystone Crossing, Indianapolis, IN 46240. Dennis Hamilton, Ed. Articles, 300 to 3,000 words, on the computer business, centering on software management: productivity, profitability, return-on-investment. Pays $50 to $500, on publication. Query.

IMPRESSIONS—15400 Knoll Trail Dr., Dallas, TX 75248. Carl Piazza, Ed. Articles for the imprinted sportswear industry, on trends, retail techniques, market information, etc. Pays $50 to $100, on publication. Query.

IN BUSINESS—Box 323, Emmaus, PA 18049. Jerome Goldstein, Ed. How-to's on marketing, advertising, and financing, 1,500 to 2,000 words, for people who run small businesses. Profiles and pieces on new trends. Pays to $200, on publication. Query.

INC.—38 Commercial Wharf, Boston, MA 02110. George Gendron, Ed. Feature articles about how owners and managers of small companies solve common problems. Pays to $1,500 on acceptance. Query.

INCOME OPPORTUNITIES—380 Lexington Ave., New York, NY 10017. Steve Wagner, Ed. Helpful articles, 2,000 to 3,000 words, on how to make money, how to run a successful business, improve sales, etc. Pays varying rates, on acceptance. Query.

INDUSTRIAL CHEMICAL NEWS—633 Third Ave., New York, NY 10017. Irvin J. Schwartz, Ed. Articles, 500 to 2,000 words, on technical and professional issues of interest to chemists working in industrial labs. Pays $150 to $600, on acceptance. Query.

INDUSTRIAL DESIGN—330 W. 42nd St., New York, NY 10036. Steven Holt, Man. Ed. Articles to 2,000 words, on product development, design management, graphic design, design history, for designers and marketing executives. Profiles of designers and corporations that use design effectively. Pays $250 to $500, on publication.

INDUSTRIAL MARKETING—See *Business Marketing.*

INFOSYSTEMS—Hitchcock Bldg., Wheaton, IL 60187. Wayne L. Rhodes, Ed. How-to articles, 6- to 8- pages, for managers in the data processing systems field. Pays negotiable rates, on publication. Query.

INSTANT PRINTER—P.O. Box 368, Northbrook, IL 60062. Dan Witte, Ed. Articles, 5 to 7 typed pages, for owners and/or managers of printing businesses specializing in retail printing: case histories, how-to's, technical pieces, interesting ideas. Opinion pieces, 1 to 2 typed pages. Photos. Pays $150 to $200 ($25 to $50 for opinion pieces), extra for photos on publication. Query preferred.

INTERFACE AGE—17000 Marquardt Ave., Cerritos, CA 90701. Les Spindle, Ed. Articles, 3,000 to 5,000 words, on microcomputer applications in the business field. Reviews of new products and computer programs. Pays $50 to $80 per published page, on publication.

KIDS FASHIONS—210 Boylston St., Chestnut Hill, MA 02167. Mary Ann Wood, Man. Ed. Articles, 1,000 to 2,000 words, with photos, on the retailing and merchandising of children's apparel and gift items. Pays from $150, on acceptance.

LEISURE TIME ELECTRONICS—124 E. 40th St., New York, NY 10016. Bill Silverman, Ed. Articles, about 1,500 words, for retailers of audio and video equipment, personal computers, and electronic games: improving business, new products and trends in the field, etc. Pays $5 per column inch, on acceptance. Query.

LOS ANGELES BUSINESS JOURNAL—3727 W. Sixth St., Suite 506, Los Angeles, CA 90020. David Yochum, Ed. Feature articles on specific industries in the five-county Los Angeles area, stressing the how-to, trends and analysis. Pays negotiable rates, on publication. Query.

LP-GAS MAGAZINE—131 W. First St., Duluth, MN 55802. Zane Chastain, Ed. Articles, 1,500 to 2,500 words, with photos, on LP-Gas dealer operations: marketing, management, etc. Photos. Pays to 15¢ a word, extra for photos, on acceptance. Query.

MADISON AVENUE MAGAZINE—369 Lexington Ave., New York, NY

10017. Stuart Emmrich, Ed. Feature articles on advertising and marketing strategy. Pays $550 to $650.

MANAGE—2210 Arbor Blvd., Dayton, OH 45439. Doug Shaw, Ed. Articles, 1,500 to 2,200 words, with photos, on management and supervision for first-line and middle managers. Pays 5¢ a word.

MEMPHIS BUSINESS JOURNAL—4515 Poplar, Suite 322, Memphis, TN 38117. Barney DuBois, Ed. Articles, to 2,000 words, on business, industry trade, agribusiness and finance in the Mid-South trade area. Pays $80 to $200, on acceptance.

MINIATURES AND DOLL DEALER—Clifton House, Clifton, VA 22024. Marla Bethel, Ed. Articles, about 2,500 words, on advertising, promotion, merchandising of miniatures and dolls and other small business concerns. Pays about $200 to $250, on publication. Query.

MODERN HEALTHCARE—750 N. Rush St., Chicago, IL 60611. Donald Johnson, Ed. Features on management, finance, building design and construction, and new technology for hospitals, nursing homes, and other health care institutions. Pays $6 per column inch, on publication. Query.

MODERN JEWELER—7950 College Blvd., Shawnee Mission, KS 66201. Joseph Thompson, Ed. Features, 6 to 7 typewritten pages, with photos, on jewelers. Pays $100 to $150, on acceptance.

MODERN TIRE DEALER—P.O. Box 5417, 110 N. Miller Rd., Akron, OH 44313. Greg Smith, Ed. Merchandising management and service articles, 1,000 to 1,500 words, with photos, on independent tire dealers and retreaders. Pays $200 to $250, on publication.

MONEY MAGAZINE—Time & Life Bldg., New York, NY 10020. Marshall Loeb, Man. Ed. Articles on various aspects of personal finance and investment. Welcomes article suggestions. Pays $2,500 and up for major articles.

MONEY MAKER—5705 N. Lincoln Ave., Chicago, IL 60659. John Manos, Ed. Informative, jargon-free articles, to 4,000 words, for beginning to sophisticated investors, on investment opportunities, market analyses and low-priced investments. Pays 20¢ a word, on acceptance. Query for assignment.

THE MONEYPAPER—2 Madison Ave., Larchmont, NY 10538. Vita Nelson, Ed. Financial news and money-saving ideas, especially those of interest to women. Brief, well-researched articles on personal finance, money management: saving, earning, investing, taxes, insurance and related subjects. Features on women's attitudes toward money and personal experiences in solving money management problems. Pays 20¢ a word, on acceptance. Query with resumé and writing sample.

MOTOR—555 W. 57th St., New York, NY 10019. Ken Zino, Ed. Articles, 700 to 3,000 words, with photos, on new trends and repair procedures in automotive service business. Pays $150 to $1000, on acceptance. Query; no unsolicited submissions.

MUSICAL MERCHANDISE REVIEW—210 Boylston St., Chestnut Hill, MA 02167. Articles, 1,000 to 2,000 words, with photos, on the retailing and merchandising of musical instruments and accessories. Pays from $150, on acceptance.

NATIONAL DAIRY NEWS—Box 951, Madison, WI 53701. Jerry Dryer, Pub. Articles, to 2,500 words, on innovative dairies, dairy processing operations, marketing successes and new dairy products for milk handlers, and makers of cheese, butter, yogurt and ice cream. Fillers, 25 to 150 words. Pays $25 to $300, $5 to $25 for fillers, on publication.

NATIONAL FISHERMAN—21 Elm St., Camden, ME 04843. James W. Fullilove, Ed. Articles, 200 to 2,000 words, aimed at commercial fishermen and boatbuilders. Pays from $2.50 per inch, extra for photos, on publication. Query preferred.

THE NATIONAL GLASS BUDGET—P.O. Box 7138, Pittsburgh, PA 15213. Liz Scott, Man. Ed. Articles, to 1,500 words, on developments in glass manufacturing, glass factories, types of glass. Personality profiles. Pays 5¢ to 10¢ a word, on publication. Query with SASE.

NATION'S BUSINESS—1615 H. St. N.W., Washington, DC 20062. Business articles 1,500 words, with management advice. Must have Washington, DC focus. Pays negotiable rates, on acceptance. Query.

NEW CAREER WAYS NEWSLETTER—P.O. Box 1142, Haverhill, MA 01830. William J. Bond, Ed. How-to-articles, 1,500 to 2,000 words, on new ways to succeed in business careers. Pays varying rates, on publication. Query with outline.

NORTHERN HARDWARE—2965 Broadmoor Valley Rd., Suite B, Colorado Springs, CO 80906. Edward Gonzales, Ed. Articles, 800 to 1,000 words, on unusual hardware stores and promotions in Northwest and Midwest. Photos. Pays 4¢ a word, extra for photos, on publication. Query.

NURSINGWORLD JOURNAL—470 Boston Post Rd., Weston, MA 02193. Ira Alterman, Ed. Articles, 500 to 1,500 words, for nurses and nurse educators, on aspects of nursing employment and other nursing issues. Photos. Pays from 25¢ per column inch, on publication.

OCCUPATIONAL HAZARDS—1111 Chester Ave., Cleveland, OH 44114. Peter J. Sheridan, Ed. Articles, 500 to 2,000 words, on industrial safety, health, fire prevention and security. Photos. Pays from 5¢ a word, on publication.

OPPORTUNITY MAGAZINE—6 N. Michigan Ave., Suite 1405, Chicago, IL 60602. Jack Weissman, Ed. Articles, 900 words, on sales psychology, sales techniques, self-improvement. Pays $20 to $40, on publication.

ORTHOPEDICS TODAY—6900 Grove Rd., Thorofare, NJ 08086. Eric M. Baloff, Ed. Articles, 500 to 2,500 words, for orthopedic specialists, on new techniques and advancement in orthopedic treatment. Photos. Pays varying rates on acceptance.

THE OSHA COMPLIANCE LETTER—24 Rope Ferry Rd., Waterford, CT 06386. James Bolger, Ed. Interview-based articles, 800 to 1,250 words, for safety professionals, on solving OSHA-related safety problems. Pays to 12¢ a word, on acceptance, after editing. Query.

PAPERBOARD PACKAGING—7500 Old Oak Blvd., Cleveland, OH 44130. Mark Arzoumanian, Ed. Articles, any length, on corrugated containers, folding cartons and setup boxes. Pays on publication. Query with outline.

PET BUSINESS—7330 N.W. 66th St., Miami, FL 33166. Bob Behme, Pub./Ed. Articles, 300 to 1,000 words, on all aspects of pet business: success stories, profiles, retail shops, manufacturers, distributors. All material must have a news slant. Photos. Pays to 10¢ a word, extra for photos, on acceptance.

PETS/SUPPLIES/MARKETING—One E. First St., Duluth, MN 55802. David D. Kowalski, Ed. Articles, 1,000 to 1,200 words, with photos, on pet shops, and pet and product merchandising. Pays 10¢ a word, extra for photos. No fiction or news clippings. Query.

PHOENIX BUSINESS JOURNAL—1817 N. 3rd St., Suite 100, Phoenix, AZ 85004. Naaman Nickell, Ed. Articles on leading and innovative businesses and business people in Arizona. Photos. Pays $2.50 to $3.25 per column inch, on publication.

PHOTO MARKETING—3000 Picture Pl., Jackson, MI 49201. Theresa Wood, Man. Ed. Articles, 500 words, on camera store successes in promotion, advertising, personnel management. Photos. Pays to 10¢ a word, extra for photos, on publication.

PHYSICIAN'S MANAGEMENT—7500 Old Oak Blvd., Cleveland, OH 44130. Bob Feigenbaum, Ed. Articles, about 2,500 to 3,000 words, on finance, investments, malpractice, and office management for primary care physicians. No clinical pieces. Pays $125 per printed page, on acceptance. Query with SASE.

P.O.B.—P.O. Box 810, Wayne, MI 48184. Jeanne Heltrick, Assoc. Ed. Technical and business articles, 1,000 to 4,000 words, for professionals and technicians in the surveying and mapping fields. Technical tips on field and office procedures and equipment maintenance. Pays $150 to $400, on publication.

POLICE PRODUCT NEWS—P.O. Box 847, Carlsbad, CA 92008. James Daigh, Ed. Reviews of new products and equipment and profiles of people in the law enforcement profession, 1,000 to 4,000 words. Fiction. Photos. Pays to $300, extra for photos, on acceptance. Writers' guidelines sent on request.

POOL & SPA NEWS—3923 W. Sixth St., Los Angeles, CA 90020. News pieces on swimming pool, spa, and hot tub industry. Photos. Pays 5¢ to 8¢ a word, extra for photos, on publication. Query.

PREMIUM/INCENTIVE BUSINESS—1515 Broadway, New York, NY 10036. Carol Herzberg, Man. Ed. Articles, 2 to 6 typewritten pages, for sales promotion executives and premium buyers, on premium offers, incentive programs, interviews. Pays on publication. Query.

THE PRESS—302 Grote St., Buffalo, NY 14207. Mary Lou Vogt, Ed. Quarterly. Short profiles, 800 to 1,200 words, on cartoonists and industry and advertising personalities, 800 to 1,200 words, for advertising executives at newspapers and ad agencies. Pieces on unusual hobbies or occupations. Travel articles. Humor. Pays 10¢ a word, on acceptance.

PRIVATE PRACTICE—Box 12489, Oklahoma City, OK 73157. Shannon Wingrove, Asst. Ed. Articles, 1,500 to 2,000 words, on state or local legislation affecting medical field. Pays $250 to $350, on acceptance.

PROGRESSIVE GROCER—1351 Washington Blvd., Stamford, CT 06902. Edgar B. Walzer, Ed. Articles, to 2,500 words, on supermarket management, merchandising and promotion. Short, 100 to 200 words, on sales and promotion ideas. Photos. Pays varying rates, on acceptance.

PUBLICATIONS, LTD. (formerly *Executive Review*)—100 N. LaSalle St., Chicago, IL 60602. Franklin E. Sabes, Pub. How-to articles; profiles of successful companies and individuals; human-interest pieces; hunting, fishing and travel articles. Reprints from business publications preferred. Pays varying rates, on publication.

RADIO-ELECTRONICS—200 Park Ave. S., New York, NY 10003. Art Kleiman, Ed. Technical articles, 1,500 to 3,000 words, on electronic equipment. Pays $50 to $500, on acceptance.

READER'S NUTSHELL—Drawer 189, Palm Beach, FL 33480. Articles, 600 to 800 words, for professional insurance agents, on specific aspects of insurance, safety, health, etc. General interest pieces. Pays 5¢ a word, on acceptance.

REEVES JOURNAL—6618 Aqueduct Ave., Van Nuys, CA 91406. Larry Dill, Ed. Articles, 1,000 to 3,000 words, with photos, on leaders in the plumbing field in the western states, solar energy applications and developments, and how-to materials. Pays 8¢ a word, extra for photos, on publication.

RESORT MANAGEMENT—4501 Mission Bay Dr., San Diego, CA 92109. Articles, 1,000 to 1,500 words, on successful resort operation and management. Photos. Query with outline.

ROBOTICS AGE—174 Concord St., Peterborough, NH 03458. Raymond G. A. Cote, Ed. Technical, tutorial pieces, on robotics technology. Pays varying rates for varying lengths of pieces, on publication.

THE ROOFER—P.O. Box 06253, Fort Myers, FL 33906. Karen S. Parker, Ed. Non-technical articles, 500 to 1,000 words, on roofing-related topics: new processes and products, energy savings, roofing concepts, etc., Safety and medical pieces; interviews with contractors. Pays negotiable rates, on publication.

RV BUSINESS—29901 Agoura Rd., Agoura, CA 91301. Sheryl Davis, Man. Ed. Articles, 1,500 to 3,000 words, on manufacturing, financing, selling and servicing recreational vehicles. Articles on legislative matters affecting the industry. Pays to $400, on acceptance.

SECURITY MANAGEMENT—1655 N. Ft. Myer Dr., Suite 1200, Arlington, VA 22209. Mary Alice Crawford, Sr. Ed. Articles, 2,500 to 3,000 words, on legislative issues related to security; case studies of innovative security applications; management topics; employee relations, training programs, etc. Pays 10¢ a word, on publication. Query.

SELLING DIRECT—6255 Barfield Rd., Atlanta, GA 30328. William Robertson, Ed. Articles, 400 to 1,800 words, for independent salespersons selling to homes, stores, industries, and businesses. Pays 10¢ a word, on publication.

SKIING TRADE NEWS—One Park Ave., New York, NY 10016. John Auran, Ed. How-to articles, 1,000 words maximum, with photos, on making profits in retail ski shops. Pays 12¢ a word, on acceptance.

SNACK FOOD MAGAZINE—131 W. First St., Duluth, MN 55802. Jerry Hess, Ed. Articles, 600 to 1,500 words, on trade news, personalities, promotions, production in snack food manufacturing industry. Short pieces; photos. Pays 12¢ to 15¢ a word, extra for photos, on acceptance. Query.

SOFTWARE NEWS—5 Kane Industrial Dr., Hudson, MA 01749. Edward J. Bride, Ed. Technical features, 1,000 to 1,200 words, for computer literate audience, on how software products can be used. Pays about $150 to $200, on publication. Query preferred.

SOLID WASTES MANAGEMENT—See *World Wastes.*

SOUVENIRS AND NOVELTIES—Suite 226–27, 401 N. Broad St.,

Philadelphia, PA 19108. Articles, 1,500 words, quoting souvenir shop managers on items that sell, display ideas, problems in selling, industry trends. Photos. Pays from $1 per column inch, extra for photos, on publication.

THE SPORTING GOODS DEALER—1212 N. Lindbergh, St. Louis, MO 63132. Articles, about 500 words, on sporting goods stores. Pays from 2¢ a word, on publication.

SUCCESSFUL FARMING—1716 Locust St., Des Moines, IA 50336. Richard Krumme, Ed. Articles, to 2,000 words, for farming families, on all areas of business farming: money management, marketing, machinery, soils and crops, livestock, and buildings. Pays from $300, on acceptance. Query first.

TEXTILE WORLD—4170 Ashford-Dunwoody Rd., N.E., Suite 420, Atlanta, GA 30319. L. A. Christiansen, Ed. Articles, 500 to 2,000 words, with photos, on manufacturing and finishing textiles. Pays varying rates, on acceptance.

TOURIST ATTRACTIONS AND PARKS—Suite 226–27, 401 N. Broad St., Philadelphia, PA 19108. Chuck Tooley, Ed. Articles, 1,500 words, on successful management of parks and leisure attractions. News items, 250 and 500 words. Pays 7¢ a word, on publication. Query.

TRAILER/BODY BUILDERS—1602 Harold St., Houston, TX 77006. Paul Schenk, Ed. Articles on engineering, sales, and management ideas for truck body and truck trailer manufacturers. Pays from $80 per printed page, on acceptance.

TRAINING, THE MAGAZINE OF HUMAN RESOURCES DEVELOPMENT—731 Hennepin Ave., Minneapolis, MN 55403. Jack Gordon, Ed. Articles, 1,500 to 2,000 words, for managers of training and development activities. Pays 5¢ to 10¢ a word, on acceptance. Query.

THE TRAVEL AGENT—2 W. 46th St., New York, NY 10036. Eric Friedheim, Ed. Articles, 1,500 words, with photos, on travel trade, for travel agents. Pays $50 to $75, on acceptance.

VENDING TIMES—545 8th Ave., New York, NY 10018. Arthur E. Yohalem, Ed. Feature and news articles, with photos, on vending machines. Pays varying rates, on acceptance. Query.

VIEW—80 Fifth Ave., New York NY 10011. Kathy Haley, Ed. Features and news pieces on trends in the television programming, marketing, and advertising business. Pays $350, after acceptance. Query required.

WESTERN INVESTOR—400 S.W. Sixth Ave., Suite 1115, Portland, OR 97204. Business and investment articles, 800 to 1,200 words, about business leaders, trends, products, etc., in the Pacific Northwest, intermountain states, Alaska and Hawaii. Pays from $50, on publication. Query first.

WESTERN OUTFITTER—5314 Bingle Rd., Houston, TX 77092. Anne DeRuyter, Ed. Articles, to 1,500 words, with photos, on merchandising western wear and equipment. Photos. Pays 8¢ a word, extra for photos, on publication. Query.

WINES & VINES—1800 Lincoln Ave., San Rafael, CA 94901. Philip Hiaring, Ed. Articles, 1,000 words, on grape and wine industry, emphasizing marketing and production. Pays 5¢ a word, on acceptance.

WISCONSIN BUSINESS JOURNAL—450 N. Sunnyslope Rd., Suite 120, Brookfield, WI 53005. Nancy Aldrich-Ruenzel, Man. Ed. Articles, 1,000 to

6,000 words, on Wisconsin business trends and developments. How-to's for executives on management, finance, marketing and real estate. Profiles of state businesses and executives. Pays negotiable rates, on acceptance. Query.

WOOD 'N ENERGY—P.O. Box 2008, Laconia, NH 03247. Kenneth Daggett, Ed. Profiles and interviews, 1,000 to 2,500 words, with retailers and manufacturers of alternative energy equipment. Fillers, 200 to 500 words. Pays $50 to $350, for articles, on publication. Query.

WORLD OIL—Gulf Publishing Co., P.O. Box 2608, Houston, TX 77001. T. R. Wright, Ed. Engineering and operations articles, 3,000 to 4,000 words, on petroleum industry exploration, drilling or producing. Photos. Pays from $50 per printed page, on acceptance. Query.

WORLD WASTES (formerly *Solid Wastes Management*)—6255 Barfield Rd., Atlanta, GA 30328. Bill Wolpin, Ed. Case studies, 1,500 to 2,500 words, with photos, of refuse haulers, landfill operators, resource recovery operations and transfer stations, with solutions to problems in field. Pays from $100 per printed page, on publication. Query preferred.

ZIP TARGET MARKETING MAGAZINE—North American Publishing Co., 401 N. Broad St., Philadelphia, PA 19108. James McCanney, Ed. Articles, 4 to 6 manuscript pages, for major mailers and mail-order advertisers, on marketing, circulation, mailing operations, fulfillment, mail-order, telemarketing, computer technology, and communications. No pieces on postal service. Pays $150 to $225, on publication.

COMPANY PUBLICATIONS

Company publications (also called house magazines or house organs) are excellent, well-paying markets for writers at all levels of experience. Thousands of these magazines are published, usually by large corporations, to promote good will, familiarize readers with the company's services and products, and interest customers in these products. In all cases, editors want to see manuscripts with the same high quality and original treatment as material published in top-circulation magazines. Writers should always read a house magazine before submitting an article; write to the editor for a sample issue (offering to pay for it) and the editorial requirements sheet. Stamped, self-addressed envelopes should be enclosed with any query or manuscript.

AIR LINE PILOT—Air Line Pilots Association International, 1625 Massachusetts Ave. N.W., Washington, DC 20036. C. V. Glines, Ed. Articles, to 3,000 words, on aviation, stressing pilot's point of view; articles on safety and air transport history; profiles of ALPA members. Pays varying rates, on acceptance. Query. Replies only if SASE is provided.

THE COMPASS—Mobil Sales and Supply Corp., 150 E. 42nd St., New York, NY 10017. R. G. MacKenzie, Ed. Articles, to 3,500 words, on the sea and deep sea trade. Photos. No fiction. Pays to $250, on acceptance. Query.

EXXON U.S.A. MAGAZINE—Exxon Company, U.S.A., P.O. Box 2180, Houston, TX 77252. Downs Matthews, Ed. Articles, 2,000 to 2,500 words, for thought leaders largely outside the oil industry, on Exxon Co.'s public affairs interests and concerns in the U.S.: environmental conservation, business economics, public energy policy, etc. Pays $1,000 to $1,500. Query first.

FRIENDS MAGAZINE—30400 Van Dyke, Warren, MI 48093. Herman G. Duerr, Exec. Ed. Bill Gray, Ed. Articles on topics of general interest, 800 to 1,200 words, for Chevrolet customers: life styles, sports, travel, food, etc.

Must be non-controversial and in good taste. Pays from $300, extra for photos, on acceptance. Query; indicate if photos are available.

THE FURROW—Deere & Company, John Deere Rd., Moline, IL 61265. George R. Sollenberger, Ed., North America. Articles and humor, to 1,500 words; researched agricultural-technical features; rural social- and economic-trend features. Pays to $1,000, on acceptance.

GO GREYHOUND—Greyhound Tower, Phoenix, AZ 85077. Juanita Soto, Publications Ass't. Human-interest travel articles, 600 to 800 words, with color photos. Pays $350, on publication. Query.

INLAND—Inland Steel Co., 30 W. Monroe, Chicago, IL 60603. Sheldon A. Mix, Man. Ed. Imaginative articles, essays, commentaries, of any length, of special interest in Midwest. Pays varying rates, on acceptance.

THE LOOKOUT—Seamen's Church Institute of New York, 15 State St., New York, NY 10004. Carlyle Windley, Ed. Articles, 750 to 1,500 words, relating to merchant marine: oddities, adventure, etc. Graphics, occasional short verse. Pays to $80 for articles with art, extra for black-and-white cover photos, on publication.

THE MODERN WOODMEN—Modern Woodmen of America, Mississippi River at 17th St., Rock Island, IL 61201. Gloria Bergh, Manager, Public Relations. Family- and community-oriented, general-interest articles; some quality fiction. Photos. Pays from $40, on acceptance. Publication not copyrighted.

RAYTHEON MAGAZINE—141 Spring St., Lexington, MA 02173. Robert P. Suarez, Ed. Articles by assignment only. Pays $750 to $1,250, on acceptance, for articles 800 to 1,200 words. Query with writing sample.

SPERRY NEW HOLLAND—Div. of Sperry Corp., New Holland, PA 17557. Gary Martin, Ed. Articles, to 1,000 words, with strong photo support, on production agriculture, research and rural human interest. Pays on acceptance.

THE WATER SKIER—American Water Ski Assn., P.O. Box 191, Winter Haven, FL 33882. Duke Cullimore, Ed. Unusual articles, to 1,500 words, and photo features, on water skiing. Pays varying rates, on acceptance. Query.

WOMEN IN BUSINESS—9100 Ward Parkway, Box 8728, Kansas City, MO 64114. Publication of the American Business Women's Association. Sharon K. Tiley, Ed. Features, 1,000 to 2,000 words, for career women from 45 to 55 years old; no profiles. Pays to $250, on acceptance. Query.

SPECIALIZED ARTICLES

HEALTH

ACCENT ON LIVING—P.O. Box 700, Bloomington, IL 61701. Raymond C. Cheever, Pub./Ed. Articles, 250 to 1,000 words, about physically disabled people—their careers, recreation and sports, self-help devices, and ideas that can make daily routine easier. Good photos a plus. Pays 10¢ a word, on publication. Query.

AMERICAN BABY—575 Lexington Ave., New York, NY 10022. Judith Nolte, Ed. Articles, 1,000 to 2,000 words, for new or expectant parents, on infant care. Pays varying rates, on acceptance.

AMERICAN FAMILY PHYSICIAN—1740 W. 92nd St., Kansas City, MO 64114. Walter H. Kemp, Man. Publisher. Illustrated articles, 1,600 to 3,200 words, on clinical topics only. Pays from $150, on publication. Query. Most material written by physicians.

AMERICAN HEALTH: FITNESS OF BODY AND MIND—80 Fifth Ave., Suite 302, New York, NY 10011. Address Editorial Dept. Features, 1,000 to 3,000 words, on recent developments in nutrition, exercise, medicine, prevention and psychology. Shorter news items on similar topics: medical advances, tooth care, consumer health, and life styles. Pays from $125 per manuscript page, on acceptance. Query.

AMERICAN JOURNAL OF NURSING—555 W. 57th St., New York, NY 10019. Mary B. Mallison, R.N., Ed. Articles, 1,500 to 2,000 words, with photos, on nursing. Pays $20 per printed page, on publication. Query.

BESTWAYS—400 Hot Springs Rd., P.O. Box 2028, Carson City, NV 89701. Barbara Bassett, Ed. Articles, 1,500 to 2,000 words, on health, food, life styles, exercise, nutrition. Pays from $75, on publication. Query.

CHILDBIRTH EDUCATOR—575 Lexington Ave., New York, NY 10022. Marsha Rehns, Ed. Articles, 2,000 words, on maternal and fetal health, childcare and teaching techniques for teachers of childbirth and baby care classes. Pays $400, on acceptance. Query.

EMERGENCY—P.O. Box 159, Carlsbad, CA 92008. James Daigh, Ed. Features on all aspects of emergency services. Pays $75 to $200, on publication. Query.

THE EXCEPTIONAL PARENT—605 Commonwealth Ave., Boston, MA 02215. Maxwell J. Schleifer, Ed. Articles, 600 to 3,000 words, with practical information for parents of disabled children. Pays on publication.

EXPECTING—685 Third Ave., New York, NY 10017. Evelyn A. Podsiadlo, Ed. Articles, 700 to 1,800 words, for expectant mothers. Pays $150 to $350, on acceptance.

HEALTH—3 Park Ave., New York, NY 10016. Articles, 800 to 2,500 words, on medicine, nutrition, fitness, emotional and psychological well-being. Pays $200 to $1,000, on acceptance. Query.

HEALTH LITERATURE REVIEW—True-to-Form Press, P.O. Box 13129, St. Paul, MN 55113. Sheila Nauman-Haight, Ed./Pub. Reviews of current and contemporary health literature; articles on health care and trends in health literature and communications. Pays 10¢ a word, for articles, only, on publication. Send for writer's guidelines. Query with credentials.

HEALTH PROGRESS—4455 Woodson Rd., St. Louis, MO 63134. Carol S. Boyer, Ed. Journal of the Catholic Health Association. Features, 1,500 to 2,000 words, on hospital management and administration. Pays by arrangement. Query.

HOSPITALS—211 E. Chicago Ave., Chicago, IL 60611. Frank Sabatino, Man. Ed. Articles, 2,000 to 3,000 words, for hospital administrators, on financing, staffing, coordinating, and providing facilities for health care services. Pays varying rates, on acceptance. Query.

LET'S LIVE—444 N. Larchmont Blvd., Los Angeles, CA 90004. Howard Kim, Man. Ed. Articles, 1,500 to 1,800 words, on preventive medicine and nutrition, alternative medicine, diet and exercise. Pays $150, on publication. Query.

NEW BODY—888 Seventh Ave., New York, NY 10106. Judy Jones, Ed. Well-researched, service-oriented articles, 1,000 to 2,000 words, on exercise, nutrition, diet and health for men and women aged 18 to 35. Writers should have some background in or knowledge of the health field. Pays $250 to $500, on publication. Query preferred.

NURSING 85—1111 Bethlehem Pike, Springhouse, PA 19477. Jeanmarie Coogan, Ed. Most articles are clinically oriented, and assigned to nursing experts. No poetry. Pays $25 to $350, on publication. Query.

NURSING HOMES—Centaur & Co., 5 Willowbrook Ct., Potomac, MD 20854. William D. Manges, Ed.-in-Chief. Articles, 1,000 to 1,500 words, of interest to administrators, managers, and supervisory personnel in nursing homes; academic and clinical pieces; book reviews, 250–300 words. Pays $100 for articles, $35 for reviews, on acceptance. Photos, graphics welcome.

NURSING JOB NEWS—See *Nursingworld Journal.*

NURSING LIFE—1111 Bethlehem Pike, Springhouse, PA 19477. Loy Wiley, Ed. Articles, 12 to 15 double-spaced pages, by nurses, lawyers, management consultants, psychologists, with practical advice for staff nurses. Pays negotiable rates, on publication. Query.

NURSINGWORLD JOURNAL—470 Boston Post Rd., Weston, MA 02193. Eileen DeVito, Man. Ed. Articles, 500 to 1,500 words, for and by nurses and nurse-educators, on aspects of current nursing issues. Pays from 25¢ per column inch, on publication.

PATIENT CARE—16 Thorndal Circle, Darien, CT 06820. Clayton Raker Hasser, Ed. Articles on medical care, for physicians. Pays varying rates, on publication. Query; all articles assigned.

THE PHYSICIAN AND SPORTSMEDICINE MAGAZINE—4530 W. 77th St., Minneapolis, MN 55435. Gary Legwold, Man. Ed. Articles, 500 to 3,000 words, for physicians who treat athletic injuries. Pays $50 to $750, on acceptance.

RESPIRATORY THERAPY—825 S. Barrington Ave., Los Angeles, CA 90049. Articles for respiratory therapists and technologists on management and training; social and pyschological aspects, treatment and prevention of respiratory disease. Query with resume and samples; most articles on assignment only. Pays $200 to $350 on acceptance.

RN MAGAZINE—Oradell, NJ 07649. Articles, to 2,000 words, preferably by R.N.s, on nursing, clinical care, etc. Pays 10¢ to 15¢ a word, on publication. Query.

Rx BEING WELL—800 Second Ave., New York, NY 10017. Mark Deitch, Ed. Articles, 500 to 2,000 words, providing authoritative information on prevention, fitness, nutrition, and current medical topics. No personal-experience pieces. Many articles co-authored by doctors. Pays $250 to $750, a few weeks after acceptance. Query. Send SASE for guidelines.

TIC—P.O. Box 407, N. Chatham, NY 12132. Joseph Strack, Ed. Articles, 800 to 3,000 words, for dentists: building a practice, improving office procedures, etc. Profiles, with photos of dentists' achievements in the arts, sports, business, and other fields. Pays on acceptance.

TODAY'S OR NURSE—6900 Grove Rd., Thorofare, NJ 08086. Judith B. Paquet, R.N., Ed. Short humor, 400 to 500 words, for operating room nurses. Pays 10¢ a word, on publication. Query.

VEGETARIAN TIMES—P.O. Box 570, Oak Park, IL 60603. Paul Obis, Ed. Articles, 750 to 3,000 words, on nutrition, exercise and fitness, meatless food, etc. Personal experience and historical pieces, profiles. Pays $25 to $300, on publication. Send for sample copy.

YOUR LIFE AND HEALTH—55 W. Oak Ridge Dr., Hagerstown, MD 21740. Features, 1,000 to 2,800 words, on nutrition, diet, exercise, fitness and the latest developments in medicine. Seeks upbeat articles on how to live happier and healthier lives, with emphasis on prevention and vegetarianism. Pays $100 to $300, on acceptance.

EDUCATION

AMERICAN EDUCATION—U.S. Dept. of Education, 400 Maryland Ave. S.W., Washington, DC 20202. Beverley P. Blondell, Ed. Articles, 2,000 to 3,000 words, on government policy, opinion, key issues, education programs or activities for all ages.

AMERICAN SCHOOL & UNIVERSITY—401 N. Broad St., Philadelphia, PA 19108. Dorothy Wright, Ed. Articles and case studies, 1,200 to 1,500 words, on design, construction, operation and maintenance of school and college plants. Payment varies. Query.

CAPSTONE JOURNAL OF EDUCATION—P.O. Box Q, Unversity, AL 35486. Alexia M. Kartis, Asst. Ed. Articles, to 5,000 words, on contemporary ideas in educational research.

CHANGE—4000 Albemarle St. N.W., Suite 500, Washington, DC 20016. Reports, 1,500 to 2,000 words, on programs, people and institutions of higher education. Intellectual essays, 3,000 to 5,000 words, on higher education today. Payment varies.

CLASSROOM COMPUTER LEARNING—Pitman Learning, Inc., 19 Davis Dr., Belmont, CA 94002. Holly Brady, Ed. Articles, to 3,000 words, for teachers of grades K–12, related to uses of computers in the classroom: human-interest and philosophical articles, how-to pieces, software reviews, and hands-on ideas. Payment varies, on acceptance.

EDUCATION WEEK—Suite 560, 1333 New Hampshire Ave., N.W., Washington, DC 20036. M. Matzke, Exec. Ed. Articles covering national elementary and secondary education. Pays 20¢ a word, on publication. Query.

ELECTRONIC EDUCATION—Electronic Communications, 1311 Executive Center Dr., Suite 220, Tallahassee, FL 32301. Sharon Lobello, Ed. Marjorie Blair, Senior Ed. Articles, to 2,000 words, for educators, on uses of technology in education. Fillers. Pays $150 to $300, on publication. Query preferred.

FOUNDATION NEWS—1828 L St. N.W., Washington, DC 20036. Arlie W. Schardt, Ed. Articles, to 2,000 words, on national or regional activities supported by, or of interest to, grant makers. Pays to $1,000, on acceptance. Query.

THE HORN BOOK MAGAZINE—Park Sq. Bldg., 31 St. James Ave., Boston, MA 02116. Anita Silvey, Ed. Articles, 600 to 2,600 words, on books for young readers, and related subjects, for librarians, teachers, parents, etc. Pays $20 per printed page, on publication. Query.

INDUSTRIAL EDUCATION—1495 Maple Way, Troy, MI 48084. Andrew Cummins, Ed. Instructional material, projects and how-to pieces, 500 to 1,500 words, with photos and drawings, for industrial arts, vocational and technical education classes. Pays $30 per printd page, on publication.

INSTRUCTOR—545 Fifth Ave., New York, NY 10017. Leanna Landsmann, Ed. How-to articles on elementary classroom teaching, and computers in the classroom, with practical suggestions and project reports. Pays varying rates, on acceptance.

KEY TO CHRISTIAN EDUCATION—8121 Hamilton Ave., Cincinnati, OH 45231. Virginia Beddow, Ed. Articles, 600 to 2,000 words, on Christian education; tips for teachers in the local church. Pays varying rates, on acceptance.

LEARNING—19 Davis Dr., Belmont, CA 94002. Buff Bradley, Ed. How-to, why-to and public affairs articles, 1,500 to 3,000 words, for teachers of grades K–8. Tested classroom ideas for "Swap Shop," and "Idea Place," to 600 words. Pays $50 to $300, on acceptance. Query with SASE.

MEDIA & METHODS—1511 Walnut St., Philadelphia, PA 19102. Ann Caputo, Ed. Articles, 1,200 to 1,500 words, on media, technologies, and methods used to enhance instruction and learning in junior and senior high classrooms. Pays $25 to $75, on publication. Query.

THE MINORITY ENGINEER—44 Broadway, Greenlawn, NY 11740. James Schneider, Ed. Articles, 1,000 to 5,000 words, for college students, on career opportunities in engineering, scientific and technological fields; techniques of job hunting; developments in and applications of new technologies. Interviews. Profiles. Pays 10¢ a word, after publication. Query. Same address and requirements for *The Woman Engineer.*

PHI DELTA KAPPAN—8th and Union St., Box 789, Bloomington, IN 47402. Robert W. Cole, Jr., Ed. Articles, 1,000 to 4,000 words, on educational research, service, and leadership; issues, trends, and policy. Pays $100 to $500, on publication.

SCHOOL ARTS MAGAZINE—50 Portland St., Worcester, MA 01608. David W. Baker, Ed. Articles, 800 to 1,000 words, on art education with special application to the classroom. Photos. Pays varying rates, on publication.

TEACHERS & WRITERS—5 Union Sq. W., New York, NY 10003. Ron Padgett, Ed. Firsthand articles, 3,000 to 6,000 words, on the teaching of creative and imaginative writing. Pays in copies. Query preferred.

TEACHING ENGLISH IN THE TWO-YEAR COLLEGE—Dept. of English, East Carolina University, Greenville, NC 27834. Bertie Fearing, Ed. Articles on teaching English in two-year colleges. Pays in copies.

TODAY'S CATHOLIC TEACHER—2451 E. River Rd., Suite 200, Dayton, OH 45439. Ruth A. Matheny, Ed. Articles, 600 to 800 words and 1,200 to 1,500 words, on Catholic education, parent-teacher relationships, innovative teaching, etc. Pays $15 to $75, on publication.

WILSON LIBRARY BULLETIN—950 University Ave., Bronx, NY 10452. Milo Nelson, Ed. Articles, 1,000 to 3,000 words, on library-related material, education, etc. News reports; opinion pieces, 900 words, for "Vantage Point." Photos. Pays from $100, extra for photos, on acceptance.

THE WOMAN ENGINEER—See *The Minority Engineer.*

FARMING AND AGRICULTURE

AMERICAN BEE JOURNAL—51 N. Second St., Hamilton, IL 62341. Joe M. Graham, Ed. Articles on beekeeping, for professionals. Photos. Pays 75¢ per column inch, extra for photos, on publication.

BEEF—1999 Shepard Rd., St. Paul, MN 55116. Paul D. Andre, Ed. Articles on beef cattle feeding, cowherds, stocker operations, and related phases of the cattle industry. Pays to $300, on acceptance. Query.

BUCKEYE FARM NEWS—Ohio Farm Bureau Federation, 35 E. Chestnut St., Columbus, OH 43216. Ketih M. Stimpert, Man. Ed. Articles and humor, to 1,000 words, related to agriculture. Pays on publication. Query.

COUNTRY PEOPLE—5400 S. 60th St., Greendale, WI 53129. Bob Ottum, Man. Ed. Agriculturally-related, human-interest features, 300 to 1,000 words, and shorts, one-liners and up, with accent on humor. Pays $25 to $150, on acceptance. Queries preferred.

CRANBERRIES—P.O. Box 249, Cobalt, CT 06414. Bob Taylor, Ed. Articles of interest to cranberry growers, industry processors and agricultural researchers. Pays $15 to $40, extra for photos, on publication. Query.

DAIRYLIFE NORTHWEST—P.O. Box 98, Heisson, WA 98622. Dixie Ross, Pub. Articles, 1,000 to 1,500 words, related to the Northwest dairy industry. Personal profiles of farmers, farm-oriented poetry and fillers. Pays $1.50 per column inch, on publication. Send for writer's guidelines.

THE EVENER—29th and College, Cedar Falls, IA 50613. Susan Salterberg, Man. Ed. How-to and feature articles, 300 to 3,000 words, related to draft horses, mules and oxen. Pays 3¢ to 10¢ a word, $5 to $25 for photos, on acceptance. Queries preferred.

FARM & RANCH LIVING—5400 S. 60th St., Greendale, WI 53129. Bob Ottum, Man. Ed. Articles, 2,000 words, on rural people and situations; nostalgia pieces; profiles of interesting farms and farmers, ranches and ranchers. Poetry. Pays $15 to $400, on acceptance and on publication.

FARM FUTURES—Plaza East Office Center, 330 E. Kilbourn Ave., Suite 200, Milwaukee, WI 53202. David Skoloda, Ed. Articles, to 1,500 words, on marketing of agricultural commodities, farm business issues, management success stories, and the use of commodity futures by agricultural producers. Query with outline.

FARM INDUSTRY NEWS—1999 Shepard Rd., St. Paul, MN 55116. Den Gardner, Ed. Articles for farmers, on new products, buying, machinery, equipment, chemicals, and seeds. Pays $175 to $400, on acceptance. Query.

FARM JOURNAL—Washington Sq., Philadelphia, PA 19105. Lane Palmer, Ed. Articles, 500 to 1,500 words, with photos, on the business of farming, for farmers. Pays 20¢ to 50¢ a word, on acceptance. Query.

FARM SUPPLIER—Mt. Morris, IL 61054. B. Miller, Ed. Articles, 600 to 1,800 words, preferably with color photos, on retail farm trade products: feed, fertilizer, agricultural chemicals, etc. Photos. Pays about 15¢ to 20¢ a word, on acceptance.

FARMING UNCLE—P.O. Box 91, Liberty, NY 12754. Louis Turo, Ed. Articles, 500 to 700 words, on small stock, poultry, etc. Pays 1¢ a word, on acceptance.

FARMSTEAD MAGAZINE—Box 111, Freedom, ME 04941. Lynn Ann Ascrizzi, Senior Ed. Articles, 700 to 4,000 words, on organic home gardening and small farming methods, plant and vegetable varieties, alternative cash crops, livestock, marketing and economics for the small farmer, tools, self-reliant life styles, homestyle recipes, etc. Pays 5¢ a word, on publication. Query preferred.

FLORIDA GROWER & RANCHER—723 E. Colonial Dr., Orlando, FL 32803. Frank H. Abrahamson, Ed. Articles and case histories on farmers, growers and ranchers. Pays on publication. Query; buys little freelance material.

THE FURROW—Deere & Company, John Deere Rd., Moline, IL 61265. George Sollenberger, North American Ed. Specialized illustrated articles on farming. Pays to $1,000, on acceptance.

GURNEY'S GARDENING NEWS—Gurney Seed and Nursery Co., 2nd and Capitol, Yankton, SD 57079. Janet Schoniger, Ed. Practical articles on specific gardening topics; gardener profiles. Pays $50 to $375 for articles, 700 to 2,500 words, and $30 to $100 for articles 500 to 1,500 words, on gardening projects for children, and short articles 300 to 500 words, on gardening tips, hints, methods. Query.

HARROWSMITH—Camden House Publishing Ltd., Camden East, Ont., Canada KOK 1JO. James H. Lawrence, Ed./Pub. Articles, 100 to 5,000 words, on homesteading, husbandry, organic gardening and alternative energy with a Canadian slant. Pays $25 to $1,000, on acceptance. Query.

MICHIGAN FARMER—3303 W. Saginaw, Lansing, MI 48901. David Weinstock, Assoc. Ed. Articles on Michigan farming, rural situations and problems. Pays $15 to $20 per column, on publication.

NORDEN NEWS—601 W. Cornhusker Hwy., Lincoln, NE 68501. Gary Svatos, Ed. Technical articles, 1,200 to 1,500 words, and clinical features, 500 words, on veterinary medicine. Photos. Pays $200 to $250, $100 for shorter pieces, extra for photos, on publication.

THE OHIO FARMER—1350 W. Fifth Ave., Columbus, OH 43212. Andrew L. Stevens, Ed. Articles on farming, rural living, etc., in Ohio. Pays $15 per column, on publication.

PEANUT FARMER—P.O. Box 95075, Raleigh, NC 27625. Marla Maeder, Ed. Articles, 500 to 1,500 words, on production and management practices in peanut farming. Pays $50 to $350, on publication. Limited free-lance market.

PENNSYLVANIA FARMER—704 Lisburn Rd., Camp Hill, PA 17011. Robert H. Williams, Ed. Articles on farmers in PA, NJ, DE, MD, and WV: farm operations, families, life styles, etc. Pays $1 per column inch, on publication.

THE RECORD STOCKMAN—101 Livestock Exchange Bldg., Denver, CO 80216. Dan Green, Ed. Reportage and features, 400 to 2,500 words, that cover the business of raising cattle and sheep in the U.S. Writers must know the cattle business. Photos. Pays $25 to $200 for articles, $10 to $100 for photos, on publication.

SHEEP! MAGAZINE—Box 329, Jefferson, WI 53549. Dave Thompson, Ed. Articles, to 1,500 words, on successful shepherds. B/W photos. Pays $2 per column inch, extra for photos, on publication. Query.

SMALL FARMER'S JOURNAL, *featuring Practical Horse-Farming*—P.O. Box 2805, Eugene, OR 97402. How-to's, humor, practical work horse information, livestock and produce marketing, and articles appropriate to the independent family farm. Pays negotiable rats, on publication. Query first.

SUCCESSFUL FARMING—1716 Locust St., Des Moines, IA 50336. Richard Krumme, Ed. Articles on farm management, operations, etc. Helpful hints of farm shops. Pays varying rates, on acceptance.

WALLACES FARMER—#501, 1501 42nd St., W. Des Moines, IA 50265. Monte Sesker, Ed. Features, 600 to 700 words, on farming in Iowa, methods and equipment; interviews with farmers. Pays 4¢ to 5¢ a word, on acceptance. Query.

THE WESTERN PRODUCER—Box 2500, Saskatoon, Saskatchewan, Canada S7K 2C4. Attn. Man. Ed. Articles, to 700 words, on agricultural subjects, preferably with a Canadian slant. Photos. Pays from $3 per printed inch, $15 for b&w photos, on publication.

MEDIA AND THE ARTS

THE AMERICAN ART JOURNAL—40 W. 57th St., 5th Floor, New York, NY 10019. Jane Van N. Turano, Ed. Quarterly. Scholarly articles, 2,000 to 10,000 words, on American art of the 17th through 20th centuries. Photos. Pays $200 to $400, on acceptance.

AMERICAN FILM—The American Film Institute, John F. Kennedy Center, Washington, DC 20566. Peter Biskind, Ed. Feature articles, 4,000 words, on film and television. Profiles; news items; reports. Columns, 100 to 1,500 words. Photos. Pays from $50 to $1,000. Query preferred.

AMERICAN INDIAN ART MAGAZINE—7314 E. Osborne Dr., Scottsdale, AZ 85251. Roanne P. Goldfein, Man. Ed. Detailed, specific articles, 10 typed pages, on American Indian arts—painting, carving, bead works, basketry, textiles, ceramics, jewelry, etc. Pays varying rates for articles, on publication. Query.

AMERICAN THEATRE—355 Lexington Ave., New York, NY 10017. Jim O'Quinn, Ed. Features, 500 to 4,000 words, on the theatre and theatre-related subjects. Payment negotiable, on publication. Query first.

ART NEW ENGLAND—353 Washington St., Brighton, MA 02135. Carla Munsat, Stephanie Adelman, Eds. Features, 1,200 to 1,500 words, for artists, curators, gallery directors, collectors. Reviews and art criticism, 600 words. At least 2 photos must accompany article. Pays $10 for short reviews, $50 for longer pieces, on publication. Query preferred.

ARTSATLANTIC—P.O. Box 848, Charlottetown, P.E.I., Canada C1A 7L9. Joseph Sherman, Ed. Articles, 800 to 2,500 words, on visual, performing and literary arts, crafts in Atlantic Canada. Also, "idea and concept" articles of universal appeal. Pays from 10¢ per word, on publication. Query.

ARTSLINE—P.O. Box 24287, Seattle, WA 98124. Alice Copp Smith, Ed. Features, 1,800 to 2,400 words, on theatre, dance, and other performing or visual arts in the Northwest or the U.S.; arts-related humor; short pieces, 750 to 1,000 words pay $75 to $100; longer pieces pay from $200, on acceptance. Query.

BALLET NEWS—The Metropolitan Opera Guild, 1865 Broadway, New York, NY 10023. Robert Jacobson, Ed. Articles, to 2,500 words; profiles of dancers; features on ballet past and present. Pays 11¢ a word, on publication. Query.

BLUEGRASS UNLIMITED—Box 111, Broad Run, VA 22014. Peter V. Kuykendall, Ed. Articles, to 3,500 words, on bluegrass and traditional country music. Photos. Pays 5¢ to 6¢ a word, extra for photos. Query.

BROADCASTER—7 Labatt Ave., Toronto, Ont. Canada M5A 3P2. Barbara Moes, Ed. Articles, 500 to 2,000 words, on communications business in Canada. Pays from $250, on publication. Query.

CHANNELS OF COMMUNICATIONS—304 W. 58th St., New York, NY 10019. Les Brown, Ed.-in-Chief. Articles on developments in telecommunications and their impact on society (law, politics, religion, business, education and the arts). No personality profiles or reviews, unless related specifically to their affect on viewers. Pays on acceptance. Query required.

DANCE MAGAZINE—33 West 60th St., New York, NY 10023. William Como, Ed. Features on dance, personalities, and trends. Photos. Query; limited free-lance market.

DANCE TEACHER NOW—University Mall, Suite 2, 803 Russell Blvd., Davis, CA 95616. Susan M. Wershing, Ed. Articles, 2,500 words, for professional dancers and dance teachers, on practical aspects of a dance teacher's professional life, and political or economic issues related to the dance profession. Profiles on teachers or schools. Must be thoroughly researched. Pays $100 to $300, on acceptance.

DARKROOM PHOTOGRAPHY—One Hallidie Plaza, Suite 600, San Francisco, CA 94102. Richard Senti, Ed. How-to articles, 1,000 to 2,500 words, with photos, for all levels of photographers. Pays $100 to $400. Query.

THE DRAMA REVIEW—School of the Arts, New York Univ., 51 W. Fourth St., New York, NY 10012. Michael Kirby, Articles, with photos, on contemporary, avant-garde theater, theatrical theory and history. Pays 2¢ a word, on publication.

DRAMATICS—3368 Central Pkwy., Cincinnati, OH 45225. S. Ezra Goldstein, Ed. Articles, 1,000 to 3,500 words, on the performing arts: theater, puppetry, dance, mime, one-act plays, etc. Pays $25 to $200, on acceptance.

EXHIBIT—Drawer 189, Palm Beach, FL 33480. Christine C. Provo, Ed. Articles, to 800 words, with photos, on fine arts, new movements, techniques, etc.; profiles of artists. Query.

FILM QUARTERLY—Univ. of California Press, Berkeley, CA 94720. Ernest Callenbach, Ed. Film reviews, historical and critical articles, production projects, to 5,000 words. Pays on publication. Query.

FRETS—20085 Stevens Creek, Cupertino, CA 95014. Phil Hood, Ed. Articles, 750 to 3,000 words, for musicians, on acoustic string instruments, instrument making and repair, music theory and technique. Covers jazz, folk, bluegrass, classical, etc. Profiles of musicians and instruments. Pays $125 to $300, on acceptance. Query.

FUNCTIONAL PHOTOGRAPHY—101 Crossways Park West, Woodbury,

NY 11797. Mel Konecoff, Ed. Articles on use of photography and other image-making processes in science, medicine, research, etc. Photos. Pays varying rates, on publication. Query.

GUITAR PLAYER MAGAZINE—20085 Stevens Creek, Cupertino, CA 95014. Tom Wheeler, Ed. Articles, 1,500 to 5,000 words, on guitarists, guitars, and related subjects. Pays $75 to $300, on acceptance. Buys one-time and reprint rights.

HIGH FIDELITY—825 Seventh Ave., New York, NY 10019. William Tynan, Ed. Articles, 2,500 to 3,000 words, on stereo equipment, video applications, and home-entertainment computer applications. Pays on acceptance. Query.

HORIZON—P.O. Drawer 30, Tuscaloosa, AL 35402. Articles, 1,500 to 3,500 words, on art, film, literature, photography, dance, music, theater, and other cultural happenings. Pays from $300 on publication. Query Senior Editor.

INDUSTRIAL PHOTOGRAPHY—475 Park Ave., S., New York, NY 10016. Lynn Roher, Ed. Articles on techniques and trends in current professional photography, audiovisuals, etc., for industrial photographers and executives. Query.

INTERNATIONAL MUSICIAN—1500 Broadway, New York, NY 10036. J. Martin Emerson, Ed. Articles, 1,500 to 2,000 words, for professional musicians. Pays varying rates, on acceptance. Query.

KEYBOARD MAGAZINE—20085 Stevens Creek, Cupertino, CA 95014. Tom Darter, Ed. Articles, 2,500 to 5,000 words, on keyboard instruments and players. Photos. Pays $125 to $300, on acceptance. Query.

MEDIA HISTORY DIGEST—c/o Editor & Publisher, 11 W. 19th St., New York, NY 10011. Hiley H. Ward, Ed. Articles, 1,500 to 2,000 words on the history of media for wide consumer interest. Pays varying rates, on publication. Query.

MODERN DRUMMER—1000 Clifton Ave., Clifton, NJ 07013. Ronald L. Spagnardi, Ed. Articles, 500 to 2,000 words, on drumming; how-to's, interviews. Pays $50 to $500, on publication.

MODERN RECORDING & MUSIC—1120 Old Country Rd., Plainview, NY 11803. Articles, 10 to 12 double-spaced, typed pages, on recording techniques and other topics of interest to musicians and engineers; interviews with music personalities. Query Jeff Tamarkin, Ed. Pays $200, on publication.

MUSIC MAGAZINE—56 The Esplanade, Suite 202, Toronto, Ont., Canada M5E 1A7. Articles, with photos, on musicians, conductors, and composers, for all classical music buffs. Pays $35 per 1,000 words, on publication. Query.

MUSICAL AMERICA—825 Seventh Ave., New York NY 10019. Shirley Fleming, Ed. Authoritative articles, 1,000 to 1,500 words, on classical music subjects. Pays around 15¢ a word, on acceptance.

NEW ENGLAND ENTERTAINMENT—P.O. Box 735, Marshfield, MA 02050. Paul J. Reale, Ed. News features and reviews on arts and entertainment in New England. Light verse. Pays $10 to $25, $1 to $2 for verse, on publication.

OPERA NEWS—The Metropolitan Opera Guild, 1865 Broadway, New York, NY 10023. Robert Jacobson, Ed. Articles, 600 to 3,500 words, on all aspects of opera: humorous anecdotes. Pays 12¢ a word, on publication. Query.

PERFORMANCE—1020 Currie St., Fort Worth, TX 76107. Don Waitt, Ed. Reports on the touring industry: Concert promoters, booking agents, concert venues and clubs, as well as support services, such as lighting, sound and staging companies. Pays 25¢ per column line, on publication.

PETERSEN'S PHOTOGRAPHIC—8490 Sunset Blvd., Los Angeles, CA 90069. Karen Geller-Shinn, Ed. Articles and how-to pieces, with photos, on still, video, studio and darkroom photography, for beginners and advanced amateurs. Pays $60 per printed page, on publication.

PHOTOMETHODS—One Park Ave., New York, NY 10016. Fred Schmidt, Ed. Articles, 1,500 to 3,000 words, on innovative techniques in imaging (still, film, video), working situations, and management. Pays from $75, on publication. Query.

PLAYBILL—71 Vanderbilt Ave., New York, NY 10169. Joan Alleman, Ed.-in-Chief. Sophisticated articles, 800 to 2,000 words, with photos, on theater and subjects of interest to theater-goers. Pays $100 to $500, on publication.

POPULAR PHOTOGRAPHY MAGAZINE—One Park Ave., New York, NY 10016. Arthur Goldsmith, Ed. Dir. How-to articles, 500 to 2,000 words, for amateur and professional photographers. Pays $150 to $200 per printed page (including photos). Query with outline and photos.

SATELLITE DISH MAGAZINE—P.O. Box 8, Memphis, TN 38101. Kathy Ferguson, Ed. Lively entertainment features, 1,000 to 2,000 words, on current or upcoming satellite TV programs; articles on the industry and its people. Pays $100 to $750, within thirty days of publication. Send SASE for writer's guidelines.

SHOW-BOOK WEEK—*Chicago Sun Times,* 401 N. Wabash Ave., Chicago, IL 60611. Scott Powers, Ed. Articles, interviews and profiles, to 1,000 words, on the lively and fine arts. Pays $50 to $100, on publication.

SIGHTLINES—45 John St., New York, NY 10038. Judith Trojan, Ed. Informational articles on production, distribution, and programming of 16mm films and video. Interviews. Pays 2½¢ a word, on publication. Query.

SOAP OPERA DIGEST—254 W. 31st St., New York, NY 10001. Ellen Howard, Man. Ed. Features, to 1,500 words, for people interested in daytime and nighttime soaps. Pays from $200, on acceptance. Query.

SUN TRACKS—Box 2510, Phoenix, AZ 85502. Andy Van De Voorde, Music Ed. Music section of *New Times.* Long and short features, record reviews and interviews. Pays $15 to $85, on publication. Query.

TECHNICAL PHOTOGRAPHY—101 Crossways Park West, Woodbury, NY 11797. Don Garbera, Ed. Features, 8 to 10 double-spaced pages, on applications, techniques of photography for staff photographers. Some material on film and video. Pays varying rates, on publication. Query.

THEATRE CRAFTS MAGAZINE—135 Fifth Ave., New York, NY 10010. Patricia MacKay, Ed. Articles, 500 to 2,500 words, for professionals in theatre and video design and production. Pays on acceptance. Query preferred.

VIDEO—460 W. 34th St., New York, NY 10001. Richard Jaccoma, Man. Ed. How-to and service articles on video equipment and programming. Interviews and human-interest features related to nonbroadcast television, from 800 to 1,500 words. Pays varying rates, on acceptance. Query.

HOBBIES, CRAFTS, COLLECTING

AMERICAN CLAY EXCHANGE—P.O. Box 2674, La Mesa, CA 92041. Susan N. Cox, Ed. Articles, from 400 words, for collectors and/or dealers of American-made pottery, with an emphasis on antiques and collectibles. Photos. Pays from $5 for short items, to $100 for thoroughly-researched articles, on publication. Buys all rights.

ANTIQUE MONTHLY—P.O. Drawer 2, Tuscaloosa, AL 35402. Articles, 750 to 1,200 words, on the exhibition and sales of decorative arts and antiques more than 100 years old, with photos or slides. Pays $125, on publication. Query.

THE ANTIQUE TRADER WEEKLY—Box 1050, Dubuque, IA 52001. Kyle D. Husfloen, Ed. Articles, 1,000 to 2,000 words, on all types of antiques and collector's items. Photos. Pays from $5 to $150, extra for photos, on publication. Query preferred. Buys all rights.

ANTIQUES DEALER—1115 Clifton Ave., Clifton, NJ 07013. Nancy Adams, Ed. Articles, 500 to 2,000 words, on trends, pricing, retailing hints, for antiques trade. Pays $1.50 per column inch, or $50 per page, $10 for b&w photos. Query.

ANTIQUEWEEK/TRI-STATE TRADER—P.O. Box 90, Knightstown, IN 46148. Address Robert Reed, Ed. Articles, 500 to 1,000 words, on collector's items; background on antiques, restorations, antique shops, genealogy. Auction and show reports. Photos. Pays from 30¢ an inch, $25 to $50 for indepth articles, on publication. Query.

AOPA PILOT—421 Aviation Way, Frederick, MD 21701. Magazine of the Aircraft Owners and Pilots Assn. Edward G. Tripp, Ed. Articles, to 2,500 words, with photos, on general aviation for beginning and experienced pilots. Pays to $750.

ASSETS—5 Bethpage Rd., Hicksville, NY 11801. Joseph J. Abiuso, Ed. Articles, 2,000 to 2,500 words, on assets, collectibles, and tangibles. Pays $200, on publication. Queries preferred.

BIRD WATCHER'S DIGEST—P.O. Box 110, Marietta, OH 45740. Mary B. Bowers, Ed. Articles, 600 to 3,000 words, on bird-watching experiences and expeditions; information about rare sightings; updates on endangered species. Pays to $50, on publication.

THE BLADE MAGAZINE—P.O. Box 22007, Chattanooga, TN 37422. J. Bruce Voyles, Ed. Articles, 500 to 3,000 words: Historical pieces on knives and old knife factories, etc.; interviews with knifemakers; how-to pieces. Pays from 5¢ a word, on publication.

CHESS LIFE—186 Route 9W, New Windsor, NY 12550. Frank Elley, Ed. Articles, 500 to 3,000 words, for members of the U.S. Chess Federation, on news, profiles, technical aspects of chess. Features on all aspects of chess—history, humor, puzzles, etc. Fiction, 500 to 2,000 words, related to chess. Photos. Pays varying rates, on acceptance. Query; limited freelance market.

COLLECTIBLES ILLUSTRATED—Dublin, NH 03444. Articles, to 2,000 words, on collectibles. Features on specialized fields: early auto memorabilia, Shirley Temple collectibles, etc. Department pieces: profiles, to 2,000 words; collectors' trips; profiles of specialty collectors. Photos. Pays to $400, to $300 for shorter pieces, after acceptance. Query preferred. Buys all rights, but negotiable.

COLLECTOR EDITIONS QUARTERLY—170 Fifth Ave., New York, NY 10010. Krystyna Poray Goddu, Man. Ed. Articles, 750 to 1,500 words, on collectibles: glass, porcelain, *objets d'art,* modern Americana, etc. Pays $150 to $350, on publication. Query.

CRAFTS 'N THINGS—14 Main St., Park Ridge, IL 60068. Nancy Tosh, Ed. How-to articles on all kinds of crafts projects, with instructions. Pays $50 to $200, on publication. Send manuscript with instructions and photograph of the finished item.

CREATIVE CRAFTS & MINIATURES MAGAZINE—P.O. Box 700, Newton, NJ 07860. Walter Lankenau, Man. Ed. How-to articles, 200 to 1,500 words, with photos, on adult handicrafts, miniatures and collectibles. Pays on publication.

CREATIVE IDEAS FOR LIVING (formerly *Decorating and Craft Ideas*)—P.O. Box 2522, Birmingham, AL 35201. Feature articles, 700 to 1,000 words, on good quality creative projects; personality pieces for "Life In Crafts" department; decorating articles. Rates start at $350, after acceptance. Query Ed. Katherine Pearson.

DOLLS, THE COLLECTOR'S MAGAZINE—170 Fifth Ave., New York, NY 10010. Krystyna Poray Goddu, Ed. Articles, 500 to 2,500 words, for knowledgeable doll collectors: sharply focused with a strong collecting angle, with concrete information: value, identification, dollmaking, restoration, etc. Pays $100 to $350, on publication. Query.

THE FAMILY HANDYMAN—1999 Shepard Rd., St. Paul, MN 55116. Articles for homeowners, on home systems and construction, use of tools and materials. How-to pieces detailing specific projects. Seasonal material. Pays $275 to $325 per page, on acceptance. Send for guidelines.

FINESCALE MODELER—1027 N. Seventh St., Milwaukee, WI 53233. How-to articles for people who make nonoperating scale models of aircraft, automobiles, boats, figures. Photos and drawings should accompany articles. One-page model-building hints and tips. Pays from $30 per published page, on acceptance. Query preferred.

FRANKLIN MINT ALMANAC—Franklin Center, PA 19091. Well-researched articles, 1,000 to 2,000 words, on noteworthy collectors, collectibles and collections. Pay about $500, on acceptance. Query.

GAMES—515 Madison Ave., New York, NY 10022. Articles on games and puzzles. Short humor. Puzzles, tests, brainteasers, etc. Photos. Pays varying rates, on publication. Query preferred.

GEMS AND MINERALS—P.O. Box 687, Mentone, CA 92359. Jack R. Cox, Ed. Articles, with photos, on collecting, cutting and identifying gems and minerals. How-to pieces on making jewelry. Pays 50¢ per column inch, or $15 per page, on publication. Query.

GLASS CRAFT NEWS—270 Lafayette St., Rm. 1310, New York, NY 10012. David Ostiller, Ed. Practical articles of interest to stained glass hobbyists. No historical articles. Pays $100 to $200, on publication. Query required.

HANDMADE—50 College St., Asheville, NC 28801. Sally Rudich, NB/CL Ed. Service and informational articles related to soft and hard crafts, 100 to 500 words, with visuals. Unique design tidbits, 40 to 100 words. Payment varies, on acceptance. Query required.

HOME MECHANIX (formerly *Mechanix Illustrated*)— 1515 Broadway, New York, NY 10036. Joseph Provey, Ed. How-to features and articles, 1,500 to 2,500 words, on home improvement, energy conservation, and automotive subjects. Pays $300 per printed page, on acceptance. Query.

THE HOME SHOP MACHINIST—2779 Aero Park Dr., Box 1810, Traverse City, MI 49685. Joe D. Rice, Ed. How-to articles, on precision metalworking and foundry work. Accuracy and attention to detail a must. Pays $30 per published page, extra for photos and illustrations, on publication. Send SASE for writer's guidelines.

HOMEBUILT AIRCRAFT—16200 Ventura Blvd., Suite 201, Encino, CA 91436. Steven Werner, Ed. Articles, to 2,500 words, on building and flying your own plane: pilot reports on specific aircraft; new designs in airplanes and airplane parts; news features; air show coverage; pilot experiences and proficiency. Photos. Pays $150 to $300.

JOEL SATER'S ANTIQUES AND AUCTION NEWS—P.O. Box B., Marietta, PA 17547. Denise Murphy, Ed. Factual articles, 600 to 1,500 words, on antiques and collecting. Photos. Pays $10 to $20, on publication.

LOOSE CHANGE—Mead Pub. Corp., 21176 S. Alameda St., Long Beach, CA 90810. Sue Boyce, Ed. Cover articles, 3,500 to 12,000 words, for collectors of antique gaming machines, slot machines, gambling as a hobby, modern games, etc. Shorter articles, 900 to 5,000 words, on related subjects. Pays $15 to $250, extra for photos, on acceptance. Buys all rights.

MAKE IT WITH LEATHER—Box 1386, Fort Worth, TX 76101. Earl F. Warren, Ed./Pub. How-to and leathercraft business articles, to 2,000 words, with photos and patterns. Leathercraft-related features. Pays $50 to $300, extra for illustrations and photos, on publication.

MINIATURE COLLECTOR—170 Fifth Ave., New York, NY 10010. Louise Fecher, Man. Ed. Articles, 500 to 1,200 words, with photos, on outstanding miniatures and the people who make and collect them. Original, illustrated how-to projects for making miniatures. Pays varying rates, on publication. Query.

MODEL RAILROADER—1027 N. Seventh St., Milwaukee, WI 53223. Russ Larson, Ed. Articles, with photos of layout and equipment, on model railroads. Pays $54 per printed page, on acceptance. Query.

NEW SHELTER—33 E. Minor St., Emmaus, PA 18049. Address Articles Ed. Do-it-yourself articles for suburban homeowners, 1,000 to 3,000 words, with photos, on innovative housing, alternative energy, water and resource conservation. Pays from 10¢ a word, extra for photos, on acceptance. Query preferred, with photos.

THE NEW YORK ANTIQUE ALMANAC—Box 335, Lawrence, NY 11559. Carol Nadel, Ed. Articles on antiques, shows, shops, museums, art, investments, collectibles, collecting suggestions, related humor. Photos. Pays $5 to $60, extra for photos, on publication.

PLATE WORLD—6054 W. Touhy Ave., Chicago, IL 60648. Jane Grant Tougas, Ed. Articles on artists, collectors, manufacturers, retailers of limited-edition collector's plates. Internationally oriented, with on-going Canadian market section. Pays varying rates, on publication. Query first.

POPULAR MECHANICS—224 W. 57th St., New York, NY 10019. Bill Hartford, Man. Ed. Articles, 300 to 2,000 words, on latest developments in mechanics, industry, science; features on hobbies with a mechanical slant; how-to's on home, shop, and crafts projects. Photos and sketches. Pays to $1,000, $25 to $100 for short pieces, on acceptance. Buys all rights.

THE PROFESSIONAL QUILTER—Oliver Press, 917 Lakeview Ave., St. Paul, MN 55117. Jeannine M. Spears, Ed. Articles, 500 to 1,500 words, for women in small businesses related to the quilting field: business and marketing skills, personality profiles. Graphics, if applicable; no "how-to" quilt articles. Pays $25 to $75, on publication.

RAILROAD MODEL CRAFTSMAN—P.O. Box 700, Newton, NJ 07860. William C. Schaumburg, Man. Ed. How-to articles on scale model railroading; cars, operation, scenery, etc. Pays on publication.

R/C MODELER MAGAZINE—P.O. Box 487, Sierra Madre, CA 91024. Patricia E. Crews, Ed. Technical and semi-technical how-to articles on radio-controlled model aircraft, boats and cars. Pays $25 to $450, 30 days after publication. Query.

THE ROBB REPORT—1 Acton Pl., Acton, MA 01720. Feature articles on investment opportunities, classic and collectible autos, art and antiques, home interiors, boats, travel, etc. Pays on publication. Query with SASE and published clips. Attn: Mary Frakes.

ROCKS AND MINERALS—4000 Albermarle St. N.W., Washington, DC 20016. Marie Huizing, Man. Ed. Articles, 3,000 words, on minerals. Pays in copies.

STITCH 'N SEW—2535 Ridgetop Way, Valrico, FL 33594. Carol R. Pedersen, Ed. How-tos and instructional material for any of the needle arts, to 1,000 words. Fillers, 50 to 100 words. Photos and cartoons. Pays on publication.

ULTRALIGHT AIRCRAFT—16200 Ventura Blvd., Suite 201, Encino, CA 91436. Steve Werner, Ed. Articles, 1,000 to 3,000 words, on flying, maintenance, and construction of ultralight aircraft. Photos. Pays $100 to $300, on publication. Query preferred.

ULTRALIGHT PILOT—421 Aviation Way, Frederick, MD 21701. Magazine of the Aircraft Owners and Pilots Assn. Thomas A. Horne, Ed. Articles, to 2,500 words, with photos, on ultralight flying for beginning and experienced ultralight pilots. Pays to $750, extra for photos.

WESTART—Box 1396, Auburn, CA 95603. Martha Garcia, Ed. Features, 350 to 700 words, on fine arts and crafts. No hobbies. Photos. Pays 50¢ per column inch, on publication. SASE required.

THE WINE SPECTATOR—Opera Plaza, Suite 2040, 601 Van Ness Ave., San Francisco, CA 94102. Harvey Steiman, Man. Ed. Features, 600 to 800 words, preferably with photos, on topics and people in the wine industry. Pays from $100, extra for photos, on publication. Query required.

WINE WEST—P.O. Box 498, Geyserville, CA 95441. Mildred Howie, Ed. Articles of interest to wine professionals and connoisseurs, 800 to 2,500 words. Pays $2.50 per column inch, on publication. Query required.

WINNING—15115 S. 76 E. Ave., Bixby, OK 74008. Andre Hinds, Man. Ed. Articles, 300 to 800 words, on winning contests and sweepstakes. Pays 5¢ a word, on publication.

WOODENBOAT—P.O. Box 78, Brooklin, ME 04616. Jonathan Wilson, Ed. How-to and technical articles, 4,000 words, on construction, repair and maintenance of wooden boats; design, history and use of wooden boats; and profiles of outstanding wooden boat builders and designers. Pays $6 per column inch. Query preferred.

THE WOODWORKER'S JOURNAL—P.O. Box 1629, 517 Litchfield Rd., New Milford, CT 06776. Thomas G. Begnal, Man. Ed. Original plans for woodworking projects, with detailed written instructions and at least one B/W photo of finished product. Pays $80 to $120 per published page, on acceptance.

WORKBENCH—4251 Pennsylvania Ave., Kansas City, MO 64111. Jay Hedden, Ed. Articles on do-it-yourself home improvement and maintenance projects for beginning and expert craftsmen. Complete working drawings with accurate dimensions, step-by-step instructions, lists of materials, and photos of the finished product must accompany submission. Features on how to reduce energy consumption. Pays from $125 per published page, on acceptance.

YESTERYEAR—P.O. Box 2, Princeton, WI 54968. Michael Jacobi, Ed. Articles on antiques, collectibles, and nostalgia, for readers in Wisconsin, Illinois, Iowa, Minnesota and surrounding states. Photos. Will consider regular columns on collecting or antiques. Pays from $10, on publication.

ZYMURGY—Box 287, Boulder, CO 80306. Charles N. Papazian, Ed. Articles appealing to beer lovers and homebrewers. Pays $25 to $75, for pieces 750 to 2,000 words, on publication. Query.

POPULAR & TECHNICAL SCIENCE; COMPUTERS

ANTIC, THE ATARI RESOURCE—524 2nd St., San Francisco, CA 94107. Nat Friedland, Ed. Programs and information for the Atari computer user/owner. Reviews of hardward and software, original programs, etc., 500 words. Game reviews, 400 words. Pays $50 per review, $60 per published page, on publication. Query.

ASTRONOMY—Box 92788, Milwaukee, WI 53202. Richard Berry, Ed-in-Chief. Articles on astronomy, astrophysics, space travel, research. Hobby pieces on equipment; short news items. Pays varying rates, on publication.

BEYOND—1680 N. Vine St., Suite 900, Hollywood, CA 90028. Byron Laursen, Ed. College newspaper supplement for technical and engineering schools. Science articles, 1,200 to 2,000 words. Science fiction, 2,000 to 3,500 words for nonfiction. Pays 15¢ a word, on publication. Query preferred for nonfiction.

BYTE MAGAZINE—P.O. Box 372, Hancock, NH 03449. Philip Lemmons, Ed. Features on new technology, how-to articles, and reviews of computers and software, varying lengths, for sophisticated users of personal computers. Payment is competitive. Query.

COMPUTE!—P.O. Box 5406, Greensboro, NC 27403. Richard Mansfield, Ed. Timely articles on applications, tutorials, games and programs that address the needs of the consumer computer user. Length: 500 to 6,000 words. Pays on acceptance.

COMPUTER AND SOFTWARE NEWS—425 Park Ave., New York, NY 10022. Charles J. Humphrey, Ed. Newsweekly for hardware and software retailers, distributors and suppliers. News items. Pays 15¢ per published word, on publication.

COMPUTER USER—17000 Marquardt Ave., Cerritos, CA 90701. Catherine Semar, Man. Ed. How-to articles and features on applications for Radio Shack TRS-80 computer and compatibles. Pays on acceptance and on publication. Query with photos, if available.

COMPUTERS & ELECTRONICS—One Park Ave., New York, NY 10016. Seth Alpert, Ed. Articles on personal computers and consumer electronics technology. Pays $600 to $1,200, on acceptance.

COMPUTING NOW!—Moorshead Publications, Suite 601, 25 Overlea Blvd., Toronto, Ontario, Canada M4H 1B1. Steve Rimmer, Ed. Articles, from 2,000 to 4,000 words, for large audience, ranging in skill from beginners to business users. Photos and drawings. Pays 8¢ a word, $10 to $50 for drawings, on publication. Query.

DIGITAL REVIEW—160 State St., Boston, MA 02109. Patrick Kenealy, Ed. For users of Digital Equipment (DEC) computers. How-to articles, profiles, business applications and reviews, to 3,500 words. Pays $500 to $1,500, on acceptance. Include graphics. Query first.

DISCOVER MAGAZINE—Time & Life Building, Rockefeller Center, New York, NY 10020. Uses staff-written material only.

80 MICRO—Wayne Green Communications, 80 Pine St., Peterboro, NH 03458. Address Submissions Ed. Technical articles, programs and tutorials for TRS-80 microcomputer; no general-interest articles. Pays $50 to $75 per printed page, on acceptance. Query.

ELECTRONICS WEST—2250 N. 16th St., Suite 105, Phoenix, AZ 85006. Walter J. Schuch, Ed. Profiles, articles on new products and management topics, 1,000 to 3,000 words; new items for high-tech workers. Pays 10¢ a word, on publication. Query first.

ENVIRONMENT—4000 Albemarle St. N.W., Washington, DC 20016. Jane Scully, Ed. Factual articles, 2,500 to 5,000 words, on scientific, technological and environmental policy and decision-making issues. Articles must be documented. Pays $100 to $300. Query.

THE FUTURIST—World Future Society, 4916 Elmo Ave., Bethesda, MD 20814. Edward S. Cornish, Ed. Features, 1,000 to 5,000 words, on subjects pertaining to the future; environment, education, science, technology, etc. Pays in copies.

GENETIC ENGINEERING NEWS—157 E. 86th St., New York, NY 10028. Peter Dorfman, Ed. Articles on all aspects of biotechnology; feature articles and news articles. Pays varying rates, on acceptance. Query preferred.

GEOPHYSICS: THE LEADING EDGE OF EXPLORATION—P.O. Box 702740, Tulsa, OK 74170-2740. Articles, to 5,000 words, on the successes, failures and aspirations of geophysicists and other scientists. Pays $50 to $500 for features, on publication.

HAM RADIO—Greenville, NH 03048. Rich Rosen, Ed. Articles, to 2,500 words, on amateur radio theory and construction. Pays to 5¢ a word, on publication. Query.

HARDCOPY—Box 759, Brea, CA 92621. Harry McClain, Ed. Articles, 2,000 to 3,500 words, for manufacturers, users, and distributors of Digital Equipment Corp. (DEC): how-to pieces on product and system applications, and company profiles. Must have DEC tie-in. Pays $200 to $600, thirty days after acceptance. Query first.

HOT COCO—80 Pine St., Peterborough, NH 03458. Michael Nadeau, Ed. How-to pieces, programs of games, utilities, education, etc., and reviews for Radio Shack Color Computer users. Pays $50 to $75 per printed page, on acceptance, for articles 2 to 15 double-spaced typed pages. Query.

INCIDER—80 Pine St., Peterborough, NH 03458. Articles for Apple computer users: personal experience and how-to pieces; software and hardware reviews; computer-related fiction. Fillers. Pays $100 per printed page, on acceptance. Query preferred.

THE JOURNAL OF FRESHWATER—2500 Shadywood Rd., Box 90, Navarre, MN 55392. Linda Schroeder, Ed. Articles on freshwater environment and science, for lay persons. Photos. Pays $100 to $300, extra for photos, on publication.

LINK-UP—10800 Lyndale Ave. S., Minneapolis, MN 55420. Richard Hughes, Man. Ed. How-to pieces and reviews for small-computer communications enthusiasts, 600 to 2,500 words. Photos are a plus. Pay runs from $200 to $400, on acceptance.

MACWORLD—Editorial Proposals, 555 DeHaro St., San Francisco, CA 94107. Articles relating to Macintosh personal computers; varying lengths. Query or send outline with screenshots, if applicable. Pays from $350, on acceptance. Send SASE for writer's guidelines.

MICRO COMMUNICATIONS—Miller Freeman, 500 Howard St., San Francisco, CA 94105. Mark Hall, Tech. Ed. Application articles, communications, 2,500 to 4,000 words, with photos or drawings. Pays 10¢ a word, on acceptance.

MINI-MICRO SYSTEMS—221 Columbus Ave., Boston, MA 02116. George Kotelly, Ed. Technical monthly for computer system users, manufacturers, and integrators. How-to pieces, profiles, news items, etc. Pays $35 to $100 per printed page, on publication. Query.

NIBBLE—Box 325, Lincoln, MA 01773. David P. Szetela, Man. Ed. Programs and programming methods, as well as short articles, reviews and general-interest pieces for Apple Computer users. Send short cover letter and sample program runs with manuscript. Pays $400 to $500 for articles, $20 to $250 for shorter pieces. Send SASE for writer's guidelines.

OMNI—1965 Broadway, New York, NY 10022. Dick Teresi, Exec. Ed. Articles, 2,500 to 3,500 words, on scientific aspects of the future: space colonies, cloning, machine intelligence, ESP, origin of life, future arts, lifestyles, etc. Pays $800 to $1,250, less for short features, on acceptance. Query.

ONLINE TODAY—5000 Arlington Centre Blvd., Columbus, OH 43220. Douglas G. Branstetter, Ed. Articles, 1,000 to 5,000 words, on social and political implications of the new technology; quality standards for videotex; computers and education; and computer applications in business and financial areas. Human-interest pieces. Pays $75 to $100 per printed page, on acceptance. Query.

PC AGE—8138 Foothill Blvd., Sunland, CA 91040. Jack Crone, Ed. Technical computer articles, 2,000 words, for IBM PC users. Pays 10¢ a word, on acceptance. Query. Send SASE for writer's guidelines.

PC TECH JOURNAL—The World Trade Center, Suite 211, Baltimore, MD 21202. Will Fastie, Ed. How-to pieces and reviews, for technically sophisticated computer professionals. Pays $100 to $1,000, on acceptance. Query required.

POPULAR COMPUTING—70 Main St., Peterborough, NH 03458. Richard Friedman, Exec. Ed. Articles, 1,500 to 3,000 words, for lay people, on home, small business and educational uses of personal computers. Pays $150 to $1,000 on acceptance. Query.

POPULAR SCIENCE MONTHLY—380 Madison Ave., New York, NY 10017. C. P. Gilmore, Ed. Articles, to 2,000 words, with photos, on developments in applied science and technology. Short illustrated articles on new inventions and products; photo essays, to 4 pages. Pays from $150 per printed page, on acceptance.

PORTABLE 100—Computer Communications, Inc., P.O. Box 250, Camden, ME 04843. John P. Mello, Ed. Programs and applications for users of TRS-80 Model 100 Microcomputers, 2,000 to 4,000 words. Product reviews. Pays $100 to $400 for articles, $75 to $200 for reviews, on acceptance. Query.

PUBLIC OPINION—1150 17th St. N.W., Washington, DC 20036. Karlyn H. Keene, Man. Ed. Articles, 3,000 words, analyzing current issues through use of public opinion polls. Pays to $500, on publication. Query first.

SCIENCE DIGEST—888 Seventh Ave., New York, NY 10106. Oliver S. Moore, Ed. Timely authoritative articles on key science issues, digest departments on important findings, items and special reports for the young professional.

SCIENCE 85—1101 Vermont Ave., N.W., 10th Fl., Washington, DC 20005. Allen Hammond, Ed. Short articles, 500 to 1,200 words, and features, 3,000 to 4,000 words, on developments in the sciences, including social science and economics, medicine and technology. Profiles of scientists. Book reviews. Pays $1,500 to $2,000 for features, $300 to $800 for shorter pieces, on acceptance. Query.

SEA FRONTIERS—3979 Rickenbacker Causeway, Virginia Key, Miami, FL 33149. Jean Bradfisch, Ed. Illustrated articles, 2,000 words, on scientific advances related to the sea, biological, physical, chemical, or geological phenomena, etc., for lay readers. Send SASE for guidelines. Pays $20 to $30 a page, on publication. Query.

TECHNOLOGY REVIEW—Rm. 10-140, Massachusetts Institute of Technology, Cambridge, MA 02139. John Mattill, Ed. General-interest articles, and more technical features, 1,500 to 5,000 words, on technology, the environment and society. Payment varies, on publication. Query.

TODAY—See *Online Today.*

WEATHERWISE—4000 Albemarle St. N.W., Washington, DC 20016. Linda Dove, Man. Ed. Articles, 2,500 to 5,000 words, on weather. Pays in copies.

THE POPULAR MARKET

The popular market includes the magazines that used to be called the "pulps": men's magazines, detective and mystery, science fiction, western, confession and romance magazines. Included among the men's magazines are publications seeking so-called adult material. Most of the popular magazines use fiction, and many use both stories and articles, while a few detective and adventure magazines want only factual material. Book publishers also have a continuing need for western, mystery, science fiction, romance and adventure novels; many paperback book publishers particularly are in the market for paperback originals in these areas. Writers should consult the list of *Paperback Book Publishers* for their requirements.

MEN'S AND ADULT MAGAZINES

CAVALIER—2355 Salzedo St., Coral Gables, FL 33134. Nye Wilden, Man. Ed. Maurice De Walt, Fiction Ed. Articles with photos, and fiction, 1,500 to 3,000 words, for sophisticated young men. Pays to $400 for articles, to $250 for fiction, on publication. Query for articles.

CHIC—2029 Century Park E., Suite 3800, Los Angeles, CA 90067. Richard Warren Lewis, Articles Ed. Articles, 4,500 words. Pays $750 for articles, on acceptance.

ESQUIRE—2 Park Ave., New York, NY 10016. Gene Stone, Sr. Ed. Rust Hills, Fiction Ed. Literary short stories, 1,000 to 7,000 words, for intelligent adult audience. Articles, 1,500 to 4,000 words. Pays varying rates, on acceptance. Query, with clips, for articles; submit complete manuscript and SASE for fiction.

FORUM, THE INTERNATIONAL JOURNAL OF HUMAN RELATIONS—1965 Broadway, New York, NY 10023-5965. Articles, 2,500 words, on sex-related topics, health, lifestyles, personal experiences, etc. Pays $400 to $800, on acceptance. Query.

GALLERY—800 Second Ave., New York, NY 10017. John Bensink, Ed.-in-Chief. Articles, investigative pieces, and fiction, to 4,000 words, for sophisticated men. Short humor, satire, service pieces. Photos. Pays varying rates, half on acceptance, half on publication. Query.

GEM—G&S Publications, 1472 Broadway, New York, NY 10036. Will Martin, Ed. Articles and fiction, 500 to 2,500 words, on sex-related and contemporary topics. No pornographic or obscene material. Pays varying rates, after acceptance. Same address and requirements for *BUF.*

GENESIS—770 Lexington Ave., New York, NY 10021. J. J. Kelleher, Ed.-in-Chief. Articles, 3,000 to 4,000 words; humor, 1,000 to 3,000 words; celebrity interviews, 2,500 words. Photo essays. Sexually explicit fiction, 3,000 words, with well-developed plots. Pays 30 days after acceptance. Query.

GENTLEMAN'S COMPANION—2029 Century Park E., Suite 3800, Los Angeles, CA 90067. Address Fiction Manuscripts Dept. Short stories, 2,500 to 4,000 words, with fully developed plots and characterization. Erotic scene a must (study magazine style). Pays from $300, on acceptance.

GENTLEMEN'S QUARTERLY (GQ)—350 Madison Ave., New York, NY 10017. Eliot Kaplan, Articles Ed. Articles of interest to men of style, 750 to 3,000 words. Fitness and grooming, health and nutrition, entertainment, sports, politics, food and wine, travel, money, women's views; profiles; humor; fiction. Query with outline required. Fiction, to 2,500 words: Query Adam Gopnik, Staff Ed.

HARVEY FOR LOVING PEOPLE—Suite 2305, 450 Seventh Ave., New York, NY 10001. Harvey Shapiro, Ed./Pub. Sexually-oriented articles and fiction, to 2,500 words. Pays to $200, on publication. Query for articles. No recent report.

HUSTLER—2029 Century Park E., Suite 3800, Los Angeles, CA 90067. Richard Warren Lewis, Articles Ed. Investigative articles and profiles, 5,000 words. Sex Play articles, with educational focus, 1,500 to 2,000 words. Pays from $1,200; from $350 for Sex Play pieces, on acceptance. Query.

OUI—300 W. 43rd St., New York, NY 10036. Attn.: Articles Ed. Articles, 1,200 to 2,500 words, geared to predominantly male audience, age 18–35, college educated. Hard-hitting exposés, new sexual trends, political intrigue. How-to and service articles on new or untapped trends. Query first. Modern, upbeat stories, 1,200 to 2,500 words. Sexual situations or overtones helpful, but not required. Payment varies.

PENTHOUSE—1965 Broadway, New York, NY 10023. Peter Bloch, Ex. Ed. Kathy Green, Fiction Ed. Peter McCabe, Articles Ed. General-interest or investigative articles, to 5,000 words. Sophisticated, quality fiction, 4,000 to 6,000 words, with contemporary settings and well-defined characters. Interviews, 5,000 words, with introductions. Satire, humor, and black comedy. Pays to 50¢ a word, on acceptance.

PLAYBOY—919 N. Michigan Ave., Chicago, IL 60611. James Morgan, Articles Ed. Alice K. Turner, Fiction Ed. "In nonfiction, we regularly feature politics, business and finance, sports, science and technology, topical humor, music, personality profiles, sex and relationships, and other topics that have some bearing on the up-and-coming, success-oriented lifestyles of our readers. Writers can best determine what we're looking for by reading the nonfiction we are currently publishing, and evaluating our tastes and judgment. A brief query and writing sample will get the most prompt and thorough attention from us. Average length for nonfiction: 4,000 to 5,000 words. Minimum payment is $3,000.

"As for fiction, we continue to look for well-written, well-constructed stories that will appeal to a chiefly well-informed, young male audience, and we have a standing need for the following: serious, quality stories that involve current issues or situations; adventure stories and suspense; humor; science fiction; mystery; satire. We constantly reject stories—and articles—some of high quality, simply because they are inappropriate to our publication. Fairy tales, extremely experimental stories, and outright pornography do not have a place in PLAYBOY. Average length for fiction—1,000 to 6,000 words; payment is usually $2,000 (for very short stories, $1,000).

"Submissions for our 'Ribald Classics' department should be between 900 and 1,100 words, and we require that they be derived from some actual source, and that the source be clearly and exactly stated with the date. Payment is usually $200. Enclose SASE with all material."

PLAYERS—8060 Melrose Ave., Los Angeles, CA 90046. Joe Hazel, Jr., Ed. Leslie Gersicoff, Assoc. Ed. Articles, 1,000 to 4,000 words, with photos, for black men: travel, business, entertainment, sports; interviews. Offbeat fiction of high literary quality, 1,000 to 5,000 words. No adventure stories. Humor; satire. Pays on publication.

645

DETECTIVE AND MYSTERY MAGAZINES

ALFRED HITCHCOCK'S MYSTERY MAGAZINE—380 Lexington Ave., New York, NY 10017. Cathleen Jordan, Ed. Well-plotted mystery, detective, suspense and crime fiction, 1,000 to 14,000 words. Submissions by new writers strongly encouraged. Pays 3¢ to 8¢ a word, on acceptance.

ARMCHAIR DETECTIVE—129 W. 56th St., New York, NY 10019. Michael Seidman, Ed. Articles on mystery and detective fiction; reviews, biographical sketches, etc. Pays in copies.

DETECTIVE DRAGNET—1440 St. Catherine W., Suite 625, Montreal, Quebec, Canada H3G 1S2. Dominick A. Merle, Ed. Well-researched true crime stories, 3,500 to 6,000 words, with photos, involving mystery, suspense and lots of human interest. No fiction. Include clippings describing the case, with date, location and names of victims and suspects. Pays $200 to $300, on acceptance. Same address and requirements for *Detective Cases, Detective Files, Headquarters Detective, Startling Detective,* and *True Police Cases.*

ELLERY QUEEN'S MYSTERY MAGAZINE—380 Lexington Ave., New York, NY 10017. Eleanor Sullivan, Ed. Detective, crime, mystery and spy fiction, 4,000 to 6,000 words. Suspense or straight detective stories. No sex, sadism or sensationalism. Particularly interested in new writers and "first stories." Pays 3¢ to 8¢ a word, on acceptance.

FRONT PAGE DETECTIVE—See *Inside Detective.*

HEADQUARTERS DETECTIVE—See *Detective Dragnet.*

INSIDE DETECTIVE—Reese Communications, Inc., 460 W. 34th St., New York, NY 10001. Rose Mandelsberg, Ed. Timely, true detective stories, 5,000 to 6,000 words. Individual investigative techniques for "The Sherlock Experts." No fiction. Pays $250, on acceptance. Query. Same address and requirements for *Front Page Detective.*

MASTER DETECTIVE—460 W. 34th St., New York, NY 10001. Art Crockett, Ed. Detailed articles, 5,000 to 6,000 words, with photos, on current cases (some older, solved cases considered), emphasizing human motivation and detective work. No fiction. Pays to $250, extra for photos, on acceptance. Query.

MIKE SHAYNE MYSTERY MAGAZINE—P.O. Box 178, Reseda, CA 91335. Charles E. Fritch, Ed. Detective, mystery, and suspense stories, 100 to 5,000 words. Pays 1½¢ a word, after publication.

OFFICIAL DETECTIVE STORIES—460 W. 34th St., New York, NY 10001. Art Crocket, Ed. True detective stories, 5,000 to 6,000 words, on current investigations, strictly from the investigator's point of view. No fiction. Photos. Pays $250, extra for photos, on acceptance. Query.

STARTLING DETECTIVE—See *Detective Dragnet.*

TRUE DETECTIVE—460 W. 34th St., New York, NY 10001. Art Crockett, Ed. Articles, from 5,000 words, with photos, on current police cases, emphasizing detective work and human motivation. No fiction. Pays $250, extra for photos, on acceptance. Query.

TRUE POLICE CASES—See *Detective Dragnet.*

WESTERN MAGAZINES

AMERICAN WEST—3033 N. Campbell Ave., Tucson, AZ 85719. Mae Reid-Bills, Man. Ed. Well-researched, illustrated articles, 1,000 to 3,000 words, on western America, past and present, in a lively style appealing to the intelligent general reader. Query required. Pays from $200, on acceptance.

PERSIMMON HILL—1700 N.E. 63rd St., Oklahoma City, OK 73111. Sara Dobberteen, Sr. Ed. Articles, 2,000 to 3,000 words, on Western history and art, rodeo, cowboys, ranching, and nature. Profiles, biographies. Pays from $150, on publication.

REAL WEST—Charlton Publications, Inc., Division St., Derby, CT 06418. Ed Doherty, Ed. True stories of the Old West, 1,000 to 4,000 words. Photos. Pays from 3¢ a word, on acceptance.

TRUE WEST—700 E. State St., Iola, WI 54990. Jim Dullenty, Ed. True stories, 500 to 3,000 words, with photos, about the Old West (1830–1910). Source list required. Pays 5¢ to 10¢ a word, extra for B/W photos, on acceptance. Query. Same address and requirements for *Old West.*

SCIENCE FICTION AND FANTASY MAGAZINES

AMAZING SCIENCE FICTION STORIES—Box 110, Lake Geneva, WI 53147. George Scithers, Ed. Science fiction and fantasy, to 15,000 words. Also general-interest science articles; query first on nonfiction. Pays 4¢ to 6¢ a word, on acceptance.

ANALOG SCIENCE FICTION/SCIENCE FACT—380 Lexington Ave., New York, NY 10017. Stanley Schmidt, Ed. Science fiction, with strong characters in believable future or alien setting: short stories, 2,000 to 7,500 words; novelettes, 10,000 to 20,000 words; serials, to 80,000 words. Also uses future-related articles. Pays to 7¢ a word, on acceptance. Query on serials and articles.

ANTITHESIS—See *Bifrost.*

BEYOND—1680 N. Vine St., Suite 900, Hollywood, CA 90028. Judith Sims, Ed. Science fiction, 2,000 to 3,000 words. Pays 12¢ a word, on publication. Query preferred for non-fiction.

BIFROST (formerly *Antithesis*)—687 E. Market St., Marietta, PA 17457. Ms. P. M. Spath, Exec. Ed. Fiction: science fiction, fantasy, horror. Interviews with behind-the-scenes persons in publishing, movies and theatre. Poetry. Humor; jokes. Pays in copies. Query preferred.

DIFFERENT WORLDS—P.O. Box 6302, Albany, CA 94706. Tadashi Ehara, Ed. Articles, to 5,000 words, on role-playing games: reviews, variants, source materials, etc. Pays 1¢ a word, on publication. Query preferred.

DRAGON MAGAZINE—P.O. Box 110, Lake Geneva, WI 53147. Kim Mohan, Editor-in-Chief. Articles, 1,500 to 10,000 words, on fantasy and SF role-playing games. Fiction, 1,500 to 10,000 words. Pays 4¢ a word for fiction, slightly lower for articles, on publication. Query.

EMPIRE FOR THE SF WRITER—1025 55th St., Oakland, CA 94608. Millea Kenin, Ed. Articles, 2,000 words preferred, on the craft of writing science fiction and fantasy. Cartoons, illustrations. Pays negotiable rates, on publication. Query.

FANTASY REVIEW—College of Humanities, Florida Atlantic University, Boca Raton, FL 33431. Robert A. Collins, Ed. Articles and interviews, to 5,000 words. Fantasy and science fiction, poetry. Cartoons, photos, artwork. Pays varying rates. Query preferred.

GRIMOIRE—c/o Thomas Wiloch, 8181 Wayne Rd., Apt. H2084, Westland, MI 48185. Thomas Wiloch, Ed. Fiction and poetry, to 3,000 words, on the surreal, macabre and fantastic. Collages, black and white. Query on nonfiction. Pays in copies; SASE.

THE HORROR SHOW—Phantasm Press, Star Route 1, Box 151-T, Oak Run, CA 96069. David B. Silva, Ed. Contemporary horror fiction, to 3,500 words, "with a style that keeps the reader's hand trembling as he turns the pages." Pays ¼¢ a word, on acceptance. Send SASE for guidelines.

ISAAC ASIMOV'S SCIENCE FICTION MAGAZINE—380 Lexington Ave., New York, NY 10017. Shawna McCarthy, Ed. Short, character-oriented science fiction and fantasy, to 15,000 words. Pays 5¢ to 7¢ a word, on acceptance. Send SASE for requirements.

THE MAGAZINE OF FANTASY AND SCIENCE FICTION—Box 56, Cornwall, CT 06753. Edward Ferman, Ed. Fantasy and science fiction stories, to 10,000 words. Pays 3¢ to 5¢ a word, on acceptance.

MAGICAL BLEND—Box 11303, San Francisco, CA 94101. Mary Webster, Nonfiction Ed., Lisa Shulman, Fiction Ed. Positive, uplifting pieces on spiritual exploration, lifestyles, occult, white magic and fantasy. Fiction and features to 5,000 words, poetry, 4 to 40 lines. Query preferred. Pays in copies.

OMNI—1965 Broadway, New York, NY 10023-5965. Ellen Datlow, Ed. Strong, realistic science fiction, 2,000 to 9,000 words, with real people as characters. Some fantasy. No horror, ghost or sword and sorcery tales. Pays to $2,000, on acceptance.

ORACLE—21111 Maple Ridge, Southfield, MI 48075. Dave Lillard, Ed. Action/adventure science fiction and fantasy, any length. No pornography, heavy violence, horror stories, poems or reviews. Pays 1¢ to 3¢ a word, on acceptance and after publication. Query to learn if overstocked.

OWLFLIGHT—1025 55th St., Oakland, CA 94608. Millea Kenin, Ed. Articles, to 5,000 words, on speculative science and related topics. Science fiction and fantasy, to 10,000 words. Science fiction/fantasy poetry, to 100 lines. Photographs, illustrations. Pays 1¢ a word, extra for illustrations, on publication. Query to learn if temporarily overstocked.

PANDORA—P.O. Box 625, Murray, KY 42071. Lois Wickstrom, Ed. Science fiction and speculative fantasy stories, to 5,000 words. Pays 1¢ a word, on acceptance.

ROD SERLING'S TWILIGHT ZONE MAGAZINE—800 Second Ave., New York, NY 10017. T. E. D. Klein, Ed. Fiction, to 5,000 words: human-centered fantasies of horror, suspense and the supernatural involving "ordinary people in extraordinary events." Pays about 5¢ a word, half on acceptance, half on publication.

THE SPACE GAMER—Box 18957, Austin, TX 78760. Christopher Frink, Ed. Science fiction and fantasy, to 4,000 words, with conflict theme. Articles, to 4,000 words, on science fiction and fantasy games. Illustrations. Pays to 3¢ a word for fiction, 1¢ a word for articles, extra for illustrations, on publication.

STAR* LINE—P.O. Box 491, Nantucket, MA 02554. Bob Frazier, Ed. Newsletter. Articles, short interviews, on speculative poetry, 500 to 2,500 words. Short reviews of science fiction/fantasy poetry. Poetry. Prose poems, 50 to 100 words. Short news items on the world of speculative poetry. Pays $1 to $5 for articles, $1 to $2 for reviews, $1 for ten lines of poetry (5¢ a line thereafter).

THRUST: SCIENCE FICTION IN REVIEW—8217 Langport Terrace, Gaithersburg, MD 20877. D. Douglas Fratz, Ed. Articles, interviews, 2,000 to 6,000 words, for readers familiar with SF and related literary and scientific topics. Book reviews, 100 to 800 words. Pays ½¢ to 2¢ a word, on publication. Query preferred.

THE TWILIGHT ZONE—See *Rod Serling's Twilight Zone Magazine.*

WEIRDBOOK—Box 149, Amherst Branch, Buffalo, NY 14226. W. Paul Ganley, Ed. Horror and fantasy adventure fiction, to 20,000 words. Poetry, to 15 lines. No straight science fiction. Pays from $4 per printed page, on publication. Send SASE for guidelines.

CONFESSION AND ROMANCE MAGAZINES

BRONZE THRILLS—355 Lexington Ave., New York, NY 10017. Teadra Allen, Ed. Romances, 3,000 words, written from the woman's perspective, for women age 18 to 45. Must have interesting plot and contain at least two descriptive love scenes. Pays $45 to $75, after acceptance. *Jive:* geared toward the younger woman, out on her own for the first time in her life, seeking new adventures and romance.

JIVE—See *Bronze Thrills.*

MODERN ROMANCES—215 Lexington Ave., New York, NY 10016. Jean Sharbel, Ed. Confession stories with reader-identification and strong emotional tone, 1,500 to 7,500 words. Articles for blue-collar, family-oriented women, 300 to 1,000 words. Light, romantic poetry, to 24 lines. Pays 5¢ a word, after publication. Buys all rights.

SECRETS—215 Lexington Ave., New York, NY 10016. Jean Press Silberg, Ed. Realistic, emotional confession stories, 1,500 to 10,000 words, emphasizing family, home, and love relationships. Articles on subjects of interest to blue-collar, family-oriented women. Pays 3¢ a word, on publication. Buys all rights.

TORCH ROMANCES—P.O. Box 3307, McLean, VA 22103. Address Fiction Ed. Romantic suspense short stories, 12,000 words, with sensual love scenes; avoid plots that contain murder, drugs, and excess violence. Pays flat rate or royalty. Tip sheet.

TRUE CONFESSIONS—215 Lexington Ave., New York, NY 10016. Barbara J. Brett, Ed. Timely, emotional, first-person stories, 2,000 to 10,000 words, on romance, family life, and problems of today's young blue-collar women. Love interest and love problems should be stressed. Articles, 300 to 700 words, for young wives and mothers. Pays 5¢ a word, after publication.

TRUE EXPERIENCE—215 Lexington Ave., New York, NY 10016. Helene Eccleston, Ed. Realistic first-person stories, 4,000 to 8,000 words (short shorts, to 2,000 words), on family life, love, courtship, health, religion, etc. Pays 3¢ a word, a month after publication.

TRUE LOVE—215 Lexington Ave., New York, NY 10016. Marta Mestrovic, Ed. Fresh, true first-person stories, on young love, marital problems, and topics of current interest. Pays 3¢ a word, a month after publication.

TRUE ROMANCE—215 Lexington Ave., New York, NY 10016. Susan Weiner, Ed. Timely, emotional, first-person stories, 2,000 to 7,500 words, on romance, love and problems of today's young women. Articles, 300 to 700 words, for young wives and singles. Pays 3¢ a word, a month after publication.

TRUE STORY—215 Lexington Ave., New York, NY 10016. Helen Vincent, Ed. First-person true stories, 3,000 to 12,000 words. Pays 5¢ a word, on publication.

FICTION MARKETS

GENERAL-INTEREST MAGAZINES

This list gives the fiction requirements of the general-interest magazines. See *The Popular Market* for lists of magazines using male-oriented and "adult" fiction, confession and romance stories, science fiction, and mysteries. Juvenile fiction markets are listed under *Juvenile, Teen-Age and Young Adult Magazines.* Publishers of book-length adult and juvenile manuscripts are listed under *Book Publishers.*

ALFRED HITCHCOCK'S MYSTERY MAGAZINE—380 Lexington Ave., New York, NY 10017. Cathleen Jordan, Ed. Well-plotted, plausible mystery, suspense, detection and crime stories, 1,000 to 14,000 words. Pays 3¢ to 8¢ a word, on acceptance.

ALOHA, THE MAGAZINE OF HAWAII—828 Fort Street Mall, Honolulu, HI 96813. Rita Gormley, Ed. Fiction to 4,000 words, on Hawaii and its ethnic groups. Pays 10¢ a word on publication. Query.

AMAZING SCIENCE FICTION STORIES—Box 110, Lake Geneva, WI 53147. George Scithers, Ed. Science fiction and fantasy, to 15,000 words. Pays 4¢ to 6¢ a word, on acceptance.

ANALOG: SCIENCE FICTION/SCIENCE FACT—380 Lexington Ave., New York, NY 10017. Stanley Schmidt, Ed. Science fiction, with strong characters in believable future or alien setting: short stories, 2,000 to 7,500 words; novelettes, 10,000 to 20,000 words, serials, to 70,000 words. Pays 3.5¢ to 7¢ a word, on acceptance. Query on novels.

THE ATLANTIC—8 Arlington St., Boston, MA 02116. William Whitworth, Ed. Short stories, 2,000 to 6,000 (occasionally, to 14,000) words, of highest literary quality. Pays on acceptance.

THE ATLANTIC ADVOCATE—P.O. Box 3370, Fredericton, N.B., Canada E3B 5A2. H. P. Wood, Ed. Fiction, 1,000 to 1,500 words, with regional angle. Pays 5¢ to 8¢ a word, on publication.

AUGUSTA SPECTATOR—P.O. Box 3168, Augusta, GA 30904. Fiction to 2,000 words, with Georgia or South Carolina tie-in. Pays $25, plus two copies, on publication.

BITTERSWEET—Box 266, Cornish, ME 04020. Address Ed. People-oriented fiction situated in the rural Northeast of today or yesterday, 800 to 2,000 words. Pays 2¢ a word, on publication.

BLUE & GRAY—5212 W. Broad St., Columbus, OH 43228. David E. Roth, Ed. Fiction, 1,500 to 4,000 words, relating to the Civil War period. Pays $25 to $200, on acceptance.

BOYS' LIFE—1325 Walnut Hill La., Irving, TX 75062. Robert E. Hood, Ed. Publication of Boy Scouts of America. Fiction, 1,000 to 3,200 words, for 8- to 18-year-old boys. Two-part serials, to 6,000 words. Pays from $350, on acceptance.

CALIFORNIA HORSE REVIEW—Box 646, N. Highlands, CA 95660. Kathleen Riordan, Ed. Fiction, 1,500 to 2,500 words, on horses. Pays $50 to $125, on publication. Query preferred.

CAMPUS LIFE—465 Gundersen Dr., Carol Stream, IL 60188. Gregg Lewis, Ed. General fiction and humor, reflecting Christian values and worldview (no overtly religious material), for high school and college students. Pays from $150, on acceptance. Limited free-lance market.

CAT FANCY—P.O. Box 6050, Mission Viejo, CA 92690. Linda W. Lewis, Ed. Fiction, to 3,000 words, about cats. Pays 3¢ a word, on publication.

CAVALIER—2355 Salzedo St., Coral Gables, FL 33134. Maurice DeWalt, Fiction Ed. Sexually-oriented fiction, to 3,000 words, for sophisticated young men. Pays to $300, on publication.

CHATELAINE—Maclean Hunter Bldg., 777 Bay St., Toronto, Ont., Canada M5W 1A7. Barbara West, Fiction Ed. Fiction, 3,000 to 4,500 words, on issues in contemporary women's lives: relationships, adventure, romance, humor. Canadian setting preferred. Pays from $1,500, on acceptance. Most fiction by Canadian writers.

CHESAPEAKE BAY MAGAZINE—1819 Bay Ridge Ave., Annapolis, MD 21403. Betty Rigoli, Ed. Short stories, to 12 pages; must be related to Chesapeake Bay area. Pays $75 to $85, on publication.

CHICAGO—303 E. Wacker Dr., Chicago, IL 60601. Christine Newman, Fiction Ed. Fiction, 1,000 to 5,000 words. Pays varying rates, on acceptance.

COASTAL JOURNAL—Box 84, Lanesville Sta., Gloucester, MA 01930. Randy Greenfield, Ed. Fiction, 2,500 words, relating to the New England Coast—past, present or future—or nautical history. Pays $100 to $150, on publication.

COBBLESTONE—20 Grove St., Peterborough, NH 03458. Carolyn P. Yoder, Ed. Fiction, 500 to 1,200 words, for children aged 8 to 14 years. Pays 10¢ to 15¢ a word, on publication. Send SASE for editorial guidelines with monthly themes.

COLORADO MONTHLY MAGAZINE—P.O. Box 22542, Denver, CO 80222. Peter and Eileen Wigginton, Eds. Fiction (900 to 2,000 words): reflective essays, travel and historical topics. Pays 5¢ to 10¢ a word, on publication.

COMMENTARY—165 E. 56th St., New York, NY 10022. Norman Podhoretz, Ed. Fiction, of high literary quality, on social or Jewish issues. Pays on publication.

THE COMPASS—Mobil Sales and Supply Corp., 150 E. 42nd St., New York, NY 10017. R. G. MacKenzie, Ed. Short stories, to 3,500 words, on the sea and sea trades. Pays to $250, on acceptance. Query.

651

CORVETTE FEVER—Box 55532, Ft. Washington, MD 20744. Pat Stivers, Ed. Corvette-related fiction, about 300 lines. Pays 10¢ a word, on publication.

COSMOPOLITAN—224 W. 57th St., New York, NY 10019. Betty Kelly, Fiction Ed. Fiction, on male-female relationships: shorts, 1,500 to 3,000 words; short stories, 3,000 to 4,000 words; published novels condensed to 24,000 words. Pays on acceptance.

CRICKET—Box 100, La Salle, IL 61301. Marianne Carus, Ed.-in-Chief. Fiction, 200 to 1,500 words, for 6- to 12-year-olds. Pays to 25¢ a word, on publication.

DELTA SCENE—P.O. Box B-3, Delta State Univ., Cleveland, MI 38733. Fiction, with Mississippi Delta slant, 1,500 to 2,000 words. Pays $15 to $20, after publication.

DIVER MAGAZINE—#210-1807 Maritime Mews, Granville Island, Vancouver, B.C., Canada V6H 3W7. Neil McDaniel, Ed. Fiction, related to diving/diving experiences. Humor. Pays $2.50 per column inch, on publication. Query.

DOG FANCY—P.O. Box 6050, Mission Viejo, CA 92690. Linda W. Lewis, Ed. Fiction, to 3,000 words, about dogs. Pays 3¢ a word, on publication.

DRESSAGE & CT—P.O. Box 12460, Cleveland OH 44112. Ivan Bezugloff, Jr., Ed. Humorous fiction about dressage or eventing, 1,000 to 1,500 words. Pays varying rates.

EBONY JR.!—820 S. Michigan Ave., Chicago, IL 60605. Marcia V. Roebuck-Hoard, Ed. Wholesome humor, mystery, science fiction and fantasy, 400 to 1,500 words. Pays $75 to $200, on acceptance. Buys all rights or reprints.

ELLERY QUEEN'S MYSTERY MAGAZINE—380 Lexington Ave., New York, NY 10017. Eleanor Sullivan, Ed. High-quality detective, crime, and mystery stories, 4,000 to 6,000 words. "First Stories" by unpublished writers. Pays 3¢ to 8¢ a word, on acceptance.

ESQUIRE—2 Park Ave., New York, NY 10016. Rust Hills, Fiction Ed. Tom Jenks, Assoc. Fiction Ed. Literary short stories, 1,000 to 7,000 words, for intelligent adult audience. Pays $1,000 to $1,500, on acceptance.

ESSENCE—1500 Broadway, New York, NY 10036. Susan L. Taylor, Ed.-in-Chief. Fiction, 1,500 to 3,000 words, for largely black, female readership. Pays varying rates, on acceptance.

FAMILY CIRCLE—488 Madison Ave., New York, NY 10022. Jamie Raab, Fiction Editor. "We are actively pursuing contemporary short stories by both novice and established writers. Stories that deal with relationships and family-oriented issues seem to be most popular with our readers, though we certainly will give serious consideration to well-written stories about women outside the home. Stories must have strong plots and characters with whom our readers can identify—so many of the stories submitted to us are really only character sketches or vignettes, lacking a clear point and a conclusion. Though many of these demonstrate great talent and skill, what interests us is storytelling rather than evocation of mood. We're particularly interested in short, short stories of 2,500 words or less. We pay top rates, on acceptance."

FAMILY MAGAZINE—P.O. Box 4993, Walnut Creek, CA 94596. Address Editors. Short stories, to 3,000 words, of interest to high school-educated women between 20 and 35. Pays from $100 to $300, on publication.

FARM WOMAN NEWS—P.O. Box 643, Milwaukee, WI 53201. Ruth C. Benedict, Man. Ed. Fiction, to 1,000 words, of interest to farm and ranch women. Pays $30 to $250, on publication.

FLORIDA KEYS MAGAZINE—Box 818, 6161 O/S Highway, Marathon, FL 33050. David Ethridge, Ed. Fiction, to 4,000 words. Pays varying rates. Query preferred.

GALLERY—800 Second Ave., New York, NY 10017. John Bensink, Ed.-in-Chief. Fiction, to 4,000 words, for sophisticated men. Pays varying rates, half on acceptance, half on publication. Query.

GENESIS MAGAZINE—770 Lexington Ave., New York, NY 10021. Sexually explicit fiction, 3,000 words, with well-developed plots. Pays 30 days after acceptance. Query.

GENTLEMEN'S QUARTERLY—350 Madison Ave., New York, NY 10017. Adam Gopnik, Staff Ed. Fiction, to 2,500 words. Query required.

GOLF DIGEST—495 Westport Ave., Norwalk, CT 06856. Jack McDermott, Ed. Unusual or humorous stories, to 2,000 words, about golf; golf "fables," to 1,000 words. Pays 20¢ a word, on acceptance.

GOOD HOUSEKEEPING—959 Eighth Ave., New York, NY 10019. Naome Lewis, Fiction Ed. Short stories, 2,000 to 5,000 words, with strong identification figures for women, by published writers and "beginners with demonstrable talent." Novel condensations or excerpts. Pays top rates, on acceptance.

GUN DOG—P.O. Box 68, Adel, IA 50003. Douglas M. Lidster, Man. Ed. Occasional fiction, humor, related to gun dogs and bird hunting. Pays $100 to $300, on acceptance.

HANG GLIDING—U.S. Hang Gliding Assn., P.O. Box 66306, Los Angeles, CA 90066. Gilbert Dodgen, Ed. Fiction, 2 to 3 pages, related to hang gliding. Pays to $50. Query preferred.

HICALL—1445 Boonville Ave., Springfield, MO 65802. William P. Campbell, Ed. Fiction, to 1,800 words, for 12- to 19-year-olds with strong evangelical emphasis: believable characters working out their problems according to biblical principles. Don't be preachy. Pats 3¢ a word for first rights, on acceptance.

HIGHLIGHTS FOR CHILDREN—803 Church St., Honesdale, PA 18431. Kent L. Brown, Jr., Ed. Sports, humor, adventure, and mystery stories, 900 words, for 9- to 12-year-olds. Easy rebus form, 200 to 250 words, and easy-to-read stories, to 600 words, for beginning readers. Pays from 6¢ a word, on acceptance.

INSIDE RUNNING—9514 Bristlebrook Dr., Houston, TX 77083. Joanne Schmidt, Ed. Fiction related to running. Pays $35 to $100, on acceptance.

ISAAC ASIMOV'S SCIENCE FICTION MAGAZINE—380 Lexington Ave., New York, NY 10017. Shawna McCarthy, Ed. Short science fiction and fantasies, to 15,000 words. Pays 5¢ to 7¢ a word, on acceptance. Send SASE for requirements.

JACK AND JILL—Box 567, Indianapolis, IN 46206. Christine French Clark, Ed. Fiction, to 1,200 words, for 6-to 8-year-olds. Pays about 6¢ a word, on publication.

LADIES' HOME JOURNAL—3 Park Ave., New York, NY 10016. Fiction

653

with strong identification for women. Short stories and full-length manuscripts accepted *through agents only.*

LADYCOM—1732 Wisconsin Ave., NW, Washington, DC 20007. Sheila Gibbons, Ed. Fiction, to 2,000 words, for military wives in the U.S. and overseas. Pays $75 to $250, after acceptance.

LADY'S CIRCLE—23 W. 26th St., New York, NY 10010. Rose Marshall, Ed. Emotional fiction, to 2,000 words, for homemakers. No stories about divorce or separation; light romance. Pays to $125, on publication.

LIVE—1445 Boonville Ave., Springfield, MO 65802. Kenneth D. Barney, Adult Ed. Fiction, 1,500 to 2,000 words, on applying Bible principles to everyday living. Send SASE for writers' guidelines. Pays 2¢ to 3¢ a word, on acceptance.

LOLLIPOPS, LADYBUGS, AND LUCKY STARS—Good Apple Inc., P.O. Box 299, Carthage, IL 62321-0299. Short stories, 500 to 1,200 words, preferably with moral, for children preschool to 7. Rates vary.

LUTHERAN WOMEN—2900 Queen Lane, Philadelphia, PA 19129. Terry Schutz, Ed. Fiction, 1,000 to 2,000 words, demonstrating character growth and change. Pays $35 to $50, on publication.

MCCALL'S—230 Park Ave., New York, NY 10169. Helen DelMonte, Fiction Ed. Short stories, to 3,000 words. Short-shorts, 2,000 words: Contemporary themes with strong identification for intelligent women. Family stories, love stories, humor. Pays from $2,000 for stories, $1,500 for short-shorts, on acceptance.

MADEMOISELLE—350 Madison Ave., New York, NY 10017. Eileen Schnurr, Fiction Ed. Short stories, 2,500 to 4,500 words, of high literary quality. Pays from $1,000, on acceptance.

THE MAGAZINE OF FANTASY AND SCIENCE FICTION—Box 56, Cornwall, CT 06753. Edward Ferman, Ed. Fantasy and science fiction stories, to 10,000 words. Pays 3¢ to 5¢ a word, on acceptance.

MATURE LIVING—127 Ninth Ave. N., Nashville, TN 37234. Jack Gulledge, Ed. Zada Malugen, Ass't Ed. Fiction, 925 to 1,550 words, for senior adults. Southern Baptist orientation. Pays 4¢ a word, on acceptance.

MICHIGAN, THE MAGAZINE OF THE DETROIT NEWS—615 W. Lafayette Blvd., Detroit, MI 48231. Susan Slobojan, Ed. Fiction, with Michigan slant, to 3,000 words. Pays $75 to $400, on publication. Query.

MIDSTREAM—515 Park Ave., New York, NY 10022. Joel Carmichael, Ed. Fiction on Jewish social or political issues. Pays 5¢ a word, on publication.

MIKE SHAYNE MYSTERY MAGAZINE—P.O. Box 178, Reseda, CA 91335. Charles E. Fritch, Ed. Mystery and suspense fiction, to 5,000 words. Presently overstocked. Pays 1½¢ a word, after publication.

MISSISSIPPI ARTS AND LETTERS—Box 3510, Persons Publishing, Hattiesburg, MI 39403-3510. Contemporary adult, humor, some science fiction, 2,000 to 3,000 words; Southern authors only. Pays $5 to $50, on acceptance.

MOMENT—462 Boylston St., Boston, MA 02116. Leonard Fein, Ed. Short stories, 2,000 to 4,000 words, on Jewish themes. Pays $150 to $250, on publication.

MS.—119 W. 40th St., New York, NY 10018. Address Ed. Dept., Fiction.

Short stories on women's changing self-image and status. Pays varying rates, on acceptance.

THE NATIONAL CENTURION—3180 University Ave., Suite 230, San Diego, CA 92104. Denny Fallon, Man. Ed. Humorous fiction, 2,000 to 4,000 words, with law enforcement theme. Pays $300 to $400, on publication.

NATIONAL DOLL WORLD—P.O. Box 1952, Brooksville, FL 33512. Address Karen P. Sherrer. Doll-related fiction, to 1,000 words. Pays to 5¢ a word, on publication.

NATIONAL RACQUETBALL—4350 DiPaolo Center, Dearlove Rd., Glenview, IL 60025. Chuck Leve, Ed. Fiction, related to racquetball. Pays $25 to $150, on publication.

NATIONAL SUPERMARKET SHOPPER—P.O. Box 500, Franklin Sq., NY 11010. Lee Shore, Man. Ed. Fiction to 2,500 words, supermarket-, refund-, coupon-oriented. Pays 5¢ a word, on publication.

NEW BEDFORD MAGAZINE—5 South Sixth St., New Bedford, MA 02740. Fiction, to 3,000 words, related to southeastern Massachusetts. Short humor. Pays varying rates, on publication.

THE NEW YORKER—25 W. 43rd St., New York, NY 10036. Short stories, humor and satire. Pays varying rates, on acceptance.

NORTHEAST MAGAZINE—*The Hartford Courant,* 179 Allyn St., Hartford, CT 06103. Larry Bloom, Ed. Short stories, to 5,000 words; must have Connecticut tie-in, or be universal in theme and have non-specific setting. Pays $300 to $1,000, on acceptance.

OMNI—1965 Broadway, New York, NY 10023-5965. Ellen Datlow, Fiction Ed. Strong, realistic science fiction, with real people as characters, to 9,000 words. Some contemporary hard-edged fantasy. Pays to $2,000, on acceptance.

OUI—300 W. 43rd St., New York, NY 10036. Modern, upbeat stories with unusual settings: humorous, science fiction, mystery, etc. Sexual situations or overtones helpful, but not required. Audience: 18–35, mostly but not all male. Length: 1,200 to 2,500 words. Payment varies.

OUR FAMILY—Box 249, Battleford, Sask., Canada S0M 0E0. A. Lalonde, O.M.I. Ed. Fiction, 1,000 to 3,000 words, on the struggle to live the Christian life in the face of modern-day problems. Pays 7¢ to 10¢ a word, on acceptance. Write for guidelines. Enclose *international postal reply coupons* with SASE.

PENNSYLVANIA SPORTSMAN—Box 5196, Harrisburg, PA 17110. Lou Hoffman, Ed. Fiction, 1,200 to 1,500 words, for field sports enthusiasts. Pays varying rates, on publication.

PENTHOUSE—1965 Broadway, New York, NY 10023-5965. Address Fiction Department. Quality fiction, 4,000 to 6,000 words, on contemporary themes. Pays on acceptance.

PILLOW TALK—215 Lexington Ave., New York, NY 10016. I. Catherine Duff, Ed. Short erotic fiction, to 2,000 words, for "Fantasy Forum." Pays from $150, on publication. Query.

PLAYBOY—919 N. Michigan Ave., Chicago, IL 60611. Alice K. Turner, Fiction Ed. Quality fiction, 1,000 to 10,000 words (average 6,000): suspense, adventure and sports short stories; science fiction. Active plots and strong characterization. Pays from $1,000 to $3,000, on acceptance.

PLAYERS—8060 Melrose Ave., Los Angeles, CA 90046. Joe Hazel, Fiction Ed. Offbeat fiction of high literary quality, 1,000 to 5,000 words, for black men. No adventure stories. Pays 10¢ a word for the first 500 words, 2¢ to 8¢ a word thereafter, on publication.

PLAYGIRL—3420 Ocean Park Blvd., Suite 3000, Santa Monica, CA 90405. Mary Ellen Strote, Fiction Ed. Contemporary, romantic fiction, 1,000 to 3,000 words. Pays from $500, after acceptance.

PRIME TIMES—Suite 120, 2802 International Ln., Madison, WI 53704. Journal for the National Assn. for Retired Credit Union People. Ana Maria M. Guzman, Assoc. Ed. Fiction, 2,500 to 4,000 words. Pays varying rates, on publication. Query.

RANGER RICK MAGAZINE—1412 16th St., N.W., Washington, DC 20036. Trudy Farrand, Ed. Nature-and conservation-related fiction, for 6- to 12-year-olds. Maximum: 900 words. Pays to $350, on acceptance. Buys all rights.

REDBOOK—224 W. 57th St., New York, NY 10019. Kathy Sagan, Fiction Ed. Fresh, distinctive short stories, of interest to young women, about love and love relationships, being a parent or dealing with one, friendship, careers, or confronting basic problems of contemporary life and women's issues. Pays $850 for short stories (about 9 manuscript pages), from $1,000 for short stories (10 pages, or longer). Allow 6 to 8 weeks for reply. Manuscripts without SASEs will not be returned. No unsolicited novellas or novels accepted.

ROAD KING—P.O. Box 250, Park Forest, IL 60466. George Friend, Ed. Short stories, 1,200 to 1,500 words, for and/or about truck drivers. Pays to $400, on acceptance.

ROD SERLING'S THE TWILIGHT ZONE MAGAZINE—800 Second Ave., New York, NY 10017. T.E.D. Klein, Ed. Fiction, to 5,000 words: human-centered fantasies of horror, suspense and the supernatural involving "ordinary people in extraordinary events." Pays about 5¢ a word, half on acceptance, half on publication.

ST. ANTHONY MESSENGER—1615 Republic St., Cincinnati, OH 45210. Norman Perry, Ed. Fiction that makes readers think about issues, lifestyles and values. Pays 12¢ a word, on acceptance. Query.

THE SATURDAY EVENING POST—1100 Waterway Blvd., Indianapolis, IN 46202. Jack Gramling, Fiction Ed. Upbeat short stories, 500 to 4,000 words, that lend themselves to illustration. Pays varying rates, on publication.

SCHOLASTIC SCOPE—Scholastic, Inc., 730 Broadway, New York, NY 10003. Katherine Robinson, Ed. Fiction for 15- to 18-year olds, with 4th to 6th grade reading ability. Short stories, 500 to 1,000 words, on teen-age interests and relationships; family, job and school situations. Pays good rates, on acceptance.

SEVENTEEN—850 Third Ave., New York, NY 10022. Bonni Price, Fiction Ed. High-quality fiction for young adults. Pays on acceptance.

SPORTS AFIELD—250 W. 55th St., New York, NY 10019. Tom Paugh, Ed. Fiction, on hunting, fishing, and related topics. Outdoor adventure stories. Humor. Pays top rates, on acceptance.

SPORTSCAPE—1318 Beacon St., Brookline, MA 02146. Marc Onigman, Man. Ed. Participant-sport-related fiction, with New England setting/angle, 2,000 to 3,000 words. Pays $200 to $250, on acceptance. Send complete manuscript.

STRAIGHT—8121 Hamilton Ave., Cincinnati, OH 45231. Dawn Brettschneider, Ed. Well-constructed fiction, 1,000 to 1,500 words, showing Christian teens using Bible principles in everyday life. Contemporary, realistic teen characters a must. Most interested in school, church, dating, and family life stories. Pays about 2¢ a word, on acceptance.

THE SUNDAY CAMERA MAGAZINE—Box 591, Boulder, CO 80306. Victoria Groniger, Ed. Fiction, 2,000 to 4,000 words. Pays $125 to $250, on publication.

SUNSHINE MAGAZINE—Litchfield, IL 62056. Wholesome fiction, 900 to 1,200 words; short stories for youths, 400 to 700 words. Pays to $100, on acceptance.

SWANK—888 Seventh Ave., New York, NY 10106. Dave Trilby, Fiction Ed. Graphic erotic short stories, to 2,500 words. Pays on publication.

'TEEN—8490 Sunset Blvd., Los Angeles, CA 90069. Address Fiction Dept. Short stories, 2,000 to 4,000 words: mystery, travel, adventure, romance, humor for teens. Pays from $100, on acceptance.

TODAY'S OR NURSE—6900 Grove Rd., Thorofare, NJ 08086. Humorous fiction, 300 to 500 words, about the operating room or the medical field. Pays 10¢ a word, on publication.

TORCH ROMANCES—P.O. Box 3307, McLean, VA 22103. Address Fiction Ed. Romantic suspense short stories, 12,000 words, with sensual love scenes; avoid plots that contain murder, drugs, and excess violence. Pays flat rate or royalty. Tip sheet.

VOGUE—350 Madison Ave., New York, NY 10017. Amy Gross, Features Ed. Fiction, 500 to 4,000 words. Pays on acceptance.

THE WAR CRY—799 Bloomfield Ave., Verona, NJ 07044. Fiction, 800 to 1,500 words, with strong evangelical Christian emphasis. Pays 4¢ a word, on acceptance.

WESTERN MASSACHUSETTS MAGAZINE—The Benjamin Co., P.O. Box 76, Northampton, MA 01061-0076. Michael R. Evans, Man. Ed. Fiction, 500 to 3,500 words. Pays $50 to $250, on acceptance.

WESTERN PEOPLE—Box 2500, Saskatoon, Sask., Canada S7K 2C4. Short stories, 1,000 to 2,500 words, on subjects or themes of interest to rural readers in Western Canada. Pays $40 to $150, on acceptance. *Enclose international postal reply coupons.*

WOMAN'S DAY—1515 Broadway, New York, NY 10036. Eileen Herbert Jordan, Fiction Ed. Short fiction, humorous or serious. Pays top rates, on acceptance.

WOMAN'S WORLD—P.O. Box 6700, Englewood, NJ 07631. Elinor Nauen, Fiction Ed. Fast-moving short stories, about 4,500 to 5,000 words, with light romantic theme. Mini-mysteries, 1,500 to 1,700 words, with "whodunit" or "howdunit" theme. No science fiction, fantasy or historical romance. Pays $1,000 for short stories, $500 for mini-mysteries on acceptance.

WOODMEN OF THE WORLD MAGAZINE—1700 Farnam St., Omaha, NE 68102. Leland A. Larson, Ed. Family-oriented fiction. Pays 5¢ a word, on acceptance.

YANKEE—Dublin, NH 03444. Judson Hale, Ed. Realistic short stories, to 4,000 words, with setting in or compatible with New England. Pays on acceptance.

YOUNG AMBASSADOR—Box 82808, Lincoln, NE 68501. David Lambert, Man. Ed. Fiction, to 2,000 words, for Christian teens. Pays 4¢ to 10¢ a word, on acceptance.

YOUNG MISS—685 Third Ave., New York, NY 10017. Deborah Purcell, Features/Fiction Ed. Fiction, 1,500 to 3,000 words, on topics of interest to 17-year-old girls. Pays to $700, on acceptance.

POETRY MARKETS

Markets for both serious and light verse are included in the following lists of general-interest magazines and greeting card markets. Also given is information on university presses that publish book-length collections of poetry.

Although major magazines pay good rates for poetry, the competition to break into print is very stiff, since editors use only a limited number of poems in each issue. On the other hand, college and literary magazines use a great deal of poetry, and though payment is usually modest, or in contributors' copies only, publication in these journals can establish a beginning poet's reputation, and lead to publication in the major magazines. (The listing of college, literary, and "little" magazines, which begins on page 694, includes requirements for poetry, fiction, and essays.) Poets will find a number of competitions offering cash awards for unpublished poetry in the *Literary Prize Offers* list, beginning on page 752.

Poets should also consider local newspapers as possible verse markets. Although they may not specifically seek poetry from free lancers, newspaper editors often print verse submitted to them, especially on holidays and for special occasions.

GENERAL-INTEREST MAGAZINES

ALCOHOLISM/THE NATIONAL MAGAZINE—1004 N. 105th St., Seattle, WA 98133. Anthony Whyte, Ed. Poetry, 4 to 15 lines, on recovery from alcoholism; humor. Pays $5 to $25, on publication. Guidelines available.

ALIVE! FOR YOUNG TEENS—Christian Board of Publication, Box 179, St. Louis, MO 63166. Short poems, for 12- to 15-year-olds. Pays 25¢ per line, on publication.

ALOHA, THE MAGAZINE OF HAWAII—828 Fort St. Mall, Honolulu, HI 96813. Rita Gormley, Ed. Poetry relating to Hawaii. Pays $25 per poem, on publication.

AMAZING SCIENCE FICTION STORIES—Box 110, Lake Geneva, WI 53147. George Scithers, Ed. Serious and light verse, with SF/fantasy tie-in. Pays $1.00 per line for short poems, somewhat less for longer ones, on acceptance.

THE AMERICAN LEGION MAGAZINE—P.O. Box 1055, Indianapolis, IN 46206. Kathleen Whitehead, Parting Shots Editor. Humorous verse, to 4 lines. Pays $4.50 a line, on acceptance.

THE AMERICAN SCHOLAR—1811 Q St. N.W., Washington, DC 20009. Joseph Epstein, Ed. Highly original poetry, 10 to 32 lines, for college-educated, intellectual readers. Pays $50, on acceptance.

THE ATLANTIC—8 Arlington St., Boston, MA 02116. Peter Davison, Poetry Ed. Poetry of highest quality. Limited market; only 3 to 4 poems an issue. Interest in young poets. Occasionally uses light verse. Pays excellent rates, on acceptance.

THE ATLANTIC ADVOCATE—P.O. Box 3370, Fredericton, N.B., Canada E3B 5A2. Poetry related to Canada's Atlantic provinces. Pays to $5 per column inch, on publication.

AUGUSTA SPECTATOR—P.O. Box 3168, Augusta, GA 30904. Barri Armitage, Poetry Ed. Poetry. Pays in copies.

BIRD WATCHER'S DIGEST—P.O. Box 110, Marietta, OH 45750. Mary B. Bowers, Ed. Poetry, to 30 lines, related to birds or bird watching. Pays to $15, on publication.

BOCA RATON MAGAZINE—P.O. Box 820, Boca Raton, FL 33429. Address Poetry Ed. Occasional poetry, any length, for readers in Florida and elsewhere. Pays in copies.

CAPPER'S WEEKLY—616 Jefferson St., Topeka, KS 66607. Dorothy Harvey, Ed. Traditional poetry and free verse, 4 to 16 lines. Submit up to 6 poems at a time. Pays $3 to $5, on acceptance.

CHILDREN'S PLAYMATE—P.O. Box 567, Indianapolis, IN 46206. Kathleen B. Mosher, Ed. Poetry for children, 5 to 7 years old, on good health, nutrition, exercise, safety, and humorous subjects. Pays from $5, on publication. Buys all rights.

CHRISTIAN HERALD—Chappaqua, NY 10514. David E. Kucharsky, Ed. Interdenominational. Short verse on Christian themes. Pays from $5, on acceptance.

THE CHRISTIAN SCIENCE MONITOR—One Norway St., Boston, MA 02115. Roderick Nordell, Ed., The Home Forum. Fresh, vigorous nonreligious poems of high quality, on various subjects. Short poems preferred. Pays varying rates, on acceptance. Submit no more than 5 poems at a time.

COBBLESTONE—20 Grove St., Peterborough, NH 03458. Mark Corsey, Ed. Poetry, to 100 lines, on historical subjects, for 8- to 13-year-olds. Pays $1.50 a line, on publication. Send SASE for guidelines and themes.

COMMONWEAL—232 Madison Ave., New York, NY 10016. Peter Steinfels, Ed. Catholic. Serious poetry of high quality. Pays 40¢ a line, on acceptance.

COMPLETE WOMAN—1165 N. Clark St., Chicago, IL 60610. Address Assoc. Ed. Poetry. Pays $10, on publication. SASE necessary for return of material.

COSMOPOLITAN—224 W. 57th St., New York, NY 10019. Roni Benson, Poetry Ed. Poetry about relationships, for young, active career women. Pays from $25, on acceptance.

DAILY MEDITATION—Box 2710, San Antonio, TX 78299. Ruth S. Paterson, Ed. Nonsectarian. Verse on religious subjects. Pays 14¢ a line to 16 lines, on acceptance.

DECISION—Billy Graham Evangelistic Assn., 1300 Harmon Pl., Minneapolis, MN 55403. Roger C. Palms, Ed. Poems, 5 to 24 lines, on devotional and other subjects; preferably free verse. Pays on publication.

THE DISCIPLE—Box 179, St. Louis, MO 63166. James L. Merrell, Ed. Journal of Disciples of Christ. Poetry, on religious, seasonal, and historical subjects. Pays $3 to $10, on publication.

THE EVANGEL—Dept. of Christian Education, Free Methodist Headquarters, 901 College Ave., Winona Lake, IN 46590. Vera Bethel, Ed. Free Methodist. Devotional or nature poetry, 8 to 16 lines. Pays $5, on publication.

EVANGELICAL BEACON—1515 E. 66th St., Minneapolis, MN 55423. George Keck, Ed. Denominational publication of Evangelical Free Church of America. Some poetry related to Christian faith. Pays 3¢ a word, $2.50 minimum, on publication.

FAMILY CIRCLE—488 Madison Ave., New York, NY 10022. Eleanor Lewis, Poetry Ed. Poetry to 20 lines (occasionally longer), of interest to women and families. Pays from $25, on acceptance. Submit no more than 7 poems at a time. Query.

FARM AND RANCH LIVING—5400 S. 60th St., Greendale, WI 53129. Bob Ottum, Ed. Poetry, to 20 lines, on rural people and situations. Photos. Pays $35 to $75, extra for photos, on acceptance and on publication. No recent report. Query.

FARM WOMAN NEWS—P.O. Box 643, Milwaukee WI 53201. Ruth Benedict, Man. Ed. Traditional rural poetry and light verse, 20 to 25 lines, on rural experiences, for farm and ranch women. Pays $30 to $60, on acceptance.

GOLF DIGEST MAGAZINE—495 Westport Ave., Norwalk, CT 06856. Lois Hains, Ass't. Ed. Humorous verse, 4 to 8 lines, on golf. Pays $15 to $25, on acceptance. Send SASE.

GOOD HOUSEKEEPING—959 Eighth Ave., New York, NY 10010. Serious poetry, of interest to women; send to A. Quarfoot, Poetry Ed. Light, humorous verse; send to Mary Ann Littell, Light Housekeeping Ed. Pays $5 a line, on acceptance.

GRIT—208 W. Third St., Williamsport, PA 17701. Joanne Decker, Assignment Ed. Traditional poetry and light verse, 4 to 16 lines, for readers in small-town and rural America. Pays $6 for poems up to 4 lines, 50¢ a line for each additional line, on acceptance.

HOME LIFE—127 Ninth Ave. N., Nashville, TN 37234. Reuben Herring, Ed. Southern Baptist. Short lyrical verse, humorous, marriage and family, seasonal, and inspirational. Pays to $20, on acceptance.

LADIES' HOME JOURNAL—3 Park Ave., New York, NY 10016. No unsolicited poetry; submit through an agent only.

LEATHERNECK—Box 1775, Quantico, VA 22134. Ronald D. Lyons, Ed.

Publication of U.S. Marine Corps. Marine-oriented poetry. Pays from $10, on acceptance.

McCALL'S MAGAZINE—230 Park Ave., New York, NY 10169. Address Poetry Editor. Poetry and light verse, 4 to 30 lines, of interest to women. Pays $5 a line, on acceptance.

MARRIAGE AND FAMILY LIVING—Abbey Press Publishing Div., St. Meinrad, IN 47577. Kass Dotterweich, Man. Ed. Verse, on marriage and family. Pays $15, on acceptance.

MATURE YEARS—210 Eighth Ave. S., Nashville, TN 37202. Daisy D. Warren, Ed. United Methodist. Poetry, to 14 lines, on pre-retirement, retirement, seasonal subjects, aging. No saccharine poetry. Pays $1.00 per line.

MIDSTREAM—515 Park Ave., New York, NY 10022. Joel Carmichael, Ed. Poetry, of Jewish interest. Pays $25, on publication.

THE MIRACULOUS MEDAL—475 E. Chelten Ave., Philadelphia, PA 19144. Robert P. Cawley, C.M., Ed. Catholic. Religious verse, to 20 lines. Pays 50¢ a line, on acceptance.

MODERN BRIDE—One Park Ave., New York, NY 10016. Mary Ann Cavlin, Man. Ed. Short verse of interest to bride and groom. Pays $25 to $35, on acceptance.

MODERN MATURITY—215 Long Beach Blvd., Long Beach, CA 90801. Ian Ledgerwood, Ed. Short verse, for Americans 55 years and older. Pays from $50, on acceptance.

MODERN ROMANCES—215 Lexington Ave., New York, NY 10016. Jean Sharbel, Ed. Light, romantic poetry, to 24 lines. Pays varying rates, after publication. Buys all rights.

MS.—119 W. 40th St., New York, NY 10018. Address Poetry Ed. Poetry of high quality, on feminist subjects. Pays $75, on acceptance.

THE NATION—72 Fifth Ave., New York, NY 10011. Grace Schulman, Poetry Ed. Poetry of high quality. Pays after publication.

NATIONAL ENQUIRER—Lantana, FL 33464. Jim Allan, Asst. Ed. Short poems of a philosophical or amusing nature. Pays $20, on publication. SASE required.

NEW AGE—342 Western Ave., Brighton, MA 02135. Sandy MacDonald, Senior Ed. Poetry for readers interested in self-development and awareness. Pays 10¢ a word, on publication.

NEW ENGLAND ENTERTAINMENT DIGEST—P.O. Box 735, Marshfield, MA 02050. Paul J. Reale, Ed. Light verse, of any length, related to the entertainment field. Pays $1 to $2, on publication.

THE NEW REPUBLIC—1220 19th St., N.W., Washington, DC 20036. Robert Pinsky, Poetry Ed. Poetry, of interest to liberal, intellectual readers. Pays $40, after publication.

NEW WORLD OUTLOOK—475 Riverside Dr., New York, NY 10115. Arthur J. Moore, Jr., Ed. United Methodist. Poetry, to 16 lines. Pays on publication.

THE NEW YORKER—25 W. 43rd St., New York, NY 10036. First-rate poetry and light verse. Pays top rates, on acceptance.

THE OHIO MOTORIST—P.O. Box 6150, Cleveland, OH 44101. Jerome F. Turk, Ed. Humorous verse, 4 to 6 lines, on automobile and vacation topics (foreign and domestic). Pays $10 to $15, on acceptance.

OUR FAMILY—Box 249, Dept. E., Battleford, Sask., Canada S0M 0E0. Rev. Albert Lalonde, O.M.I., Catholic. Verse, for family men and women. Pays 75¢ to $1.00 a line, on acceptance. Send self-addressed envelope with International Reply Coupons (or 37¢) for guidelines.

PENTECOSTAL EVANGEL—1445 Boonville, Springfield, MO 65802. Robert C. Cunningham, Ed. Journal of Assemblies of God. Religious and inspirational verse, 12 to 30 lines. Pays to 40¢ a line, on publication.

PLAYBOY—919 N. Michigan Ave., Chicago, IL 60611. Address Party Jokes Editor. Limericks only. No light or serious verse. Pays $50, on acceptance. Jokes cannot be returned.

PURPOSE—616 Walnut Ave., Scottdale, PA 15683. James E. Horsch, Ed. Poetry, 3 to 12 lines, with uplifting Christian angle. Pays $5 to $15, on acceptance.

ROLL CALL: THE NEWSPAPER OF CAPITOL HILL—201 Massachusetts Ave. N.E., Washington, DC 20002. Light, humorous satire on Congress or politics. Pays on acceptance.

ST. JOSEPH'S MESSENGER—P.O. Box 288, Jersey City, NJ 07303. Sister Ursula Marie Maphet, Ed. Light verse and traditional poetry, 4 to 40 lines. Pays $5 to $15, on publication.

THE SATURDAY EVENING POST—1100 Waterway Blvd., Indianapolis, IN 46202. Address Post Scripts Ed. Light verse and humor. Pays $15, on publication.

SCOPE—426 S. Fifth St., Box 1209, Minneapolis, MN 55440. Constance Lovaas, Ed. Publication of the American Lutheran Church Women. Limited free-lance market for poetry. Pays $10 to $20, on acceptance.

SCORE, CANADA'S GOLF MAGAZINE—43 Madison Ave., Toronto, Ont., Canada M5R 2S2. Poetry, to 50 words, on the Canadian golf scene. Pays to $20, on publication.

SEVENTEEN—850 Third Ave., New York, NY 10022. Poetry, to 20 lines, by teens. Submit up to 5 poems. Pays $15, after acceptance.

STRAIGHT—8121 Hamilton Ave., Cincinnati, OH 45231. Religious poetry by teenagers only. Shorter poems have best chance. Pays on acceptance.

UNITED METHODIST REPORTER—P.O. Box 221076, Dallas, TX 75222. Spurgeon M. Dunnam III, Editor. Religious verse, 4 to 12 lines. Pays $2, on acceptance.

WESTERN PEOPLE—P.O. Box 2500, Saskatoon, Sask., Canada S7K 2C4. Mary Gilchrist, Man. Ed. Short poetry, for Western Canadians. Pays on acceptance. Send SAE with International Reply Coupons.

YANKEE—Dublin, NH 03444. Jean Burden, Poetry Ed. Serious poetry of high quality, to 30 lines. Pays $35 per poem for all rights, $25 for first rights, on publication.

POETRY SERIES

The following university presses publish book-length collections of poetry by writers who have never had a book of poems published. Each has specific rules for submission, so before submitting any material, be sure to write well ahead of the deadline dates for further information. Some organizations sponsor competitions in which prizes are offered for book-length collections of poetry; see *Literary Prize Offers* list on page 752.

THE ALABAMA PRESS POETRY SERIES—Dept. of English, Drawer AL, Univ. of Alabama, University, AL 35486. Address Thomas Rabbitt or Dara Wier. Considers unpublished book-length collections of poetry for publication as part of the Alabama Press Poetry Series. Submissions accepted during the months of September, October, and November only.

UNIVERSITY OF GEORGIA PRESS POETRY SERIES—Athens, GA 30602. Poets who have never had a book of poems published may submit book-length poetry manuscripts for possible publication. Open during the month of September each year.

WESLEYAN UNIVERSITY PRESS—110 Mt. Vernon St., Middletown, CT 06547. Considers unpublished book-length poetry manuscripts by poets who have never had a book published for publication in the Wesleyan New Poets Series. There is no deadline.

GREETING CARD MARKETS

Greeting card companies often have their own specific requirements for submitting ideas, verse, and artwork. The National Association of Greeting Card Publishers, however, gives the following general guidelines for submitting material: Verses and messages should be typed, double-spaced, each one on 3 × 5 or 4 × 6 card. Use only one side of the card, and be sure to put your name and address in the upper left-hand corner. Keep a copy of every verse or idea you send. (It's also advisable to keep a record of what you've submitted to each publisher.) Always enclose a stamped, self-addressed envelope, and do not send out more than ten verses or ideas in a group to any one publisher.

The National Association of Greeting Card Publishers brings out a booklet for free lancers, *Artists and Writers Market List,* with the names, addresses, and editorial guidelines of greeting card companies. This may be obtained free, by sending a self-addressed, stamped envelope to the Association at 600 Pennsylvania Ave., S.E. #300, Washington, DC 20003.

ABBEY PRESS—St. Meinrad, IN 47577. Attn: P. A. Ledford, Prod. Dir. Long, poetic verses that begin on front of card and continue on inside. All occasions: birthday, friendship, get well, sympathy, congratulations, thank you, etc. Special occasions: Christmas, Easter, Valentine, St. Patrick's, Mother's Day, Father's Day. Pays $30 to $50.

AMBERLEY GREETING CARD COMPANY—P.O. Box 36159, Cincinnati, OH 45236. Ned Stern, Ed. Humorous studio greeting card ideas, for birthday, illness, friendship, congratulations, miss you, thank you, retirement, apology, goodbye. Risqué and nonrisqué humor. No seasonal cards. Pays $40. Buys all rights.

AMERICAN GREETINGS CORPORATION—10500 American Rd., Cleveland, OH 44144. Overstocked.

ARTFORMS CARD CORP.—725 County Line Rd., Deerfield, IL 60015. Attn: Bluma Marder. Verse, suitable for Jewish market. Formal for holiday cards and humorous for get well, birthdays, etc. Pays $15 to $25.

BLUE MOUNTAIN ARTS, INC.—P.O. Box 4549, Boulder, CO 80306. Attn: Editorial Staff, Dept. TW. Poetry and prose: inspirational (non-religious) and sensitive. No artwork. No rhymed verse. Send SASE. Pays $150, on publication.

BRETT-FORER GREETINGS, INC.—105 E. 73rd St., New York, NY 10021. Ideas and designs for whimsical everyday and Christmas lines. Pays from $20 per idea, on acceptance.

CURRENT, INC.—P.O. Box 2559, Colorado Springs, CO 80901. Nancy P. McConnell, Product Editor. Humorous greeting cards—puns, studio or sweet humor (two to four lines) for all occasions. Include design suggestions. Pays $10 per item, on acceptance.

DRAWING BOARD GREETING CARDS (formerly *The Drawing Board, Inc.*)—8200 Carpenter Freeway, Dallas, TX 75222. Jimmie Fitzgerald, Edit. Director. General and studio card ideas. Pays $30 to $80.

D. FORER & COMPANY, INC.—105 E. 73rd St., New York, NY 10021. Ideas and designs for whimsical everyday and Christmas lines. Pays from $20 per idea, on acceptance. No recent report.

FRAN MAR GREETING CARDS, LTD.—Box 1057, Mt. Vernon, NY 10550. Stationery and pad concepts. Party invitations. Thank you notes. Pays $25 per idea, within 30 days of acceptance.

FRAVESSI-LAMONT, INC.—11 Edison Pl., Springfield, NJ 07081. Address Editor. Short verse, mostly humorous or sentimental; cards with witty prose. No Christmas material. Pays varying rates, on acceptance.

FREEDOM GREETING CARD COMPANY—P.O. Box 715, Bristol, PA 19007. Submit to Jay Levitt. Verse, traditional, humorous, and love message. Zodiac and inspirational poetry for all occasions. Pays $1 a line, on acceptance. Query.

GALLANT GREETINGS CORPORATION—2654 West Medill, Chicago, IL 60647. Ideas for humorous and serious greeting cards. Pays $30 per idea, in 45 days.

HALLMARK CARDS, INC.—P.O. Box 580, Contemporary #303, Kansas City, MO 64141. *Contemporary (Studio) Cards.* No artwork. Send to Contemporary Free-Lance Editor. *Hallmark Editions;* no free-lance material. *Hallmark General Verse and Prose;* no freelance material.

THE KEATING LINE, INC.—27–08 40th Ave., Long Island City, NY 11101. Attn: Arwed H. Baenisch, A.D. Formal verse for all occasions. Everyday and seasonal.

LEANIN' TREE PUBLISHING CO.—Box 9500, Boulder, CO 80301. Address Editorial Assistant. Verse with a western flavor or theme, friendship and inspirational verse, Christian verse for holiday and friendship cards, and short love poems. Pays $35, on publication. Send SASE for guidelines first (required).

THE MAINE LINE COMPANY—P.O. Box 418, Rockport, ME 04856.

Unusual humor cards, especially those written from a woman's point of view. Enclose SASE with submission. Pays $25 to $50 per card, on publication. Send return envelope with three first-class stamps for copy of editorial guidelines.

ALFRED MAINZER, INC.—27-08 40th Ave., Long Island City, NY 11101. Arwed H. Baenisch, Art Dir. Everyday, Christmas, Mother's Day, Father's Day, Valentine's Day, Easter verses. Rates vary. Query.

MARK I—1733 W. Irving Park Rd., Chicago, IL 60613. Attn: Alex H. Cohen. Verse should be stimulating or contemporary with either a humorous or sensitive feeling. Interested in all occasions. Pays $50 for verse ideas. Query with SASE.

MISTER B GREETING CARD CO.—3305 N. W. 37th St., Miami, FL 33142. Harry W. Gee, Ed. Humorous, risqué or novelty ideas, and serious conventional or sentimental material, no more than 4 lines: Anniversary, Birthday, Get Well, Friendship, Mother's Day, Valentine's Day, Christmas, Jewish, and Special Captions. Spanish and French captions with translations of same. Rates vary.

OATMEAL STUDIOS—Box 138, Rochester, VT 05767. Attn: Helene Lehrer. Humorous and clever ideas needed for birthdays, anniversary, get well, etc., also, Valentine's Day, Christmas, Mother's Day, Father's Day, etc. Pays $25 to $50.

PARAMOUNT CARDS INC.—Box 678, Pawtucket, RI 02862. Attn: Dolores Riccio. Prose and verse for sensitivity, humorous, and general cards. Send SASE for guidelines. Pays varying rates, on acceptance.

RED FARM STUDIOS—P.O. Box 347, 334 Pleasant St., Pawtucket, RI 02862. Informal cards, for graduations, weddings, birthdays, get-wells, anniversaries, friendship, new baby, retirement, Christmas, and sympathy. No studio humor. Pays varying rates.

REED STARLINE CARD CO.—3331 Sunset Blvd., Los Angeles, CA 90026. Lissa Stevens, Ed. Whimsical and short humorous studio card copy, conversational in tone, for sophisticated adults; no verse or jingles. Everyday copy, for birthday, friendship, get well, anniversary, thank you, travel, congratulations. Submit material for fall holidays in January; for Valentine's Day and St. Patrick's Day in February; and for Easter, Mother's Day, Father's Day in July. Pays $40 per idea, on acceptance.

ROUSANA CARDS—28 Sager Pl., Hillside, NJ 07205. Attn: Bob Weist. Verse, for everyday and all seasons. Humor ideas, including fun compliments, soft sophistication, puns and twists.

VAGABOND CREATIONS, INC.—2560 Lance Dr., Dayton, OH 45409. George F. Stanley, Jr., Ed. Greeting cards with graphics only on cover (no copy) and short tie-in copy punch line on inside page: birthday, everyday, Valentine, Christmas, and graduation. Mildly risqué humor with *double entendre* acceptable. Ideas for humorous buttons and illustrated theme stationery. Pays $15, on acceptance.

WARNER PRESS PUBLISHERS—Anderson, IN 46018. Jane Hammond, Product Editor. Prose sensitivity, insp. poems, and verse card ideas, religious themes. Submit Christmas material in July and August, other material in June and July. Pays $1 a line, on acceptance.

WILLIAMHOUSE-REGENCY, INC.—28 W. 23rd St., New York, NY 10010. Submit to Diane Carol Brandt. Captions for wedding invitations. Pays varying rates, on acceptance. Query with SASE.

FILLERS AND HUMOR

Magazines noted for their excellent filler departments, plus a cross-section of representative publications using fillers and short humor pieces, follow. However, almost all magazines use some type of filler material, and writers can find dozens of markets by studying copies of magazines at a library or newsstand.

Many magazines do not acknowledge or return filler material, and in such cases, writers may assume that after 90 days have passed from the time of submission, a filler may be submitted to another market.

ACCENT—Box 2315, 1720 Washington Blvd., Ogden, UT 84404. Peggie Bingham, Ed. Money-saving tips and short how-to's for travelers. Also, good humor pieces, 200 to 500 words. Pays 15¢ a word, on acceptance. Query with SASE.

ALCOHOLISM/THE NATIONAL MAGAZINE—1004 N. 105th, Seattle, WA 98133. "Coffee Break Page": short, true-experience pieces, jokes and anecdotes relating to alcoholism, for professionals in the alcoholism treatment field and recovering alcoholics. Nominal payment.

ALIVE! FOR YOUNG TEENS—Christian Board of Publication, P.O. Box 179, St. Louis, MO 63166. Mike Dixon, Ed. Puzzles, riddles, daffy definitions; poetry, to 20 lines. Pays to $10, 25¢ a line for poetry, on publication.

AMERICAN BAR ASSOCIATION JOURNAL—33 W. Monroe St., Chicago, IL 60603. Laurence Bodine, Assoc. Ed. Humor, related to the legal field, to 750 words. Pays $100 to $300, $25 for a "War Stories" item on acceptance. Query.

AMERICAN CLAY EXCHANGE—P.O. Box 2674, La Mesa, CA 92041. Short items on American-made pottery. Pays $5, on publication.

THE AMERICAN FIELD—222 W. Adams St., Chicago, IL 60606. W. F. Brown, Ed. Short fact items and anecdotes on outdoor sports and field trials for bird dogs. Pays varying rates, on acceptance.

THE AMERICAN LEGION MAGAZINE—Box 1055, Indianapolis, IN 46206. Ward A. Beckham, Parting Shots Ed. Short, funny anecdotes appealing to military/naval, veterans, older readers; one- or two-line gags; humorous verse, to 4 lines. No sex, religion, or ethnic humor. Pays $15 for anecdotes and gags, $5 a line for verse, on acceptance.

THE AMERICAN ROSE MAGAZINE—P.O. Box 30,000, Shreveport, LA 71130. Fillers on home rose gardening. Pays in copies.

AMERICAS—General Secretariat Bldg., OAS, 1889 F St., N.W., Washington, D.C. 20006. A. R. Williams, Man. Ed. Short pieces on Latin American personalities, 800 words. Pays varying rates, on publication.

ARIZONA—P.O. Box 1950, Phoenix, AZ 85001. Sunday magazine of *The Arizona Republic.* Humor, 300 to 1,000 words, both on general-interest subjects and relating to Arizona. Pays on publication.

ARTSLINE—P.O. Box 24287, Seattle, WA 98124. Arts-related fillers. Pays on acceptance.

THE ATLANTIC—8 Arlington St., Boston, MA 02116. Sophisticated humorous or satirical pieces, 1,000 to 3,000 words. Some light poetry. Pays varying rates, on acceptance.

ATLANTIC SALMON JOURNAL—1435 St. Alexandre, Suite 1030, Montreal, Quebec, Canada H3A 2G4. Joanne Eidinger, Ed. Fillers, 50 to 100 words, on salmon politics, conservation, and nature. Pays on publication.

BIKEREPORT—Bikecentennial, P.O. Box 8308, Missoula, MT 59807. Daniel D'Ambrosio, Ed. News shorts from the bicycling world for "In Bicycle Circles." Pays $25 to $65 per published page, on publication.

BIRD WATCHER'S DIGEST—P.O. Box 110, Marietta, OH 45750. Mary Bowers, Ed. Fillers, 200 to 250 words, for bird watchers. Cartoons. Pays $5, $10 for cartoons, on publication.

BOYS' LIFE—1325 Walnut Hill Lane, Irving, TX 75062. Robert Hood, Ed. How-to features, to 400 words, with photos, on hobbies, crafts, science, outdoor skills, etc. Pays from $150.

BUSINESS NH—177 E. Industrial Dr., Manchester, NH 03103. John Milne, Ed. Fillers, 300 to 650 words, on business and economic topics. Pays on publication.

BUSINESS VIEW OF SOUTHWEST FLORIDA—P.O. Box 1546, Naples, FL 33939. Business-related puzzles. Pays varying rates, on publication.

CAPPER'S WEEKLY—616 Jefferson St., Topeka, KS 66607. Dorothy Harvey, Ed. Informal articles, 300 to 500 words, on human-interest, personal experiences, for women's section, "In the Heart of the Home." Household hints, recipes, jokes. Pays varying rates, on publication.

CASHFLOW—1807 Glenview, Glenview, IL 60025. Vince DiPaolo, Ed. Fillers, to 1,000 words, on varied aspects of finance, for treasury managers in public and private institutions. Pays on publication.

CATHOLIC DIGEST—P.O. Box 64090, St. Paul, MN 55164. Features, to 300 words, on instances of kindness rewarded, for "Hearts Are Trumps." Stories about conversions, for "Open Door." Reports of tactful remarks or actions, for "The Perfect Assist." Accounts of good deeds, for "People Are Like That." Humorous pieces on parish life, for "In Our Parish." Amusing signs, for "Signs of the Times." Jokes; fillers. Include source. Pays $4 to $50, on publication.

CHEVRON USA—P.O. Box 6227, San Jose, CA 95150. Mark Williams, ED. Quarterly. True, previously unpublished anecdotes, 50 to 250 words, on travel and leisure in the United States. Pays $25, on publication.

CHIC—2029 Century Park E., Suite 3800, Los Angeles, CA 90067. Visual fillers, short humor with visuals, 100 to 200 words, for "Odds and Ends" section. Pays on acceptance.

CHICKADEE—59 Front St. E., Toronto, Ont., Canada M5E 1B3. Humorous poetry about animals and about the seasons for children, 10 to 15 lines. Pays on publication.

CHILD LIFE—P.O. Box 567, Indianapolis, IN 46206. Steve Charles, Ed. Puzzles, games, mazes, and rebuses, on health or safety-related subjects, for children 7 to 9 years. Pays $10 to $15, on publication.

CHILDREN'S PLAYMATE—1100 Waterway Blvd., P.O. Box 567, Indianapolis, IN 46206. Kathleen Mosher, Ed. Puzzles, games, mazes for 5- to 7-year-olds, emphasizing health, safety, nutrition. Pays about 4¢ a word (varies on puzzles), on publication.

CHRISTIAN HERALD—40 Overlook Dr., Chappaqua, NY 10514. David

Kucharsky, Ed. Poetry and true anecdotes, to 24 lines, on Christian/church themes. Pays $5 to $15, after acceptance.

CHRISTIAN LIFE—396 E. St. Charles Rd., Wheaton, IL 60188. Karen Tornberg, News Ed. News items, to 200 words, on trends, ideas, unique personalities/ministries, and events of interest to Christians. Photos. Pays $5 to $15, on publication. Short pieces, 500 to 800 words, of interest to women: handicrafts, recipes, true adventures. Must have some spiritual application. Send to Jan Franzen. Pays $15 to $20.

THE CHURCH MUSICIAN—127 Ninth Ave. N., Nashville, TN 37234. W. M. Anderson, Ed. For Southern Baptist music leaders. Humorous fillers with a music slant. No clippings. Pays around 4¢ a word, on acceptance. Same address and requirements for *Glory Songs* (for adults), and *Opus One* and *Opus Two* (for teen-agers).

COLLECTIBLES AND ANTIQUES GAZETTE—P.O. Drawer 450, Hollywood, FL 33022. Short items on collectibles, antiques, rare books. Pays $2, on publication.

COLUMBIA—Box 1670, New Haven, CT 06507. Elmer Von Feldt, Ed. Journal of the Knights of Columbus. Humor and satire, to 1,000 words; captionless cartoons. Pays $200, $25 for cartoons, on acceptance.

COLUMBIA JOURNALISM REVIEW—700 Journalism Bldg., Columbia Univ., New York, NY 10027. Gloria Cooper, Man. Ed. Amusing mistakes in news stories, headlines, photos, etc. (original clippings required), for "Lower Case." Pays $10, on publication.

COSMOPOLITAN—224 W. 57th St., New York, NY 10019. Anecdotal essays, 650 words, for "Outrageous Opinions." Pays $300, on acceptance.

CYCLE WORLD—1499 Monrovia Ave., P.O. Box 1757, Newport Beach, CA 92663. Allan Girdler, Ed. Humor, 1,500 to 2,000 words, of interest to motorcycle enthusiasts. Racing reports, 400 to 600 words, with photos. News items on motorcycle industry, legislation, trends. Pays $75 to $100 per printed page, on publication.

CYCLIST—20916 Higgins Court, Torrance, CA 90501. John Francis, Ed. Shorts on bicycle racing, training, travel, etc. Pays 50¢ a word, on acceptance.

DOWN EAST—Camden, ME 04843. Anecdotes about Maine, to 1,000 words, for "I Remember." Humorous anecdotes, to 300 words, for "It Happened Down East." Pays $10 to $50, on acceptance.

DYNAMIC YEARS—215 Long Beach Blvd., Long Beach, CA 90802. Lorena F. Farrell, Ed. Short items for "Questions You've Asked," "To Your Health," "After Hours," "Personal Notebook," "Changing Gears," and "Dynamic Americans." Humorous, sophisticated pieces, 200 words, on social issues and topics of interest to mid-life readers, for "Voice of Experience." Pays $350 for "Voice of Experience," $150 for short items, on acceptance. No fillers.

EBONY—820 S. Michigan Ave., Chicago, IL 60605. John H. Johnson, Ed./Pub. "Speaking of People," short features, to 200 words, on blacks in traditionally non-black jobs. Cartoons. Pays $50 for cartoons, on publication.

EBONY, JR.!—820 S. Michigan Ave., Chicago, IL 60605. Marcia V. Roebuck-Hoard, Ed. Riddles, games, jokes and puzzles, with emphasis on black heritage. Pays $5 to $25, on acceptance.

668

ELECTRONIC GAMES—460 W. 34th St., New York, NY 10001. Fillers and short humor, 500 to 1,500 words, on electronic games. Query. Pays on acceptance.

THE ELKS MAGAZINE—425 W. Diversey Pkwy., Chicago, IL 60614. Herbert Gates, Ed. General interest, nostalgia and humor, 1,500 to 3,000 words, for a family audience. Non-political satire. No fillers. Pays from 10¢ a word, on acceptance.

EXPECTING—685 Third Ave., New York, NY 10017. E. Podsiadlo, Ed. Anecdotes about pregnancy, for "Happenings." Pays $10, on publication.

FAMILY CIRCLE—488 Madison Ave., New York, NY 10022. Ideas or suggestions on homemaking, education, and community betterment, for "Readers' Idea Exchange." Pays $50. Unpublished entries cannot be returned or acknowledged. Query.

FARM AND RANCH LIVING—5400 S. 60th St., Greendale, WI 53129. Bob Ottum, Man. Ed. Fillers on rural people and living, 200 words. Pays from $15, on acceptance and on publication.

FARM WOMAN NEWS—P.O. Box 643, Milwaukee, WI 53201. Ruth C. Benedict, Man. Ed. Short verse, 20 to 25 lines, and fillers, to 250 words, on the rural experience, for farm and ranch women. Pays from $35, on publication.

FATE—500 Hyacinth Pl., Highland Park, IL 60035. Mary Margaret Fuller, Ed. Factual fillers, to 200 words, on strange or psychic happenings. True stories, to 300 words, on psychic or mystic personal experiences. Pays $1 to $10.

FIELD & STREAM—1515 Broadway, New York, NY 10036. Duncan Barnes, Ed. Fillers on hunting, camping, fishing, etc., 500 to 1,000 words, for "How It's Done," and "Did You Know?" Cartoons. Pays $250 for "How It's Done," $350 for "Did you Know?," $100 for cartoons, on acceptance.

FLARE—777 Bay St., Toronto, Ont., Canada M5W 1A7. Jane Hess, Assoc. Ed. Career-related items, profiles, 100 to 150 words, for young Canadian working women aged 18 to 34. Pays on acceptance. Query.

FLOWER & GARDEN—4521 Pennsylvania Ave., Kansas City, MO 64111. Rachel Snyder, Ed. Short, how-to home gardening and landscaping pieces by writers experienced in growing plants. Pays varying rates, on acceptance. Query preferred.

FLY FISHERMAN—Harrisburg, PA 17105. Tom Meade, Assoc. Ed. Fillers, 100 words, on how to and where to go fly fishing. Pays from $35, on acceptance.

FRONTIER MAGAZINE—Inflight Publishing Co., P.O. Box 1002, 4100 S. Parker Rd., Aurora, CO 80014. Frontier Airlines' inflight magazine. Short pieces, 300 to 1,000 words, on travel, aviation and general-interest subjects. Pays on acceptance and on publication. Query preferred.

GALLERY—800 Second Ave., New York, NY 10017. John Bensink, Ed.-in-Chief; Marc Lichter, Man. Ed. Short humor, satire, and short service features for men. Pays varying rates, on acceptance and on publication. Query.

GAMEPLAY—P.O. Box 979, Crystal Lake, IL 60014. Jake Jaquet, Ed. Short items on game-related topics. Pays 4¢ to 6¢ a word, on acceptance.

GAMES—515 Madison Ave., New York, NY 10022. Jacqueline Damian, Ed. Puzzles, word and number games, riddles, codes, mazes, trivia, and other games. Short articles on puzzles and games. Humor pieces and short fiction. Pays varying rates, on publication.

GLAMOUR—350 Madison Ave., New York, NY 10017. Articles, 1,000 to 1,200 words, for "Viewpoint" section: opinion pieces for women. Pays $500, on acceptance. Send SASE.

GOLF DIGEST—495 Westport Ave., Norwalk, CT 06856. Jerry Tarde, Senior Features Ed. Short fact items, anecdotes, quips, jokes, light verse related to golf. True humorous or odd incidents, to 200 words. Pays from $25, on acceptance.

GOLF MAGAZINE—380 Madison Ave., New York, NY 10017. George F. Peper, Ed. Fillers to 750 words, on golf. Pays from $25, on acceptance.

GOOD HOUSEKEEPING—959 Eighth Ave., New York, NY 10019. Mary Ann Littell, Asst. Ed. Light verse and very short humorous prose. Pays from $10 to $100, and from $5 a line for verse.

GRIT—208 W. Third St., Williamsport, PA 17701. Joanne Decker, Assignment Ed. Brief anecdotal features, from 30 words, on interesting, amusing, heartwarming, and inspiring subjects. Humorous verse. Pays 12¢ a word for prose, $6 for four lines of verse.

GUIDEPOSTS—747 Third Ave., New York, NY 10017. Inspirational anecdotes, to 250 words. Pays $10 to $50, on acceptance.

HEALTH & CARE—1500 Adams Ave., Suite 105, Costa Mesa, CA 92626. Sherry Angel, Ed. Personal essays on health, book reviews, 300 to 600 words, crossword puzzles, games. Short, original hospital humor. Pays from $100, $25 for hospital humor, on acceptance.

HEALTH LITERATURE REVIEW—P.O. Box 8029, St. Paul, MN 55113. Tammy Rognlie, Man. Ed. Humorous stories or jokes, 25 to 50 words, on health topics. Pays on publication.

HOME LIFE—127 Ninth Ave. N., Nashville, TN 37234. Reuben Herring, Ed. Southern Baptist. Personal-experience pieces, 100 to 500 words, on Christian marriage, and family relationships. Pays 4¢ a word, on acceptance.

HOME MECHANIX (formerly *Mechanix Illustrated*)—1515 Broadway, New York, NY 10036. Joseph Provey, Ed. Single photos with captions and tips for shortcuts in shop, garage or home. Pays $50 to $75, on acceptance.

INFLIGHT—P.O. Box 2315, Ogden UT 84404. Wayne DeWald, Ed. Humor, for male, business-oriented audience. Pays 15¢ a word, on acceptance. Query.

INSIDE WOMEN'S TENNIS—1604 Union St., San Francisco, CA 94123. Joseph Page, Ed. Fillers and crossword puzzles with women's tennis data. Pays $25, on publication.

JACK & JILL—1100 Waterway Blvd., P.O. Box 567, Indianapolis, IN 46206. Christine French Clark, Ed. Poems, puzzles, games, science and craft projects, for 6- to 8-year-olds, with health or holiday themes. Instructions for activities should be clearly written, accompanied by diagrams and a list of needed materials. Pays varying rates, on publication.

LADIES' HOME JOURNAL—"Last Laughs," 3 Park Ave., New York, NY 10016. Brief anecdotes and poems about the funny business of being a woman today. Pays $25. Submissions cannot be acknowledged or returned.

LAUGH FACTORY—400 S. Beverly Dr., #214, Beverly Hills, CA 90212. Jamie Masada, Pub. Jokes and cartoons. Restrictions: no four-letter words and nothing too off-color. Pays negotiable rates, on publication.

LONG ISLAND'S NIGHTLIFE MAGAZINE—1770 Deer Park Ave., Deer Park, NY 11729. Bill Ervolino, Ed. Topical humor, 1,000 to 2,000 words, and fillers, on entertainment, leisure, personalities on Long Island. Pays from $50, on publication. Query preferred.

LOOSE CHANGE—Mead Publishing Corp., 21176 S. Alameda St., Long Beach, CA 90810. Daniel R. Mead, Ed. Short pieces of interest to collectors of antique gaming machines and coin-operated slot machines. Pays from $5, on acceptance.

MATURE LIVING—127 Ninth Ave. N., MSN 140, Nashville, TN 37234. Nostalgia, 875 words, for "I Remember When . . ." Brief, humorous, original items, for "Cracker Barrel." Profiles of senior adults, 25 lines with photos. Pays after acceptance. Send SASE for guidelines.

MATURE YEARS—201 Eighth Ave., S., Nashville, TN 37202. Daisy D. Warren, Ed. Poems, cartoons, puzzles, jokes, anecdotes, to 300 words, for older adults. Pays 4¢ a word, on acceptance.

MECHANIX ILLUSTRATED—See *Home Mechanix.*

MID-WEST OUTDOORS—111 Shore Dr., Hinsdale, IL 60521. Gene Laulunen, Ed. Where to and how to fish in the Midwest, 200 to 1,500 words, with 2 photos. Pays $15 to $35, on publication.

MODERN BRIDE—One Park Ave., New York, NY 10016. Mary Ann Cavlin, Man. Ed. Humorous pieces, 500 to 1,500 words, and poetry, for brides. Pays on acceptance.

MODERN MATURITY—215 Long Beach Blvd., Long Beach, CA 90802. Ian Ledgerwood, Ed. Money-saving ideas and how-to items; jokes; quizzes, graphic puzzles; narrative math problems, etc. Submit seasonal material 6 months in advance. Pays from $15, on acceptance. Query.

MODERN PHOTOGRAPHY—825 Seventh Ave., New York, NY 10019. Julia Scully, Ed. How-to pieces, 200 to 300 words, with photos, on photography. Pays $50 to $100, on acceptance.

MODERN ROMANCES—215 Lexington Ave., New York, NY 10016. Short items, to 300 words, for "Little Things (That Say 'I Love You')" and "Our Family Tradition." Pays $25, thirty days after month of publication.

NATIONAL ENQUIRER—Lantana, FL 33464. Jim Allan, Asst. Ed. Short, humorous fillers, witticisms, anecdotes, tart comments. Original items preferred, but others considered if source and date given. Short poems of a philosophical or amusing nature. Pays $20, on publication. Self-addressed, stamped envelope required.

NATIONAL REVIEW—150 E. 35th St., New York, NY 10016. William F. Buckley, Ed. Satire, to 900 words. Pays $35 to $100, on publication.

NATIONAL SUPERMARKET SHOPPER—American Coupon Club, P.O. Box 500, Franklin Square, NY 11010. Lee Shore, Man. Ed. Fillers, 50 to 250 words, on the use of coupons and refunds, smart shopping, consumerism, and money-savers. Pays $5 to $10, on publication. Buys all rights.

NEW ENGLAND MONTHLY—P.O. Box 446, Haydenville, MA 01039. Daniel Okrent, Ed. Shorts, 400 to 1,000 words, on various aspects of life and culture in the six New England states. Pays $100 to $350, on acceptance.

THE NEW YORKER—25 W. 43rd St., New York, NY 10036. Amusing mistakes in newspapers, books, magazines, etc. Pays from $5, extra for headings and tag lines, on acceptance.

NEW YORK'S NIGHTLIFE MAGAZINE—1770 Deer Park Ave., Deer Park, NY 11729. Bill Ervolino, Ed. Topical humor, 1,000 to 2,000 words, and fillers, on entertainment, leisure, personalities in New York. Pays from $50, on publication. Query preferred.

OHIO FISHERMAN—1570 Fishinger Rd., Columbus, OH 43221. Short, do-it-yourself fishing-related tidbits, 250 to 500 words. Pays varying rates, on acceptance.

THE OHIO MOTORIST—P.O. Box 6150, Cleveland, OH 44101. F. Jerome Turk, Ed. Humorous verse, 4 to 6 lines, on motoring and vacation topics. Pays $10 to $15, on acceptance.

OMNI—1965 Broadway, New York, NY 10023. Douglas Colligan, Senior Ed. Opinion pieces, to 800 words, on aspects of the future: science and technology, the arts, lifestyles. Humor and satire. Pays from $500, on acceptance.

OPUS ONE and **OPUS TWO**—See *The Church Musician.*

ORBEN'S CURRENT COMEDY—1200 N. Nash St., Apt. 1122, Arlington, VA 22209. Robert Orben, Ed. Original, funny, performable one-liners and brief jokes on news, fads, topical subjects, etc., especially for speakers. Pays $5, after publication. SASE required.

ORGANIC GARDENING—33 E. Minor St., Emmaus, PA 18049. Jack Ruttle, Planning Ed. Fillers, 100 to 500 words, on gardening experiences; how-to's, solutions of problems, etc. Photos of lawn art. Cartoons, cartoon ideas. Gardening riddles. Horticultural "bloopers" in local newspapers, etc. Pays $25 to $200, on publication.

OUTDOOR AMERICA—1800 N. Kent St., Suite 806, Arlington, VA 22209. Humor, 1,500 words, on natural resource conservation issues. Pays 5¢ to 10¢ a word, on publication.

OUTDOOR LIFE—380 Madison Ave., New York, NY 10017. Clare Conley, Ed. Short instructive items and 1-pagers on hunting, fishing, camping gear, boats, outdoor equipment. Photos. Pays on acceptance.

PARENTS—685 Third Ave., New York, NY 10017. Short items on solutions of child care-related problems for "Parents Exchange." Pays $20, on publication

PARISH FAMILY DIGEST—200 Noll Plaza, Huntington, IN 46750. Patrick R. Moran, Ed. Family- or parish-oriented humor. Anecdotes, 250 words, of unusual parish experiences, for "Our Parish." Pays $5 to $12.50, on acceptance.

PENNYWHISTLE PRESS—Box 500-P, Washington, DC 20044. Anita Sama, Ed. Short fillers, puzzlers, word games, humorous stories, for 6- to 12-year-olds. Pays varying rates, on acceptance.

PENTHOUSE—1965 Broadway, New York, NY 10023. Peter Bloch, Articles Ed. Kathy Green, Fiction Ed. Satire, humor, black comedy. Pays to 50¢ a word, on acceptance.

PEOPLE IN ACTION—P.O. Box 2315, Ogden, UT 84404. Profiles, 500 to 700 words, on anyone who likes to cook, for "Celebrity Chef." Must be accompanied by recipe and color transparency. Query. Pays 15¢ a word, extra for photos, on acceptance.

PLAYBOY—919 N. Michigan Ave., Chicago, IL 60611. Address Party Jokes Editor, After Hours Editor, or Ribald Classics Editor. Jokes; short original material on new trends, lifestyles, personalities; humorous news items. Pays $50 for jokes, $50 to $350 for "After Hours" items, on publication. "Ribald Classics" (900 to 1,100 words) must be derived from some actual source that's clearly and exactly stated with the date. No stories from overly familiar sources (such as Boccaccio and Chaucer), nor tales that have already appeared in the magazine. Pays $200.

PLAYGIRL—3420 Ocean Park Blvd., Suite 3000, Santa Monica, CA 90405. Moe Bryant, Cartoon Ed. Sophisticated cartoons dealing positively with women and women's issues. Pays $75, on publication.

POPULAR MECHANICS—224 W. 57th St., New York, NY 10019. Bill Hartford, Man. Ed. How-to pieces, from 300 words, with photos and sketches, on home improvement and shop and craft projects. Pays $25 to $100, on acceptance. Buys all rights.

POPULAR SCIENCE MONTHLY—380 Madison Ave., New York, NY 10017. A. W. Lees, Group Ed. One-column fillers, 350 words, with photo or sketch if demo necessary: general workshop ideas, maintenance tips for home and car. Pays from $100; $50 for ideas for "Taking Care of Your Car" and "Wordless Workshop," $200 for "Computer Adventures," $250 for "Adventures in Alternative Energy," on acceptance.

POWDER, THE SKIER'S MAGAZINE—Box 1028, Dana Point, CA 92629. Pat Cochran, Man. Ed. Humorous pieces. Product reports. Pays $225 per printed page, on publication. Query with published clips.

PROCEEDINGS—U.S. Naval Institute, Annapolis, MD 21402. Clayton R. Barrow, Jr., Ed. Short humorous anecdotes for members of Navy, Marine Corps, and Coast Guard profession. Pays $25, on acceptance.

READER'S DIGEST—Pleasantville, NY 10570. Anecdotes, for "Life in These United States," "Humor in Uniform," "Campus Comedy" and "All in a Day's Work." Pays $300, on publication. Short items for "Toward More Picturesque Speech." Pay $40, $35 for reprints. Anecdotes for "Laughter, the Best Medicine," "Personal Glimpses," etc. Pays $20 per two-column line ($35 for reprints). No submissions acknowledged or returned. Consult anecdote page in each issue for additional guidelines.

ROAD KING—P.O. Box 250, Park Forest, IL 60466. Address Features Ed. Trucking-related cartoons for "Loads of Laughs"; anecdotes to 200 words, for "Trucker's Life." Pays $25 for cartoons, $25 for anecdotes, on publication. SASE required.

ROLL CALL—201 Mass. Ave. N.E., Washington, DC 20002. Sidney Yudain, Ed. Humorous items on Congress; anecdotes; quips. Pays on acceptance.

RX BEING WELL—800 Second Ave., New York, NY 10017. Fillers, 300

673

to 500 words, on health, nutrition, sports medicine, disease prevention, and related topics. Pays a few weeks after acceptance.

SACRAMENTO—P.O. Box 2424, Sacramento, CA 95811. Humor for "Fools Rush In," 850 to 1,750 words. "City Lights," interesting and unusual people, places, and behind-the-scenes news items, 75 to 250 words. All material must have California tie-in. Pays on acceptance.

THE SATURDAY EVENING POST—1100 Waterway Blvd., Indianapolis, IN 46202. Ted Kreiter, Exec. Ed. Humor and satire, 1,500 to 2,000 words; cartoons, jokes, for "Post Scripts," short quizzes. Pays varying rates, on publication.

SCIENCE 85—1101 Vermont Ave., 10th Fl., N.W., Washington, DC 20005. Susan Williams, Ass't. Ed. Short features on the science of sports, news items, scientific discoveries, and scientific curiosities and mysteries. Pays $150 to $800, on acceptance. Query.

SCORE, CANADA'S GOLF MAGAZINE—287 MacPherson Ave., Toronto, Ont., Canada M4V 1A4. Fillers, 50 to 100 words, related to Canadian golf scene. Pays $10 to $25, on publication.

SHENANDOAH/VIRGINIA TOWN & COUNTRY—See *The Virginian*.

SKIING MAGAZINE—One Park Ave., New York, NY 10016. Alfred H. Greenberg, Ed.-in-Chief. Articles, to 600 words, on skiing; humorous vignettes, fillers on skiing oddities. Pays from 15¢ a word, on acceptance. Query.

SLIMMER—3420 Ocean Park Blvd., Suite 3000, Santa Monica, CA 90405. Kathleen Dantini, Art Dir. Sophisticated cartoons dealing with diet and exercise. Pays $50, on publication.

SMALL FARMER'S JOURNAL—P.O. Box 2805, Eugene, OR 97402. Humor, 500 to 1,000 words, for farmers who use horses on the farm. Pay rates vary, on publication.

SMALL WORLD—Volkswagen of America, Troy, MI 48099. Ed Rabinowitz, Ed. Anecdotes, to 100 words, about Volkswagen owners' experiences; cartoons, humorous photos of Volkswagens. Pays from $15, on acceptance.

SNOWMOBILE—715 Florida Ave., Suite 306, Minneapolis, MN 55426. C. J. Ramstad, Ed. Dick Hendricks, Man. Ed. Short humor and cartoons on snowmobiling and winter snowmobiling, "Personality Plates" sighted. Pays varying rates, on publication.

SOUTHERN EXPOSURE—P.O. Box 531, Durham, NC 27702. Michael Yellin, Ed. Fillers on civil rights, black politics, nuclear power, utility reform, labor education and organizing, land use, southern women, etc. Pays from $50, on publication.

SPORTS AFIELD—250 W. 55th St., New York, NY 10019. Unusual, useful tips, 100 to 500 words, for "Almanac" section: hunting, fishing, camping, boating, etc. Photos. Pays $10 per column inch, on publication.

SPORTS PARADE—1720 Washington Blvd., Ogden, UT 84404. Wayne DeWald, Ed. Short pieces, 200 to 400 words, of wide appeal to sports fans, on any participant sport. Pays 15¢ a word, on acceptance. Query.

SUNDAY DIGEST—850 N. Grove Ave., Elgin, IL 60120. Inspirational anecdotes, short humor (500 words). Writers guidelines on request. Pays 7¢ to 10¢ a word, on acceptance.

TAMPA BAY MONTHLY—2502 Rocky Point Rd., Suite 295, Tampa, FL 33607. Shorts, 300 to 1,200 words, on Tampa area. Pays good rates, on publication. Query.

TEENAGE—P.O. Box 948, Lowell, MA 01853. Jokes and humorous fillers for older teenagers. Categories: "A for Effort," "Excuses, Excuses," "Bloopers and Head Aches," and "Great Moments in High School." Pays $25, on publication. Send c/o Insanity Please Editor.

TODAY'S CHRISTIAN PARENT—8121 Hamilton Ave., Cincinnati, OH 45231. Mildred Mast, Ed. Refreshing insights into everyday happenings in the family; short items on Christian living, for "Happenings at Our House." Ideas for family devotions. Appropriate short sayings and anecdotes, serious or humorous. Pays varying rates, on acceptance. Self-addressed, stamped envelope required for return of material.

TODAY'S OR NURSE—6900 Grove Rd., Thorofare, NJ 08086. Judith B. Paquet, Ed. Short humor, 500 words, for operating room nurses. Pays 10¢ a word, on publication. Query.

TOUCH—Box 7244, Grand Rapids, MI 49510. Carol Smith, Man. Ed. Fillers, puzzles, for Christian girls aged 8 to 14. Pays 2¢ a word, on acceptance.

TRAILER BOATS—P.O. Box 2307, Gardena, CA 90248. Jim Youngs, Ed. Fillers and humor, preferably with illustrations, on boating and related activities. Pays 7¢ to 10¢ a word, on publication.

TRUE CONFESSIONS—215 Lexington Ave., New York, NY 10016. Barbara J. Brett, Ed. Warm, inspirational first-person fillers, 300 to 700 words, about love, marriage and family life for "The Feminine Side of Things." Pays after publication. Buys all rights.

TRUE STORY—215 Lexington Ave., New York, NY 10016. Short personal-experience pieces for "Women Are Wonderful." Kids' cute sayings; light verse. Pays from 5¢ a word, on publication.

THE VIRGINIAN (formerly *Shenandoah/Virginia Town & Country*)—P.O. Box 8, New Hope, VA 24469. Hunter S. Pierce, IV, Ed. Dir. Fillers relating to Virginia and adjacent region of the South. Anecdotes and nostalgic pieces preferred. Pays varying rates, on publication. Include SASE.

WESTART—Box 1396, Auburn, CA 95603. Martha Garcia, Ed. Features and current news items, 350 to 500 words, on fine arts. No hobbies. Pays 50¢ per column inch, on publication.

THE WESTERN BOATMAN—16427 S. Avalon, P.O. Box 2307, Gardena, CA 90248. Humor and jokes, 100 to 300 words, for boating enthusiasts in the West. Pays 10¢ a word, on publication.

WESTERN MASSACHUSETTS MAGAZINE—P.O. Box 76, Northampton, MA 01061-0076. Michael R. Evans, Man. Ed. Fillers, 50 to 200 words, on interesting Western Massachusetts information. Pays from $20, on acceptance.

WINE WEST—P.O. Box 498, Geyserville, CA 95441. Fillers and short humor related to the wine industry. Pays $2.50 per column inch, on publication.

WINNING—15115 S. 76 E. Ave., Bixby, OK 74008. Short pieces, 600 to 900 words, on winning contest sweepstakes, positive thinking, hobbies, and creative ways to make money. Pays 5¢ a word, on publication.

675

WOMAN—1115 Broadway, New York, NY 10010. Sherry Amatenstein, Ed. Short newsbreaks on medical and legal advances for women for "Let's Put Our Heads Together." Pays on acceptance. Query.

WOMAN'S DAY—1515 Broadway, New York, NY 10036. Short items on instructive family experiences and tips, for "Neighbors"; practical suggestions for homemakers. Pays $50, on publication.

WOMEN'S SPORTS AND FITNESS—310 Town and Country Village, Palo Alto, CA 94301. Short pieces, on nutrition, beauty, health, and new products for the active woman; timely sports-related news items; short profiles of up-and-coming female athletes or other female sports figures; book reviews; opinion pieces. Pays from $25, on publication.

WOOD 'N ENERGY—P.O. Box 2008, Laconia, NH 03247. Kenneth Daggett, Ed. Fillers, 200 to 500 words, related to wood and coal heating and other alternative energy sources. Pays on publication.

YACHTING—P.O. Box 1200, 5 River Rd., Cos Cob, CT 06807. Deborah Meisel, Asst. Ed. Fillers, for yachtsmen interested in powerboats and sailboats. Pays on acceptance.

YOGA JOURNAL—1054 University Ave., Berkeley, CA 94704. Stephan Bodian, Ed. Humor, 250 to 1,000 words, with a yoga slant. Pays from $15, on publication.

YOUNG MISS—685 Third Ave., New York, NY 10017. Phyllis Schneider, Ed. First-person, humorous fillers, to 850 words, on any aspect of adolescence: early or late blooming, boy-girl relationships, school, part-time jobs, getting along with siblings, dieting, etc. Serious fillers, to 850 words, on typical teen concerns: shyness, loneliness, popularity, self-confidence, etc. Teen quotes. Professional advice. Pays on acceptance.

JUVENILE, TEEN-AGE AND YOUNG ADULT MAGAZINES

JUVENILE MAGAZINES

ACTION—Dept. of Christian Education, Free Methodist Headquarters, 901 College Ave., Winona Lake, IN 46590. Vera Bethel, Ed. Stories, 1,000 words for 9- to 11-year-olds. How-to features, 200 to 500 words. Verse. Seasonal material. Pays $25 for stories, $15 for features with photos or sketch. $5 for poetry, on publication.

AHOY! THE CHILDREN'S MAGAZINE—P.O. Box 5174, Armdale, Nova Scotia B3L 4M7 Canada. Mr. Dana Phillip Doiron, Ed. Articles and fiction, 1,000 to 1,800 words, for children 8 to 12 years old. Pays $30 to $70, on acceptance. Enclose international reply coupons for return of material.

CHICKADEE—The Young Naturalist Foundation, 59 Front St., E. Toronto, Ont., Canada M5E 1B3. Janis Nostbakken, Ed. Animal and adventure stories, 500 to 1,000 words, for children aged 3 to 8. Also, puzzles, activities and observation games, 50 to 300 words. Pays varying rates, on publication. Send complete manuscript and International postal coupons. No outlines.

CHILD LIFE—1100 Waterway Blvd., P.O. Box 567, Indianapolis, IN 46206. Steve Charles, Ed. Articles, 500 to 1,200 words, especially on health and nutrition, safety, and exercise, for 7- to 9-year-olds. General fiction and humor stories, to 1,600 words. Health-related puzzles, Photos. Pays about 4¢ a word, extra for photos, on publication. Buys all rights.

CHILDREN'S DIGEST—1100 Waterway Blvd., P.O. Box 567, Indianapolis, IN 46206. Kathleen B. Mosher, Ed. Health publication for children aged 8 to 10. Informative articles, 500 to 1,200 words, and fiction (especially realistic, adventure, mystery, and humorous), 500 to 1,800 words, with health, safety, exercise, nutrition, or hygiene as theme. Historical and biographical articles. Poetry. Pays 4¢ a word, from $5 for poems, on publication. Buys all rights.

CHILDREN'S PLAYMATE—Editorial Office, 1100 Waterway Blvd., P.O. Box 567, Indianapolis, IN 46206. Kathleen B. Mosher, Ed. Humorous and health-related short stories, about 600 words, for 5- to 7-year-olds. Simple science articles and how-to crafts pieces with brief instructions. "All About" features, about 500 words, on health, nutrition, safety, and exercise. Poems. Pays about 4¢ a word, $5 minimum for poetry, on publication.

THE CHRISTIAN SCIENCE MONITOR—One Norway St., Boston, MA 02115. Marilyn Gardner, Ed., "For Children" Page. Feature articles, fiction, and poetry, written by children up to 12 years old. Pays to $25, $5 for short articles and poems.

CLUBHOUSE—Berrien Springs, MI 49103. Elaine Meseraull, Ed. Action-oriented Christian stories: features, 1,000 to 1,200 words; "Story Cubes" and "Thinker Tales" (parables), about 800 words. Children in stories should be wise, brave, funny, kind, etc. Pays to $35 for features, $25 for parables, on acceptance.

COBBLESTONE—20 Grove St., Peterborough, NH 03458. Carolyn Yoder, Ed. Theme-Related biographies, and short accounts of historical events, to 1,200 words, for children aged 8 to 13 years. Fiction, 500 to 1,200 words. Poetry, to 100 lines. Photos. Pays 10¢ to 15¢ a word for prose, to $1.50 a line for poetry, on publication. Send SASE for editorial guidelines with monthly themes.

CRICKET—Box 100, La Salle, IL 61301. Marianne Carus, Ed.-in-Chief. Articles and fiction, 200 to 1,500 words, for 6- to 12-year-olds. Poetry, to 30 lines. Pays to 25¢ a word, to $3 a line for poetry, on publication. Send SASE for guidelines. Overstocked.

DASH—Christian Service Brigade, Box 150, Wheaton, IL 60189. Address David Leight. Articles, to 1,500 words, for 8- to 11-year-old boys, on Christian lifestyles, current events. Photo and photo essays. Cartoons. Adventure fiction. Pays 5¢ to 10¢ a word on publication.

DISCOVERIES—6401 The Paseo, Kansas City, MO 64131. Elizabeth M. Huffman, Ed. Stories, to 1,000 words, for 3rd to 6th graders, with Christian emphasis. Poetry, 4 to 20 lines. Cartoons. Pays 3.5¢ a word (2¢ a word for reprints), 25¢ a line for poetry (minimum of $2), on acceptance.

EBONY JR.!—820 S. Michigan Ave., Chicago, IL 60605. Marcia V. Roebuck-Hoard, Ed. Articles, 500 to 1,500 words, on careers, for 6- to 12-year-olds. Biographies of prominent blacks, in adventure-story format. Wholesome humor, mystery, science fiction and fantasy, 400 to 1,500 words. Verse, 5 to 50 words; riddles, games, jokes and puzzles, with emphasis on black heritage. Pays $75 to $200 for articles and fiction, $15 to $100 for poetry, $5 to $25 for fillers, on acceptance. Buys all rights or reprints.

ELECTRIC COMPANY MAGAZINE—See *3-2-1 Contact.*

677

ENTER MAGAZINE—See *3-2-1 Contact.*

THE FRIEND—50 E. North Temple, 23rd Fl., Salt Lake City, UT 84150. Vivian Paulsen, Man. Ed. Stories and articles, 1,000 to 1,200 words. "Tiny tot" stories, 300 to 700 words. Pays from 7¢ a word, from 45¢ a line for poetry, on acceptance.

HEALTH EXPLORER—1100 Waterway Blvd., P.O. Box 567, Indianapolis, IN 46206. Steve Charles, Ed. Articles, 1,000 words, for children aged 9 to 11, on nutrition, diet, exercise, disease and health fads, with emphasis on ways to improve and maintain health. Pays about 4¢ a word, on publication.

HIGHLIGHTS FOR CHILDREN—803 Church St., Honesdale, PA 18431. Kent L. Brown, Ed. Fiction and articles, to 900 words, for 3- to 12-year-olds. Fiction should have strong plot, believable characters, story that holds reader's interest from beginning to end. No crime or violence. For articles, cite references used and qualifications. Easy rebus-form stories. Easy-to-read stories, 400 to 600 words, with strong plots. Pays from 6¢ a word, on acceptance.

HUMPTY DUMPTY'S MAGAZINE—1100 Waterway Blvd., P.O. Box 567, Indianapolis, IN 46206. Christine French Clark, Ed. Health publication for children ages 4 to 6. Easy-to-read fiction, to 600 words, some with health and nutrition, safety, exercise, or hygiene as theme; humor and light approach preferred. Crafts with clear, brief instructions. Short poems. Stories-in-rhyme. Pays about 4¢ a word, from $5 for poems, on publication. Buys all rights.

JACK AND JILL—Box 567, Indianapolis, IN 46206. Christine French Clark, Ed. Articles, 500 to 1,000 words, for 6- to 8-year-olds, on sports, nature, science, health, safety, exercise. Features 1,000 to 1,200 words, on history, biography, life in other countries, etc. Fiction, to 1,200 words. Short poems, games, puzzles, projects. Photos. Pays about 4¢ a word, extra for photos, varying rates for fillers, on publication.

ODYSSEY—625 E. St. Paul Ave., Milwaukee, WI 53202. Nancy Mack, Ed. Features, 750 to 2,000 words, on astronomy, spacecraft, for 8- to 12-year-olds. Photos. Pays $100, extra for photos, on publication. Query.

ON THE LINE—616 Walnut, Scottdale, PA 15683. Helen Alderfer, Ed. Religious articles, 500 to 750 words, for 10- to 14-year-olds. Fiction, 800 to 1,200 words. Poetry, puzzles, cartoons. Pays to 4¢ a word (to 2¢ a word for reprints), on acceptance.

OUR LITTLE FRIEND—P.O. Box 7000, Mountain View, CA 94039. Louis Schutter, Ed. Seventh-day Adventist. Stories, 500 to 1,000 words, for 2- to 6-year-olds. Verse, 8 to 12 lines. Puzzles. Photos. Pays 1¢ a word, 10¢ a line for verse, on acceptance.

OWL—The Young Naturalist Foundation, 59 Front St., E. Toronto, Ont., Canada M5E 1B3. Sylvia Funston, Ed. Articles, 500 to 1,000 words, for children aged 8 to 12, on animals, science, people, places, experiments, etc. Should be informative but not preachy. Pays varying rates, on publication. Send brief outline and International reply coupons.

PENNYWHISTLE PRESS—Box 500-P, Washington, DC 20044. Anita Sama, Ed. Short fiction, 850 words for 8- to 12-year-old children, 400 words for 5- to 8-year-olds. Puzzles and word games. Payment varies, on publication.

PLAYS, THE DRAMA MAGAZINE FOR YOUNG PEOPLE—120 Boylston St., Boston, MA 02116. Elizabeth Preston, Man. Ed. Needs one-act plays, programs, skits, creative dramatic material, suitable for school productions at junior high, middle and lower grade levels. Plays with one set preferred. Uses comedies, dramas, satires, farces, melodramas, dramatized classics, folktales and fairy tales, puppet plays. Pays good rates, on acceptance. Send SASE for manuscript specification sheet. Buys all rights.

PRIMARY TREASURE—P.O. Box 7000, Mountain View, CA 94039. Louis Schutter, Ed. Seventh-day Adventist. Stories, 600 to 1,200 words, for 7- to 9-year-olds. Verse, 8 to 12 lines. Puzzles. Photos. Pays 1¢ a word, 10¢ a line for verse, on acceptance.

RADAR—8121 Hamilton Ave., Cincinnati, OH 45231. Margaret Williams, Ed. Articles, 400 to 650 words, on nature, hobbies, crafts. Short stories, 900 to 1,100 words: mystery, sports, school, family, with 12-year-old as main character; serials of 2,000 words. Christian emphasis. Poems to 12 lines. Pays to 2¢ a word, to 35¢ a line for poetry, on acceptance. Send SASE for guidelines and sample issue.

RANGER RICK—1412 16th St. N.W., Washington, DC 20036. Trudy Farrand, Ed. Articles, to 900 words on wildlife, conservation, natural sciences, and nature crafts, for 6- to 12-year-olds. Nature-related fiction welcome. Features on children involved with nature. Games and puzzles. Pays to $350, on acceptance. Buys all rights.

SESAME STREET MAGAZINE—See *3-2-1 Contact.*

STONE SOUP, THE MAGAZINE BY CHILDREN—Box 83, Santa Cruz, CA 95063. Gerry Mandel, Ed. Stories, poems, plays, book reviews by children under 13. Pays in copies.

STORY FRIENDS—Mennonite Publishing House, Scottdale, PA 15683. Marjorie Waybill, Ed. Stories, 350 to 800 words, for 4- to 9-year-olds, on Christian faith and values in everyday experiences. Quizzes, riddles. Poetry. Pays to 3¢ a word, to $5 per poem, on acceptance.

3-2-1 CONTACT—Children's Television Workshop, 1 Lincoln Plaza, New York, NY 10023. Jonathan Rosenbloom, Ed. Entertaining articles, 600 to 1,000 words, on all aspects of science, scientists, and children who are learning about or practicing science for 8- to 12-year-olds. Pays $75 to $300, on acceptance. No fiction. Also publishes *Enter Magazine, Electric Company Magazine,* and *Sesame Street Magazine.* Query.

TOUCH—Box 7244, Grand Rapids, MI 49510. Carol Smith, Man. Ed. Upbeat fiction and features, 1,000 to 1,500 words for Christian girls age 8 to 14; personal life, nature, crafts. Poetry; fillers, puzzles. Pay 2¢ word, extra for photos, on acceptance. Query for theme with SASE.

TRAILS—Box 788, Wheaton, IL 60189. LoraBeth Norton, Ed. Publication of Pioneer Ministries. Christian articles and fiction, to 1,500 words, for 7- to 12-year-old children. Quizzes, games, crafts. Pays about 3¢ a word, on acceptance.

TURTLE MAGAZINE FOR PRESCHOOL KIDS—1100 Waterway Blvd., Box 567, Indianapolis, IN 46206. Beth Wood Thomas, Ed. Stories about safety, exercise, health, and nutrition, for preschoolers. Fiction, 600 words. Simple poems. Stories-in-rhyme; easy-to-read stories, to 500 words, for beginning readers. Pays about 4¢ a word, on publication. Buys all rights.

WEE WISDOM—Unity Village, MO 64065. Colleen Zuck, Ed. Character-building stories, to 800 words, for 6- to 12-year-olds. Pays 3¢ to 4¢ per word, on acceptance.

WONDER TIME—6401 The Paseo, Kansas City, MO 64131. Evelyn J. Beals, Ed. Stories, 200 to 600 words, for 6- to 8-year-olds, with Christian emphasis to correlate with Sunday School curriculum. Features, to 300 words, on nature, crafts, etc. Poetry, 4 to 12 lines. Pays 3½¢ a word, from 25¢ a line for verse, $2.50 minimum, on acceptance.

YABA WORLD—5301 S. 76th St., Greendale, WI 53129. Jean Yeager, Ed. Articles, 1,500 words, on Young American Bowling Alliance league or tournament bowling. Profiles; how-to's. Photos. Pays $25 to $100, extra for photos, on acceptance. Query preferred.

YOUNG CRUSADER—1730 Chicago Ave., Evanston, IL 60201. Michael Vitucci, Ed. Character-building stories, 600 to 800 words, for 6-to 12-year-olds. Pays ½¢ a word, on publication.

YOUNG JUDEAN—50 W. 58th St., New York, NY 10019. Mordecai Newman, Ed. Articles, 500 to 1,000 words, with photos, for 9- to 12-year-olds, on Israel, Jewish holidays, Jewish-American life, Jewish history. Fiction, 800 to 1,500 words, on Jewish themes. Poetry, from 8 lines. Fillers, humor, reviews. Pays $10 per printed page.

TEEN-AGE, YOUNG ADULT MAGAZINES

ALIVE!—Christian Board of Publication, Box 179, St. Louis, MO 63166. Mike Dixon, Ed. Fiction, to 1,200 words, for junior-high-age young people. First-person articles, to 1,200 words, with photos, on interesting youths, projects and activities. Poetry, to 16 lines. Cartoons, puzzles, brain-teasers. Pays 2¢ a word, extra for photos, 25¢ a line for poetry, extra for cartoons, on publication.

ALIVE NOW!—P.O. Box 189, Nashville, TN 37202. Mary Ruth Coffman, Ed. Short essays, 250 to 400 words, with Christian emphasis. Poetry, one page. Photos. Pays $5 to $20, on publication.

AMERICAN NEWSPAPER CARRIER—P.O. Box 15300, Winston-Salem, NC 27103. Marilyn Rollins, Ed. Light fiction, 1,800 to 2,000 words, for 14- to 17-year-old newspaper carriers; mystery, adventure, etc. Inspirational articles, editorials. Pays $10 to $25, on acceptance.

THE BLACK COLLEGIAN—1240 S. Broad, New Orleans, LA 70125. James Borders, Ed. Articles, 500 to 2,500 words, on career opportunities, job hunting, financial aid, and other issues concerning Black students. Pays $25 to $350, on publication.

BOP—7060 Hollywood Blvd., Suite 720, Hollywood, CA 90028. Kerry Laufer, Ed. Interviews and features, 1,000 to 2,000 words, for teenage girls, on stars popular with teenagers. Fillers, jokes. Photos. Pays varying rates, on acceptance. Query preferred.

BOYS' LIFE—1325 Walnut Hill Lane, Irving, TX 75062. Robert E. Hood, Ed. Publication of Boy Scouts of America. Articles, 300 to 1,500 words, and fiction, 1,000 or 2,500 to 3,200 words, for 8- to 18-year-old boys. Photos. Pays from $250 for articles, from $350 for fiction, on acceptance. Query for articles.

CAMPUS LIFE—465 Gundersen Dr., Carol Stream, IL 60188. Gregg Lewis, Ed. Articles reflecting Christian values and world view, for high school and college students. Humor and general fiction. Photo essays, cartoons. Pays from $150, on acceptance. Limited free-lance market.

THE CHRISTIAN ADVENTURER—P.O. Box 850, Joplin, MO 64802. Rosmarie Foreman, Ed. Fiction, 1,500 to 1,800 words, for 13- to 19-year-olds, on Christian living. Fillers. Pays 1¢ a word, quarterly.

CIRCLE K MAGAZINE—3636 Woodview Trace, Indianapolis, IN 46268. Chuck Jonak, Exec. Ed. In-depth features on subjects of interest to service-minded college students, and family-related subjects: communication, housing, nutrition, future jobs, community involvement, etc. B/W photos. Pays $150 to $275, on acceptance. Query preferred.

CURRENT CONSUMER & LIFESTUDIES—3500 Western Ave., Highland Park, IL 60035. Margaret Mucklo, Ed. Practical, well-researched articles, 1,000 to 1,200 words, for high school students, on family living, interpersonal relationships, and consumer topics. Pays $100, on publication. Queries only; no unsolicited manuscripts accepted.

ENTER—Children's Television Workshop, 1 Lincoln Plaza, New York, NY 10023. Jim Lewis, Senior Ed. "We buy human-interest articles, profiles of kids and adults using computers and new technology in interesting ways, as well as computer programs, word hunts, computer-related puzzles or games, and fiction. We pay $300 to $500 for features, 1,000 to 1,500 words, on acceptance."

EXPLORING—1325 Walnut Hill Ln., Irving, TX 75062. Scott Daniels, Exec. Ed. Publication of Boy Scouts of America. Articles, 500 to 1,800 words, for 15- to 21-year-olds, on education, careers, Explorer post activities (hiking, canoeing, camping), and program ideas for Explorer post meetings. No controversial subjects. Pays $150 to $400, on acceptance. Query. Send SASE for guidelines.

FREEWAY—Box 632, Glen Ellyn, IL 60138. Cindy Atoji, Ed. First-person true stories, trend pieces, how-to's, personality profiles, and humor, to 1,000 words, with photos, for 15- to 21-year-olds. Christian emphasis. Pays to 8¢ a word.

GRIT—Williamsport, PA 17701. Joanne Decker, National Ed. Articles, 300 to 500 words, with photos, on young people involved in unusual hobbies, occupations, athletic pursuits, and personal adventures. Pays 12¢ a word, extra for photos, on acceptance.

HICALL—1445 Boonville Ave., Springfield, MO 65802. William P. Campbell, Ed. Articles, 500 to 1,000 words, and fiction, to 1,800 words, for 12- to 19-year olds; strong evangelical emphasis. Pays on acceptance.

IN TOUCH—Box 2000, Marion, IN 46952. Articles, 1,200 to 1,500 words, on contemporary issues, athletes and singers from conservative Christian perspective, for 13- to 18-year-olds. Pays 2¢ to 3¢ a word. Send SASE for guidelines and sample copy. No queries.

KEYNOTER—3636 Woodview Trace, Indianapolis, IN 46268. Melinda A. Dunlevy, Ed. Articles, 1,000 to 2,500 words, for high school leaders: general-interest features; self-help; pieces on contemporary teen-age problems. Photos. Pays $75 to $200, extra for photos, on acceptance. Query preferred.

681

LIGHTED PATHWAY—922 Montgomery Ave., Cleveland, TN 37311. Hoyt E. Stone, Ed. Human-interest and inspirational articles, 1,200 to 1,600 words, for teen-agers. Short pieces, 600 to 800 words. Fiction, 1,500 to 1,800 words. Pays 2¢ to 4¢ a word, on acceptance.

THE NATIONAL FUTURE FARMER—Box 15160, Alexandria, VA 22309. Michael Wilson, Man. Ed. Articles, to 1,000 words, preferably with photos, for agriculture students aged 14 to 21, on activities of Future Farmers of America, new developments in agriculture, and general-interest subjects. Pays from 4¢ a word, on acceptance. Query.

NEW ERA—50 E. North Temple, Salt Lake City, UT 84150. Brian Kelley, Ed. Articles, 150 to 3,000 words, and fiction, to 3,000 words, for young Mormons. Poetry. Photos. Pays 3¢ to 10¢ a word, 25¢ a line for poetry, on acceptance. Query.

NUTSHELL—505 Market St., Knoxville, TN 37902. Keith Bellows, Group Ed. Self-help and feature articles, 1,500 to 3,000 words, on subjects of interest to college students. Photos. Pays 10¢ to 20¢ a word, extra for photos, on acceptance. Send SASE for guidelines.

PROBE—1548 Poplar Ave., Memphis, TN 38104. Timothy C. Seanor, Ed. Southern Baptist. Articles, to 1,500 words, for 12- and 17-year-old-boys, on teen problems, current events. Photo essays on Baptist sports personalities. Pays 3½¢ a word, extra for photos, on acceptance.

SCHOLASTIC SCOPE—730 Broadway, New York, NY 10003. Katherine Robinson, Ed. For 15- to 18-year-olds with 4th to 6th grade reading ability. Realistic fiction, 400 to 1,200 words, and plays, to 6,000 words, on teen problems. Profiles, 400 to 800 words, of interesting teenagers, with black and white photos. Pays $100 for 500- to 600-word articles and short stories, from $150 for longer pieces, on acceptance.

SEVENTEEN—850 Third Ave., New York, NY 10022. Midge Turk Richardson, Ed. Articles, to 2,500 words, on subjects of interest to teens. Sophisticated, well-written fiction, 2,500 to 3,500 words, for young adults. Poetry, to 15 lines, by teens. Short news and features, to 750 words, for "Mini-Mag." Articles, 1,000 words, by teens, for "Your Words." Short pieces, to 200 words, by teens, for "Free for All." Pays varying rates, on acceptance.

SPRINT—850 N. Grove St., Elgin, IL 60120. Kristine Miller Tomasik, Ed. Feature articles, 800 to 1,000 words, for junior high Sunday school students, on church/community projects involving teens, teen problems, and personalities. Fiction, 1,000 to 1,200 words, with realistic characters and dialogue. Poetry. Photos. Pays to $100, extra for photos, on acceptance. Submit seasonal material one year in advance. Buys all rights. Query for nonfiction.

STRAIGHT—8121 Hamilton Ave., Cincinnati, OH 45231. Dawn Brettschneider, Ed. Devotional pieces, features on current situations and issues, humor, for Christian teens. Well constructed fiction, 1,000 to 1,500 words, showing teens using Christian principles. Poetry, by teen-agers. Cartoons, photos. Pays about 2¢ a word, on acceptance.

'TEEN MAGAZINE—8490 Sunset Blvd., Los Angeles, CA 90069. Overstocked.

TEEN POWER—Box 632, Glen Ellyn, IL 60138. Christopher Grant, Ed. First person (as told to), true teen experience stories with Christian insights and conclusion, 1,100 words. Include photos. Pays 4¢ to 7¢ a word, extra for photos, on acceptance.

TEENAGE—P.O. Box 948, Lowell, MA 01853. Bill Weber, Ed.-in-Chief. Articles, profiles, interviews, short news reports, essays, humor, celebrity interviews, 500 to 2,000 words, on topics of vital interest to sophisticated teens: sex, relationships, college, careers, sports and fitness, dating, health, money, computers, drugs and alcohol, examples of achievement and leadership among peers, advice on "making it" in the adult world. Some preference given to high school and college-age writers; fiction accepted only from students. Pays $25 to $500, on acceptance.

TIGER BEAT—105 Union Ave., Cresskill, NJ 07626. Nancie S. Martin, Ed. Articles, to 4 pages, on young people in show business and music industry. Teen romance fiction, to 1,000 words. Self-help articles. Pays varying rates, on acceptance. Query. Unsolicited manuscripts sent without SASE will not be returned.

TIGER BEAT PRESENTS ROCK!—105 Union Ave., Cresskill, NJ 07626. Nancie S. Martin, Ed. Articles, to 4 pages, on well-known pop and rock stars. Pays varying rates, on acceptance. Query with SASE.

VENTURE—Box 150, Wheaton, IL 60189. Address David Leight. Articles, 1,500 words, for 12- to 18-year-old boys, on Christian living, contemporary issues. Adventure fiction, true stories. Photos, photo essays; cartoons. Pays 5¢ to 10¢ a word, on publication.

WRITING!—3500 Western Ave., Highland Park, IL 60035. Bonnie Bekken, Ed. Interviews, 1,200 words, for "Writers at Work" department, for high school students. Pays $100, on publication. Query.

YOUNG AMBASSADOR—Box 82808, Lincoln, NE 68501. David Lambert, Man. Ed. Articles and fiction, to 1,800 words, for Christian teens. B/W photos and color slides. Pays 4¢ to 10¢ a word, extra for photos, on publication.

YOUNG AND ALIVE—4444 S. 52nd St., Lincoln, NE 68506. Richard Kaiser, Ed. Feature articles and fiction, 800 to 1,400 words, for blind and visually impaired young adults, on adventure, biography, camping, health, hobbies, and travel. Photos. Pays 3¢ to 5¢ a word, extra for photos, on acceptance. Write for guidelines.

YOUNG MISS—685 Third Ave., New York, NY 10017. Phyllis Schneider, Ed.-in-Chief. Features, 1,500 to 2,000 words, on topics of interest to 12- to 17-year-old girls: personal growth, relationships, dilemmas unique to adolescence, etc. Address queries to Deborah Purcell, Features/Fiction Ed.

RELIGIOUS AND DENOMINATIONAL MAGAZINES

ADVANCE—1445 Boonville Ave., Springfield, MO 65802. Gwen Jones, Ed. Articles, 1,200 words, slanted to ministers, on preaching, doctrine, practice; how-to-do-it features. Pays 2¢ to 3¢ a word, on acceptance.

683

AGLOW MAGAZINE—P.O. Box 1, Lynnwood, WA 98046. Gwen Weising, Man. Ed. Articles, 1,000 to 2,000 words, written in first person by women of all ages: either a testimony of or teaching about Jesus as Savior, as baptizer in the Holy Spirit, as healer, or as guide and strength in everyday circumstances. Pays to 8¢ a word, on acceptance.

AMERICA—106 W. 56 St., New York, NY 10019. George W. Hunt, S.J., Ed. Articles, 1,000 to 2,500 words on current affairs, family life, literary trends. Pays $75 to $150, on acceptance.

AMERICAN BIBLE SOCIETY RECORD—1865 Broadway, New York, NY 10023. Clifford P. Macdonald, Man. Ed. Material related to work of American Bible Society: translating, publishing, distributing. Pays on acceptance. Query.

AMIT WOMAN—817 Broadway, New York, NY 10003. Micheline Ratzerdorfer, Ed. Articles, 1,000 to 2,000 words, of interest to Jewish women: Middle East, Israel, history, holidays, travel. Pays to $50, on publication.

ANNALS OF ST. ANNE DE BEAUPRÉ—P.O. Box 1000, St. Anne de Beaupré, Quebec, Canada G0A 3C0. Roch Achard, C.Ss.R., Ed. Articles, 1,100 to 1,200 words, on Catholic subjects and on St. Anne. Pays 2¢ to 4¢ a word, on acceptance.

BAPTIST LEADER—P.O. Box 851, Valley Forge, PA 19482-0851. L. Isham, Ed. Articles, 750 to 1,600 words, on church-school work. Photos.

BREAD—6401 The Paseo, Kansas City, MO 64131. Gary Sivewright, Ed. Church of the Nazarene. Devotional, Bible study and Christian guidance articles, to 1,200 words, for teen-agers. Religious short stories, to 1,500 words; inspirational poetry, to 20 lines. Pays from 3¢ a word for prose, 25¢ per line for poetry, on acceptance.

BRIGADE LEADER—Box 150, Wheaton, IL 60189. David R. Leight, Man. Ed. Inspirational articles, 1,000 to 1,800 words, for Christian men who help boys. Pays $60 to $150. Query only.

CATECHIST—2451 E. River Rd., Dayton, OH 45439. Patricia Fischer, Ed. Informational and inspirational articles, 1,200 to 1,500 words, for Catholic teachers, coordinators, and administrators in religious education programs. Pays $25 to $75, on publication.

CATHOLIC DIGEST—P.O. Box 64090, St. Paul, MN 55164. Address Articles Ed. Articles, 2,000 to 2,500 words, on Catholic and general subjects. Fillers, to 300 words, on instances of kindness rewarded, for "Hearts Are Trumps"; accounts of good deeds, for "People Are Like That." Pays from $200 for original articles, $100 for reprints, on acceptance; $4 to $50 for fillers, on publication.

CATHOLIC LIFE—35750 Moravian Dr., Fraser, MI 48026. Robert C. Bayer, Ed. Articles, 600 to 1,200 words, on Catholic missionary work in Hong Kong, India, Latin America, Africa, etc. Photos. No fiction or poetry. Pays 4¢ a word, extra for photos, on publication.

CATHOLIC NEAR EAST MAGAZINE—1011 1st Ave., New York, NY 10022. Regina J. Clarkin, Ed. Articles, 1,000 to 1,800 words, on countries and culture of the Near East, and on the Eastern rites of the Church. Photos; color slides preferred. Pays 10¢ a word, on publication. Query.

CATHOLIC TWIN CIRCLE—6404 Wilshire Blvd., Suite 900, Los Angeles, CA 90048. Mary Louise Frawley, Ed. Stories and interviews of interest to Catholics, 1,000 to 1,500 words, with photos. Strict attention to Catholic doctrine required. Enclose SASE. Pays 8¢ a word, on publication.

CHARISMA—174 W. Comstock Ave., Suite 100, Winter Park, FL 32789. Howard Earl, Submissions Ed. Charismatic Christian articles, 2,000 to 3,000 words, for developing the spiritual life. Photos. Pays varying rates, on publication. Query.

CHESAPEAKE SHALOM—P.O. Box 789, Severna Park, MD 21146. Lee Irwin, Ed. General interest articles, 500 to 1,500 words, on Jewish life and leisure in the Chesapeake Bay region, as well as pieces on Jewish issues and "heartwarming" anecdotes of Jewish-American life. Pays $5 to $15, $2 to $10 for poetry, on publication.

CHRISTIAN BOOKSELLER—396 E. St. Charles Rd., Wheaton, IL 60188. Karen M. Ball, Ed. Articles, 1,500 to 2,000 words, for Christian booksellers, librarians, publishers, and suppliers, Interviews with Christian authors and recording artists. Photos with articles only. Pays $10 to $100, on publication. Query.

THE CHRISTIAN CENTURY—407 S. Dearborn St., Chicago, IL 60605. James M. Wall, Ed. Ecumenical. Articles, 1,500 to 2,500 words, with a religious angle, on political and social issues, international affairs, culture, the arts. Poetry, to 20 lines. Photos. Pays about $25 per printed page, extra for photos, on publication.

CHRISTIAN HERALD—Chappaqua, NY 10514. David Kucharsky, Ed. Interdenominational. Articles, personal-experience pieces, to 1,500 words, on biblically-oriented topics. Short verse. Pays from 10¢ a word for full-length features, from $10 for short pieces, after acceptance. Query first.

CHRISTIAN HOME—Box 189, 1908 Grand Ave., Nashville, TN 37202. Articles, 90 to 1,600 words, on parenting, marriage, and devotional life. Fiction, 1,000 to 1,800 words, Pays 4¢ to 5¢ a word, on acceptance.

CHRISTIAN LIFE MAGAZINE—396 E. St. Charles Rd., Wheaton, IL 60188. Janice Franzen, Exec. Ed. Articles, 1,500 to 2,500 words, on evangelical subjects, Christian living, and Christians in politics, sports, and entertainment. Photos. Fiction, 1,500 to 2,500 words, on problems faced by Christians. Pays to $150, on publication.

CHRISTIAN LIVING—850 N. Grove Ave., Elgin, IL 60102. Anne E. Dinnan, Assoc. Ed. Weekly paper for evangelical and mainline Christian teens. Articles, and fiction, to 1,200 words, that challenge, interest, and inspire teens to spiritual growth. Taboos: obscenity, sexual scenes, heavy moralizing and preachiness. Pays 6¢ to 9¢ a word, on acceptance.

CHRISTIAN SINGLE—127 Ninth Ave. N., Nashville, TN 37234. Cliff Allbritton, Ed. Articles, 600 to 1,200 words, on leisure activities, inspiring personal experiences, for Christian singles. Humor. Pays 4¢ a word, on acceptance. Query.

CHRISTIANITY TODAY—465 Gundersen Dr., Carol Stream, IL 60188. V. Gilbert Beers, Ed. Doctrinal, social issues and interpretive essays, 1,500 to 3,000 words, from evangelical Protestant perspective. Pays $300 to $500, on acceptance.

CHURCH ADMINISTRATION—127 Ninth Ave. N., Nashville, TN 37234, George Clark, Ed. Southern Baptist. How-to articles, 750 to 1,500 words, on administrative planning, staffing, organization and financing. Pays 4¢ a word, on acceptance.

CHURCH & STATE—8120 Fenton St., Silver Spring, MD 20910. Joseph L. Conn, Man. Ed. Articles, 600 to 2,600 words, on religious liberty and church-state relations issues. Pays varying rates, on acceptance. Query.

CHURCH EDUCATOR—765 Penarth Ave., Walnut, CA 91789. Robert C. Davidson, Ed. Articles, 200 to 3,000 words, with a "person-centered" approach to Christian education. How-to's for adult and juvenile Christian education. Pays from 3¢ to 5¢ a word, on publication.

THE CHURCH HERALD—1324 Lake Drive S.E., Grand Rapids, MI 49506. John Stapert, Ed. Reformed Church in America. Articles, 500 to 1,500 words, on Christianity and culture, politics, marriage and home. Children's stories. Pays 3¢ to 4¢ a word, on acceptance.

THE CHURCH MUSICIAN—127 Ninth Ave. N., Nashville, TN 37234. W. M. Anderson, Ed. Humorous fillers with a musical slant, for southern Baptist music leaders. No clippings. Pays about 4¢ a word, on acceptance. Same address and requirements for *Glory Songs* (for adults), and *Opus One* and *Opus Two* (for teen-agers).

THE CHURCHMAN—1074 23rd Ave. N., St. Petersburg, FL 33704. Edna Ruth Johnson, Ed. Articles, to 1,000 words, which offer humanistic approach to religion, ethics, and education. Pays in copies. Sample copy sent on request.

THE CIRCUIT RIDER—P.O. Box 801, Nashville, TN 37202. Richard Peck, Ed. Articles for United Methodist Pastors, 800 to 1,600 words. Pays $25 to $100, on acceptance. Query, with SASE, preferred.

COLUMBIA—Box 1670, New Haven, CT 06507. Elmer Von Feldt, Ed. Knights of Columbus. Articles, 2,500 to 3,500 words, for Catholic families. Must be accompanied by color photos or transparencies. No fiction. Pays to $750 for articles and photos, on acceptance.

COMMENTARY—165 E. 56th St., New York, NY 10022. Norman Podhoretz, Ed. Articles, 5,000 to 7,000 words, on contemporary issues, Jewish affairs, social sciences, religious thought, culture. Serious fiction; book reviews. Pays on publication.

COMMONWEAL—232 Madison Ave., New York, NY 10016, Peter Steinfels, Ed. Catholic. Articles, to 3,000 words, on political, religious, social and literary subjects. Pays 2¢ a word, on acceptance.

CONTEMPORARY CHRISTIAN MAGAZINE—P.O. Box 6300, Laguna Hills, CA 92654. Articles that reflect a Christian lifestyle for "baby boom" generation, with a Christian world view of the arts, especially contemporary forms of music. Personality features, interviews and profiles of contemporary Christians; news, social and spiritual articles. Reviews. Pays 8¢ a word, on publication. Query required. Send for guidelines.

DAILY MEDITATION—Box 2710, San Antonio, TX 78299. Ruth S. Paterson, Ed. Inspirational nonsectarian articles, 650 to 2,000 words. Fillers, to 350 words; verse, to 20 lines, Pays ½¢ to 1½¢ a word, 14¢ a line for verse, on acceptance.

DECISION—Billy Graham Evangelistic Association, 1300 Harmon Pl., Minneapolis, MN 55403. Roger C. Palms, Ed. Articles, Christian testimonials,

1,800 to 2,200 words. Poems, 4 to 24 lines, preferably free verse; narratives, 200 to 800 words. Pays varying rates, on publication.

THE DISCIPLE—Box 179, St. Louis, MO 63166. James L. Merrell, Ed. Disciples of Christ. Articles on Christian living; devotionals, 150 words. Poetry; short humor. Pays $10 to $25 for articles, $2 to $10 for poetry, on publication.

DISCOVERIES—6401 The Paseo, Kansas City, MO 64131. Libby Huffman, Ed. Fiction for children, grades 3 to 6, 800 to 1,000 words, defining Christian experiences and demonstrating Christian values and beliefs. Pays 3½¢ a word for first rights, 2¢ a word for second rights, on acceptance. Query.

ENGAGE/SOCIAL ACTION MAGAZINE—100 Maryland Ave. N.E., Washington, DC 20002. Lee Ranck, Ed. Articles, 1,500 to 2,000 words, on social issues, for church-oriented audience.

THE EPISCOPALIAN—1930 Chestnut St., Philadelphia, PA 19103. Judy Foley, Man. Ed. Articles to 2,000 words, that show Episcopalians solving problems; action stories; profiles. Pays $25 to $100, on publication.

THE EVANGEL—901 College Ave., Winona Lake, IN 46590. Vera Bethel, Ed., Free Methodist. Personal-experience articles, 1,000 words. Short, devotional items, 300 to 500 words. Fiction, 1,200 words, on Christian solutions to problems. Serious poetry, 8 to 12 lines. Pays $25 for articles, $35 to $40 for fiction, $5 for poetry, on publication. Return postage required.

EVANGELICAL BEACON—1515 E. 66th St., Minneapolis, MN 55423. George Keck, Ed. Evangelical Free Church. Articles, 250 to 1,750 words, on religious topics; testimonials; pieces on current issues from an evangelical perspective; short inspirational and evangelistic devotionals. Pays 3¢ a word, on publication. Send SASE for writers' guidelines.

FRIENDS JOURNAL—1501 Cherry St., Philadelphia, PA 19102. Vinton Deming, Editor-Manager. Articles, to 2,500 words. Pays in copies. Query.

THE FUNDAMENTALIST JOURNAL—Langehorn Plaza, Lynchburg, VA 24514. Deborah Huff, Ed. Articles, 800 to 2,500 words, that examine matters of contemporary interest to all Fundamentalists; new articles, profiles, human-interest pieces; moral and religious issues; Bible stories. Pays 10¢ a word, on publication.

GLORY SONGS—See *The Church Musician.*

GOOD NEWS BROADCASTER—Box 82808, Lincoln, NE 68501. Norman A. Olson, Man. Ed. Articles, to 1,500 words, on relating biblical truths to daily living. Photos. Pays 4¢ to 10¢ a word (3¢ a word for reprints), extra for photos, on acceptance. Query.

GOSPEL HERALD—616 Walnut Ave., Scottdale, PA 15683. Daniel Hertzler, Ed. Mennonite. Articles, to 1,500 words, on Christian experience. Poetry, to 10 lines. Pays on acceptance. Query for articles.

GUIDE—Review and Herald Publishing Co., 55 W. Oak Ridge Dr., Hagerstown, MD 21740. Stories and articles, 1,000 to 2,500 words, and poetry, to 12 lines, for Christian youth, ages 10 to 15. Pays 3¢ to 4¢ a word, on acceptance.

GUIDEPOSTS—747 Third Ave., New York, NY 10017. True first-person stories, 250 to 1,500 words, stressing how faith in God helps people cope with life. Anecdotal fillers, to 250 words. Pays $100 to $400, $10 to $25 for fillers, on acceptance.

687

HIS—P.O. Box 1450, Downers Grove, IL 60515. David Neff, Ed. Scripture-oriented articles, to 2,000 words, on Christian living in college, for students and faculty. Fiction. Humor. Biography. Pays 2¢ to 5¢ a word, on acceptance.

HOME LIFE—127 Ninth Ave. N., Nashville, TN 37234. Reuben Herring, Ed. Southern Baptist. Articles, preferably personal-experience, and fiction, to 2,000 words, on Christian marriage, parenthood, and family relationships. Human-interest pieces, 200 to 500 words; cartoons and short verse. Pays to 4¢ a word, on acceptance.

INSIDE—226 S. 16th St., Philadelphia, PA 19102. Jane Biberman, Ed. Articles, 1,500 to 3,000 words, and fiction, 2,000 to 3,000 words, of interest to Jewish men and women. Pays $100 to $500, on acceptance. Query.

INSIGHT—55 West Oak Ridge Dr., Hagerstown, MD 21740. Dan Fahrbach, Ed. Seventh-day Adventist. Personal-experience narratives and articles, to 1,800 words, for high school and college students. Parables; shorts. Pays 4¢ to 8¢ a word, extra for photos, on acceptance. Query.

INTERACTION—1333 S. Kirkwood Rd., St. Louis, MD 63122. Martha S. Jander, Acting Ed. Articles, 1,500 to 2,000 words, for Lutheran Sunday School teachers. Pays $5 to $35, on publication. Limited free-lance market.

THE JEWISH MONTHLY—B'nai B'rith, 1640 Rhode Island Ave. N.W., Washington, DC 20036. Marc Silver, Ed. Shorts, 200 to 800 words, and articles, 1,000 to 3,500 words, on contemporary Jewish topics. Pays 10¢ to 20¢ a word, on publication.

KEY TO CHRISTIAN EDUCATION—8121 Hamilton Ave., Cincinnati, OH 45231. Virginia Beddow, Ed. Articles, with photos, on teaching methods, and success stories, for workers in Christian education. Pays varying rates, on acceptance.

LIBERTY MAGAZINE—6840 Eastern Ave. N.W., Washington, DC 20012. Roland R. Hegstad, Ed. Timely articles, to 2,500 words, and photo essays, on religious freedom and church-state relations. Pays 6¢ to 8¢ a word, on acceptance. Query.

LIGHT AND LIFE—901 College Ave., Winona Lake, IN 46590. Lyn Cryderman, Ed. Fresh, lively articles about practical Christian living, and sound treatments of vital issues facing the Evangelical in contemporary society. Pays 3¢ a word, on publication. Query.

LIGUORIAN—Liguori, MO 63057. Rev. Norman J. Muckerman, Ed. Francine O'Connor, Man. Ed. Catholic. Articles and short stories, 1,500 to 2,000 words, on Christian values in modern life. Pays 7¢ to 10¢ a word, on acceptance. Buys all rights.

LIVE—1445 Boonville Ave., Springfield, MO 65802. Kenneth D. Barney, Adult Ed. Sunday school paper for adults. Fiction, 1,500 to 2,000 words, and articles, 1,000 to 1,500 words, on applying Bible principles to everyday living. Pays 2¢ to 3¢ a word, on acceptance. Send SASE for guidelines first.

THE LIVING LIGHT—United States Catholic Conference, Dept of Education, 1312 Massachusetts Ave. N.W., Washington, DC 20005. Mariella Frye, M.H.S.H., Ed. Theoretical and practical articles, 1,500 to 4,000 words, on religious education, catechesis and pastoral ministry. Pays $15 per printed page, on publication.

LIVING WITH CHILDREN—127 Ninth Ave. N., Nashville, TN 37234. SuAnne Bottoms, Ed. Articles, 800, 1,450 or 2,000 words, on parent-child relationships, told from a Christian perspective. Pays 4¢ a word, after acceptance.

LIVING WITH PRESCHOOLERS—127 Ninth Ave., N., Nashville, TN 37234. SuAnne Bottoms, Ed. Articles, 800, 1,450 or 2,000 words, and fillers, to 300 words, for Christian families. Pays 4¢ a word, on acceptance.

LIVING WITH TEENAGERS—127 Ninth Ave. N., Nashville, TN 37234. Articles, told from a Christian perspective; first-person approach preferred. Poetry, 4 to 16 lines. Photos. Pays 4¢ a word, on acceptance.

THE LOOKOUT—8121 Hamilton Ave., Cincinnati, OH 45231. Mark A. Taylor, Ed. Articles, 1,000 to 1,500 words, on families and people overcoming problems by applying Christian principles. Inspirational or humorous shorts, 500 to 800 words, fiction. Pays 4¢ to 6¢ a word, on acceptance.

THE LUTHERAN—2900 Queen Ln., Philadelphia, PA 19129. Edgar R. Trexler, Ed. Articles, to 2,000 words, on Christian ideology, personal religious experiences, family life, church and community. Pays $75 to $250, on acceptance. Query.

LUTHERAN STANDARD—426 S. Fifth St., Box 1209. Minneapolis, MN 55440. Lowell G. Almen, Ed. Articles, 500 to 1,000 words, on social, economic and political aspects of church and Christian living; human-interest items; personality profiles. Pays from 10¢ a word, on acceptance.

LUTHERAN WOMEN—2900 Queen Ln., Philadelphia, PA 19129. Terry Schutz, Ed. Articles, preferably with photos, on subjects of interest to Christian women. No recipes, homemaking hints. Fiction, 1,000 to 2,000 words, on personal growth and change. Short poems. Pays to $50 for articles, $35 to $40 for fiction, on publication.

MARRIAGE AND FAMILY LIVING—Division of Abbey Press, St. Meinrad, IN 47577. Kass Dotterweich, Man. Ed. Expert advice, personal experience articles, 2,000 to 2,500 words, on marriage and family relationships. Family humor, 1,000 to 2,000 words. Pays 7¢ a word, on acceptance.

MATURE LIVING—127 9th Ave. N., Nashville, TN 37234. Jack Gulledge, Ed. General-interest pieces, travel articles, nostalgia and fiction, under 1,000 words, for Christian senior adults 60 years and older. Also, profiles recognizing a senior adult for an accomplishment or interesting or unusual experience, to 25 lines; must include a B/W action photo. Brief, humorous items for "Cracker Barrel." Pays 4¢ a word, $10 for profiles, $5 for "Cracker Barrel," on acceptance. Buys all rights.

MATURE YEARS—201 Eighth Ave. S., Nashville, TN 37203. Daisy D. Warren, Ed. United Methodist. Articles on retirement or related subjects, 1,500 to 2,000 words. Humorous and serious fiction, 1,500 to 1,800 words, for adults. Poetry, to 14 lines. Pays 4¢ a word, 50¢ a line for poetry, on acceptance.

MESSENGER OF THE SACRED HEART—661 Greenwood Ave., Toronto, Ont., Canada M4J 4B3. Write M. Pujolas. Articles and short stories, about 1,500 words, for American and Canadian Catholics. Pays from 2¢ a word, on acceptance.

MIDSTREAM—515 Park Ave., New York, NY 10022. Joel Carmichael, Ed. Jewish-interest articles and book reviews. Fiction, to 3,000 words, book excerpts, and poetry. Pays 5¢ a word, on publication.

THE MIRACULOUS MEDAL—475 E. Chelten Ave., Philadelphia, PA 19144. Robert P. Cawley, C.M., Edit. Director. Catholic. Fiction, to 2,000 words. Religious verse, to 20 lines. Pays from 2¢ a word for fiction, from 50¢ a line for poetry, on acceptance.

MODERN LITURGY—160 E. Virginia St., #290, San Jose, CA 95112. Ken Guentert, Ed. Creative material for Catholic worship services; religious parables, to 1,000 words; how-to's, essays on worship, 750 to 1,600 words. Plays. Poetry. Pays 3¢ a word, after publication.

MOMENT—462 Boylston St., Boston, MA 02116. Nechama Katz, Assoc. Ed. Sophisticated articles and some fiction, 2,000 to 5,000 words, on Jewish topics. Pays $150 to $400, on publication.

MOMENTUM—National Catholic Educational Assn., Suite 100, 1077 30th St., NW, Washington, DC 20007. Patricia Feistritzer, Ed. Articles, 500 to 2,000 words, on outstanding programs, issues and research in education. Book reviews. Pays 2¢ a word, on publication. Query.

MOODY MONTHLY—2101 W. Howard, Chicago, IL 60645. Mike Umlandt, Man. Ed. Articles, 1,200 to 1,800 words, on the Christian experience in school, the home and the workplace. Pays 5¢ to 10¢ a word, on acceptance. Query.

MUSICLINE—P.O. Box 6300, Laguna Hills, CA 92653. Thom Granger, Ed. Christian music trade articles, 500 to 1,000 words. Pays 8¢ a word, on publication.

THE NATIONAL CHRISTIAN REPORTER—See *The United Methodist Reporter.*

NEW ERA—50 E. North Temple, Salt Lake City, UT 84150. Brian Kelly, Ed. Articles, 150 to 3,000 words, and fiction, to 3,000 words, for young Mormons. Poetry; photos. Pays 5¢ to 10¢ a word, 25¢ a line for poetry, on acceptance. Query.

NEW WORLD OUTLOOK—475 Riverside Dr., Rm. 1351, New York, NY 10115. Arthur J. Moore, Ed. Articles, 1,500 to 2,500 words, on Christian missions, religious issues and public affairs. Poetry, to 16 lines. Pays on publication.

OBLATES MAGAZINE—15 S. 59th St., Belleville, IL 62222. Address Linda Lehr. Articles, 500 to 600 words, for older Christian Americans. Poetry, to about 16 lines. Pays $60 for articles, $25 for poetry, on acceptance. Send for free sample copy and guidelines.

OPUS ONE AND OPUS TWO—See *The Church Musician.*

OUR FAMILY—Box 249, Dept. E., Battleford, Sask., Canada S0M 0E0. Albert Lalonde, O.M.I., Ed. Articles, 1,000 to 3,000 words, for Catholic family readers, on modern society, family, marriage, current affairs. Fiction, 1,000 to 3,000 words. Humor, verse. Pays 7¢ to 10¢ a word for articles, 75¢ to $1 a line for poetry, on acceptance. Send SASE with Canadian postage for guidelines.

OUR SUNDAY VISITOR—Huntington, IN 46750. Robert Lockwood, Ed. In-depth features, 1,000 to 1,500 words, on the Catholic Church in America today. Pays $100 to $150, on acceptance.

PARISH FAMILY DIGEST—Noll Plaza, Huntington, IN 46750. Patrick R. Moran, Ed. Articles, to 1,000 words, fillers, and humor, for Catholic families and parishes. Pays 5¢ a word, on acceptance. Query first.

THE PENTECOSTAL EVANGEL—1445 Boonville Ave., Springfield, MO 65802. Richard Champion, Ed. Assemblies of God. Religious personal-experience and devotional articles, 500 to 1,000 words. Verse, 12 to 30 lines. Pays 2¢ to 3¢ a word, on publication.

THE PRESBYTERIAN SURVEY—341 Ponce de Leon Ave., NE., Atlanta, GA 30365. Vic Jamison, Ed. Articles, to 1,500 words, of interest to members of the Presbyterian Church or ecumenical individuals. Pays $25 to $200, on acceptance. Query.

PRESENT TENSE—165 E. 56th St., New York, NY 10022. Murray Polner, Ed. Serious articles, 2,000 to 3,000 words, with photos, on news concerning Jews throughout the world; first-person encounters and personal-experience pieces. Literary-political reportage. Contemporary themes only. Pays $100 to $200, on publication. Query.

THE PRIEST—200 Noll Plaza, Huntington, IN 46750. Articles, to 2,500 words, on life and ministry of priests, current theological developments, etc., for priests and seminarians.

PURPOSE—616 Walnut Ave., Scottdale, PA 15683. James E. Horsch, Ed. Articles, 350 to 1,200 words, on Christian themes, with good photos; pieces of history, biography, science, hobbies, from a Christian perspective. Fiction 1,200 words, on Christian problem solving. Poetry, 3 to 12 lines. Pays 5¢ a word, 75¢ to $1 per line for poetry, extra for photos, on acceptance.

QUEEN—26 S. Saxon Ave., Bay Shore, NY 11706. James McMillian, S.M.M., Ed. Publication of Montfort Missionaries. Articles and fiction, 1,000 to 2,000 words, relating to the Virgin Mary. Pays varying rates on acceptance.

THE RECONSTRUCTIONIST—270 W. 89th St., New York, NY 10024. Dr. Jacob Staub, Ed. Articles and fiction, 2,000 to 3,000 words, relating to Judaism. Poetry. Pays $15 to $25, on publication.

ST. ANTHONY MESSENGER—1615 Republic St., Cincinnati, OH 45210. Norman Perry, O.F.M., Ed. Catholic. Articles, 2,500 to 3,500 words, on personalities, major movements, education, family, and social issues. Human-interest pieces. Humor. Fiction. Pays from 12¢ a word, on acceptance. Query on non-fiction.

ST. JOSEPH'S MESSENGER—P.O. Box 288, Jersey City, NJ 07303. Sister Ursula Maphet, Ed. Inspirational articles, 500 to 1,000 words, and fiction, 1,000 to 1,500 words. Verse, 4 to 40 lines. Pays 1¢ a word. Query.

SCOPE—426 S. Fifth St., Box 1209, Minneapolis, MN 55440. Constance Lovaas, Ed. American Lutheran Church Women. Educational and inspirational articles for women in careers, the home, church, and community. Human-interest pieces, 500 to 1,000 words. Poetry and fillers. Pays moderate rates, on acceptance.

SEEK—8121 Hamilton Ave., Cincinnati, OH 45231. Leah Ann Crussell, Ed. Articles and fiction, to 1,200 words, on inspirational and controversial topics and timely religious issues. Christian testimonials. Pays up to 2½¢ a word, on acceptance.

SHARING THE VICTORY—8701 Leeds Rd., Kansas City, MO 64129. Skip Stogsdill, Ed. Articles and profiles, to 800 words, for coed Christian athletes and coaches in high school and college. Pays from $25, on publication. Queries required.

SH'MA—Box 567, Port Washington, NY 11050. Eugene B. Borowitz, Ed. Articles, 750 to 2,000 words, on ethics, Zionism, and Jewish living. Pays in copies.

SIGNS OF THE TIMES—P.O. Box 7000, Boise, ID 83707. Seventh-day Adventists. Devotionals, to 1,200 words. Pays on acceptance.

SISTERS TODAY—St. John's Abbey, Collegeville, MN 56231. Sister Mary Anthony Wagner, O.S.B., Ed. Articles, 500 to 3,500 words, on Roman Catholic theology, religious issues for women and the Church. Poetry, to 34 lines. Pays $5 per printed page, $10 per poem, on publication. Send articles to Editor at St. Benedict's Convent, St. Joseph, MN 56374. Send poetry to Sister Audrey Synnott, R.S.M., 1437 Blossom Rd., Rochester, NY 14610.

SOCIAL JUSTICE REVIEW—3835 Westminster Pl., St. Louis, MO 63108. Harvey J. Johnston, Ed. Articles, 2,000 to 3,000 words, on social problems in light of Catholic teaching and current scientific studies. Pays 2¢ a word, on publication.

SPIRITUAL LIFE—2131 Lincoln Rd. N.E., Washington, DC 20002-1199. Christopher Latimer, O.C.D., and Steven Payne, O.C.D., Co-editors. Professional religious journal. Religious essays, 3,000 to 5,000 words, on spirituality in contemporary life. Pays from $50, on acceptance. Guidelines available.

SPIRITUALITY TODAY—Aquinas Institute, 3642 Lindell Blvd., St. Louis, MO 63108. Christopher Kiesling, O.P., Ed. Quarterly. Biblical, liturgical, theological, ecumenical, historical, and biographical articles of critical, probing kind, 4,000 words, about the challenges of contemporary Christian life. No poetry. Pays from 1¢ a word, on publication. Guidelines available upon request.

STANDARD—6401 The Paseo, Kansas City, MO 64131. Address Ed. Articles, 300 to 2,000 words: true experiences, devotional fillers; poetry to 20 lines; fiction, 1,500 to 2,000 words, with Christian emphasis but not preachy; fillers, cryptograms on Scripture verses or inspiring quotes, cartoons in good taste. Pays 3½¢ a word, on acceptance.

SUNDAY DIGEST—850 N. Grove Ave., Elgin, IL 60120. Judy C. Couchman, Ed. Articles, to 1,500 words, on Christian faith in contemporary life; inspirational and how-to articles; free-verse poetry. Anecdotes, 500 words. Pays from 7¢ a word, on acceptance.

SUNDAY SCHOOL COUNSELOR—1445 Boonville Ave., Springfield, MO 65802. Sylvia Lee, Ed. Articles, 1,000 to 1,500 words, on teaching and Sunday school people, for local Sunday school teachers. Pays 3¢ to 5¢ a word, on acceptance.

SUNSHINE MAGAZINE—Litchfield, Il 62056. Address Ed. Inspirational articles, to 600 words. Short stories, 1,000 words and juveniles, 400 words. No heavily religious material or "born-again" pieces. Pays varying rates, on acceptance.

TEENS TODAY—Nazarene Publishing House, 6401 The Paseo, Kansas City, MO 64131. Gary Sivewright, Ed. Short stories that deal with teens demonstrating Christian principles, 1,200 to 1,500 words. Pays 3½¢ a word, on acceptance.

THEOLOGY TODAY—Box 29, Princeton, NJ 08542. Hugh T. Kerr, Ed. Articles, to 3,500 words, or to 1,500 words, on theology, religion and related social issues. Literary criticism. Pays $35 to $50, on publication.

TODAY'S CHRISTIAN PARENT—8121 Hamilton Ave., Cincinnati, OH 45231. Mildred D. Mast, Ed. Articles, to 1,000 words, on application of Christian principles in child-rearing and aspects of family living; problems and pleasures of parents, grandparents. Serious or humorous fillers. Timely articles on moral issues, social situations, ethical dilemmas; refreshing insights for everyday happenings in the home. Pays to 2½¢ a word, after acceptance. Include SASE.

THE UNITED CHURCH OBSERVER—85 St. Clair Ave. E., Toronto, Ont., Canada M4T 1M8. Factual articles, 1,500 to 2,500 words, on religious trends, human problems, social issues. No poetry. Pays from 10¢ a word, after publication. Query.

UNITED EVANGELICAL ACTION—P.O. Box 28, Wheaton, IL 60189. Don Brown, Ed. National Assn. of Evangelicals. News-oriented expositions and editorials, 750 to 1,000 words, on current events of concern and consequence to the evangelical church. Pays about 7¢ to 10¢ a word, on publication. Query with writing samples.

THE UNITED METHODIST REPORTER—P.O. Box 221076, Dallas, TX 75222. Spurgeon M. Dunnam III, Ed. John Lovelace, Man. Ed. United Methodist. Religious features, to 500 words. Religious verse, 4 to 12 lines; puzzles. Photos. Pays 4¢ a word, on acceptance. Send for guidelines. Same address and requirements for *The National Christian Reporter* (interdenominational).

UNITED SYNAGOGUE REVIEW—155 Fifth Ave., New York, NY 10010. Rabbi Marvin S. Wiener, Ed. Articles, 1,000 to 1,500 words, on synagogue programs and projects, Jewish worship services, rituals, etc. Pays after publication. Query.

UNITY MAGAZINE—Unity School of Christianity, Unity Village, MO 64065. Pamela Yearsley, Ed. Inspirational and metaphysical articles, 500 to 2,500 words. Pays 2¢ to 5¢ a word, on acceptance.

VIRTUE—P.O. Box 850, Sisters, OR 97759. Articles for Christian women. Query only, except for pieces for "One Woman's Journal" and "In My Opinion." Material sent without SASE will not be returned.

VISTA—Box 2000, Marion, IN 46952. Adult fiction, 1,200 to 1,500 words, on Christian living. Devotional and first-person articles; poetry. Anecdotes of spiritual significance, 200 to 500 words. Filler trivia items, 50 to 150 words. Pays 2¢ to 3¢ a word.

THE WAR CRY—799 Bloomfield Ave., Verona, NJ 07044. Henry Gariepy, Ed. Articles, 800 to 1,600 words, related to the Bible and modern-day life. Fiction, 800 to 1,500 words, with strong evangelical Christian emphasis. Some poetry. Pays 4¢ a word, on acceptance.

WORKING FOR BOYS—St. John's H. S., Main St., Shrewsbury, MA 01545. Brother Alois, C.F.X., Assoc. Ed. Fiction and nonfiction, to 1,200 words, for elementary school children, parents: human-interest, how-to, travel, religion, sports. Verse, to 24 lines. No pictures or puzzles. Pays 4¢ a word, 40¢ a line for poetry, on acceptance.

WORLDWIDE CHALLENGE—Arrowhead Springs, San Bernardino, CA 92414. Dave Boehi, Ed. Features, 1,200 to 2,000 words, on spiritual growth, for readers familiar with the "Campus Crusade for Christ." Personality pieces. Inspirational fiction. Pays to $75 for features, on publication. No unsolicited manuscripts; query.

THE YOUNG SOLDIER—The Salvation Army, 799 Bloomfield Ave., Verona, NJ 07044. Dorothy Hitzka, Ed. Articles, 600 to 800 words, for children 6 to 12. Must carry a definite Christian message, or teach a Biblical truth. Fiction, 600 to 800 words. Some poetry. Fillers, puzzles, etc. Pays 3¢ a word, $3 to $5 for fillers, puzzles, on acceptance.

YOUTHWORKER—1224 Greenfield Dr., El Cajon, CA 92021. Noel Becchetti, Ed. Articles, 2,500 to 3,000 words, for ministers of the Christian church who work with teens. Pays $100, on acceptance. Query.

COLLEGE, LITERARY, AND LITTLE MAGAZINES

FICTION, NONFICTION, POETRY

The thousands of literary journals, little magazines, and college quarterlies being published today offer a receptive market for novices and pros alike; editors are always on the lookout for traditional and experimental fiction, poetry, essays, reviews, short articles, criticism, and satire, and as long as the material is well-written, the fact that a writer is a beginner doesn't adversely affect his chances for acceptance.

Most of these smaller publications have small budgets and staffs, so they may be slow in their reporting time—several months is not unusual. In addition, they usually pay only in copies of the issue in which published work appears, and some—particularly college magazines—do not read manuscripts during the summer.

Publication in the literary journals can, however, lead to recognition by editors of large-circulation magazines, who read the little magazines in their search for new talent. There is also the possibility of having one's work chosen for reprinting in one of the prestigious annual collections of work from the little magazines.

Because the requirements of these journals differ widely, it is always important to study recent issues before submitting work to one of them. Copies of magazines on this list may be in a large library, or a writer may send a postcard to the editor, and ask the price of a sample copy. Always enclose a return envelope, with sufficient postage for the return of the manuscript.

For a complete list of literary and college publications and little magazines, writers may consult such reference works as *The International Directory of Little Magazines and Small Presses,* published annually by Dustbooks (P.O. Box 100, Paradise, CA 95969).

THE AGNI REVIEW—P.O. Box 229, Cambridge, MA 02138. Sharon Dunn, Ed. Short stories and poetry. Pays in copies.

ALASKA QUARTERLY REVIEW—Dept. of English, Univ. of Alaska, 3211 Providence Dr., Anchorage, AK 99508. Address Eds. Short stories, novel excerpts, poetry (traditional and unconventional forms). Submit manuscripts between August 15 and May 15. Pays in copies.

THE ALTADENA REVIEW—P.O. Box 212, Altadena, CA 91001. Robin Shectman, Ed. High quality poetry, any form. Interviews, to 3,500 words; reviews, 700 to 1,500 words. Illustrations. Pays in copies.

THE AMERICAN BOOK REVIEW—P.O. Box 188, Cooper Sta., New York, NY 10003. Charles Russell, Exec. Ed. Book reviews, 750 to 1,200 words. Pays in copies.

THE AMERICAN POETRY REVIEW—1616 Walnut St., Rm. 405, Philadelphia, PA 19103. Address the Eds. High-quality modern poetry. Pays $1 a line.

AMERICAN QUARTERLY—303 College Hall, Univ. of Pennsylvania, Philadelphia, PA 19104. Richard R. Beeman and Janice Radway, Eds. Scholarly essays, 5,000 to 10,000 words, on any aspect of U.S. culture. Pays in copies.

THE AMERICAN SCHOLAR—1811 Q St. N.W., Washington, DC 20009. Joseph Epstein, Ed. Articles, 3,500 to 4,000 words, on science, politics, literature, the arts, etc. Book reviews. Pays $350 for articles, $100 for reviews, on publication.

ANTAEUS—18 W. 30th St., New York, NY 10001. Daniel Halpern, Ed. Short stories, essays, documents, parts-of-novels, poems. Submissions accepted from October 1 to May 1 only. Pays on publication.

THE ANTIGONISH REVIEW—St. Francis Xavier Univ., Antigonish, N.S., Canada. George Sanderson, Ed. Poetry; short stories, essays, book reviews, 1,800 to 2,500 words. Pays in copies.

ANTIOCH REVIEW—P.O. Box 148, Yellow Springs, OH 45387. Robert S. Fogarty, Ed. Timely articles, 2,000 to 8,000 words, on social sciences, literature, and humanities. Quality fiction. Poetry. Pays $10 per printed page, on publication.

APALACHEE QUARTERLY—DDB Press, P.O. Box 20106, Tallahassee, FL 32316. Monica Faeth, Barbara Hamby, Rich Johnson, and Allen Woodman, Eds. Fiction, to 30 manuscript pages; poems (3 to 5); essays. Pays in copies.

ARIZONA QUARTERLY—Univ. of Arizona, Tucson, AZ 85721. Albert F. Gegenheimer, Ed. Literary essays; regional material; general-interest articles. Fiction, to 3,500 words. Poetry (up to 30 lines)—any form or subject matter. Pays in copies.

BALL STATE UNIVERSITY FORUM—Ball State Univ., Muncie, IN 47306. Dick A. Renner and Frances Mayhew Rippy, Eds. Short stories and general-interest articles, 500 to 4,000 words. One-act plays. Poetry. Pays in copies.

THE BELLINGHAM REVIEW—412 N. State St., Bellingham, WA 98225. Knute Skinner and Stanley Hodson, Eds. Fiction, to 5,000 words. Poetry of all kinds. Short dramas. Submit manuscripts between September 15 and June 1. Pays in copies plus subscription.

BELOIT POETRY JOURNAL—Box 154, RFD 2, Ellsworth, ME 04605. First-rate contemporary poetry, of any length or mode. Pays in copies. Write for guidelines.

BERKELEY POETS COOPERATIVE—P.O. Box 459, Berkeley, CA 94701. Charles Entrekin, Ed. Poetry, all forms; no restrictions. Submissions accepted from April 1 to August 1 and from October 1 to February 1. Pays in copies.

THE BLACK COLLEGIAN—1240 S. Broad St., New Orleans, LA 70125. James Borders, Ed. Articles, to 2,000 words, on experiences of black students, careers, and how-to subjects. Pays on publication. Query.

BLACK MARIA—P.O. Box 25187, Chicago, IL 60625. Feminist. Short stories and experimental fiction, to 3,500 words. Poetry of any form. Articles; essays; B&W photos. Pays in copies.

THE BLACK WARRIOR REVIEW—P.O. Box 2936, University, AL 35486. Will Blythe, Ed. Serious fiction, reviews, interviews, and essays. Poetry. Pays in copies and annual awards.

THE BLOOMSBURY REVIEW—P.O. Box 8928, Denver, CO 80201. Marilyn Auer, Assoc. Ed.; Carol Arenberg, Senior Ed.; Ray Gonzalez, Poetry Ed. Book reviews, publishing features, interviews, essays, poetry, up to 800 words. Pays $5 to $15, on publication.

BLUELINE—Blue Mountain Lake, NY 12812. Alice Gilborn, Ed. Essays, fiction, to 2,500 words, on Adirondack region or similar areas. Poetry, to 44 lines. No more than 5 poems per submission. Pays in copies.

BOOK FORUM—38 E. 76th St., New York, NY 10021. Essays, 800 to 1,600 words, on books, writers, art, politics, etc. Interviews. Book reviews assigned. Pays $25 to $100, on acceptance. Query.

BOSTON REVIEW—991 Massachusetts Ave., Cambridge, MA 02138. Nicholas Bromell, Ed. Reviews and essays, 1,500 to 3,000 words, on literature, art, music, film, photography. Original fiction, to 5,000 words. Poetry. Pays $40 to $150.

BOUNDARY 2—SUNY—Binghamton, NY 13901. Experimental short stories; sections from longer experimental fiction; poetry; translations; criticism. Pays in copies.

BUCKNELL REVIEW—Bucknell Univ., Lewisburg, PA 17837. Harry R. Garvin, Ed. Interdisciplinary journal in book form. Scholarly articles on arts, science, and letters. Pays in copies.

CALLIOPE—Creative Writing Program, Roger Williams College, Bristol, RI 02809. Martha Christina, Ed. Short stories and experimental fiction, to 2,500 words; interviews. Poetry (query first to find out about thematic issues). Pays in copies. No submissions April through July.

CALYX, A JOURNAL OF ART & LITERATURE BY WOMEN—P.O. Box B, Corvallis, OR 97339. M. Donnelly, Man. Ed. Fiction, 5,000 words, reviews, 250 to 1,000 words, by women. Pays in copies. Include short bio with submission.

THE CANADIAN FICTION MAGAZINE—Box 946, Sta. F., Toronto, Ontario, Canada M4Y 2N9. High-quality short stories, novel excerpts, and experimental fiction, to 5,000 words, by Canadians. Interviews with Canadian authors; translations. Pays $10 per page, on publication.

THE CAPILANO REVIEW—Capilano College, 2055 Purcell Way, North Vancouver, B.C., Canada V7J 3H5. Ann Rosenberg, Ed. Fiction; poetry; drama; visual arts. Pays $10 to $40.

CAROLINA QUARTERLY—Greenlaw Hall 066A, Univ. of North Carolina, Chapel Hill, NC 27514. Marc Manganaro, Ed. Innovative fiction, to 7,000 words, by new or established writers. Poetry (no restrictions on length, though limited space makes inclusion of works of more than 300 lines impractical). Pays $3 per printed page for fiction, $5 per poem, on acceptance.

THE CATHARTIC—P.O. Box 1391, Ft. Lauderdale, FL 33302. Patrick M. Ellingham, Ed. All styles of poetry, any length. Reviews of small press books of poetry. Pays in copies and cash awards.

CEDAR ROCK—1121 Madeline, New Braunfels, TX 78130. David C. Yates, Ed. Poetry, conventional and free verse. Submit 3 or 4 poems at a time.

Pays $2 to $200. Fiction, 800 to 2,500 words—adventure stories, satire, humor, suspense, science-fiction, and experimental. Address fiction submissions to John O'Keefe, Fiction Ed. 732 W. Coll, New Braunfels, TX 78130. Pays $20 to $250. Guidelines available.

THE CENTENNIAL REVIEW—110 Morrill Hall, Michigan State Univ., East Lansing, MI 48824-1036. Linda Wagner, Ed. Articles, 2,000 to 3,000 words, on sciences and humanities. Pays with subscription.

THE CHARITON REVIEW—Northeast Missouri State Univ., Kirksville, MO 63501. Jim Barnes, Ed. High-quality fiction, to 6,000 words. Modern and contemporary translations. Book reviews. Pays $5 per printed page for fiction.

THE CHICAGO REVIEW—Univ. of Chicago, Chicago, IL 60637. Steve Heminger and Steve Schroer, Eds. Essays; interviews; reviews; fiction; translations; poetry. Pays in copies plus subscription.

CIMARRON REVIEW—Oklahoma State Univ., Stillwater, OK 74078. Jeanne Adams Wray, Man. Ed. Articles, 1,500 to 2,500 words, on history, philosophy, political science, etc. Serious contemporary fiction. Pays in copies.

COLORADO-NORTH REVIEW—Univ. Center, Univ. of Northern Colorado, Greeley, CO 80639. Address Ed. Fiction, to 20 typed pages; poetry; graphic art. Include biographical sketch with submission. Pays in copies.

COLORADO STATE REVIEW—English Dept., 322 Eddy, Colorado State Univ., Fort Collins, CO 80523. Fiction submissions accepted from August 1 to December 31; poetry from January 1 to April 30 every year.

COLUMBIA, A MAGAZINE OF POETRY & PROSE—404 Dodge, Columbia Univ., New York, NY 10027. Address Eds. Fiction, 5 to 15 typed pages. Poetry (1 to 4 typed pages). Submit poems in batches of 5 or less. Pays in copies. Annual award.

CONFRONTATION—Dept. of English, Long Island Univ., Brooklyn, NY 11201. Martin Tucker, Ed. Serious fiction, 750 to 6,000 words. Crafted poetry, 20 to 200 lines. Pays $5 to $40, on publication.

CREDENCES—420 Capen Hall, SUNY, Buffalo, NY 14260. Robert Bertholf, Ed. Interviews; essays; reviews; fiction, to 25 typed pages. Long poems. Pays in copies and cash.

THE CRISIS—N.A.A.C.P., 186 Remsen St., Brooklyn, NY 11201. Maybelle Ward, Ed. Dir. Articles, to 1,500 words, on civil rights, problems and achievements of blacks and other minorities. Pays in copies.

CRITICAL INQUIRY—Univ. of Chicago Press, Wieboldt Hall, 1050 E. 59th St., Chicago, IL 60637. W. J. T. Mitchell, Ed. Critical essays that offer a theoretical perspective on literature, music, visual arts, popular culture, etc. Pays in copies.

CROTON REVIEW—P.O. Box 277, Croton-on-Hudson, NY 10520. Quality short-short fiction (to 14 pages), poetry (to 75 lines), and literary essays. Submissions accepted from September to February only. Pays in copies and modest honorarium.

CUMBERLAND POETRY REVIEW—P.O. Box 120128, Acklen Sta., Nashville, TN 37212. Address Eds. High-quality poetry and criticism. No restrictions on form, style or subject matter. Pays in copies.

DENVER QUARTERLY—Univ. of Denver, Denver, CO 80208. Eric Gould, Ed. Literary, cultural essays and articles; poetry; book reviews; fiction. Pays $5 per printed page, after publication.

DESCANT—Texas Christian Univ., T.C.U. Sta., Fort Worth, TX 76129. Betsy Colquitt and Harry Opperman, Eds. Critical articles, to 3,000 words, on modern literature. Fiction, to 6,000 words. Poetry, to 40 lines; no restriction on form or subject. Pays in copies. Submit manuscripts during academic year only.

THE DEVIL'S MILLHOPPER—Rt. 3, Box 29, Elgin, SC 29045. Jim Peterson, Ed. Poetry, any length. Pays in copies.

EPOCH—245 Goldwin Smith Hall, Cornell Univ., Ithaca, NY 14853. Serious fiction. Poetry. Pays in copies.

EVENT—Kwantlen College, Box 9030, Surrey, B.C., Canada V3T 5H8. Dale Zieroth, Ed. Short stories; novellas; plays. Pays modest rates, after publication.

FAT TUESDAY—808¾ N. Detroit St., Los Angeles, CA 90046. F. M. Cotolo, Ed. Annual. Short fiction, poetry, parts-of-novels, paragraphs, crystal thoughts of any dimension—up to 5 pages. Pays in copies.

FICTION INTERNATIONAL—English Dept. San Diego State Univ., San Diego, CA 92182. Harold Jaffe and Larry McCaffery, Eds. Wide range of work considered—from formalism to committed realism. Query for submission deadlines. Pays in copies.

THE FIDDLEHEAD—Dept. of English, Univ. of New Brunswick, Fredericton, N.B., Canada E3B 5A3. Serious fiction, 2,500 words, preferably by Canadians. Pays about $10 per printed page, on publication.

FIELD—Rice Hall, Oberlin College, Oberlin, OH 44074. Stuart Friebert, David Young, Eds. Serious poetry, any length, by established and unknown poets; essays on poetics by poets. Translations by qualified translators. Pays $15 to $25 per page, on publication.

FOUR QUARTERS—La Salle College, Philadelphia, PA 19141. John C. Kleis, Ed. Critical articles, 1,500 to 6,000 words, on writers and literary arts; "think pieces" on history, politics, the arts. Short stories. Poetry, 8 to 32 lines. Some shorter poems used as fillers. Pays $5 for poems, $25 for fiction and nonfiction, on publication. No submissions in July or August.

FRONT STREET TROLLEY—2125 Acklen Ave., Nashville, TN 37212. Molly McIntosh, Ed. Poetry, satirical and serious, any length, preferably by Southern writers. Short stories and reviews. Pays in copies.

GARGOYLE—P.O. Box 3567, Washington, DC 20007. Gretchen Johnsen, Poetry Ed. Poetry, average 10 to 35 lines. Fiction. Pays in copies.

THE GEORGIA REVIEW—Univ. of Georgia, Athens, GA 30602. Stanley W. Lindberg, Ed.; Stephen Corey, Asst. Ed. Short fiction; interdisciplinary essays on arts and the humanities; book reviews; poetry. No submissions in June, July, and August.

GRAIN—Box 1885, Saskatoon, Sask., Canada S7K 3S2. Brenda Riches, Ed. Short stories, about 10 typed pages. Songs, essays, and drama. Poetry (send no more than 6). Pays $30 to $100 for prose; $20 per poem, on publication.

GREAT LAKES REVIEW—Central Michigan Univ., Box 122, Anspach Hall, Mt. Pleasant, MI 48859. Martha H. Brown, Ronald Primeau, Eds. Reviews and scholarly articles, 10 to 15 typed pages, on history, literature, etc., of Midwest. Short stories. Pays in copies.

GREAT RIVER REVIEW—211 W. 7th St., Winona, MN 55987. Fiction and creative prose, 2,000 to 10,000 words. Quality contemporary poetry; send 4 to 8 poems. Special interest in Midwestern writers and themes.

THE GREENFIELD REVIEW—R.D. 1, Box 80, Greenfield Center, NY 12833. Joseph Bruchac III, Ed. Contemporary poetry, any length, by established and new poets, third world writers. Translations. Pays in copies.

GREEN'S MAGAZINE—P.O. Box 3236, Regina, Sask., Canada S4P 3H1. David Green, Ed. Fiction, 1,500 to 4,000 words. Poetry, to 40 lines. Pays in copies.

THE GREENSBORO REVIEW—Univ. of North Carolina, Greensboro, NC 27412. Lee Zacharias, Ed. Semi-annual. Poetry and fiction. Submissions read in September, October, January, and February. Pays in copies.

HAWAII REVIEW—Dept. of English, Univ. of Hawaii, 1733 Donaghho Rd., Honolulu, HI 96882. Quality fiction, poetry, interviews, and literary criticism reflecting both regional and universal concerns.

HELICON NINE, THE JOURNAL OF WOMEN'S ARTS AND LETTERS—P.O. Box 22412, Kansas City, MO 64113. Poetry and fiction about women. Query preferred.

HOME PLANET NEWS—Box 415, Stuyvesant Sta., New York, NY 10009. Enid Dame, Donald Lev, Eds. Lively, energetic poetry, to 100 lines; shorter poems preferred. Pays in copies and one-year subscription.

HUDSON REVIEW—684 Park Ave., New York, NY 10021. Frederick Morgan, Paula Deitz, Eds. Fiction, to 10,000 words, of high literary quality. Essays on literature, the arts, culture, reviews. Pays 2½¢ a word, on publication.

INDIANA REVIEW—316 N. Jordan Ave., Bloomington, IN 47405. Jane Hilberry, Erin McGraw, Eds. Fiction with an emphasis on style. Poems that are well executed and ambitious. Pays $5 a page for poetry; fiction is eligible for annual fiction contest.

INLET—Dept. of English, Virginia Wesleyan College, Norfolk, VA 23502. Joseph Harkey, Ed. Short fiction, 500 to 3,000 words (short lengths preferred). Poems of 4 to 40 lines; all forms and themes. Address poetry to H. Rick Hite, Assoc. Ed. Submit between September and March. Pays in copies.

INTERNATIONAL POETRY REVIEW—Box 2047, Greensboro, NC 27402. Evalyn P. Gill, Ed. Contemporary poetry and translations (with original). Pays in copies.

INVISIBLE CITY—P.O. Box 2853, San Francisco, CA 94126. John McBride, Paul Vangelisti, Eds. Reviews, translations, especially contemporary European literature.

THE IOWA REVIEW—EPB 308, Univ. of Iowa, Iowa City, IA 52242. David Hamilton, Ed. Essays, poems, stories, reviews. Pays $10 a page for fiction and nonfiction, $1 a line for poetry, on publication.

JAM TO-DAY—P.O. Box 249, Northfield, VT 05663. Don Stanford and Judith Stanford, Eds. High-quality fiction and poetry, particularly from unknown and little-known writers. Pays $5 per printed page for fiction, $5 per poem, plus copies.

JAPANOPHILE—Box 223, Okemos, MI 48864. Earl R. Snodgrass, Ed. Fiction, to 10,000 words, with a Japanese setting. Each story should have at least one Japanese character and at least one non-Japanese. Pays to $20, on publication. Annual contest.

KANSAS QUARTERLY—Dept. of English, Kansas State Univ., Manhattan, KS 66506. Articles on history, art and folklore of Midwest area. Fiction. Poetry. Pays in copies. Annual awards. Query for articles.

KARAMU—Dept. of English, Eastern Illinois Univ., Charleston, IL 61920. John Guzlowski, Ed. Traditional or experimental fiction. Poetry. Pays in copies.

LIGHT YEAR—Bits Press, Dept. of English, Case Western Reserve Univ., Cleveland, OH 44106. Robert Wallace, Ed. Annual. "The best funny, witty, or merely levitating verse being written." No restrictions on style or length. Pays to $7.50 per poem, plus copies, on publication. Material will not be returned unless accompanied by SASE.

LILITH—250 W. 57th St., New York, NY 10019. Susan Weidman Schneider, Ed. Fiction, 1,500 to 2,000 words, on issues of interest to Jewish women. Pays in copies.

THE LIMBERLOST REVIEW—P.O. Box 771, Hailey, ID 83333. Richard Ardinger, Ed. Poetry, any style or form. Alternate issues devoted to the works of one or two poets in the form of a chapbook. Pays in copies.

LITERARY MAGAZINE REVIEW—English Dept., Kansas State Univ., Manhattan, KS 66506. Reviews of literary magazines, 1,000 to 1,500 words, for writers and readers of contemporary literature. Pays in copies. Query preferred.

THE LITERARY REVIEW—Fairleigh Dickinson Univ., Madison, NJ 07940. Martin Green, Harry Keyishian, Walter Cummins, Eds. Serious fiction; poetry; reviews; essays on literature. Pays in copies.

THE LITTLE BALKANS REVIEW—601 Grandview Heights Terrace, Pittsburg, KS 66762. Fiction, to 5,000 words; articles, to 6,000 words; and poetry (prefer Kansas slant). Illustrations. Pays in copies.

MAGAZINE—P.O. Box 806, Venice, CA 90291. Alexandra Garrett, Jocelyn Fisher, Eds. Contemporary fiction and reviews. Overstocked with poetry. Pays in copies.

THE MALAHAT REVIEW—Univ. of Victoria, P.O. Box 1700, Victoria, B.C., Canada V8W 2Y2. Constance Rooke, Ed. Fiction, poetry, and some articles and translations. Pays $12.50 per poem or $30 per 1,000 words of prose, on acceptance.

MASSACHUSETTS REVIEW—Memorial Hall, Univ. of Massachusetts, Amherst, MA 01003. Literary criticism; articles on public affairs; scholarly disciplines. Short fiction. Poetry. No submissions between June and October. Pays modest rates, on publication.

MENDOCINO REVIEW—Box 888, Mendocino, CA 95460. Fiction and nonfiction, to 2,500 words, and poetry. Pays in copies.

MICHIGAN QUARTERLY REVIEW—3032 Rackham Bldg., Univ. of

Michigan, Ann Arbor, MI 48109. Laurence Goldstein, Ed. Scholarly essays on all subjects; fiction; poetry. Pays $5 a page, on acceptance.

MID-AMERICAN REVIEW—Dept. of English, Bowling Green State Univ., Bowling Green, OH 43403. Robert Early, Ed. High-quality fiction, articles, and reviews of contemporary writing. Fiction to 20,000 words. Reviews, articles, 500 to 2,500 words. Pays $5 per printed page, on publication.

MIDWAY REVIEW—S.W. Area Cultural Council, Suite 134, 3400 W. 111th St., Chicago, IL 60655. Peter S. Cooper, Ed. Fiction, 2,000 to 8,000 words, reviews and art-related articles, 500 to 5,000 words, contemporary poetry, and one act plays, 5,000 to 10,000 words. Pays $5 to $25, within 30 days of publication.

MIDWEST QUARTERLY—Pittsburg State Univ., Pittsburg, KS 66762. James B. Schick, Ed. Scholarly articles, 2,500 to 5,000 words, on contemporary issues. Pays in copies.

MILKWEED CHRONICLE—Box 24303, Minneapolis, MN 55424. Emilie Buchwald, Ed. Poems that reflect a unique voice. No overtly religious or political material. Pays $5 for poems, $25 for essays (500 to 1,000 words), on publication.

THE MINNESOTA REVIEW—Dept. of English, Oregon State Univ., Corvallis, OR 97331. Fred Pfeil, Ed. Poetry, fiction, essays, reviews. Pays in copies.

MISSISSIPPI REVIEW—Center for Writers, Univ. of Southern Mississippi, Southern Sta., Box 5144, Hattiesburg, MS 39406. Serious fiction, poetry, criticism. Pays in copies.

THE MISSISSIPPI VALLEY REVIEW—Dept. of English, Western Illinois Univ., Macomb, IL 61455. Forrest Robinson, Ed. Short fiction, to 20 typed pages. Poetry; send 3 to 5 poems. Pays in copies.

THE MISSOURI REVIEW—Dept. of English, 231 Arts & Science, Univ. of Missouri-Columbia, Columbia, MO 65211. Greg Michalson, Man. Ed. Poems, of any length. Fiction and essays. Pays $5 to $10 per printed page, on publication.

MODERN HAIKU—P.O. Box 1752, Madison, WI 53701. Robert Spiess, Ed. Articles, any length, on haiku. Haiku. $125 in awards in each issue.

MONTHLY REVIEW—155 W. 23rd St., New York, NY 10011. Paul M. Sweezy, Harry Magdoff, Eds. Serious articles, 5,000 words, on politics and economics, from independent socialist viewpoint. Pays $50 on publication.

THE MOVEMENT—Box 19458, Los Angeles, CA 90019. Anja Leigh, Ed. Articles, of varying lengths, on human insight, events of human interest. Pays in copies. Query preferred.

MOVING OUT—P.O. Box 21879, Detroit, MI 48221. Quality poetry, fiction, and art by women; submit 4 to 6 poems at a time. Pays in copies.

MSS—State Univ. of New York, Binghamton, NY 13901. L. M. Rosenberg, Joanna Higgins, Eds. Short stories, novellas, essays, poems, illustrations, any length. Tri-quarterly. Pays negotiable rates.

MUNDUS ARTIUM—Univ. of Texas at Dallas, Box 688, Richardson, TX 75080. Rainer Schulte, Ed. Short fiction, translations, interdisciplinary essays on the humanities. Pays in copies.

NEGATIVE CAPABILITY—6116 Timberly Rd. N., Mobile, AL 36609. Sue Walker, Ed. Poetry, any length. Pays in copies. Annual Eve of St. Agnes poetry competition.

NEW MEXICO HUMANITIES REVIEW—Box A, New Mexico Tech, Socorro, NM 87801. Poetry, any length, any themes; southwestern and native American themes welcome. Pays with subscription.

NEW ORLEANS REVIEW—Loyola Univ., New Orleans, LA 70118. John Mosier, Ed. Literary or film criticism, to 6,000 words. Serious fiction and poetry.

THE NEW RENAISSANCE—9 Heath Rd., Arlington, MA 02174. Louise T. Reynolds, Ed. Well-crafted stories (occasionally experimental), excerpts from novels, 3 to 35 pages. Essays, reviews, interviews, 4 to 25 pages; articles, 10 to about 20 pages. Quality poetry, translations. Submit 3 to 5 poems. No haiku. Query for nonfiction. Do not submit in July or August. Allow 5 months for reply. Pays from $13, after publication.

THE NEW SOUTHERN LITERARY MESSENGER—400 S. Laurel St., Richmond, VA 23220. Chales Lohmann, Ed. Quarterly. Short stories, satire, contemporary history, 1,000 to 5,000 words. One-act plays and short film scripts. Poetry. Pays $5 for one-time reprint rights, plus one copy, on publication. Send for guidelines.

NIMROD—2210 S. Main St., Tulsa, OK 74114. Quality poetry and fiction, experimental and traditional. Pays in copies. Annual awards for poetry and fiction. Send for guidelines.

THE NORTH AMERICAN REVIEW—University of Northern Iowa, Cedar Falls, IA 50614. Peter Cooley, Poetry Ed. Poetry of high quality. Overstocked in fiction until October 1984. Pays 50¢ a line for poetry, on publication.

NORTH COUNTRY ANVIL—Box 37, Millville, MN 55957. Steven and Barbara Whipple, Literary Eds. Political articles, interviews, criticism, related to productive living, peace and plenitude, and spiritual values in Minnesota. Poetry and fiction. Pays in copies.

THE NORTH DAKOTA QUARTERLY—Box 8237, Univ. of North Dakota, Grand Forks, ND 58202. Nonfiction essays in the humanities. Some fiction and poetry. Limited market. Pays in copies.

NORTHWEST MAGAZINE—*The Sunday Oregonian,* Portland, OR 97201. Traditional and experimental poetry, by Northwest poets. Pays $5, after publication.

NORTHWEST REVIEW—369 PLC, Univ. of Oregon, Eugene, OR 97403. John Witte, Ed. Serious fiction and poetry. Reviews. Pays in copies.

OBSIDIAN—Dept. of English, Wayne State Univ., Detroit, MI 48202. Alvin Aubert, Ed. Short fiction, poetry and plays, interviews, reviews, scholarly articles, on black authors and their work. Pays in copies.

THE OHIO JOURNAL—164 W. 17th Ave., Columbus, OH 43210. William Allen, Ed. Short stories, poetry, book reviews. No submissions during the summer. Pays in copies.

THE OHIO REVIEW—Ellis Hall, Ohio Univ., Athens, OH 45701. Short stories, poetry, essays, reviews. Pays from $5 per page, plus copies, on publication.

THE ONTARIO REVIEW—9 Honey Brook Dr., Princeton, NJ 08540. Raymond J. Smith, Ed. Poetry and fiction. No unsolicited manuscripts.

OUTERBRIDGE—A-323, College of Staten Island, 715 Ocean Terr., Staten Island, NY 10301. Charlotte Alexander, Ed. Short stories, reviews, parts-of-novels, poetry. Special focus issues: urban, rural, Southern, etc. Pays in copies.

PACIFIC REVIEW—Dept. of Eng. and Comparative Lit., San Diego State Univ., San Diego, CA 92182. Fiction, essays and reviews, 3,000 to 5,000 words, and poetry, any length. Pays in copies.

PANDORA—P.O. Box 625, Murray, KY 42071. Lois Wickstrom, Ed. Science fiction and speculative fantasy stories, to 5,000 words. Pays 1¢ a word, on acceptance.

PARABOLA—150 Fifth Ave., New York, NY 10011. Lorraine Kisly, Ed. Non-academic articles, 3,000 to 5,000 words, on mythology, comparative religion, the arts, in relation to contemporary life. Book reviews. *No* unsolicited fiction. Some poetry. Pays varying rates, on publication. Query. Study magazine before submitting.

PARIS REVIEW—541 E. 72nd St., New York, NY 10021. Address Fiction and Poetry Eds. Fiction and poetry of high literary quality. Pays on publication.

PARNASSUS—205 W. 89th St., New York, NY 10024. Herbert Leibowitz, Ed. Critical essays and reviews on contemporary poetry. International in scope. Pays in cash and copies.

PARTISAN REVIEW—Boston Univ., 121 Bay State Rd., Boston, MA 02215. William Phillips, Ed. Serious fiction, poetry and essays. Payment varies.

PASSAGES NORTH—William Bonifas Fine Arts Center, Escanaba, MI 49829. Elinor Benedict, Ed. Quality short fiction and contemporary poetry. Pays in copies.

PAVEMENT—Threepenny Poetry, Student Activities Center, Iowa Memorial Union, Univ. of Iowa, Iowa City, IA 52242. Gary Duer, Ed. Poetry. Pays in copies.

PERMAFROST—English Dept., UAF, Fairbanks, AK 99708. Poetry, fiction, essays, translations and reviews. Pays in copies.

PIEDMONT LITERARY REVIEW—P.O. Box 3656, Danville, VA 24543. David Craig, Ed. Fiction, to 2,000 words. Poems, of any length and style. Special interest in young poets. Pays in copies. Submit up to 5 poems at a time.

PIG IRON—P.O. Box 237, Youngstown, OH 44501. Rose Sayre, Jim Villani, Eds. Fiction and nonfiction, to 8,000 words. Poetry, to 100 lines. Pays $2 per published page, on publication.

PINCHPENNY—4851 Q St., Sacramento, CA 95819. Tom Miner, Elizabeth Goossens, Ed. Hard-hitting, contemporary poetry. New writers welcome. Pays in copies.

PLAINS POETRY JOURNAL—Box 2337, Bismarck, ND 58502. Jane Greer, Ed. Traditional poetry; no "greeting card"-type verse. No subject is taboo. Pays in copies.

PLOUGHSHARES—Box 529, Cambridge, MA 02139. Address Fiction or Poetry Ed. Serious fiction, to 7,000 words. Poetry. Pays $10 to $100, on publication. Query.

POEM—c/o English Dept., U.A.H., Huntsville, AL 35899. Robert L. Welker, Ed. Serious poetry, any length. Pays in copies.

POET AND CRITIC—Dept. of English, Iowa State Univ., Ames, IA 50011. Michael Martone, Ed. Poetry, essays on contemporary poetry. Pays in copies.

POET-LORE—4000 Albemarle St. N.W., Washington, DC 20016. Susan Davis, Man. Ed. Traditional and experimental poetry. Translations, reviews. Pays in copies. Annual contest.

POETRY—P.O. Box 4348, 601 S. Morgan St., Chicago, IL 60680. Joseph Parisi, Acting Ed. Poetry of highest quality. Pays $1 a line, on publication.

POETRY NEWSLETTER—Dept. of English, Temple Univ., Philadelphia, PA 19122. Richard O'Connell, Ed. Quarterly. Poetry and translations. Pays in copies.

THE POETRY REVIEW—The Poetry Society of America, 15 Gramercy Park, New York, NY 10003. Poetry, criticism and translations. Pays $10 per printed page, on publication. Must enclose SASE.

PRAIRIE SCHOONER—201 Andrew Hall, Univ. of Nebraska, Lincoln, NE 68588. Hugh Luke, Ed. Short stories, poetry and essays, to 6,000 words. Pays in copies.

PRIMAVERA—1212 E. 59th St., Chicago, IL 60637. Stories, poems and personal essays, to 30 typed pages, by or about women. Send no more than 6 poems at a time. Pays in copies.

PRISM INTERNATIONAL—E459-1866 Main Hall, Dept. of Creative Writing, Univ. of British Columbia, Vancouver, B.C., Canada V6T 1W5. Richard Stevenson, Ed.-in-Chief. Bill Hurst, Fiction Ed. Anne Henderson, Drama Ed. High-quality fiction, poetry, drama, and literature in translation. Pays $15 per published page, on publication. Quarterly.

PROOF ROCK—P.O. Box 607, Halifax, VA 24558. Don Conner, Ed. Fiction, to 2,500 words. Poetry, to 32 lines. Reviews. Pays in copies. Sample copies available.

PUDDING—2384 Hardesty Dr. South, Columbus, OH 43204. Jennifer Groce Welch, Ed. Poems—especially free verse and experimental—with fresh language, concrete images, and specific detail. Short articles about poetry and creative writing efforts in human services.

PULPSMITH—5 Beekman St., New York, NY 10038. Harry Smith, General Ed. Literary genre fiction; mainstream mystery, SF, westerns. Short lyric poems, sonnets, ballads. Essays and articles. Pays $35 to $100 for fiction, $20 to $35 for poetry, on acceptance.

QUARRY WEST—Porter College, Univ. of California, Santa Cruz, CA 95064. Timothy Fitzmaurice, Ed. Biannual. Fiction, poetry, short plays, and articles on poetics and aesthetic theory. Submissions between September and May. Pays in copies.

QUEEN'S QUARTERLY—Queens Univ., Kingston, Ont., Canada K7L 3N6. Articles, to 6,000 words, on a wide range of topics, and fiction, to 5,000 words. Poetry: send no more than 6 poems. Pays to $100, on publication.

RED CEDAR REVIEW—Dept. of English, Morrill Hall, Michigan State Univ., East Lansing, MI 48825. Fiction, 4,000 to 8,000 words. Poetry. Interviews; book reviews. Pays in copies. Query.

RIVERSIDE QUARTERLY—Box 863-388 Wildcat Station, Plano, TX 75086. Science fiction and fantasy, to 3,500 words. Reviews, criticism, poetry. Send fiction to Redd Boggs, Box 1111, Berkeley, CA 94701, and poetry to Sheryl Smith, 40425 Chapel Way, Fremont, CA 94536. Pays in copies.

SAN FERNANDO POETRY JOURNAL—18301 Halstead St., Northridge, CA 91324. Richard Cloke, Ed. Quality poetry, 20 to 100 lines, with social content; scientific, philosophic and historical themes. Pays in copies.

SAN JOSE STUDIES—San Jose State Univ., 174 Administration Bldg., San Jose, CA 95152. Selma Burkom, Ed. Poetry; fiction. Pays in copies. Annual award.

SANDS—17302 Club Hill Dr., Dallas, TX 75248. Joyce Meier, Ed. Quality fiction with good narrative. Poetry, essays, translations. Pays in copies.

SCANDINAVIAN REVIEW—127 E. 73rd St., New York, NY 10021. Fiction and poetry, translated from Scandinavian languages. Essays on Scandinavia. Pays to $100, on publication.

SCRIVENER—McGill Univ., Arts B-20, 853 Sherbrooke St. W., Montreal, Quebec, Canada H3A 2T6. Dan Pope, Ed. Biannual. Short stories, 1 to 30 pages; reviews of Canadian books, 300 to 1,000 words; poetry. Pays in copies.

SECOND WAVE—Box 344, Cambridge A, Cambridge, MA 02139. Articles, fiction, poetry and reviews, with radical, socialist and anarchist feminist perspectives. Pays in copies.

SENECA REVIEW—Hobart & William Smith Colleges, Geneva, NY 14456. Deborah Tall, Ed. Poetry. Pays in copies.

SEVEN—3630 N.W. 22, Oklahoma City, OK 73107. James Neill Northe, Ed. Serious poetry, in any form. Pays $5, on acceptance. Query. Annual contest. Guidelines available.

SEWANEE REVIEW—Sewanee, TN 37375. George Core, Ed. Fiction, to 7,500 words. Serious poetry, to 40 lines, of highest quality. Pays about $10 per printed page for fiction, 60¢ per line for poetry, on publication. Buys all rights. For fiction, send cover letter with manuscript.

SING HEAVENLY MUSE! WOMEN'S POETRY & PROSE—P.O. Box 14059, Minneapolis, MN 55414. Short stories and essays, to 5,000 words. Poetry. Pays small honorarium, plus copies, on publication.

SLIPSTREAM—Box 2071, New Market Sta., Niagara Falls, NY 14301. Robert Borgatti, Dan Sicoli, and Livio Farello, Eds. Fiction, 2 to 25 pages, and contemporary poetry, any length. Pays in copies.

SMACKWARM—Writer's Workshop, ASH 212, Univ. of Nebraska, at Omaha, Omaha, NE 68182. Short stories, to 15 pages, and contemporary poetry. Pays in copies.

SMALL PRESS REVIEW—Box 100, Paradise, CA 95969. Len Fulton, Ed. News pieces and reviews, to 250 words, about small presses and little magazines. Pays in copies.

SNOWY EGRET—205 S. Ninth St., Williamsburg, KY 40769. Humphrey A. Olsen, Alan Seaburg, Eds. Poetry to 10,000 words, related to natural history. Fiction and nonfiction, about 3,000 words, related to natural history. Pays $2 per page, on publication. Send fiction to Alan Seaburg, Ed., 67 Century St., W. Medford, MA 02155.

SONORA REVIEW—Dept. of English, Univ. of Arizona, Tucson, AZ 85721. Marvin Diogenes, Catherine Catellani, Eds. Fiction, poetry, reviews and short critical articles. Pays in copies. Annual prizes for fiction and poetry.

SOUTH CAROLINA REVIEW—c/o Dept. of English, Clemson Univ., Clemson, SC 29631. Carol Johnston, Man. Ed. Short stories, 3,000 to 5,000 words. Poetry. Criticism. Pays in copies.

SOUTH DAKOTA REVIEW—Box 111, Univ. Exchange, Vermillion, SD 57069. John R. Milton, Ed. Exceptional fiction, 3,000 to 5,000 words, and poetry, 10 to 25 lines. Critical articles, especially on American literature, Western American literature, theory and esthetics, 3,000 to 5,000 words. Pays in copies.

SOUTHERN HUMANITIES REVIEW—Auburn Univ., Auburn, AL 36849. Patrick D. Morrow, James P. Hammersmith, Eds. Short stories, poetry, essays, criticism, 3,500 to 5,000 words. Pays in copies.

SOUTHERN POETRY REVIEW—Dept. of English, Univ. of North Carolina, Charlotte, NC 28223. Robert W. Grey, Ed. Poems. No restrictions on style, length or content.

SOUTHERN REVIEW—43 Allen Hall, Louisiana State Univ., Baton Rouge, LA 70803. Lewis P. Simpson, James Olney, Eds. Fiction, and essays, 4,000 to 8,000 words. Serious poetry of highest quality. Pays $12 a page for prose, $20 a page for poetry, on publication.

SOUTHWEST REVIEW—Southern Methodist Univ., Dallas, TX 72575. Charlotte T. Whaley, Ed. Short stories, book reviews and articles, 3,000 to 5,000 words. Poetry. Pays on publication.

THE SOUTHWESTERN REVIEW—English Dept., Univ. of Southwestern Louisiana, Box 4691, Lafayette, LA 70504. Annual. Fiction and poetry, by regional writers. Pays in copies.

SOU'WESTER—Dept. of English, Southern Illinois Univ. at Edwardsville, Edwardsville, IL 62026. Dickie Spurgeon, Ed. Fiction, to 10,000 words. Poetry, especially poems over 100 lines. Pays in copies.

SPECTRUM—U.C.S.B., Box 14800, Santa Barbara, CA 93106. Short stories, articles on literature, memoirs. Poetry, to 100 lines. Send no more than 5 poems per submission. Pays in copies and awards.

THE SPIRIT THAT MOVES US—P.O. Box 1585 TW, Iowa City, IA 52244. Morty Sklar, Ed. Biannual. Fiction, poetry, that is expressive rather than formal or sensational. Each issue focuses on a specific theme—query. Pays $10 to $20 for fiction and nonfiction, $5 for poems, on publication.

STONE COUNTRY—P.O. Box 132, Menemsha, MA 02552. Judith Neeld, Ed. High-quality contemporary poetry in all genres. Pays in copies. Annual award.

STONY HILLS: NEWS & REVIEWS OF THE SMALL PRESS—Weeks Mills, New Sharon, ME 04955. Diane Kruchkow, Ed. Reviews of small press books and magazines nationwide, to 500 words. Some short poetry. Pays in copies. Query on nonfiction preferred.

STORY QUARTERLY—P.O. Box 1416, Northbrook, IL 60062. Short stories and interviews. Pays in copies.

STUDIES IN AMERICAN FICTION—English Dept., Northeastern Univ., Boston, MA 02115. James Nagel, Ed. Reviews, 750 words; scholarly essays, 2,500 to 6,500 words, on American fiction. Pays in copies.

SUN DOG—406 Williams Bldg., English Dept., Florida State Univ., Tallahassee, FL 32306. Allen Woodman, Ed. Rick Lott, Poetry Ed. Fiction. Poetry. Awards $100 for best fiction and poems in each issue when funds are available.

TAR RIVER POETRY—Dept. of English, East Carolina Univ., Greenville, NC 27834. Peter Makuck, Ed. Poems, all styles. Submit between September and May. Pays in copies.

TAURUS—Box 28, Gladstone, OR 97027. Bruce Combs, Ed. Quarterly. Fresh, earnest, and energetic poetry. Pays in copies.

TELESCOPE—P.O. Box 16129, Baltimore, MD 21218. Jack Stephens, Julia Wendell, Eds. Triannual. Fiction and nonfiction, 10 to 30 pages. Poetry—send no more than 10 poems at a time. Pays 50¢ a line for poetry, $3 a page for prose, on acceptance. Most issues focus on a specific theme; query for details.

TERRA POETICA—Dept. of Modern Languages and Literatures, SUNY at Buffalo, Buffalo, NY 14260. Jorge Guitart, Ed. Poetry: non-English originals and their English translations. Pays in copies. Query preferred.

THE TEXAS REVIEW—English Dept., Sam Houston State Univ., Huntsville, TX 77341. Paul Ruffin, Ed. Fiction, poetry, articles, to 20 typed pages. Reviews. Pays in copies.

THE THREEPENNY REVIEW—P.O. Box 9131, Berkeley, CA 94709. Wendy Lesser, Ed. Fiction, to 1,000 words. Poetry, to 40 lines. Essays, on books, theater, film, dance, music, art, television, and politics, 1,500 to 3,000 words. Pays $25 to $50, on publication.

TOUCHSTONE—P.O. Box 42331, Houston, TX 77042. Bill Laufer, Pub. Quarterly. Fiction, 750 to 2,000 words: mainstream, fantasy, mystery, experimental, historical. Interviews, essays, reviews. Poetry, 2 to 34 lines. Pays in copies.

TRANSLATION—The Translation Center, 307A Mathematics Bldg., Columbia Univ., New York, NY 10027. Frank MacShane, Dir. Diane G. H. Cook, Man. Ed. Semiannual. New translations of contemporary foreign poetry and prose.

TRIQUARTERLY—1735 Benson Ave., Northwestern Univ., Evanston, IL 60201. Serious, aesthetically informed and inventive poetry and prose, for an international and literate audience. Pays $12 per page.

THE UNIVERSITY OF PORTLAND REVIEW—Univ. of Portland, Portland, OR 97203. Thomas H. Faller, Ed. Scholarly articles and contemporary fiction, 500 to 2,500 words. Poetry. Book reviews. Pays in copies.

THE UNIVERSAL BLACK WRITER—P.O. Box 5, Radio City Sta., New York, NY 10101. Linda Cousins, Ed. How-to articles, 1,000 to 1,500 words, for

Black writers. Fiction, 1,000 words, geared toward same audience. Profiles of Black writers and institutions. Poetry to 2 pages. Pays in copies.

UNIVERSITY OF WINDSOR REVIEW—Dept. of English, Univ. of Windsor, Windsor, Ont., Canada N9B 3P4. Eugene McNamara, Ed. Short stories, poetry, criticism, reviews. Pays $10 to $25, on publication.

UNMUZZLED OX—105 Hudson St., New York, NY 10013. Michael Andre, Ed. Interviews, literary criticism, reviews, parts-of-novels. Poetry. Include cover letter with submissions. Pays in copies.

THE VILLAGER—135 Midland Ave., Bronxville, NY 10708. Amy Murphy, Ed. Fiction, 900 to 1,500 words: mystery, adventure, humor, romance. Short, preferably seasonal poetry. Pays in copies.

VIRGINIA QUARTERLY REVIEW—One W. Range, Charlottesville, VA 22903. Quality fiction and poetry. Serious essays and articles, 3,000 to 6,000 words, on literature, science, politics, economics, etc. Pays $10 per page for prose, $1 per line for poetry, on publication.

WASCANA REVIEW—c/o Dept. of English, Univ. of Regina, Regina, Sask., Canada S4S 0A2. John Chamberlain, Ed. Short stories, 2,000 to 6,000 words; critical articles; poetry. Pays $3 per page, after publication.

WASHINGTON REVIEW—P.O. Box 50132, Washington, DC 20004. Mary Swift, Ed. Poetry; articles on literary, performing and fine arts in the Washington, D.C. area, 1,000 to 2,500 words. Fiction, to 1,000 words. Pays in copies.

WEBSTER REVIEW—Webster Univ., Webster Groves, MO 63119. Nancy Schapiro, Ed. Fiction; poetry; interviews; essays; translations. Pays in copies.

WEST BRANCH—English Dept., Bucknell Univ., Lewisburg, PA 17837. Karl Patten, Robert Taylor, Eds. Poetry and fiction. Pays in copies.

WEST COAST POETRY REVIEW—1335 Dartmouth Dr., Reno, NV 89509. Bruce McAllister, Assoc. Ed. Experimental fiction, avant-garde poetry. Criticism of poetry. Pays in copies.

WESTERN HUMANITIES REVIEW—Univ. of Utah, Salt Lake City, UT 84112. Jack Garlington, Ed. Robert Shapard, Man. Ed. Articles on the humanities; fiction; poetry; book and film reviews. Pays $150 for fiction, to $50 for poems, on acceptance.

THE WINDLESS ORCHARD—Dept. of English, Indiana-Purdue Univ., Ft. Wayne, IN 46805. Robert Novak, Ed. Contemporary poetry. Pays in copies.

WINEWOOD JOURNAL—P.O. Box 339, Black Hawk, CO 80422. Kate Aiello, Ed. Poetry; short stories; essays; reviews. Pays in copies.

WISCONSIN REVIEW—Box 276, Dempsey Hall, Univ. of Wisconsin, Oshkosh, WI 54901. Luke Gabrilska, Senior Ed. Fiction, to 4,000 words. Quality poems. Pays in copies.

WRITERS FORUM—Univ. of Colorado, Colorado Springs, CO 80933-7150. Alex Blackburn, Ed. Annual. Mainstream and experimental fiction, 1,000 to 10,000 words. Poetry (1 to 5 poems per submission). Send material January through August. Pays in copies.

YALE REVIEW—1902A Yale Sta., New Haven, CT 06520. Kai Erikson, Ed. Serious poetry, to 200 lines and fiction, 3,000 to 5,000 words. Pays in copies.

THE DRAMA MARKET

REGIONAL AND UNIVERSITY THEATRES

Community, regional and civic theatres and college dramatic groups offer the best opportunities today for playwrights to see their plays produced, whether for staged production, or for dramatic readings. Indeed, aspiring playwrights who can get their work produced by any of these have taken an important step toward breaking into the competitive dramatic field—many well-known playwrights received their first recognition in the regional theatres. Payment is generally not large, but regional and university theatres usually buy only the right to produce a play, and all further rights revert to the author. Since most directors like to work closely with the authors on any revisions necessary, theatres will often pay for the playwright's expenses while in residence during rehearsals. The thrill of seeing your play come to life on the stage is one of the pleasures of being on hand for rehearsals and performances.

Aspiring playwrights should query college and community theatres in their region to find out which ones are interested in seeing original scripts. Dramatic associations of interest to playwrights include the Dramatists Guild and Theatre Communications, Inc. The latter publishes the annual *Dramatists Sourcebook.*

Some of the theatres on the following list require that playwrights submit all or some of the following with scripts—cast list, synopsis, resumé, recommendations, return postcard—and with scripts and queries, self-addressed, stamped envelopes (SASE) must *always* be enclosed. Playwrights may also wish to register their material with the U.S. Copyright Office. For additional information about this, write Register of Copyrights, Library of Congress, Washington, DC 20559.

ACADEMY THEATRE—1137 Peachtree St., N.E., Atlanta, GA 30309. Frank Wittow, Artistic Dir. One-act and full-length dramas, and adaptations with new approaches that go beyond the conventions of naturalism; 6 to 8 cast members unless actors can play multiple roles. Simple settings. Pays negotiable rates. Query first.

ACTORS THEATRE OF LOUISVILLE—316 W. Main St., Louisville, KY 40202. Jon Jory, Artistic Dir. One-act and full-length dramas and comedies. Send manuscript, cast list, and SASE to "New Plays Program." Reports in 3 to 6 months. Payment varies.

ALASKA REPERTORY THEATRE—705 W. 6th Ave., Suite 201, Anchorage, AK 99501. Robert Farley, Artistic Dir. Full-length dramas, comedies, and adaptations. Queries only; include SASE.

ALLEY THEATRE—615 Texas Ave., Houston, TX 77002. Beth Sanford and Trent Jenkins, Literary Advisors. No unsolicited manuscripts. Submit synopsis of full-length comedies, dramas and adaptations.

ALLIANCE THEATRE COMPANY—1280 Peachtree St. N.E., Atlanta, GA 30309. Sandra Deer, Lit. Man. Dramas, comedies, children's plays. Submit manuscript with SASE. Reporting time: 3 months. Royalty basis.

AMAS REPERTORY COMPANY—1 E. 104th St., New York, NY 10029. Rosetta LeNoire, Artistic Dir. Original full-length musicals for adults and children. No complex sets. Enclose manuscript with cast list, cassette tape of score, and SASE. No payment.

AMERICAN CONSERVATORY THEATRE—450 Geary St., San Francisco, CA 94102. Janice Hutchins, Director, Plays-in-Progress. Plays with good characterization and structure, for production and staged readings. No payment, but offers residency for duration of rehearsals and performances. Allow up to six months for report. Office closed June–Sept.

AMERICAN JEWISH THEATER—c/o 92nd St., YM-YWHA, 1395 Lexington Ave., New York, NY 10028. Address Robert Blumenfeld. Full-length comedies, dramas, musicals and adaptations. Plays should have direct or indirect Jewish theme. Send manuscript with SASE. No payment. Allow 2 months for reply.

AMERICAN PLACE THEATRE—111 W. 46th St., New York, NY 10036. Address Lit. Man. Full-length dramas. Do not favor commercial comedies or musicals. Inexpensive set. Send manuscript with synopsis and SASE. Allow 4 to 6 months for reply.

AMERICAN REPERTORY THEATRE—64 Brattle St., Cambridge, MA 02138. Jonathan Marks, Lit. Man. No unsolicited manuscripts. Submit one-page description of play and SASE.

AMERICAN STAGE COMPANY—P.O. Box 1560, St. Petersburg, FL 33731. Victoria Holloway, Artistic Dir. Full-length comedies and dramas. Send synopsis with short description of cast and production requirements with self-addressed postcard. Pays negotiable rates. Submit material November through January.

THE APPLE CORPS.—601 W. 51st St., New York, NY 10019. Address Robert Coles. All types of plays. Send manuscript with SASE. Payment varies. No recent report.

ARENA STAGE—6th and Maine Ave., S.W., Washington, DC 20024. Full-length comedies, dramas, musicals and adaptations. John Glore, Lit. Man. Submit one-page synopsis with resume and recommendations. No unsolicited manuscripts. Pays varying rates. Workshops and readings offered. Allow 2 to 4 months for reply.

ARIZONA THEATRE COMPANY—P.O. Box 1631, Tucson, AZ 85702. Gary Gisselman, Artistic Director. Full-length dramas, comedies, and musicals, for production and stage readings. Submissions preferred in January and February. Pays on royalty basis.

ARKANSAS ARTS CENTER CHILDREN'S THEATRE—Box 2137, Little Rock, AR 72203. Bradley Anderson, Art. Dir. Seeks solid, professional (full length or one-act) scripts. Original, and, particularly, adapted work from contemporary and classic literature. Pays flat rate.

ASOLO STATE THEATRE—P.O. Drawer E, Sarasota, FL 33578. John Ulmer, Artistic Dir. Full-length dramas, comedies, musicals, and children's plays. Small stage. Pays royalty or varying rates. Readings and workshops offered.

ASPEN PLAYWRIGHTS CONFERENCE (a division of the *American Theater Company in Aspen*)—Box 9438, Aspen, CO 81612. Full-length and one-act dramas, comedies for small cast; few sets. Submit fall of each year.

AT THE FOOT OF THE MOUNTAIN—2000 S. 5th St., Minneapolis, MN 55454. Judith Katz, Lit. Man. Full-length and one-act plays of all types, with particular interest in scripts by and about women. Submit manuscript with synopsis, return postcard, and SASE (best time to submit: early spring). Reports in 4 to 6 months. Pays on royalty basis.

710

BACK ALLEY THEATRE—15231 Burbank Blvd., Van Nuys, CA 91411. Laura Zucker, Producing Dir. Full-length plays. Submit manuscript with SASE and resume. Reports in 2–3 months. Pays $500, and travel/expenses for playwright to attend rehearsals.

BARTER THEATER—P.O. Box 867, Abingdon, VA 24210. Rex Partington, Producing Dir. Full-length dramas, comedies, adaptations, musicals and children's plays, for full workshop and reading productions. Allow 6 to 8 months for report. Payment rates negotiable.

BEAR REPUBLIC THEATRE—P.O. Box 1137, Santa Cruz, CA 95061. Michael Griggs, Art. Dir. Full-length and one-act scripts, particularly bilingual and children's plays; social and political topics. Query first. Reports in two months. Pays on production.

BERKELEY REPERTORY THEATRE—2025 Addison St., Berkeley, CA 94704. Carole Braverman, Lit. Man. Besides main season, produces *Playworks*—five staged readings of new plays in second stage. Enclose SASE. Reporting time: 4 to 6 months. No sit-coms.

BERKELEY STAGE COMPANY—Box 2327, Berkeley, CA 94702. Robert MacDougall, Lit. Man. Full-length comedies, dramas, and musicals; 8 to 10 cast members; unit set. Send manuscript with synopsis, cast list, resume, and SASE. Pays $35 for first performance, $15 for each additional showing, at the end of run. No recent report.

BOARSHEAD: MICHIGAN PUBLIC THEATRE—425 S. Grand Ave., Lansing, MI 48933. Richard Thomsen, Artistic Dir. Full-length comedies and dramas. Midwestern origin/theme preferred. Pays negotiable rates.

BURBAGE THEATRE ENSEMBLE—10508 W. Pico Blvd., Los Angeles, CA 90064. Ivan Spiegal, Art. Dir. Full-length comedies, dramas, and musicals. Query first. Six-month reporting time. Pays negotiable rates.

CALDWELL PLAYHOUSE—P.O. Box 277, Boca Raton, FL 33432. Full-length comedies, dramas, for cast of up to 8. Send manuscript with short biographical sketch, between October and March. Pays negotiable rates. Offers workshops.

CAST THEATRE—804 El Centro Ave., Los Angeles, CA 90038. Address Lit. Man. Full-length dramas, comedies, and musicals, preferably with one abstract set, 10 to 12 cast members. Submit manuscript with resumé and SASE. Pays $50 a week against 5% of box office.

CENTER STAGE—700 N. Calvert St., Baltimore, MD 21202. Jackson Phippin, Assoc. Artistic Dir. Full-length and one-act comedies, dramas, musicals, adaptations and children's plays. No unsolicited manuscripts. Send synopsis, resume, cast list, recommendations and production history, with return postcard and SASE, in late spring. Pays varying rates. Offers workshops and readings. Allow 4 months for reply.

CHELSEA THEATER CENTER, INC.—407 W. 43rd St., 3rd Fl., New York, NY 10036. Full-length translations of little-known classics; contemporary European plays; American plays of distinction; adaptations; contemporary musicals. Pays on percentage basis. Query with synopsis and SASE.

CHILDREN'S THEATRE OF RICHMOND, INC.—6317 Mallory Drive, Richmond, VA 23226. One-acts and musicals for children 5 to 12, 45 minutes to one hour. Pays on royalty basis. Query with synopsis and score between October and March.

711

CINCINNATI PLAYHOUSE IN THE PARK—Box 6537, Cincinnati, OH 45206. Michael Burnham, Lit. Man. Full-length comedies, dramas, musicals, adaptations and cabarets. Rarely accepts unsolicited manuscripts. Send synopsis with cast list, resume, recommendations and return postcard. Pays negotiable rates and travel expenses. Allow 6 months to a year for reply.

CIRCLE IN THE SQUARE—1633 Broadway, New York, NY 10019. Theodore Mann, Art. Dir. Robert Pesola, Lit. Advisor. Full-length comedies, dramas, and musicals, suitable for thrust and arena staging. Send query with one page synopsis; 3-month reporting time. Pays negotiable rates.

CIRCLE REPERTORY COMPANY—161 Ave. of Americas, New York, NY 10013. B. Rodney Marriott, Assoc. Art. Dir. New plays by American writers; manuscripts accepted through agents only.

CLEVELAND PLAYHOUSE—8500 Euclid Ave., P.O. Box 1989, Cleveland, OH 44106. Arthur Knight, Literary Asst. Full-length dramas, comedies, and adaptations. Query with synopsis. Pays on royalty basis.

COMMON GROUND THEATRE ENSEMBLE—P.O. Box 7126, Ann Arbor, MI 48107. Elise Bryant, Artistic Dir. Full-length comedies, dramas, musicals and adaptations. Interested in plays on labor and feminist issues. Send manuscript with cast list and synopsis. Pays negotiable rates. Offers workshops and readings.

A CONTEMPORARY THEATRE—100 West Roy St., Seattle, WA 98119. Address Barry Pritchard. Full-length plays of all kinds, for adults and children. Small musicals. Pays on royalty basis.

COUNTRY PLAYHOUSE—12802 Queensbury, Town and Country Village, Houston, TX 77024. Address John Newell. Full-length and one-act dramas, comedies, and non-musicals. Submit manuscript with synopsis, resume, and return postcard. Pays varying rates.

THE CRICKET THEATRE—Hennepin Center for the Arts, 528 Hennepin Ave., Minneapolis, MN 55403. Address Lit. Man. Full-length comedies and dramas for cast up to 6; single or unit set. Send manuscript with return postcard and SASE. Six-month reporting time. Pays on contract basis, plus travel and residence expenses.

CROSSROADS THEATRE CO.—320 Memorial Pkwy., New Brunswick, NJ 08901. Lee Richardson, Art. Dir. Full-length and one-act dramas, comedies, musicals and adaptations; experimental pieces; one man/one woman shows. Queries only, with synopsis, cast list, resume and SASE.

DENVER CENTER THEATRE COMPANY—1050 13th St., Denver, CO 80204. Peter Hackett, Assoc. Art. Dir. Full-length and one-act comedies, dramas, musicals and adaptations. Send manuscript with synopsis, resumé, return postcard and SASE. Pays negotiable rates. Special interest in regional material.

DETROIT REPERTORY THEATRE—13103 Woodrow Wilson Ave., Detroit, MI 48238. Barbara Busby, Lit. Man. Full-length comedies, and dramas. Enclose SASE. Pays royalty. Annual contest.

EAST WEST PLAYERS—4424 Santa Monica Blvd., Los Angeles, CA 90029. Alberto Isaac, Lit. Man. Full-length comedies, dramas and musicals, dealing with Asian American issues and/or including important roles for Asian actors. Cast up to 15. Send manuscript with synopsis, cast list, resume and SASE. Pays varying rates. Offers workshops and readings. Allow 3 months for reply.

712

EMPIRE STATE INSTITUTE FOR THE PERFORMING ARTS—Empire State Plaza, Albany, NY 12223. Barbara R. Maggio, Lit. Man. Full-length and one-act plays and musicals (preferably unproduced) on any subject. Submit manuscript and synopsis. Pays negotiable rates.

THE EMPTY SPACE THEATRE—Merrill Place, 1st Ave. S. and S. Jackson, Seattle, WA 98104. M. Burke Walker, Art. Dir. Unsolicited scripts accepted from WA, OR, WY, MT and ID only for annual conference: brochure available on request. Outside five-state NW region: scripts accepted through agents or established theater groups only.

ENSEMBLE STUDIO THEATRE—549 W. 52nd St., New York, NY 10019. Stuart Spencer, Lit. Man. Full-length and one-act dramas and comedies, for cast of up to 12; small stage. Send manuscript with cast list, return postcard and SASE. Pays $1,000 for full-length, $175 for one-acts.

EQUITY LIBRARY THEATRE—165 W. 46th St., New York, NY 10036. Rebecca Kreinen, Producer. Full-length plays, including musicals, previously unproduced. Limited facilities. Send manuscript with resume, postcard and SASE, in April and May. No payment.

THE FAMILY—50 E. 7th St., New York, NY 10003. Attn. Patrick I. Honde. Full-length and one-act dramas and musicals. Submit manuscript with synopsis, return postcard and resume. Pays small fee.

FLORIDA STUDIO THEATRE—1241 North Palm Ave., Sarasota, FL 33566. Richard Hopkins, Art. Dir. Full-length comedies, dramas and musicals, preferably with small cast. Pays varying rates. Enclose return postcard.

FOLGER THEATRE GROUP—201 E. Capitol St., S.E., Washington, DC 20003. Bob Stevens, Lit. Man. New versions or adaptations of classics. Payment rates negotiable. Query with SASE.

FORCE TEN PRODUCTIONS, INC.—1 W. 72nd St., No. 44, New York, NY 10023. Carol Drechsler, Dir. of Dev. Full-length comedies and dramas, for Off-Broadway and Broadway theatre, with casts up to 12. Query with synopsis and SASE. No payment.

GEVA THEATRE—168 Clinton Ave. S., Rochester, NY 14604. Ann Patrice Carrigan, Lit. Dir. Full-length and one-act dramas, comedies and musicals. Submit manuscript with SASE. Pays on percentage basis.

THE GOODMAN THEATRE—200 South Columbus Dr., Chicago, IL 60603. Gregory Mosher, Artistic Dir. No unsolicited manuscripts. Query through agent or other playwright.

THE GUTHRIE THEATRE—725 Vineland Pl., Minneapolis, MN 55403. Mark Bly, Lit. Man. Full-length comedies, dramas, and adaptations. Manuscripts accepted only from recognized theatrical agents. Query with detailed synopsis, cast size, resume, return postcard and recommendations. Pays negotiable rates, and travel/residency expenses. Offers readings. Reports in 1 to 2 months.

HARTFORD STAGE COMPANY—50 Church St., Hartford, CT 06103. Constance Congdon, Lit. Man. Full-length plays of all types, for cast up to 12. No unsolicited manuscripts; submit through agent or send synopsis and 10 pages of sample dialogue. Pays varying rates.

HARTMAN THEATER COMPANY—307 Atlantic St., Stamford, CT 06901. Edwin Sherin, Artistic Dir. Full-length comedies, dramas and musicals. No unsolicited manuscripts. Query with synopsis, return postcard and SASE. Offers workshops and readings. Reports in 3 to 4 months.

713

HIPPODROME THEATRE—25 S.E. Second Place, Gainesville, FL 32601. Gregory Haush, Artistic Director. Full-length plays, with unit sets and casts up to 15. Submit in summer and fall. Enclose return postcard and synopsis.

HOLLYWOOD ACTORS THEATRE—P.O. Box 27429, Los Angeles, CA 90027. Ron Bastone, Art. Dir. Full-length comedies and dramas, for cast of 6 to 15 actors; single or unit set preferred. Send manuscript with synopsis, cast list, resumé, and SASE. Pays 20% of gross receipts.

HONOLULU THEATRE FOR YOUTH—Box 3257, Honolulu, HI 96801. John Kauffman, Art. Dir. Plays, 60 to 90 minutes playing time, for young people/family audiences. Adult casts. Contemporary issues, Pacific themes, etc. Unit sets, small cast. Query or send manuscript with synopsis, cast list and SASE. Royalties negotiable.

HUDSON GUILD THEATRE—441 W. 26th St., New York, NY 10001. David Kerry Heefner, Producing Dir. Full-length comedies, dramas and adaptations, for single or simple set, and cast to 10. Enclose SASE. Pays $750. Workshops and readings offered.

ILLINOIS THEATRE CENTER—400 Lakewood Blvd., Park Forest, IL 60466. Steve S. Billig, Artistic Dir. Full-length comedies, dramas, musicals and adaptations, for unit/fragmentary sets, and cast to 6. Send manuscript with recommendations and return postcard. Pays negotiable rates. Workshops and readings offered.

THE INDEPENDENT EYE—208 East King St., Lancaster, PA 17602. Conrad Bishop, Artistic Dir. Full-length comedies and dramas, for simple set and cast to 8. Send synopsis and resume first. Pays about $35 per performance. Reports in 6 months. Offers staged readings.

INVISIBLE THEATRE—1400 N. First Ave., Tucson, AZ 85719. Christine Meisser, Lit. Man. Full-length comedies, dramas, musicals and adaptations, for cast to 10; simple set. Send manuscript with cast list, return postcard and SASE. Pays on percentage basis.

JACKSONVILLE UNIVERSITY THEATRE—Jacksonville Univ., Jacksonville, FL 32211. Davis Sikes, Artistic Dir. Unproduced full-length and one-act dramas and comedies. Send manuscript with synopsis, cast list, return postcard, and SASE. Pays $1,000 and production.

JEWISH REPERTORY THEATRE—344 E. 14th St., New York, NY 10003. Ran Avni, Artistic Dir. Full-length comedies, dramas, musicals, children's plays and adaptations, with cast to 10, relating to the Jewish experience. Pays varying rates. Enclose return postcard.

THE JULIAN THEATRE—953 DeHaro St., San Francisco, CA 94107. Address New Plays. Full-length comedies and dramas with a social statement. Send 5 to 10 page scene, synopsis, cast description, and SASE. Pays on contractual basis. Allow 2 to 9 months for reply. Workshops and readings offered.

KARAMU HOUSE, INC.—2355 E. 89th St., Cleveland, OH 44106. Full-length and one-act plays of all kinds, for workshop and reading productions. Reports in 3 months. Payment rates negotiable.

KENYON FESTIVAL THEATER—P.O. Box 404, Gambier, OH 43022. Address Thomas G. Dunn, Producing Dir. Full-length and one-act comedies and dramas, with unit or one set, and cast to 12. Send manuscript with synopsis, cast list, SASE and return postcard. Pays on royalty basis.

L.A. PUBLIC THEATRE—8105 W. 3rd St., Los Angeles, CA 90048. Peg Yorkin, Art. Dir. Comedies, dramas; full-length and one-act. Submit script, cast list, and synopsis. Reporting time: six months.

LAMB'S PLAYERS THEATRE—500 Plaza Blvd., P.O. Box 26, National City, CA 92050. Address Script Search Committee. All types of full-length plays, for small cast; arena staging. Send manuscript with cast list and synopsis. Pays $500 to $1,000.

LOOKING GLASS THEATRE—175 Matthewson St., Providence, RI 02903. Pamela Messore, Artistic Dir. One-act, participation style children's plays, with cast to 5. Send manuscript with return postcard and SASE. Pays negotiable rates. Allow 6 weeks for reply.

LOS ANGELES ACTORS' THEATRE—514 S. Spring St., Los Angeles, CA 90013. Adam Leipzig, Dramaturg. Full-length comedies, dramas, musicals and adaptations; special interest in plays with social/political content. Query with synopsis, cast list and SASE. Pays advance against 4% or 5%, at time of production, and travel and residence expenses.

MCCADDEN PLACE THEATRE—1157 N. McCadden Place, Los Angeles, CA 90038. Address Joy O'Neil, Artistic Dir. Full-length and one-act comedies, dramas and adaptations. Send manuscript with cast list, synopsis, resume, return postcard and SASE. Pays varying rates.

MCCARTER THEATRE COMPANY—91 University Pl., Princeton, NJ 08540. Robert Lanchester, Assoc. Art. Dir. Full-length comedies and dramas. Send manuscript with cast list and SASE. Pays negotiable rates.

MAGIC THEATRE—Bldg. D, Fort Mason, San Francisco, CA 94123. Martin Esslin, Dramaturg. Full-length and one-act comedies and dramas, for cast to 10; simple set. Send manuscript with SASE. Pays on royalty basis.

MANHATTAN THEATRE CLUB—321 E. 73rd St., New York, NY 10021. Address Jonathan Alper. Full-length and one-act comedies, dramas and musicals. No unsolicited manuscripts. Send synopsis with cast list, resume, recommendations and return postcard. Pays negotiable rates. Allow 6 months for reply. Offers workshops and readings.

MEGAW THEATRE, INC.—17601 Saticoy St., Northridge, CA 91325. Address Marcia Steil. Full-length comedies and dramas, with cast of 7 to 10, and unit set. Send manuscripts with synopsis, cast list, resume, recommendations, return postcard and SASE. Pays on contractual basis. Offers readings.

MIDWEST PLAYLABS—c/o The Playwrights' Center, 2301 Franklin Ave. E., Minneapolis, MN 55406. One-act and full-length comedies and dramas, by playwrights associated with the Midwest only. Submit scripts with synopsis, cast list, and SASE between Jan. 1 and March 15. Pays stipend, room and board, and partial travel.

THE NEGRO ENSEMBLE COMPANY—165 W. 46th St., Suite 800, New York, NY 10036. Douglas Turner Ward, Art. Dir. Full-length comedies, dramas, musicals and adaptations pertaining to Black life and the Black experience. Submit March through May. Pays on royalty basis. Enclose return postcard. No recent report.

THE NEIGHBORHOOD GROUP THEATRE—420 W. 42nd St., New York, NY 10036. Kathryn Ballou, Art. Dir. Full-length comedies, dramas, and adaptations; special interest in plays about the South. Simple sets. Send manuscript with synopsis, cast list, return postcard, and SASE. Nominal payment.

NEW DRAMATISTS—424 W. 44th St., New York, NY 10036. Workshop for playwrights living in New York City. Submit two original, full-length, nonmusical scripts, along with resume, bio, and statement outlining goals. Playwrights from outside New York City may apply only if recommended by theatre professional from a regional theatre. Deadline for applications: November 1 annually. Send for guidelines.

NEW TUNERS/PERFORMANCE COMMUNITY—1225 W. Belmont Ave., Chicago, IL 60657. George H. Gorman, Dramaturg. Full-length musicals only, for cast to 15; no wing/fly space. Send manuscript with cassette tape of score, cast list, resume and return postcard. Pays on a royalty basis.

NEW YORK SHAKESPEARE FESTIVAL—425 Lafayette St., New York, NY 10003. Gail Merrifield, Dir. of New Plays and Musicals Dept. Bill Hart, Lit. Man. Plays, musical works for the theatre, translations, and adaptations. Submit manuscript with synopsis and SASE. Enclose cassette with musicals.

NORTHLIGHT REPERTORY THEATRE—2300 Green Bay Rd., Evanston, IL 60201. Jimmy Bickerstaff, Asst. Art. Dir. Full-length plays, music-theatre, translations, and adaptations for cast to 10; small theatre. Synopses only. Royalties, fees and compensations negotiable.

ODYSSEY THEATRE ENSEMBLE—12111 Ohio Ave., Los Angeles, CA 90025. Ron Sossi, Artistic Dr. Full-length comedies, dramas, musicals, and adaptations: provocative subject matter, or plays that stretch and explore the form and possibilities of theatre. Send manuscript with synopsis and return postcard. Pays variable rates. Allow 2 to 6 months for reply. Workshops and readings offered.

OLD GLOBE THEATRE—Simon Edison Center for the Performing Arts, Box 2171, San Diego, CA 92112. Address Andrew Traister. Full-length comedies and dramas with casts up to ten, and single set. Send cast list and synopsis with script.

EUGENE O'NEILL THEATER CENTER—Suite 901, 234 W. 44th St., New York, NY 10036. Annual competition to select new stage and television plays for development at organization's Waterford, Ct. location. Submit entries between Sept. 15 and Dec. 1, 1985, for 1986 conference. Send SASE for rules to National Playwright's Conference, c/o above address. Pays $350, plus travel/living expenses during conference.

PENNSYLVANIA STAGE COMPANY—837 Linden St., Allentown, PA 18101. Pamela K. Pepper, Lit. Man. Full-length plays with cast to 8; one set. Full-length musicals, with unit set and cast to 18. Send manuscript with synopsis, cast list and return postage. Pays negotiable rates. Allow 3 months for reply. Offers readings.

PEOPLE'S LIGHT AND THEATRE COMPANY—39 Conestoga Rd., Malvern, PA 19355. Alda Cortese, Lit. Man. Full-length and one-act comedies and dramas, for cast to 10; unit set preferred. Send synopsis with 10 pages of dialogue, cast list and SASE. Pays negotiable rates.

PLAYHOUSE ON THE SQUARE—2121 Madison Ave., Memphis, TN 38104. Jackie Nichols, Artistic Dir. Full-length comedies, dramas, and musicals, with unit or single set, and cast to 15. Send manuscript with resume, return postcard and SASE. Pays $500. Workshops or readings offered.

PLAYS IN PROGRESS AT THE A.C.T.—450 Geary St., San Francisco, CA 94102. Janice Hutchins, Dir. Full-length and one-act comedies and dramas for small cast. Send manuscript with SASE, Sept.-May. Closed in summer. Pays on royalty basis.

716

PLAYWRIGHTS HORIZONS—416 W. 42nd St., New York, NY 10036. Address Literary Dept. Full-length comedies, dramas, and musicals. Send synopsis and SASE. Pays varying rates.

PLAYWRIGHTS' PLATFORM—43 Charles St., Boston, MA 02114. David Moore, Jr., Dir. Script development workshops and public readings for New England playwrights. Full-length and one-act plays of all kinds, especially innovative in form/theme. Residents of New England: Send scripts with short synopsis, resumé, return postcard and SASE.

PORTLAND STAGE COMPANY—Box 4876 DTS, Portland, ME 04112. Barbara Rosoff, Art. Dir. Full-length comedies, dramas, and musicals, for cast to 10. Send synopsis with return postcard. Pays $1,500 and 4-week residency if play is produced.

RAFT THEATER—432 W. 42nd St., New York, NY 10036. Attn. Daniel Lauria. Full-length and one-act comedies and dramas, for cast to 8; unit set. Send manuscript with cast list and SASE. Pays good rates; one year option.

THE RESTON REPERTORY TELEVISION THEATRE—P.O. Box 3615, Reston, VA 22090. Sharon Cohen, Exec. Producer. Full-length comedies and dramas, with small cast preferred. Pays on percentage basis. Allow 3 to 4 months for reply. Readings offered. Enclose SASE.

THE ROAD COMPANY—Box 5278 EKS, Johnson City, TN 37603. Robert H. Leonard, Artistic Dir. Full-length and one-act comedies, dramas with social/political relevance to small town audiences. Send synopsis, cast list, and production history, if any. Pays negotiable rates. Reports in 6 to 12 months.

SOHO REPERTORY THEATRE—19 Mercer St., New York, NY 10013. Jerry Engelbach, Artistic Dir. Full-length dramas, musicals, adaptations and mixed media works for thrust stage. No unsolicited manuscripts. Send brief synopsis, cast list, and resume. Send for guidelines. Pays $100. Readings offered.

SOUTH COAST REPERTORY—655 Town Center Dr., Box 2197, Costa Mesa, CA 92626-1197. Jerry Patch, Lit. Man. Full-length comedies and dramas. Query with synopsis, resume and return postcard. Pays percent of gross, and travel/living expenses.

STAGE ONE: THE LOUISVILLE CHILDREN'S THEATRE—721 W. Main St., Louisville, KY 40202. Moses Goldberg, Artistic Director. Children's plays for adult actors to perform. Pays varying rates. Allow 3 to 4 months for reply. Enclose SASE.

STUDIO ARENA THEATRE—710 Main St., Buffalo, NY 14202. Kathryn Long, Dramaturg. Full-length dramas, comedies, and adaptations. Query with synopsis. Pays negotiable rates.

MARK TAPER FORUM—135 N. Grand Ave., Los Angeles, CA 90012. Plays, preferably full-length, on any subject, for production in thrust theater or flexible theater. Pays on royalty basis. Query first.

THEATRE AMERICANA—Box 245, Altadena, CA 91001. Full-length comedies, dramas and musicals. Send manuscript with cast list and SASE. No payment. Allow 3 to 6 months for reply.

THEATRE AT ST. CLEMENT'S—423 W. 26th St., New York, NY 10036. Lynn M. Thomson, Lit. Man. Full-length dramas and comedies. Send manuscript with SASE. 3-4 months reporting time. Pays negotiable rates. No recent report.

THEATRE BY THE SEA—125 Bow St., Portsmouth, NH 03801. Tom Celli, Art Dir. Full-length comedies, dramas, musicals, and adaptations, with casts up to 15. Payment rates negotiable. Enclose resume, cast list, and synopsis.

THEATRE FOR YOUNG PEOPLE—Univ. of North Carolina, Greensboro, NC 27412. Tom Behm, Art. Dir. Full-length children's plays. Submit manuscript with SASE, Dec.—April. Pays $15 to $25 per performance.

THEATRE OF THE ARTS PRODUCTIONS, LTD.—T.A.P. Ltd., P.O. Box 1833T, Detroit, MI 48231. Address Michael J. Klier. Full-length dramas, comedies, and musicals, for casts up to 6 and 1 or 2 sets. Pays varying rates.

THE THEATRE-STUDIO—750 Eighth Ave., Rm. 500, New York, NY 10036. Ann Raychel, Art. Dir. Full-length and one-act dramas, comedies, musicals and adaptations. Send manuscript with SASE. No payment.

THEATRE THREE—2800 Routh St., Dallas, TX 75201. Address Norma Young, Artistic Dir., or Jac Alder. Full-length comedies and dramas, for New Play Festival. Offers readings.

THEATREWORKS/USA (PART)—131 W. 86th St., New York, NY 10024. Barbara Miller, Promotional Director. Comedies, dramas, musicals or plays for young people, particularly historical musicals, for casts up to 6 (can double). Set should be good, simple and portable. Pays $1,500 to $2,000. Send resume, recommendations, cast list, and synopsis (to 50 words).

13TH STREET REPERTORY COMPANY—50 W. 13th St., New York, NY 10011. Address Play Reading Committee. One-act dramas, musicals and children's plays, with cast to 9 and simple set. Send synopsis, return postcard and SASE with manuscript. No payment. Allow 3 to 6 months for reply. Workshops or readings offered.

UNIVERSITY OF ALABAMA THEATRE—115 Music and Speech Bldg., P.O. Box 6386, University, AL 35486. Thomas J. Taylor, Art. Dir. Full-length and one-act comedies, dramas, and musicals. Send manuscript with SASE. Payment varies. Reports in 2 to 3 months. Readings.

VIRGINIA MUSEUM THEATRE—Boulevard and Grove, Richmond, VA 23221. Tom Markus, Artistic Dir. Full-length comedies, dramas and musicals. Send synopsis, cast list and SASE with manuscript. Submit in late spring. No payment. Allow 6 to 12 months for reply.

WILLIAMSTOWN THEATRE FEST—Box 517, Williamstown, MA 01267. Address Literary Manager. Full-length dramas and comedies. Submit September through February. No payment.

WISDOM BRIDGE THEATRE—1559 W. Howard St., Chicago, IL 60626. Address Douglas Finlayson. Full-length and one-act dramas and comedies. Must enclose synopsis and SASE with manuscript. Pays negotiable rates.

WOOLLY MAMMOTH THEATRE COMPANY—1317 G St. N.W., Washington, D.C. 20005. Howard Shalwitz, Art. Dir. Innovative scripts for full-length plays; cast to 12. Submit synopsis with SASE. Pays on performance.

GARY YOUNG MIME THEATRE—9613 Windcroft Way, Rockville, MD 20854. Gary Young, Artistic Director. Mime and comedies, for children and adults, 1 minute to 90 minutes in length; casts of 1 or 2, and portable set. Pays varying rates. Enclose return postcard, resume, recommendations, cast list and synopsis.

718

RADIO THEATRES

R. BEAN'S VOICE THEATRE—467 Sidney St., Madison, WI 53703. Gene Becker, Assoc. Prod. Radio theatre. 15-minute to half-hour radio dramas, mysteries, comedies, adventure, horror, and suspense, etc. Pays $100 to $500 for half-hour script, no later than ten days after completion of final production. Send SASE for "Writers' Format."

NATIONAL RADIO THEATRE OF CHICAGO—600 N. McClurg Ct., Suite 502-A, Chicago, IL 60611. Yuri Rasovsky, Producer. Original radio scripts. Pays varying rates. Write for guidelines.

TALKING INFORMATION CENTER—Library Plaza, Marshfield, MA 02050. Grace Rudolph, Producing Director. Half-hour radio scripts for cast to 8; simple sound effects. Send manuscript with SASE. Guidelines available. Non-profit radio station: no pay, but playwright may become involved in production.

PLAY PUBLISHERS

ART CRAFT PLAY COMPANY—Box 1058, Cedar Rapids, IA 52406. Three-act comedies and one-act comedies or dramas, with one set, for production by junior and senior high schools. Pays on royalty basis or by outright purchase.

WALTER H. BAKER COMPANY—100 Chauncy St., Boston, MA 02111. Scripts for amateur production: one-act plays for competition, children's plays, religious drama, full-length plays for high school production. Three- to four-month reading period. Include SASE.

CHILD LIFE MAGAZINE—P.O. Box 567, Indianapolis, IN 46206. Plays, 700 and 1,600 words, for classroom or living-room production by children 8 to 11 years. Pays about 4¢ a word, on publication. Buys all rights.

CHILDREN'S PLAYMATE MAGAZINE—1100 Waterway Blvd., P.O. Box 567, Indianapolis, IN 46206. Kathleen B. Mosher, Ed. Plays, 200 to 600 words, for children 5 to 7: special emphasis on health, nutrition, exercise, and safety. Pays about 4¢ a word, on publication.

CONTEMPORARY DRAMA SERVICE—Meriwether Publishing, Ltd., Box 7710, 885 Elkton Dr., Colorado Springs, CO 80933. Arthur Zapel, Ed. Easy-to-stage comedies, skits, one-acts, musicals, puppet scripts, full-length plays for schools and churches. Adaptations of classics, and improvisational material for classroom use. Comedy monologues and duets. Chancel drama for Christmas and Easter church use. Enclose synopsis. Pays by fee arrangement or on royalty basis.

THE DRAMATIC PUBLISHING COMPANY—4150 N. Milwaukee Ave., Chicago, IL 60641. Full-length and one-act plays, musical comedies for amateur and stock groups. Must run at least thirty minutes. Pays on royalty basis. Address Sara Clark. Reports within 8 to 10 weeks.

DRAMATICS—3368 Central Pkwy., Cincinnati, OH 45225. S. Ezra Goldstein, Ed. One-act and full-length plays, for high school production. Pays $40 to $150, on acceptance.

ELDRIDGE PUBLISHING COMPANY—Franklin, OH 45005. Kay Myerly, Edit. Dept. Three-act and one-act plays for schools, churches, community groups, etc., especially comedies. Christmas comedies. Best to submit in summer. Pays varying rates, on acceptance.

719

SAMUEL FRENCH, INC.—45 W. 25th St., New York, NY 10010. Lawrence R. Harbison, Ed. Full-length plays for dinner, community, stock, college and high school theatres. One-act plays (30 to 45 minutes). Children's plays, 45 to 60 minutes. Pays on royalty basis.

HEUER PUBLISHING COMPANY—Drawer 248, Cedar Rapids, IA 52406. C. Emmett McMullen, Ed. One-act comedies and dramas for contest work; three-act comedies with one interior setting, for high school production. Pays on acceptance.

INSTRUCTOR—545 Fifth Ave., New York, NY 10017. Leanna Landsmann, Ed. Plays, 700 to 2,000 words, for elementary school children. Holiday and seasonal plays only. Send six months in advance. Pays $50 to $100, on acceptance.

PERFORMANCE PUBLISHING—978 N. McLean Blvd., Elgin, IL 60120. Virginia Butler, Ed. One- and three-act plays, musicals and children's plays. Pays on royalty basis. Return postage required.

PIONEER DRAMA SERVICE—P.O. Box 22555, Denver, CO 80222. Shubert Fendrich, Ed. and Pub. Full-length plays and musicals for the educational market, children's theatre plays to be produced by adults for children, and old-fashioned melodrama. "No unproduced plays, one-acts, or plays which have a largely male cast." Pays on a royalty basis. Buys all rights.

PLAYS, THE DRAMA MAGAZINE FOR YOUNG PEOPLE—120 Boylston St., Boston, MA 02116. Elizabeth Preston, Man. Ed. One-act plays, with simple settings, for production by young people, 7 to 17; holiday plays, comedies, dramas, skits, dramatized classics, farces, puppet plays, melodramas, dramatized folktales, and creative dramatics. Maximum lengths: lower grades, 10 double-spaced pages; middle grades, 15 pages; junior and senior high, 20 pages. Casts may be mixed, all-male or all-female; plays with one act preferred. Manuscript specification sheet available on request. Queries suggested for adaptations. Pays good rates, on acceptance. Buys all rights.

SCHOLASTIC SCOPE—730 Broadway, New York, NY 10003. Katherine Robinson, Ed. For ages 15 to 18 with 4th to 6th grade reading ability. Plays, to 6,000 words, on problems of contemporary teenagers, relationships between people in family, job and school situations. Some mysteries, comedies, and science fiction; plays about minorities. Pays good rates, on acceptance.

THE TELEVISION MARKET

The almost round-the-clock television offerings available for viewers on commercial and educational television stations—greatly expanded by the mushrooming cable TV offerings—may understandably lead free-lance writers to believe that opportunities to sell scripts or program ideas are infinite.

But unfortunately the realities of the television marketplace are generally quite different from this fantasy. With few exceptions, direct submissions of scripts, no matter how good they are, are not considered by producers or programmers, and in general free-lance writers can achieve success in this almost-closed field by concentrating on getting their fiction (short and in novel form) and nonfiction published in magazines or books, combed diligently by television producers for possible adaptations. A large percentage of the material offered over all types of networks (in addition to the motion pictures made

720

in Hollywood or especially for TV) is in the form of adaptations of what has appeared in print.

Writers who want to try their hand at writing directly for this very limited market should be prepared to learn the special techniques and acceptable format of script writing. Also, experience in playwriting and a knowledge of dramatic structure gained through working in amateur, community, or professional theatres can be helpful, though TV is a highly specialized and demanding field, with unique requirements and specifications.

This section of the *Handbook* includes the names of the TV shows scheduled for broadcast during the 1984–85 season, and names and addresses of the production companies responsible for these shows. The lists should not be considered either complete or permanent. A more complete list of shows and production companies may be found in *Ross Reports Television,* published monthly by Television Index, Inc., 150 Fifth Ave., New York, NY 10011. The cost is $3.00 ($3.21 for New York residents) prepaid for each issue (including first-class postage).

Because virtually all of the producers of these shows tell us that they will read only scripts (and queries) submitted through recognized agents, we've included a list of agents who have indicated to us that they are willing to read queries from writers about television scripts. The names and addresses of other literary and dramatic agents can be found in *Literary Market Place* (Bowker), available in most libraries. A list of agents can also be obtained by sending a self-addressed, stamped envelope to Society of Authors' Representatives, P.O. Box 650, Old Chelsea Station, New York, NY 10113. Before submitting scripts to producers or to agents, authors should query to learn whether they prefer to see the material in television script form, or as an outline or summary.

Writers may wish to register their story, treatment, series format, or script with the Writers Guild of America. This registration doesn't confer statutory rights, but it does supply evidence of authorship which is effective for five years (and is renewable after that). To register material a writer should send one copy of his work, along with a $10 fee, to the Writers Guild of America Registration Service, 8955 Beverly Blvd., Los Angeles, CA 90048. Writers can also register dramatic material with the U.S. Copyright Office—for further information, write Register of Copyrights, Library of Congress, Washington, DC 20559. The Copyright Office is mainly used for book manuscripts, plays, music or lyrics, which the Writer's Guild will not register.

TELEVISION SHOWS

THE "A" TEAM (NBC)—Stephen J. Cannell Productions.

AIRWOLF (CBS)—Universal Television.

ALICE (CBS)—Warner Brothers Television.

ALL MY CHILDREN (ABC)—ABC Productions.

ANOTHER WORLD (NBC)—Benton & Bowles, Inc.

AS THE WORLD TURNS (CBS)—Compton Advertising for Proctor and Gamble.

BENSON (ABC)—Witt-Thomas-Harris Productions.

BERRENGER'S (NBC)—Lorimar Productions.

PUNKY BREWSTER (NBC)—NBC Productions.

CAGNEY & LACEY (CBS)—Barney Rosenzweig Productions/Orion Television.

CAPITOL (CBS)—John Conboy Productions.

CHARLES IN CHARGE (CBS)—Universal Television.

CHEERS (NBC)—Paramount Television.

THE BILL COSBY SHOW (NBC)—Carsey-Werner Company.

COVER UP (CBS)—Glen A. Larson Productions.

DALLAS (CBS)—Lorimar Productions.

DAYS OF OUR LIVES (NBC)—Corday Productions, Inc.

DIFF'RENT STROKES (NBC)—Tandem Productions, Inc.

DREAMS (CBS)—Centerpoint Productions.

THE DUKES OF HAZZARD (CBS)—Warner Brothers Television.

DYNASTY (ABC)—Aaron Spelling Productions.

THE EDGE OF NIGHT (ABC)—Benton & Bowles, Inc.

E/R (CBS)—Embassy Television.

THE FACTS OF LIFE (NBC)—Embassy Television.

FALCON CREST (CBS)—Lorimar Productions.

THE FALL GUY (ABC)—Glen A. Larson Productions.

FAMILY TIES (NBC)—Paramount Television.

FINDER OF LOST LOVES (ABC)—Aaron Spelling Productions.

GENERAL HOSPITAL (ABC)—ABC Entertainment.

GIMME A BREAK (NBC)—Alan Landsburg Productions.

GLITTER (ABC)—Aaron Spelling Productions.

THE GUIDING LIGHT (CBS)—Compton Advertising (for Proctor & Gamble).

MIKE HAMMER (CBS)—Columbia Pictures Television.

HARDCASTLE & MCCORMICK (ABC)—Stephen J. Cannell Productions.

HAWAIIAN HEAT (ABC)—Universal Television.

HILL STREET BLUES (NBC)—MTM Enterprises.

T.J. HOOKER (ABC)—Columbia Pictures Television.

HOT PURSUIT (NBC)—NBC Productions.

HOTEL (ABC)—Aaron Spelling Productions.

MATT HOUSTON (ABC)—Aaron Spelling Productions.

HUNTER (NBC)—Stephen J. Cannell Productions.

IT'S YOUR MOVE (NBC)—Embassy Television.

THE JEFFERSONS (CBS)—Embassy Televison.

KATE & ALLIE (CBS)—Alan Landsburg Productions.

KNIGHT RIDER (NBC)—Glen A. Larson Productions.

722

KNOT'S LANDING (CBS)—Lorimar Productions.

THE LOVE BOAT (ABC)—Aaron Spelling Productions.

LOVING (ABC)—Dramatic Creations, Inc.

MAGNUM, P.I. (CBS)—Universal Television.

MAKING OUT (NBC)—Lorimar Productions.

MIAMI VICE (NBC)—Universal Television.

MURDER, SHE WROTE (CBS)—Universal Television.

NBC'S SATURDAY NIGHT LIVE (NBC)—NBC-TV.

NEWHART (CBS)—MTM Enterprises.

NIGHT COURT (NBC)—Warner Brothers Television.

ONE LIFE TO LIVE (ABC)—ABC-TV.

PAPER DOLLS (ABC)—Leonard Goldberg Productions with MGM/UA.

PARTNERS IN CRIME (NBC)—Carson Productions, Ltd.

RIPTIDE (NBC)—Stephen J. Cannell Productions.

RYAN'S HOPE (ABC)—ABC Productions.

ST. ELSEWHERE (NBC)—MTM Enterprises.

SANTA BARBARA (NBC)—Dobson Productions.

SCARECROW AND MRS. KING (CBS)—Warner Brothers Television.

SEARCH FOR TOMORROW (NBC)—Compton Advertising (for Proctor & Gamble).

SILVER SPOONS (NBC)—Embassy Television.

SIMON & SIMON (CBS)—Universal Television.

REMINGTON STEELE (NBC)—MTM Enterprises.

STREET HAWK (ABC)—Universal Television.

THREE'S A CROWD (ABC)—NRW Co/Bergmann-Taffner.

TRAPPER JOHN, M.D. (CBS)—Don Brinkley Productions/20th Century Fox Television.

V (NBC)—Warner Brothers Television.

WEBSTER (ABC)—Paramount Television.

WHO'S THE BOSS (ABC)—Embassy Television.

THE YOUNG AND THE RESTLESS (CBS)—Columbia Pictures Television.

TELEVISION PRODUCERS

ABC ENTERTAINMENT—4151 Prospect Ave., Los Angeles, CA 90027.

ABC PRODUCTIONS—101 W. 67th St., New York, NY 10023.

ABC-TV—56 W. 66th St., New York, NY 10023.

723

BENTON & BOWLES, INC.—909 Third Ave., New York, NY 10022.

STEPHEN J. CANNELL PRODUCTIONS—7083 Hollywood Blvd., Hollywood, CA 90028.

CARSEY-WERNER PRODUCTIONS—NBC Studios, 1268 E. 14th St., Brooklyn, NY 11230.

CARSON PRODUCTIONS—4123 Radford Ave., Studio City, CA 91604.

CBS ENTERTAINMENT—51 W. 52nd St., New York, NY 10019.

CENTERPOINT PRODUCTIONS—3575 Cahuenga Blvd., W., Suite 455, Los Angeles, CA 90068.

COLUMBIA PICTURES TELEVISION—300 Colgems Sq., Burbank, CA 91505.

COMPTON ADVERTISING—625 Madison Ave., New York, NY 10022.

JOHN CONBOY PRODUCTIONS—CBS-TV, 7800 Beverly Blvd., Los Angeles, CA 90036.

CORDAY PRODUCTIONS, INC.—Colgems Sq., Burbank, CA 91505.

DOBSON PRODUCTIONS—NBC Studio 11, 3000 W. Alameda Ave., Burbank, CA 91523.

DRAMATIC CREATIONS—320 W. 66th St., New York, NY 10023.

EMBASSY TELEVISION—100 Universal City Plaza, Universal City, CA 91608.

ALAN LANDSBURG PRODUCTIONS—1554 S. Sepulveda Blvd., Los Angeles, CA 90025.

GLEN A. LARSON PRODUCTIONS—10201 W. Pico Blvd., Los Angeles, CA 90064.

LORIMAR PRODUCTIONS—3970 Overland Ave., Culver City, CA 90230.

MGM-UA TELEVISION—10202 W. Washington Blvd., Culver City, CA 90230.

MTM ENTERPRISES—4024 Radford Ave., Studio City, CA 91604.

NBC PRODUCTIONS—NBC Television, 3000 W. Alameda Ave., Burbank, CA 91523.

NBC-TV—30 Rockefeller Plaza, New York, NY 10020.

NRW CO./BERGMANN-TAFFNER—5746 Sunset Blvd., Hollywood, CA 90028.

ORION ENTERPRISES—1875 Century Park East, Los Angeles, CA 90067.

PARAMOUNT TELEVISION—5555 Melrose Ave., Los Angeles, CA 90038.

AARON SPELLING PRODUCTIONS—1041 N. Formosa Ave., Hollywood, CA 90046.

SUNSET GOWER STUDIOS—1438 N. Gower, Hollywood, CA 90028.

TANDEM PRODUCTIONS—100 Universal City Plaza, Universal City, CA 91608.

20TH CENTURY-FOX TELEVISION—10201 W. Pico Blvd., Los Angeles, CA 90064.

UNIVERSAL TELEVISION—100 Universal City Plaza, Universal City, CA 91608.

WARNER BROTHERS TELEVISION—4000 Warner Blvd., Burbank, CA 91505.

WITT-THOMAS-HARRIS PRODUCTIONS—1438 Gower, Los Angeles, CA 90028.

TELEVISION SCRIPT AGENTS

ACT 48 MANAGEMENT—1501 Broadway, New York, NY 10036. Reads queries and treatments accompanied by SASEs.

LEE ALLAN AGENCY—4571 N. 68th St., Milwaukee, WI 53218. Reads queries.

HOWARD T. BRODY—P.O. Box 291423, Davie, FL 33329. Reads queries and scripts.

THE CALDER AGENCY—4150 Riverside Dr., Burbank, CA 91505. Reads queries and synopses.

BILL COOPER ASSOCIATES—224 W. 49th St., New York, NY 10022. Will look at developed ideas for comedies, dramas, for TV, theatre, and motion pictures.

LIL CUMBER ATTRACTIONS—6515 Sunset Blvd., Hollywood, CA 90028. Reads queries with SASEs.

D.J. ENTERPRISES—339 S. Franklin St., Allentown, PA 18102. Reads queries, scripts and treatments.

HOLLYWOOD TALENT AGENCY—213 Brock Ave., Toronto, Ont., M6K 2L8, Canada. Reads queries, scripts and treatments.

ANSLY Q. HYMAN—3123 Cahuenga Blvd., W., Los Angeles, CA 90068. Reads queries and scripts accompanied by SASEs.

JAFFE REPRESENTATIVES—140 7th Ave., New York, NY 10011. Reads queries and treatments.

WILLIAM KERWIN AGENCY—1605 N. Cahuenga Blvd., #202, Hollywood, CA 90028. Reads queries.

ARCHER KING, LTD.—1440 Broadway, #2100, New York, NY 10018. Reads queries and treatments.

OTTO R. KOZAK LITERARY AGENCY—33 Bay St., East, Atlantic Beach, NY 11561. Reads queries.

LUCY R. KROLL AGENCY—390 W. End Ave., New York, NY 10024. Reads queries accompanied by SASE.

KRATZ & CO.—210 5th Ave., New York, NY 10010. Reads queries and treatments.

L. HARRY LEE LITERARY AGENCY—Box 203, Rocky Point, NY 11778. Reads queries accompanied by SASE only.

RICK LEED—c/o Hesseltine/Baker Associates, 165 W. 46th St., #409, New York, NY 10036. Reads queries.

LONDON STAR PROMOTIONS—7131 Owensmouth Ave., #C116, Canoga Park, CA 91303. Reads queries and treatments.

PROFESSIONAL AUTHOR'S LITERARY SERVICES—4237-2 Keanu St., Honolulu, HI 96816. Reads queries.

RHODES LITERARY AGENCY—140 W. End Ave., New York, NY 10023. Reads queries.

SUZANNE SHELTON—CNA Associates, 8721 Sunset Blvd., #202, Los Angeles, CA 90069. Reads queries accompanied by SASEs only.

VAMP TALENT AGENCY—713 E. La Loma, #1, Somis, CA 93066. Reads queries, treatments and scripts, accompanied by SASEs.

VASS TALENT AGENCY—1017 N. La Cienega Blvd., #305, Los Angeles, CA 90069. Reads queries, treatments, and scripts.

ERIKA WAIN AGENCY—1418 N. Highland Ave., #102, Hollywood, CA 90028. Reads queries.

DAN WRIGHT c/o Ann Wright Representatives, Inc.,—136 E. 57th St., New York, NY 10022. Reads queries.

WRITERS & ARTISTS AGENCY—11726 San Vicente Blvd., Los Angeles, CA 90049. Reads queries.

BOOK PUBLISHERS

Four lists are included here: hardcover book publishers (although many of these have paperback subsidiaries as well); publishers of paperback originals; romance publishers; and university presses, which publish a limited number of scholarly and specialized books.

Royalty rates for hardcover books usually start at 10% of the retail price of the book, and increase after a certain number of copies have been sold. Paperbacks generally have a somewhat lower rate, about 5% to 8%. It is customary for the publishing company to pay the author a cash advance against royalties when the book contract is signed or when the finished manuscript is received.

Book manuscripts may be sent by first-class mail, but the most inexpensive and commonly used method at present is by "Special Fourth Class Rate-Manuscript." For a summary of postal regulations for the "Special Fourth Class Rate-Manuscript," see the chapter on *Manuscript Preparation and Submission* in this book and for rates, details of insurance, etc., inquire at your local post office. Be sure to enclose a self-addressed, stamped envelope (SASE) with any submission to a book publisher.

HARDCOVER BOOK PUBLISHERS

ABBEY PRESS—St. Meinrad, IN 47577. Rev. Keith McClellan, Pub. Nonfiction. Christian materials on marriage and family living. Royalty basis. Query with table of contents and writing sample.

ABINGDON PRESS—201 Eighth Ave. S., P.O. Box 801, Nashville, TN 37202. Ronald P. Patterson, Edit. Dir. Religious books, juveniles, general nonfiction. Query with outline and sample chapters.

HARRY N. ABRAMS, INC. (Subsidiary of *Times Mirror Co.*)—100 Fifth Ave., New York, NY 10011. Art and other heavily illustrated books. Pays varying rates. Query.

ACADEMIC PRESS, INC. (Subsidiary of *Harcourt Brace Jovanovich*)— HBJ Building, Orlando, FL 32887. Address Erwin V. Cohen, Ed. Dept. Scientific books for professionals; college science texts. Royalty basis. Query.

ACADEMY CHICAGO, PUBLISHERS—425 N. Michigan Ave., Chicago, IL 60601. Anita Miller, Ed. General fiction; mysteries. History; biographies; books by and about women. Royalty basis. Query. SASE required.

ADDISON-WESLEY PUBLISHING CO.—Reading, MA 01867. General Publishing Group: Adult nonfiction on current topics: education, health, psychology, computers, professions, human resources, business, etc. Royalty basis.

ALASKA NORTHWEST PUBLISHING CO.—130 2nd Ave. S., Edmonds, WA 98020. Jean Chapman, Chief Book Ed. Nonfiction, 10,000 to 100,000 words, with an emphasis on natural resources and history of Alaska. Northwestern Canada and Pacific Northwest: how-to books; biographies; cookbooks; nutrition; gardening; humor; nature; guidebooks. *Juveniles:* Picture books, easy-to-read books, and how-to books, with regional themes. Send query or sample chapters with outline. Royalty basis.

ANDERSON WORLD, INC.—1400 Stierlin Rd., Mountain View, CA 94043. Richard Benyo, Ed. Dir. Books on health and fitness subjects, 50,000 to 100,000 words. Royalty basis. Query; enclose SASE.

ARBOR HOUSE PUBLISHING CO.—235 E. 45th St., New York, NY 10017. Eden Collinsworth, Pub. General fiction and nonfiction. Royalty basis. Query.

ARCO PUBLISHING, INC.—215 Park Ave. S., New York, NY 10003. William Mlawer, Educational Books; Madelyn Larsen, Consumer Books. Nonfiction, originals and reprints, from 50,000 words. Career guides, test preparation, how-to's, young adult, science, needlecraft. No fiction, poetry, humor, history, biography, personal accounts. Pays on royalty basis or by outright purchase. Query with outline. Return postage required.

ATHENEUM PUBLISHERS (Subsidiary of *The Scribner Book Companies*)—115 Fifth Ave., New York, NY 10003. Thomas A. Stewart, Vice-President and Ed.-in-Chief. General nonfiction; biography, history, current affairs, belles-lettres; juveniles, from picture books through young-adult. *Argo Books:* science fiction and fantasy for children and adults; send complete manuscripts or sample chapters and outline. *Escapade:* Juvenile mysteries, 25,000 to 30,000 words. No unsolicited adult fiction. Royalty basis.

THE ATLANTIC MONTHLY PRESS—8 Arlington St., Boston, MA 02116. Fiction, biography, history, belles-lettres, poetry, general nonfiction, children's books. Royalty basis. Query.

727

AUGSBURG PUBLISHING HOUSE—Box 1209, 426 S. Fifth St., Minneapolis, MN 55440. Roland Seboldt, Dir. of Book Development. Fiction and nonfiction, for adults, children and teens, on Christian themes. Royalty basis.

BACKCOUNTRY PUBLICATIONS, INC.—P.O. Box 175, Woodstock, VT 05091. Christopher Lloyd, Ed. Outdoor recreational books and regional guidebooks, 150 to 300 manuscript pages, on hiking, walking, canoeing, bicycling, and fishing. Royalty basis.

BAEN BOOKS—Baen Enterprises, 8 W. 36th St., New York, NY 10018. Elizabeth Mitchell, Sr. Ed. Jim Baen, Pres. High-tech science fiction; innovative fantasy. Query with synopsis and sample chapters. Royalty basis.

BAKER BOOK HOUSE—P.O. Box 6287, Grand Rapids, MI 49506. Daniel Van't Kerkhoff, Ed. Religious nonfiction, academic and popular. Royalty basis.

A.S. BARNES & CO., INC.—9601 Aero Dr., San Diego, CA 92123. Modeste Williams, Ed. Dir. General nonfiction for adults; contemporary issues, U.S. history, sports, etc. Royalty basis. Query with synopsis and outline or table of contents.

BEACON PRESS—25 Beacon St., Boston, MA 02108. Marie Cantlon, Sr. Ed. General nonfiction: world affairs, sociology, psychology, women's studies, political science, art, literature, philosophy, religion. No fiction or poetry. Royalty basis. Query. Return postage required.

BETTER HOMES AND GARDENS BOOKS—See *Meredith Corporation.*

THE BOBBS-MERRILL CO., INC.—630 Third Ave., New York, NY 10017. Margaret B. Parkinson, Ed.-in-Chief. Nonfiction: how-to's, finance, self-improvement, cookbooks, psychology, medicine; biography, autobiography of entertainment and world figures. Query. Royalty basis.

THOMAS BOUREGY & CO., INC.—22 E. 60th St., New York, NY 10022. Rita Brenig, Ed. Light, wholesome, well-plotted romances, modern Gothics, westerns, and nurse romances, 50,000 to 60,000 words. Send one-page synopsis. SASE required.

BRADBURY PRESS, INC. (An affiliate of *Macmillan, Inc.*)—2 Overhill Rd., Scarsdale, NY 10583. Richard Jackson, Ed. Juvenile and young adult fiction. Royalty basis.

GEORGE BRAZILLER, INC.—One Park Ave., New York, NY 10016. Literature, history, philosophy, science, art, social science; fiction. Royalty basis. No unsolicited manuscripts.

BROADMAN PRESS—127 Ninth Ave. N., Nashville, TN 37234. Tom Clark, Supervisor. Religious and inspirational fiction and nonfiction. Royalty basis. Query.

CAPRA PRESS—P.O. Box 2068, Santa Barbara, CA 93120. Noel Young, Ed. Nonfiction: how-to, biography, nature, popular science, nutrition, western outdoor guides. Royalty basis, no advance. Query with outline.

CAROLRHODA BOOKS—241 First Ave. N., Minneapolis, MN 55401. Susan Pearson, Ed. Picture books, fiction, nonfiction for elementary children. Outright purchase. Send SASE for guidelines.

CARROLL AND GRAF PUBLISHERS, INC.—260 Fifth Ave., New York, NY 10001. Kent E. Carroll, Exec. Ed. General fiction and nonfiction. Royalty basis. Query with SASE.

CBI PUBLISHING CO.—See *Van Nostrand Reinhold Co., Inc.*

CELESTIAL ARTS—P.O. Box 7327, Berkeley, CA 94707. Nonfiction, 25,000 to 80,000 words, on all subjects. No fiction or poetry. Query Paul Reed. Royalty basis.

CHATHAM PRESS—P.O. Box A, Old Greenwich, CT 06807. Roger H. Lowie, Man. Dir. Books on the Northeast coast, New England and the ocean. Royalty basis. Query with outline, sample chapters, illustrations and SASE large enough for return of material.

CHILDRENS PRESS—1224 W. Van Buren St., Chicago, IL 60607. Fran Dyra, Ed. Dir. Juvenile fiction and nonfiction, 50 to 10,000 words, for supplementary use in classrooms. Query first. Picture books, 50 to 1,000 words. Royalty basis or outright purchase.

CHILTON BOOK CO.—201 King of Prussia Rd., Radnor, PA 19089. Alan F. Turner, Edit. Dir. Business, and business applications for computers, crafts and hobbies, automotive. Royalty basis. Query with outline, sample chapter, and return postage.

CHRONICLE BOOKS—870 Market St., San Francisco, CA 94102. Larry L. Smith, Ed. Nonfiction: West Coast regional recreational guides, regional histories, natural history, art and architecture. Royalty basis.

CITADEL PRESS—See *Lyle Stuart, Inc.*

CLARION BOOKS (Juvenile imprint of *Ticknor & Fields, a Houghton Mifflin* company)—52 Vanderbilt Ave., New York, NY 10017. James C. Giblin, Ed. Juvenile fiction and nonfiction, picture books, for ages 4 and up. Royalty basis. Query preferred on manuscripts of more than 20 pages. Publishes approximately 30–35 hardcover titles a year.

COMPUTE! PUBLICATIONS, INC.—P.O. Box 5406, Greensboro, NC 27403. How-to computer books; specializes in machine specific publications. Query preferred. Royalty basis.

CONTEMPORARY BOOKS—180 N. Michigan Ave., Chicago, IL 60601. N. Crossman, Exec. Ed. General nonfiction: fitness, self-help; how-to; practical business; nutrition; sports guides. Royalty basis. Query with outline and sample chapter.

DAVID C. COOK PUBLISHING CO.—850 N. Grove Ave., Elgin, IL 60120. Joe Hertel, Book Division Manager; Catherine L. Davis, Man. Ed./ Books. Religious children's/juveniles only. Royalty and work-for-hire basis. Query with chapter-by-chapter synopsis and two sample chapters. Unsolicited manuscripts returned unopened. Label envelope "query." SASE required.

COWARD, MCCANN (Div. of *Putnam Publishing Group*)—200 Madison Ave., New York, NY 10016. Fiction and nonfiction through agents only.

CREATIVE EDUCATION INC.—1422 W Lake St., Minneapolis, MN 55408. Ann Redpath, Ed. Nonfiction for children aged 5 to 12. No textbooks. Mostly flat fee basis, some royalty.

THE CROSSING PRESS—P.O. Box 640, Trumansburg, NY 14886. Elaine Gill, John Gill, Pubs. How-to books, feminist, gay, natural food cookbooks. Fiction. Royalty basis.

THOMAS Y. CROWELL—See *Harper & Row.*

CROWN PUBLISHERS, INC.—One Park Ave., New York, NY 10016. Betty A. Prashker, Ed.-in-Chief. Alan Benjamin, Dir., Children's Books. Fiction and general nonfiction. Royalty basis. Query letters only: Address Ed. Dept.; no unsolicited manuscripts. SASE required.

JONATHAN DAVID PUBLISHERS, INC.—68-22 Eliot Ave., Middle Village, NY 11379. Alfred J. Kolatch, Ed.-in-Chief. General nonfiction—how-to, sports, cooking and food, self-help, etc.—and nonfiction on Judaica. Royalty basis or outright purchase. Query with outline, sample chapter, and resumé.

DELACORTE PRESS(Div. of *Dell Publishing Co., Inc.*)—245 E. 47th St., New York, NY 10017. Jackie Farber, Ed. of adult fiction and nonfiction. George Nicholson, *Books for Young Readers* Ed. General fiction and nonfiction. *Books for Young Readers:* Contemporary fiction for students through secondary school. Royalty basis. Query with outline; no unsolicited manuscripts.

DELAIR PUBLISHING CO.—420 Lexington Ave., New York, NY 10170. Louise T. Apfelbaum, Ed. General nonfiction: cookbooks; food; home improvement; health and popular medical books; self-help; women's interest. Illustrated juveniles, to age 9. Query or send outline and sample chapters and SASE. Royalty basis.

DEMBNER BOOKS—1841 Broadway, New York, NY 10023. S. Arthur Dembner, Pres. Self-help, lifestyle, reference and other nonfiction; good fiction. Royalty basis. Query with outline, sample chapters, and SASE large enough for return of material.

DEVIN-ADAIR PUBLISHERS, INC.—6 N. Water St., Greenwich, CT 06830. C. de la Belle Issue, Pub. J. Andressi, Ed. Books on conservative affairs, Irish topics, Americana, computers, self-help, health, ecology. Royalty basis. Query with outline, sample chapters, and SASE.

DIAL BOOKS FOR YOUNG READERS (Div. of *E. P. Dutton, Inc.*)—Two Park Ave., New York, NY 10016. Picture books; easy-to-read books; middle-grade readers; young adult fiction and nonfiction. Submit complete manuscripts for fiction; outline and sample chapters for nonfiction. Royalty basis. Enclose SASE.

THE DIAL PRESS (Imprint of *Doubleday*)—245 Park Ave., New York, NY 10167. General fiction and nonfiction. Query with sample chapter.

DILLON PRESS—242 Portland Ave. S., Minneapolis, MN 55415. Uva Dillon, Ed.-in-Chief. Juvenile nonfiction: science, natural science, biographies, health, nutrition, doing and learning activities, new approaches to sports, and in-depth writing about the states and regions of the U.S. Royalty basis. Complete manuscript preferred. SASE required. *Gemstone Books:* Fiction for grades K-12: mystery, adventure, romance, science fiction, fantasy, history, sports, etc. Contemporary stories about lifestyles and experiences of today's young people. No folktales. Send complete manuscript with SASE.

DODD, MEAD & CO.—79 Madison Ave., New York, NY 10016. Allen Klots, Jerry Gross, Cynthia Vartan, Nancy Crawford, Sr. Eds. Margaret Norton, Sr. Ed. for mystery and suspense. Joe Ann Daly, Dir., Children's Books. General fiction and nonfiction: biography, history, belles-lettres, travel, mystery. Juveniles. Royalty basis. Query.

DOUBLEDAY AND CO., INC.—245 Park Ave., New York, NY 10167. General fiction and nonfiction. No poetry, short stories or children's books.

Complete manuscripts to Patrick LoBrutto, Science Fiction Ed. Mysteries to Michele Tempesta, Mystery/Suspense Ed. Address Editorial Dept. 195 with SASE; send for "How to Tell Doubleday About Your Book."

E.P. DUTTON, INC.—2 Park Ave., New York, NY 10016. General fiction, nonfiction; query with outline and sample chapters. *Lodestar Books,* Virginia Buckley, Ed. Dir., young adult fiction and nonfiction—submit proposals for nonfiction, complete manuscripts for fiction. Royalty basis. Send queries to Editorial Dept.

EAST WOODS PRESS—429 East Blvd., Charlotte, NC 28203. Sally McMillan, Ed. Outdoor and travel books; cookbooks; self-help and how-to books; sports; trail guides; childcare. Royalty basis. Query with sample chapters.

WM. B. EERDMANS PUBLISHING COMPANY, INC.—255 Jefferson Ave., S.E., Grand Rapids, MI 49503. Jon Pott, Ed.-in-Chief. Protestant theological nonfiction; American history; some fiction. Royalty basis.

EMC CORP.—300 York Ave., St. Paul, MN 55101. Rosemary J. Barry, Ed. Fiction, nonfiction, with high-interest, low vocabulary material. Fiction, to 6,000 words, with a top vocabulary level of 5th grade. Royalty basis. No unsolicited manuscripts accepted.

ENSLOW PUBLISHERS—Bloy St. & Ramsey Ave., Box 777, Hillside, NJ 07205. R. M. Enslow, Jr., Ed./Pub. Specialized nonfiction. Children's nonfiction. Royalty basis. Query first.

PAUL S. ERIKSSON, PUBLISHER—Battell Bldg., Middlebury, VT 05753. General nonfiction; some fiction. Royalty basis. Query.

ESCAPADE—See *Atheneum Publishers.*

FACTS ON FILE PUBLICATIONS—460 Park Ave. S., New York, NY 10016. Eleanor Schoenebaum, Edit. Dir. Reference and trade books on business, science, consumer affairs, the performing arts, etc. Query with outline and sample chapter. Royalty basis.

FARRAR, STRAUS & GIROUX—19 Union Sq. W., New York, NY 10003. General fiction, nonfiction, juveniles. Address queries to Editorial Dept.

FREDERICK FELL PUBLISHERS, INC.—386 Park Ave., S., New York, NY 10016. Mercer Warriner, Ed.-in-Chief. Nonfiction: business, crafts, health, etc. Royalty basis. Query by letter or with outline and sample chapters. SASE required.

FLEET PRESS CORPORATION—160 Fifth Ave., New York, NY 10010. S. Schiff, Ed. General nonfiction; sports and how-to. Royalty basis. Query; no unsolicited manuscripts.

FORTRESS PRESS—2900 Queen Lane, Philadelphia, PA 19129. Harold W. Rast, Th.D., Exec. Ed. Serious, nonfiction works, from 100 pages, on theology and religion, for the academic or lay reader. Royalty basis. Query preferred.

FOUR WINDS PRESS (An imprint of *Macmillan Children's Books*)—866 Third Ave., New York, NY 10022. Judith R. Whipple, Publisher. Juveniles: picture books, fiction and nonfiction for all ages. Unsolicited material welcome. Send SASE with all submissions.

THE FREE PRESS—See *Macmillan Publishing Co.*

GARDEN WAY PUBLISHING COMPANY—Storey Communications, Schoolhouse Rd., Pownal, VT 05261. Roger M. Griffith, Ed. How-to books on gardening, cooking, building, etc. Royalty basis or outright purchase. Query with outline and sample chapter.

GEMSTONE BOOKS—See *Dillon Press.*

THE K. S. GINIGER CO., INC.—235 Park Ave. S., New York, NY 10003. General nonfiction; reference and religious. Royalty basis. Query with SASE; no unsolicited manuscripts.

THE GLOBE PEQUOT PRESS—Old Chester Rd., Box Q, Chester, CT 06412. Linda Kennedy, Vice-Pres./Publications Dir. Nonfiction about New England and the Northeast. Travel guidebooks a specialty. Royalty basis. Query with a sample chapter, contents, and one-page synopsis. SASE a must.

GOLDEN PRESS—See *Western Publishing Co., Inc.*

THE STEPHEN GREENE PRESS/THE LEWIS PUBLISHING CO.—(Div. of *Viking Penguin, Inc.*)—15 Muzzey St., Lexington, MA 02173. General nonfiction; social science. Royalty basis.

GREENWILLOW BOOKS—See *William Morrow and Co., Inc.*

GROSSET AND DUNLAP, INC. (Div. of *Putnam Publishing Group*)—51 Madison Ave., New York, NY 10010. Juveniles: picture books, concept books, for ages 3 to 12. Popular science books for ages 8-12. No unsolicited manuscripts.

GROVE PRESS, INC.—196 W. Houston St., New York, NY 10014. Barney Rosset, Ed. General fiction and nonfiction. Royalty basis. Query with outline and sample chapter. SASE required.

HAMMOND INCORPORATED—Maplewood, NY 07040. Dorothy Bacheller, Ed. Nonfiction: reference, cooking, travel. Payment varies. Query with outline and sample chapters. SASE required.

HARCOURT BRACE JOVANOVICH—1250 Sixth Ave., San Diego, CA 92101. Adult trade nonfiction and fiction. *Books for Professionals:* test preparation guides and other student self-help materials. *Miller Accounting Publications, Inc.:* professional books for practioners in accounting and finance; college accounting texts. Juvenile fiction and nonfiction: for beginning readers through young adults, especially contemporary young adult novels and nonfiction with commercial appeal; query Kathleen Krull, Sen. Ed. for Children's Books. Query; unsolicited manuscripts accepted.

HARPER & ROW—10 E. 53rd St., New York, NY 10022. Fiction, nonfiction, biography, economics, etc.: address Trade Dept. College texts: address College Dept. Paperback originals: address Paperback Dept. *Harper Junior Books Group:* juvenile fiction, nonfiction, and picture books. *Thomas Y. Crowell Co., Publishers:* juveniles, etc. *J. B. Lippincott Co.:* juveniles, picture books, etc. All three imprints publish from preschool to young adult titles. Religion, theology, etc.: address Religious Books Dept., 1700 Montgomery St., San Francisco, CA 94111. No unsolicited manuscripts; query only. Royalty basis.

HARVEST HOUSE PUBLISHERS—1075 Arrowsmith, Eugene, OR 97402. Eileen L. Mason, Ed. Nonfiction—how-to's, educational, health—with evangelical theme. No biographies, history or poetry. Query first. SASE required.

HEARST BOOKS—See *William Morrow and Co., Inc.*

732

D.C. HEATH & COMPANY—125 Spring St., Lexington, MA 02173. Textbooks for schools and colleges. Professional books (*Lexington Books* division). Query Bruce Zimmerli, College; Robert Marshall, School; Robert Bovenschulte, Lexington Books.

HERALD PRESS—616 Walnut Ave., Scottdale, PA 15683. Paul M. Schrock, Book Editor. Christian books for adults and children (age 9 and up): inspiration, Bible study, self-help, devotionals, current issues, peace studies, church history, missions and evangelism, family life and Christian ethics. Send one-page summary and sample chapter. Royalty basis.

HOLIDAY HOUSE, INC.—18 E. 53rd St., New York, NY 10022. Margery S. Cuyler, Vice Pres. General juvenile and young-adult fiction and nonfiction. Royalty basis. Query with outline and sample chapter.

HOLT, RINEHART AND WINSTON—521 Fifth Ave., New York, NY 10175. Accepts no unsolicited material.

HOUGHTON MIFFLIN COMPANY—2 Park St., Boston, MA 02108. Linda Glick Conway, Man. Ed. Contemporary fiction: historical suspense and science fiction. Nonfiction: history, natural history, biography. Poetry. Query with SASE. Children's Book Division, address Walter Lorraine: picture books, fiction and nonfiction for all ages. Query for nonfiction, complete manuscripts for fiction. Royalty basis.

H. P. BOOKS—P.O. Box 5367, Tucson, AZ 85703. Rick Bailey, Pub. Illustrated how-to's, 50,000 to 80,000 words, on cooking, gardening, photography, etc. Royalty basis. Query.

ICARUS PRESS—P.O. Box 1225, South Bend, IN 46624. Bruce Fingerhut, Ed. General nonfiction; biography; history; sports; travel; regional. Royalty basis or outright purchase. Query preferred.

IDEALS PUBLISHING—11315 Watertown Plank Rd., Milwaukee, WI 53226. Patricia Pingrey, Dir., Publishing. Children's books, cookbooks. Flat fee basis.

INNER TRADITION/DESTINY BOOKS—377 Park Ave. S., New York, NY 10016. Lisa Sperling, Ed. Nonfiction, on spiritual subjects, astrology, Eastern mysticism, wholistic health, diet, nutrition. Cookbooks. Royalty basis. Query required.

KEATS PUBLISHING, INC.—27 Pine St., Box 876, New Canaan, CT 06840. An Keats, Ed. Nonfiction: health, inspiration, how-to. Royalty basis. Query.

ROBERT R. KNAPP, PUBLISHER—Box 7234, San Diego, CA 92107. Professional reference and textbooks in the humanities and social sciences. Royalty basis. Query.

ALFRED A. KNOPF, INC.—201 E. 50th St., New York, NY 10022. Ashbel Green, Vice-Pres. and Senior Ed. Frances Foster, Juvenile Ed. Distinguished fiction and general nonfiction. Juvenile fiction and nonfiction; picture books, 3,000 to 5,000 words. Royalty basis. Query.

JOHN KNOX PRESS—341 Ponce de Leon Ave., N.E., Atlanta, GA 30365. Walter C. Sutton, Ed. Books that inform, interpret, challenge and encourage Christian faith and life. Royalty basis. Send SASE for "Guidelines for a Book Proposal."

LEXINGTON BOOKS—See *D. C. Heath & Company*.

THE LINDEN PRESS (Div. of *Simon & Schuster*)—1230 Ave. of the Americas, New York, NY 10020. Joni Evans, Pub. and Ed.-in-Chief. Marjorie Williams and Allen Peacock, Sr. Eds. Quality fiction and nonfiction, 75,000 to 125,000 words. Royalty basis. Query with a synopsis or outline and writing sample.

J. B. LIPPINCOTT COMPANY—See *Harper & Row*.

LITTLE, BROWN AND COMPANY—34 Beacon St., Boston, MA 02106. Address Ed. Dept., Trade Division or Children's Books, Trade Division. Fiction, general nonfiction, sports books, juveniles; divisions for law, medical and college texts. Royalty basis. Submissions only from authors who have previously published a book or have published in professional or literary journals, newspapers or magazines. Query first.

LODESTAR BOOKS—See *E. P. Dutton, Inc.*

LOTHROP, LEE & SHEPARD CO.—See *William Morrow & Co.*

MCGRAW-HILL BOOK CO.—1221 Ave. of the Americas, New York, NY 10020. Fiction and nonfiction through agents only.

DAVID MCKAY COMPANY—2 Park Ave., New York, NY 10017. James Loutitt, Pres. and Ed. General nonfiction. Unsolicited manuscripts neither acknowledged nor returned.

MACMILLAN PUBLISHING CO., INC.—866 Third Ave., New York, NY 10022. General Books Division: General and genre fiction, general nonfiction—how-to, current affairs, biography, business, religious, juveniles. College texts and professional books in social sciences, humanities, address *The Free Press*. Royalty basis.

MADRONA PUBLISHERS, INC.—P.O. Box 22667, Seattle, WA 98122. Sara Levant, Acquisitions Ed. General-interest nonfiction trade books (no poetry, children's books or fiction). Royalty basis.

RICHARD MAREK PUBLISHERS—See *St. Martin's/Marek*.

MEREDITH CORP., BOOK GROUP (*Better Homes and Gardens Books*)—1716 Locust St., Des Moines, IA 50336. Gerald M. Knox, Ed. Address The Editors. Books on gardening, crafts, health, decorating, etc. Outright purchase. Query with outline and sample chapter.

JULIAN MESSNER (Div. of *Simon & Schuster*)—1230 Ave. of the Americas, New York, NY 10020. Jane Steltenpohl, Sr. Ed. High-interest, curriculum-oriented nonfiction. General nonfiction for junior and senior high, about 52,000 words; Iris Rosoff, Ed.-in-Chief. Wendy Barish, Ed. Dir. Royalty basis.

MILLER ACCOUNTING PUBLICATIONS, INC.—See *Harcourt Brace Jovanovich*.

MOREHOUSE-BARLOW CO., INC.—78 Danbury Rd., Wilton, CT 06897. Stephen S. Wilburn, Ed. Dir. Theology, history of religion, etc. Royalty basis or outright purchase. Query with outline, contents, and sample chapter.

WILLIAM MORROW AND CO., INC.—105 Madison Ave., New York, NY 10016. Sherry Arden, Pub. Adult fiction and nonfiction. No unsolicited manuscripts. *Morrow Quill Paperbacks:* James D. Landis, Publisher. Trade paperbacks. Adult fiction and nonfiction. No unsolicited manuscripts. *Morrow Junior Books:* David Reuther, Ed.-in-Chief. Children's books for all ages.

Greenwillow Books: Susan Hirschman, Ed.-in-Chief. Children's books for all ages. Picture books. *Lothrop, Lee & Shepard Co.:* Dorothy Briley, Ed.-in-Chief. Juvenile fiction and nonfiction. Royalty basis. Query. *Hearst Books:* Joan B. Nagy, Ed. Dir. General nonfiction. No unsolicited manuscripts.

THE MOTHER EARTH NEWS BOOKS—105 Stoney Mountain Rd., Hendersonville, NC 28791. Barbara S. Henderson, Ed. Dir. Books on homebuilding and shelter, gardening, crafts, energy, cooking, health and nutrition, sideline businesses, do-it-yourself projects, household management, and other self-help and back-to-basics topics. Payment negotiated on an individual basis. Enclose SASE with all submissions; reports in two to three months.

THE MOUNTAINEERS BOOKS—715 Pike St., Seattle, WA 98101. Ann Cleeland, Man. Ed. Nonfiction on mountaineering, backpacking, canoeing, bicycling, skiing. Field guides, regional histories, biographies of mountaineers; accounts of expeditions. Nature books. Royalty basis. Submit sample chapters and outline.

THE MYSTERIOUS PRESS—129 W. 56th St., New York, NY 10019. Donna Horowitz, Man. Ed. Mystery/suspense novels. Query with synopsis. SASE required.

NAL BOOKS (Div. of *New American Library*)—1633 Broadway, New York, NY 10019. Michaela Hamilton, Ed. Dir. Fiction and nonfiction books. Manuscripts and proposals accepted only from agents or upon personal recommendation.

NATUREGRAPH PUBLISHERS—P.O. Box 1075, Happy Camp, CA 96039. Barbara Brown, Ed. Nonfiction: natural history, outdoor living, land and gardening, Indian lore, crafts and how-to. Royalty basis. Query.

THOMAS NELSON INC.—Nelson Place at Elm Hill Pike, Nashville, TN 37214. Lawrence M. Stone, Ed. Religious adult nonfiction. Royalty basis. Query with outline and sample chapters.

NEW REPUBLIC BOOKS/HOLT, RINEHART AND WINSTON—1220 19th St., N.W., Washington, DC 20036. Steve Wasserman, Ed.-in-Chief. Books on politics, Washington affairs, culture, the arts. Royalty basis. Query.

NEW YORK GRAPHIC SOCIETY BOOKS/LITTLE, BROWN AND CO.—34 Beacon St., Boston, MA 02106. Books of fine arts and photography. Query with outline or proposal and vita. Royalty basis.

NORTH POINT PRESS—P.O. Box 6475, Albany, CA 94706. Thomas Christensen, Asst. Ed. Nonfiction: anthropology, philosophy, non-academic criticism, "literary" travel, and biography. Serious fiction. No poetry. Royalty basis. Query. SASE required.

W. W. NORTON & COMPANY, INC.—500 Fifth Ave., New York, NY 10110. Fiction and nonfiction. Royalty basis. Query with synopsis, 2 to 3 chapters, and resume. SASE required.

OAK TREE PUBLICATIONS—9601 Aero Dr., San Diego, CA 92123. Adult nonfiction: current social, adult and parenting concerns. Juvenile nonfiction, for ages 7 to 11: unique craft, activity, and science books; fiction. Young adult (ages 12 to 16) nonfiction and fiction; no historical biographies or mystery-adventures. Royalty basis. Query with synopsis, outline and credentials. SASE required.

101 PRODUCTIONS—834 Mission St., San Francisco, CA 94103. Jacqueline Killeen, Ed. Nonfiction: gardening, domestic arts, travel. Royalty basis. Query; no unsolicited manuscripts.

OPEN COURT PUBLISHING COMPANY—Box 599, La Salle, IL 61301. Scholarly books. Elementary textbooks. Royalty basis. Query.

OXFORD UNIVERSITY PRESS—200 Madison Ave., New York, NY 10016. Authoritative books on literature, history, philosophy, etc.; college textbooks, medical, and reference books; paperbacks. Royalty basis. Query.

OXMOOR HOUSE, INC.—Box 2262, Birmingham, AL 35202. John Logue, Ed. Nonfiction on southern subjects; art and craft books. Royalty basis.

PACIFIC SEARCH PRESS—222 Dexter Ave., N., Seattle, WA 98109. Carolyn J. Theadgill, Dir. Nonfiction, 200 or more manuscript pages. Crafts, natural history, travel, outdoor recreation, cooking. Queries are preferred. Pays on royalty basis.

PANTHEON BOOKS (Div. of *Random House*)—201 E. 50th St., New York, NY 10022. Address Daniel Cullen or Helena Franklin. Nonfiction: academic level for general reader on history, political science, sociology, etc.; picture books; folklore. Some fiction. Royalty basis. Query; no unsolicited manuscripts.

PARENTS MAGAZINE PRESS—685 Third Ave., New York, NY 10017. Stephanie Calmenson, Ed. Dir. Humorous picture books, 400 to 600 words, for 3- to 6-year-olds. SASE required.

PARKER PUBLISHING COMPANY, INC.—West Nyack, NY 10994. James Bradler, Pres. Self-help and how-to books, 65,000 words: health, money opportunities, business, etc. Royalty basis.

PELICAN PUBLISHING CO., INC.—1101 Monroe St., Gretna, LA 70053. James L. Calhoun, Exec. Ed. General nonfiction: Americana, architecture, how-to, travel, cookbooks, inspirational, motivational, children's, etc. Royalty basis.

PELION PRESS—See *The Rosen Publishing Group.*

PERSEA BOOKS, INC.—225 Lafayette St., New York, NY 10012. Karen Braziller, Ed. Dir. Scholarly fiction; nonfiction; poetry. Royalty basis or outright purchase. Query only.

PHALAROPE BOOKS—See *Steeple Books.*

PHILOMEL BOOKS (Div. of *Putnam Publishing Group*)—51 Madison Ave., New York, NY 10010. Query Christine Grenz. General fiction, nonfiction, picture books for juveniles.

THE PILGRIM PRESS—132 W. 31 St., New York, NY 10001. Larry E. Kalp, Pub. Religious and general-interest nonfiction. Royalty basis. Query with outline and sample chapters.

PLENUM PUBLISHING CORP.—233 Spring St., New York, NY 10013. Linda Greenspan Regan, Ed. Nonfiction, 200 to 300 pages, on scientific and social scientific topics. Royalty basis. Query required.

POSEIDON PRESS (Imprint of *Pocket Books*)—1230 Ave. of the Americas, New York, NY 10020. Ann Patty, Editor-in-Chief. General fiction and nonfiction. Royalty basis. Query.

CLARKSON N. POTTER, INC.—One Park Ave., New York, NY 10016. Carol Southern, Ed. Dir. General trade books. Submissions accepted through agents only.

PRAEGER PUBLISHERS (Div. of *CBS Educational and Professional Publishing Group*)—521 Fifth Ave., New York, NY 10017. Ron Chambers, Ed. Dir. General nonfiction; scholarly and reference books. Royalty basis. Query with outline.

PRENTICE-HALL, INC.—Englewood Cliffs, NJ 07632. Lynne A. Lumsden, Vice-President and Editorial Dir., Publishing Division. Nonfiction, how-to books and software. Barbara Francis, Ed.-in-Chief, Children's Books Division. Fiction and nonfiction. College books; textbooks; business and professional books. Royalty basis. Query first.

PRESIDIO PRESS—31 Parmaron Way, Novato, CA 94947. California regional fiction with military background; nonfiction with contemporary military history; from 50,000 words. Royalty basis. Query.

PRUETT PUBLISHING COMPANY—2928 Pearl, Boulder, CO 80301. Gerald Keenan, Man. Ed. Non-fiction: railroadiana, Western Americana, recreational guides with Western orientation. Royalty basis. Query.

G. P. PUTNAM'S SONS (Div. of *Putnam Publishing Group*)—200 Madison Ave., New York, NY 10016. General fiction and nonfiction. No unsolicited manuscripts or queries.

QUEST BOOKS (Imprint of *The Theosophical Publishing House*)—306 W. Geneva Rd., P.O. Box 270, Wheaton, IL 60189. Shirley Nicholson, Senior Ed. Nonfiction books on Eastern and Western religion and philosophy, holism, healing, meditation, yoga, astrology, Royalty basis. Query.

RAINTREE PUBLISHERS INC.—205 W. Highland Ave., Milwaukee, WI 53203. Address Ed. Dept. Juveniles: information and reference books; nonfiction picture books. Outright purchase or royalty basis. Query.

RAND MCNALLY & COMPANY—Editorial Dept., Box 7600, Chicago, IL 60680. Adult nonfiction: travel, geographically related subjects. Juvenile picture books. Royalty basis or outright purchase. Query with SASE (required).

RANDOM HOUSE, INC.—201 E. 50th St., New York, NY 10022. Jason Epstein, Ed.-in-Chief. G. Harrison, Ed.-in-Chief, Juvenile Books; Stuart Flexner, Ed.-in-Chief, Reference Books. General fiction and nonfiction; reference and college textbooks; juvenile fiction and nonfiction, picture books, easy-to-read material. Royalty basis. Query with three chapters and outline for nonfiction; complete manuscript for fiction.

RAWSON ASSOCIATES (Div. of *The Scribner Book Cos.*)—115 Fifth Ave., New York, NY 10003. Kennett L. Rawson, Pres. General nonfiction and fiction. Royalty basis. Query.

REGNERY GATEWAY—360 West Superior, Chicago, IL 60610. Nonfiction, average of 70,000 words in length: politics, business, religion, science, etc. Royalty basis. Query first.

FLEMING H. REVELL COMPANY—Old Tappan, NJ 07675. Gary A. Sledge, V.P. and Ed.-in-Chief. Inspirational and devotional religious books. Royalty basis.

RODALE PRESS, BOOK DIVISION—33 E. Minor St., Emmaus, PA 18049. Richard Huttner, Acquisitions Ed. Nonfiction: health, nutrition, alternative energy, gardening; etc. Royalty basis or outright purchase. Query.

THE ROSEN PUBLISHING GROUP, INC.—29 E. 21st St., New York, NY 10010. Roger Rosen, Pres. Ruth C. Rosen, Ed. Young adult books, to 40,000 words, on vocational guidance, journalism, theater, etc. *Pelion Press:* music, art, history. Pays varying rates.

RUTLEDGE BOOKS—300 Mercer St., Suite 32M, New York, NY 10003. Hedy Caplan, Man. Ed. General and graphic-oriented adult nonfiction; cookbooks; sports books. Royalty basis. Query with outline.

ST. MARTIN'S/MAREK—175 Fifth Ave., New York, NY 10010. Fiction: suspense, mystery, historical; general nonfiction: history, political science, biography. Royalty basis. Query before submitting.

SCHOCKEN BOOKS—200 Madison Ave., New York, NY 10016. Emile Capouya, Man. Dir. General nonfiction: history, Judaica, women's studies, etc. Royalty basis. Query.

SCOTT, FORESMAN & COMPANY—1900 E. Lake Ave., Glenview, IL 60025. Richard T. Morgan, Pres. Elementary, secondary, and college textbooks and materials; lifelong learning, electronic material. Royalty basis.

CHARLES SCRIBNER'S SONS—115 Fifth Ave., New York, NY 10003. Jacek W. Galazka, Dir. of Trade Publishing. Fiction; general nonfiction, especially science, business, health. Juvenile Ed., Clare Costello. Royalty basis. Query first.

SEAVER BOOKS—333 Central Park W., New York, NY 10025. Jeannette W. Seaver, Pub. Trade Fiction, nonfiction. Accepts no unsolicited manuscripts. Royalty basis. Query.

SIERRA CLUB BOOKS—2034 Fillmore St., San Francisco, CA 94115. Nonfiction: environment, natural history, the sciences; outdoors and regional guidebooks; juvenile fiction and nonfiction. Royalty basis. Query with SASE.

SIMON & SCHUSTER INC.—1230 Ave. of the Americas, New York, NY 10020. Michael V. Korda, Ed.-in-Chief. General nonfiction; biography, popular science. Fiction. Royalty basis. Query; no unsolicited manuscripts.

STANDARD PUBLISHING—8121 Hamilton Ave., Cincinnati, OH 45231. Address Marge Miller. Fiction: based on Bible or with moral tone. Nonfiction: biblical, Christian education. Conservative evangelical. Query preferred.

STEEPLE BOOKS—Prentice Hall, Inc., Englewood Cliffs, NY 07632. Mary E. Kennan, Ed. Nonfiction religious books. Royalty basis. Send query with completed manuscripts (200 to 300 pages) and SASE. *Phalarope Books*— Series in natural history.

STEIN AND DAY—Scarborough House, Briarcliff Manor, NY 10510. Address Editorial Dept. Adult general fiction and nonfiction. Royalty basis. Query with outline and sample chapter for nonfiction; descriptive letter, up to two pages, for fiction. No unsolicited manuscripts. SASE required.

STEMMER HOUSE—2627 Caves Rd., Owings Mills, MD 21117. Barbara Holdridge, Ed. Adult and juvenile fiction and nonfiction. Royalty basis. Query.

STERLING PUBLISHING CO., INC.—2 Park Ave., New York, NY 10016. Burton Hobson, Pres. How-to, self-help, hobby, woodworking, craft, and sports books. Royalty basis or outright purchase. Query with outline, table of contents, sample chapter, and sample of illustration.

LYLE STUART, INC.—120 Enterprise Ave., Secaucus, NJ 07094. Allan J. Wilson, Ed. General fiction and nonfiction. *Citadel Press* division: biography, film, history, limited fiction. Royalty basis. Query; no unsolicited manuscripts.

SUMMIT BOOKS—1230 Ave. of the Americas, New York, NY 10020. General-interest fiction and nonfiction of high literary quality. No category books. Royalty basis. Query with outline for nonfiction; query with SASE and several chapters for fiction.

SWALLOW PRESS—P.O. Box 2080, Chicago, IL 60690. Self-help, history, biography. Contemporary novels. No unsolicited poetry or fiction. Royalty basis.

TAB BOOKS INC.—Blue Ridge Summit, PA 17214. Raymond A. Collins, Vice-Pres., Edit. Dept. Nonfiction: electronics, computer, how-to, aviation, solar and energy, science and technology, back to basics, automotive, marine and outdoor life. Royalty basis or outright purchase. Query.

TAPLINGER PUBLISHING CO.—132 W. 22nd St., New York, NY 10011. Bobs Pinkerton, Roy Thomas, Eds. General nonfiction: history, art, etc. Royalty basis.

JEREMY P. TARCHER, INC.—9110 Sunset Blvd., Los Angeles, CA 90069. Jeremy P. Tarcher, Ed.-in-Chief. General nonfiction. Royalty basis. Query with outline, sample chapter and SASE.

TEN SPEED PRESS—P.O. Box 7123, Berkeley, CA 94707. Jacqueline Wan, Ed. Self-help and how-to on careers, recreation, etc.; natural science, history, cookbooks. Query with outline and sample chapters. Royalty basis.

TEXAS MONTHLY PRESS—Box 1569, Austin, TX 78767. Scott Lubeck, Ed. Dir. Fiction, nonfiction, related to Texas or the Southwest: 60,000 words. Royalty basis.

TICKNOR & FIELDS (Subsidiary of *Houghton Mifflin Company*)—52 Vanderbilt Ave., New York, NY 10017. General nonfiction and fiction. Royalty basis.

TIMES BOOKS (Div. of *Random House*)—130 Fifth Ave., New York, NY 10011. Jonathan B. Segal, Ed.-in-Chief. General nonfiction and selected fiction. No unsolicited manuscripts or queries accepted.

TROLL ASSOCIATES—320 Rt. 17, Mahwah, NJ 07430. M. Francis, Ed. Juvenile fiction and nonfiction. Royalty basis or outright purchase. Query preferred.

TYNDALE HOUSE—336 Gundersen Dr., Box 80, Wheaton, IL 60187. Wendell Hawley, Ed.-in-Chief. Christian. Juvenile and adult fiction and nonfiction on subjects of concern to Christians. Submit complete manuscripts. Royalty basis.

UNIVERSE BOOKS—381 Park Ave. S., New York, NY 10016. Louis Barron, Vice-Pres. and Ed. Dir. Art, ballet, how-to, history, music, natural history, social science, etc. Royalty basis. Query with SASE.

VAN NOSTRAND REINHOLD INC. (Incorporating *CBI Publishing Co.*)—135 W. 50th St., New York, NY 10020. J. Gill, Pres. Nonfiction: how-to; technical scientific, and reference subjects. Royalty basis.

THE VANGUARD PRESS, INC.—424 Madison Ave., New York, NY 10017. Bernice Woll, Ed. Adult and juvenile fiction and nonfiction. Royalty basis. Query with sample chapters.

VIKING PENGUIN, INC.—40 W. 23rd St., New York, NY 10010. *The Viking Press:* Adult fiction and nonfiction. *Viking Junior Books:* Juveniles. *Penguin Books:* Paperback reprints and originals. Royalty basis. Query letters only, with SASE.

WALKER AND COMPANY—720 Fifth Ave., New York, NY 10019. Beth Walker, Man. Ed. Adult and romantic suspense, men's action, mysteries. Regency romances, and westerns. Royalty basis. Query with synopsis.

WANDERER BOOKS (Div. of *Simon & Schuster, Inc.*)—1230 Ave. of the Americas, New York, NY 10020. Wendy Barish, Ed. Dir. General-interest juveniles, for 8- to 14-year-olds. Nonfiction. Flat fee and royalty basis. Query with outline and sample chapter for nonfiction.

FREDERICK WARNE & CO., INC.—2 Park Ave., New York, NY 10016. Address Ed. Dept. Juvenile and young-adult books. No manuscripts accepted without previous query. Royalty basis.

FRANKLIN WATTS, INC.—387 Park Ave. S., New York, NY 10016. Jeanne Vestal, Edit. Dir. Juvenile nonfiction. College-level history and social sciences. Royalty basis. Query. SASE required.

WESTERN PUBLISHING CO., INC.—850 Third Ave., New York, NY 10022. Doris Duenewald, Pub., Children's Books; Jonathan B. Latimer, Pub., Adult Books: Ronne Peltzman, Ed.-in-Chief, Children's Books. Adult nonfiction: family-oriented, how-to's, etc. Children's books, fiction and nonfiction: picture books, storybooks, concept books, novelty books. Royalty basis and outright purchase. Query. Same address and requirements for *Golden Press*.

WINCHESTER PRESS—220 Old New Brunswick Rd., CN 1332, Piscataway, NJ 08854. Bob Elman, Consulting Ed. Nonfiction: outdoors, how-to, etc. Royalty basis. Query.

WINSTON PRESS—430 Oak Grove, Minneapolis, MN 55403. Miriam Frost, Man. Ed., Trade Books. Nonfiction, from 120 manuscript pages: religion; self help; popular appeal. Royalty basis. Submit table of contents and one or two sample chapters.

WORKMAN PUBLISHING CO., INC.—1 W. 39th St., New York, NY 10018. General nonfiction. Normal contractual terms based on agreement.

YANKEE BOOKS—Main St., Dublin, NH 03444. Clarissa Silitch, Ed. Books relating to New England: Cooking, crafts, old-time skills adapted to today's materials. New England travel, gardening, nature, nostalgia, folklore and popular history, etc. No scholarly history, highly technical work, or off-color humor. Regional New England fiction also considered. Royalty basis. Query or send complete manuscript.

CHARLOTTE ZOLOTOW BOOKS (Imprint of *Harper & Row*)—10 E. 53rd St., New York, NY 10022. Juvenile fiction and nonfiction "with integrity of purpose, beauty of language, and an out-of-ordinary look at ordinary things." Royalty basis.

THE ZONDERVAN CORPORATION—1415 Lake Dr., S.E., Grand Rapids, MI 49506. Julie Ackerman Link, Manuscript Review Ed. Nonfiction books with an evangelical Christian viewpoint: self-help; general nonfiction;

Bible study; devotional and gift. Fiction, with a religious theme. Juvenile adventure novels, for children aged 10 to 14. Royalty basis. Query with outline and sample chapter.

PAPERBACK BOOK PUBLISHERS

ACE BOOKS (Imprint of *Berkley Publishing Group*)—200 Madison Ave., New York, NY 10016. Science fiction and fantasy. Pays on royalty basis or by outright purchase. No unsolicited manuscripts.

APPLE BOOKS—See *Scholastic, Inc.*

ARCHWAY PAPERBACKS (Imprint of *Simon and Schuster*)—1230 Ave. of the Americas, New York, NY 10020. Fiction for ages 8—15, including adventure, suspense, romance, humor, science fiction, fantasy, animals, sports, and young adult novels. *Which Way Books:* multiple-plot series for children grades 3-6. *Follow Your Heart Romances:* multiple–plot romances for girls in grade 5 and up. Query with outline and SASE. Royalty basis.

ARCSOFT PUBLISHERS—P. O. Box 132, Woodsboro, MD 21798. Anthony Curtis, Pres. Nonfiction on personal computing for laymen, general and public consumers, beginners and novices. Outright purchase and royalty basis. Query.

AVON BOOKS—1790 Broadway, New York, NY 10019. Page Cuddy, Ed. Dir. Modern fiction; historical romances; general nonfiction, 60,000 to 200,000 words. Science fiction, 75,000 to 100,000 words. Royalty basis. Query with synopsis, sample chapters, and SASE. *Camelot Books:* Ellen Krieger, Sen. Ed. Fiction and nonfiction for 5- to 12-year-olds. Pays on royalty basis. Query. *Flare Books:* Ellen Krieger, Sen. Ed. Fiction and nonfiction for 12-year-olds and up. Royalty basis. Query.

BALLANTINE BOOKS—201 E. 50th St., New York, NY 10022. Robert Wyatt, Ed.-in-Chief. Accepts no unsolicited material for general fiction and nonfiction lines.

BANTAM BOOKS, INC.—666 Fifth Ave., New York, NY 10103. Lou Aronica, Coordinator, Science Fiction/Fantasy; Judy Gitenstein, Ed. Dir., Young Readers Books; Carolyn Nichols, *Loveswept;* Linda Grey, Ed. Dir., Adult Fiction and Nonfiction. General and educational fiction and nonfiction, 75,000 to 100,000 words. No unsolicited manuscripts. *Dark Forces:* see listing under *Southbury Press.*

BERKLEY PUBLISHING GROUP—200 Madison Ave., New York, NY 10016. Roger Cooper, Vice-Pres./Ed. Dir. General interest fiction and nonfiction: science fiction; suspense and espionage novels; romance. Submit through agent only. Publishes both reprints and originals.

BETHANY HOUSE PUBLISHERS—6820 Auto Club Rd., Minneapolis, MN 55438. Address Ed. Dept. Fiction, nonfiction. Religious. Royalty basis. Query required.

BETTERWAY PUBLICATIONS—White Hall, VA 22987. Robert F. Hostage, Sr. Ed. Nonfiction for adults: parenting, family health, small and home-based business interests. How-to books for teens and young adults. Royalty basis.

CAMELOT BOOKS—See *Avon Books.*

741

CHARTER BOOKS (Imprint of *Berkley Publishing Group*)—200 Madison Ave., New York, NY 10016. Roger Cooper, V.P., Ed. Dir. Adventure, espionage and suspense fiction, women's contemporary fiction, family sagas and historical novels. Westerns, male action/adventure, and cartoon books. No unsolicited manuscripts. Pays on royalty basis or by outright purchase.

CLOVERDALE PRESS—133 Fifth Ave., New York, NY 10003. Ben Baglio, Ed. Book packager. Young adult and juvenile fiction. Popular writing on computers, all age levels. No unsolicited manuscripts. Query with resumé.

CONCORDIA PUBLISHING HOUSE—3558 S. Jefferson Ave., St. Louis, MO 63118. Practical nonfiction with moral or religious values. Very little fiction. No poetry. Royalty basis. Query.

DARK FORCES—See *Southbury Press*.

DAW BOOKS, INC.—1633 Broadway, New York, NY 10019. Donald A. Wollheim, Pub. and Ed. Science fiction and fantasy, 50,000 to 80,000 words. Royalty basis.

DELL PUBLISHING CO., INC.—245 E. 47th St., New York, NY 10017. *Dell Books:* family sagas, historical romances, sexy modern romances, war action, occult/horror/psychological suspense, true crime, men's adventure. *Delta:* general-interest nonfiction, psychology, feminism, health, nutrition, child care, science. *Juvenile Books: Yearling* (kindergarten through 6th grade; no unsolicited manuscripts); and *Laurel-Leaf* (grades 7 through 12; no unsolicited manuscripts). *Purse Books:* miniature paperbacks about 60 pages in length, on topics of current consumer interest. Submissions policy: Send four-page narrative synopsis for fiction, or an outline for nonfiction. Enclose SASE. Don't send any sample chapters, artwork, or manuscripts. Address submissions to the appropriate Dell division and add Editorial Dept.—Book Proposal.

DELTA BOOKS—See *Dell*.

DOUBLEDAY—245 Park Ave., New York, NY 10017. Loretta Barrett, Exec. Ed. Adult trade books: fiction, sociology, psychology, philosophy, women's, etc. Query.

FAWCETT BOOKS GROUP—See *Ballantine Books*.

THE FEMINIST PRESS—Box 334, Old Westbury, NY 11568. Reprints of significant lost fiction or autobiography by women; reprints of other classic feminist texts; feminist biography; women's studies for classroom adaptation. Royalty basis.

FIRESIDE BOOKS (Imprint of *Simon & Schuster*)—1230 Ave. of the Americas, New York, NY 10020. General nonfiction. Royalty basis or outright purchase. Submit outline and one chapter.

FLARE BOOKS—See *Avon Books*.

GOLD EAGLE BOOKS (Imprint of *Worldwide Library*)—225 Duncan Mill Rd., Don Mills, Ont., Canada M3B 3K9. Mark Howell, Ed. Formula action-adventure novels. "Work for hire" bonus basis. Query with 3 chapters and outline.

HARLEQUIN BOOKS—225 Duncan Mill Rd., Don Mills, Ont., Canada M3B 3K9. Romances. See complete listing under *Romance Publishers*.

JOHNSON BOOKS, INC.—1880 S. 57th Ct., Boulder, CO 80301. Michael McNierney, Ed. Nonfiction: western history and archaeology, how-to, nature, outdoor sports and recreation, regional. Royalty basis. Query.

JOVE BOOKS—200 Madison Ave., New York, NY 10016. Roger Cooper, Ed.-in-Chief. Fiction and nonfiction. No unsolicited manuscripts.

JUNIPER BOOKS (Imprint of *Fawcett Books*)—201 E. 50th St., New York, NY 10022. Leona Nevler, Ed.-in-Chief. Novels, mystery and suspense, for teens, from 50,000 words. Query first. Pays on royalty basis.

LAUREL-LEAF BOOKS—See *Dell Publishing Co., Inc.*

MEADOWBROOK PRESS—18318 Minnetonka Blvd., Deephaven, MN 55391. Kathe Grooms, Ed. Dir. Books on infant and child care; maternity; health; travel; consumer interests. Fiction: juvenile mysteries. Royalty basis and outright purchase. Query. SASE required.

MENTOR BOOKS—See *New American Library.*

JOHN MUIR PUBLICATIONS—P. O. Box 613, Santa Fe, NM 87501. Jeanne Flannery, Project Coordinator. General nonfiction: gardening, computers, how-to, sports, travel, auto-related, etc. Royalty basis. Query with outline and sample chapters.

NEW AMERICAN LIBRARY—1633 Broadway, New York, NY 10019. Pat Taylor, Ed. *Signet Books:* Commercial fiction: historicals, sagas, thrillers, romances, action/adventure. Nonfiction: self-help, how-to, etc. *Plume Books:* Nonfiction: hobbies, business, health, cooking, child care, psychology, etc. *Mentor Books:* Nonfiction originals for high school and college market. Royalty basis. Query with outline and sample chapters.

PACER BOOKS FOR YOUNG ADULTS (Imprint of *The Putnam Publishing Group*)—51 Madison Ave., New York, NY 10010. Eve Siskind, Ed. Young adult novels, 40,000 to 60,000 words, in all genres—mystery, humor, non-formula romance, adventure, and fantasy. Query, with plot summary, age of characters, setting, or submit complete manuscript. Royalty or flat fee basis.

PENGUIN BOOKS (Div. of *Viking/Penguin, Inc.*)—40 W. 23rd St., New York, NY 10010. Kathryn Court, Edit. Dir. Adult fiction and nonfiction. No original poetry or juveniles. Royalty basis. Query with synopsis and sample chapter.

PINNACLE BOOKS, INC.—1430 Broadway, New York, NY 10018. Sondra Ordover, Ed.-in-Chief. Popular and commercial fiction, historical and contemporary romance, romantic adventure, thriller and humor. Query with SASE. No unsolicited manuscripts.

PLUME BOOKS—See *New American Library.*

POCKET BOOKS (Div. of *Simon & Schuster, Inc.*)—1230 Ave. of the Americas, New York, NY 10020. Address Editorial Department. Some originals. Query with outline. No unsolicited manuscripts.

POINT—See *Scholastic, Inc.*

PRICE/STERN/SLOAN PUBLISHERS, INC.—410 N. La Cienega Blvd., Los Angeles, CA 90048. Short, humorous "non-books." Royalty basis or outright purchase. Query.

PURSE BOOKS—See *Dell Publishing Co., Inc.*

REWARD BOOKS (Subsidiary of *Prentice-Hall, Inc.*)—Englewood Cliffs, NJ 07632. Ted Nardin, Manager. Nonfiction: self-help, real estate, selling, business, health, etc. Royalty basis. No recent report.

743

SCHOLASTIC, INC.—730 Broadway, New York, NY 10003. Brenda Bowen, Assoc. Ed.—Trade. *Point:* young adult fiction, for readers age 12 and up. *Apple Books:* Fiction for readers age 9 to 12. Submit complete manuscripts with covering letter and SASE. Royalty basis. *Wildfire* and *Sunfire:* See listing under *Romance Publishers.*

SIGNET BOOKS—See *New American Library.*

SILHOUETTE BOOKS—See listing under *Romance Publishers.*

SIMON & SCHUSTER—1230 Ave. of the Americas, New York, NY 10020. Barbara Gess, Group Man. Ed., Adult Trade Paperback Div. Nonfiction; cooking, self-help, how-to, humor, health and beauty, baby and child care and development, sports, music, and other general interest topics. Royalty and flat fee basis. Send outline and sample chapters.

SOUTHBURY PRESS—P.O. Box 162, Southbury, CT 06488. Lorraine Bruck, Projects Coordinator. Book packager. Young adult supernatural/occult books for Bantam's *Dark Forces* series and YA historical romances. Query. SASE required. Overstocked.

STERLING PAPERBACKS—2 Park Ave., New York, NY 10016. General nonfiction, 50,000 to 90,000 words: how-to, self-help, health, hobbies, etc. Royalty basis or outright purchase. Query with outline and table of contents.

TIMBRE BOOKS (Imprint of *Arbor House*)—235 E. 45th St., New York, NY 10017. Helen Eisenbach, Ed. Mgr. Adult trade paper. Nonfiction: business, music, sports, food, health, and humor, biography, reference. Submit manuscripts or detailed outline with sample chapters. Royalty basis.

TROUBADOR PRESS—One Sutter St., Suite 205, San Francisco, CA 94104. Juvenile illustrated nonfiction and fiction, especially games, activity, paper doll, coloring and cut-out books. Royalty basis or outright purchase. Query with outline and SASE.

WARNER BOOKS—666 Fifth Ave., New York, NY 10103. Bernard Shir-Cliff, Ed.-in-Chief. Fiction: historical romance, contemporary women's fiction, unusual big-scale horror and suspense. Controversial nonfiction, self-help and how-to-books. Royalty basis. Query with sample chapters. Also publishes trade paperbacks and hardcover titles.

WHICH WAY BOOKS—See *Archway Paperbacks.*

WILSHIRE BOOK COMPANY—12015 Sherman Rd., North Hollywood, CA 91605. Specialized nonfiction: Inspirational, self-help; calligraphy, advertising, mail order, sports, health, horses, etc. Royalty basis. Query with synopsis or outline. SASE required.

WOODBRIDGE PRESS PUBLISHING HOUSE—Box 6189, Santa Barbara, CA 93111. Howard B. Weeks, Ed. Nonfiction: health, gardening, nutrition, humor, cooking. Royalty basis. Query with outline and sample chapters.

YEARLING BOOKS—See *Dell Publishing Co., Inc.*

ROMANCE BOOK PUBLISHERS

BESTSELLERS—Worldwide Library, 225 Duncan Mill Rd., Don Mills, Ont. M3B 3K9 Canada. Jennifer Campbell, Sen. Ed. Mainstream romantic fiction, historical or contemporary. Submit complete manuscript of 100,000 to 150,000 words. Send for tip sheet.

CANDLELIGHT ECSTASY ROMANCES—Dell Publishing Co., Inc., 245 E. 47th St., New York, NY 10017. Lydia E. Paglio, Ed. Sensuous, realistic contemporary romantic novels, 50,000 to 60,000 words, set in the United States. *Ecstasy Supreme Romances:* 85,000 to 100,000 words, with more complex plots, more fully developed characterizations; not necessarily confined to the United States. Query with 2- to 4-page synopsis only.

CAPRICE—Ace Books, 200 Madison Avenue, New York, NY 10016. Romances for teenagers, 50,000 to 60,000 words. Royalty basis.

DESIRE—See *Silhouette Books.*

DREAM YOUR OWN ROMANCE STORIES—Wanderer Books, 1230 Ave. of the Americas, New York, NY 10020. Wendy Barish, Ed.-in-Chief. Romances for juveniles, 8 and up. Overstocked.

ECSTASY SUPREME—See *Candlelight Ecstasy.*

FIRST LOVE—See *Silhouette Books.*

FOLLOW YOUR HEART ROMANCES—Archway Paperbacks, 1230 Ave. of the Americas, New York, NY 10020. Catherine Crean, Ed. Asst. Multiple plot romances for girls in grades 5 and up. Query with summary for two complete tracks, and SASE.

HARLEQUIN AMERICAN ROMANCES—919 Third Ave., 15th Floor, New York, NY 10022. Hilari Cohen and Debra Matteucci, Sen. Eds. Contemporary romances, 70,000 to 75,000 words, with American settings, American characters. Submit complete manuscript. Send for tip sheet.

HARLEQUIN INTRIGUE—Harlequin Books, 919 Third Ave., New York, NY 10022. Debra Matteucci and Hilari Cohen, Sen. Eds. Contemporary romances, with intricate, twisting plots, 70,000 to 75,000 words. Submit query letter, proposal (3 chapters and detailed outline), or complete manuscript. Send for tip sheet.

HARLEQUIN ROMANCES AND HARLEQUIN PRESENTS—Harlequin Books, 225 Duncan Mill Rd., Don Mills, Ont., Canada M3B 3K9; Maryan Gibson, Sr. Ed. Contemporary romance novels, 55,000 to 60,000 words, with North American or exotic settings, varying in style, plot and characters from the traditional and gentle to the more sophisticated and sensuous. Send complete manuscript or first fifty pages and short synopsis. Send for tip sheet.

HARLEQUIN SUPERROMANCES—Worldwide Library, 225 Duncan Mill Rd., Don Mills, Ont., Canada M3B 3K9. Lauren Baumen, Sr. Ed. Contemporary romances, 85,000 words, with North American or foreign setting. New authors: Send as much of completed manuscript as possible or a minimum of three chapters and long synopsis. Published authors: same, plus copy of published work. Send for tip sheet.

HARLEQUIN TEMPTATION—Harlequin Books, 225 Duncan Mill Rd., Don Mills, Ont., Canada M3B 3K9. Kay Meierbachtol, Man. Ed. Contemporary romantic fantasies, 60,000 to 65,000 words, with sensual love scenes presented tastefully. Send for tip sheet.

LOVESWEPT—Bantam Books, Inc., 666 Fifth Ave., New York, NY 10019. Carolyn Nichols, Ed. Dir. Highly sensual, adult contemporary romances. Query.

MAGIC MOMENTS—New American Library, 1633 Broadway, New York, NY 10019. Cindy Kane, Ed. Contemporary teen romances, 45,000 to

50,000 words. No tip sheet. Submit detailed outline and three or more sample chapters. Royalty basis.

MAKE YOUR DREAMS COME TRUE—Warner Books, 666 Fifth Ave., New York, NY 10103. Kathy Simmons, Man. Ed. Multiple-plot young adult romances. Query with detailed outline and sample chapter. Flat fee.

MOONSTONE—Cloverdale Press, 133 Fifth Ave., 6th Floor, New York, NY 10003. Teen-age romantic suspense novels. Query first. Write for tip sheet. Distributed by Pocket Books, with Pocket imprint.

RAPTURE ROMANCES—New American Library, 1633 Broadway, New York, NY 10019. Mary Anne Gartland, Ed. Contemporary romances, 55,000 words, for adult women. Royalty basis. Query with 4- to 6-page synopsis and sample chapters or complete manuscript. SASE required. Send for tip sheet.

RHAPSODY ROMANCES—Harvest House Pubs., 1075 Arrowsmith, Eugene, OR 97402. Adult contemporary romance fiction. Query with complete manuscript, 42,000 words, or partials of 50 to 70 pages. SASE required.

SCHOLASTIC, INC.—730 Broadway, New York, NY 10003. Ann Reit, Ed. Contemporary romance lines for girls 12 to 15 years old, 40,000 to 45,000 words: *Wildfire,* realistic problems of girls in first or early relationships; *Sunfire,* American historical romances, 85,000 words. Query with outline and three sample chapters. Write for tip sheets.

SECOND CHANCE AT LOVE—The Berkley Publishing Group, 200 Madison Ave., New York, NY 10016. Ellen Edwards, Sr. Ed. Contemporary romances, 60,000 words, with mature, experienced heroines who find the happiness that was missing in previous relationships or marriages. Royalty basis. Query with synopsis. Send for tip sheet.

SERENADE AND SERENADE/SAGA ROMANCES—Zondervan Publishing House, 749 Templeton Dr., Nashville, TN 37205. Anne W. Severance, Ed. Inspirational romances, 60,000 words, for Christian readers. *Serenade:* contemporary. *Serenade/Saga:* historical. Royalty basis. Send sample chapter, outline, synopsis and biographical sketch. Send for tip sheet.

SILHOUETTE BOOKS—300 E. 42nd St., 6th Fl., New York, NY 10017. Karen Solem, Ed.-in-Chief. *Silhouette Romances:* contemporary romances, 53,000 to 56,000 words. *Special Edition:* 75,000 to 80,000 words, sophisticated contemporary romances. *Desire:* extremely sensuous romances, 55,000 to 65,000 words. *Silhouette Intimate Moments:* 75,000 to 85,000 words, sensuous, sophisticated contemporary romances. *First Love* (for 11- to 16-year-old girls): 50,000 to 55,000 words. Write for tip sheets. *Silhouette Inspiration:* romances, 55,000 to 60,000 words, of hope and faith, with Christian background. Send query letter, two-page synopsis, and SASE to Assoc. Ed. Rosalind Noonan.

STARLIGHT—Doubleday & Co., Inc., 245 Park Ave., New York, NY 10167. Veronica Mixon, Ed. Hardback. Contemporary adult romances, 70,000 to 75,000 words, with no overt sex, but reflecting the contemporary lifestyles of everyday life for young women in America. Minority heroes and heroines welcomed. Royalty basis. Send complete manuscript with outline.

SUNFIRE—See *Scholastic, Inc.*

TEMPTATIONS—Dell Publishing Co., Inc., 1 Dag Hammarskjold Plaza, 245 E. 47th St., New York, NY 10017. No unsolicited material accepted.

TO HAVE AND TO HOLD—The Berkley Publishing Group, 200 Madison Ave., New York, NY 10016. Ellen Edwards, Sr. Ed. Contemporary romances,

60,000 words, centered around married couples and the joys and challenges of married life. Royalty basis. Query with synopsis. Send for tip sheet.

TURNING POINTS—New American Library, 1633 Broadway, New York, NY 10019. Teen romances. No unsolicited material accepted.

TWO BY TWO ROMANCES—Riverview Books Inc., 200 Riverview Ave., Tarrytown, NY 10591. Louise Colligan, Pub. Two romance novels in one; one story from the male and one from the female point of view. Query with published clips. Royalty basis. Published by Warner Books.

WILDFIRE—See *Scholastic, Inc.*

YOUNG LOVE—Dell Publishing Co., Inc., 245 E. 47th St., New York, NY 10017. Contemporary romances for teens, in which the heroines are at least 14 years old. Royalty basis. Write for tip sheet.

UNIVERSITY PRESSES

University presses generally publish books of a scholarly nature or of specialized interest by authorities in a given field. Many publish only a handful of titles a year. Always query first. Do not send any manuscripts until you have been invited to do so by the editor.

BRIGHAM YOUNG UNIVERSITY PRESS—209 University Press Bldg., Provo, UT 84602.

BUCKNELL UNIVERSITY PRESS—Lewisburg, PA 17837.

CAMBRIDGE UNIVERSITY PRESS—32 East 57th St., New York, NY 10022.

THE CATHOLIC UNIVERSITY OF AMERICA PRESS—620 Michigan Ave., N.E., Washington, DC 20064.

COLORADO ASSOCIATED UNIVERSITY PRESS—University of Colorado, 1424 15th St., Boulder, CO 80302.

COLUMBIA UNIVERSITY PRESS—562 West 113th St., New York, NY 10025.

DUKE UNIVERSITY PRESS—Box 6697, College Station, Durham, NC 27708.

DUQUESNE UNIVERSITY PRESS—101 Administration Bldg., Pittsburgh, PA 15219.

FORDHAM UNIVERSITY PRESS—Box L, Bronx, NY 10458.

GEORGIA STATE UNIVERSITY, SCHOOL OF BUSINESS ADMINISTRATION, PUBLISHING SERVICES DIVISION—University Plaza, Atlanta, GA 30303.

HARVARD UNIVERSITY PRESS—79 Garden St., Cambridge, MA 02138.

INDIANA UNIVERSITY PRESS—10th and Morton Sts., Bloomington, IN 47401.

THE JOHNS HOPKINS UNIVERSITY PRESS—Baltimore, MD 21218.

KENT STATE UNIVERSITY PRESS—Kent, OH 44242.

LOUISIANA STATE UNIVERSITY PRESS—Baton Rouge, LA 70803.

LOYOLA UNIVERSITY PRESS—3441 North Ashland Ave., Chicago, IL 60657.

MEMPHIS STATE UNIVERSITY PRESS—Memphis, TN 38152.

MICHIGAN STATE UNIVERSITY PRESS—1405 South Harrison Rd., East Lansing, MI 48824.

THE M.I.T. PRESS—28 Carleton St., Cambridge, MA 02142.

NEW YORK UNIVERSITY PRESS—Washington Sq., New York, NY 10003.

OHIO STATE UNIVERSITY PRESS—Hitchcock Hall, Rm. 316, 2070 Neil Ave., Columbus, OH 43210.

OHIO UNIVERSITY PRESS—Scott Quadrangle, Athens, OH 45701.

OREGON STATE UNIVERSITY PRESS—101 Waldo Hall, Corvallis, OR 97331.

THE PENNSYLVANIA STATE UNIVERSITY PRESS—215 Wagner Bldg., University Park, PA 16802.

PRINCETON UNIVERSITY PRESS—Princeton, NJ 08540.

RUTGERS UNIVERSITY PRESS—30 College Ave., New Brunswick, NJ 08903.

SOUTHERN ILLINOIS UNIVERSITY PRESS—Box 3697, Carbondale, IL 62901.

SOUTHERN METHODIST UNIVERSITY PRESS—Dallas, TX 75275.

STANFORD UNIVERSITY PRESS—Stanford, CA 94305.

STATE UNIVERSITY OF NEW YORK PRESS—State Univ. Plaza, Albany, NY 12246.

SYRACUSE UNIVERSITY PRESS—1011 East Water St., Syracuse, NY 13210.

TEMPLE UNIVERSITY PRESS—Broad and Oxford Sts., Philadelphia, PA 19122.

UNIVERSITY OF ALABAMA PRESS—Drawer 2877, University, AL 35486.

UNIVERSITY OF ARIZONA PRESS—Box 3398, College Station, Tucson, AZ 85722.

UNIVERSITY OF CALIFORNIA PRESS—2223 Fulton St., Berkeley, CA 94720.

UNIVERSITY OF CHICAGO PRESS—5801 Ellis Ave., Chicago, IL 60637.

UNIVERSITY OF GEORGIA PRESS—Athens, GA 30602.

UNIVERSITY OF ILLINOIS PRESS—Urbana, IL 61801.

UNIVERSITY OF MASSACHUSETTS PRESS—Box 429, Amherst, MA 01002.

UNIVERSITY OF MICHIGAN PRESS—Ann Arbor, MI 48106.

UNIVERSITY OF MINNESOTA PRESS—2037 University Ave., S.E., Minneapolis, MN 55455.

UNIVERSITY OF MISSOURI PRESS—107 Swallow Hall, Columbia, MO 65201.

UNIVERSITY OF NEBRASKA PRESS—901 North 17th St., Lincoln, NE 68588.

UNIVERSITY OF NEW MEXICO PRESS—Albuquerque, NM 87131.

UNIVERSITY OF NOTRE DAME PRESS—Notre Dame, IN 46556.

UNIVERSITY OF OKLAHOMA PRESS—1005 Asp Ave., Norman, OK 73019.

UNIVERSITY OF PITTSBURGH PRESS—127 North Bellefield Ave., Pittsburgh, PA 15260.

UNIVERSITY OF SOUTH CAROLINA PRESS—USC Campus, Columbia, SC 29208.

UNIVERSITY OF TENNESSEE PRESS—Communications Bldg., Knoxville, TN 37916.

UNIVERSITY OF UTAH PRESS—Bldg. 513, Salt Lake City, UT 84112.

UNIVERSITY OF WASHINGTON PRESS—Seattle, WA 98195.

UNIVERSITY OF WISCONSIN PRESS—Box 1379, Madison, WI 53701.

THE UNIVERSITY PRESS OF KENTUCKY—Lafferty Hall, Lexington, KY 40506.

UNIVERSITY PRESS OF MISSISSIPPI—3825 Ridgewood Rd., Jackson, MS 39211.

THE UNIVERSITY PRESS OF NEW ENGLAND—Box 979, Hanover, NH 03755.

THE UNIVERSITY PRESS OF VIRGINIA—Box 3608, University Sta., Charlottesville, VA 22903.

THE UNIVERSITY PRESSES OF FLORIDA—15 N.W. 15th St., Gainesville, FL 32603.

WAYNE STATE UNIVERSITY PRESS—5959 Woodward Ave., Detroit, MI 48202.

WESLEYAN UNIVERSITY PRESS—55 High Street, Middletown, CT 06457.

YALE UNIVERSITY PRESS—302 Temple St., New Haven, CT 06511.

SYNDICATES

Syndicates are business organizations that publish nothing themselves, but buy material from writers and artists to sell to newspapers all over the country and the world. Authors are paid either a percentage of the gross proceeds, or an outright fee.

Of course, features by people well known in their fields have the best chance of being syndicated. In general, syndicates want columns that have been popular in a local newspaper, perhaps, or magazine. Since most syndicated fiction has been published previously in magazines or books, beginning fiction writers should try to sell their stories to magazines before submitting them to syndicates.

Always query syndicates before sending manuscripts—their needs change frequently.

CANADA WIDE FEATURE SERVICE—333 King St. E., Toronto, Ontario, M5A 3X5, Canada. Glenn-Stewart Garnett, Ed. Interviews with well-known celebrities and international political figures, 1,500 to 2,000 words, with photos. Pays 50% of gross, on publication.

CONTEMPORARY FEATURES SYNDICATE—P.O. Box 1258, Jackson, TN 38301. Lloyd Russell, Ed. Articles, 1,000 to 3,000 words: how to, back-to-nature, money-savers, travel, business, etc. Self-help pieces, 1,000 to 10,000 words. Pays from $25, on acceptance.

CURIOUS FACTS FEATURES—6B Ridge Ct., Lebanon, OH 45036. Donald Whitacre, Ed. Nonfiction, to 500 words, and fillers to 50 words, for average reader; strange, true and unknown facts and oddities. Pays 50%, on publication.

FACING SOUTH—Box 531, Durham, NC 27702. Jocelyn Moody, Ed. Articles, to 700 words, on oral history, nostalgia, profiles: emphasis on individuals whose creativity, courage, or dissent illustrate positive southern values of community, pride in the land, helping others. Pays $50 a column, on publication.

FEATURES ASSOCIATES—P.O. Box 9144, San Rafael, CA 94912. Peter Menkin, Ed. Articles, 150 to 650 words; special interest in second rights. Pays 50%.

FICTION NETWORK—Box 5651, San Francisco, CA 94101. Fiction, to 5,000 words (preferably 2,500 or shorter). One submission per author; submit manuscript unfolded. SASE required. Pays royalty basis. Allow 12 weeks for response.

FIELD NEWSPAPER SYNDICATE—See *News America Syndicate.*

HARRIS & ASSOCIATES—615 Carla Way, La Jolla, CA 92037. Dick Harris, Ed. Sports and family-oriented features, to 1,200 words; fillers and short humor, 500 to 800 words. Queries preferred. Pays varying rates.

HERITAGE FEATURES SYNDICATE—214 Mass. Ave., NE, Washington, DC 20002. Andrew Seamans, Sr., Man. Ed. Public policy news features; syndicates weekly by-lined columns and editorial cartoons. Query with SASE a must.

HISPANIC LINK NEWS SERVICE—1420 N St., NW, Washington, DC 20005. Hector Ericksen-Mendoza, Ed. Trend articles, general features, hispanic focus, 650 to 700 words; editorial cartoons. Pays $25 for op/ed column and cartoons, on acceptance. Send SASE for writers' guidelines.

THE HOLLYWOOD INSIDE SYNDICATE—Box 49957, Los Angeles, CA 90049. John Austin, Director. Feature material, 750 to 1,000 words, on TV and motion picture personalities. Story suggestions for 3-part series. Pieces on unusual medical and scientific breakthroughs. Pays on percentage basis for features, negotiated rates for ideas, on acceptance.

INTERNATIONAL MEDICAL TRIBUNE SYNDICATE—600 New Hampshire Ave., Suite 700, NW, Washington, DC 20037. Health and medical news, features, 250 to 1,000 words; technical accuracy and clarity a must. Pays 15¢ to 20¢ a word.

KING FEATURES SYNDICATE—235 E. 45th St., New York, NY 10017. James D. Head, Ed. Columns, comics; most contributions on contract for regular columns. Feature articles for Sunday newspaper supplement "Sunday Woman"; query Merry Clark, Ed.

LONGHORN PRODUCTIONS—21213 Hawthorne Blvd., Suite 5208, Torrance, CA 90509. Michael Granada, Ed. Cindy Gonzalez, Women's Ed. Nationally-slanted original features, 1,500 to 3,000 words, and columns, 600 to 1,000 words. Fillers, short humor, trivia, etc. Particularly interested in items for adult men; topical subjects. Pays $5 to $75 per insertion per newspaper, on acceptance for features, on monthly basis for other material. Query required, with SASE.

LOS ANGELES TIMES SYNDICATE—Times Mirror Sq., Los Angeles, CA 90053. Cartoons, comics, features and columns. Query for articles, either one-shots or series.

NATIONAL CATHOLIC NEWS SERVICE—1312 Massachusetts Ave. N.W., Washington, DC 20005. Richard W. Daw, Director and Ed.-in-Chief. Articles on the Catholic Church and Catholic issues; photos. Pays to 5¢ a word, after publication.

NATIONAL NEWS BUREAU—2019 Chancellor St., Philadelphia, PA 19103. Articles, 500 to 800 words, on subjects of national interest: interviews, consumer news, how-to's, travel pieces, reviews, opinion columns, etc. Pays on publication.

NEW YORK TIMES SYNDICATION SALES—200 Park Ave., New York, NY 10166. Susan G. Sawyer, Man. Ed. Previously published articles only, to 2,000 words. Query with published article or tear sheet. Pays 40%, on publication.

NEWS AMERICA SYNDICATE—1703 Kaiser Ave., Irvine, CA 92714. Leighton McLaughlin, Ed. Columns, comic strips, panel cartoons, serials.

NEWSPAPER ENTERPRISE ASSOCIATION, INC.—200 Park Ave., New York, NY 10166. David Hendin, Vice Pres. and Ed. Director. Ideas for new concepts in syndicated columns, comic strips, and panels. No single stories or stringers. Payment by contractual arrangement.

OCEANIC PRESS SERVICE—P.O. Box 6538, Buena Park, CA 90622-6538. John R. West, General Manager. Buys reprint rights on previously published novels, self-help, and how-to books; interviews with celebrities; illustrated features on celebrities, family, health, beauty, personal relations, etc.; cartoons, comic strips. Pays on acceptance. Query.

RELIGIOUS NEWS SERVICE—104 W. 56th St., New York, NY 10019. Gerald A. Renner, Ed. and Director. Religious news stories and features. Photos on religious subjects. Pays 3¢ a word, extra for photos, on acceptance.

SELECT FEATURES OF NEWS AMERICA SYNDICATE—1703 Kaiser Blvd., P.O. Box 19620, Irvine, CA 92714. Doris Richetti, Man., Select Features. Articles and series dealing with lifestyle trends, psychology, health, beauty, fashion, finance, jobs; personality profiles. Query or send complete manuscript. Pays varying rates, on publication.

SINGER COMMUNICATIONS INC.—3164 W. Tyler Ave., Anaheim, CA 92801. Jane Sherrod, Ed. U.S. and/or foreign reprint rights to romantic short stories, historical and romantic novels, published during last 25 years. Biography, women's-interest material, all lengths. Interviews with celebrities. Illus-

olumns, humor. Cartoons, comic strips. Pays on percentage basis or by purchase.

ITH NEWS SERVICE—P.O. Box 385, Slate Hill, NY 10973. George A. Smith, Ed.-in-Chief. Articles, 1,500 to 2,500 words, on government, national issues, and health. Profiles and human-interest pieces. Fillers, 25 to 150 words. Pays varying rates, on acceptance.

SPOTLIGHT INTERNATIONAL—146 E. 89th St., #1R, New York, NY 10128. Address Bert Goodman. Magazine features, with b&w or color slides, 1,000 to 3,000 words; upbeat, controversial compelling entertainment, investigative, profiles, etc. Pays 75% for first rights, 50% for second rights, on publication. Query preferred.

TRANSWORLD FEATURE SYNDICATE, INC.—275 Seventh Ave., 21st Fl., New York, NY 10001. Raymond F. Whelan, Chief Operating Officer. Feature material for overseas and North American markets. Query.

TRIBUNE MEDIA SERVICES—720 N. Orange Ave., Orlando, FL 60812. Michael Armrion, Ed. Continuing columns, comic strips, features, electronic data bases.

UNITED FEATURE SYNDICATE—200 Park Ave., New York, NY 10166. David Hendin, Vice President. Creative, professional columns and comics. No one-shots or series. Payment by contractual arrangement.

UNITED PRESS INTERNATIONAL—1400 Eye St., NW, Washington, DC 20005. Ron Cohen, Man. Ed. Seldom accepts free-lance material.

LITERARY PRIZE OFFERS

Each year many important prize contests are open for free-lance writers. The short summaries given below are intended merely as guides. Closing dates, requirements, and rules are tentative. No manuscript should be submitted to any competition unless the writer has first checked with the Contest Editor and received complete information about a particular contest.

Send a stamped, self-addressed envelope with all requests for contest rules and application forms.

ACADEMY OF AMERICAN POETS—177 E. 87th St., New York, NY 10128. Offers Walt Whitman Award: Publication and $1,000 cash prize for a book-length poetry manuscript by a poet who has not yet published a volume of poetry. Closes in November.

ACTORS THEATRE OF LOUISVILLE—316 W. Main St., Louisville, KY 40202. Conducts the Great American Play Contest, with prize of $7,500 for full-length, previously unproduced play. Also offers prize of $1,000 for a one-act play. Closes in April.

ALLIANCE THEATRE/ATLANTA CHILDREN'S THEATRE—1280 Peachtree St., N.E., Atlanta, GA 30309. Conducts ACT Guild Playwriting Contest, with $1,000 prize for previously unproduced one-act children's play. Closes in June.

THE AMERICAN ACADEMY AND INSTITUTE OF ARTS AND LETTERS—633 W. 155 St., New York, NY 10032. Offers Richard Rodgers Production Award, which consists of subsidized production in New York City by a non-profit theater for a musical, play with songs, thematic review, or any comparable work other than opera. Closes in November.

AMERICAN HEALTH MAGAZINE—80 Fifth Ave., New York, NY 10011. Offers prize of $2,000, plus publication, for short story about an intense physical experience. Closes in December.

ASSOCIATED WRITING PROGRAMS—Old Dominion University, Norfolk, VA 23508. Conducts Annual Award Series in Short Fiction, the Novel, and Nonfiction. In each category the prize is book publication and a $1,000 honorarium. Closes in December. Offers the Edith Shiffert Prize in Poetry: $1,000 cash prize and publication by the University Press of Virginia for an unpublished book-length collection of poetry. Closes in December. Sponsors the Short Short Fiction Competition, with prizes of $1,000, $500, and $250 for short fiction. Closes in October. Also offers Anniversary Awards, with grand prize of $1,000, two second prizes of $500 each, and four third prizes of $250 each for unpublished, original poems. Closes in April.

BEAR REPUBLIC THEATER—Pacific Coast Performing Arts Foundation, P.O. Box 1137, Santa Cruz, CA 95061. Conducts Playwriting Competition, with prize of $500, plus possible production, for previously unproduced play written by resident of California. Closes in April.

BEVERLY HILLS THEATRE GUILD—Playwright Award Competition, c/o Marcella Meharg, 2815 N. Beachwood Dr., Los Angeles, CA 90068. Conducts Playwriting Competition, with $3,000 prize for unproduced and unpublished full-length play. Closes in November.

THE CALDWELL PLAYHOUSE—P.O. Box 277, Boca Raton, FL 33432. Conducts Playwriting Contest, with prize of $1,000 and production for original, unproduced full-length play. Closes in April of even-numbered years.

CBS INC. AND THE FOUNDATION OF THE DRAMATISTS GUILD—FDG/CBS New Plays Program, The Foundation of the Dramatists Guild, 234 W. 44th St., New York, NY 10036. Sponsor New Plays Program, in which five different theaters select five new plays for production. Winning playwrights also receive prizes of $5,000 each. Closes in September.

CHICAGO MAGAZINE—303 E. Wacker Dr., Chicago, IL 60601. Offers Nelson Algren Award: $5,000, plus publication, for unpublished short story by writer living in the U.S. Closes in January.

CHOCOLATE BAYOU THEATRE COMPANY—1823 Lamar, Houston, TX 77010. John R. Pearson, Symposium Coordinator. Sponsors Preston Jones New Play Symposium, a five-week residency program for playwrights, to develop their plays. Travel expenses, room and board, and $500 stipend are offered to the playwrights whose original scripts are selected for development. Closes in February.

COMMUNITY CHILDREN'S THEATER—8021 E. 129th Terrace, Grandview, MO 64030. Address Blanche Sellens. Offers an award of $500, plus production, for unpublished hour-long play for children. Closes in January.

COURT THEATRE—The University of Chicago, 5706 S. University Ave., Chicago, IL 60637. Offers Sergel Drama Prize: $1,500 for full-length unpublished and unproduced play. Closes in June of odd-numbered years.

EUGENE V. DEBS FOUNDATION—Dept. of History, Indiana State University, Terre Haute, IN 47809. Offers Bryant Spann Memorial Prize of $750 for published or unpublished article or essay on themes relating to social protest or human equality. Closes in April.

DELACORTE PRESS—Dept BFYR, 1 Dag Hammarskjold Plaza, New York, NY 10017. Sponsors Delacorte Press Prize for an outstanding first young adult novel. The prize consists of one Delacorte Hardcover and Dell paperback contract, an advance of $4,000 on royalties, and a $1,000 cash prize. Closes in December.

FOREST A. ROBERTS-SHIRAS INSTITUTE—Forest Roberts Theatre, Northern Michigan Univ., Marquette, MI 49855. Dr. James A. Panowski, Dir. Conducts annual Playwriting Competition, with prize of $1,000, plus production, for an original, full-length, previously unproduced and unpublished play. Closes in November.

THE FOUNDATION OF THE DRAMATISTS GUILD—234 W. 44th St., New York, NY 10036. Sponsors Young Playwrights Festival. Playwrights under 19 years of age may submit scripts; winning plays will be given full stage productions or staged readings. Closes in July.

HIGHLIGHTS FOR CHILDREN—803 Church St., Honesdale, PA 18431. Conducts Contest for Juvenile Fiction, with cash prizes and production for short stories. Closes in February.

HOUGHTON MIFFLIN COMPANY—2 Park St., Boston, MA 02108. Offers Literary Fellowship for fiction or nonfiction project of exceptional literary merit written by American author. Work under consideration must be unpublished and in English. Fellowship consists of $10,000, of which $2,500 is an outright grant and $7,500 is an advance on royalties. There is no deadline.

ILLINOIS STATE UNIVERSITY—Dept of Theatre, Illinois State Univ., Normal, IL 61761. Address John W. Kirk. Sponsors Fine Arts Competition, with prize of $1,000, plus production, for previously unpublished and unproduced full-length play. Closes in October.

JACKSONVILLE UNIVERSITY—Annual Playwriting Contest, Dept. of Theatre Arts, College of Fine Arts, Jacksonville Univ., Jacksonville, FL 32211. Davis Sikes, Dir. Conducts playwriting contest, with prize of $1,000 and production, for original, previously unproduced script (full-length or one-act). Closes in January.

JEWISH COMMUNITY CENTER THEATRE—3505 Mayfield Rd., Cleveland Heights, OH 44118. Dorothy Silver, Dir. of Cultural Arts. Offers cash award of $1,000 and a staged reading for an original, previously unproduced full-length play on some aspect of the Jewish experience. Closes in December.

CHESTER H. JONES FOUNDATION—P.O. Box 43033, Cleveland, OH 44143. Conducts the National Poetry Competition, with more than $1,800 in cash prizes (including a first prize of $1,000) for poems. Closes in March.

LANDERS THEATRE—311 E. Walnut St., Springfield, MO 65806. Address Mick Denniston, Managing Director. Offers Playwright Award of $2,500, plus production, for unproduced, full-length play by U.S. citizen. Closes in December.

LINCOLN COLLEGE—Lincoln, IL 62656. Address Janet Overton. Offers Billee Murray Denny Poetry Award for original poem by poet who has not previously published a volume of poetry. First prize of $1,000, 2nd prize of $450, and 3rd prize of $200 are offered. Closes in May.

754

LITTLE THEATRE OF ALEXANDRIA—600 Wolfe St., Alexandria, VA 22314. Address One-Act Playwriting Chairman. Conducts Weisbrod National One-Act Playwriting Competition, with cash prizes for unpublished unproduced one-act plays. Closes in June.

MADEMOISELLE MAGAZINE—350 Madison Ave., New York, NY 10017. Sponsors Fiction Writers Contest, with first prize of $1,000, plus publication, and second prize of $500, for short fiction. Closes in March.

MS. MAGAZINE—119 W. 40th St., New York, NY 10018. Sponsors annual College Fiction Contest for short story by college student. Prize is publication and electronic typewriter. Closes in May.

NATIONAL ENDOWMENT FOR THE ARTS—Washington, DC 20506. Address Director, Literature Program. The National Endowment for the Arts offers fellowships to writers of poetry, fiction, scripts, and other creative prose. Deadlines vary; write for guidelines.

NATIONAL FOUNDATION FOR JEWISH CULTURE—122 E. 42nd St., New York, NY 10168. Sponsors Berman Playwriting Award, with $500 cash prize for original play on some aspect of Jewish life. Closes in February.

NATIONAL PLAY AWARD—P.O. Box 71011, Los Angeles, CA 90071. National Play Award consists of a $7,500 cash prize, plus $5,000 for production, for an original, previously unproduced play. Closes in October of odd-numbered years.

NATIONAL POETRY SERIES—18 W. 30th St., New York, NY 10001. Address Megan Ratner, Coordinator. Sponsors Annual Open Competition for unpublished, book-length poetry manuscript. The prize is publication. Closes in February.

NEW DRAMATISTS—424 W. 44th St., New York, NY 10036. Thomas Dunn, Exec. Dir. Sponsors non-performance workshops, unrehearsed studio readings, and mainstage readings for playwrights. Applicants must submit two original, full-length, non-musical scripts, along with resumé, biographical note, and statement outlining goals. Playwrights outside New York City must have the recommendation of a theatre professional. Closes in November.

THE NEW ENGLAND THEATRE CONFERENCE—50 Exchange St., Waltham, MA 02154. First prize of $500 and second prize of $250 are offered for unpublished and unproduced one-act plays in the John Gassner Memorial Playwriting Award Competition. Closes in April.

OGLEBAY INSTITUTE—Oglebay Park, Wheeling, WV 26003. Sponsors Towngate Theatre Playwriting Contest, with prize of $300, production, and travel expenses for original, unproduced play. Closes in January.

O'NEILL THEATER CENTER—234 W. 44th St., Suite 901, New York, NY 10036. Offers stipends of $350 each, staged readings, and room and board at the National Playwrights Conference, for new stage and television plays. Closes in December.

THE PARIS REVIEW—541 E. 72nd St., New York, NY 10021. Sponsors Aga Khan Prize for Fiction: $1,000, plus publication, for previously unpublished short story. Closes in June. Also sponsors Bernard F. Connors Prize: $1,000, plus publication, for previously unpublished poem. Closes in May.

PEN AMERICAN CENTER—568 Broadway, New York, NY 10012. Sponsors PEN/Nelson Algren Award: stipend of $1,000, plus one-month residency at Edward Albee Foundation's summer residence on Long Island, for uncom-

755

pleted novel or collection of short stories by an American writer who needs assistance to complete the work. Closes in November. Sponsors Renato Poggioli Translation Award: $3,000 grant for a translator working on his or her first book-length translation from Italian into English. Closes in February.

PHILLIPS EXETER ACADEMY—Exeter, NH 03833. Offers Bennett Fellowship—$4,800, plus room and board for the academic year—to an individual pursuing a career as a writer. Selection is based primarily on the quality of the manuscript (fiction or poetry, preferably a work in progress) submitted. Duties: residence for academic year while working on the manuscript; informal availability to students. Closes in December.

PIONEER DRAMA SERVICE—2172 S. Colorado Blvd., P.O. Box 22555, Denver, CO 80222. Offers Pioneer Drama Playwriting Award: $1,000 advance against royalties, plus publication, for a previously produced full-length or children's play suitable for educational theater. Closes in March.

PLAYHOUSE ON THE SQUARE—2121 Madison Ave., Memphis, TN 38104. Address Jackie Nichols. Conducts Mid-South Playwriting Contest, with $500 prize, for unproduced, full-length play. Southerners are given preference. Closes in April.

THE PLAYMAKERS—P.O. Box 5745, Tampa, FL 33675. Conducts a playwriting competition, with a cash prize of $2,000, plus travel and accommodation expenses during production, for previously unproduced full-length play by an American playwright. Closes in April.

THE PLAYWRIGHTS' CENTER—2301 Franklin Ave., E., Minneapolis, MN 55406. Offers Jerome Playwrights-in-Residence Fellowships to promising playwrights. The fellowship includes a $4,100 stipend and a one-year residency. The playwrights receive written criticism of their plays, and their work is given company and staged readings. Closes in April.

POETRY SOCIETY OF AMERICA—15 Gramercy Park, New York, NY 10003. Conducts annual contests—The Celia B. Wagner Memorial Award, the John Masefield Memorial Award, and the Elias Lieberman Student Poetry Award—in which cash prizes are offered for unpublished poems. Contests close in December.

RADIO DRAMA AWARDS—3319 W. Beltline Hwy., Madison, WI 53713. Norman Michie, Exec. Producer. Wisconsin Public Radio conducts annual Radio Drama Awards competition for original scripts by writers in Illinois, Iowa, Michigan, Minnesota, and Wisconsin. Prizes for thirty-minute radio scripts are professional production and cash awards of $500 (first prize), $300 (second), and $200 (third). Closes in January.

REDBOOK MAGAZINE—224 W. 57th St., New York, NY 10019. Conducts Short Short Story Contest for writers over 18 years of age. First prize is $1,000, plus publication. Second prize of $500 and third prize of $300 are also offered. Closes in May.

THE SAN FRANCISCO FOUNDATION—Awards Office, 500 Washington St., 8th Fl., San Francisco, CA 94111. Sponsors Joseph Henry Jackson Award: $2,000 grant for an unpublished work-in-progress (fiction, nonfiction, or poetry), written by a resident of northern California or Nevada. Also sponsors James D. Phelan Award: $2,000 grant for an unpublished work-in-progress (fiction, nonfiction, poetry, or drama), written by a resident of California. Closes in January.

756

CHARLES SCRIBNER'S SONS—115 Fifth Ave., New York, NY 10003. Offers Scribner Crime Novel Award: Publication, $5,000 advance on royalties, and $2,500 advertising and promotion budget for full-length mystery novel by a writer who has not yet published a novel. Closes in September. Also sponsors the Maxwell Perkins Prize: Publication, a $5,000 advance on royalties, and a $5,000 advertising and promotion budget for a book-length fiction manuscript on some aspect of American life, written by U.S. citizen or resident who has not yet published a novel. Closes in September. Sponsors Scribner Science Writing Prize: Publication, $5,000 advance on royalties, and a $5,000 advertising and promotion guarantee for an unpublished work of nonfiction (full-length treatment or collection of essays) involving natural history, the physical sciences, or the sciences of man. Only writers who are American citizens or permanent residents of the U.S. and who have not previously published a science book for general readers are eligible. Closes in March.

SEVENTEEN MAGAZINE—850 Third Ave., New York, NY 10022. Sponsors short story contest, with prizes of $500, $300, and $200, plus six honorable mentions of $50 each, for short fiction by teenagers aged 13 to 19. Closes in July.

SIERRA REPERTORY THEATRE—P.O. Box 3030, Sonora, CA 95370. Offers Cummings/Taylor Award of $350, plus production, for original, previously unpublished, unproduced full-length play or musical. Closes in May.

SINCLAIR RESEARCH LTD.—50 Staniford St., Boston, MA 02114. Conducts annual contest for Sinclair Prize for Fiction (£5,000—approximately $7,500—plus publication) for a previously unpublished novel of social or political significance. Write for required entry form; manuscripts must be sent to Sinclair's offices in Great Britain. Closes in July.

SOURCE THEATRE COMPANY—1809 14th St., N.W., Washington, DC 20009. Address Keith Parker, Literary Manager. Conducts National Playwriting Competition for an original, unproduced one-act or full-length play. Cash prize of $250 and production are offered for the winning script. Closes in April.

SOUTHERN ILLINOIS UNIVERSITY AT CARBONDALE—Dept. of Theater, Carbondale, IL 62901. Christian H. Moe, Director. Sponsors International Play Competition, with a first prize of $1,000, and possible production, for unpublished, unproduced full-length play. Closes in March.

SUNSET CENTER—P.O. Box 5066, Carmel, CA 93921. Richard Tyler, Director. Offers prize of up to $2,000 for an original, unproduced full-length play in its annual Festival of Firsts Playwriting Competition. Closes in August.

SYRACUSE UNIVERSITY PRESS—1600 Jamesville Ave., Syracuse, NY 13210. Address Director. Sponsors John Ben Snow Prize: $1,000, plus publication, for unpublished book-length manuscript about New York State, especially upstate or central New York. Closes in December.

TEXAS WOMAN'S UNIVERSITY—Dept. of Music and Drama, P.O. Box 23865, Denton, TX 76204. Conducts Margo Jones Playwriting Competition, in which a prize of $1,000, plus production, is offered for a full-length, unpublished and unproduced play for and about women. Closes in February.

UNICORN THEATRE—3514 Jefferson, Kansas City, MO 64111. Sponsors National Playwright Competition, with a first prize of $1,000, plus travel and residency while in production, for an original, unpublished and unproduced full-length play or musical. Closes in May.

U.S. NAVAL INSTITUTE—Annapolis, MD 21402. Address Membership Department. Conducts Arleigh Burke Essay Contest, with prizes of $1,500, $1,000, and $750, plus publication, for essays on the advancement of professional, literary, and scientific knowledge in the naval and maritime services, and the advancement of the knowledge of sea power. Closes in December.

UNIVERSITY OF ALABAMA AT BIRMINGHAM—School of Humanities, Dept. of Theatre and Dance, University Sta., Birmingham, AL 35294. Rick J. Plummer, Director. Conducts Ruby Lloyd Apsey Playwriting Competition, with $500 cash prize, plus production and travel expenses, for previously unproduced full-length play. Closes in January.

UNIVERSITY OF CINCINNATI—Elliston Poetry Collection, 646 Central Library, Univ. of Cincinnati, Cincinnati, OH 45221. Offers the George Elliston Poetry Prize, which consists of publication by the Ohio State University Press and a standard royalty contract, for a book-length poetry manuscript by a poet who has not yet published a book. Closes in December.

UNIVERSITY OF HAWAII—Kennedy Theatre, Univ. of Hawaii, 1770 East-West Rd., Honolulu, HI 96822. Conducts annual Kumu Kahua Playwriting Contests with cash prizes for original plays dealing with some aspect of the Hawaiian experience. Closes in January.

UNIVERSITY OF HAWAII PRESS—2840 Kolowalu St., Honolulu, HI 96822. Sponsors Pacific Poetry Series competition, with prize of publication and royalty contract, for unpublished book-length poetry manuscript. Closes in March.

UNIVERSITY OF IOWA—Iowa School of Letters Award, English-Philosophy Bldg., Univ. of Iowa, Iowa City, IA 52242. Offers Iowa School of Letters Award—$1,000, plus publication—for book-length collection of short stories by writer who has not yet had a book published.

UNIVERSITY OF MASSACHUSETTS PRESS—Juniper Prize, Univ. of Massachusetts Press, c/o Mail Rm., Amherst, MA 01003. Offers Juniper Prize of $1,000, plus publication, for book-length manuscript of poetry. Closes in October.

UNIVERSITY OF MISSOURI PRESS—200 Lewis Hall, Columbia, MO 65211. Breakthrough Editor. Conducts competition for Breakthrough Series: Authors who have not yet published a book are eligible to submit complete manuscripts of poetry, short fiction, or drama; the prize is publication. Closes in March.

UNIVERSITY OF PITTSBURGH PRESS—Pittsburgh, PA 15260. Sponsors Drue Heinz Literature Prize—$5,000, plus publication and royalty contract—for unpublished collection of short stories. Closes in August. Also sponsors Agnes Lynch Starrett Poetry Prize—$1,000, plus publication and royalty contract—for book-length collection of poems by poet who has not yet published a volume of poetry. Closes in April.

UNIVERSITY OF WISCONSIN-PARKSIDE—Fine Arts Division, Box No. 2000, Kenosha, WI 53141. Address Rhoda-Gale Pollack, Chairman. Conducts Playwriting Competition, with $1,000 award, plus production, for full-length unpublished and unproduced original play. Closes in October.

UNIVERSITY OF WISCONSIN PRESS—Poetry Series, 114 N. Murray St., Madison, WI 53715. Ronald Wallace, Admin. Offers Brittingham Prize in Poetry: $500, plus publication, for unpublished book-length poetry manuscript. Closes in October.

758

WAGNER COLLEGE—Staten Island, NY 10301. Conducts contest for Stanley Drama Award, in which a prize of $1,000 is offered for an original full-length play that has not been professionally produced or published. Closes in June.

WALT WHITMAN CENTER FOR THE ARTS AND HUMANITIES—2nd and Cooper Sts., Camden, NJ 08102. Sponsors the annual Camden Poetry Award: $1,000, plus publication, for an unpublished book-length collection of poetry. Closes in September.

WORD WORKS—P.O. Box 42164, Washington, DC 20015. Offers the Washington Prize of $1,000 for unpublished poem by American poet. Closes in November.

YALE UNIVERSITY PRESS—Box 92A, Yale Sta., New Haven, CT 06520. Conducts Yale Series of Younger Poets Competition, in which the prize is publication of a book-length manuscript of poetry, written by a poet under 40 who has not previously published a volume of poems. Closes in February.

CREATIVE ARTS COLONIES

A creative arts colony can offer a writer isolation and a quiet place to concentrate upon his or her work without the distractions of everyday life. Colonies vary in size—some provide space for as many as thirty or forty writers at one time, others can accommodate only three or four—and length of residencies varies from one week to several months. These programs have strict admissions policies, and require a formal application or letter of intent, with resumé, writing samples, and letters of recommendation. It's a good idea to write for application information first, enclosing a stamped, self-addressed envelope (SASE).

CENTRUM FOUNDATION—The Centrum Foundation sponsors residencies of two or three months at Fort Worden State Park, a Victorian fort on the Strait of Juan De Fuca in Washington. Nonfiction, fiction, and poetry writers may apply for residency awards, which include stipend of $600 a month. Application deadline is in early December; send letter explaining the project, short biographical note, and writing sample of 20 pages of more. For details, send SASE in fall, to Carol Jane Bangs, Director of Literature Program, Centrum Foundation, Fort Worden State Park, P.O. Box 1158, Port Townsend, WA 98368.

CUMMINGTON COMMUNITY OF THE ARTS—Residential program in the Berkshires offers uninterrupted time, studio space for emerging and established writers. For more information, send SASE to Cummington Community of the Arts, Cummington, MA 01026.

DORLAND MOUNTAIN COLONY—Novelists, playwrights, and poets may apply for one- to two-month residencies at the Dorland Preserve, a wildlife sanctuary in the Palomar Mountains of Southern California. Cottages, firewood, and kerosene are provided at no cost. Application deadlines are March 1 and September 1. For further information and application forms, send

SASE to J. Patrick Liteky, Resident Director, Dorland Mountain Colony, P.O. Box 6, Temecula, CA 92390.

DORSET COLONY HOUSE—Writers and playwrights are offered low-cost room and board at the Colony House in Dorset, Vermont. Periods of residency are 3 to 6 weeks, and are available between October 1 and June 1. Applications deadlines are September 15, December 15, and February 15 for the periods immediately following the deadlines. For more information, send SASE to John Nassivera, Director, Dorset Colony House, Dorset, VT 05251.

FINE ARTS WORK CENTER IN PROVINCETOWN—Fellowships, living and studio space at the Fine Arts Work Center on Cape Cod, for writers to work independently. Residencies are for seven months; apply before the February 1 deadline. For details, send SASE to Jim Potter, Director, Fine Arts Work Center, Provincetown, MA 02657.

THE WILLIAM FLANAGAN MEMORIAL CREATIVE PERSONS CENTER—The Edward F. Albee Foundation sponsors one month residencies for writers at the William Flanagan Memorial Creative Persons Center on Montauk, Long Island. The center is open between May 15 and October 15. Applications will be accepted from January 1 to April 1. For further information, send self-addressed, stamped envelope to The William Flanagan Memorial Creative Persons Center, c/o Edward F. Albee Foundation, Inc., 14 Harrison St., New York, NY 10013.

THE HAMBIDGE CENTER—Two-week to two-month residencies are offered to writers at the Hambidge Center in the Northeast Georgia mountains. Send SASE for application form to Mary C. Nikas, Exec. Director, Residency Program, The Hambidge Center, P.O. Box 33, Rabun Gap, GA 30568.

THE MACDOWELL COLONY—Studios, room and board at the MacDowell Colony of Peterborough, New Hampshire, for writers to work without interruption in woodland setting. Selection is competitive. Apply at least six months in advance of season desired; residencies are usually 5 to 6 weeks. For details and admission forms, send SASE to Admissions Coordinator, The MacDowell Colony, 100 High St., Peterborough, NH 03458.

THE MILLAY COLONY FOR THE ARTS—At Steepletop in Austerlitz, New York—former home of Edna St. Vincent Millay—studios, living quarters, and meals are provided to writers at no cost. Residencies are for one month. Application deadlines are February 1, May 1, and September 1. To apply, send SASE to The Millay Colony for the Arts, Inc., Steepletop, Austerlitz, NY 12017.

MONTALVO CENTER FOR THE ARTS—Three-month, low-cost residencies at the Villa Montalvo in the foothills of the Santa Cruz Mountains south of San Francisco, for writers working on specific projects. Send self-addressed envelope and 37¢ stamp for application forms to Montalvo Residency Program, P.O. Box 158, Saratoga, CA 95071.

RAGDALE FOUNDATION—Low-cost living and working space are offered to writers at the Ragdale Foundation, near Chicago. All meals are provided, and financial assistance is available. Residencies range from one week to two months, year round. For more information, send SASE to Selection Committee, Ragdale Foundation, 1260 N. Green Bay Rd., Lake Forest, IL 60045.

UCROSS FOUNDATION—Residencies, two weeks to four months, at the Ucross Foundation in the foothills of the Big Horn Mountains in Wyoming, for writers to concentrate on their work without interruptions. There are two sessions per year, January through May and August through December. Application deadlines are October 1 and March 1. For more information, send SASE to Director, Residency Program, Ucross Foundation, Ucross Route, Box 19, Clearmont, WY 82835.

VIRGINIA CENTER FOR THE CREATIVE ARTS—Residencies of one to three months at the Mt. San Angelo Estate in Sweet Briar, Virginia, for writers to work without distraction. Apply at least three months in advance. A limited amount of financial assistance is available. Open year round. For more information, send SASE to William Smart, Director, Virginia Center for the Creative Arts, Sweet Briar, VA 24595.

HELENE WURLITZER FOUNDATION OF NEW MEXICO—Rent-free and utility-free studios at the Helene Wurlitzer Foundation in Taos, New Mexico, are offered to creative writers. Length of residency varies, but is usually three months. For details, write to Henry A. Sauerwein, Jr., Exec. Director, The Helene Wurlitzer Foundation of New Mexico, Box 545, Taos, NM 87571.

YADDO—Artists, writers, and composers are invited for short-term residencies at the Yaddo estate in Saratoga Springs, New York. Although there is no fixed charge, voluntary contributions are encouraged. Requests for applications should be sent with SASE before January 15 or August 1 to Curtis Harnack, Exec. Director, Yaddo, Box 395, Saratoga Springs, NY 12866.

STATE ARTS COUNCILS

State Arts Councils sponsor grants, fellowships, and other programs for writers. To be eligible for funding, a writer *must* be a resident of the state in which he is applying. For more information, write to the addresses listed below.

ALABAMA STATE COUNCIL ON THE ARTS AND HUMANITIES
Barbara George, Programs Coordinator
323 Adams Ave.
Montgomery, AL 36130

ALASKA STATE COUNCIL ON THE ARTS
Jean Palmer, Grants Officer
619 Warehouse Ave., Suite 220
Anchorage, AK 99501

ARIZONA COMMISSION ON THE ARTS
Carol Kean Kennedy, Education Director
2024 N. 7th St., Suite 201
Phoenix, AZ 85006

OFFICE OF ARKANSAS STATE ARTS AND HUMANITIES
Amy Aspell, Executive Director
Suite 200
225 E. Markham St.
Little Rock, AR 72201

CALIFORNIA ARTS COUNCIL
Roberta Blogg, Public Information Officer
1901 Broadway, Suite A
Sacramento, CA 95818-2492

COLORADO COUNCIL ON THE ARTS AND HUMANITIES
Ellen Sollod, Executive Director
770 Pennsylvania St.
Denver, CO 80203

CONNECTICUT COMMISSION ON THE ARTS
Address Grant Program
340 Capital Ave.
Hartford, CT 06106

DELAWARE STATE ARTS COUNCIL
Cecelia Fitzgibbon, Administrator
Carvel State Building
820 N. French St.
Wilmington, DE 19801

FLORIDA ARTS COUNCIL
Chris Doolin
Dept. of State
Div. of Cultural Affairs
The Capitol
Tallahassee, FL 32301

GEORGIA COUNCIL FOR THE ARTS AND HUMANITIES
2082 E. Exchange Place, Suite 100
Tucker, GA 30084

HAWAII STATE FOUNDATION ON CULTURE AND THE ARTS
Sarah M. Richards, Executive Director
335 Merchant St., Rm. 202
Honolulu, HI 96813

IDAHO COMMISSION ON THE ARTS
Joan Lolmaugh, Executive Director
304 W. State St.
Boise, ID 83720

ILLINOIS ARTS COUNCIL
Mary Lee O'Brien, Artists' Services Coordinator
111 N. Wabash Ave., Rm. 720
Chicago, IL 60602

INDIANA ARTS COMMISSION
Tom Schorgl, Executive Director
32 E. Washington St., 6th Fl.
Indianapolis, IN 46204

IOWA STATE ARTS COUNCIL
Marilyn Parks, Grants Coordinator
State Capitol Complex
Des Moines, IA 50319

KANSAS ARTS COMMISSION
Max Wilson, Assistant Director and Chief Grants Officer
112 West 6th St., 4th Floor
Topeka, KS 66603

762

KENTUCKY ARTS COUNCIL
Nash Cox, Director
Berry Hill, Louisville Rd.
Frankford, KY 40601

LOUISIANA COUNCIL FOR MUSIC AND PERFORMING ARTS, INC.
Literature Program Associate
7524 St. Charles Ave.
New Orleans, LA 70118

MAINE STATE COMMISSION ON THE ARTS AND HUMANITIES
Stuart Kestenbaum
State House, Station 25
Augusta, ME 04330

MARYLAND STATE ARTS COUNCIL
Linda Vlasak, Program Director
Artists-in-Education and Poets-in-the-Schools
15 W. Mulberry St.
Baltimore, MD 21201

MASSACHUSETTS COUNCIL ON THE ARTS AND HUMANITIES
Pat Dixon, Literature Program Director
1 Ashburton Place, Rm. 1305
Boston, MA 02108

MICHIGAN COUNCIL FOR THE ARTS
E. Ray Scott, Executive Director
1200 Sixth Ave., 4th Floor
Detroit, MI 48226

COMPAS: WRITERS IN THE SCHOOLS
Molly LaBerge, Director
308 Landmark Center
75 W. 5th St.
St. Paul, MN 55102

MINNESOTA STATE ARTS BOARD
John Maliga, Program Director
Artist Assistance Program
432 Summit Ave.
St. Paul, MN 55102

MISSISSIPPI ARTS COMMISSION
Mrs. Theo Inman, Director, Artists-in-Education
Box 1341
Jackson, MS 39205

MISSOURI ARTS COUNCIL
Kim A. Bozark, Program Administrator for Literature
Wainwright Office Complex
111 N. 7th St., Suite 105
St. Louis, MO 63101

MONTANA ARTS COUNCIL
Program Director, Artist Services
35 S. Last Chance Gulch
Helena, MT 59620

NEBRASKA ARTS COUNCIL
Rebecca Blunk, Associate Director, Programs
1313 Farnam On-the-Mall
Omaha, NE 68102-1873

NEVADA STATE COUNCIL ON THE ARTS
Jacqueline Belmont, Executive Director
329 Flint St.
Reno, NV 89501

NEW HAMPSHIRE COMMISSION ON THE ARTS
Sally Gaskill, Grants and Touring Arts Coodinator
Phenix Hall, 40 N. Main St.
Concord, NH 03301

NEW JERSEY STATE COUNCIL ON THE ARTS
Noreen M. Tomassi, Literary Arts Coordinator
109 W. State St.
Trenton, NJ 08625

NEW MEXICO ARTS COMMISSION
Santa Fe Poets-in-the Schools Program
224 E. Palace Ave.
Santa Fe, NM 87501

NEW YORK STATE COUNCIL ON THE ARTS
Gregory Kolovakos, Director, Literature Program
915 Broadway
New York, NY 10003

NORTH CAROLINA ARTS COUNCIL
Lida Lowrey, Literature Program
Dept. of Cultural Resources
Raleigh, NC 27611

NORTH DAKOTA COUNCIL ON THE ARTS
Vern Goodin, Program Director
Black Building, Suite 606
Fargo, SD 58102

OHIO ARTS COUNCIL
727 E. Main St.
Columbus, OH 43205

STATE ARTS COUNCIL OF OKLAHOMA
Ellen Binkley, Assistant Director
Jim Thorpe Bldg., Rm. 640
Oklahoma City, OK 73105

OREGON ARTS COMMISSION
835 Summer St., N.E.
Salem, OR 97301

PENNSYLVANIA COUNCIL ON THE ARTS
Peter Carnahan, Literature and Theatre Programs
Mack Granderson, Artists-in-the-Schools Program
Room 216, Finance Bldg.
Harrisburg, PA 17120

RHODE ISLAND STATE COUNCIL ON THE ARTS
Iona B. Dobbins, Executive Director
312 Wickenden St.
Providence, RI 02903

SOUTH CAROLINA ARTS COMMISSION
Steve Lewis, Director, Literary Arts Program
1800 Gervais St.
Columbia, SC 29201

SOUTH DAKOTA ARTS COUNCIL
Artists-in-Schools Coordinator
108 W. 11th St.
Sioux Falls, SD 57102

TENNESSEE ARTS COMMISSION
505 Deaderick St., Suite 1700
Nashville, TN 37219

TEXAS COMMISSION ON THE ARTS
P.O. Box 13406, Capitol Station
Austin, TX 78711

UTAH ARTS COUNCIL
G. Barnes, Literary Arts Coordinator
617 East South Temple
Salt Lake City, UT 84102

VERMONT COUNCIL ON THE ARTS
Geof Hewitt, Grants Coordinator
136 State St.
Montpelier, VT 05602

VIRGINIA COMMISSION ON THE ARTS
Peggy J. Baggett, Executive Director
James Monroe Bldg., 17th Floor
Richmond, VA 23219

WASHINGTON STATE ARTS COMMISSION
Lee Bassett, Artists-in-Residence Program
110 9th and Columbia Bldg., MS GH-11
Olympia, WA 98504

WEST VIRGINIA ARTS AND HUMANITIES DIVISION
Dept. of Culture and History
The Cultural Center, Capitol Complex
Charleston, WV 25305

WISCONSIN ARTS BOARD
107 S. Butler St.
Madison, WI 53703

WYOMING COUNCIL ON THE ARTS
Joy Thompson, Executive Director
Capitol Complex
Cheyenne, WY 82001

ORGANIZATIONS FOR WRITERS

AMERICAN MEDICAL WRITERS ASSOCIATION
5272 River Rd., Suite 410
Bethesda, MD 20816
Lillian Sablack, *Executive Director*

Any person actively interested in or professionally associated with any medium of medical communication is eligible for membership. The annual dues for Active Members are $55.

AMERICAN SOCIETY OF JOURNALISTS AND AUTHORS
1501 Broadway, Suite 1907
New York, NY 10036
Marci Vitous-Hurwood, *Executive Secretary*
Membership is open to qualified professional free-lance writers of nonfiction; qualification of applications are judged by the Membership Committee. Initiation fee is $50 and annual dues are $95.

AMERICAN TRANSLATORS ASSOCIATION
109 Croton Avenue
Ossining, NY 10562
Rosemary Malia, *Staff Administrator*
Membership is open to any person actively engaged in translating, interpreting, or professionally related work *(Active Member),* or to any person or organization interested in the objectives of the Association *(Associate Member).* Dues for individuals are $50 annually.

THE AUTHORS GUILD, INC.
234 West 44th Street
New York, NY 10036
A writer who has published a book in the last seven years with an established publisher, or one who has published several magazine pieces with periodicals of general circulation within the last eighteen months, may be eligible for active, voting membership. A new writer—for example, one who has had a contract offer from an established book publisher—may be eligible for associate membership, on application to the Membership Committee. Dues are $60 a year, which includes membership in The Authors League of America.

THE AUTHORS LEAGUE OF AMERICA, INC.
(Authors Guild and Dramatists Guild)
234 West 44th St.
New York, NY 10036
The Authors League of America is a national organization of over 12,000 authors and dramatists, representing them on matters of joint concern, such as copyright, taxes, and freedom of expression. Membership in the League is restricted to authors and dramatists who are members of The Authors Guild, Inc. and The Dramatists Guild, Inc. Matters such as contract terms and subsidiary rights are in the province of the two guilds.

THE DRAMATISTS GUILD, INC.
234 West 44th Street
New York, NY 10036
David E. LeVine, *Executive Director*
The Dramatists Guild, the professional association of playwrights, composers, and lyricists, promotes the interests of authors of stage works. It protects their rights in such works and strives to improve the conditions under which they are created. All theater writers (produced or not) are eligible for Active or Associate membership; non-writers interested in the Guild may become Subscribing members.

MYSTERY WRITERS OF AMERICA, INC.
150 Fifth Avenue
New York, NY 10011
Mary A. Frisque, *Executive Secretary*

There are four classifications of membership in MWA: 1) *Active*—for anyone who has made a sale in the field of mystery, suspense, or crime writing (book, magazine, newspaper, motion picture, radio, television). Only *Active* members may vote or hold office. 2) *Associate*—for non-writers who are allied to the mystery field: editors, publishers, critics, literary agents, motion picture, radio or television producers. 3) *Corresponding*—for writers living outside the United States. *Corresponding* members do not need to be American citizens. 4) *Affiliate*—for new writers who have not as yet made a sale, or non-writers who are mystery enthusiasts.

Annual dues are $40; $15 for *Corresponding* members.

NATIONAL ASSOCIATION OF SCIENCE WRITERS, INC.
P.O. Box 294
Greenlawn, NY 11740

Anyone who is actively engaged in the dissemination of science information, and has two years or more of experience in this field, is eligible to apply for membership. Active members must be principally engaged in reporting science through newspapers, magazines, television, or other media that reach the public directly. Associate members report science through limited-circulation publications, and other special media. Annual membership dues are $45.

THE NATIONAL WRITERS CLUB
1450 S. Havana, Suite 620
Aurora, CO 80012
Donald E. Bower, *Director*

The National Writers Club is a nonprofit representative organization of new and established writers, poets, and playwrights, founded in 1937, serving free-lance writers throughout the U.S. and Canada. Membership includes a subscription to the bimonthly newsletter, *Authorship*. Professional dues are $50 annually, plus a $15 initiation fee.

P.E.N. AMERICAN CENTER
568 Broadway
New York, NY 10012
Karen Kennerly, *Executive Secretary*

P.E.N. American Center is an independent association of writers—poets, playwrights, essayists, editors and novelists—that promotes and maintains intellectual cooperation among men and women of letters in the United States and abroad in the interest of literature, exchange of ideas, freedom of expression, and good will.

The criteria for membership are the publication of two books of literary merit in the United States, and nomination by a P.E.N. member. There are two classifications of dues. Dues: $45 per year (includes invitations to P.E.N. events, auto rental discount, and eligibility for group health insurance).

THE POETRY SOCIETY OF AMERICA
15 Gramercy Park
New York, NY 10003
Dennis Stone, *Administrative Director*

Founded in 1910, The Poetry Society of America seeks through a variety of programs to gain a wider audience for American poetry. The Society offers 17 annual prizes for poetry, and many contests are open to non-members as well as members. Also sponsors workshops, free public poetry readings, publication of the semiannual *The Poetry Review,* and a Newsletter. Dues for all classes of membership are the same—$20 annually.

PRIVATE EYE WRITERS OF AMERICA
1811 E. 35th St.
Brooklyn, NY 11234
Robert J. Randisi, *Vice President*
Writers who have published a work of fiction—short story, novel, television or movie screenplay—with a private eye as the central character are eligible to join the organization as active members. Serious devotees of the P.I. story may become associate members. Dues are $15 for active members, $10 for non-active. Present annual Shamus Award for best in P.I. fiction.

SCIENCE FICTION WRITERS OF AMERICA
P.O. Box H
Wharton, NJ 07885
Peter D. Pautz, *Executive Secretary*
Any writer who has sold a work of science fiction or fantasy is eligible for membership in the Science Fiction Writers of America. For membership information and applications, writers should apply to the address above. Dues are $40 per year for actives, $25 for affiliates, plus $7.50 installation fee for new affiliates. Quarterly SFWA Bulletin available to non-members for $10/4 issues.

SOCIETY OF AMERICAN TRAVEL WRITERS
1120 Connecticut Ave., Suite 940
Washington, DC 20036
Ken Fischer, *Administrative Coordinator*
Membership in the Society of American Travel Writers is by invitation. Active Membership is limited to salaried travel editors, writers, broadcasters, or photographers; and to those who are employed as free lancers in any of the above areas and with a sufficient steady volume of published or distributed work about travel to satisfy the Membership Committee. Associate Membership is open to persons regularly engaged in public relations within the travel industry. Initiation fee for Active members is $100, for Associate members, $200. Annual dues for Active members are $75, for Associate members, $140.

SOCIETY OF CHILDREN'S BOOK WRITERS
P.O. Box 296, MAR Vista Station
Los Angeles, CA 90066
Lin Oliver, *Executive Director*
Full memberships are open to those who have had at least one children's book or story published. Associate memberships are open to all those with an interest in children's literature, whether or not they have published. Yearly dues are $30 for both full and associate members.

SOCIETY FOR TECHNICAL COMMUNICATION
815 15th St., N.W.
Washington, DC 20005
William C. Stolgitis, *Executive Director*
The Society for Technical Communication is a professional organization dedicated to the advancement of the theory and practice of technical communication in all media. The membership represents every discipline associated with technical communication, including technical writers and editors, publishers, artists and draftsmen, researchers, educators, and audiovisual specialists. There are about 80 chapters in the United States, Canada, and other countries.

WESTERN WRITERS OF AMERICA, INC.
P.O. Box 1645
Yakima, WA 98907
Jean Mead, *Secretary-Treasurer*

Western Writers of America is a non-profit organization of writers of fiction, nonfiction, and poetry pertaining to the traditions, legends, development and history of the American West. Its chief purpose is to promote a more widespread distribution, readership and appreciation of the West and its literature. Dues are $40 a year. Sponsors annual Spur Awards contest.

WRITERS GUILD OF AMERICA, EAST, INC.
555 W. 57th St.
New York, NY 10019
Mona Mangan, *Executive Director*

WRITERS GUILD OF AMERICA, WEST, INC.
8955 Beverly Blvd.
Los Angeles, California 90048
Naomi Gurian, *Executive Director*
The Writers Guild of America (East and West) represents writers in the fields of radio, television, and motion pictures.
In order to qualify for membership, a writer must fulfill current requirements for employment or sale of material in one of these three fields.
The basic dues are $25 a quarter. In addition, there are quarterly dues based on a percentage of the writer's earnings in any of the fields over which the Guild has jurisdiction. The initiation fee is $1,500.

AMERICAN LITERARY AGENTS

Most literary agents do not usually accept new writers as clients. Since the agent's only income is a percentage—10% to 20%—of the amount he receives from the sales he makes for his clients, he must have as clients writers who are selling fairly regularly to good markets. Always query an agent first. Do not send any manuscripts until the agent has asked you to do so. The following list is only a partial selection of representative agents. Addresses which include zip codes in parentheses are located in New York City (the majority of agents on this list are in New York). A list of agents can also be obtained by sending a stamped, self-addressed envelope to Society of Authors' Representatives, P.O. Box 650, Old Chelsea Sta., New York, NY 10113 or Independent Literary Agents Assn., Inc., 21 W. 26th St., New York, NY 10010.

MAXWELL ALEY ASSOCIATES, 145 E. 35 St. (10016)

ALLEN & YANOW LITERARY AGENCY, Box 5158, Santa Cruz, CA 95063

MARCIA AMSTERDAM, 41 W. 82 St. (10024)

GEORGES BORCHARDT, 136 E. 57 St. (10022)

BRANDT & BRANDT LITERARY AGENTS, INC., 1501 Broadway (10036)

CURTIS BROWN, LTD., 575 Madison Ave. (10022)

JANE JORDAN BROWNE, MULTIMEDIA PRODUCT DEVELOPMENT, INC., 410 S. Michigan Ave., Rm. 828, Chicago, IL 60605

PEMA BROWNE LTD., 185 E. 85 St. (10028)

KNOX BURGER ASSOCIATES, LTD., 39½ Washington Sq. S. (10012)

RUTH CANTOR, 156 Fifth Ave. (10010)

MARIA CARVAINIS AGENCY, INC., 235 West End Ave. (10023)

HY COHEN LITERARY AGENCY LTD., 111 W. 57 St. (10019)

MOLLY MALONE COOK LITERARY AGENCY, Box 338, Provincetown, MA 02657

ROBERT CORNFIELD LITERARY AGENCY, 145 W. 79 St. (10024)

LIZ DARHANSOFF, 1220 Park Ave. (10028)

JOAN DAVES, 59 E. 54 St. (10022)

ANITA DIAMANT, 310 Madison Ave. (10017)

JOSEPH ELDER AGENCY, 150 W. 87 St., 6D (10024)

JOHN FARQUHARSON, LTD., 250 W. 57 St., Suite 1914 (10107)

THE FROMMER PRICE LITERARY AGENCY, INC., 185 E. 85 St. (10028)

SANFORD J. GREENBURGER ASSOCIATES, 55 Fifth Ave. (10003)

J DE S ASSOCIATES, INC., Shagbark Rd., Wilson Point, S. Norwalk, CT 06854

MICHAEL LARSEN/ELIZABETH POMADA, LITERARY AGENTS, 1029 Jones St., San Francisco, CA 94109

THE ADELE LEONE AGENCY, 52 Riverside Dr., 6A (10024)

ELLEN LEVINE LITERARY AGENCY, INC., Suite 1205, 432 Park Ave. S. (10016)

THE STERLING LORD AGENCY, 660 Madison Ave. (10021)

BARBARA LOWENSTEIN ASSOCIATES, 250 W. 57 St. (10019)

DONALD MACCAMPBELL, INC., 12 E. 41 St. (10017)

MRS. RENATE B. MCCARTER, 823 Park Ave. (10021)

HELEN MCGRATH AND ASSOCIATES, 1406 Idaho Court, Concord, CA 94521

JET LITERARY ASSOCIATES, INC., 124 E. 84 St., Suite 4A (10028)

VIRGINIA KIDD LITERARY AGENTS, Box 278, 538 E. Hartford St., Milford, PA 18337

HARVEY KLINGER, INC., 301 W. 53 St. (10019)

BILL KRUGER LITERARY SERVICES, P.O. Box 40887, St. Petersburg, FL 33743

PETER LAMPACK AGENCY, INC., 551 Fifth Ave., Suite 2015 (10017)

THE LANTZ OFFICE, INC., 888 Seventh Ave. (10019)

MCINTOSH & OTIS, INC., 475 Fifth Ave. (10017)

HAROLD MATSON CO., INC., 276 Fifth Ave. (10001)

MEWS BOOKS LTD., 20 Bluewater Hill, Westport, CT 06880

MARTHA MILLARD LITERARY AGENCY, 357 W. 19 St. (10011)

WILLIAM MORRIS AGENCY, 1350 Ave. of Americas (10019)

HAROLD OBER ASSOCIATES, INC., 40 E. 49 St. (10017)

FIFI OSCARD ASSOCIATES, INC., 19 W. 44 St. (10036)

RAY PEEKNER LITERARY AGENCY, 3210 S. 7th St., Milwaukee, WI 53215

RODNEY PELTER, 129 E. 61 St. (10021)

SIDNEY E. PORCELAIN AGENCY, Box 69, Brigantine, NJ 08203

PAUL R. REYNOLDS, INC., 12 E. 41 St (10017)

MARIE RODELL-FRANCES COLLIN LITERARY AGENCY, Suite 2004, 110 W. 40th St. (10018)

ROSENSTONE & WENDER, 3 E. 48 St. (10017)

GLORIA SAFIER, INC., 667 Madison Ave. (10021)

JOHN SCHAFFNER ASSOCIATES, INC., 425 E. 51 St. (10022)

PHILIP G. SPITZER LITERARY AGENCY, 1465 Third Ave. (10028)

AUSTIN WAHL AGENCY, LTD., 53 W. Jackson Blvd., Suite 342 Monadnock Bldg., Chicago, IL 60604

MARY YOST ASSOCIATES, INC., 59 E. 54 St. (10022)

SUSAN ZECKENDORF ASSOCIATES, INC., 171 W. 57 St. (10019)

INDEX TO MARKETS

773